# AMNESTY INTERNATIONAL REPORT 2015/16

## THE STATE OF THE WORLD'S HUMAN RIGHTS

WITHDRAWN

# AMNESTY INTERNATIONAL

Amnesty International is a global movement of more than 7 million people who campaign for a world where human rights are enjoyed by all. Our vision is for every person to enjoy all the rights enshrined in the Universal Declaration of Human Rights and other international human rights standards.

Amnesty International's mission is to conduct research and take action to prevent and end grave abuses of all human rights – civil, political, social, cultural and economic. From freedom of expression and association to physical and mental integrity, from protection from discrimination to the right to housing – these rights are indivisible.

Amnesty International is funded mainly by its membership and public donations. No funds are sought or accepted from governments for investigating and campaigning against human rights abuses. Amnesty International is independent of any government, political ideology, economic interest or religion. Amnesty International is a democratic movement whose major policy decisions are taken by representatives from all national sections at International Council Meetings held every two years. Check online for current details.

First published in 2016 by Amnesty International Ltd Peter Benenson House, 1 Easton Street, London WC1X 0DW United Kingdom

© Amnesty International 2016

Index: POL 10/2552/2016

ISBN: 978-0-86210-492-4

A catalogue record for this book is available from the British Library.

Original language: English

This report documents Amnesty International's work and concerns through 2015.

The absence of an entry in this report on a particular country or territory does not imply that no human rights violations of concern to Amnesty International have taken place there during the year. Nor is the length of a country entry any basis for a comparison of the extent and depth of Amnesty International's concerns in a country.

# CONTENTS
# ANNUAL REPORT 2015/16

# ABBREVIATIONS

**ASEAN**
Association of Southeast Asian Nations

**AU**
African Union

**CEDAW**
UN Convention on the Elimination of All Forms of Discrimination against Women

**CEDAW COMMITTEE**
UN Committee on the Elimination of Discrimination against Women

**CERD**
International Convention on the Elimination of All Forms of Racial Discrimination

**CERD COMMITTEE**
UN Committee on the Elimination of Racial Discrimination

**CIA**
US Central Intelligence Agency

**ECOWAS**
Economic Community of West African States

**EU**
European Union

**EUROPEAN COMMITTEE FOR THE PREVENTION OF TORTURE**
European Committee for the Prevention of Torture and Inhuman or Degrading Treatment or Punishment

**EUROPEAN CONVENTION ON HUMAN RIGHTS**
(European) Convention for the Protection of Human Rights and Fundamental Freedoms

**ICC**
International Criminal Court

**ICCPR**
International Covenant on Civil and Political Rights

**ICESCR**
International Covenant on Economic, Social and Cultural Rights

**ICRC**
International Committee of the Red Cross

**ILO**
International Labour Organization

**INTERNATIONAL CONVENTION AGAINST ENFORCED DISAPPEARANCE**
International Convention for the Protection of All Persons from Enforced Disappearance

**LGBTI**
Lesbian, gay, bisexual, transgender and intersex

**NATO**
North Atlantic Treaty Organization

**NGO**
Non-governmental organization

**OAS**
Organization of American States

**OSCE**
Organization for Security and Co-operation in Europe

**UK**
United Kingdom

**UN**
United Nations

**UN CONVENTION AGAINST TORTURE**
Convention against Torture and Other Cruel, Inhuman or Degrading Treatment or Punishment

**UN REFUGEE CONVENTION**
Convention relating to the Status of Refugees

## UN SPECIAL RAPPORTEUR ON FREEDOM OF EXPRESSION
UN Special Rapporteur on the promotion and protection of the right to freedom of opinion and expression

## UN SPECIAL RAPPORTEUR ON RACISM
Special Rapporteur on contemporary forms of racism, racial discrimination, xenophobia and related intolerance

## UN SPECIAL RAPPORTEUR ON TORTURE
Special Rapporteur on torture and other cruel, inhuman or degrading treatment or punishment

## UN SPECIAL RAPPORTEUR ON VIOLENCE AGAINST WOMEN
Special Rapporteur on violence against women, its causes and consequences

## UNHCR, THE UN REFUGEE AGENCY
Office of the United Nations High Commissioner for Refugees

## UNICEF
United Nations Children's Fund

## UPR
UN Universal Periodic Review

## USA
United States of America

## WHO
World Health Organization

# PREFACE

The *Amnesty International Report 2015/16* documents the state of the world's human rights during 2015.

The foreword, five regional overviews and a survey of 160 countries and territories highlight the suffering endured by many, be it through conflict, displacement, discrimination or repression. The Report also highlights the strength and extent of the human rights movement, and surveys the progress made in the safeguarding and securing of human rights.

While every attempt is made to ensure accuracy, information may be subject to change without notice.

# AMNESTY INTERNATIONAL REPORT 2015/16

## FOREWORD AND REGIONAL OVERVIEWS

# FOREWORD

"The fact that we are seeing so many new crises breaking out without any of the old ones getting resolved, clearly illustrates the lack of capacity and political will to end conflict, let alone to prevent it. The result is an alarming proliferation of unpredictability and impunity."

António Guterres, UN High Commissioner for Refugees

The past year severely tested the international system's capacity to respond to crises and mass forced displacements of people, and found it woefully inadequate. More people are currently displaced and seeking refuge worldwide than at any point since the Second World War. This is partly fuelled by the continuing armed conflict in Syria, where more than half of the population has now fled beyond the country's borders or been internally displaced. So far attempts to resolve the conflict have simply served to highlight global and regional divisions.

Multilateral initiatives to respond to the outpouring of refugees, including the UN Regional Refugee and Resilience Plan, have in recent months been jostled by the sheer weight of the crisis into stronger co-ordination across Egypt, Iraq, Jordan, Lebanon and Turkey. Governments in Europe, Canada and the USA, where public perceptions of refugees were shaken by the gut-wrenching media image of the drowned body of Syrian toddler Alan Kurdi, were forced to react to the public outcry and the calls to welcome refugees and end the crisis.

Yet both in Syria's regional neighbourhood and in western countries, significant gaps in institutional responses to crisis and conflict were exposed. Although some countries in the region accepted a large number of Syrian refugees, many governments both within and outside the Middle East and North Africa region remained unwilling to increase their intake of refugees to meaningful levels. Burden- and responsibility-sharing continued to be tremendously lopsided, and provision of resources lagged well behind the rapidly unfolding crisis. Meanwhile, the human rights of many families and individuals on the move were violated, including through criminalization of asylum-seekers, refoulement, push-backs and removal to other territories, and through various state actions that amounted to denial of access to an asylum process.

As the world struggled to respond to the large numbers leaving Syria, the war raging within the country crystallized urgent concerns around the application of international human rights and humanitarian law that Amnesty International and others have consistently raised for years. The Syrian conflict has become a byword for the inadequate protection of scores of civilians at risk, and more broadly for the systemic failure of institutions to uphold international law.

Even as we live in the hope that current efforts will yield peace in Syria, over the years the war in the country has also highlighted the impunity gap that ensues when the five permanent members of the UN Security Council use their veto to block credible and proportionate action to end war crimes and crimes against humanity, and to impede accountability when such crimes are being or have been committed. Syria's dire human rights situation has demonstrated the weakness of systems of civilian protection during armed conflicts. In the Syrian crisis, and more widely with the actions of the armed group calling itself Islamic State (IS), we see the results of reckless arms trading over decades, and the deadly impact this has on civilians. The conflict has also highlighted the retreat of responsibility for refugee protection, as countries bickered about "border protection" and "migration management" rather than taking decisive action to save lives.

Even then, emblematic as it might have been, Syria's civil war was but one of the many conflicts that contributed to the unprecedented global number of refugees, migrants and internally displaced people. Armed conflicts continued in countries including Afghanistan, Iraq, Libya, Pakistan and Yemen. Across several borders, IS displayed a gross disregard for civilian lives, forcing thousands to flee. In Africa, state and non-state actors committed serious violations and abuses of human rights in Burundi, Cameroon, Central African Republic, northeastern Nigeria, Somalia and South Sudan, including in some cases attacks directed at civilians and civilian infrastructure. These situations have all led to significant numbers of people fleeing their homes to seek refuge elsewhere. Conflicts in Israel and the Occupied Palestinian Territories and Ukraine continued to claim civilian lives as all parties violated international humanitarian and human rights law. And while the Americas welcomed positive developments in the decades-old Colombian conflict – where, even then, accountability might be sacrificed in a political deal – violence continued to subvert human rights and institutions in countries including Brazil, Mexico and Venezuela.

That we reached this nadir in the year when the UN turned 70, its formation having beckoned nations to come together to "save succeeding generations from the scourge of war" and to "reaffirm faith in fundamental human rights", poses a simple but grim challenge: is the international system of law and institutions adequate for the urgent task of protecting human rights?

In the *Amnesty International Report* of 1977, we welcomed the first meeting of the UN Human Rights Committee, and noted that it represented one of "a number of developments at the UN in areas important to Amnesty International's human rights concerns". We added to that developments in areas such as the fight against torture. Over the years, Amnesty International has helped to foster a critical commitment to the system of international human rights law and international humanitarian law. Yet the shortcomings of that system have never been more apparent than they are today.

Among the various threats to human rights surveyed in this year's report, we highlight here two related themes. The first clear theme of the past year is that the international system was not robust in the face of hard knocks and challenges. As the cracks began to show, we realized that the system of international protection of human rights itself needs to be protected.

In 2015, there were several threats to mechanisms for human rights protection. Regional human rights protection and accountability in Africa and the Americas came under internal threat. In addition, governments in Africa hampered co-operation with the ICC while claiming to be strengthening African systems, even though they continued to fail to ensure that domestic and regional mechanisms brought justice. Emerging mechanisms in the Middle East and North Africa did not sufficiently promote a vision of universal human rights. Asia's fledgling system remained largely ineffectual. Meanwhile the European system was under threat, both from the possibility of losing the support of some states and from a massive backlog of cases requiring justice and accountability.

Multilateral protections such as the UN Refugee Convention and the UN Convention against Torture, and specialized mechanisms such as those protecting people in peril at sea, did not succeed in preventing or containing humanitarian crises, nor in protecting civilians against gross human rights violations, much less in fostering accountability for atrocities.

Barbarous attacks on people from Beirut to Bamako and Yola, from Tunis to Paris and elsewhere, also raised questions about the role of international human rights law to counter threats posed by non-state actors – violent armed groups in particular.

Amnesty International calls for a renewed commitment to the protection of the international human rights system. To make the international system adequate for its task, states must protect the system itself.

This must include voluntary restraint in the UN Security Council members' use of the veto in situations of mass atrocity crimes; effective implementation of human rights norms across all instruments of international human rights law; respect for international humanitarian law; refraining from actions that undermine human rights systems, including attacks against or withdrawal of support from them; and alignment of regional human rights mechanisms with the universal standards of the international system.

The second overriding theme of the past year is closely related. At their roots, several of the crises of the past year were set in motion by the resentments and conflicts that often follow the brutal crushing of dissent by states, or when states repress that enduring quest of every person to live in dignity with their rights upheld.

Whether it be the Andaman Sea crisis in May that saw thousands of refugees and migrants adrift at sea without food or water, or the killing and forcible disappearance of human rights defenders working to protect people's rights to land and livelihoods in Latin America and the Caribbean: in these and many other cases, the brutal repression of dissent and the denial of people's basic rights – including economic, social and cultural rights – as well as the failure by states to protect the human rights of all, often spawn societal tensions, the by-products of which, in turn, stretch international protection systems beyond their limits. The most palpable recent example of the link between system failure

and governments' repression of dissent and failure to protect human rights is the "Arab Spring", which half a decade ago changed the face of the Middle East and North Africa region.

Five years on from one of the most dynamic demonstrations of people power the world has ever seen, governments are using increasingly calculated means to crush dissent, not just in the Middle East, but globally. Particularly disconcerting is the ample evidence that repression has now become as sophisticated as it is brutal.

While 2011 saw the deaths of more than 300 people at the hands of security forces during Egypt's "January 25 revolution", and more than 50 protesters killed in Yemen's "Bloody Friday", the swing of the police truncheon in the public square may not make the news headline so readily today. Yet in this report, Amnesty International documents the continuing and widespread use of excessive force against dissenters and demonstrators, in addition to extrajudicial executions and forced disappearances, across the globe. Five years ago, systematic round-ups and torture in the Syrian town of Tell Kalakh marked an early manifestation of the backlash by states in the region against dissent and popular protest. In the intervening years, torture has continued in that part of the world, and elsewhere too, often finding cover in the lingual sophistry of so-called "enhanced interrogation techniques" – those dissembling horrors hatched before the "Arab Spring" in the context of the so-called "war on terror".

Often, repression was almost routine and, time and again, was packaged as a necessity for achieving national security, law and order, and the protection of national values. The authorities in numerous countries repressed freedom of expression online and cracked down on dissenters using a range of tools, including arbitrary arrests and detentions, torture and other ill-treatment, and the death penalty.

Meanwhile, a legal case by Amnesty International uncovered Orwellian levels of surveillance by some states, particularly focused on the lives and work of human rights defenders. Today, states' continuing development of new methods of repression to keep abreast of advancing technology and connectivity is a major threat to freedom of expression.

Following advocacy by organizations including Amnesty International, the UN mandated a new special procedure, the Special Rapporteur on the right to privacy in the digital age. The work of the Special Rapporteur will be important in the coming months to help develop clear human rights-respecting norms in this area.

The crackdown by states on dissent, protest and outspokenness has expanded since those epoch-making popular expressions of the people's voice that began five years ago. Amnesty International calls on states to respect the human rights of individuals and groups to organize, assemble and express themselves, to hold and share, through any medium, opinions that governments may disagree with, and for all to be protected equally before the law.

As well as being vital for individual freedom, rights that protect the work and space of human rights defenders do, in their turn, protect the system of human rights itself. The signs of hope that we saw in 2015 were the result of the ongoing advocacy, organizing, dissent and activism of civil society, social movements and human rights defenders.

To give just three examples from the past year: the presence of human rights and accountability elements in the UN Sustainable Development Goals; action in May to prevent forced evictions on the Regional Mombasa Port Access Road project in Kenya; and the release of Filep Karma, a Papuan prisoner of conscience in Indonesia, as a result of 65,000 messages written on his behalf by supporters from around the world.

These outcomes were not borne of the benevolence of states. Nor will, in future, such signs of hope be sustained by state actors alone. But governments must allow the space and freedom for human rights

defenders and activists to carry out their essential work. Amnesty International therefore calls upon states to ensure that the resolution adopted in November by the UN General Assembly to protect the rights of human rights defenders is implemented with accountability and transparency, including the naming and shaming of states that fail to uphold these rights.

Beyond the moment that the last full stop was inked on that resolution, not one more human rights defender, nor a member of their family, should have their life taken by a state, or be without the protection of a state. Not one more should be harassed, nor be at risk.

As the world's largest organization of human rights defenders, we present to you this report of the state of human rights during the past year. While the report captures the above themes and others, its pages cannot convey the full human misery of the topical crises of this last year, notably the refugee crisis – even now exacerbated in this northern winter. In such a situation, protecting and strengthening systems of human rights and civilian protection cannot be seen as optional. It is literally a matter of life and death.

*Salil Shetty, Secretary General*

# AFRICA REGIONAL OVERVIEW

With the African Union (AU) declaring 2016 as the Year of Human Rights in Africa, many across the continent and beyond hoped that Africa's leaders, regional institutions and the international community would show the determination and political will to make significant headway in addressing entrenched human rights challenges.

Such hopes were not without foundation. As conflict, political instability, authoritarian regimes, poverty and humanitarian disasters continued to deny many their rights, security and dignity, Africa was also presented with real opportunities. Social and economic developments were evident in many countries and relatively peaceful political transitions were achieved in others. The adoption of historic commitments regionally and globally – including the AU's Agenda 2063 and the UN Sustainable Development Goals (SDGs) – offered the potential to realize the rights enshrined in the African Charter on Human and Peoples' Rights (African Charter) and international human rights instruments.

Nevertheless, throughout 2015, serious violations and abuses of international humanitarian and human rights law in the context of conflicts remained a major challenge. Protracted conflicts in the Central African Republic (CAR), Democratic Republic of Congo (DRC), Sudan, South Sudan and Somalia caused thousands of civilian deaths and left millions living in fear and insecurity. Burundi faced a political crisis and escalating violence.

In west, central and east Africa – including in Cameroon, Chad, Kenya, Mali, Nigeria, Niger and Somalia – armed groups such as al-Shabaab and Boko Haram perpetrated constant violence, with tens of thousands of civilians killed, thousands abducted and millions forced to live in fear and insecurity, both within and outside conflicts.

Many governments responded to these security threats with disregard for international humanitarian law and human rights. Military and security operations in Nigeria and Cameroon were marked by mass arbitrary arrests, incommunicado detentions, extrajudicial executions, and torture and other ill-treatment. Similar patterns of human rights violations were observed in Niger and Chad.

Impunity remained a key cause and driver of conflicts and instability. Despite some progress, there was little or no accountability for crimes under international law committed by security forces and armed groups in countries as disparate as Cameroon, CAR, DRC, Nigeria, Somalia, South Sudan and Sudan. Internationally, some states and the AU also continued their political efforts to undermine the independence of the International Criminal Court (ICC), and to ensure immunity from prosecution for serving heads of state, even when accused of crimes against humanity and other crimes under international law. South Africa failed to arrest and surrender Sudan's President al-Bashir to the ICC in June, in a betrayal of the hundreds of thousands of victims killed during the Darfur conflict.

Many civil society organizations, human rights defenders, journalists and political opponents operated in an increasingly hostile environment, with laws aimed at restricting civic space in the name of national security, counter-terrorism, public order and regulation of NGOs and media. Civic space remained closed in countries such as Eritrea, Ethiopia and The Gambia and deteriorated in others, with freedoms of expression, association and peaceful assembly increasingly restricted. Peaceful assemblies were disrupted with brutal and excessive force, including in Angola, Burkina Faso, Burundi, Chad, the Republic of Congo, DRC, Ethiopia, Guinea, South Africa, Togo and Zimbabwe. In South Africa, excessive force was used as a "clean-up" operation to remove undocumented immigrants.

Elections and political transitions triggered widespread violations and repression. Many countries saw bans on protests, attacks on demonstrators by security forces, and arbitrary arrests and harassment of political opponents, human rights defenders and journalists.

The humanitarian crisis endured by the region continued as the Ebola epidemic that spread across West Africa in 2014 continued to claim lives in Guinea, Liberia and Sierra Leone.

Yet there were signs of hope and progress. Social and economic developments continued to unfold in many countries and offered real optimism in addressing some of the structural causes of poverty, including inequality, climate change, conflict and accountability deficits. Several states achieved some of the UN Millennium Development Goals and Africa played a critical role in the adoption of the SDGs.

Some measures taken by the AU Peace and Security Council, as well as sub-regional bodies, to address violent conflicts in the region demonstrated a growing move from indifference to engagement. Despite capacity limitations, a lack of coherent approaches and concerns about the adequacy of measures to address human rights violations and impunity, the AU and regional bodies took notable steps – from mediation to peacekeeping – in response to crises and conflicts.

Several regional human rights norms and standards were also developed. In November, the African Commission on Human and Peoples' Rights (African Commission) adopted a General Comment on Article 4 (right to life) of the African Charter. The AU Special Technical Committee on Legal Affairs (STC) also considered and approved the Draft Protocol on the Rights of Older Persons in Africa, initially developed by the African Commission. Regrettably, the STC declined to approve the Draft Protocol on the Abolition of the Death Penalty in Africa.

More countries also opened up their human rights records for review. Periodic reports on implementation of the African Charter were submitted by Algeria, Burkina Faso, Kenya, Malawi, Namibia, Nigeria and Sierra Leone.

There were reforms and positive measures in several countries. In Mauritania, a new law defined torture and slavery as a crime against humanity and banned secret detention. Sierra Leone ratified the Protocol to the African Charter on Human and Peoples' Rights on the Rights of Women in Africa. There were signs of improvement in Swaziland – including the release of prisoners of conscience and political prisoners – although repressive legislation continued to be used to suppress dissent.

A watershed moment for international justice took place in Senegal when the trial against former Chadian President Hissène Habré opened in July – the first time a court in one African state had tried the former leader of another.

## CONFLICT – COSTS AND VULNERABILITY

Violent conflicts and insecurity affected many countries, resulting in large-scale violations and characterized by lack of accountability for atrocities. Ongoing conflicts in CAR, DRC, Nigeria, Somalia, South Sudan and Sudan were marked by crimes under international law and persistent violations and abuses of humanitarian and human rights law, committed by both government forces and armed groups. Gender-based and sexual violence was widely reported and children were abducted or recruited as child soldiers.

Despite coordinated military advances against Boko Haram, the armed group continued attacking civilians in Chad, Niger, Nigeria and Cameroon. Its catalogue of abuses included suicide bomb attacks in civilian areas, summary executions, abductions, torture and recruitment of child soldiers.

The impact of Boko Haram's abuses was exacerbated by states' unlawful and heavy-handed response. Amnesty International released a report during the year outlining war crimes and possible crimes against humanity committed by the Nigerian military during its fight against Boko Haram – including more than 8,200 people murdered, starved, suffocated or tortured to death – and calling for senior members of the military to be investigated for war crimes.

In the Far North region of Cameroon, government security forces carried out mass arbitrary arrests, detentions and extrajudicial executions, as well as the enforced disappearances of at least 130 men and boys from two villages on the border with Nigeria. In Niger – where the government decreed and extended a state of emergency in the entire Diffa region, which was still in place at the end of the year – the authorities' response included extreme restrictions on movement, as well as the forced return of thousands of Nigerian refugees. In Chad, a restrictive anti-terrorism law was passed, and the security forces carried out arbitrary arrests and detentions.

A major humanitarian crisis involving mass displacement and civilian casualties continued to unfold in Sudan's armed conflicts in Darfur, South Kordofan and Blue Nile, as all parties committed violations of international humanitarian law and other violations and abuses of international human rights law. Government forces continued indiscriminate bombings, destruction of civilian settlements and obstruction of humanitarian access to civilians.

Despite the signing of a peace agreement in August, the conflict in South Sudan – characterized by deliberate attacks against civilians – continued. Both parties carried out mass killings of civilians, destruction of civilian property, obstruction of humanitarian aid, widespread gender-based and sexual violence, and recruitment of child soldiers. The AU Commission of Inquiry on South Sudan found evidence of systematic war crimes and crimes against humanity, as well as human rights violations and abuses committed by both warring parties.

Despite a de-escalation of violence since the deployment of the multidimensional UN peacekeeping operation, renewed violence and instability in CAR in September and October resulted in civilian deaths, destruction of property and displacement of more than 42,000 people. At least 500 inmates, most of them detained in relation to ongoing investigations into crimes committed in the context of the conflict, escaped from the prison in the capital, Bangui, in a mass break in September.

In central and southern Somalia, civilians continued to face indiscriminate and targeted attacks amidst continuing armed conflict between forces from the Somali Federal Government and the AU Mission in Somalia on one side and al-Shabaab on the other. All parties to the conflict committed violations of international humanitarian law and serious violations and abuses of international human rights law.

## A CRISIS FOR REFUGEES AND MIGRANTS

The bloodshed and atrocities of Africa's conflict zones played a major role in fuelling and sustaining a global refugee crisis, causing millions of women, men and children to flee from their homes in gruelling, risky and often fatal bids to reach safety in their own country or elsewhere.

The conflicts in Sudan and South Sudan alone were responsible for millions of displacements. During the year, around one-third of South Kordofan's population of approximately 1.4 million people were internally displaced, and an estimated 223,000 people were displaced in Darfur, bringing the total number of those internally displaced in the region to 2.5 million. An estimated 60,000 people were additionally displaced due to intermittent fighting between the Sudan People's Liberation Army (SPLA)-North and government forces in Blue Nile state.

A further 2.2 million people were displaced by the conflict in South Sudan during the year, with 3.9 million people facing severe food insecurity.

Huge numbers of people were internally displaced or became refugees after fleeing areas affected by violence from Boko Haram. In Nigeria alone, more than two million people have been forced to flee their homes since 2009. Hundreds of thousands of refugees from Nigeria and CAR were living in harsh conditions in crowded camps in Cameroon and Niger, where in May government forces of Niger and Cameroon forced thousands of refugees back to Nigeria, accusing them of bringing Boko Haram attacks to the area. In Chad, hundreds of thousands of refugees from Nigeria, CAR, Sudan and Libya continued to live in difficult conditions in crowded refugee camps.

More than 1.3 million Somalis were internally displaced during the year. Globally, there were more than 1.1 million Somali refugees. Yet states hosting Somali asylum-seekers and refugees – including Saudi Arabia, Sweden, the Netherlands, Norway, the UK and Denmark – continued to pressure Somalis to return to Somalia, claiming that security had improved in the country.

Kenya's government threatened to close Dadaab, the world's largest refugee camp, presenting the move as a security measure following an attack by al-Shabaab. Against a backdrop of harassment of Somali and other refugees by Kenyan security services, the authorities threatened to forcibly return around 350,000 refugees to Somalia. This would put thousands of lives at risk and violate Kenya's obligations under international law.

Countless numbers of refugees and migrants – displaced not only by conflict but also by political persecution or the need to secure a better livelihood – faced intolerance, xenophobia, abuses and violations. Many languished in camps that failed to provide proper access to water, food, health care, sanitation or education, and many fell prey to human trafficking networks.

More than 230,000 people fled Burundi's deteriorating political, social and economic situation to neighbouring countries. Thousands continued to flee Eritrea to escape indefinite National Service, which amounts to forced labour. Eritreans caught trying to escape the country were arbitrarily detained without charge or trial, frequently in harsh conditions and without access to lawyers. A "shoot to kill" policy was in place for anyone

evading capture and trying to cross into Ethiopia. Those who managed to leave Eritrea faced numerous dangers on routes through Sudan, Libya and the Mediterranean to reach Europe, including hostage-taking for ransom by armed groups and criminal gangs.

In Malawi, unregistered migrants were kept in detention beyond the expiry of their custodial sentences, with limited prospect of being released or deported. At least 100 such detainees, mostly from Ethiopia, were held in overcrowded prisons at the end of the year.

An ongoing failure by the South African government to establish a systematic programme of prevention and protection resulted in widespread and violent xenophobic attacks against migrants and refugees, including on their businesses.

## IMPUNITY FOR CRIMES UNDER INTERNATIONAL LAW

Impunity for serious human rights violations and abuses – especially those committed in the context of armed conflicts – continued to deprive people of truth and justice, and contributed to further instability and abuses. Most governments – including in Cameroon, CAR, Nigeria, Somalia, South Sudan and Sudan – showed little progress towards tackling the entrenched accountability gap, with those suspected of responsibility for crimes under international law rarely held to account.

Despite promises by Nigeria's new President to investigate crimes under international law and other serious human rights violations and abuses committed by the military and Boko Haram, no meaningful action was taken. The government failed to hold its own forces to account, and prosecuted few people suspected of being Boko Haram members. However, the Office of the Prosecutor of the ICC identified eight potential cases involving crimes against humanity and war crimes: six involving Boko Haram and two involving the Nigerian security forces.

Despite the publication on 26 October of the report by the AU Commission of Inquiry on South Sudan, and the signing of a peace agreement in August which laid the foundation for the AU's decision to set up a hybrid court, there was no progress towards its establishment. The Hybrid Court on South Sudan was announced as an African-led and Africa-owned legal mechanism.

In April, CAR's National Transitional Council took a positive step towards establishing an accountability mechanism by adopting a law to establish a Special Criminal Court. There was little progress in establishing the Court, however, which is expected to investigate and prosecute those responsible for war crimes and crimes against humanity committed in the country since 2003.

South Africa's government failed to fulfil its international legal obligations in June when Sudan's President al-Bashir – visiting Johannesburg for an AU Summit – was allowed to leave the country. Two open ICC arrest warrants had been laid against him for his alleged role in genocide, crimes against humanity and war crimes in Darfur, and a court order from South Africa's high court also prohibited him from leaving. South Africa's failure to act saw it join a long list of states that have failed to arrest and surrender President al-Bashir to the ICC to face trial. In a worrying development, the African National Congress was reported to have resolved in October that South Africa should withdraw from the ICC. No steps had been taken by the end of the year.

President Ouattara of Côte d'Ivoire stated in April that there would be no more transfers to the ICC, despite the ICC's outstanding arrest warrant for former First Lady Simone Gbagbo for alleged crimes against humanity.

Some states and the AU continued with political efforts to interfere with or undermine the independence of the ICC, and to ensure immunity from prosecution for serving heads of state even when accused of crimes against humanity and other international crimes. The AU Assembly adopted a resolution in June which reiterated its previous calls for termination or suspension of ICC proceedings against Deputy President Ruto of Kenya and President al-Bashir of Sudan. In November, Kenya's government attempted to influence the 14th session of the Assembly of States Parties (ASP) – the political oversight body of the ICC – as part of its attempt to undermine the trial of Deputy President Ruto, by threatening to withdraw from the ICC. The government of Namibia also threatened to withdraw from the ICC in November.

More positively, the DRC took a significant step in November when the Senate voted in favour of adopting domestic legislation for implementation of the Rome Statute of the ICC. During the $14^{th}$ session of the ASP in November, many African states parties to the Rome Statute of the ICC voiced strong commitment to the ICC and denied support to proposals that could undermine its independence.

A significant step towards justice for victims of the Lord's Resistance Army (LRA) was achieved in January following the transfer of Dominic Ongwen, alleged former LRA commander, to the ICC. The beginning in July of the trial of Hissène Habré in Senegal – with the accused charged with crimes against humanity, torture and war crimes committed during his tenure between 1982 and 1990 – was a major positive development in Africa's long fight against impunity.

## REPRESSION OF DISSENT IN THE CONTEXT OF ELECTIONS AND TRANSITIONS

Fifteen general or presidential elections took place across the continent during the year, many forming the backdrop for human rights violations and restrictions. In countries including Burundi, the Republic of Congo, Côte d'Ivoire, DRC, Ethiopia, Guinea, Sudan, Tanzania, Togo, Uganda and Zambia there were bans on protests, attacks on demonstrators, and arbitrary arrests of political opponents, human rights defenders and journalists.

Ethiopia's general election in May was marred by restrictions on civil society observing the elections, use of excessive force against peaceful demonstrators, and harassment of political opposition observers. Security officers beat, injured and killed people at polling stations, and four members and leaders of political opposition parties were extrajudicially executed.

In Guinea, tensions around the electoral process led to violence between supporters of different political parties, and between protesters and security forces, the latter often using excessive and lethal force to police demonstrations.

Presidential and parliamentary elections in Sudan saw President al-Bashir re-elected amid reports of fraud and vote-rigging, with low voter turnout and opposition political parties boycotting the elections. Sudan's authorities intensified their suppression of freedom of expression as the elections approached, repressing the media, civil society and opposition political parties, and arresting dozens of political opponents.

In countries including Burkina Faso, Burundi, DRC and the Republic of Congo, attempts by political incumbents to stay in power for a third term sparked protests and subsequent state violence. In Burundi, protests were violently suppressed by the security forces and there was a marked increase in torture and other ill-treatment, especially against those opposed to President Nkurunziza's re-election bid. From September onwards, the situation deteriorated even further; killings on a near-daily basis, including extrajudicial executions, and arbitrary arrests and disappearances became routine. More than 400 people were killed between April and December.

In Burkina Faso in September, members of the Presidential Guard (RSP) attempted a coup and took political leaders hostage, including the President and Prime Minister, triggering public protests. Before being forced to withdraw by the army, the RSP used excessive and sometimes lethal force in a bid to suppress protests.

In The Gambia, relatives of those suspected of involvement in a failed coup in December 2014 were arbitrarily arrested and detained by law enforcement agencies. Three soldiers suspected of being involved were sentenced to death. Political instability in Lesotho continued following an attempted coup in 2014.

Dissent and basic human rights were suppressed in DRC and Uganda, linked to presidential elections scheduled for 2016. As pressure intensified on the DRC President Kabila to not seek another term after 14 years in power, the authorities increasingly targeted human rights defenders and journalists and violently disrupted demonstrations. In Uganda – where President Museveni will seek a fifth term in office in elections due in February 2016 – police arbitrarily arrested political opposition leaders, including presidential candidates, and used excessive force to disperse peaceful political gatherings.

## SHRINKING CIVIC SPACE AND ATTACKS ON HUMAN RIGHTS DEFENDERS

Outside the context of elections, many governments stifled dissent and muzzled rights to freedom of expression. Peaceful assemblies were often disrupted with excessive force. Many civil society organizations and human rights defenders faced an increasingly hostile environment, including through use of laws aimed at restricting civic space.

Such patterns of increasing restrictions took place in a wide spectrum of countries, including Angola, Burundi, Cameroon, Chad, the Republic of Congo, Côte d'Ivoire, Equatorial Guinea, Gambia, Kenya, Lesotho, Mauritania, Niger, Rwanda, Senegal, Sierra Leone, Somalia, Swaziland, Togo, Uganda, Zambia and Zimbabwe.

In Angola, there was an increase in crackdown on dissent and outright violations of fundamental freedoms, including through the arbitrary detention of activists peacefully calling for public accountability of leadership.

In Eritrea, thousands of prisoners of conscience continued to suffer arbitrary detentions. There was no space for opposition political parties, activism, independent media or academic freedom.

In South Sudan, the space for journalists,

human rights defenders and civil society to operate without intimidation or fear continued to decline significantly.

Restrictions on the rights to freedoms of expression, association and assembly increased in Mauritania, and activists were jailed for holding anti-slavery rallies. Senegal's authorities continued to ban demonstrations by supporters of political parties and human rights defenders, and to prosecute peaceful demonstrators.

In Tanzania, journalists faced harassment, intimidation and arrests. Four bills were introduced to Parliament that collectively codified unwarranted restrictions to freedom of expression.

In Zambia, police continued to implement the Public Order Act, restricting freedom of assembly. Zimbabwe's authorities gagged freedom of expression, including through crackdowns involving arrests, surveillance, harassment and intimidation of those campaigning for the licensing of community radio stations.

## DISCRIMINATION AND MARGINALIZATION

Although 2015 was the AU's "Year of Women's Empowerment and Development towards Africa's Agenda 2063", women and girls frequently suffered abuse, discrimination and marginalization in many countries – often because of cultural traditions and norms, and the institutionalization of gender-based discrimination through unjust laws. In conflicts and countries hosting large numbers of displaced people and refugees, women and girls were subjected to rape and other forms of sexual violence. Positively, countries including Burkina Faso, Madagascar and Zimbabwe launched national campaigns to end child marriages.

Abuses – including persecution and criminalization – of people who are or are perceived to be lesbian, gay, bisexual, transgender and intersex (LGBTI) were ongoing in many countries, including Cameroon, Nigeria, Senegal and South Africa.

Malawi accepted a UN Universal Periodic Review recommendation to take measures to protect LGBTI people against violence and to prosecute the perpetrators, and agreed to guarantee effective access to health services. However, it rejected recommendations to repeal provisions in the Penal Code criminalizing consensual same-sex conduct between adults.

The African Commission granted observer status to the South Africa-based LGBTI rights organization, the Coalition of African Lesbians (CAL), during its 56th Ordinary Session held in The Gambia. However, at a subsequent AU Summit in South Africa, the Executive Council of the AU declined to approve the Commission's activity report until it withdrew the observer status granted to CAL – raising fears that the Commission may be forced to withdraw the decision.

Despite condemnation by the President, there was a sharp increase in killings and other attacks on people with albinism in Malawi by individuals and gangs seeking body parts to sell for use in witchcraft. In Tanzania, the government failed to ensure adequate safety measures for people living with albinism; a young girl was reportedly killed for body parts, and reported cases involved abduction, mutilation and dismemberment.

## LOOKING AHEAD

Events throughout the year demonstrated the extent and depth of Africa's human rights challenges, as well as the urgent need for international and regional institutions to protect millions of lives and to address the global refugee crisis by taking a stronger, clearer and more consistent approach to tackling conflict.

The year also underlined the desperate need for African states to tackle impunity at home and abroad – including by withdrawing from politicized attacks on the ICC. Effective accountability for human rights violations and crimes under international law could be transformative for countries across Africa.

Alongside the Year of Human Rights in Africa, 2016 will mark the 35th anniversary of the adoption of the African Charter, the 30th anniversary of the Charter's entry into force and the 10<sup>th</sup> anniversary of the establishment of the African Court. With such auspicious anniversaries looming, the challenge for most African leaders is to listen to and work with the continent's growing human rights movement.

# AMERICAS REGIONAL OVERVIEW

Events in 2015 underscored the magnitude of the human rights crisis facing the Americas region. A mix of discrimination, violence, inequality, conflict, insecurity, poverty, environmental damage and failure to ensure justice for violations of human rights threatened the protection of human rights and fundamental freedoms in the region.

Although most states supported and ratified human rights standards and treaties, the promise of rights remained hollow for millions, confirming a two-year trend of regression on human rights.

A pervasive culture of impunity allowed perpetrators of human rights abuses to operate without fear of the consequences, denied truth and redress to millions, and weakened the rule of law. Impunity was frequently sustained by weak, under-resourced and corrupt security and justice systems, compounded by a lack of political will to ensure their independence and impartiality.

Throughout the year, the authorities repeatedly relied on a militaristic response to social and political problems, including the growing influence of criminal networks and the impact of multinational corporations on people's rights.

At the same time, levels of lethal violence across the region remained extremely high. Latin America and the Caribbean were home to eight of the 10 most violent countries in the world, and four of these – Brazil, Colombia, Mexico and Venezuela – accounted for one in four violent killings worldwide. Only 20 out of 100 homicides in Latin America resulted in a conviction; in some countries, the share was even lower. Violent crime was particularly widespread in El Salvador, Guyana, Honduras, Jamaica, Trinidad and Tobago and Venezuela.

The increasing influence of transnational corporations and their involvement in human rights abuses – especially in the extractive and other industries related to the appropriation of territory and natural resources, mainly in land claimed by and belonging to Indigenous Peoples, other ethnic minorities and peasant farmers – continued to threaten human rights across the region.

A growing number of socio-environmental conflicts bred violence and human rights violations. Human rights defenders and activists working to protect land, territory and natural resources were increasingly exposed to killings, enforced disappearance and other criminal acts. In Honduras, local civil society organizations faced violent attacks and threats by private security guards with ties to powerful landowners. In Brazil, dozens of people were killed in conflicts over land and natural resources.

Discussions at the Organization of American States (OAS) to finalize a proposed American Declaration on the Rights of Indigenous Peoples were hampered by barriers to the effective participation of Indigenous Peoples and by some states' efforts to weaken the draft. Indigenous representatives withdrew from negotiations after several states insisted on the inclusion of provisions that would, in practice, endorse national laws that disregard the protection of Indigenous Peoples' rights.

Meanwhile, insecurity, violence and economic hardship in Mexico and Central America drove a growing number of people, in particular unaccompanied children, to leave their homes and cross borders in search of better living conditions and an escape from violence.

Human rights defenders continued to be targeted for their work. Standing up for human rights was often a dangerous and even lethal choice, as many governments oversaw an erosion of civic space and the criminalization of dissent.

Unfolding human rights crises at the national level included Mexico, which was plagued by thousands of complaints of torture and other ill-treatment and reports of extrajudicial executions; the whereabouts of at least 27,000 people remained unknown at the end of the year. Although September marked the first anniversary of the enforced disappearance of 43 students from the Ayotzinapa teacher training college, one of Mexico's most alarming human rights violations in recent history, investigations remained flawed.

In Venezuela, a year after huge demonstrations that left 43 people dead, hundreds injured and dozens tortured or otherwise ill-treated, no one had been found guilty of the crimes committed – nor had charges been dropped against those arbitrarily detained by the authorities. Despite a reduction in protests at the end of the year, the government's intolerance of dissent often led to human rights defenders facing threats, harassment and attacks, and security forces continued to use excessive force to suppress protests. Attacks on opposition politicians and activists raised concerns about the fairness of congressional elections. Luis Manuel Diaz, a local opposition politician in Guárico state, was shot dead during a rally before the elections.

The situation of sexual and reproductive rights in Paraguay, particularly the case of a 10-year-old girl who became pregnant after being repeatedly raped – allegedly by her stepfather – attracted global attention, underscoring the need to repeal the country's draconian anti-abortion law. The authorities refused to allow an abortion, despite evidence that the girl's life was at risk from the pregnancy.

The human rights situation in Cuba was at a crossroads. The year was marked by warming international relations – with the country taking part in the Summit of the Americas for the first time, as well as historic meetings between the Cuban and US presidents and a state visit by Pope Francis – and advances such as the release of prisoners of conscience. Yet the authorities stifled dissent and continued to arbitrarily detain thousands of people simply for expressing their views peacefully.

In Brazil, infrastructure construction for the 2016 Olympic Games led to ongoing evictions of people from their homes in Rio de Janeiro, often without adequate notification, financial compensation or resettlement.

The year saw positive developments too. In Colombia, peace talks between the government and the Revolutionary Armed Forces of Colombia (FARC) continued to make significant progress, raising expectations that the country's 50-year-long armed conflict may soon end.

Jamaica's government finally established a Commission of Enquiry into human rights violations committed during the 2010 state of emergency, when security forces killed 76 people, including 44 who were alleged to have been extrajudicially executed. The President of Peru ratified a national mechanism for the prevention of torture and set up a national register of victims of forced sterilization during the 1990s.

The USA accepted many recommendations made under the UN Universal Periodic Review (UPR) process following an examination of its human rights record, repeating that it supported calls for the closure of the US detention centre in Guantánamo Bay, Cuba, for the ratification of the UN Convention on the Rights of the Child and the UN Convention on the Elimination of All Forms of Discrimination against Women (CEDAW), and for accountability for torture. However, none of the recommendations had been implemented at the end of the year.

## PUBLIC SECURITY AND HUMAN RIGHTS

Increasing violence and influence of non-state actors – including criminal networks and transnational corporations operating with impunity – continued to challenge governments' ability to protect human rights. Efforts to control criminal networks, including the occasional use of armed forces, led to grave human rights violations and undue restrictions on freedoms of expression and peaceful assembly.

Excessive use of force by the police and

other security forces was reported in countries including the Bahamas, Brazil, Chile, the Dominican Republic, Ecuador, Guyana, Jamaica, Trinidad and Tobago and Venezuela.

Brazil's security forces often used excessive or unnecessary force to suppress protests. Killings during police operations remained high and were rarely investigated; a lack of transparency often made it impossible to ascertain the exact number of people killed. Off-duty police officers reportedly carried out unlawful killings as part of death squads operating in several cities. In Mexico, a number of reported shoot-outs involving the police or military showed signs of extrajudicial executions.

Nationwide anti-government protests in Ecuador throughout the year were marked by clashes between the security forces – who reportedly used excessive force and made arbitrary arrests – and protesters.

In Peru, people opposing extractive industry projects were victims of intimidation, excessive use of force and arbitrary arrests. Seven protesters were shot and killed in circumstances suggesting that security officials used excessive force.

Across the USA, at least 43 people died after police used Tasers on them. There were protests at the excessive use of force by police in a number of cities. The authorities again failed to track the exact number of people killed by law enforcement officials each year.

In Venezuela, public security operations to tackle high crime rates raised concerns of excessive use of force, including possible extrajudicial executions, as well as arbitrary arrests and forced evictions of suspected criminals and their families.

## ACCESS TO JUSTICE AND THE FIGHT TO END IMPUNITY

The denial of meaningful access to justice for scores of people seriously undermined human rights, particularly among deprived and marginalized communities.

Impunity was pervasive in Honduras,

fostered by an ineffective criminal justice system that – together with corruption and human rights violations by police officers – created a lack of trust in law enforcement and justice institutions. The government announced it would tackle corruption and impunity by forming an initiative with the OAS to reform the justice system.

In Chile, cases of police violence and human rights violations involving members of the security forces continued to be investigated by military courts, despite concerns about the impartiality and independence of such tribunals and commitments by the authorities to reform the military justice system.

There was an ongoing lack of political will to confront unresolved human rights violations, including thousands of political killings and enforced disappearances in the second half of the 20th century, and to ensure the rights to truth, justice and reparation.

In Bolivia, measures to ensure truth, justice and full reparation for victims of human rights violations during past military and authoritarian regimes were limited, although the authorities committed to creating a truth commission. Public trials were held in Argentina for crimes against humanity perpetrated during the military regime of 1976-1983, with eight new convictions handed down. However, those from the civil, business and legal sectors who were complicit in human rights violations and crimes under international law had yet to be brought to justice.

In Chile, there were over 1,000 active cases of human rights violations committed in the past; victims' organizations condemned the slow progress in establishing the truth about thousands of victims of enforced disappearance. However, charges were brought against several former military officers, including for the abduction and killing of singer and political activist Victor Jara in 1973.

A Guatemala City appeals court declared that a 1986 amnesty decree did not apply to crimes against humanity and genocide in

Guatemala, meaning that a case against former President and army commander-in-chief José Efraín Rios Montt could proceed.

In Panama, the trial of former President Manuel Noriega for the enforced disappearance of Heliodoro Portugal was suspended after Manuel Noriega's lawyer appealed against his charge, arguing that the trial would violate the terms of his extradition. It was unclear whether the trial would proceed.

In Haiti, after the death in 2014 of former President Jean-Claude Duvalier, an investigation into allegations of crimes against humanity committed during his tenure (1971-1986) made little progress.

## TORTURE AND OTHER ILL-TREATMENT

Despite strong anti-torture laws and mechanisms across the region, torture and other ill-treatment remained widespread; the authorities failed to prosecute perpetrators or to provide adequate reparation to victims. Cruel, inhuman and degrading treatment was common in prisons or at the time of arrest, and was mainly used against criminal suspects to inflict punishment or to extract confessions.

In Argentina, reports of torture – including beatings with cattle prods, near asphyxiation with plastic bags, submersion and prolonged isolation – were not investigated and there was no system in place to protect witnesses. Torture victims in Bolivia were deterred from seeking justice and reparation due to the lack of an independent mechanism to record and investigate allegations of abuse.

Mexico came under international scrutiny in March, when the UN Special Rapporteur on torture and other cruel, inhuman or degrading treatment or punishment presented a report to the UN Human Rights Council, detailing the generalized nature of torture and the impunity among police and other security forces.

Torture and other ill-treatment were endemic in Brazil's prisons, including against boys and girls.

Prison conditions – including overcrowding, violence and a lack of food and water – were particularly harsh in the Bahamas, Bolivia, Brazil, Haiti, Jamaica, the USA and Venezuela.

## REFUGEES, ASYLUM-SEEKERS AND MIGRANTS

In an escalating humanitarian crisis, migrants and refugees – especially large numbers of unaccompanied children and adolescents – crossing Central America and Mexico faced serious human rights violations as they attempted to gain entry to the USA, and were often detained in harsh conditions. They were frequently killed, abducted or faced extortion by criminal gangs, who often operated in collusion with the authorities. Women and girls were at particular risk of sexual violence and human trafficking.

In the USA, tens of thousands of families and unaccompanied children were apprehended when attempting to cross the southern border during the year. Families were detained for months – many in facilities lacking proper access to medical care, sanitation, water and legal counsel – as they pursued claims to remain in the country.

Elsewhere, migrants and their descendants faced pervasive discrimination, with states doing little to tackle entrenched exclusion.

Despite the implementation of a law intended to address their situation, many people of Haitian descent in the Dominican Republic remained stateless after their Dominican nationality had been arbitrarily and retroactively removed by a Constitutional Court judgment in 2013. After the Dominican authorities announced that deportations of irregular migrants would resume in June, tens of thousands of Haitian migrants decided to return to Haiti, mainly for fear of violence, expulsion or xenophobic behaviour from employers or neighbours; hundreds settled in makeshift camps at the border.

In the Bahamas, there were allegations of arbitrary arrests and abuses against migrants. Parliament approved migration reforms that could potentially prevent the children of irregular migrants born in the Bahamas from obtaining Bahamian nationality, at the risk of rendering individuals stateless.

In July, the UN Human Rights Committee called on Canada to report back within a year on a range of human rights concerns relating to migrants and refugees. In a positive development, the new government announced that cuts to the Interim Federal Health Program for refugees and asylum-seekers would be reversed and health coverage restored.

Nearly 2,000 Colombian nationals – including refugees and asylum-seekers – were deported from Venezuela in August, with no opportunity to challenge their expulsion or gather their belongings. In some cases children were separated from parents. Scores of people were forcibly evicted or had their houses destroyed, and some detainees were ill-treated.

In December, the Inter-American Commission on Human Rights expressed concern over the vulnerability of more than 4,500 Cuban migrants stranded on the Costa Rica-Nicaragua border, amid allegations of abuses by Nicaraguan authorities; the Commission called on Central American states to allow safe and legal migration to Cubans travelling overland to the USA.

## INDIGENOUS PEOPLES' RIGHTS

Even though every state in the region has endorsed the 2007 UN Declaration on the Rights of Indigenous Peoples, human rights violations – including attacks, excessive use of force and killings – remained a daily reality for Indigenous Peoples across the region, threatening their rights over their land, territory and natural resources, their culture and even their own existence.

Poverty, exclusion, inequality and discrimination continued to affect thousands, including in Argentina, Bolivia, Canada, Chile, Colombia, Mexico, Paraguay and Peru. State and non-state actors – including businesses and landowners – continued to forcibly displace Indigenous Peoples from their own lands in the pursuit of economic development.

Development projects, including by the extractive industry, saw Indigenous Peoples repeatedly denied meaningful consultation and free, prior and informed consent, which threatened their culture and environment and led to the forced displacement of entire communities.

Attacks on members of Indigenous communities in Brazil were widespread and those responsible were rarely brought to justice. An amendment to the Constitution which transferred responsibility for demarcating Indigenous land from the executive to the legislative branch of the government threatened to have a negative impact on Indigenous Peoples' access to land. The amendment was pending approval by the Senate at the end of the year.

Paraguay's Supreme Court rejected a second attempt by a landowner to nullify the country's 2014 expropriation law, which was passed to return their land to the Sawhoyamaxa community. A resolution to a complaint filed by the community against the occupation of their land by the landowner's employees was still pending at the end of the year.

Ecuador's authorities failed to fully implement the 2012 ruling of the Inter-American Court of Human Rights in favour of the Kichwa People of Sarayaku, including the complete removal of explosives left on their land and the issuing of legislation to regulate Indigenous Peoples' right to free, prior and informed consent over laws, policies and measures that affect their livelihoods.

## HUMAN RIGHTS DEFENDERS AT RISK

Across the region, a pattern of threats and attacks against human rights defenders, lawyers, judges, witnesses and journalists continued, and there was an increasing trend of judicial systems being misused to repress human rights defenders. Progress in investigating such abuses or bringing perpetrators to justice was rare.

Being a human rights defender carried with it the risk of abuses and violence in many countries in the Americas. Those taking action to tackle impunity and defend women's and Indigenous Peoples' rights were at particular risk of reprisals.

Human rights defenders in Colombia were at serious risk of attack, mainly by paramilitaries.

In Venezuela, human rights defenders routinely faced verbal attacks from the authorities. Cuba's authorities imposed severe restrictions on basic freedoms, with thousands of reported cases of harassment of government critics as well as arbitrary arrests and detentions. Human rights defenders and others who openly criticized government policies in Ecuador faced attacks, fines and unfounded criminal charges; media outlets continued to receive fines under a communication law that was potentially being used to undermine freedom of expression. Authorities in Bolivia discredited the work of NGOs, including human rights defenders, and also applied strict regulation for NGOs to obtain registration.

Human rights defenders in Guatemala – especially Indigenous leaders and protesters defending environmental and land rights and opposing hydroelectric and mining megaprojects – faced continuous attacks, threats, harassment and intimidation.

In Honduras, against the backdrop of a general climate of violence and crimes, human rights defenders – particularly women – faced threats and attacks which were rarely investigated, as well as judicial harassment. Congress approved a law which could be an important step to protect human rights defenders and journalists, among other groups, although a group of civil society organizations expressed concerns about the vagueness and lack of transparency of the draft implementation regulations, and asked for the approval to be postponed by several months.

Measures to protect human rights defenders were often weakly applied or ignored entirely. Brazil's National Programme for the Protection of Human Rights Defenders failed to deliver the protection promised in its provisions, and its implementation was hampered by insufficient resources. Cases of threats, attacks and killings targeting human rights defenders went largely uninvestigated and unpunished. In Mexico, the federal Mechanism for the Protection of Human Rights Defenders and Journalists lacked resources and co-ordination, leaving human rights defenders and journalists inadequately protected; impunity for attacks and violence remained.

## RIGHTS OF WOMEN AND GIRLS

A pattern of increasing violence against women continued to be one of the principal human rights challenges across the region. Little progress was made in addressing this, with states failing to prioritize the protection of women and girls from rape, threats and killings and to hold perpetrators to account. Legislation was slow to be implemented.

High levels of gender-based violence were reported in Guatemala, Guyana, El Salvador, Jamaica and Trinidad and Tobago, among other countries. Implementation of 2007 legislation criminalizing such abuses in Venezuela remained slow, due to a lack of resources. In the USA, Native American and Alaska Native women continued to experience disproportionate levels of violence, being 2.5 times more likely to be raped or sexually assaulted than other women in the country. In El Salvador, 475 women were murdered between January and October – an increase from 294 in 2014.

Violations of sexual and reproductive rights had a significant impact on women's and girls' health. By the end of the year, seven countries in the region – Chile, the Dominican Republic, El Salvador, Haiti, Honduras, Suriname and Nicaragua – still had a total ban on abortion, or lacked an explicit legal provision to protect the woman's life. In Chile, a bill to decriminalize abortion under certain circumstances was pending before Congress at the end of the year. In the Dominican Republic, the Constitutional Court struck down reforms to the Penal Code which decriminalized abortion in certain cases. In Peru, a bill to decriminalize abortion for victims of rape was rejected by a congressional constitutional commission.

In Argentina, women and girls faced obstacles in accessing legal abortion. In Brazil, new legislation and constitutional amendments threatened sexual and reproductive rights and women's rights. Some bills proposed to criminalize abortion in all circumstances, or would effectively prevent access to safe and legal abortion.

Even when access to abortion services was legal in certain cases in other countries, protracted judicial procedures made access to safe abortion virtually impossible, particularly for those unable to pay for private abortion services. Restricted access to contraception and information on sexual and reproductive issues remained a concern, especially for the most marginalized women and girls.

In Bolivia, high rates of maternal mortality, particularly in rural areas, remained a concern.

All parties to the conflict in Colombia – security forces, paramilitaries and guerilla groups – were responsible for crimes of sexual violence; very few of the alleged perpetrators were brought to justice.

## RIGHTS OF LESBIAN, GAY, BISEXUAL, TRANSGENDER AND INTERSEX PEOPLE

LGBTI people faced ongoing discrimination and violence across the region, despite progress in some countries on legislation prohibiting discrimination on the grounds of sexual orientation and gender identity.

There were violent and unresolved murders of several transgender women in Argentina, as well as reports of hate crimes – including murder and rape – against LGBTI people in the Dominican Republic. Violence and discrimination towards LGBTI people remained a concern in El Salvador, Guyana, Honduras, Trinidad and Tobago, and Venezuela.

Consensual sex between men remained criminalized in Jamaica, where homelessness and displacement of LGBTI youths and a failure to investigate threats and harassment against LGBTI people persisted. However, in a positive development, a gay pride celebration was held for the first time, with the Minister of Justice calling for tolerance during the event and expressing his support for the right of LGBTI people to express themselves peacefully.

## ARMED CONFLICT

In Colombia, ongoing peace talks between the government and the FARC offered the best chance in more than a decade to put a definitive end to the region's longest-running internal armed conflict. However, during the year both sides committed crimes under international law as well as serious human rights violations and abuses, principally against Indigenous Peoples, Afro-descendant and peasant farmer communities, and human rights defenders.

Security forces, guerrilla groups and paramilitaries perpetrated unlawful killings, forced displacement, enforced disappearances, death threats and crimes of sexual violence with almost total impunity. Children continued to be recruited as combatants by guerrilla groups and paramilitaries. Relatives of victims of human rights violations who campaigned for justice, as well as members of human rights organizations helping them, faced death threats and other serious human rights abuses.

A ceasefire by the FARC from July and the government's suspension of aerial bombardments against FARC positions seemed to alleviate some of the worst effects of the conflict on civilians in rural areas.

In September, the two sides announced they had reached an agreement on transitional justice and announced that a peace deal would be signed by March 2016. However, doubts remained over whether the agreement, which was not made public until December – coupled with legislation that could enable suspected human rights abusers to evade justice – would guarantee victims' right to truth, justice and reparation in line with international law.

## COUNTER-TERROR AND SECURITY

By the end of the year, no one had been brought to justice for human rights violations – including torture and other ill-treatment as well as enforced disappearance – committed in the secret detention and interrogation programme operated by the Central Intelligence Agency (CIA) after the 11 September 2001 attacks in the USA.

Over a year after the publication of the declassified summary of a report by the Senate Select Committee on Intelligence into the CIA programme, the full report remained top secret, thus facilitating impunity. Most, if not all, of the detainees held as part of the programme were subjected to enforced disappearance and to conditions of detention and/or interrogation techniques which violated the prohibition of torture and other cruel, inhuman or degrading treatment.

Detainees were still held at Guantánamo, most of them without charge or trial and some still facing trial by military commission, under a system falling short of international fair trial standards.

## DEATH PENALTY

The USA was once again the only country in the region to carry out executions. Yet there were signs that the worldwide trend towards abolition of capital punishment was slowly but steadily gaining ground there too. The Nebraska legislature voted to abolish the death penalty, although the repeal was on hold at the end of the year after opponents petitioned to have the issue put to the popular vote in 2016. Pennsylvania's state governor announced a moratorium on executions; moratoriums also remained in force in Washington State and Oregon.

# ASIA-PACIFIC REGIONAL OVERVIEW

Even as rapid social and economic change continued in the Asia-Pacific region, the human rights situation often remained bleak. The increasing trend towards repression and injustice threatened the protection of human rights in the region.

A recurring and central threat to people's rights was states' failure to ensure accountability, with impunity often entrenched and widespread, denying justice and sustaining human rights violations including torture and other ill-treatment. Impunity also fuelled suffering in armed conflicts, such as in Afghanistan and Myanmar, and perpetuated injustice by failing to ensure reparations for past conflicts, as in Indonesia.

In many countries there was a serious disconnect between governments and the people. People, particularly youth, frequently felt newly empowered to speak out for their rights, often aided by affordable communications technologies and platforms, including social media. Governments, in contrast, often sought to shield themselves from accountability or criticism, while some – such as those of China, Cambodia, India, Malaysia, Thailand and Viet Nam – intensified their crackdown on key freedoms. Severe restrictions on the rights to freedom of expression, association and peaceful assembly continued in Laos, where authorities further tightened control of civil society groups.

Despite a global trend towards abolition, the death penalty also continued in several countries in the region, including extensively in China and Pakistan. Indonesia resumed executions, Maldives threatened to do so, and there was a surge of executions in Pakistan after a moratorium on the execution of civilians was lifted in December 2014.

However, there were also some positive steps as Fiji became the world's 100th fully abolitionist country and Mongolia's parliament passed a new criminal code removing the death penalty for all crimes.

Millions of refugees and asylum-seekers faced harsh conditions across the Asia-Pacific region, and countries as disparate as Australia and China violated international law by forcibly returning people to countries where they would face a real risk of serious violations. A major humanitarian and human rights crisis occurred in the Bay of Bengal and Andaman Sea, where people smugglers and traffickers abandoned thousands of refugees and migrants at sea, with states initially turning them away or being slow to mount search and rescue operations.

Specifically, in Nepal the devastating earthquake of 25 April and its aftershocks caused more than 8,000 deaths and 22,000 injuries, and displaced more than 100,000 people. The government refused to waive costly and time-consuming customs duties and procedures for health and relief supplies, leaving thousands in desperate need. A new Constitution, rushed through in the earthquake's aftermath, was marked by human rights shortcomings. A federalist structure was rejected by ethnic groups, leading to violent protests and confrontations. The security forces resorted to excessive, unnecessary or disproportionate force in several clashes with protesters, leading to dozens of deaths.

Extreme repression and systematic violation of almost all human rights overshadowed life in the Democratic People's Republic of Korea (North Korea), and those who fled the country reported an increase in arbitrary arrests. Reduced daily rations severely threatened the right to adequate food, and hundreds of thousands of people continued to languish in prison camps and detention facilities where torture and other ill-treatment was widespread and forced labour routine.

China's geopolitical influence continued to grow, but an appalling internal human rights situation prevailed. Under the pretext of enhancing national security, the government increased repression by drafting or enacting an unprecedented series of laws and regulations with the potential to silence dissent and crack down on human rights defenders. The authorities also stepped up their controls over the internet, mass media and academia.

The run-up to Myanmar's general elections in November – the first since a quasi-civilian government came to power in 2011 after almost five decades of military rule – was marred by the political disenfranchisement of minority groups, in particular the persecuted Rohingya, and ongoing conflicts in northern Myanmar. Nevertheless, the landslide election victory for the National League for Democracy, led by former prisoner of conscience Aung San Suu Kyi, was a historic moment offering hope for human rights change. The real test of whether this will happen is yet to come.

As the military rulers of Thailand delayed their plans for political transition, the country experienced a continuing backslide in meeting its human rights obligations. Restrictions on human rights – in particular relating to freedoms of expression and assembly – which the authorities had promised would be temporary after taking power in a military coup in 2014, were in fact retained and strengthened.

A new government came to power in Sri Lanka in January, bringing constitutional reforms and promises of improved human rights protection. Many serious challenges remained, however, including the use of arbitrary arrest and detention, torture and other ill-treatment, enforced disappearances and deaths in custody. A longstanding climate of impunity for abuses by both sides in Sri Lanka's armed conflict that ended in 2009 was still largely unaddressed.

There were other smaller signs of progress in the region, even if sometimes fragile and halting. These included tentative steps towards addressing widespread torture and other ill-treatment in Afghanistan, India and Sri Lanka.

## INCREASING ACTIVISM AND SUPPRESSION OF PUBLIC PROTESTS

A rise in human rights activism that had emerged in the Asia-Pacific region in recent years continued. Protests and other actions, however, were frequently overshadowed by authorities' efforts to curtail freedoms of expression, association and peaceful assembly, including through force and violence.

People were intimidated and harassed as they exercised their right to freedom of peaceful assembly in Viet Nam; in July, security forces beat and intimidated peaceful activists attempting to take part in a hunger strike in solidarity with prisoners of conscience. In Maldives, hundreds of political opponents of the government taking part in peaceful protests were arrested and detained, and in Malaysia organizers of and participants in peaceful protests were criminalized.

In Cambodia, a 2014 crackdown on the right to freedom of peaceful assembly was reinforced by criminal convictions for demonstrators. In July, 11 opposition members and activists were found guilty on far-fetched charges of insurrection. They had taken part in a demonstration in the capital, Phnom Penh, in July 2014 that resulted in clashes with security forces. No credible evidence was produced that linked the men to the violence.

Prison sentences imposed on two activists in Thailand for staging a play were part of a pattern in which the military authorities made unprecedented use of the country's Lèse-Majesté Law to target freedom of expression. The authorities continued to outlaw "political meetings" of five or more people, and introduced legislation requiring demonstrators to seek permission from the police/authorities, or face imprisonment. Students and activists carrying out small-scale symbolic and peaceful demonstrations often experienced excessive force or arrests and charges.

A brutal police crackdown on largely peaceful student protests in Myanmar was subsequently followed by mass arrests and widespread harassment of student leaders and all those associated with the protests. They included Phyoe Phyoe Aung, leader of the All Burma Federation of Student Unions.

A series of protests were held in the Republic of Korea (South Korea) over the government's response to the 2014 Sewol ferry disaster that caused more than 300 deaths. Although most protests were peaceful, police blockaded street rallies in the capital, Seoul, marking the tragedy's first anniversary in April, and used unnecessary force against participants on a vigil walk in memory of the victims.

## REPRESSION OF DISSENT

Many governments in the Asia-Pacific region demonstrated an entrenched intolerance of dissent and resorted to draconian restrictions on human rights.

May marked the first anniversary of the military declaring martial law and seizing power in Thailand. The authorities adopted harsh measures, abused the judicial system and entrenched their powers to stamp out peaceful dissent or criticism of military rule. They displayed ongoing intolerance of peaceful dissent, arbitrarily arresting students and anti-coup activists, and holding academics, journalists and parliamentarians in secret detention or without charge or trial in military camps. Individuals faced unfair trials in military courts for speaking out against the military takeover. Authorities penalized scores of individuals for Facebook comments and statements deemed to be insulting towards the monarchy, with courts handing down sentences of up to 60 years' imprisonment.

North Korea's government refused to allow any political parties, independent newspapers or independent civil society organizations to operate, and barred almost all nationals from international mobile telephone services. Yet many people took risks to make international calls. People living close to the border with China took advantage of the unofficial private economy and accessed smuggled mobile phones connected to Chinese networks to contact people outside North Korea – exposing themselves to surveillance, arrest

and detention.

In Cambodia, human rights defenders were jailed and the authorities exacerbated existing arbitrary restrictions on the rights to freedom of expression and peaceful assembly by increasing arrests for online activity. The new Law on Associations and Non-Governmental Organizations was signed into law despite protests from civil society that it threatened to undermine the right to freedom of association; it remained unclear how the law would be implemented.

In Viet Nam, the state controlled the media and judiciary as well as political and religious institutions; dozens of prisoners of conscience remained imprisoned in harsh conditions after unfair trials. There was an increase in reports of harassment, short-term arbitrary detentions and physical attacks on members of civil society.

In July, China's authorities launched a massive crackdown against human rights lawyers that persisted throughout the rest of the year. Activists as well as human rights defenders and their families were systematically subjected to harassment, intimidation, arbitrary arrest and violence.

The space for civil society, human rights defenders and freedom of expression also shrank across South Asia. Pakistan remained one of the world's most dangerous countries for journalists as targeted attacks, including killings, by armed groups continued against media workers, and the government failed to provide adequate protection. Bangladesh became increasingly dangerous for those speaking their own minds, with a pattern of repression of freedom of expression that included the killing of several secularist bloggers and publishers. NGOs also faced legislative restrictions for criticizing the authorities in Bangladesh and Pakistan. In India, authorities used restrictive foreign funding laws to repress NGOs critical of the government.

Human rights defenders in Afghanistan were targeted with impunity and suffered violence by state and non-state actors. Non-state actors were accused of involvement in grenade attacks, bombings and killings of human rights defenders. Parliament amended a mass media law that could further limit freedom of expression. After the Taliban seized control of Kunduz province in September, there were reports of mass killings, rapes and searches for media workers and women human rights defenders named on a hit list.

Elsewhere, governments demonstrating an intolerance of public criticism included the government of Japan, where a law on official secrets that could excessively restrict the right to access information held by the authorities came into effect in December 2014. South Korea's government broadened the application of the National Security Law to additional groups such as politicians, a move that could further curtail freedom of expression. Indonesia's authorities used an internet law to criminalize certain forms of freedom of expression, resulting in individuals being convicted and imprisoned simply for sharing their opinions online.

Restrictions on peaceful activism and dissent in Myanmar intensified, with scores of prisoners of conscience detained and hundreds of people facing charges for peacefully exercising their rights to freedom of expression and assembly. They included student protesters, political activists, media workers and human rights defenders, in particular land and labour activists.

Media outlets faced restrictions in Malaysia, and activists were intimidated and harassed. A Federal Court ruling confirming the constitutionality of the repressive Sedition Act – used to arbitrarily arrest and detain scores of human rights defenders and others in recent years – further undermined freedom of expression.

## TORTURE AND OTHER ILL-TREATMENT

Torture and other ill-treatment was reported in numerous countries in the region, including Fiji, Indonesia, Malaysia, Mongolia, Nepal, North Korea, the Philippines, Thailand, Timor-Leste and Viet Nam. Impunity for those responsible was common.

Torture and other ill-treatment remained widespread in China during detention and interrogation.

Afghanistan's government took steps towards establishing a national action plan to eliminate torture; the intelligence agency issued an order reiterating a ban on its use, although torture and other ill-treatment by security officers remained prevalent throughout the prison system.

In India, torture and other ill-treatment in custody, including cases of deaths from torture, were reported. In a positive move, the Supreme Court directed states to install closed-circuit television in all prisons to prevent torture and other violations, while the government stated it was considering amending the Penal Code to specifically recognize torture as a crime.

Torture and other ill-treatment of detainees, including sexual violence, continued to be reported in Sri Lanka, as did suspicious deaths in custody. Impunity persisted for earlier cases. However, the new government promised the UN Human Rights Council that it would issue clear instructions to all security forces that torture and other ill-treatment is prohibited and that those responsible would be investigated and punished.

## ARMED CONFLICT

Armed conflict in parts of the Asia-Pacific region continued. Increasing insecurity, insurgency and criminal activity in Afghanistan saw civilians injured and killed by the Taliban and other armed groups, as well as by pro-government forces. Accountability for unlawful killings by pro-government forces and armed groups was virtually non-existent.

In October, US forces bombed a hospital run by the NGO Médecins sans Frontières in the city of Kunduz, killing 22 staff and patients and triggering calls for an independent investigation. The Taliban targeted civilians or attacked indiscriminately, and briefly took control of most of Kunduz province.

Allegations of violations – including rape and other crimes of sexual violence – were made against members of the Myanmar army, particularly in Kachin and northern Shan states, where the armed conflict entered a fifth year. Both state and non-state actors were accused of violations of international humanitarian law and human rights abuses, in a climate of impunity.

In India, armed groups continued to perpetrate abuses against civilians, including in Jammu and Kashmir as well as central India. However, in August a historic peace framework agreement was reached in northeastern India between the government and the influential armed group National Socialist Council of Nagaland (Isak-Muivah faction).

Armed violence continued in Thailand's three southern provinces of Pattani, Yala and Narathiwat, as well as parts of Songkhla.

## IMPUNITY

A chronic and entrenched failure to ensure justice and accountability for past and present human rights violations and abuses was a major problem in a wide range of countries in the Asia-Pacific region.

Impunity for violations by security forces in India persisted, and legislation granting virtual immunity from prosecution for the armed forces remained in force in Jammu and Kashmir and parts of northeastern India.

In Cambodia, impunity continued for violations during policing of demonstrations, including deaths caused by unnecessary or excessive use of force in previous years. Unresolved cases included 16-year-old Khem Saphath, last seen in January 2014. He was feared to have been the victim of enforced disappearance and was reportedly among at least five people shot during a government crackdown. The Khmer Rouge tribunal heard for the first time evidence on charges of genocide in a case against Nuon Chea, the former second-in-command of the Khmer Rouge, and against Khieu Samphan, the head of state during the Khmer Rouge era.

Indonesia marked the 50th anniversary of the 1965 mass human rights violations, when – following a failed coup – the military systematically attacked members of the Indonesian Communist Party and suspected sympathizers. There was a continuing failure to ensure truth, justice and reparation for appalling human rights violations and the deaths of an estimated 500,000 to one million people. The year 2015 also marked the 10th anniversary of the end of Indonesia's devastating decades-long Aceh conflict between Indonesian government forces and the pro-independence Free Aceh Movement (Gerakan Aceh Merdeka), in which between 10,000 and 30,000 people were killed. Despite evidence that violations by security forces may amount to crimes against humanity – and that both sides may have committed war crimes – little has been done to ensure justice.

There was, however, progress towards accountability in Sri Lanka. A UN investigation into alleged abuses committed during the final years of the country's armed conflict, including enforced disappearances and military attacks targeting civilians, concluded that these abuses, if established before a court of law, could amount to war crimes and/or crimes against humanity. It recommended reforms to address ongoing violations and the establishment of a hybrid court to address crimes under international law, with which the government signalled agreement.

## PEOPLE ON THE MOVE

Refugees and asylum-seekers continued to face significant hardship in the Asia-Pacific region and beyond. People smuggling and human trafficking in the Bay of Bengal exposed thousands of refugees and migrants to serious abuse on board boats. Some people were shot on the boats, thrown overboard and left to drown, or died from starvation, dehydration or disease. People were beaten, sometimes for hours, for moving, begging for food or asking to use the toilet.

A crisis unfolded in the Bay of Bengal and Andaman Sea in May, triggered by Thailand's crackdown on human trafficking and the smugglers' and traffickers' subsequent abandonment of people at sea, causing an unknown number of deaths and leaving thousands of refugees and migrants stranded for weeks and lacking food, water and medical care.

Indonesia, Malaysia and Thailand initially pushed overcrowded vessels back from their shores and prevented thousands of desperate people from disembarking, while regional governments were slow in setting up search and rescue operations. Following international criticism, Indonesia and Malaysia permitted people to land and accommodated them on a temporary basis. Nevertheless, hundreds or even thousands of people remained unaccounted for, and may have died or been sold for forced labour. By the end of the year, there were serious unanswered questions about a long-term solution for the survivors, as – despite Indonesia devoting resources to housing thousands of refugees and asylum-seekers, and helping to fulfil their basic needs – the government had not clarified whether they could stay beyond May 2016.

As a result of the ongoing insecurity and armed conflict in Afghanistan, nearly 3 million Afghans were refugees, mostly living in Iran and Pakistan, and almost 1 million Afghans were internally displaced in their own country, often in harsh conditions in makeshift camps.

Australia displayed an ongoing harsh approach towards refugees and asylum-seekers. Measures included pushing back boats, *refoulement*, and mandatory and indefinite detention, including in off-shore processing centres in Papua New Guinea and Nauru. In March, an independent review of the Nauru centre documented allegations of rape and other sexual assault. In October, the authorities announced that asylum-seekers would no longer be detained at the centre, which would become an open facility, and that the remaining 600 asylum claims would be processed "within a week". By December processing had still not been completed.

Migrant workers were abused and discriminated against in several countries. North Korea dispatched at least 50,000 people to work in countries such as Libya, Mongolia, Nigeria, Qatar and Russia, often in poor safety conditions and for excessive hours; they received wages via the North Korean government, who made significant deductions.

## RISING RELIGIOUS AND ETHNIC INTOLERANCE

Some authorities colluded in, or failed to address, an increasing trend of religious and ethnic intolerance, exclusion and discrimination. Abuses were reported in countries in the Asia-Pacific region including Laos, Myanmar, Pakistan, Sri Lanka and Viet Nam.

The authorities in Indonesia failed to ensure that all religious minorities were protected and allowed to practise their faith free from fear, intimidation and attack. A community of Shi'a Muslims – forcibly evicted in 2013 from temporary shelter in East Java – remained in limbo throughout 2015; they had previously been forcibly evicted from their home village in 2012 after attacks by an anti-Shi'a mob. Local authorities prevented them from returning unless they converted to Sunni Islam. Elsewhere, local authorities in Aceh province tore down Christian churches, with mob violence forcing around 4,000 people to flee to North Sumatra province.

Freedom of religion was systematically stifled in China. A government campaign to demolish churches and take down Christian crosses in Zhejiang province intensified and persecution of Falun Gong practitioners included arbitrary detention, unfair trials, imprisonment and torture and other ill-treatment. The government maintained extensive controls over Tibetan Buddhist monasteries. The regional government in the predominantly Muslim Xinjiang Uighur Autonomous Region enacted new regulations to more tightly control religious affairs and ban all unauthorized religious practice.

In India, authorities failed to prevent many incidents of religious violence, and sometimes contributed to tensions through polarizing speeches. Mobs attacked Muslim men they suspected of stealing, smuggling or slaughtering cows; and scores of artists, writers and scientists protested against what they said was a climate of growing intolerance.

## DISCRIMINATION

Discrimination remained a concern in numerous countries, with the authorities frequently failing to act effectively to protect people.

Pervasive caste-based discrimination and violence continued in India, and dominant castes continued to use sexual violence against Dalit and Adivasi women and girls. There was some progress when the lower house of Parliament passed an amendment to the Scheduled Castes and the Scheduled Tribes (Prevention of Atrocities) Act, recognizing new offences and requiring that special courts be established to try them, and stipulating that victims and witnesses receive protection.

In Nepal, discrimination – including on the basis of gender, caste, class, ethnic origin and religion – was rife, while in Australia Indigenous Peoples were jailed at a disproportionate rate.

Lesbian, gay, bisexual, transgender and intersex (LGBTI) people faced widespread discrimination and same-sex conduct remained criminalized in many countries. However, a ward in the capital Tokyo became Japan's first municipality to pass an ordinance to distribute certificates that recognize same-sex unions, while India's upper house of Parliament passed a bill to protect transgender people's rights.

## RIGHTS OF WOMEN AND GIRLS

Women across the Asia-Pacific region were frequently subjected to violence, abuse and injustice, including gender-based discrimination and violations and abuses of sexual and reproductive rights.

In Nepal, gender-based discrimination resulted in a range of negative impacts on women from marginalized groups. These included limiting the ability of women and girls to control their sexuality and make choices related to reproduction, such as to challenge early marriage or to ensure adequate antenatal and maternal health care. Stigma and discrimination by police officials and authorities in India continued to deter women from reporting sexual violence, and most states still lacked standard operating procedures for the police to address violence against women.

Sexual and other gender-based violence remained pervasive in Papua New Guinea, where there were also ongoing reports of violence and killing of women and children following accusations of sorcery. The government took little preventative action.

## DEATH PENALTY

Despite some progress in the Asia-Pacific region towards reducing the use of the death penalty in recent years, several countries still applied the punishment, including in ways contrary to international human rights laws and standards. Executions were resumed in some countries.

Pakistan reached the shameful milestone of executing more than 300 people since the lifting of a moratorium on the execution of civilians in December 2014, following a terrorist attack.

In August, India's Law Commission recommended that the death penalty be abolished for all crimes except terrorism-related offences and "waging war against the state".

Amendments to China's Criminal Law came into effect, reducing the number of crimes punishable by death. Although state media claimed that this was in line with the government's policy of executing fewer people, the changes failed to bring the law in line with international human rights laws and standards on use of the death penalty. Statistics on how the punishment is used continued to be classified as state secrets.

A new Criminal Code abolishing the death penalty for all crimes was adopted by Mongolia's Parliament, to take effect from September 2016.

# EUROPE AND CENTRAL ASIA REGIONAL OVERVIEW

2015 was a turbulent year in the Europe and Central Asia region, and a bad one for human rights. It opened with fierce fighting in eastern Ukraine and ended with heavy clashes in eastern Turkey. In the EU, the year was bookended by armed attacks in and around Paris, France, and dominated throughout by the plight of the millions of people, most of them fleeing conflict, who arrived on Europe's shores. Against this backdrop, respect for human rights regressed across the region. In Turkey and across the former Soviet Union, leaders increasingly abandoned respect of human rights altogether, as they strengthened their control of the media and further targeted their critics and opponents. In the EU, the regressive trend took a different form. Fuelled by lingering economic uncertainty, disenchantment with establishment politics and growing anti-EU and anti-immigrant sentiment, populist parties made significant electoral inroads. In the absence of principled leadership, the place of human rights as a cornerstone of European democracies looked shakier than ever. Sweeping anti-terrorism measures and proposals to restrict the inflow of migrants and refugees were typically announced with all the customary human rights caveats, but they were increasingly stripped of their content.

In the UK, the ruling Conservative Party put forward proposals to repeal the Human Rights Act; in Russia, the Constitutional Court was given the power to overrule the decisions of the European Court of Human Rights; in Poland, the ruling Law and Justice Party pushed through measures restricting the oversight of the Constitutional Court within months of its election. Increasingly diminished on the international stage, EU member states turned a blind eye to human rights violations that they would once have strongly condemned, as they sought to cut economic deals and enlist the support of third countries in their efforts to combat terrorism and keep refugees and migrants at bay.

Although there was progress on equality for lesbian, gay, bisexual, transgender and intersex (LGBTI) people (in most Western European countries at least) and the European Commission continued to tackle the systemic discrimination against Roma, almost all underlying trends across the region offered a bleak outlook for the state of human rights in 2016.

## THE REFUGEE CRISIS

The defining image of the year was that of Alan Kurdi, a three-year-old Syrian boy, lying on a Turkish beach. Either side of his tragic death in September, over 3,700 refugees and migrants lost their lives trying to reach Europe's shores, as EU member states struggled to deal with the impact of a global refugee crisis on Europe. While Turkey was hosting over 2 million Syrian refugees, and Lebanon and Jordan a further 1.7 million between them, 1 million refugees and migrants, many of them refugees from Syria, entered the EU irregularly during the year. However, the EU, the world's richest political bloc with a total population of over 500 million people, singularly failed to come up with a coherent, humane and rights-respecting response to this challenge.

The year began inauspiciously, with European leaders declining to replace the Italian Navy's Mare Nostrum search and rescue operation with an adequate alternative, despite ample evidence of continuing migratory pressure on the central Mediterranean route. It took the death of more than 1,000 refugees and migrants in a series of incidents off the Libyan coast over one weekend in mid-April to finally prompt a rethink. At a hastily convened summit, EU leaders agreed to expand EU border agency Frontex's maritime border control Operation Triton, while a number of countries, including the UK and Germany, dispatched additional naval vessels to the region. The results were positive: according to the International Organization for Migration, death rates along the central Mediterranean route declined by 9% compared to 2014, but still stood at 18.5 deaths for every 1,000 travellers. The number of refugees and migrants dying in the Aegean Sea increased considerably, however, reaching over 700 by the end of the year; this represented around 21% of all deaths in the Mediterranean in 2015, compared to 1% in 2014.

The increase in deaths in the Aegean Sea reflected the sharp rise in irregular sea arrivals in Greece, from the summer onward. In the absence of safe and legal avenues of entry to EU countries, over 800,000 people, overwhelmingly refugees fleeing conflict or persecution in Syria, Afghanistan, Eritrea, Somalia and Iraq, made the dangerous crossing to Greece. Only 3% of those entering Greece irregularly crossed via the largely fenced-off land border.

The logistical and humanitarian challenges presented by such large numbers utterly defeated Greece's already ailing reception system. As hundreds of thousands of refugees and migrants left Greece and marched on through the Balkans, most of them aiming to reach Germany, the so-called "Dublin regime" – the EU system for allocating responsibility for the processing of asylum applications across member states – broke down too. The funnelling of refugees and asylum-seekers to just a few external border countries, essentially Greece and Italy, made it impossible to uphold a system allocating the primary responsibility for processing asylum claims to the first EU country the applicant entered. The Schengen Agreement – which abolished border controls across internal EU borders – also showed signs of cracking, as Germany, Austria, Hungary, Sweden and Denmark suspended its provisions.

As the crisis grew, EU leaders organized summit after summit, but to no avail. While the European Commission vainly sought to propose constructive measures for the redistribution of asylum-seekers and the organization of reception facilities along the route, EU member states for the most part vacillated or actively obstructed potential solutions. Only Germany showed leadership commensurate with the scale of the challenge.

Little effort was made to increase safe and legal avenues of entry for refugees into the EU. Member states agreed to an EU-wide resettlement scheme for 20,000 refugees from across the globe proposed by the European Commission in May. UNHCR, the UN refugee agency, had put the number of Syrian refugees in need of resettlement and other forms of humanitarian admission at 400,000, but other than Germany, hardly any EU countries offered to resettle more than a few thousands of them.

European leaders also struggled to agree on and implement an effective mechanism to redistribute arriving refugees and migrants across the EU. At a summit in May, EU leaders voted to approve a relocation scheme for 40,000 asylum-seekers from Italy and Greece, in the face of fierce opposition from a number of Central European countries. In September, the scheme was extended by a further 120,000, including the relocation of 54,000 asylum-seekers from Hungary. Never enough in the first place, the scheme foundered in the face of logistical challenges and the reluctance of recipient states to meet the targets they committed to: only around 200 asylum-seekers had been transferred from Italy and Greece by the end of the year, while Hungary declined to participate.

As pressure mounted, Balkan countries alternated between closing their borders and simply ushering refugees and migrants through. Border guards used teargas and batons to beat back crowds as Macedonia briefly closed its border in August and Hungary permanently sealed its border with Serbia in September. By the end of the year, a more or less orderly corridor, passing through Macedonia, Serbia, Croatia, Slovenia and Austria, was in place, amounting to an ad hoc response to the crisis that remained entirely contingent on Germany's continued willingness to accept incoming asylum-seekers and refugees. Thousands were still sleeping rough, as authorities along the route struggled to provide adequate shelter.

Hungary led the way in refusing to engage with pan-European solutions to the refugee crisis. Having seen a sharp increase in arriving refugees and migrants at the start of the year, Hungary turned its back on collective efforts and decided to seal itself off. It constructed over 200km of fencing along its borders with Serbia and Croatia and adopted legislation rendering it almost impossible for refugees and asylum-seekers entering via Serbia to claim asylum. "We think all countries have a right to decide whether they want to have a large number of Muslims in their countries", Hungarian Prime Minister Viktor Orbán said in September.

Public opinion across Europe ranged from indifference or hostility to strong shows of solidarity. The shocking scenes of chaos and need along the Balkan route prompted countless individuals and NGOs to plug the gaps in the humanitarian assistance provided to refugees and migrants. However, European leaders overwhelmingly chose to listen to vocal anti-immigrant sentiment and concerns over the loss of national sovereignty and security threats. As a result, the only policies they could agree on were measures to strengthen "Fortress Europe".

As the year progressed, European summits increasingly focused on measures designed to keep refugees and migrants out or hasten their return. EU leaders agreed to create a common list of "safe" countries of origin, to which asylum-seekers could be returned after expedited proceedings. They agreed to strengthen the capacity of Frontex to carry out expulsions. Most significantly, they started to look to countries of origin, and especially transit, to restrict the flow of refugees and migrants to Europe. The outsourcing of the EU migration controls to third countries reached its peak with the signing of a Joint Action Plan with Turkey in October. The deal essentially involved Turkey agreeing to limit the flow of refugees and migrants to Greece by strengthening its border controls, in exchange for 3 billion euros of aid for its resident refugee population and, unofficially, the turning of a blind eye to its growing list of human rights indiscretions. It ignored the fact that despite Turkey's broadly positive reception of over 2 million Syrian refugees, many still lived in dire poverty, while those from other countries had little prospect of ever being recognized as refugees on account of Turkey's woefully inadequate asylum system. Towards the end of the year, evidence emerged of Turkey forcibly returning refugees and asylum-seekers detained in its western border provinces to Syria and Iraq, further highlighting that the EU was limiting the influx of refugees and migrants at the expense of their human rights.

As the year drew to a close, around 2,000 people were still entering Greece daily. While reception capacity on the Greek islands and further along the Balkan route had increased and reception conditions improved, they remained woefully incommensurate with the scale of the challenge. With no sign of the number of arriving migrants and refugees decreasing significantly in 2016, the EU was no closer to finding sustainable, rights-respecting solutions for those seeking sanctuary within its borders than at the start of the year.

## ARMED VIOLENCE

In January and February, heavy fighting resumed in Ukraine's eastern region of Donbass, as Russian-backed separatists in the self-proclaimed Donetsk People's Republic and Luhansk People's Republic sought to advance and straighten their frontline. Amid heavy military losses, Ukrainian forces ceded control over the long-contested Donetsk airport and the area around the town of Debaltseve, with heavy shelling by both sides resulting in numerous civilian casualties. By the end of the year, the UN estimated that the death toll for the conflict exceeded 9,000 people, including

2,000 civilians, many of whom appeared to have died as a result of indiscriminate rocket and mortar fire. War crimes and other violations of international humanitarian law included the torture and other ill-treatment of detainees by both sides, and the summary execution of captives by separatist forces. While the conflict had subsided by the end of year as a fragile ceasefire took hold, the prospect of accountability for the crimes committed remained remote. On 8 September, Ukraine accepted the jurisdiction of the International Criminal Court (ICC) with respect to alleged crimes committed in its territory since 20 February 2014, but no progress was made on the ratification of the Rome Statute of the ICC. While a few criminal investigations into suspected abuses by Ukrainian forces – mostly by paramilitary groups – were opened by Ukrainian authorities, there had been no convictions by the end of the year. Total impunity persisted in the Donetsk and Luhansk regions, where a more pervasive lawlessness took hold.

Accountability for the abuses committed in the course of the 2013-2014 pro-European demonstrations in the capital Kyiv ("EuroMaydan") also proved elusive. In November, the Prosecutor General's Office reported that investigations into over 2,000 criminal incidents related to EuroMaydan were ongoing, with criminal proceedings instigated against 270 individuals. The trial of two former riot police (Berkut) officers on charges of manslaughter and abuse of authority began but no convictions were secured for EuroMaydan-related crimes during the year. An International Advisory Panel set up by the Council of Europe to monitor investigations into EuroMaydan published two reports in April and November, both of which deemed the investigations inadequate.

While accountability for past human rights abuses continued to stall, some progress was made in instituting structural reforms to Ukraine's notoriously corrupt and abusive law enforcement agencies; a law backed by the Council of Europe creating a new agency to investigate offences by public officials, including torture and other ill-treatment, was finally adopted. Ukraine took its first tentative steps towards institutional reform, but the Donbass region remained far from stable and, like Crimea, a black hole for unmonitored human rights abuses.

While the conflict in Ukraine subsided, heavy clashes erupted in Turkey as the ever uncertain peace process with the Kurdistan Workers' Party (PKK) collapsed in July. By the end of the year, over 100 people were reported killed in the course of law enforcement operations in urban areas that took on an increasingly militarized aspect. There were numerous reports of excessive use of force and extrajudicial executions by Turkish forces. Law enforcement operations were typically conducted under round-the-clock curfews, often lasting several weeks, during which residents had their water and electricity cut and were unable to access medical treatment or food. The significant escalation in human rights violations largely escaped international censure, as Turkey successfully leveraged its crucial role in relation to the Syrian conflict and the refugee crisis to dampen criticism of its domestic actions.

## FREEDOMS OF EXPRESSION, ASSOCIATION AND ASSEMBLY

The respect for freedoms of expression, association, and peaceful assembly deteriorated across the former Soviet Union. Government control over the media, internet censorship, the curbing of protest and the criminalization of the legitimate exercise of these freedoms intensified almost everywhere.

In Russia, the steady squeeze on government critics gathered pace, as repressive laws enacted in the aftermath of Vladimir Putin's return to the presidency were applied. By the end of the year, over 100 NGOs were included, most of them compulsorily, on the Ministry of Justice's list of "foreign agents". Not a single NGO succeeded in legally challenging its inclusion on the list. The Human Rights Centre (HRC) Memorial was one of a number of NGOs to be fined for failing to brand its publications with the toxic label "foreign agent", paving the way for criminal prosecution of its leaders in the future. The law, whose purpose was to discourage NGOs from receiving foreign funding and discredit those that did, was supplemented in May by a new law enabling authorities to designate foreign organizations as "undesirable" if deemed to pose a "threat to the country's constitutional order, defence or state security". The target appeared to be foreign donor organizations, in particular US ones. By the end of the year, four US-based donors had been declared "undesirable", rendering their continued operations in Russia – and any co-operation with them – illegal. The authorities further extended their control over the media and the internet. Thousands of websites and pages were blocked by government regulators, often in violation of the right to freedom of expression. Restrictions on freedom of peaceful assembly also intensified and the number of public protests declined. For the first time, four peaceful protesters were prosecuted under a 2014 law which criminalized the repeated breach of the law on assemblies.

In Azerbaijan, the prominent NGO leaders arrested in 2014 were predictably convicted on a range of trumped-up charges. At the end of the year, at least 18 prisoners of conscience, including human rights defenders, journalists, youth activists and opposition politicians, remained behind bars. Leyla Yunus, president of the Institute for Peace and Democracy, and her husband and co-worker Arif Yunus were released towards the end of 2015, although they still faced spurious treason charges.

The human rights situation in Kazakhstan also regressed. The new Criminal Code that came into effect in January retained the offences of inciting social and other "discord". Four criminal investigations were opened under the vaguely worded offence, including against activists Yermek Narymbaev and Serkzhan Mambetalin after they posted extracts from an unpublished book deemed to denigrate the Kazakh people on their Facebook page. They remained in pre-trial detention at the end of the year. Drawing inspiration from Russia and sharing the same suspicion of foreign NGO funding, Kazakhstan adopted amendments to the Law on Non-Profit Organizations, creating a central "operator" to raise funding and administer state and non-state funds to NGOs, including foreign funding, for projects and activities that comply with a limited list of issues approved by the government. Kyrgyzstan also toyed with adoption of a "foreign agents" law along Russian lines; a draft bill was put before Parliament with strong backing from President Atambaev, but was withdrawn "for further discussion" in June. Parliament also got to a third reading on a law criminalizing "fostering positive attitude" towards "non-traditional sexual relations", before it too was withdrawn for additional consultation.

Tajikistani President Emomali Rahmon was granted lifetime immunity from prosecution and the title "leader of the nation", while Uzbekistan and Turkmenistan remained fundamentally unchanged in their deeply repressive rules. Georgia and Ukraine continued to offer broadly free environments, but neither without their wobbles. In Ukraine, it became increasingly dangerous to voice pro-Russian views: pro-Russian journalist Oles Buzina was shot dead by two masked gunmen in April, while journalist Ruslan Kotsaba became Ukraine's first prisoner of conscience for five years when he was remanded in custody on charges of treason in February. Following the adoption in May of four so-called "decommunization laws" banning the use of communist and nazi symbols, the Ministry of Justice initiated proceedings to ban the Communist Party of Ukraine. In Georgia, the opposition party United National Movement and several NGOs accused the government of orchestrating a protracted legal battle between an ousted former shareholder and the current owners of pro-opposition TV station Rustavi 2. In

November, the Tbilisi City Court ordered the replacement of the station's director general and chief financial officer.

Elsewhere in Europe, perhaps the most significant human rights regression took place in Turkey. Against the backdrop of two successive parliamentary elections which resulted in an outright majority for the ruling Justice and Development Party (AK), the increasingly autocratic rule of its former leader and current President Recep Tayyip Erdoğan, and the breakdown of the peace process with the PKK, freedom of expression suffered further. Countless unfair criminal prosecutions under criminal defamation and counter-terrorism laws targeted political activists, journalists and other critics of public officials or government policy. Particular targets were pro-Kurdish commentators and supporters of media outlets associated with former AK Party ally Fethullah Gülen. People expressing criticism of the President, particularly through social media channels, were increasingly prosecuted. Over 100 cases of criminal defamation under article 299 for "insulting the President" were initiated by the President and sanctioned by the Ministry of Justice.

Critical media outlets and journalists were subjected to immense pressure. Journalists were regularly dismissed by editors for their critical reporting and comment. News websites, including large swathes of the Kurdish press, were blocked on unclear grounds by administrative orders, aided by a compliant judiciary. Journalists were harassed and assaulted by police while covering stories in the predominantly Kurdish south-east. Media outlets linked to Fethullah Gülen were systematically targeted, and either taken off air or taken over by government administrators.

Sensitive protests continued to be disrupted. May Day demonstrations were banned for the third year in a row and Istanbul's annual Gay Pride was violently dispersed for the first time in over a decade. Reports of excessive use of force by law enforcement agents breaking up protests were frequent, particularly in the south-east.

## COUNTER-TERROR AND SECURITY

The year began with violent attacks in Paris against journalists at the satirical weekly *Charlie Hebdo* and against a Jewish supermarket, resulting in 17 deaths and an outpouring of solidarity both in France and abroad. Another series of attacks in and around Paris on 13 November killed a further 130 people. The attacks gave fresh impetus – in France in particular, but also elsewhere in Europe – to a raft of measures that threatened human rights. These included measures targeting those travelling or intending to travel abroad to commit or otherwise pursue ill-defined terrorism-related acts; sweeping new surveillance powers; extended powers of arrest with reduced procedural guarantees; and "counter-radicalization" measures that would potentially repress freedom of expression and discriminate against certain groups.

Some of the most significant developments took place in the area of surveillance, as a range of states adopted or tabled measures granting intelligence and law enforcement agencies almost unfettered access to electronic communications. In France, Parliament approved two laws on surveillance that provided extensive executive powers to monitor people's communications and internet use, including by way of indiscriminate mass interception of internet traffic. The second law, adopted in October, paved the way for the use of mass surveillance techniques on communications in and out of the country, in the pursuit of an undefined list of objectives, including promoting foreign policy, economic and scientific interests. None of the new surveillance measures required prior judicial authorization, instead granting limited and occasional powers to an administrative authority to advise the Prime Minister.

Switzerland adopted a new surveillance law which granted sweeping powers to the Federal Intelligence Service to intercept data on internet cables entering or leaving Switzerland, access metadata, internet histories and content of emails, and use government spyware. The Dutch government put forward a bill that would in effect legalize the bulk collection of telecoms data, including internal communications without prior judicial approval. The UK government proposed a new Investigatory Powers Bill which would authorize intelligence services to intercept all communications in and out of the country, and oblige phone and internet companies to hand over customers' internet and phone histories – all with insufficient judicial control.

While European governments threatened the right to privacy, a number of key international court decisions laid down markers for what is likely to be a fiercely contested and highly litigated issue in the years ahead. In December, in *Roman Zakharov v. Russia*, the Grand Chamber of the European Court of Human Rights highlighted the need for prior individual suspicion and meaningful judicial scrutiny for any surveillance-related interference with the right to privacy to be considered necessary and proportionate.

After the landmark Digital Ireland case rendered in 2014, the Court of Justice of the European Union also delivered another key ruling. In October, it invalidated the 15-year-old "safe harbour agreement" between the USA and the EU, which allowed private companies to transfer personal data between the two, on the assumption of an essentially equivalent level of protection of fundamental rights relating to personal data in the USA and in EU law. Following the revelations of the extent of the US surveillance programme by Edward Snowden, the Court concluded that "the United States authorities were able to access the personal data transferred from the Member States to the United States and process it in a way [that was] beyond what was strictly necessary and proportionate to the protection of national security."

The increasing use of exceptional right-threatening counter-terrorism measures since the 11 September 2001 attacks on the USA found particularly vivid expression in France in the wake of the November attacks. A state of emergency introducing a range of measures including the ability to carry out warrantless house searches, forcing people to remain in specific locations and the power to dissolve associations or groups broadly described as participating in acts that breach public order, was declared for an initial period of 12 days and then extended by three months. In the space of just a few weeks, French authorities conducted 2,700 warrantless house searches, resulting in just two terrorism-related investigations being opened (but another 488 for unrelated offences); assigned 360 people to fixed residency; and closed down 20 mosques and numerous Muslim associations. Throughout the year, the authorities initiated a spate of prosecutions under vague "apology for terrorism" legislation, several of them in apparent breach of the right to freedom of expression.

France was not alone, however. Proposals for new counter-terrorism laws in the aftermath of the November attacks were tabled in countries across the region, including Belgium, Luxembourg, Netherlands, and Slovakia. In all these countries, new proposals included lengthening the time period permitted for pre-charge detention for persons suspected of terrorism-related offences on a lower standard of proof than "reasonable suspicion".

Throughout the year, European states worked on the adoption of legislation to curtail and criminalize travelling or preparing to travel abroad for the vaguely defined purpose of committing or otherwise pursuing terrorism-related acts, following on from the adoption in 2014 of the UN Security Council Resolution 2178. In December, the EU Commission tabled a proposal for a new directive that would introduce a prohibition on travel and acts associated with travel for the purpose of committing acts of terrorism abroad into the national legislation of member states. This followed and referred to the adoption earlier in the year under the auspices of the Council of Europe of a treaty containing similar measures. These laws, and others introduced to tackle the so-called "foreign fighters" phenomenon, threatened to various extents a range of human rights guarantees. In several countries, and the UK in particular, these measures went hand in glove with a wider set of measures designed to prevent and identify "violent extremism" that risked discriminating against and stigmatizing Muslims.

# MIDDLE EAST AND NORTH AFRICA REGIONAL OVERVIEW

For millions of people across the Middle East and North Africa region, 2015 brought calamity and unremitting misery. Armed conflicts in Syria, Iraq, Yemen and Libya continued to cause countless civilian deaths and injuries and forced displacement that in the case of Syria was on a truly epic scale. Elsewhere, government authorities clamped down on dissent and tightened controls citing the threat to public safety posed by armed groups that carried out a rash of bomb and other attacks in countries across the region and beyond.

## ARMED CONFLICT

In Syria, Yemen and large areas of Iraq and Libya continuing armed conflicts saw government and non-state forces repeatedly commit war crimes and serious human rights abuses with impunity, killing and injuring thousands of civilians and driving millions from their homes and into despair and destitution. Fighting forces showed little or no regard for the lives of civilians and ignored the legal obligation of all parties – both state and non-state – to spare civilians.

The most severe of these armed conflicts continued to rage in Syria, causing widespread devastation and loss of life, while also severely impacting on Syria's neighbours and other countries in the region and beyond. By the end of the year, according to the UN, more than 250,000 people had been killed in Syria since the government's brutal repression of popular protests and demands for reform that began in 2011. Civilians continued to bear the brunt of the conflict. Millions continued to be forcibly displaced; by the end of 2015, an additional 1 million people had fled Syria, swelling the number of refugees – mostly in Turkey, Lebanon and Jordan – to 4.6 million. Thousands sought to gain entry to Europe via perilous sea crossings from Turkey, and more than 7.6 million people were internally displaced within Syria. Some had been forcibly displaced several times.

Throughout 2015, forces loyal to Syrian President Bashar al-Assad continued to bomb and shell opposition-held civilian areas without restraint, killing and injuring thousands. They also reportedly used chemical agents in some attacks. They continued to target medical facilities and to besiege civilian areas controlled by armed opposition groups, trapping their remaining civilian inhabitants and condemning them to starvation and utter deprivation while exposing them to repeated shelling and bombing. At the same time, non-state armed groups also carried out unlawful killings and indiscriminately shelled government-held areas. Large areas of Syria, like much of northern Iraq, were controlled by the armed group calling itself Islamic State (IS), whose forces also continued to commit war crimes and crimes against humanity, while brazenly advertising their abuses over the internet as a propaganda and recruitment tool. In areas it controlled, such as al-Raqqa in Syria and Mosul in Iraq, IS ruthlessly enforced its own narrow interpretation of Islam and deterred opposition with summary killings and other cruel punishments. In Iraq, in particular, IS continued to target Shi'a Muslims and members of the Yazidi and other minorities; more than a dozen mass graves were found in areas of Iraq formerly held by IS that contained the mortal remains of Yazidis whom IS forces had summarily killed. Many Yazidi women and girls remained missing after being captured by IS fighters and forced into sexual slavery. In Iraq, IS forces captured Ramadi, capital of the predominantly Sunni Anbar province, in May, driving out government forces and causing thousands of people to flee south towards the capital Baghdad. After capturing the city, IS forces conducted a wave of killings of civilians and members of the security forces, disposing of bodies by dumping them into the Euphrates River. They imposed strict dress and behaviour codes and punished alleged infractions with execution-style public killings; IS forces reportedly killed dozens of men they alleged were gay by throwing them from the roofs of buildings. IS forces also destroyed religious and cultural artefacts, including at the UNESCO World Heritage site at Palmyra in Syria.

The Iraqi government sought to recapture Ramadi and other IS-controlled areas of the north and east, initially augmenting its security forces with mainly Shi'a militias previously responsible for sectarian killings and other serious human rights abuses, and by calling in air strikes by a US-led international coalition and assistance from Iran. As they advanced, government forces indiscriminately shelled areas held or contested by IS, killing and injuring civilians. In December, the Iraqi army, supported by US-led international coalition air strikes and Sunni tribal fighters, but not Shi'a militias, recaptured Ramadi. The Iraqi authorities continued to detain thousands of mostly Sunni Muslims without trial as alleged terrorism suspects and subjected them to torture and other ill-treatment with impunity; many others were sentenced to death or long prison sentences after grossly unfair trials before courts that commonly convicted defendants on the basis of torture-tainted "confessions".

In Yemen, an array of contending forces spread misery and mayhem throughout the country. Early in the year, Huthi forces belonging to the northern Zaidi Shi'a minority, who took control of the capital Sana'a in September 2014, swept southward, supported by forces loyal to former President Ali Abdullah Saleh, threatening Yemen's second and third largest cities, Taiz and the Red Sea port city of Aden. Huthi forces fired explosive weapons indiscriminately into civilian areas of Yemen and across the border into Saudi Arabia; attacked hospitals and medical workers; recklessly exposed civilians to risk by launching attacks from the vicinity of homes, hospitals and schools; deployed anti-personnel landmines that pose an ongoing risk to civilians; used lethal force against protesters; closed down NGOs, and abducted and detained journalists and other critics.

On 25 March, a military coalition of nine Arab states led by Saudi Arabia intervened in the conflict at the request of Yemeni President Abd Rabbu Mansour Hadi, who had taken refuge in the Saudi Arabian capital Riyadh as Huthi forces advanced, and with the aim of restoring President Hadi and his government to power. The coalition launched a campaign of air strikes against the Huthis and areas that they controlled or contested, imposed a partial air and sea blockade and deployed ground troops in support of Yemeni anti-Huthi forces. While some coalition attacks targeted military objectives, many others were indiscriminate, disproportionate or appeared to be deliberately directed against civilians and civilian objects, including schools, hospitals and roads, particularly in Yemen's northern Sa'da governorate, the Huthis' main base. In some areas, coalition aircraft also dropped US-made cluster munitions, despite the international prohibition on the use of these inherently indiscriminate weapons, endangering civilians' lives.

Armed groups opposed to the Huthis, including IS, summarily killed captured Huthi fighters and carried out suicide and other attacks targeting civilians. IS bomb attacks on two Shi'a mosques on 20 March killed more than 140 people, all or mostly civilians, and wounded hundreds of others.

By the end of the year, Yemen's armed conflict had killed more than 2,700 civilians, according to the UN, and forcibly displaced more than 2.5 million people, creating a humanitarian crisis.

The Yemeni conflict was not the only one in which international forces became direct participants. In both Iraq and Syria a US-led international military coalition of Western and Arab states used aircraft and drones to target

IS forces and some other armed groups, sometimes causing civilian casualties. In Syria, Russia's armed forces intervened to support the al-Assad government, despite its mounting record of human rights violations, launching air strikes and cruise missile attacks against areas held by opposition forces as well as against IS targets; by the end of the year, these attacks were reported to have killed hundreds of civilians.

Libya, too, remained mired in armed conflict four years after the fall of Mu'ammar al-Gaddafi's regime. Two rival governments and parliaments vied for supremacy, one based in the east that was internationally recognized and backed by the Operation Dignity military coalition, and the other, supported by the Libya Dawn coalition of Western-based armed militias and other forces, in the capital Tripoli. Elsewhere, armed groups pursuing their own ideological, regional, tribal, economic and ethnic agendas fought for control, including local affiliates of IS and al-Qa'ida.

The various forces ranged against each other committed serious violations of the laws of war, including direct attacks on civilians, including medical workers, and indiscriminate or disproportionate attacks, as well as unlawful killings, abductions, arbitrary detention, torture and other serious abuses. IS-affiliated forces in the Libyan cities of Sirte and Derna carried out public killings, floggings and amputations, and targeted foreign nationals of other faiths. In February, an IS-affiliated armed group published graphic video footage on the internet showing its mass killing of 21 mostly Egyptian Coptic Christian migrants abducted several weeks earlier, sparking a retaliatory air strike by Egyptian war planes.

In December, representatives of Libya's two rival governments signed a peace deal brokered by the UN, committing to end the violence and form a national unity government. It offered at least some hope to Libya's beleaguered population at the end of a year that saw some 600 civilians killed in the armed conflict and almost 2.5 million

people in need of humanitarian assistance and protection, although the agreement excluded various armed groups and militias and did not bring an end to hostilities.

Elsewhere in the region, major, deep-rooted problems remained. The year saw no progress towards resolving the Israeli-Palestinian conflict even if it did not again flare into open warfare. Israel maintained its relentless land, sea and air blockade of Gaza, suffocating reconstruction there after the devastation caused by the 2014 armed conflict. In the occupied West Bank, Israel continued to promote illegal settlements and severely restricted the movement of Palestinians using an array of military checkpoints, barriers and a fence/wall stretching hundreds of kilometres. Thousands of Palestinians who opposed Israel's military occupation or engaged in protests against it were arrested and detained, with hundreds held under renewable administrative orders that empowered the authorities to detain them indefinitely without charge or trial; others were shot by Israeli troops who regularly used excessive force against Palestinian protesters. Tension rose sharply in the last quarter of the year amid a spate of stabbing and other attacks on Israelis by lone Palestinians. Israeli soldiers and police responded with lethal force including, at times, in circumstances when individuals posed no imminent threat to life. Israeli forces killed at least 156 Palestinians from the Occupied Palestinian Territories, including children, mostly in the last quarter of the year, some in apparent extrajudicial executions.

In January, Palestinian President Mahmoud Abbas declared Palestine's accession to the Rome Statute and accepted the ICC's jurisdiction over crimes within its mandate committed within the Occupied Palestinian Territories since June 2014. However, neither the Palestinian national unity government under President Abbas nor the Hamas de facto administration in Gaza took any steps to investigate war crimes, including indiscriminate rocket and mortar attacks, summary killings, and other serious abuses by Palestinian armed groups during the 2014 armed conflict with Israel, or to hold to account Palestinian security officials responsible for unlawful detentions and torture. Israel, likewise, failed to conduct independent investigations into the extensive war crimes and other violations of international law that its forces committed in Gaza during the 2014 armed conflict, or to hold to account those responsible for unlawful killings in the West Bank and torture and other ill-treatment of detainees.

## REFUGEES, INTERNALLY DISPLACED PEOPLE AND MIGRANTS

The human cost of the armed conflicts in Syria, Iraq, Yemen and Libya in 2015 was immeasurable, although the continuing surge in refugees fleeing these countries and the even greater number of people who were internally displaced within them gave some indication. By the end of the year, the four conflicts had together created more than 5 million refugees and asylum-seekers and more than 13.5 million internally displaced persons (IDPs), according to UNHCR, the UN refugee agency. Elsewhere, such as in Iran, state repression also fuelled a continuing flow of refugees seeking protection abroad.

The impact of the refugee crisis fell most heavily on states within the Middle East and North Africa region. At the end of the year, Lebanon hosted well over 1 million refugees from Syria – they comprised between a quarter and a third of Lebanon's total population – and Jordan hosted in excess of 641,800 refugees from Syria. The presence of so many refugees placed an enormous strain on the host countries' resources, a strain that was only partly alleviated by faltering international humanitarian assistance and support, and presented huge social and security challenges. In both Lebanon and Jordan the authorities took measures to staunch the flow of new arrivals, tightening controls at official and informal border crossing points, blocking the entry of certain categories of people, notably members of Syria's long-standing Palestinian refugee community, and toughening residency requirements for those already admitted. More than 12,000 refugees from Syria, denied entry to Jordan, remained in a remote desert area on the Jordanian side of the border with Syria in desperate conditions. Meanwhile, in December, Jordanian authorities deported more than 500 Sudanese refugees and asylum-seekers to Sudan, where they were at risk of human rights violations, in contravention of the international principle of *non-refoulement*.

Life remained very tough and uncertain even for those who escaped Syria and the other countries enmeshed in armed conflict, due to the hardships and insecurity they encountered as refugees. These difficulties propelled hundreds of thousands of refugees to expose themselves to new risks as they sought to find greater security further afield, particularly in EU countries. Huge numbers departed, particularly from Libya and Turkey, which alone hosted around 2.3 million refugees from Syria, to attempt dangerous sea crossings to Italy and Greece, often in overcrowded, unseaworthy vessels provided by extortionate people traffickers. Many made it and gained entry to the relative safety of Europe, where they faced a decidedly mixed reception as EU states bickered about who should bear responsibility for them and what should be each state's "fair share" of refugees. Countless others, however, lost their lives at sea attempting that stage of their journey, including many infants and other children.

In addition to the more than 1 million refugees from Syria who swelled its population, Lebanon also continued to host several hundred thousand Palestinian refugees, decades after the conflicts with Israel that led them to flee their homes. They were afforded protection by the Lebanese authorities but remained subject to discriminatory laws and policies that denied them property inheritance rights, access to free public education and certain categories of paid employment.

Migrants, as well as refugees and those

internally displaced, remained particularly vulnerable to abuse in a number of countries. In Algeria and Morocco, migrants from countries in sub-Saharan Africa were liable to arrest and summary expulsion. In Libya, Tripoli-based authorities held up to 4,000 migrants and other undocumented foreign nationals in indefinite detention in facilities where they faced torture or other ill-treatment, and other refugees, asylum-seekers and migrants faced serious abuses, including discrimination and labour exploitation. In Israel, the authorities denied asylum-seekers from Eritrea and Sudan access to a fair refugee determination process, detained more than 4,200 at desert detention facilities by the end of the year, and pressured others to leave Israel "voluntarily" or face indefinite detention.

Migrant workers, many from South and Southeast Asia, also continued to face severe levels of exploitation and abuse in the oil and gas-rich countries of the Gulf, where the *kafala* sponsorship system tied them to their employers and they were inadequately protected under labour law. In Qatar, where 90% of the workforce were migrant workers, the government largely failed to implement reforms it had promised in 2014; many construction workers remained exposed to unsafe living and working conditions and thousands of domestic workers, mostly women, faced numerous abuses ranging from low pay and excessive working hours to physical assault, forced labour and human trafficking. In Kuwait, however, a new law for the first time gave migrant domestic workers a right to one rest day each week and 30 days' annual paid leave.

## REPRESSION OF DISSENT

Governments across the Middle East and North Africa region remained intolerant of criticism and dissent and curtailed rights to freedom of expression, association and peaceful assembly. In Algeria and Morocco, state authorities used widely drawn criminal insult and/or defamation laws to prosecute and imprison online and other critics, as did

the Egyptian authorities and the governments of Bahrain, Kuwait, Oman and the United Arab Emirates (UAE). In these Gulf states, those targeted included individuals accused of harming their countries' relations with Saudi Arabia by posting comments considered disrespectful to Saudi Arabia's late King or criticizing its military intervention in Yemen. In Qatar, a poet continued to serve a 15-year prison term for writing and reciting lines that the authorities deemed offensive to the country's Emir. In Jordan, dozens of journalists and activists faced prosecution under Penal Code provisions that prohibit criticism of the King and government institutions and under an anti-terrorism law amended in 2014 that criminalized criticism of foreign leaders or states.

In Iran, the international agreement relating to the country's nuclear programme and the easing of financial and economic sanctions did not yield any let-up in state repression. The authorities continued to curtail freedom of speech and rights to association and assembly, blocking access to Facebook, Twitter and other social media websites, jamming foreign broadcasts, and arresting, detaining and imprisoning journalists, human rights defenders, trade unionists, artists and others who voiced dissent, including three opposition political leaders held without charge or trial since 2009.

Authorities in Saudi Arabia also brooked no criticism or dissent and harshly punished those who dared advocate reform or speak out in support of human rights. Blogger Raif Badawi remained in prison serving the 10-year sentence he received in 2014 after a court convicted him of "insulting Islam" and violating the Cyber-crime law by setting up the Free Saudi Liberals Network website, which the authorities closed. The court also sentenced him to a flogging of 1,000 lashes. Dr Zuhair Kutbi, arrested in July, was detained for months, then tried and imprisoned after he advocated constitutional monarchy as a form of government in a television interview.

In Egypt, the government continued the

relentless crackdown on the Muslim Brotherhood that began when the army ousted Mohamed Morsi from the presidency in July 2013, widening it to encompass their other critics and opponents, as well as advocates of human rights and political reform. The authorities held thousands of detainees on political grounds; by the end of the year, at least 700 had been held without sentence by courts for longer than the two-year legal maximum. Thousands of others faced unfair mass trials before criminal or military courts, which handed down mass prison sentences and death sentences. Some detainees were subjected to enforced disappearance. The authorities rejected any criticism of the crackdown on dissent, noting the threat posed by armed groups that launched increasingly deadly attacks on security forces, state officials and civilians.

All across the region, national judicial systems were weak, lacked independence and failed to ensure due process and uphold the right to a fair trial, especially in cases against those perceived to be government critics or opponents. Throughout 2015, courts in countries including Bahrain, Iran, Iraq, Jordan, Saudi Arabia and UAE, as well as those in Egypt, continued to hand down sentences of imprisonment and death after convicting defendants in unfair trials; rather than being fearless upholders of justice, such courts operated as mere instruments of state repression.

## DEATH PENALTY

The death sentence was widely used across the region, including in states such as Algeria, Lebanon, Morocco and Tunisia that have not carried out any executions for years. By contrast, the governments of Iran, Iraq and Saudi Arabia remained among the world's foremost executioners, with Iran being at the forefront of a disturbing spike in executions. Between them, they carried out hundreds of executions despite clear evidence that many of those executed had been sentenced to death after unfair trials or for offences, such as drugs-related crimes, that did not cause

loss of life or fell below the threshold of "most serious crimes". Juvenile offenders were among those executed in Iran and facing execution in Saudi Arabia.

## TORTURE AND OTHER ILL-TREATMENT

Torture and other ill-treatment of detainees remained common and widespread throughout the Middle East and North Africa region. It was used to extract information and "confessions" and to punish and terrorize victims and to intimidate others. Those who perpetrated torture almost always did so with impunity; courts rarely took serious notice of defendants' allegations of torture in pre-trial detention and governments rarely conducted independent investigations into torture or took measures to safeguard detainees, although most countries have ratified the UN Convention against Torture. In Syria, government forces continued to use torture systematically, causing countless further deaths of detainees. In Egypt, security forces frequently assaulted detainees at time of arrest and thereafter subjected them to beatings, electric shocks and painful stress positions. Iranian courts continued to impose punishments that violate the prohibition of torture and other cruel, inhuman or degrading treatment or punishment, included flogging, blinding, stoning and amputations.

## IMPUNITY AND ACCOUNTABILITY

Government forces and non-state armed groups committed war crimes, other violations of international humanitarian law and serious human rights abuses with impunity in Syria, Iraq, Yemen and Libya, and there was no accountability for similar crimes and abuses committed by Israeli forces and Palestinian armed groups during their 2014 conflict and in previous conflicts. In Algeria, it remained a crime to campaign for justice for victims of serious abuses by state forces during the internal armed conflict of the 1990s. In Lebanon, no progress was made in ascertaining the fate of thousands who were forcibly disappeared or went missing during and in the aftermath of the civil war that ended two decades ago. In Egypt, the authorities failed to investigate and ensure accountability for the killings of hundreds of protesters by the security forces since June 2013.

In May, Tunisia's Truth and Dignity Commission, appointed following the "Jasmine Revolution" of 2011, began hearing testimonies as part of its investigations into past human rights violations. However, the Commission remained weakened by corruption allegations and resignations while a new draft law threatened to scupper any prospect that it could ensure accountability for economic crimes committed during the regime that held power until 2011. In Libya, Tripoli authorities sentenced former Gaddafi-era officials to long prison terms or death for alleged war crimes and other offences committed during the 2011 uprising and ensuing armed conflict. Their trial was marred by irregularities; the authorities failed to comply with an ICC demand that they hand over Saif al-Islam al-Gaddafi, son of Mu'ammar al-Gaddafi; instead, they put him on trial and sentenced him to death.

## DISCRIMINATION – MINORITIES

Religious and ethnic minorities continued to face discrimination in several countries. In Iran, Baha'is, Sufis, Yaresan (Ahl-e Haq), Sunni Muslims, Christian converts from Islam, and Shi'a Muslims who became Sunni were imprisoned or prevented from freely practising their faith. Minority rights activists belonging to Iran's disadvantaged ethnic groups including Ahwazi Arabs, Azerbaijani Turks, Baluchis and Kurds, were given harsh prison sentences, and remained disproportionately subject to the death penalty. In Saudi Arabia, discrimination against the Shi'a minority remained entrenched and Shi'a leaders and activists were detained and, in some cases, sentenced to death in unfair trials. In Kuwait, the government continued to withhold citizenship from over 100,000 Bidun, claiming that they were illegal residents although many were born and had lived all their lives in Kuwait,

and Bidun rights activists faced arrest and prosecution. In Israel, Palestinian citizens faced discrimination in many areas, especially housing and land rights.

## FORCED EVICTIONS

Israeli authorities continued to demolish Palestinian homes in the West Bank, including East Jerusalem, that they said were built without virtually unobtainable Israeli permits, forcibly evicting their occupants, and punished the families of Palestinians who attacked Israelis by destroying their homes. They also demolished the homes of Palestinian citizens of Israel mostly in Bedouin villages in the Negev/Naqab region. In Egypt, the military carried out forced evictions to create a security "buffer" zone along the country's border with the Gaza Strip.

## WOMEN AND GIRLS

Women and girls continued to face discrimination under the law and in practice in all countries in the Middle East and North Africa region; in many, they also faced high levels of sexual and other violence. Personal status laws commonly accorded women fewer rights than men in relation to divorce, custody of children and inheritance, while several countries' nationality laws barred women married to foreign spouses, unlike men with foreign spouses, from passing on their nationality to their children.

In Jordan, women continued to receive inadequate protection against violence including so-called "honour" crimes. The government revised legislation that allowed rapists to escape prosecution if they married their victim, except in cases where the victim is aged between 15 and 18. In Bahrain, a new law afforded greater protection to victims of domestic violence but only after the country's parliament voted down an article that would have criminalized marital rape. In Saudi Arabia, women were allowed for the first time to vote and stand in municipal elections but they continued to be prohibited from driving. Iran's Parliament approved the general principles of a draft law that undermines women's right to decide freely whether and when to marry, divorce and have children, and debated other draft laws that threaten to further entrench discrimination against women, including one that would block access to information about contraception and outlaw voluntary sterilization. Women in Iran also remained subject to compulsory "veiling" (*hijab*) laws and to harassment, violence and imprisonment by the police and paramilitary forces that enforced such laws.

Women and girls comprised half the population of the region and made an enormous contribution to every society within it, yet they were denied equality with men in virtually all facets of life. No country had a woman head of state, very few women held high political office or senior diplomatic posts, and women were totally or largely absent from the judiciary, particularly its highest levels. This was unsurprising given the continuing prevalence of stereotypical and discriminatory attitudes towards women and their human rights. The most public and extreme manifestation of such prejudice and misogyny were the crimes, including rape, forced marriage, sexual slavery and summary killing, committed against women and girls by IS forces, particularly in Iraq. But throughout the region, the prevalence of gender-based violence and lack of redress for survivors was anything but exceptional.

By the end of 2015, the heady hopes of political and human rights reform that the mass popular uprisings of the Arab Spring had aroused across the region four years earlier had been all but totally dashed. Instead of political and social reform, economic advance and greater protection of human rights, the region was gripped by armed conflict, tightening state repression, abuse of rights, and the threat of attack by armed groups. Yet, amid the gloom and despair, thousands of valiant individuals – human rights defenders, medical workers and volunteers, lawyers, journalists, community activists and others – showed through their actions that the hopes expressed in 2011 remain alive, deep-seated and anything but an empty dream.

# AMNESTY
# INTERNATIONAL
# REPORT 2015/16

## A-Z COUNTRY ENTRIES

# AFGHANISTAN

**Islamic Republic of Afghanistan**
Head of state and government: **Muhammad Ashraf Ghani Ahmadzai**

There was growing insecurity with insurgency and criminal activity worsening across the country. The first three months of 2015 were the most violent of any equivalent period on record. The UN Assistance Mission in Afghanistan (UNAMA) recorded 1,592 civilians killed and 3,329 injured in the first six months of 2015, while 70% of civilian casualties were attributed to Taliban and other armed insurgent groups, and 16% to pro-Afghan government forces. The Taliban increasingly attacked soft and civilian targets. In September the Taliban took control of most of Kunduz province, and the government reported that some 20,000 people were internally displaced due to the conflict. The majority did not receive any humanitarian assistance from the government. The Ministry of Women's Affairs registered thousands of cases of violence against women in the last nine months of the year. Threats, intimidation and attacks by a range of perpetrators against human rights defenders continued in a climate of impunity, with the government failing to investigate cases and bring those suspected of criminal responsibility to trial. The Afghan Parliament amended the Mass Media Law which journalists and human rights groups feared would further restrict freedom of expression. Afghanistan continued to apply the death penalty, often after unfair trials.

## BACKGROUND

On 19 April the unity government completed its cabinet which received the Parliament's vote of confidence. On 30 June the government launched its first National Action Plan relating to UN Security Council Resolution 1325 on Women, Peace and Security. It enshrined the government's pledges to increase women's role in the four pillars of Resolution 1325: participation, protection, prevention, and relief and recovery.

On 29 July the government proclaimed that Mullah Omar, the Taliban leader, died in April 2013 in Pakistan. Following this announcement a string of attacks occurred in the capital, Kabul, between 7 and 10 August. Mullah Akhtar Mohammad Mansoor, Mullah Omar's deputy since 2010, was announced as his successor. In his first public statement as the new leader on 1 August, he called for Taliban unity and continued jihad, while characterizing reports of a peace process as enemy propaganda. In May, the Ministry of Interior estimated that there were some 7,180 foreign fighters across Afghanistan, the majority of whom were associated with armed groups Tehreek-e-Taliban Pakistan and the Islamic Movement of Uzbekistan.

There were reports of the emergence of the group Islamic State (IS) in at least four provinces of Afghanistan, although the extent to which groups operating under its banner had any affiliation to IS in Syria was unclear.

## ABUSES BY INTERNATIONAL AND AFGHAN FORCES, AND BY PRO-GOVERNMENT ARMED GROUPS

Civilian casualties resulting from operations by international military forces decreased considerably, owing to the withdrawal of US/International Security Assistance Force (ISAF) combat forces.

However, attacks by pro-government forces, particularly the Afghan national security forces (ANSF), resulted in an increasing number of civilian casualties in the first six months of 2015, according to UNAMA. Of a total of 4,921 civilian casualties, 796 were allegedly caused by pro-government forces – a 60% rise compared to the same period in 2014.

There were reports of violations carried out by the Afghan Local Police (ALP), including intimidation, beatings, illegal detention, targeted killings and child rape. In September the *New York Times* reported that the US military ignored complaints by its personnel of the sexual abuse of young boys by ALP commanders on its bases.

Accountability for unlawful killings by pro-government forces and groups was virtually non-existent, although President Ghani pledged to take steps to reduce civilian casualties.

On 3 October US forces bombed a hospital run by Médecins sans Frontières (MSF) in Kunduz province in the north, killing 40 people, including 14 hospital staff, and destroying parts of the building. MSF called for an independent investigation into the bombing.

## ABUSES BY ARMED GROUPS

Attacks by the Taliban and other armed insurgent groups continued to cause the majority of civilian casualties. UNAMA attributed 70% of civilian deaths and injuries between 1 January and 30 June to attacks carried out by armed groups (3,436 civilian casualties, including 1,213 dead and 2,223 injured, representing a 3% decrease from the same period in 2014). The Taliban claimed responsibility for incidents causing over 1,000 civilian casualties, and UNAMA attributed an additional 971 civilian casualties to Taliban-affiliated commanders. UNAMA documented 10 civilian casualties caused by groups associated with IS, primarily in the east.

Most civilian casualties attributed to the Taliban and other armed groups were the result of violations of international humanitarian law, amounting to war crimes. The Taliban and other armed groups continued deliberate attacks on civilians and civilian objects, using weapons such as pressure plate improvised explosive devices (IEDs). According to its official statements, the Taliban reinstated their policy of deliberately targeting individuals associated with the government or seen by them as "pernicious".

Eleven NGO-run clinics and nine public schools were closed down in Nangahar province due to threats from IS, according to the International NGO Safety Organization (INSO). INSO recorded 150 attacks on aid workers, resulting in 33 deaths, 33 injuries and 82 abductions over nine months in 2015.

Civilians continued to be subject to killings, hostage-taking and arbitrary punishments by armed groups as a result of trials by *ad hoc* justice structures. These did not exhaust all judicial guarantees, in violation of international humanitarian law.

On 23 February, 30 civilians, mostly members of the Hazara community, were abducted by armed groups in Zabul province. On 11 May, 19 were released in exchange for relatives of Uzbek insurgents, held in government prisons. The fate of the remaining 11 was unknown at the end of the year.

On 10 April the bodies of five Afghan employees of the NGO Save the Children were found in Uruzgan province. They had been abducted on 1 March in an attempt to exchange them for Taliban prisoners.

On 28 September, the Taliban took control of Kunduz city, releasing nearly 700 prisoners, among them at least 100 Taliban members. Much public and private property was destroyed, including that of media organizations. Reports of rapes and unlawful killings were rife.

## HUMAN RIGHTS DEFENDERS

Threats, intimidation and attacks against human rights defenders continued in a climate of impunity, with the government failing to investigate cases and bring those suspected of criminal responsibility to justice. Human rights defenders suffered bombings, grenade attacks and assassinations by state and non-state actors. Women participating in public life were at greater risk of discrimination and violence than men because they were perceived as defying cultural and social norms.

On 8 January Senator Rohgul Khairzad was seriously injured when her car was fired upon by unknown assailants. She was previously attacked in 2013 by Taliban insurgents who fired at her car, killing her seven-year-old daughter and brother; her 11-year-old daughter was left paralyzed.

On 16 February Angiza Shinwari, a provincial council member in Nangahar province and defender of women's rights, died following a targeted bomb attack on her vehicle which also killed her driver and injured four others. No one claimed responsibility and no arrests were made.

On 28 September the Taliban took control of Kunduz province in a surprise attack. There were reports of house-to-house searches for media personnel and women human rights defenders allegedly named on a hit-list. Many women human rights defenders fled the city, while others were forced into hiding.

## REFUGEES AND INTERNALLY DISPLACED PEOPLE

Afghanistan continued to produce vast numbers of refugees and internally displaced persons, second only to Syria. According to UNHCR, the UN refugee agency, nearly three million Afghans were refugees, the majority of whom were living in Iran and Pakistan. Nearly one million Afghans were internally displaced in Afghanistan.

The armed conflict, insecurity and natural disasters were the main causes of displacement in Afghanistan. Despite the launch by the government of the National Internally Displaced People Policy in February 2014, at the end of 2015 many thousands of people were still living in camps and makeshift shelters, where overcrowding, poor hygiene and harsh weather conditions increased the prevalence of communicable and chronic diseases such as malaria and hepatitis.

According to the UN Office for Coordination of Humanitarian Affairs (OCHA), in the first six months of 2015 some 103,000 people were reportedly displaced mainly because of the armed conflict and insecurity across Afghanistan. The government reported that some 20,000 people were internally displaced as a result of the conflict in Kunduz province in September.

## VIOLENCE AGAINST WOMEN AND GIRLS

The government took steps to improve women's participation in governance. On 21 March President Ghani and Abdullah Abdullah, Chief Executive Officer of Afghanistan, announced four women among the nominees to lead the Ministry of Women's Affairs, the Ministry of Higher Education, the Ministry of Labour, Social Affairs, Martyrs and Disabled, and the Ministry of Counter Narcotics.

By 20 August, 75 police women councils (PWCs) had been established – 45 in Ministry of Interior directorates and Kabul police districts, and 30 in provinces. The PWCs were introduced in December 2014 by the Ministry of Interior with the aim of strengthening and building capacity among female police officers. On 14 September the Afghan cabinet approved the Regulation Against Sexual Harassment of Women and Girls, which criminalizes and penalizes certain acts of sexual harassment of women. At the end of the year the Ministry of Women's Affairs (MOWA) was drafting a further regulation to prevent discrimination in the workplace, due to be sent to the Ministry of Justice for review in 2016. Following a presidential decree of 2 January, 144 women and girls who had been detained for so-called "moral" crimes were released.

The Ministry of Women's Affairs registered more than 4,000 cases of violence against women in the last nine months of the year. Violence against women was severely under-reported in Afghanistan due to insecurity, lack of a functioning government or judiciary, and traditional practices which combined to discourage victims and their families from reporting violence.

On 12 February, police in Balkh arrested six people in connection with the marriage of an 11-year-old girl.

On 19 March, Farkhunda Malikzada was killed by a mob near the Shah-e Du Shamshira shrine in Kabul after being falsely accused of burning a copy of the Qur'an. A primary court in Kabul sentenced four men to death for her murder, while others received prison sentences. On 2 July an appeal court overruled the four death sentences and reduced them to prison sentences of between 10 and 20 years.

On 9 August a woman accused of adultery was hanged during a tribal court hearing by the Taliban in Badakhshan province.

## FREEDOM OF EXPRESSION
Journalists in Afghanistan continued to face violence and censorship by state and non-state actors. Some journalists were killed during attacks, while others were forced to leave their homes and seek sanctuary elsewhere. Nai, a media watchdog in Afghanistan, reported 73 cases of attacks against journalists and media workers, with the majority being committed by government representatives, including police and security agencies, as well as elected officials. The government failed to investigate those suspected of responsibility for attacks against journalists and media workers. On 28 January Parliament amended the Mass Media Law and limited media freedom, which journalists and human rights groups feared would further restrict freedom of expression.

## TORTURE AND OTHER ILL-TREATMENT
On 4 May the government established a working committee to launch a National Action Plan for the elimination of torture. On 25 June the National Directorate of Security, Afghanistan's intelligence agency, issued an order reiterating the prohibition on torture, particularly its use during police interrogations. Despite these developments, torture and other ill-treatment, as well as incommunicado detention, remained prevalent throughout the prison system, while the authorities continued to arrest and detain individuals arbitrarily without due process. Individuals were frequently detained for acts that were not offences under Afghan law. They included so-called "moral" crimes such as "running away", which affected mainly women and girls. Prison conditions remained below international standards with overcrowding, insufficient food and water and poor sanitation facilities.

While conflict-related detainees held in US custody were transferred to the Afghan authorities in December 2014, a lack of accountability for illegal detentions, ill-treatment and torture of detainees by US personnel in Afghanistan persisted.

## DEATH PENALTY
Afghanistan continued to apply the death penalty, often after unfair trials. By the end of the year, results were still awaited of the review of nearly 400 death row cases ordered by President Ghani in 2014.

On 28 February Raees Khudaidad was hanged at Pul-e-Charkhi prison in Kabul, after being charged with murder, kidnapping and armed robbery.

# ALBANIA

Republic of Albania
Head of state: **Bujar Nishani**
Head of government: **Edi Rama**

**Roma and Egyptian communities were denied adequate housing and subjected to forced evictions. Thousands of Albanians, driven by poverty, sought asylum in the EU. Protection against domestic violence remained inadequate.**

## BACKGROUND
The European Commission in November required Albania to protect fundamental rights, reform the judiciary and combat corruption and organized crime before talks on EU membership could commence. In June, a parliamentary committee reported widespread corruption among police, prosecutors and the judiciary. In December around 50,000 people joined opposition-led protests against government corruption and rising poverty.

A law introduced in May enabled the subjects of surveillance by the communist-era state security service (Sigurimi) to access their files.

## ENFORCED DISAPPEARANCES

The authorities made no progress in bringing to justice those responsible for the enforced disappearance in 1995 of Remzi Hoxha, an ethnic Albanian from Macedonia, or in establishing the whereabouts of his remains. Former state security agent Ilir Kumbaro, convicted in 2012 for the torture and subsequent death of Remzi Hoxha, remained at large after absconding from an extradition hearing in the UK.

In March, an Office of Missing Persons was established to locate the remains of Albanians forcibly disappeared under the communist government between 1944 and 1991.

## FREEDOMS OF EXPRESSION AND ASSEMBLY

Media independence was compromised by self-censorship, government pressure on media outlets and threats against journalists. Journalist Aurora Koromani received police protection in June after receiving threats believed to originate from the armed group Islamic State (IS), following her investigations into IS recruitment in Albania. Several other journalists sought asylum in the EU and Norway on the basis that the authorities were unable to protect them.

Civil society activist Nderim Lushi was convicted in December of organizing an illegal assembly and inciting violence "against the constitutional order" after a peaceful demonstration in May in Kukës which called on the government to cancel electricity debts and encouraged citizens not to leave Albania. Police had used excessive force against demonstrators.

## VIOLENCE AGAINST WOMEN AND GIRLS

State police reported 1,696 cases of family violence in the first six months of the year, giving rise to 993 requests for civil protection orders. Of 406 requests submitted to courts in the capital Tirana between January and August, only 118 were granted, with 251 applicants withdrawing their application, or not attending court due to pressure from their abusers or family members. In Tirana between January and June, defendants were convicted of family violence in 185 out of 190 prosecutions; most had pleaded guilty.

## HOUSING RIGHTS

Many Roma and Egyptians, as well as young people leaving social care, failed to meet the income threshold required to access social housing. Many Roma were unable to regularize their homes under the 2014 law on the legalization of property, which allowed "illegal constructions" to be demolished. In July, 70 mainly Romani families' houses were demolished in Selita, Tirana, during a forced eviction in advance of road construction.

## IMPUNITY

In June the prosecutor found that the failure of former State Police director Hysni Burgaj and his deputy Agron Kuliçaj to execute arrest warrants for members of the Republic Guard, who were alleged to have shot and killed four protesters in an anti-government demonstration in January 2011, was not a criminal offence. Despite convictions for the deaths of three protesters, impunity persisted in the case of the fourth, Aleks Nika.

## TORTURE AND OTHER ILL-TREATMENT

Ill-treatment of suspects in police stations was widespread; police and medical staff failed in their duty to report such incidents.

In July, the Ombudsperson reported on chronic overcrowding and inadequate conditions and health care in places of detention.

## REFUGEES AND ASYLUM-SEEKERS

Albania remained a transit country for migrants and refugees. Thousands of Albanians applied for asylum in EU countries, including 54,762 in Germany, which rejected 99% of their claims; thousands were deported back to Albania from Germany and Sweden.

# ALGERIA

People's Democratic Republic of Algeria
Head of state: **Abdelaziz Bouteflika**
Head of government: **Abdelmalek Sellal**

**The authorities restricted freedoms of expression, association and assembly, arresting, prosecuting and imprisoning peaceful protesters, activists and journalists. Legislators amended the Penal Code to protect women from violence. Perpetrators of torture and other serious human rights abuses in the 1990s continued to evade justice. Courts handed down death sentences; no executions were carried out.**

## BACKGROUND

In January, unprecedented protests took place in southern Algeria against fracking – the hydraulic fracture of rock to extract shale gas.

In July, at least 25 people were killed and others were injured in communal violence in the M'zab Valley, 600km south of the capital Algiers.

There were clashes between the security forces and armed opposition groups in various areas, according to media reports. The authorities stated that the security forces killed 109 alleged members of armed groups while disclosing few details of the circumstances in which they were killed. The armed group al-Qa'ida in the Islamic Maghreb (AQIM) said it carried out an attack in the northern province of Ain Defla in July that killed 14 soldiers.

The authorities persisted in their refusal to allow visits to Algeria by some UN human rights bodies and experts, including those with mandates on torture, counter-terrorism, enforced disappearances and freedom of association.[1]

## FREEDOM OF ASSEMBLY

In January, the authorities responded to protests against unemployment in the southern city of Laghouat by arresting peaceful activists and protesters, including those protesting in solidarity with detained activists. Some of those arrested were prosecuted on charges including participation in "unarmed gatherings", including Mohamed Rag, Belkacem Khencha and other members of the National Committee for the Defence of the Rights of the Unemployed (CNDDC), who received prison terms of between one and two years, some of which were reduced on appeal. In March, a court in the southern city of El Oued sentenced five peaceful protesters to prison terms of up to four months. At the end of the year, they remained at liberty pending an appeal to Algeria's High Court.[2] In October, a court in Tamanrasset sentenced seven protesters to one-year prison terms; six had their prison terms suspended on appeal.[3]

The authorities continued to enforce a ban on all demonstrations in Algiers. In February, security forces prevented a peaceful gathering in support of anti-fracking demonstrators by arresting people as they arrived at the protest location and detaining them for several hours.

In June, police forcibly dispersed a peaceful protest by members of SOS Disparus, a group campaigning on behalf of victims of enforced disappearance during the internal armed conflict of the 1990s, including elderly relatives of those who disappeared and whose fate the authorities have never disclosed.

## FREEDOM OF EXPRESSION

The authorities prosecuted journalists, cartoonists, activists and others on insult, defamation and other similar charges.

In February, a court in Oran convicted Mohamed Chergui of insulting the prophet Muhammad after Mohamed Chergui's employer, the newspaper *El Djoumhouria*, complained about an article he submitted based on foreign academic research about Islam. He received a three-year prison term and a fine of 200,000 Algerian dinars (around US$1,900) in his absence. His prison term was later reduced to a one-year suspended sentence, against which he appealed.

In March, a court in El Oued sentenced anti-corruption and CNDDC activist Rachid Aouine to a fine of 20,000 Algerian dinars (around US$190) and six months' imprisonment – reduced to four months on appeal – after it convicted him of "incitement to an unarmed gathering". The charge related to a sarcastic comment that he had posted on Facebook.[4]

Journalist, Abdelhai Abdessamia was released on bail in September after more than two years in pre-trial detention. He worked for the *Djaridati* and *Mon Journal* newspapers until the authorities shut them down in 2013 for reporting on President Bouteflika's health. Authorities accused him of helping to smuggle the newspapers' editorial director out of Algeria to Tunisia. Following his arrest in 2013, judicial police held Abdelhai Abdessamia in arbitrary detention for six days, in breach of Algerian law, before handing him over to the national gendarmerie and military security for interrogation.

In October, security forces arrested activist Hassan Bouras, a leading member of the Algerian League for the Defence of Human Rights (LADDH), in the western city of El Bayadh. He remained in detention at the end of the year while under investigation for "insulting a public institution" and "inciting citizens or inhabitants to take up arms against the authority of the state or against each other", charges that could incur the death penalty.[5]

In November, a court in El Oued sentenced cartoonist Tahar Djehiche to a six-month prison term and a fine of 500,000 Algerian dinars (around US$4,600) for "insulting" President Bouteflika and "inciting" others to join a shale gas protest in a comment Tahar Djehiche made on his Facebook page. He had previously been cleared by a court of first instance. At the end of the year, he remained at liberty pending an appeal before the High Court.[6]

## FREEDOM OF ASSOCIATION

Associations seeking legal registration under Law 12-06, including Amnesty International Algeria, were left in limbo by the authorities, who failed to respond to registration applications. The law, which took effect in 2012, imposes wide-ranging and arbitrary restrictions on the registration of associations and makes it a crime, punishable by up to six months' imprisonment and a fine, to belong to an unregistered, suspended or dissolved association.

## HUMAN RIGHTS DEFENDERS

In August, Italian authorities arrested Algerian human rights lawyer Rachid Mesli, founder of the Geneva-based human rights NGO Alkarama and a political refugee in Switzerland. His arrest came after Algerian authorities requested his extradition on charges of providing phones and cameras to terrorist groups, for which they had convicted him in his absence based on a previous "confession" that he said had been obtained by torture. Italy's judicial authorities placed him under house arrest for more than three weeks before lifting the restriction and allowing him to return to Switzerland.[7]

In December, local authorities banned a training event in Algiers for members of the Maghreb Co-ordination of Human Rights Organizations, including human rights defenders from Algeria, Morocco, Tunisia and Mauritania.

## JUSTICE SYSTEM

In July, the government decreed amendments to the Code of Criminal Procedure, broadening the range of alternatives to pre-charge and pre-trial detention. Suspects were granted a specific right of access to lawyers during pre-charge detention, but not during interrogation.

Following deadly clashes in the northern Saharan region, the security forces arrested 25 people in Ghardaia in July, including Kameleddine Fekhar and other activists supporting the autonomy of the M'zab region, and placed them in pre-trial detention for investigation on suspicion of terrorism and inciting hatred. They remained in detention at the end of the year.

## WOMEN'S RIGHTS
In December, legislators amended the Penal Code, criminalizing physical violence against a spouse and indecent assaults on women carried out in public.[8] However, women remained inadequately protected against gender-based violence in the absence of a comprehensive law, while the Penal Code continued to give immunity from criminal prosecution to men who rape girls under the age of 18 if they marry their victim.

## IMPUNITY
2015 marked the 10th anniversary of the Charter on Peace and National Reconciliation, under which the security forces obtained immunity from prosecution for crimes committed during the internal armed conflict of the 1990s and subsequently, and public criticism of their conduct during the conflict was criminalized. The authorities continued to fail to investigate thousands of enforced disappearances and other serious human rights violations and abuses, bring perpetrators to justice, and provide effective remedies to victims' families. Families of those forcibly disappeared who continued to seek truth and justice were subject to surveillance and repeated summons for questioning by the security forces.

## REFUGEES' AND MIGRANTS' RIGHTS
Sub-Saharan African refugees and migrants continued to enter Algeria irregularly, mostly through the southern borders. Algerian security forces arrested migrants and asylum-seekers, in particular at the southern borders. In April, the Algerian army arrested around 500 sub-Saharan migrants near the border with Niger, according to press reports. The Algerian authorities reported that nationals of Niger within the group were then "voluntarily" returned to Niger in co-operation with Nigerien authorities.

## DEATH PENALTY
Courts imposed dozens of death sentences, mostly on murder and terrorism charges, including in cases dating back to the internal armed conflict of the 1990s. No executions have been carried out since 1993.

1. The UN Human Rights Council needs to put in place effective measures to evaluate and follow up on non-co-operation with Special Procedures (IOR 40/1269/2015)
2. Algeria: Halt repression of fracking and unemployment protesters (MDE 28/2122/2015)
3. Algeria: End relentless targeting of government critics (MDE 28/2951/2015)
4. Algeria: Halt repression of fracking and unemployment protesters (MDE 28/2122/2015)
5. Algeria: End relentless targeting of government critics (MDE 28/2951/2015)
6. Algeria: End relentless targeting of government critics (MDE 28/2951/2015)
7. Algerian human rights defender at risk of extradition must be released immediately (MDE 28/2313/2015)
8. Algeria: Global reform needed to combat gender-based violence (MDE 28/3044/2015)

# ANGOLA

Republic of Angola
Head of state and government: **José Eduardo dos Santos**

Freedoms of expression, association and assembly were severely restricted. At least 16 prisoners of conscience were in detention; 15 of them were placed under house arrest on 18 December. The authorities used criminal defamation laws and state security legislation to harass, arbitrarily arrest and detain individuals for peacefully expressing their views, and to restrict press freedom. The government passed a new law restricting the activities of NGOs.

## BACKGROUND
The global drop in the price of oil during 2015 negatively affected the economy.

Security forces used excessive force against people who criticized the government, exposed corruption or denounced human rights violations. The space for the exercise of the rights to freedom of expression, peaceful assembly and association shrank as human rights defenders and government critics were arrested and subjected to criminal prosecutions by an increasingly politicized judiciary.

When its human rights record was assessed under the Universal Periodic Review (UPR) in 2014, Angola had accepted 192 of the 226 recommendations made and stated that it would give further consideration to the remaining 34 recommendations, including many related to freedoms of expression, association and peaceful assembly. In March 2015, Angola rejected these recommendations, including recommendations to refrain from using criminal defamation laws to restrict the right to freedom of expression.

## PRISONERS OF CONSCIENCE

The authorities continued to imprison government critics, human rights defenders, political activists and journalists. At the end of the year, at least 16 prisoners of conscience were in detention, 15 under house arrest.

On 14 September human rights defender José Marcos Mavungo was sentenced to six years' imprisonment on charges of rebellion, a state security crime. He had been involved in organizing a peaceful demonstration on 14 March, the day he was arrested, and was accused of association with a group of men found with explosives and flyers the day before the demonstration. No evidence of this association or of José Marcos Mavungo's involvement in producing the flyers was presented, nor were the other men brought to trial.

Fifteen male youth activists were arrested and detained by security forces between 20 and 24 June in the capital, Luanda, in connection with a peaceful meeting they attended to discuss politics and governance concerns under the presidency of José

Eduardo dos Santos.[1] They were formally charged on 16 September with preparatory acts of rebellion and of plotting against the President. Two women activists were charged with the same crimes, but were not detained. Lawyers for the 15 were only officially informed of the charges on 30 September, beyond the 90 days' pre-trial detention period permitted by law. The charges, which are considered state security crimes, each carry a penalty of up to three years' imprisonment. Three activists faced additional charges: Manuel Nito Alves, for illegal change of name (maximum penalty one month's imprisonment); Luaty Beirão for falsification of documents (maximum penalty eight years' imprisonment); and Osvaldo Caholo for theft of documents (maximum penalty eight years' imprisonment).

Four of the 15 activists went on hunger strike on 20 September for several days to protest against their unlawful detention. On 9 October, Luaty Beirão, who had remained on hunger strike, was transferred to the prison hospital of São Paulo, where he accepted an intravenous saline drip on 11 October but no solid food.[2] On 15 October, he was transferred to a private hospital in Luanda. He ended his hunger strike after 36 days.

The trial of the activists started on 16 November and breached numerous international fair trial standards, including the right to a public hearing and the right to be tried without undue delay.[3] On 18 December, the 15 activists were placed under house arrest. The trial was scheduled to continue on 11 January 2016.

## FREEDOM OF ASSEMBLY

Although by law demonstrations do not require authorization, the authorities frequently refused to allow them to take place. When demonstrations did take place, police often arbitrarily arrested and detained peaceful protesters. On a number of occasions police detained and beat protesters before leaving them many kilometres away from where they were seized.

On 29 July, police in Luanda beat and

arrested participants at a peaceful protest calling for the release of the 15 youth activists detained in June.

On 8 August, protesters peacefully demanding the release of the 15 youth activists were assaulted by armed police who used batons and dogs against them and beat several of the protesters. Several people were briefly detained before being released without charge. Those protesting included the mothers and wives of some of the detained activists.

On 11 October, supporters of the 15 youth activists held a vigil at Sagrada Família Church in Luanda. According to those who took part, the police arrived at the vigil with guns, water cannons and dogs. To avoid conflict with the police, the participants cut the vigil short. The next day another vigil was held, and several people were briefly detained by the police before being released without charge.

Attorney Arão Bula Tempo, Chair of the Cabinda Bar Association, was detained on 14 March in the province of Cabinda and conditionally released on 13 May. On 22 October he was formally charged with attempting to collaborate with foreigners to constrain the Angolan state (maximum penalty five years' imprisonment) and rebellion (maximum penalty 12 years' imprisonment). Both offences are classified as crimes against the security of the state. The charges were based on an allegation that Arão Bula Tempo had invited journalists from the Republic of Congo to cover a demonstration organized by José Marcos Mavungo (see above). Arão Bula Tempo's health deteriorated towards the end of the year and he wished to seek health care outside Cabinda province. However, he was not allowed to leave Cabinda. These restrictions violated Arão Bula Tempo's right to freedom of movement and his right to the highest attainable standard of health.[4] No date had been set for his trial by the end of the year.

# FREEDOM OF EXPRESSION

The authorities continued to use criminal defamation laws and state security laws to suppress peaceful expression of opinions, especially those critical of the government.

Rafael Marques de Morais, an anti-corruption and human rights journalist, was convicted of slanderous denunciation in May. The conviction was based on allegations of criminal conduct he made after the publication of his 2011 book, *Blood Diamonds*, in which he accused military generals and two mining companies of complicity in human rights abuses committed in the diamond fields of Lundas province. He was sentenced to six months' imprisonment, suspended for two years. His lawyers lodged an appeal before the Supreme Court in June, but it had not been heard by the end of 2015. (The average time for an appeal to be heard is two years.)

# FREEDOM OF ASSOCIATION

The government enacted a new law covering the registration of NGOs, Presidential Decree 74/15 of 23 March. The law imposed rigorous restrictions on how organizations must register and report their finances. The new law's provisions could stifle the ability of NGOs and other civil society organizations to organize and operate. Under the new decree, the Public Prosecutor's Office is empowered to suspend the activities of national and international NGOs on suspicion of money laundering, or illegal or harmful acts against Angola's sovereignty and integrity. In addition, Article 15 limits the ability of NGOs to receive and utilize resources and to carry out their activities as they determine best to achieve their objectives. The ability to seek, receive and utilize funding is a critical component of the right to freedom of association.

---

1. Angola: Detained activists must be immediately released (News story, 22 June)
2. Angola: Prisoner of conscience in critical condition must be released immediately (News story, 20 October)
3. Angola: Kangaroo court undermines judicial independence as trial of

4. Urgent Action, Angola: Further information: Two activists still face 10-15 years in jail (AFR 12/2039/2015)

# ARGENTINA

**Argentine Republic**
Head of state and government: **Mauricio Macri**
(replaced Cristina Fernández de Kirchner in November)

Women and girls faced obstacles in accessing legal abortions. Discrimination against Indigenous Peoples remained a concern. People suspected of committing crimes during the military dictatorship (1976 to 1983) stood trial. Reports of torture and other ill-treatment were not investigated.

## BACKGROUND

The presidential elections dominated the political landscape during the year. Mauricio Macri was elected President after a second ballot on 22 November.

## SEXUAL AND REPRODUCTIVE RIGHTS

The Ministry of Health published a new protocol for the implementation of legal abortions in line with a 2012 ruling by the Supreme Court. The protocol had not received ministerial endorsement by the end of the year. More than half of jurisdictions lacked comprehensive hospital protocols that would guarantee access to legal abortion when a pregnancy is the result of rape or poses a risk to the health or life of the woman or girl.

A woman from a deprived neighbourhood in Tierra del Fuego was released on bail after being charged in 2013 with having a clandestine abortion. She had faced restrictions in accessing a legal abortion in her locality. The outcome of the trial was pending at the end of the year.

## RIGHTS OF LESBIAN, GAY, BISEXUAL, TRANSGENDER AND INTERSEX PEOPLE

In September, a well-known Argentinian LGBTI activist, Daiana Sacayán, was found dead in her apartment. She was the third transgender woman – after Marcela Chocobar and Coty Olmos – to have died in violent circumstances in one month. By the end of the year nobody had been charged over their deaths.

## INDIGENOUS PEOPLES' RIGHTS

Although the Constitution recognizes the rights of Indigenous Peoples to their ancestral lands and to participate in the management of natural resources, these rights were rarely respected.

Félix Díaz, leader of La Primavera community (Potae Napocna Navogoh) in Formosa Province, continued to face criminal proceedings in three separate cases on charges dating from 2010 of illegal occupation of land, resistance to authority and theft. He denied the allegations. In June the defence called for the decision to try him for allegedly seizing land to be overturned. However, by the end of the year the decision was still pending.

In October, Relmu Ñamku, leader of the Mapuche community of Winkul Newen in Neuquén Province, was tried on disproportionate charges for resisting unlawful eviction from her ancestral territory. She was acquitted of the charge of attempting to murder a police officer. It was the first criminal trial in the region to include an intercultural jury and a simultaneous interpretation into Mapuzungun, the native language of the Mapuche.

## TRANSITIONAL JUSTICE

Public trials were held for crimes against humanity perpetrated during the military regime between 1976 and 1983. There were eight new convictions, bringing the total number of those sentenced between 2006 and 2015 to 142.

There was little progress in bringing to justice those from the civil, business and legal sectors. According to the Public Prosecutor's Office, questions about responsibility remained even in cases where significant evidence had been gathered. To date, only one member of the judiciary and two businessmen have been convicted.

On 23 September, the Chamber of Deputies passed a bill to the Senate proposing the creation of a commission, with representatives from both the Chamber and Senate, to identify economic and financial interests that had colluded with the military dictatorship.

## IMPUNITY

The investigation into the death in January of Alberto Nisman, prosecutor in the case of the 1994 attack on the Jewish Mutual Association of Argentina (AMIA) building in the capital, Buenos Aires, in which 85 people were killed, continued at the end of the year.

In August, the public hearing into the cover-up of the investigation into the 1994 AMIA attack began. Among those accused of the cover-up were a former judge and prosecutor and high-ranking officials, including former President Carlos Menem. The main case relating to the attack has been stalled since 2006 when a judge issued orders for the capture and extradition of eight Iranian nationals and a Lebanese national for questioning. Four of these orders remained in force and the subject of an Interpol "red alert". Iran refused the extradition requests for the eight Iranians.

## TORTURE AND OTHER ILL-TREATMENT

There were reports of the use of torture during arrest and in prisons in the provinces of Buenos Aires, Santa Fe and Chubut. Methods included the use of electrified cattle prods, near-asphyxiation with a plastic bag or by submersion in water, and prolonged isolation.

Reports of torture and other ill-treatment were not investigated and Argentina still lacked a national system for recording information relating to reports of torture. There was no system in place to protect witnesses to torture. There were further delays in establishing the National System for the Prevention of Torture.

# ARMENIA

**Republic of Armenia**
Head of state: **Serzh Sargsyan**
Head of government: **Hovik Abrahamyan**

**Largely peaceful protests were repeatedly disrupted, including with the use of excessive force by police, which led to yet more and larger protests. Protest organizers faced arrest and criminal prosecution on questionable charges. An anti-government protester was reported attacked and beaten. Torture and other ill-treatment, and impunity enjoyed by the perpetrators, remained a concern. New provisions for alternative civilian service, introduced into law in 2013, were made available for conscientious objectors.**

## BACKGROUND

In a referendum on 6 December, Armenians voted for constitutional amendments that transferred executive power from the presidency to parliament. However, concerns were raised by the opposition that this could also allow the incumbent President to remain in power after his second term.

## FREEDOM OF ASSEMBLY

The year was marked by growing public discontent and widespread protests around a range of social and political issues, and the authorities' attempts to clamp down on their organizers and participants. The two issues prompting the strongest protests across the country were a planned rise in electricity prices, and the constitutional amendments that would allow the President to remain in power beyond the second term, in June and in October respectively.

On 21 September, Smbat Hakobian, a member of a political group critical of the government, was severely beaten after returning from an anti-government demonstration in Yerevan, sustaining head injuries and broken ribs. Police opened an investigation and detained three men as suspects. An investigation into a similar attack against three protesters in 2014 reached no conclusion in 2015.

### Excessive use of force
On repeated occasions, police targeted peaceful protesters and largely peaceful gatherings with excessive force and arrests. Activists taking part in anti-government protests continued to face risk of violence from police and pro-government groups.

On 15 January, police blocked thousands from marching towards the Russian Consulate in Gyumri, to protest against the murder of a family of six by a Russian soldier. According to eyewitness reports, clashes ensued after police in riot gear used truncheons and fired tear gas and stun grenades, while the protesters threw stones in response. Police detained 21 people and released them the following day. Nine protesters and three police officers were reported wounded. Investigation into the incident was opened but was still ongoing at the end of the year.

On 19 June, thousands started a multi-day sit-in protest in the centre of the capital, Yerevan, prompted by the government's announcement of a planned increase in electricity tariffs. On 23 June, approximately 500 demonstrators marched towards the Presidential Administration building, and blocked the road in front of the police cordon. Police used excessive force to disperse them, including dousing people with water cannon. In response, some protesters threw water bottles but otherwise the crowd remained peaceful; 237 people were detained and then released without charge. Police also used excessive force against several journalists, confiscating and damaging their equipment, for which they later issued an official apology. Investigation into the incident was still ongoing at the end of the year.[1]

## FREEDOM OF EXPRESSION
Five members of the Founding Parliament opposition movement were arrested on charges of planning mass unrest after they announced their plans to hold an anti-government rally on 24 April, the day which Armenians marked as the centenary anniversary of the Armenian genocide. This was despite the fact that the organizers had secured official permission to hold the rally. On 9 April, a court in Yerevan ruled to remand them for two months. They were released on 4 May, following mass protests in Yerevan, but the criminal proceedings against them were not closed.

## TORTURE AND OTHER ILL-TREATMENT
Torture and other ill-treatment in police custody and in prisons, as well as impunity for the perpetrators, remained a concern. Local human rights groups highlighted the practice by which law enforcement officials suspected of using torture were often removed temporarily from their positions and later re-appointed to the same, or higher, position in a different police department.

## RIGHTS OF LESBIAN, GAY, BISEXUAL, TRANSGENDER AND INTERSEX PEOPLE
On 17 May, some 100 activists marked the International Day against Homophobia and Transphobia in a closed venue.

Discrimination against LGBTI individuals remained a concern, in the absence of gender-specific anti-discrimination legislation and amid widespread reports of hate speech.

## CONSCIENTIOUS OBJECTORS
Armenia started implementing the legal amendments from 2013 on alternative civilian service, allowing conscripted conscientious objectors to work in public service instead of serving in the armed forces.

---

1. Armenia: Investigate alleged police abuses after protesters doused with water cannon and arrested (News story, 23 June)

# AUSTRALIA

**Australia**
Head of state: **Queen Elizabeth II, represented by Sir Peter Cosgrove**
Head of government: **Malcolm Turnbull (replaced Tony Abbott in September)**

Australia jailed Indigenous people at a disproportionate rate to non-Indigenous people; some children were detained with adults. Australia continued its hard-line policies towards asylum-seekers, including pushing back boats, *refoulement*, and mandatory and indefinite detention, as well as offshore processing on Nauru and in Papua New Guinea. Those assessed as refugees on Nauru were denied the right to settle in Australia and offered temporary visas or residency in Cambodia. Papua New Guinea had yet to finalize a temporary visa, to be granted to those recognized as refugees, leaving many people in a legal limbo unable to leave Manus Island. Staff and contractors who complained about human rights violations at immigration detention facilities could face criminal proceedings under new legislation. New "security" legislation extended data interception powers and a law was passed stripping dual nationals of their Australian citizenship for terrorism-related activities.

## INDIGENOUS PEOPLES' RIGHTS

Indigenous children were 24 times more likely to be detained than non-Indigenous children. As the age of criminal responsibility in Australia is 10, laws allowed for children aged 10 and 11 to be detained in every jurisdiction in violation of the UN Convention on the Rights of the Child. Australia detained children with adults in Queensland and provided limited separation between detained children and adult prisoners in at least one detention centre in the Northern Territory.

The Western Australian government widened existing mandatory sentencing by introducing mandatory sentences for aggravated home burglaries for adults and children aged 16 and 17, and by tightening the mandatory sentencing counting rules for non-violent home burglaries.

Indigenous adults were 14 times more likely than non-Indigenous adults to be incarcerated and deaths in custody continued. In May, an Indigenous man in the Northern Territory died of heart failure in a police watch house, three hours after being taken into custody on suspicion of drinking alcohol in a regulated place. The coroner criticized the paperless arrest system under which the man was taken into custody as "manifestly unfair" in its disproportionate impact on Indigenous people, who were more likely to be targeted by the laws. Three prisoners died in two Western Australia prisons during September, November and December, adding to the list of deaths in custody yet to be heard by the Western Australian Coroner. One prisoner died in a New South Wales prison in December.

In June, the Federal government handed responsibility for essential and municipal services in remote Indigenous communities to state governments. The Western Australian Premier stated that up to 150 communities may be closed as a result; widespread protests ensued. Following the protests the Western Australian government initiated a consultation process.

## REFUGEES AND ASYLUM-SEEKERS

Australia continued its punitive approach to asylum-seekers arriving by boat by pushing them back at sea, returning them to countries of origin without proper assessment of asylum claims, creating a risk of *refoulement*, or by transferring them to Australian-run facilities in Nauru or Papua New Guinea's Manus Island.

By 30 November, 926 people were detained in Papua New Guinea and 543 people remained in the "open" facility on Nauru, including 70 children.

In March, the government released an independent review of the Nauru centre, which documented allegations of rape and sexual assault – including of children – as well as cases of harassment and physical assault (see Nauru entry). The Australian government accepted all of the recommendations but despite this in August a Senate report stated conditions were "not adequate, appropriate or safe". In October the Nauru government announced that asylum-seekers would no longer be detained in the centre, which would become an open facility. It also announced that the remaining 600 asylum claims would be processed "within a week". By the end of December processing still had not been completed.

In June, four refugees were transferred to Cambodia as part of a deal signed in September 2014 where Australia paid an additional A$40 million (US$28 million) in aid to Cambodia, as well as a further A$15 million (US$10.5 million) for specific expenses, to relocate refugees there from its offshore immigration processing centre on Nauru. While one of the four agreed to return from Cambodia to Myanmar in October, a fifth man was transferred to Cambodia from Nauru in November.

Also in June, Indonesian officials alleged Australia paid people-smugglers US$31,000 in May to return to Indonesia a boat carrying 65 asylum-seekers. A Senate Inquiry was ongoing at the end of the year.

Australia continued its policy of indefinite mandatory detention, with 1,852 people detained in onshore immigration detention centres as of 1 December. They included 104 children, despite the government's pledge in August 2014 to end the detention of children.

In July the government introduced the Border Force Act 2015, which includes prison sentences for government staff and contractors, including health and child welfare professionals, who speak out about human rights abuses in immigration detention.

It also proposed legislation that would allow immigration detention employees to use force, including lethal force, against any individual in detention, while removing judicial oversight.

In August the government announced that since December 2013 it had pushed back 20 boats, carrying a combined total of 633 people, including one directly to Vietnam in July. In November, another boat carrying 16 asylum-seekers was reportedly pushed back to Indonesia.

In September the government announced that it would resettle an additional 12,000 Syrian refugees in response to the crisis in the Middle East.

## COUNTER-TERROR AND SECURITY

Parliament passed legislation stripping those with dual nationality of their Australian citizenship on the basis of suspicion of involvement in terrorist-related activities. Australian dual nationals risked losing citizenship without any criminal conviction and with limited procedural safeguards.

Legislation was passed authorizing the mass surveillance of personal metadata.

## INTERNATIONAL SCRUTINY

In November, Australia's human rights record was assessed for the second time under the UN Universal Periodic Review. Australia received criticism for its failure to ratify the Optional Protocol to the UN Convention against Torture and its failure to address Indigenous incarceration rates. Australia received recommendations to introduce a Human Rights Act and to end mandatory detention of asylum-seekers.

# AUSTRIA

Republic of Austria
Head of state: **Heinz Fischer**
Head of government: **Werner Faymann**

**Over 85,000 people sought asylum in the country by the end of November – a remarkable increase on previous years. Thousands of asylum-seekers in the reception centre of Traiskirchen were left to sleep in inadequate facilities, with poor medical care and a lack of protection for unaccompanied minors. The government**

took insufficient steps to address ill-treatment and neglect in the penal and preventive detention systems. The authorities' failure to respond adequately to reports of ill-treatment by the police persisted. Gaps in the Anti-Discrimination law remained.

## REFUGEES, ASYLUM-SEEKERS AND MIGRANTS

Tens of thousands of refugees, asylum-seekers and migrants entered Austria during the year, the majority of whom then travelled to Germany. In one weekend in September, more than 15,000 refugees and migrants entered Austria from Hungary. As of the end of November, approximately 85,500 people had requested asylum in Austria in 2015, compared with 23,861 in the same period in 2014.

The authorities struggled to offer adequate reception conditions. By mid-August, over 4,000 asylum-seekers were hosted in the reception centre of Traiskirchen in extremely poor conditions, with over 2,000, including children, sleeping outdoors. Access to medical care was insufficient. Many unaccompanied minors were left without protection. In October, a constitutional law came into force, expanding the government's powers and allowing it to identify sites to host asylum-seekers should provincial authorities fail to do so in a timely manner. Amendments to the asylum law, which were proposed by the government in November to introduce temporary asylum and limit family reunification, were pending at the end of the year.

The length of the asylum procedure, often lasting several years, remained a problem.

## PRISON CONDITIONS

The authorities failed to promptly and effectively respond to cases of ill-treatment and neglect of detainees in penal and preventive detention systems. Medical and mental health care remained inadequate. In March, criminal proceedings were dropped against staff for the prolonged neglect in Stein prison of a 74-year-old man. Related disciplinary proceedings were dropped in June. A taskforce on preventive detention established in 2014 by the Minister of Justice published its report in January, recommending measures to address the growing number of people in preventive detention, and its increasing length and frequent imposition for minor offences.

In July, the European Court of Human Rights found that a 16-month delay in dealing with an application for release from a psychiatric institution submitted by a convicted offender in May 2006 constituted a violation of the right to liberty.

## POLICE AND SECURITY FORCES

There were reports that police used excessive force on several occasions. Victims of torture and other ill-treatment continued to experience difficulties in obtaining justice and reparation. Complaints of ill-treatment by the police were often followed by an inadequate response by both the police and the judicial system.

The government continued to refuse to create a compulsory identification system for police officers.

## DISCRIMINATION

Following a ruling by the Constitutional Court in December 2014, legislation banning same-sex couples from adopting children other than each other's biological children, ceased to be in force at the end of the year. In February, new legislation was enacted to allow women in a same-sex relationship to access reproductive medicine.

Discriminatory differences remained between marriage and registered partnerships regarding the minimum age, naming rights and separation, among others. Marriage remained exclusively reserved for heterosexual partners, and registered partnerships for same-sex couples.

The government failed to amend the Anti-Discrimination Law to ensure equal protection against all forms of discrimination in the access to goods and services – including on the basis of religion and belief, age and sexual orientation.

## COUNTER-TERROR AND SECURITY
In March, a Police State Protection bill was proposed, expanding the powers of the Federal Office for the Protection of the Constitution and the Fight against Terrorism, without adequate oversight by independent authorities. The adoption of the bill was pending at the end of the year.

# AZERBAIJAN

**Republic of Azerbaijan**
Head of state: **Ilham Aliyev**
Head of government: **Artur Rasizade**

**The crackdown on civil society and persecution of political dissent continued. Human rights organizations remained unable to resume their work. At least 18 prisoners of conscience remained in detention at the end of the year. Reprisals against independent journalists and activists persisted both in the country and abroad, while their family members also faced harassment and arrests. International human rights monitors were barred and expelled from the country. Reports of torture and other ill-treatment persisted.**

## BACKGROUND
The national currency lost a third of its value in US dollar terms after the government devalued it in response to plummeting oil prices. The economy remained heavily dependent on oil, leading to considerable price hikes and falling real income.

In June, the first European Games, a major international sporting event intended to showcase Azerbaijan, were held in the capital, Baku. They came at considerable economic cost, amid reports of the government pressuring businesses for financial contributions and salary reductions for public sector employees.

The ruling New Azerbaijan party comfortably won Parliamentary elections on 1 November. The main opposition parties boycotted the elections due to constant harassment by the authorities. The OSCE Office for Democratic Institutions and Human Rights (ODIHR) cancelled its election monitoring mission because of restrictions imposed by the government, while the OSCE representation in Baku had discontinued its operations in July.

International human rights monitors were barred and expelled from the country. Human Rights Watch and Amnesty International delegates were refused entry and expelled on arrival, as were several international journalists during the European Games. In September, the government cancelled a visit planned by the European Commission to the country, after the European Parliament called on the government to release imprisoned human rights defenders. In October, the Council of Europe withdrew from the joint working group on human rights issues in Azerbaijan, in protest at the deteriorating human rights situation.

## FREEDOM OF ASSOCIATION
Leading human rights NGOs were unable to resume their work, as a result of the freezing of their assets and ongoing harassment – including criminal prosecution – of their members. Several NGO leaders remained in prison while others were forced into exile for fear of persecution.

After 10 months spent inside the Swiss Embassy to avoid prosecution on trumped-up charges, the founder and leader of the Institute for Reporters' Freedom and Safety (IRFS), Emin Huseynov, was allowed to leave the country on 12 June but was stripped of his citizenship. The IRFS office had been raided and sealed off by the authorities in 2014, and its online broadcasting channel, Obyektiv TV, taken off air.

## PRISONERS OF CONSCIENCE
At least 18 government critics, including prominent human rights defenders, remained behind bars on fabricated charges at the end

of the year.

Following their arrest in 2014, four NGO leaders were sentenced to lengthy prison sentences on trumped-up charges of embezzlement, illegal entrepreneurship, tax evasion and abuse of authority. Rasul Jafarov, founder of the Human Rights Club, was sentenced to six and a half years' imprisonment on 16 April; Intigam Aliyev, head of the Legal Education Society, to seven and a half years on 22 April; Leyla Yunus, president of the Institute for Peace and Democracy, and her husband and co-worker Arif Yunus to eight and a half and seven years respectively on 13 August. Leyla and Arif Yunus were given conditional sentences on appeal on 9 December, and both released. Investigative reporter Khadija Ismayilova, also under arrest since 2014, was sentenced to seven and a half years' imprisonment on 1 September.

Prisoners of conscience Bashir Suleymanli, co-founder of the Election Monitoring and Democracy Studies Centre, and opposition activist Orkhan Eyyubzade were released under a presidential pardon on 18 March.

## FREEDOM OF EXPRESSION

All mainstream media remained under government control; independent outlets faced harassment and closure. Independent journalists continued to face intimidation, harassment, threats and violence.

On 26 January, deputy chair of the IRFS Gunay Ismayilova was attacked by an unidentified man in the lobby of her apartment building in Baku. An investigation into the incident was still ongoing at the end of the year.

In May, Radio Free Europe/Radio Liberty decided to close its office in Baku. It had been raided and searched by the authorities in December 2014, and remained sealed since.

On 8 August, Rasim Aliyev, journalist and chair of the IRFS, was severely beaten by a group of men in Baku and died in hospital the following day. He had reported receiving threats on social media related to his

Facebook post on a famous footballer. Six men were arrested and charged in connection with his death.

On 16 September, police apprehended two reporters from Meydan TV, an independent, online Azeri-language media outlet. Aytaj Ahmadova was released after questioning but Shirin Abbasov was held incommunicado for two days and sentenced to 30 days' administrative detention for allegedly resisting police; he served his full sentence.

On 8 December, Fuad Gahramanli, deputy chairman of the opposition Popular Front Party, was arrested in connection with his posts on Facebook criticizing the government and calling for peaceful protest and resistance. He was remanded for three months as a criminal suspect, accused of calling for government overthrow and incitement of religious hatred.

### Arrests of journalists' relatives

Relatives of media workers who work from abroad and are critical of the government faced harassment by the authorities. On 13 February, police detained Elgiz Sadigli, brother of Tural Sadigli, a blogger who had participated in a street protest in Berlin during President Ilham Aliyev's visit to Germany. Elgiz Sadigli was remanded for two months on drug-related charges and then released following international outcry.

In June, Meydan TV exiled director and former prisoner of conscience Emin Milli reported receiving threats from the authorities following his disapproving coverage of the European Games. On 23 July, his brother-in-law Nazim Aghabayov was arrested on drug-related charges and placed in detention. His cousin, Polad Abdullayev, was arrested on 27 July and released within a few days after several relatives wrote an open letter repudiating Emin Milli's work.

In July, police arrested three relatives of Ganimat Zahid, an exiled journalist and former prisoner of conscience, who runs the Turkey-based TV SAAT, a broadcasting channel available online. His nephew and cousin were arrested on 19 and 22 July for resisting police orders and released after serving 25 and 30 days respectively of administrative detention. Another nephew was arrested on 22 July and charged with drug possession.

On 13 October, police arrested and remanded Vakil and Raji Imanovs, brothers of Meydan TV exiled editor Gunel Movlud, in two separate raids in different parts of the country, also on drug-related charges.

## FREEDOM OF ASSEMBLY

Peaceful street protests were prevented or dispersed by police using violence.

On 22 August, several hundred residents of the city of Mingechevir gathered peacefully to protest against the death of a man in police custody. They were violently dispersed by tear gas and sound bombs, and chased and beaten by baton-wielding riot police.

## TORTURE AND OTHER ILL-TREATMENT

Torture and other ill-treatment continued to be committed with impunity for the perpetrators, in the absence of effective investigations and prosecutions.

Prisoner of conscience Ilgar Mammadov told his lawyer that on 16 October he had been knocked onto the floor, kicked and punched by two prison guards and the head of prison, who warned that he would not leave prison alive. His lawyer noticed injuries and bruises on his head and neck when visiting him the next day.

# BAHAMAS

Commonwealth of the Bahamas
Head of state: **Queen Elizabeth II, represented by Marguerite Pindling**
Head of government: **Perry Gladstone Christie**

**There were allegations of arbitrary arrests and abuses against migrants. Deaths in custody were reported. Impunity for allegations of police abuses remained the norm.**

## BACKGROUND

A controversial migratory reform was adopted, putting thousands of migrants and their children born in the Bahamas at risk of human rights abuses.

The homicide rate steadily increased in recent years, in a context of high unemployment and a weak justice system. According to the local press, 110 murders were recorded in 2015 as of September, a 25% increase compared with the same period in 2014.

## EXCESSIVE USE OF FORCE

Excessive use of force, including killings, by security forces continued to be reported, often in circumstances suggesting that they may have been extrajudicial executions.

On 14 August, Bahamian-Haitian Nixon Vaximar was killed by police at his home in the Gamble Heights community on the island of New Providence. According to his family, he was sleeping and unarmed when police burst into his house and shot him dead.

## MIGRANTS' RIGHTS

In March, the Ministry of Education issued a school registration policy requiring every child to prove their regular status in the country to attend school, in violation of the Bahamas' human rights obligations.[1]

On 20 March, the Inter-American Commission on Human Rights (IACHR) held a hearing to discuss the situation of migrants' rights in the Bahamas.

Local activists working with migrants reported regular round-ups of migrants by immigration officials, raising concerns over arbitrary arrests, detention and deportation of migrants and their descendants.

In June, Haitian migrant Jean-Marie Justilien was shot in the neck by an immigration officer during an attempt to arrest undocumented migrants, and was detained and charged with illegal entry into the country. On 2 December, a court found him not guilty; his lawyer reported that he was arbitrarily deported to Haiti on 7 December, without having been issued a deportation order and with no possibility to challenge the decision in court.

### Discrimination – stateless persons
In May, the Parliament approved migration reforms that could potentially prevent the children of undocumented migrants born in the Bahamas from accessing Bahamian nationality, at the risk of rendering individuals stateless.

## PRISON CONDITIONS
In February, the IACHR requested the adoption of precautionary measures for persons held in the Carmichael Road Detention Centre. This followed concerns on inhumane conditions of detention, including extreme overcrowding and a lack of appropriate medical attention that could affect prisoners' right to life and physical integrity.

Deaths in custody continued to be reported, raising further alarms over the lack of appropriate oversight mechanisms, in particular in police lock-ups.

## JUSTICE SYSTEM
Despite the authorities' efforts to reform the justice system in recent years, the capacity of the Bahamas to prosecute and convict in criminal cases remained a concern. In June, the Attorney General reported that 600 cases were backlogged in the Supreme Court.

1. Bahamas: Amnesty International seeks clarification to the authorities on migration reforms (AMR 14/1264/2015)

# BAHRAIN

Kingdom of Bahrain
Head of state: **King Hamad bin 'Issa Al Khalifa**
Head of government: **Shaikh Khalifa bin Salman Al Khalifa**

**The government continued to curtail freedoms of expression, association and assembly and cracked down further on online and other dissent. Opposition leaders remained imprisoned; some were prisoners of conscience. Torture and other ill-treatment remained common. Scores were sentenced to long prison terms after unfair trials. Authorities stripped at least 208 people of their Bahraini nationality. Eight people were sentenced to death; there were no executions.**

## BACKGROUND
Tension remained high between the minority Sunni-dominated government and the opposition, which was supported mainly by the Shi'a majority population. There were frequent protests by Shi'a demanding the release of imprisoned opposition leaders, to which the security forces often responded with excessive force. The police were targeted in several bomb explosions; one killed two police officers on the island of Sitra in July, and another killed an officer in the village of Karannah in August.

In March, Bahrain joined the Saudi Arabia-led coalition that engaged in the armed conflict in Yemen (see Yemen entry).

The authorities constructed new facilities in Dry Dock Prison to hold children aged 15 to 18, transferring 300 juvenile offenders from Jaw Prison to Dry Dock in May.

In June, the US government lifted its embargo on arms sales to the Bahrain National Guard and Bahrain Defence Forces, and in August approved a US$150 million deal to supply military aircraft parts, ammunition and communications equipment to Bahrain.

A joint statement signed by 35 countries at the UN Human Rights Council in September expressed serious concern about human rights violations in Bahrain including imprisonment of those exercising their rights to freedom of expression, assembly and association, and lack of accountability.

## FREEDOMS OF EXPRESSION AND ASSOCIATION
The authorities severely curtailed the rights to freedom of expression and association, and

arrested and prosecuted political and religious activists who criticized the government through social media or at public gatherings. Others were prosecuted and convicted for criticizing the late King Abdullah of Saudi Arabia and the Saudi-led air strikes in Yemen. The authorities continued to detain prisoners of conscience sentenced after unfair trials in previous years. Several prisoners of conscience were released after completing their sentences.

In March, the Shura Council approved amendments to Article 364 of the Penal Code which would increase the penalty for "insulting parliament, the Shura Council, security forces, judges or public interest" to two years' imprisonment, and increase the maximum prison sentence for publicly encouraging others to "defame" to three years' imprisonment, or longer for defamation in the media; the amendments had not been enacted by the end of the year. In September, the Cabinet approved regulations which would penalize media outlets for "spreading false or damaging information that could affect foreign relations".

Police rearrested prominent human rights defender Nabeel Rajab in April for posts on Twitter about torture in Jaw Prison and Saudi-led air strikes in Yemen, and in May an appeal court confirmed his earlier six-month sentence for "publicly insulting official institutions". In July, the authorities released him under a royal pardon, four days after the European Parliament adopted a resolution urging the government to release him and other prisoners of conscience. He remained banned from leaving Bahrain.

In October, a court upheld the conviction of activist Zainab al-Khawaja and reduced her three-year prison sentence to one year for "insulting the King" by ripping up a photo of the King in court in October 2014. A court also upheld her convictions for "destroying government property" and "insulting a public official".

The authorities summoned and interrogated some political opposition leaders, and prosecuted and imprisoned others on vague charges. In June, Sheikh 'Ali Salman, Secretary General of the main opposition party, Al-Wefaq National Islamic Society, received a four-year prison term after an unfair trial on charges that included "public incitement to loathing and contempt of a sect of people which will result in disrupting public order".

In July, a month after his release from prison under a royal pardon, security authorities arrested Ebrahim Sharif, the former Secretary General of the National Democratic Action Society (Wa'ad) party, and charged him with "inciting hatred and contempt of the regime" and attempting to overthrow the regime "by force and illegal means". His trial was ongoing at the end of the year.

A court sentenced Fadhel Abbas Mahdi Mohamed, Secretary General of the Unitary National Democratic Assemblage (al-Wahdawi) party, to five years in prison in June for "spreading false information" after the party said the Saudi-led air strikes in Yemen were a violation of international law.

The authorities continued to prevent or restrict visits to Bahrain by international human rights groups, including Amnesty International.

## FREEDOM OF ASSEMBLY

The authorities continued to ban all demonstrations in the capital, Manama, but protests continued in Shi'a villages demanding the release of political prisoners. The security forces frequently used excessive force, including tear gas and shotguns, to disperse protesters, injuring some protesters and bystanders. They also arrested and beat protesters. Some protesters received prison sentences.

In January, a police officer shot a protester carrying a photo of opposition leader Sheikh 'Ali Salman at close range in the village of Bilad al-Qadeem. In November, a court acquitted the officer.

## DEPRIVATION OF NATIONALITY

The authorities revoked the nationality of Bahrainis convicted of terrorism-related offences or other illegal acts, stripping at least 208 people, including nine children, of their citizenship during the year, rendering many stateless. An appeal court reinstated the nationality of nine individuals.

In January, the Interior Ministry revoked the citizenship of 72 of the 208 people, including human rights defenders and former MPs, as well as Bahrainis allegedly fighting with the armed group Islamic State (IS). One of the 72 was deported; others were told to surrender their passports and identification cards and commit to regularizing their legal status as foreigners, or leave Bahrain. Some filed a court appeal against the decision but this was rejected in December.

## TORTURE AND OTHER ILL-TREATMENT

Torture and other ill-treatment of detainees, mainly suspects in security or terrorism-related cases, remained rife, particularly within the Criminal Investigations Directorate (CID). Police and other security officials also beat or otherwise abused people when arresting them and transporting them to police stations. At Jaw Prison, detainees faced repeated beatings, were required to sleep in tents and were denied any communication with their families for several weeks after the security forces used tear gas and shotguns to quell a disturbance at the prison in March.

Human rights defender Hussain Jawad, Chairman of the European-Bahraini organization for Human Rights, said he was blindfolded, handcuffed behind his back, denied access to a toilet, beaten and threatened with sexual abuse while under interrogation by CID officers after his arrest in February. Although the Public Prosecution Office ordered his release, CID officers took him back into detention and again tortured him until he "confessed" to receiving money to support and finance subversive groups. He later refuted this confession and lodged a complaint of torture with the Special Investigations Unit (SIU), the institution in charge of investigating police abuses. The SIU subsequently closed the investigation citing a lack of evidence. In December, a court sentenced Hussain Jawad to two years in prison.

## UNFAIR TRIALS

Hundreds of people were convicted in unfair trials on charges of rioting, illegal gathering or committing terrorism-related offences. Many defendants in terrorism cases were convicted largely on the basis of "confessions" that they said interrogators had forced them to make under torture; some received death sentences.

Abbas Jamil al-Samea' and two other men were sentenced to death in February, convicted of a bombing in March 2014. Their trial, in which seven co-defendants were sentenced to life imprisonment, was unfair: the court failed to adequately investigate their allegations of torture and other ill-treatment by CID interrogators; they were denied access to their lawyers until their trial began; their lawyers were not permitted to see the full case file, and their requests to cross-examine prosecution witnesses were ignored.

## IMPUNITY

A climate of impunity persisted. The authorities failed to hold senior officials accountable for torture and other human rights violations committed during and since the 2011 protests. The few investigations that led to prosecutions of some low-ranking police officers resulted in lenient sentences or acquittals.

In April, a court acquitted a police officer of causing the death of Fadhel Abbas Muslim Marhoon, who was shot in the head in January 2014. The officer was sentenced to three months in prison for injuring Sadeq al-Asfoor, who was with Fadhel Abbas, by shooting him in the stomach. The SIU appealed against the three-month sentence.

In November, the Court of Cassation ordered the retrial of two police officers convicted of causing the death in custody of

'Ali 'Issa al-Saqer in 2011. An appeal court had reduced their 10-year prison sentences to two years in September 2013.

In June, six police officers received prison sentences ranging from one to five years for causing the death in custody of Hassan al-Shaikh in November 2014.

## WOMEN'S RIGHTS

In April, parliament voted down an article in the new Domestic Violence Protection Law (Law 17 of 2015) that would have criminalized marital rape. The law, which was enacted in August, empowered the Public Prosecution Office and courts to issue protection orders of up to three months for victims of domestic violence, and set a penalty of three months' imprisonment for breaches of the order involving violence.

## DEATH PENALTY

The death penalty remained in force for murder, terrorism-related offences and other crimes, including drugs offences. The courts sentenced eight people to death, some after unfair trials, and commuted two death sentences to life imprisonment. There were no executions.

# BANGLADESH

People's Republic of Bangladesh
Head of state: **Abdul Hamid**
Head of government: **Sheikh Hasina**

**Dozens of people were killed when passenger buses and other vehicles were attacked with petrol bombs in the context of anti-government campaigns. Hundreds of opposition supporters were detained for various periods, at times on politically motivated grounds. Independent media came under severe pressure and freedom of expression was restricted. At least nine secularist bloggers and publishers were attacked, five of whom died from their injuries. More than 40 people were subjected to enforced disappearance.**

## BACKGROUND

An anti-government campaign led by the opposition Bangladesh Nationalist Party (BNP) between January and March turned violent as hundreds of buses and other vehicles were attacked, allegedly by demonstrators using petrol bombs. Dozens of passengers were killed and scores more injured. No one directly involved in the attacks was brought to justice.

Police arrested senior members of the BNP and charged them with arson. They included Mirza Fakhrul Islam Alamgir, the party's acting Secretary General, who was frequently arrested during the year for periods of weeks or months before being released.

Hundreds of opposition members were detained for days or months before being released. Some were charged with arson.

A number of foreign nationals were targeted for attacks by unidentified assailants. Between 28 September and 18 November, an Italian aid worker and a Japanese national were shot dead; an Italian doctor survived a gun attack.

A 13-year-old boy, Samiul Islam Rajon, was beaten to death in public in July after being accused of theft, prompting strong public criticism of the neglect suffered by children living on the street. The government ordered an investigation into the killing shortly afterwards.

At least 16 people accused of mass human rights violations during the 1971 Independence War were on trial at the end of the year. Well-documented killings by pro-independence forces were not addressed by the authorities.

## FREEDOM OF EXPRESSION

Independent media outlets critical of the authorities came under severe pressure. In October the government warned business enterprises that they would be penalized if they advertised in *Prothom-Alo* and the *Daily Star*, two leading newspapers known for their critical stance.

In November, a parliamentary standing committee recommended that the anti-corruption NGO Transparency International should be deregistered in Bangladesh for criticizing the Parliament.

A court in Dhaka imposed charges of contempt of court against 49 civil society activists who criticized its trials as unfair.

Authorities blocked social media messaging and other communications applications in November, in what constituted restrictions on freedom of expression.

Bloggers expressing secular views were attacked, reportedly by Islamist groups. In February, Avijit Roy was hacked to death by men wielding machetes. His wife, Rafida Ahmed Bonya, survived. By August, three other bloggers, Washiqur Rahman, Niloy Neel and Ananta Bijoy Das, had been hacked to death. In October, a publisher of secularist literature was hacked to death, and a publisher and two secularist writers survived an attack. Government authorities, including the Prime Minister, accused the bloggers and publishers of offending religious feelings in their writings.

## ENFORCED DISAPPEARANCES

Members of the security forces in plain clothes arrested dozens of people and later denied knowledge of their whereabouts. A survey of national newspapers conducted by the human rights organization Ain O Salish Kendra indicated the enforced disappearance of at least 43 individuals, including two women, between January and September. Of the 43, six were later found dead; four were released after their abduction; and five were found in police custody. The fate and whereabouts of the other 28 was unknown.

Trials continued against three Rapid Action Battalion officers charged with abducting and killing seven people in April 2014. No members of security forces or officials implicated in other cases of enforced disappearance were brought to justice.

## TORTURE AND OTHER ILL-TREATMENT

While torture and other ill-treatment in police custody was widespread, torture complaints were rarely investigated. In March, senior police authorities complained publicly about the legal safeguards against torture, calling on the government to decriminalize torture in time of war, threat of war, internal political instability or public emergency, or when torture is ordered by a superior or a public authority.

## CHITTAGONG HILL TRACTS

A government memorandum issued in January placed severe restrictions on people wishing to visit or organize events in the Chittagong Hill Tracts, in breach of the government's obligation to respect the rights of Indigenous Peoples, as well as freedom from discrimination and freedoms of movement, peaceful assembly and association.

## VIOLENCE AGAINST WOMEN AND GIRLS

According to the Bangladesh National Women Lawyers Association, more than 240 complaints of rape were reported in the media between January and May. Human rights groups said while reported incidents of rape had risen in recent years, the conviction rate was extremely low, mainly due to the lack of timely and effective investigations. Many women and girls were reluctant to report rape to the authorities. Survivors of rape were required to prove that force was used against them, including having to undergo a physical examination.

## DEATH PENALTY

At least 198 people were sentenced to death, including six men convicted of killing Samiul Islam Rajon (see above). They also included Oishee Rahman, sentenced to death for killing her parents in 2013. Her lawyers argued that she was under the age of 18 at the time of the alleged murder and therefore not subject to the death penalty, but the court upheld a medical examination that concluded she was 19.

The International Crimes Tribunal (ICT), a Bangladeshi court established to investigate the events of the 1971 independence war, sentenced four more people to death. The proceedings of the Tribunal were marked with severe irregularities and violations of the right to a fair trial. Challenges to the jurisdiction of the court continued to be barred due to a constitutional provision. Statements from prosecution witnesses shown by the defence to have been false were still used as evidence in court. Affidavits by defence witnesses that the accused was too far from the site of the offence to be involved were not admitted. The government prevented defence witnesses abroad from attending trials by denying visas. Appeals processes were marked by similar flaws.

Despite repeated calls by Amnesty International and other human rights organizations to stop executions after unfair trials and flawed appeal hearings, three prisoners were executed in 2015, bringing the number of executions after ICT trials to four.

# BELARUS

**Republic of Belarus**
Head of state: **Alyaksandr Lukashenka**
Head of government: **Andrey Kabyakou**

**Legislation severely restricting freedoms of expression, association and peaceful assembly remained in place. Journalists continued to face harassment. Several prisoners convicted in politically motivated trials in previous years were released but compelled to regularly report their movements and activities to police. At least two people were sentenced to death, but no executions were reported. Harassment and persecution of human rights defenders continued, as did discrimination, harassment and violence against members of sexual minorities.**

## BACKGROUND

In October, President Alyaksandr Lukashenka comfortably won his fifth consecutive term in office, against a backdrop of state-controlled media as well as harassment and reprisals against political opponents.

Internationally mediated talks on the conflict in eastern Ukraine, hosted in the capital, Minsk, aided Belarus' diplomatic efforts to improve relations with the EU. In October, the EU suspended its longstanding sanctions against senior Belarusian officials, with the exception of four security officers believed to be linked to enforced disappearances of political activists in earlier years.

The national currency lost over 50% of its value against the US dollar, and the economy was projected to contract by around 4%, largely due to the economic downturn in Russia, its principal trading partner.

## DEATH PENALTY

Belarus retained the death penalty. No executions were reported, but on 18 March Syarhei Ivanou was sentenced to death. The Supreme Court rejected his appeal on 14 July. On 20 November, the Hrodna Regional Court handed down a death sentence to Ivan Kulesh.[1]

On 1 April, the UN Human Rights Committee adopted the view that the execution of Aleh Hryshkautsou in 2011 constituted a violation of his right to life; that he had not received a fair trial; and that his confession had been obtained under duress.

## PRISONERS OF CONSCIENCE

In August, prisoners of conscience Mikalai Statkevich and Yury Rubtsou were released by a presidential order, along with other activists, Mikalai Dzyadok, Ihar Alinevich, Yauhen Vaskovich and Artsyom Prakapenka, who had been imprisoned following politically motivated trials. However, their convictions were not quashed and they were placed under considerable restrictions, including "prophylactic supervision". Former presidential candidate Mikalai Statkevich therefore was prevented from standing in forthcoming elections, and was ordered to regularly report his movements and activities to the police for the following eight years. Failure to comply could lead to heavier restrictions and new criminal charges. Similar restrictions, for shorter periods of time, were imposed on the other five released activists.

## FREEDOM OF EXPRESSION

The media remained under tight government control, and independent media outlets and journalists routinely faced harassment.

Freelance journalists who contributed to foreign media were required to obtain accreditation from the Ministry of Foreign Affairs, which was regularly refused or indefinitely delayed. Kastus Zhukouski, who worked for Poland-based Belsat TV, was fined three times for working without accreditation, most recently on 9 July, and three more times in previous years, by the Central District Court and the Zheleznodorozhnyi District Court in Homel, as well as the Rahachou District Court. According to independent media watchdog Index on Censorship, since January at least 28 freelance journalists were issued fines of between 3 and 7.8 million roubles (US$215-538) for working without accreditation.

Under the vaguely worded amendments to the Law on Mass Media passed in December 2014, the Ministry of Information was given the power to compel internet providers to block access to specific online resources, without a court order. On 27 March, access to the websites of human rights organization Vyasna and of independent news platforms Belarusian Partisan and Charter '97 was blocked under this provision.

Between 2 and 5 October, the websites of news agencies BelaPAN and Naviny.by became inaccessible following a hacker's attack, after they published reports of students being forced to take part in a public prayer service attended by the President.

On 11 August, activists Vyachaslau Kasinerau, Yaraslau Uliyanenkau, Maksim Pyakarski and Vadzim Zharomski, and one unnamed Russian national, were detained in Minsk for putting up graffiti "Belarus must be Belarusian" and "Revolution of consciousness". They were released on 31 August after agreeing not to disclose details of the investigation. Because of the political nature of these phrases, they were charged with the crime of "malicious hooliganism" and may face up to six years in prison if convicted. Vyachaslau Kasinerau sustained a broken jaw during the detention by police and was hospitalized. Their trial was still pending at the end of the year.

## FREEDOM OF ASSEMBLY

The Law on Mass Events, under which any assembly or public protest is regarded as unlawful unless expressly permitted by the authorities, continued to be regularly applied.

On 27 September, a street assembly in the town of Baranavichy, which had been organized in support of presidential candidate Tatsyana Karatkevich and sanctioned by the authorities, was joined by some 30 football fans on their way to a football match. Shortly after they started chanting "Long live Belarus!", police arrived at the scene and took them away in vans. The remaining protesters were allowed to carry on.

On 30 September, a court in Minsk issued fines of between 5.4 and 9 million roubles (US$300-500) to Mikalai Statkevich and Uladzimir Nyaklyaeu, both of them presidential candidates in 2010, and leader of the United Civic Party Anatol Lyabedzka, for organizing an "unsanctioned" protest in connection with the forthcoming election. Other peaceful protesters were similarly arrested and fined during the year.

## FREEDOM OF ASSOCIATION AND HUMAN RIGHTS DEFENDERS

Article 193.1 of the Criminal Code, which prohibits activities by unregistered organizations (political parties and religious groups, as well as NGOs), remained in place.

Elena Tonkacheva, a prominent human rights defender and Chair of the Board of the Center for Legal Transformation, was ordered to leave Belarus and barred from re-entering the country for three years. A Russian national, she had been a resident of Belarus since 1985. The order was issued on 5 November 2014 and referred to repeated traffic offences; Elena Tonkacheva repeatedly tried to appeal it, without success. Minsk City Court dismissed her final appeal on 19 February, forcing her to leave by 21 February.

Leanid Sudalenka, head of human rights NGO Homel Centre for Strategic Litigation, received at least two death threats via email in March, which the authorities refused to investigate. On 8 April, police searched his home and office, and on 14 April a criminal case was opened against Leanid Sudalenka himself. The authorities accused him of distributing pornography from his email account, but he claimed it had been hacked. Leanid Sudalenka believed these were reprisals for his work in helping victims of human rights violations take complaints to the UN Human Rights Committee. The latest complaint was submitted on 28 February by Olga Haryunou, whose son had been secretly executed on 22 October 2014 and who demanded to know the location of his grave.

## RIGHTS OF LESBIAN, GAY, BISEXUAL, TRANSGENDER AND INTERSEX PEOPLE

Members of sexual minorities continued to face routine discrimination, harassment and violence.

Mikhail Pischevsky, who had been beaten by anti-LGBTI activists as he was leaving a gay party at a club in Minsk on 25 May 2014, died on 27 October of complications caused by his severe head injuries. Only one of his attackers was convicted and sentenced to two years and eight months' imprisonment for hooliganism and negligence, and released under presidential pardon in August, having served 11 months of his sentence.

---

1. Second known death sentence in Belarus in 2015: Ivan Kulesh (EUR 49/2926/2015)

# BELGIUM

Kingdom of Belgium
Head of state: **King Philippe**
Head of federal government: **Charles Michel**

---

**The government introduced several proposals to combat terrorism that raised human rights concerns. The number of asylum-seekers spiked in the second half of the year. Their asylum claims could not be registered promptly by authorities and as a result hundreds of people remained without shelter.**

## COUNTER-TERROR AND SECURITY

The parliament adopted new measures to counteract terrorism, in particular the criminalization of travelling into or out of Belgium with the purpose of perpetrating a terrorism-related offence, the expansion of the grounds for stripping a person of Belgian nationality or refugee status if convicted for offences related to terrorism, and new measures to combat violent "extremism". As with previously adopted measures to counteract terrorism, the authorities did not carry out an evaluation of the compliance of the new measures with human rights standards.

In November, in the aftermath of the attacks in Paris, France, the Prime Minister proposed further measures.

In December, the Council of Ministers approved proposals concerning some of the announced measures. They included the extension of pre-charge detention from 24 to 72 hours and the power to carry out searches at any time in investigations of terrorism-related offences. They also included the establishment of a database of Belgian nationals or residents who have attempted to travel or have travelled abroad to fight in armed conflicts or with armed groups labelled as terrorist organizations by the government.

## TORTURE AND OTHER ILL-TREATMENT

In June, the European Court of Human Rights

ruled that extraditing Abdallah Ouabour to Morocco, where he was convicted for supporting a terrorist organization, would violate his right to be free from inhuman and degrading treatment. In July, the Court of Cassation ordered the retrial of Abdallah Ouabour, Lahoucine El-Haski and Khalid Bouloudodie. The men were convicted in 2006 and 2007 for terrorism-related offences in Belgium. However, the legal proceedings had relied on evidence that might have been obtained through the use of torture in Morocco.

## REFUGEES AND ASYLUM-SEEKERS

The number of asylum-seekers spiked between July and September. Due to the limited capacity of the Immigration Office, hundreds of asylum-seekers were unable to register their claims on the day of their arrival and, as a consequence, were not provided with shelter. About 500 reportedly camped in sub-standard conditions in front of the Immigration Office. In September, the Council of Europe Commissioner for Human Rights called on Belgium to speed up the registration procedure and increase reception capacity. On 16 October, the government announced plans to open eight new reception centres with an overall capacity of 1,600 places.

The government agreed to resettle 550 refugees from Syria and the Democratic Republic of the Congo. In October, the implementation phase started for the resettlement of the first 300 refugees.

## PRISON CONDITIONS

According to official statistics published in March, the prison population was 113% of the capacity, significantly lower than in previous years. However, in some specific facilities the overcrowding rate was reported to be much higher.

Despite the opening of a specialized forensic psychiatric centre in 2014, the majority of offenders with mental illnesses remained detained in regular prisons, where insufficient care and treatment were provided.

## DEATHS IN CUSTODY

In June, seven police officers, a psychiatrist and the director of a medical facility which refused treatment, were convicted for the death of Jonathan Jacob, who died in 2010 after being physically assaulted by police while in custody.

## VIOLENCE AGAINST WOMEN AND GIRLS

In July, the French community government adopted a new four-year plan aimed at combating violence against women and domestic violence, with a strong focus on sexual violence. On 11 December, federal authorities presented a National Plan to combat gender-based violence.

## DISCRIMINATION

In June, the European Court of Human Rights communicated the case *Belkacemi and Oussar v. Belgium* to the government. The plaintiffs alleged that the prohibition on wearing the full-face veil, enforced since 2011 in Belgium, violated their human rights.

Despite the government's commitment to reform the law on legal gender recognition, transgender people continued to be required to comply with inhuman and degrading treatments, including sterilization, as a precondition to obtaining legal recognition of their gender.

# BENIN

**Republic of Benin**
Head of state: **Thomas Boni Yayi**
Head of government: **Lionel Zinsou**

There were rising tensions in the capital Cotonou and other towns ahead of legislative elections. The attempted arrest of a political opponent led to two days of protests and clashes between protesters and security forces in Cotonou. Freedom of expression remained under threat as protests were banned after elections; a journalist reported receiving threats. Prisons remained overcrowded.

## BACKGROUND

Legislative elections were held in April, with the Cowry Forces for an Emerging Benin (FCBE), a coalition of 50 parties supporting President Boni Yayi, becoming the largest group in the National Assembly, with 33 out of 83 seats. The National Assembly elected political opponent Adrien Houngbédji as its president. Presidential elections were scheduled to take place in February 2016; President Boni Yayi pledged that he would not seek a third term.

## FREEDOMS OF EXPRESSION AND ASSEMBLY

In May, the Minister of the Interior banned all protests until the end of the electoral process. President Boni Yayi filed a complaint against opposition deputy Armand-Marie Candide Azannaï for slander. An attempt to arrest him sparked clashes between protesters, the police and the army in Cotonou.

Demonstrators were dispersed using tear gas and about 10 people were injured. More than 20 people were arrested on charges of rebellion, vandalism and violence for their participation in the protests and riots between 4 and 6 May. Other demonstrations were also banned by police and gendarmerie in other cities, including Azovè, southwestern Benin.

In May, journalist Ozias Sounouvou reported receiving anonymous arrest threats after criticizing the President for hindering press freedom.

In June, 12 students at Abomey-Calavi University who were protesting against the elimination of exam resits were beaten and arrested by security forces, before being released a few days later. The protests were initially peaceful; some protesters burned tyres and set a firetruck alight following the use of excessive force by police.

In August, journalist Boris Tougan was arrested for compromising state security after he published an article asserting that the country's participation in the regional force fighting the armed group Boko Haram was solely intended to help President Boni Yayi stay in power. He was detained without charge for five days before being released unconditionally.

## PRISON CONDITIONS

Prisons remained overcrowded. The Cotonou prison held 1,130 detainees despite a maximum capacity of 500, resulting in harsh conditions of detention. In May, all detention centres in the country failed to provide prisoners with food for three days, after the state failed to pay its contractors.

## DEATH PENALTY

Despite the country's ratification in 2012 of the Second Optional Protocol to the ICCPR aiming at the abolition of the death penalty, the government had yet to adopt laws removing the death penalty from its national legislation.

# BOLIVIA

**Plurinational State of Bolivia**
Head of state and government: **Evo Morales Ayma**

**Truth, justice and full reparation for victims of human rights violations committed during past military regimes were still pending. Insufficient steps were taken to guarantee full enjoyment of sexual and reproductive rights. Discredit from the authorities of the work of NGOs, including human rights defenders, paired with strict regulation to obtain registration remained a concern.**

## BACKGROUND

Justice remained out of reach, mainly for those without economic means. Allegations of corruption, political interference and delays in the administration of justice further dampened trust in the system.

In July, the CEDAW Committee urged Bolivia to take steps within two years to prevent violence against women, ensure education and access to information on sexual and reproductive rights and amend national laws to decriminalize abortion, among other recommendations.

## IMPUNITY

Measures to ensure truth, justice and full reparation for victims of human rights violations committed during past military and authoritarian regimes (1964-1982) were very limited. The authorities took no concrete steps to establish a truth commission following a commitment made in March following a public hearing at the Inter-American Commission of Human Rights.[1] A bill that was presented by victims' organizations to the Plurinational Legislative Assembly to create such a commission was pending at the end of the year.

In July, the Public Ministry announced the creation of a genetic data bank to identify the remains of potential victims of enforced disappearance. It is estimated that around 150 people were forcibly disappeared during the military regimes. The Public Ministry called on the relatives of victims of enforced disappearances to undertake blood tests to establish possible matches.

No progress was made to ensure full and fair reparation to victims of past human rights violations after the qualification process ended in 2012.

## TORTURE AND OTHER ILL-TREATMENT

The absence of an independent mechanism to record and investigate allegations of torture deterred victims from pursing justice. No efforts were made to ensure the full independence of the national preventive mechanism against torture, dependent on the Ministry of Justice. The regulation of this mechanism was pending at the end of the year.

In June Juan Bascope lodged a complaint of torture, death threats and discrimination that he was subjected to while in detention in 2014 in Maripiri in the Yungas region. He was accused of killing three members of the security forces and a doctor during a joint police and military operation against illegal coca plantations in the municipality of Apolo in 2013. He was detained and brought before a judge three days later. However, no investigation is known to have been initiated into his complaint, despite violent injuries.

## SEXUAL AND REPRODUCTIVE RIGHTS

High rates of maternal mortality, particularly in rural areas, limited access to modern contraceptives, including emergency contraception, and a high rate of teenage pregnancies remained a concern.[2]

Despite a resolution issued by the Ministry of Health in January, the 2014 Plurinational Constitutional Court ruling that abolished the requirement of judicial authorization for abortion in cases of rape was not implemented.

## INDIGENOUS PEOPLES' RIGHTS

In March the government issued a supreme decree to modify the 2007 regulation on consultation and participation in hydrocarbon activities. The decree contained new rules, including strict deadlines and a methodology to be set up by the authorities, which could obstruct the rights of Indigenous Peoples to consultation and free, prior and informed consent over projects that affect them.

In April charges against 12 police officers for excessive use of force during a peaceful march against the construction of a road through the Isiboro-Sécure Indigenous Territory and National Park (TIPNIS) in 2011 were dismissed. The trial of six other police officers whose charges remained had not begun at the end of 2015.

## HUMAN RIGHTS DEFENDERS

In September the authorities announced that 38 NGOs were considered "irregular" because they had not submitted the necessary documents to confirm their identity in line with a 2013 regulation. A decision by the Plurinational Constitutional Court submitted by the Ombudsman against that regulation was pending. The Ombudsman raised the regulation's potential breach to the right of assembly and the principle of non-discrimination of some of its articles.

In August the Vice-President discredited the work of four local organizations for criticizing government plans, and threatened international NGOs based in the country with expulsion should they get involved in what the authorities consider domestic politics.

## PRISON CONDITIONS
Inadequate sanitary facilities, poor access to health and food provision and overcrowding in prison remained a concern. Research by the Pastoral Penitenciaria found that there were almost 14,000 prisoners in 2015, for a maximum capacity of 5,000. Delays in concluding trials within a reasonable time and the excessive use of pre-trial detention were the main reasons for overcrowding.

1. Bolivia: Derecho a la verdad, justicia, reparación de las víctimas de las violaciones graves de derechos humanos cometidas durante los gobiernos militares de Bolivia (1964-1982) (AMR 18/1291/2015)
2. Bolivia: Briefing to the UN Committee on the Elimination of Discrimination Against Women (AMR 18/1669/2015)

# BOSNIA AND HERZEGOVINA

Bosnia and Herzegovina
Head of state: **Rotating presidency – Bakir Izetbegović, Dragan Čović, Mladen Ivanić**
Head of government: **Denis Zvizdić (replaced Vjekoslav Bevanda in March)**

**Violations of the right to freedom of expression as well as discrimination against Jews and Roma continued to occur. Access to justice and reparation for past crimes remained limited due to a lack of commitment to adopt, and secure adequate resources for, state-wide programmes.**

## BACKGROUND
The Council of Ministers of Bosnia and Herzegovina (BiH) and the government of the Federation of BiH, one of the constituent entities, were formed at the end of March, five months after the 2014 general elections. The Stabilisation and Association Agreement (SAA) between the EU and BiH entered into force on 1 June.

## FREEDOM OF EXPRESSION
In February, the National Assembly of Republika Srpska adopted a Law on Public Peace and Order that brought the internet and social networks into its definition of "public space". Concerns were raised by NGOs and the OSCE Representative on Freedom of the Media over the possibility of individuals being prosecuted for their online activities, on charges of breaching public peace and order.

Threats and attacks against journalists persisted. In October, an arson attack was carried out on the car of a journalist from a local radio station. Targeted cyber attacks on news websites continued. Only 15% of court cases relating to attacks against journalists were resolved in the past 10 years.

## DISCRIMINATION
The 2009 judgment of the European Court of Human Rights in the case of *Sejdić-Finci v. BiH,* which found the power-sharing arrangements set out in the Constitution to be discriminatory, remained unimplemented. Under the arrangements, citizens such as Jews and Roma who do not declare themselves as belonging to one of the three constituent peoples of the country (Bosniaks, Serbs and Croats) are excluded from running for legislative and executive office. In June, the implementation of the judgment was removed as a requirement for the signing of the SAA, leaving little hope of the decision being implemented.

## CRIMES UNDER INTERNATIONAL LAW
Proceedings continued at the International Criminal Tribunal for the former Yugoslavia against former General Ratko Mladić for genocide, crimes against humanity and violations of the laws or customs of war, including at Srebrenica. A verdict in the case against former Bosnian Serb leader Radovan Karadzić was still pending at the end of the year.

In May, the Parliamentary Assembly of

Bosnia and Herzegovina adopted a set of amendments to the Criminal Code. The amendments introduced enforced disappearance as a separate crime and provided a clearer definition of acts of torture. Additionally, the amendments aligned the definition of war crimes of sexual violence with international standards by excluding the need to demonstrate use of force as a requirement to qualify the crime as such. However, entity courts and courts in the Brčko District continued to apply the former Criminal Code, leading to the ineffective prosecution of such crimes at the sub-state level, to which cases were increasingly being transferred.

Legislation that would enable effective reparation, including a comprehensive programme for victims of crimes under international law, and free legal aid services to victims of torture and civilian victims of war, remained absent. The harmonization of entity laws regulating the rights of civilian victims of war was still not completed.

About half of the over 500 people who were charged with war crimes in the past 10 years were indicted in the last two years. However, this notable progress was halted by the EU decision to stop funding the cost of services and courts prosecuting war crimes until the new Justice Sector Reform Strategy for 2014-2018 was adopted in September. The process was delayed as Republika Srpska, unlike the country's other two political units, refused to adopt the Strategy. In December, it announced its decision to suspend co-operation with the State Court of Bosnia and Herzegovina, further limiting effective investigations into and prosecutions of those suspected of responsibility for war crimes and who may be hiding on Republika Srpska territory.[1] An agreement on a joint action plan to implement the Strategy was still pending at the end of the year.

In June, a Bosnian court granted the first ever financial compensation to a victim of wartime rape and sentenced the perpetrators, two former Bosnian Serb soldiers, to 10-year prison sentences. Previously, victims were required to pursue compensation claims in civil proceedings, which required them to reveal their identity.

In November, the heads of the Serbian and Bosnian governments signed a protocol on co-operation in the search for missing persons. In BiH, over 8,000 people remained missing from the war.

1. Bosnia and Herzegovina: 20 years of denial and injustice (News story, 14 December)

# BRAZIL

**Federative Republic of Brazil**
Head of state and government: **Dilma Rousseff**

**Serious human rights violations continued to be reported, including killings by police and the torture and other ill-treatment of detainees. Young black men from *favelas* (shanty towns) and marginalized communities were at particular risk. The security forces often used excessive or unnecessary force to suppress protests. Conflict over land and natural resources resulted in the killings of dozens of people. Rural communities and their leaders continued to face threats and attacks by landowners, especially in the north and northeast of the country. Lesbian, gay, bisexual, transgender and intersex (LGBTI) people continued to face discrimination and violence. Civil society opposition to new legislation and constitutional amendments that threatened to set back sexual and reproductive rights, women's rights and children's rights intensified; young people and women were prominent in these mobilizations. Brazil did not present itself as a candidate for re-election to a seat on the UN Human Rights Council.**

## PUBLIC SECURITY

Public security and the high rates of homicides among black youth remained a major concern. The government failed to present a concrete national plan to reduce homicides in the country, despite having announced in July that it would do so. According to a Brazilian Forum on Public Security report covering 2014, more than 58,000 people were victims of homicides; the number of police officers killed showed a small decrease of 2.5% over the previous year to 398; and more than 3,000 people were killed by the police, an increase of around 37% over 2013.

## UNLAWFUL KILLINGS

In 2015, killings during police operations remained high, but a lack of transparency in most states made it impossible to ascertain the exact number of people killed as a result of these operations. In the states of Rio de Janeiro and São Paulo there was a significant increase in the number of people killed by police officers while on duty, continuing the trend observed in 2014. Killings by police officers while on duty were rarely investigated and there were frequent reports that the officers involved sought to alter the crime scene and criminalize the victim. Officers frequently attempted to justify the killings as acts of self-defence, claiming the victim had resisted arrest.

In September, a 13-year-old boy was killed during a police operation in Manguinhos and a 16-year-old boy was shot dead in Maré, both *favelas* of Rio de Janeiro.[1]

In February, 12 people were shot dead and four others injured by Military Police officers during an operation in the neighbourhood of Cabula in the city of Salvador in the northeastern state of Bahia. Residents reported feeling threatened and fearful at the frequent presence of Military Police after the killings. An investigation by the Civil Police concluded that the Military Police officers acted in self-defence. However, organizations working on the case found strong evidence suggesting that the 12 people were extrajudicially executed. The Public Prosecutor's Office condemned the actions of the Military Police officers involved in the killings and called into question the impartiality of the Civil Police investigation.[2]

Eduardo de Jesus Ferreira, a 10-year-old boy, was killed by Military Police officers outside his home in the Complexo do Alemão neighbourhood, Rio de Janeiro, on 2 April. Police officers tried to alter the crime scene and remove his body, but were prevented from doing so by the family and neighbours. Eduardo's mother and family had to leave the city following death threats.

Five young black men aged between 16 and 25 years old were shot dead in the neighbourhood of Costa Barros in Rio de Janeiro on 29 November by military police officers from the 41st Military Police Battalion. The car in which the men were seated was shot more than 100 times by police officers.

There were reports that off-duty officers carried out unlawful killings as part of death squads operating in a number of cities.

In Manaus in the northern state of Amazonas, 37 people were killed in a single weekend in July. In Osasco, a city in the metropolitan area of São Paulo, 18 people were killed in one night and initial investigations indicated the involvement of Military Police officers.

In February, 29-year-old Vitor Santiago Borges was shot by members of the armed forces in Maré *favela*. He was paralyzed as a result of his injuries. The authorities failed to provide him or his family with adequate assistance or to conduct a full and impartial investigation into the shooting. The army had been performing policing duties in the community since April 2014. Soldiers were deployed to Maré ahead of the World Cup and were supposed to have left soon after the event ended. However, they continued to carry out law enforcement functions in the community until June 2015. Residents reported a number of human rights violations by the military forces during this period, including physical violence and shootings.

## IMPUNITY

Police responsible for unlawful killings enjoyed almost total impunity. Out of 220 investigations into police killings opened in

2011 in the city of Rio de Janeiro, by 2015 only one case had led to a police officer being charged. As of April 2015, 183 of these investigations remained open.[3]

The National Congress established two Parliamentary Commissions of Investigation, one in the Senate and the other in the House of Representatives, to investigate the high rates of homicides of black youth. At the same time, a law to amend the current Disarmament Law in order to allow greater access to firearms gained momentum in the National Congress. Brazil did not ratify the Arms Trade Treaty.

A Parliamentary Commission of Investigation was established in October in Rio de Janeiro's state assembly. Its investigation into police killings was due to be completed in May 2016. The Civil Police of Rio de Janeiro announced that all cases of police killings would be investigated by the Homicides Divisions.

## PRISON CONDITIONS, TORTURE AND OTHER ILL-TREATMENT

In March, the President nominated 11 experts to the National Mechanism to Prevent and Fight Torture. The group is part of the National System to Prevent and Fight Torture and its mandate will include visiting and inspecting places of detention.

Severe overcrowding, degrading conditions, torture and violence remained endemic in prisons. No concrete measures were taken by the authorities to overcome serious overcrowding and harsh conditions in Pedrinhas prison in the northeastern state of Maranhão. In October, it came to light that in 2013, an inmate of Pedrinhas had been killed, grilled and partially eaten by other inmates.

Prisoner revolts were reported in a number of states. In the state of Minas Gerais, three detainees were killed during a prison revolt in the Teofilo Otoni facility in October and two in similar circumstances in Governador Valadares prison in June. In October, there were disturbances in Londrina prison in the southern state of Paraná.

## CHILDREN'S RIGHTS

The juvenile justice system also suffered from severe overcrowding and degrading conditions. There were numerous reports of torture and violence against both boys and girls and a number of minors died in custody during the year.

In August, the House of Representatives approved an amendment to the Constitution reducing the age at which children can be tried as adults from 18 to 16 years. The amendment was awaiting approval by the Senate at the end of the year. If passed, it will violate a number of Brazil's obligations under international human rights law to protect the rights of the child.

## FREEDOM OF ASSEMBLY

A protest held on 29 April in the state of Paraná against changes in the rules governing teachers' social security benefits and retirement was met with unnecessary or excessive use of force by Military Police. Police used tear gas and rubber bullets to disperse protesters. More than 200 protesters were injured and at least seven people were briefly detained. The Public Defender's Office and the Public Prosecutor's Office took legal action against the government as a result of the incident. The case was pending at the end of the year.[4]

In October, the Senate approved a bill making terrorism a separate crime in the Criminal Code. There were fears that if passed in its current form, the law could be used to criminalize protesters and label them as "terrorists". The bill was pending final approval by the House of Representatives at the end of the year.

## HOUSING RIGHTS

Since Rio de Janeiro was chosen in 2009 to host the 2016 Olympic Games, thousands of people have been evicted from their homes in connection with the building of infrastructure for the event. Many families did not receive proper notification, sufficient financial compensation or adequate resettlement. Most of the 600 families of the community of Vila

Autódromo, located near the future Olympic Park, were evicted by the municipality. In June, members of the municipal guards assaulted remaining residents who were peacefully protesting against the evictions. Five residents were injured, including Maria da Penha Macena who sustained a broken nose. At the end of the year, the remaining residents were living in the shadow of ongoing demolition work and without access to basic services such as electricity and water.

In the city of Rio de Janeiro, the majority of condominiums that were part of the "My house, my life" housing programme for low-income families were controlled by *milícias* (organized criminal groups largely made up of former or off-duty police, firemen and military agents) or organized criminal gangs. This put thousands of families at risk of violence, many of whom were forced out of their homes as a result of intimidation and threats.

## HUMAN RIGHTS DEFENDERS

The National Programme for the Protection of Human Rights Defenders failed to deliver the protection promised in its provisions. Lack of resourcing continued to hamper implementation, leaving defenders at risk, and the absence of a legal framework in the Programme also undermined its effectiveness. A bill to create a legal framework to support the co-ordination of federal and state governments in the protection of defenders was pending before Congress at the end of the year.

Conflicts over land and natural resources continued to result in dozens of deaths each year. Rural communities and their leaders were threatened and attacked by landowners, especially in the northern and northeastern regions. In October, five people were killed in Vilhena in the state of Rondônia in the context of land conflicts in the area.

Raimundo Santos Rodrigues, also known as José dos Santos, was shot and killed on 25 August in the city of Bom Jardim in the state of Maranhão. His wife, who was with him at the time, was shot and injured. Raimundo Santos Rodrigues was a member of the Board of the Biological Reserve of Gurupi, an environmentally protected area of the Amazon forest in the state of Maranhão. He had reported and campaigned for several years against illegal logging and deforestation in the Amazon and worked to defend the rights of his community. He was also a member of the Rural Workers Union of Bom Jardim. He had received several death threats, which had been repeatedly reported to the authorities by the Land Church Commission and a local human rights organization. However, no action had been taken to protect him.

Cases of threats, attacks and killings targeting human rights defenders were rarely investigated and remained largely unpunished. There were concerns that those responsible for the killing in October 2010 of Flaviano Pinto Neto, a leader of the Charco Quilombola community in Maranhão state, would not be brought to justice. Despite a thorough investigation, in October the courts dismissed the charges against the accused and blamed the victim for his own death. At the end of the year it was unclear whether this decision would be appealed against by the Public Prosecutor's Office.

The 5 November collapse of the Samarco company mining dam, controlled by Vale and BHP Billiton in the state of Minas Gerais, was considered to be Brazil's biggest ever environmental disaster. It resulted in deaths and injuries and other serious human rights violations including insufficient access to clean water and safe housing for affected families and communities, and lack of reliable information. The river of toxic sludge also violated the right to livelihood of fishermen and other workers who depend directly or indirectly on the waters of the Rio Doce river.

## INDIGENOUS PEOPLES' RIGHTS

The demarcation process of Indigenous Peoples' lands continued to make extremely slow progress, despite the fact that the federal government had both the legal authority and the financial means to progress implementation. Several cases remained pending at the end of the year. Attacks against members of Indigenous communities remained widespread and those responsible were rarely brought to justice.

There was increasing concern at the dramatically deteriorating situation of the Guarani-Kaiowá community of Apika'y in Mato Grosso do Sul. An eviction order that could have left the community homeless was temporarily suspended in August. However, at the end of the year, the risk of eviction remained.[5]

On 29 August, local ranchers attacked the Indigenous community of Ñanderú Marangatú in the municipality of Antonio João, state of Mato Grosso do Sul. One man, Simião Vilhalva, was killed and several women and children were injured. No investigation was initiated into the attack and no measures were put in place to protect the community from further violence.

An amendment to the Constitution transferring responsibility for demarcating Indigenous lands from the executive to the legislature, where the agribusiness lobby is very strong, was approved by a special Commission of the House of Representatives in October. The amendment was awaiting approval by a Plenary of the House at the end of the year. If passed, it would have a significant negative impact on Indigenous Peoples' access to land.

## SEXUAL AND REPRODUCTIVE RIGHTS

New legislation and constitutional amendments under discussion in Congress posed a serious threat to sexual and reproductive rights and women's rights. At the end of the year, the National Congress was considering bills that proposed to criminalize abortion in all circumstances, for example the so-called Bill of the Unborn Child. Another proposal would effectively prevent access to safe and legal abortions in the public health system even in those cases currently allowed under Brazilian legislation, such as when the woman's life is at risk or the pregnancy is a result of rape. If passed, the measure would also end emergency assistance to victims of rape.

1. Brazil: Police operation kills two and injures others (AMR 19/2424/2015)
2. Brazil: Twelve people killed by Military Police (AMR 19/002/2015)
3. Brazil: "You killed my son" – homicides by the Military Police in the city of Rio de Janeiro (AMR 19/2068/2015)
4. Brazil: Military police attack protesting teachers (AMR 19/1611/2015)
5. Brazil: Indigenous community faces forced eviction (AMR 19/2151/2015)

# BULGARIA

Republic of Bulgaria
Head of state: **Rosen Plevneliev**
Head of government: **Boyko Borisov**

Allegations of push-backs of refugees and migrants by border police persisted, the reception conditions of asylum-seekers remained poor and there was no integration plan for recognized refugees. Local and national authorities continued to forcibly evict Roma. The amendment of hate crime legislation stalled.

## REFUGEES, ASYLUM-SEEKERS AND MIGRANTS

A fourfold increase in the number of refugees and migrants entering through the border with Turkey was registered in 2015, following a significant drop in 2014 after the introduction of border protection measures.

The authorities announced a plan to extend the current 33km fence on the border by 60km, to divert the migration flows to official border crossings. However, NGOs reported that people in search of international protection who were trying to enter Bulgaria through checkpoints were rejected. An extensive surveillance system, including sensors and thermal cameras, remained in place at the border with Turkey.

In October, an Afghan asylum-seeker died after a warning shot fired by a police officer at the Bulgarian-Turkish border ricocheted on a nearby bridge and hit him. The Bulgarian Helsinki Committee (BHC) expressed concerns over inconsistencies between the authorities' and witnesses' versions. The investigation launched by the Prosecutor's Office was ongoing at the end of the year.

There continued to be no integration plan for recognized refugees and other beneficiaries of international protection. Although the government adopted the National Strategy on Migration, Asylum and Integration for 2015-2020 in June, it failed to follow it up with an Action Plan that would implement the Strategy.

Concerns persisted over the reception conditions of asylum-seekers, in particular with regard to food, shelter and access to health care and sanitary goods. In January, the monthly allowance of 65 leva (€33) for asylum-seekers in reception centres was stopped. The BHC filed a complaint, arguing that the removal of the allowance violated national legislation.

NGOs documented allegations of summary push-backs of refugees and migrants by Bulgarian police at the border with Turkey.[1] In March, two Iraqi Yazidis died of hypothermia on the Turkish side of the border, after allegedly being severely beaten by Bulgarian police. The authorities denied the allegations, and the Ministry of Interior's investigation into the case was discontinued as the authorities said they were unable to establish the location of the incident. No other investigation into cases of push-backs was pending at the end of the year.

## HOUSING RIGHTS – FORCED EVICTIONS OF ROMA

Despite the constitutional right to housing, housing legislation in Bulgaria does not explicitly prohibit forced evictions, nor does it establish safeguards in line with international human rights standards. Authorities continued to forcibly evict Romani communities from informal settlements. Some were relocated to inadequate housing, while others were rendered homeless.

In May-June, following anti-Roma demonstrations, local and national authorities announced a plan to demolish Romani houses in the Kremikovtzi settlement in the village of Gurmen and the Orlandovzi neighbourhood in Sofia. Between June and September, 14 households were demolished in Gurmen. In July, following a request by NGOs for interim measures, the European Court of Human Rights advised the government not to proceed with the evictions unless adequate alternative housing was provided. However, following the demolitions, around 60 Roma, including elderly people, at least one pregnant woman and two disabled children, were left homeless. There was no genuine consultation to identify alternatives to planned evictions and adequate resettlement options. In September, the UN High Commissioner for Human Rights urged Bulgaria to halt such human rights violations. At the end of the year, 96 Roma households in the Kremikovtzi settlement remained at risk of eviction.[2]

In August, the homes of 46 Romani families – including children and single mothers – were demolished without prior notice in the Maksuda neighbourhood in the town of Varna. An estimated 400 people, 150 of them children, were rendered homeless in severe weather conditions. Only a few people were offered temporary housing in an overcrowded and inadequate social centre.

On 15 September, the authorities announced the demolition of four Roma houses in the town of Peshtera. However, they stalled after the European Court of Human Rights indicated that the authorities should not proceed unless adequate alternative housing was available.

## DISCRIMINATION – HATE CRIMES

In June, the Council of Europe Commissioner for Human Rights raised concerns over the high levels of racism and intolerance against several groups including refugees, asylum-seekers and migrants, who remained particularly vulnerable to violence and harassment.

Hate crimes against Roma, Muslims, Jews and other ethnic and religious minorities continued to be largely prosecuted as acts motivated by "hooliganism", rather than under the criminal law provisions specifically enacted for "racist and xenophobic hate crimes".[3]

In May, the European Court of Human Rights found in *Karahhmed v. Bulgaria* that the authorities' failure to prevent the disruption by a group of violent protesters of a Muslim Friday prayer in 2011 amounted to a violation of the right to freedom of religion or belief.

The government did not follow up on earlier steps to amend hate crime legislation, which in its current state does not provide for explicit protection against hate crimes perpetrated on the basis of age, disability, gender or sexual orientation. In March, the Parliament adopted a bill which extended the scope of the protection against discrimination on grounds of sex to transgender people, although this only applied to "legal reassignment cases".

## TORTURE AND OTHER ILL-TREATMENT

National and international organizations, including the European Committee for the Prevention of Torture and the Council of Europe Commissioner for Human Rights, criticized the juvenile justice system as inadequate and called for a comprehensive reform.

The Commissioner for Human Rights, following a visit in February, raised concerns over the slow pace of the deinstitutionalization (the transfer from psychiatric institutions to community-based care) of children and adults with disabilities. He also criticized the overrepresentation of Roma children, poor children and children with disabilities in such institutions, as well as reports of physical and psychological violence by staff and among children.

Following a visit in 2014, the Committee for the Prevention of Torture called for urgent and effective actions to address longstanding concerns over the ill-treatment of people – including juveniles and women – both by police and in prison, over inter-prisoner violence, overcrowding, poor health care, low staffing levels, excessively harsh discipline,

segregation among prisoners and a lack of contact with the outside world.

1. Bulgaria: It's time to address the allegations of abuse of refugees and migrants by the police (EUR 15/3058/2015)
2. Bulgaria: Further information: Romani families remain at risk of forced eviction (EUR 15/2334/2015)
3. Bulgaria: Missing the point: Lack of adequate investigation of hate crimes in Bulgaria (EUR 15/0001/2015)

# BURKINA FASO

Burkina Faso
Head of state: **Roch Marc Christian Kaboré (replaced Michel Kafando on 29 December)**
Head of government: **Yacouba Isaac Zida**

**During protests following an attempted coup in September, Presidential Guard (RSP) soldiers killed 14 protesters and bystanders and injured hundreds of others. Freedoms of expression and assembly were restricted and human rights defenders, protesters and journalists faced ill-treatment and intimidation. The interim government was reinstated and investigations were opened into the September coup and crimes committed during the 2014 unrest. Levels of early and forced marriage remained high. Access to sexual and reproductive rights was limited.**

## BACKGROUND

Transitional authorities governed the country after President Blaise Compaoré fell from power in October 2014 following protests over his attempts to change the Constitution. In April, the Transitional Parliament adopted a new electoral code that disqualified supporters of the 2014 constitutional amendment from running for office in 2015. In September, a National Commission on Reconciliation and Reform made several recommendations including the adoption of a new Constitution, the abolition of the death penalty and the disbanding of the RSP.

In September, members of the RSP

attempted a coup, and took the interim President, Prime Minister and other government members hostage, triggering widespread protests. The RSP used excessive force against protesters and bystanders before withdrawing under pressure from the national army. The RSP was later disbanded and those suspected of involvement in the attempted coup arrested. In November, the Transitional Parliament modified the Constitution limiting the Presidential mandate to two terms of five years and removing amnesty for former presidents. Roch Marc Christian Kaboré was elected President in the same month, ending the one-year transition. In December, Salif ou Diallo was elected President of the National Assembly.

## EXCESSIVE USE OF FORCE

During the September coup, peaceful protests were repressed; the RSP used excessive force to prevent people from assembling. Fourteen unarmed people were shot dead, including six who were shot in the back while running away from security forces.[1] The RSP chased and fired shots in densely populated areas, leading to deaths and hundreds of injuries. Among the victims was 16-year-old Jean-Baptiste Yoda, who was shot dead while running with two others. A pregnant woman was also shot in the stomach while standing in her doorway in the Nonsin neighbourhood of the capital, Ouagadougou. The bullet pierced her uterus and hit the unborn baby. Both mother and child survived following medical intervention.

## TORTURE AND OTHER ILL-TREATMENT

Prisoners alleged that they were subjected to torture and other ill-treatment in police custody in Ouagadougou. One detainee alleged that he was tortured for six days at Ouagadougou's central police station; his hands were handcuffed to his ankles, a wooden bar was put underneath his knees and he was suspended in a squatting position from between two tables.

In September, the RSP physically assaulted protesters and bystanders. A witness filmed five people, including a child, being forced to lie down and beaten with belts with metal buckles. Six RSP soldiers whipped a member of the Balai Citoyen social movement as he lay on the ground. Jean Jacques Konombo, photographer for *Les Editions Sidwaya*, was kicked and beaten with a belt by more than six RSP soldiers until he lost consciousness. His camera and phone were destroyed.

## FREEDOMS OF EXPRESSION AND ASSOCIATION

In September, Parliament adopted legislation leading to the repeal of the law punishing press offences with prison sentences. Later that month, there were restrictions on freedom of expression, including attacks on journalists, political figures and human rights defenders during the coup. At least 10 journalists and media stations including Radio Omega, Savane FM and Laafi were also attacked; cameras and other material were destroyed or confiscated. At the Radio Omega station, RSP soldiers fired bullets in the air, set staff motorbikes alight and threatened to burn the station down. The studio of Serge Bambara ("Smockey"), leader of Balai Citoyen, was also attacked with an anti-tank rocket and computers and materials stolen.

## IMPUNITY

Judicial authorities opened investigations into the killings of four people following excessive or lethal force by security forces, including the RSP, during the October 2014 unrest.[2] However, no one had been charged or tried for these crimes under international law by the end of 2015. In September, Commissions of Inquiry were established to investigate the 2014 killings and those suspected of involvement in the September coup. Neither had yet been tasked with investigating human rights violations relating to the killings of protesters and bystanders in 2015.

## MILITARY TRIBUNAL

Military officers including generals, as well as civilians, were arrested in Ouagadougou following the September coup and charged with offences including threatening state security, crimes against humanity and murder. More than 50 people, including General Djibril Bassolé and General Gilbert Dienderé, were due to be tried by a military tribunal. Two journalists, Adama Ouédraogo and Caroline Yoda, were also charged for complicity to threaten state security.

General Dienderé also faced charges in connection with the murder of former President Thomas Sankara, including assassination and possession of a dead body, while in December an international arrest warrant was also issued against former President Blaise Compaoré for his suspected role in this murder. Authorities said that an extradition request would be sent to Côte d'Ivoire.

In the same month, three former members of the RSP were charged in connection with the murder of Norbert Zongo, a journalist who was assassinated in 1998, and more than 15 RSP members were arrested for their suspected involvement in a plan to help Generals Bassolé and Dienderé escape from prison.

## WOMEN'S RIGHTS

Women's and girls' access to sexual and reproductive health information, services and goods were limited, resulting in just 17% of women reporting using contraception. Cost, distance to health centres and pharmacies, lack of information and negative male attitudes towards contraception remained the main barriers obstructing access.

Early and forced marriage was a serious concern, with over 52% of girls being married before the age of 18, around 10% before they were 15 years old. The government failed to fulfil its obligations to prevent forced and early marriages, as well as to guarantee the protection of girls and women at risk through the provision of information on, and access to, safety. Perpetrators of forced and early marriage were not held to account. Dozens of women and girls told Amnesty International that they were victims of forced and early marriage, including a 13-year-old girl who

walked more than 160km over three days to escape being forced by her father to marry a 70-year-old man who already had five wives.

In October the Transitional Parliament adopted a law on the prevention and sanction of violence against women and girls and the provision of support for victims. The law also criminalized and provided for sanctions for forced and early marriage and sexual violence.

## DEATH PENALTY

A bill aiming to abolish the death penalty had not been examined by Parliament at the end of the year.

1. Burkina Faso: No amnesty for soldiers who killed unarmed civilians (News story, 14 October)
2. Burkina Faso: "Just what were they thinking when they shot at people?" (AFR 60/001/2015)

# BURUNDI

Republic of Burundi
Head of state and government: **Pierre Nkurunziza**

**The government increasingly restricted the rights to freedom of expression, association and peaceful assembly. Protests by members of the political opposition, civil society and others against the President's decision to stand for a third term were violently repressed by the security forces, in particular the police and national intelligence services (SNR). Demonstrators were met with excessive force by the police and those detained were tortured and otherwise ill-treated by the SNR. Security forces also attacked independent media premises. There were several cases of unlawful killings of perceived opponents of the President.**

## BACKGROUND

In February, the head of the SNR, General Godefroid Niyombare, warned President Nkurunziza not to seek a third term in office, predicting that doing so would be seen as a violation of the Arusha Accords and the Constitution. Days later, he was dismissed by the President.

In March, several high-ranking members of the ruling National Council for the Defense of Democracy-Forces of Defense of Democracy (CNDD-FDD) publicly called on President Nkurunziza not to seek a third term. They were subsequently expelled from the party.

Despite similar calls from the Catholic Church, civil society, the political opposition and many regional and international actors, the CNDD-FDD selected President Nkurunziza on 25 April as their candidate for the 2015 presidential elections. The decision sparked protests in the capital, Bujumbura, and other parts of the country. Protests were violently repressed and protesters responded with violence.

On 5 May, the Constitutional Court upheld President Nkurunziza's candidacy, a day after the Court's vice-president had fled the country, having accused the government of putting pressure on the judges.

On 13 May, a group of generals attempted to overthrow the government while President Nkurunziza was in Dar-es-Salaam, Tanzania, attending a regional heads of state summit on Burundi. The attempted coup failed. Several officers fled the country and security forces loyal to the President arrested others.

Legislative elections were held in June and presidential elections in July. Pierre Nkurunziza won the election and was sworn in on 20 August. The security forces continued their clampdown on perceived opponents. Three military installations in Bujumbura and one in Bujumbura Rural were attacked before dawn on 11 December. Systematic violations were carried out in the cordon and search operations that followed.

Efforts by the East African Community, the AU and the UN failed to bring together Burundian stakeholders in an externally mediated dialogue to resolve the crisis, with talks that reopened on 28 December soon stalling. The decision of the AU Peace and Security Council to send a prevention and protection mission was rejected by the government.

After months of instability, the political, social and economic situation deteriorated. The International Monetary Fund stated that the economy would shrink by more than 7% in 2015 as the country's tax revenue collector, *Office Burundaise des Recettes*, registered losses due to the crisis.

Many of Burundi's development partners, such as Belgium, the Netherlands and the USA, partially or completely stopped their projects. The EU initiated a dialogue with the Burundian authorities under Article 96 of the Cotonou Agreements to re-evaluate its future co-operation with the government. According to UNICEF, 80% of social sector ministries had previously been reliant on external aid.

More than 230,000 people fled to neighbouring countries. The fragile cohesion between different ethnic groups resulting from the implementation of the Arusha Accords was destabilized by the political crisis. Incendiary rhetoric from high-level officials increased tensions towards the end of the year.

## FREEDOMS OF ASSEMBLY AND ASSOCIATION

In the run-up to the elections, activities by political opposition parties and civil society organizations were restricted. In March, the then Mayor of Bujumbura issued a directive authorizing public meetings organized by the ruling political party only. On 17 April, more than 100 people were arrested during a rally against President Nkurunziza's candidacy. On 24 April, a day before the CNDD-FDD was due to select its presidential candidate, the Minister of Interior banned all demonstrations.

Despite these measures, many protested in the streets of Bujumbura against President Nkurunziza's re-election bid. Demonstrations by political opposition groups were violently suppressed by security forces; those organized by the ruling political party or in support of President Nkurunziza's candidacy went ahead without interference.

## FREEDOM OF EXPRESSION – JOURNALISTS AND MEDIA

The government restricted international journalists' access to demonstrations. In a number of incidents, officials made threats against members of international media outlets.

### Attacks on media organizations

On 26 April, government officials stormed Radio Publique Africaine (RPA), which was broadcasting live from the protests. On the same day, authorities prevented four private radio stations from broadcasting beyond Bujumbura. On 27 April, authorities shut down the studio of la Maison de la Presse, a common space for media outlets to hold joint shows on special occasions.

On 13-14 May, security forces partially or completely destroyed the premises of four private media outlets: RPA, Radio Television Renaissance, Radio Isanganiro and Radio Bonesha. The government accused them of supporting the attempted coup against President Nkurunziza. Radio Television Rema, a pro-government media outlet, was partially destroyed by unidentified armed individuals.

### Harassment of journalists

Burundian journalists were targeted and received threats from the authorities.[1] Most fled and sought refuge in neighbouring countries.

Bob Rugurika, managing director of RPA and a well-known journalist, was arrested and detained on 20 January after broadcasting investigative reports about the September 2014 killing of three elderly Italian nuns in Bujumbura. He was charged with complicity in the killing, obstructing the course of justice through violating confidentiality of a criminal investigation, harbouring a criminal and lack of public solidarity. He was released on bail on 18 February.[2]

In its report on the demonstrations against President Nkurunziza's third term bid, a Commission of Inquiry established by the government accused some journalists from the private media of having links to people behind the attempted coup. In November, the Prosecutor requested the extradition of five journalists. RPA's accounts were frozen and cars seized in December.

## EXCESSIVE USE OF FORCE

The government's response to the protests failed to comply with regional and international standards.[3] Police used excessive or lethal force against protesters, including by firing live bullets during demonstrations.

## ARBITRARY ARRESTS AND DETENTION

The UN Office of the High Commissioner for Human Rights (OHCHR) reported that at least 3,496 people were arrested in relation to the political crisis. Many were detained following their participation in peaceful protests against President Nkurunziza's third term. Many detainees were denied visits from their families or lawyers.

In certain instances, members of the ruling party's youth wing, Imbonerakure, were involved in the arrests of perceived opponents of President Nkurunziza, including protesters. Among those detained, UNICEF identified 66 children charged with "involvement in armed groups".

## IMPUNITY

2015 was marked by an increased tolerance of impunity.

### Security forces

There was concern that members of the security forces involved in human rights violations during public demonstrations were not held to account. The General Director of Police stated in July that five police officers were under investigation. The Prosecutor General announced an investigation into allegations of extrajudicial executions during the 11 December search operations.

### Imbonerakure

The government failed to investigate allegations of intimidation and harassment of individuals by the Imbonerakure, such as those documented by the OHCHR in Burundi.

### Extrajudicial executions

The government failed to investigate or suspend members of security forces accused of extrajudicial executions.

The Appui pour la Protection des Institutions (API), a police unit of the presidential guard, committed human rights violations, including extrajudicial executions of political opponents. API was reported to have been involved in the killing of Zedi Feruzi, president of the opposition party Union for Peace and Democracy-Zigamibanga. He was killed with one of his bodyguards on 23 May. On 7 September, Patrice Gahungu, spokesperson of the same party, was shot dead by unidentified armed men.

Members of API were also said to have been involved in the killing of Vénérant Kayoya and Léonidas Nibitanga on 26 April in Cibitoke neighbourhood, Bujumbura, as well as the 15 May killing of Faustin Ndabitezimana, a nurse and member of the Front for Democracy in Burundi, an opposition party in Buterere, Bujumbura.

On 13 October, cameraman Christophe Nkezabahizi and his wife and two children, and Evariste Mbonihankuye, an employee of the International Organization of Migration, were killed in Bujumbura. An OHCHR investigation indicated possible API involvement, although the prosecutor's office accused a group of youths.

Following the attacks on military installations on 11 December, Burundian security forces carried out cordon and search operations in so-called opposition neighbourhoods, during which they systematically killed dozens of people. There were reports of bodies being buried in mass graves. Witnesses cited the involvement of API and the anti-riot brigade, alongside regular police units.[4]

## TORTURE AND OTHER ILL-TREATMENT

The use of torture and other ill-treatment by security forces increased, especially against those opposed to President Nkurunziza's re-election bid. Cases of torture and other ill-treatment were reported in official detention centres, mainly at SNR headquarters, and an unofficial detention centre known as "Chez Ndadaye" in Bujumbura. Security forces used techniques including beating detainees with metal bars, wooden sticks and military belts. Some victims were submerged in dirty water and others put in rooms covered with glass shards or forced to sit in acid.[5]

The authorities had not conducted any investigation or brought to account any members of the intelligence service or police in relation to these acts by the end of the year.

## UNLAWFUL KILLINGS

At least two high-ranking members of the security forces were killed in targeted attacks by men in uniform. On 2 August, General Adolphe Nshimirimana, considered to be close to President Nkurunziza, was shot dead in Bujumbura. Following investigations, four army officers appeared before a court in Bujumbura on 2 September, accused of his murder.

On 15 August, Jean Bikomagu, retired Colonel and former Chief of Staff during the civil war, was shot dead at his residence in Bujumbura by armed men. The government indicated that investigations were ongoing but no findings had been made public by year's end. On 11 September, the current Chief of Staff survived an armed attack against his convoy in Bujumbura.

Almost daily from September, dead bodies were found in the streets of Bujumbura and occasionally in other parts of the country. According to the OHCHR, at least 400 people were killed between April and mid-December, including members of the ruling political party, the CNDD-FDD.

## HUMAN RIGHTS DEFENDERS

Civil society's opposition to President Nkurunziza's third term through its campaign "Stop the third term" led to increased harassment and intimidation against human rights defenders. Government officials referred to them as leaders or supporters of an insurrectional movement. Many of them were named in the government's Commission of Inquiry report on the protests. Many fled the country or were in hiding in Burundi at the end of the year. In November, the government suspended the activities of several NGOs and froze their accounts, as well as those of three leading activists.

On 3 August, leading human rights defender Pierre Claver Mbonimpa survived an attempted killing by unidentified armed men while returning home.[6] His son-in-law, Pascal Nshimirimana, was shot dead at his house in Bujumbura on 9 October. On 6 November, Welly Fleury Nzitonda, Pierre Claver's son, was killed after being arrested by the police. The authorities had not investigated these attacks or brought anyone to account by the end of the year.

---

1. Burundi: Media clampdown intensifies in aftermath of coup attempt (Press Release, 12 June)
2. Burundi: Further information: Prominent journalist released: Bob Rugurika (AFR 16/1134/2015)
3. Braving bullets: Excessive force in policing demonstrations in Burundi (AFR 16/2100/2015)
4. "My children are scared": Burundi's deepening human rights crisis (AFR 16/3116/2015)
5. Burundi: Just tell me what to confess to – torture by police and intelligence services since April 2015 (AFR 16/2298/2015)
6. Burundi: Shooting of human rights activist increases climate of fear (News story, 6 August)

# CAMBODIA

**Kingdom of Cambodia**
Head of state: **King Norodom Sihamoni**
Head of government: **Hun Sen**

Arbitrary restrictions on the rights to freedom of expression and peaceful assembly continued. A law came into force severely threatening the right to freedom of association. Impunity continued for human rights violations in the policing of demonstrations in 2013 and 2014, including deaths resulting from the unnecessary and excessive use of force. Political activists and human rights defenders were jailed and arrests for online activity increased. Flagrant violations of the UN Refugee Convention, including *refoulements*, took place.

## BACKGROUND

Prime Minister Hun Sen succeeded the long-serving president of the ruling Cambodia People's Party (CPP), Chea Sim, who died in June.

Political tensions continued between the CPP and the opposition Cambodian National Rescue Party (CNRP), despite the two respective leaders announcing a "culture of dialogue" in April. Negotiations between the two parties led to an agreement on a new Law on the National Election Committee, amendments to the Law on the Election of Members of the National Assembly, and the release of imprisoned political activists and human rights defenders in April. The legal changes were widely criticized for restricting freedom of expression. In July, political tensions between the two parties re-escalated over an opposition campaign on alleged Vietnamese border encroachment.

In November, an arrest warrant was issued for CNRP leader Sam Rainsy for a 2011 conviction for defamation and incitement to discrimination. He received a two-year prison sentence that was never enforced. In December, Sam Rainsy was summonsed on charges of being an accomplice in a forgery case against opposition Senator Hong Sok Hour.

The mandates of the UN Special Rapporteur on the situation of human rights in Cambodia and the local UN Human Rights Commissioner office were both renewed for two years. The UN provided assistance in drafting an Access to Information Law. The National Police announced that a law on state secrets was being drafted.

The expression of anti-Vietnamese sentiment remained prevalent, with CNRP leaders continuing to use the term *yuon*, widely considered derogatory.

In September, the General Department of Immigration stated that it had deported 1,919 illegal migrant workers, 90% of whom were Vietnamese.

Local human rights groups continued to receive complaints about new land disputes affecting thousands of families and involving well-connected military and political figures.

## FREEDOM OF ASSEMBLY

In April, 10 women land activists, arrested and convicted in November 2014 for the peaceful exercise of their right to freedom of assembly, were released after being pardoned by the King. Nine others – five CNRP activists, three monks and one woman whose family were involved in a land dispute – were released on bail. The releases were part of the dialogue reached between the CPP and CNRP.

In July, 11 CNRP officials and members were convicted of leading and participating in an insurrection and sentenced to between seven and 20 years' imprisonment. The charges arose from a demonstration in July 2014 that resulted in clashes between security forces and opposition supporters. The convictions were not supported by evidence to link the 11 to the insurrection allegations. Charges also remained in place against seven opposition MPs arrested and released in the aftermath of the demonstration. One of those convicted, Ouk Pich Samnang, was sentenced to an

additional two years' imprisonment on charges arising from a separate demonstration in October 2014 when he was violently attacked by security forces.

In August, three activists from conservation NGO Mother Nature – Try Sovikea, Sun Mala and Sim Samnang – were arrested amid a campaign to prevent alleged illegal sand dredging in Koh Kong province. The three men faced two years in prison if convicted on allegations that they threatened to destroy a dredging vessel. In October, Vein Vorn, a community representative in Koh Kong, was arrested on charges related to his peaceful activism against a major dam project. In August, two monks, Dev Tep and Chea Vanda, who had participated in several demonstrations since the 2013 election, including opposition-led demonstrations concerning alleged border encroachment by Viet Nam, were defrocked and arrested on charges of drug possession, forgery and making death threats, which they claimed were fabricated.

## IMPUNITY

No one was held to account for a range of violations by security forces in the course of a violent crackdown on freedom of peaceful assembly over 2013 and 2014, including at least six killings resulting from the unnecessary or excessive use of force during that period.[1] Despite announcing official investigations in the wake of those events, no findings were published into the crackdown that resulted in serious injuries to scores of people and the enforced disappearance of 16-year-old Khem Saphath.

In August, former governor of Bavet city in Svay Rieng province, Chhouk Bandith (who was convicted in his absence and sentenced to 18 months' imprisonment in June 2013 on minor charges for shooting into a crowd of demonstrating workers in 2012 and injuring three women) turned himself in after the Prime Minister called for his arrest.

## FREEDOM OF ASSOCIATION

In August, King Sihamoni signed into law the

controversial Law on Associations and Non-Government Organizations (LANGO) despite a sustained campaign by civil society for the law to be dropped on the grounds that it violates the right to freedom of association. By the end of the year, it remained unclear how the law would be implemented.

Tripartite discussions involving the government, unions and employers' representatives on a controversial draft Trade Union Law continued behind closed doors with government representatives refusing to publish newer versions of the draft.

## FREEDOM OF EXPRESSION

A year after the creation of a "Cyber War Team" within the Council of Ministers whose function was to "investigate, collect, analyze and compile all forms of … news [and] to inform the public with the aim to protect the government's stance and prestige", there was an upsurge in criminal charges for online expression.

In August, opposition Senator Hong Sok Hour was arrested on forgery and incitement charges for posting a video online which included an edited article from a 1979 treaty between Cambodia and Viet Nam concerning the shared border. Days later, a student was arrested on incitement charges after stating on Facebook that he planned to initiate a "colour revolution" at an unspecified date in the future. Both men were held in detention despite a presumption in the Criminal Procedure Code in favour of bail.

In December, further arrest warrants were issued in the Hong Sok Hour case for CNRP leader Sam Rainsy and two men responsible for his Facebook page, Sathya Sambath and Ung Chung Leang. All three men went into self-imposed exile.

A draft Cybercrimes Law leaked to the public in 2014, which included a series of provisions that would criminalize online expression, remained pending.

In July, Ny Chakrya, head of monitoring for the Cambodia Human Rights and Development Association (ADHOC, the oldest human rights organization in Cambodia), was summoned for questioning on a series of charges arising from comments he made about judicial conduct in a case involving the arrest of villagers engaged in a land dispute.

## REFUGEES AND ASYLUM-SEEKERS

In violation of the UN Refugee Convention and international human rights law, Cambodia forcibly returned 45 minority ethnic Jarai asylum-seekers to Viet Nam in February. At least 36 other Montagnards – a term used loosely to refer to mostly Christian indigenous minority groups in Viet Nam – were also returned over the course of the year after Cambodia refused to register their asylum claims.[2]

In June, four refugees arrived in Cambodia from Nauru as part of a A$40 million (US$28 million) deal with Australia, which is counter to the object and purpose of the Refugee Convention.

## ENFORCED DISAPPEARANCES

Two years after he was last seen in January 2014 with an apparent gunshot wound to his chest at a demonstration on the outskirts of Phnom Penh, the fate or whereabouts of 16-year-old Khem Saphath remained unclarified.

## INTERNATIONAL JUSTICE

In September, the Extraordinary Chambers in the Courts of Cambodia (ECCC, Khmer Rouge tribunal) heard for the first time evidence on charges of genocide in the second case against Nuon Chea, former second-in-command of the Khmer Rouge, and Khieu Samphan, former head of state.

---

1. Taking to the streets: Freedom of peaceful assembly in Cambodia (ASA 23/1506/2015)

2. Cambodia: Refoulement and the question of "voluntariness" (ASA 23/2157/2015)

# CAMEROON

**Republic of Cameroon**
Head of state: **Paul Biya**
Head of government: **Philémon Yang**

The armed group Boko Haram disrupted the lives of thousands of people in northern Cameroon, committing crimes under international law including unlawful killings, attacks against civilian objects, misappropriation of property and assets, looting and abductions. In an attempt to prevent Boko Haram from capturing territory, security forces carried out arbitrary arrests, detentions, enforced disappearances and extrajudicial executions of suspected members of the group. Hundreds of thousands of refugees from Nigeria and the Central African Republic continued to live in precarious conditions. Freedoms of expression, association and assembly continued to be restricted. Human rights defenders were intimidated and harassed, including by government agents. Lesbian, gay, bisexual, transgender and intersex (LGBTI) people continued to face discrimination, intimidation and harassment, although arrests and prosecutions declined from previous years. An anti-terrorism law promulgated on 23 December 2014 infringed basic rights and freedoms, and extended the scope of the death penalty to a broader set of crimes.

## BACKGROUND

There was continuing instability in the country as a result of violence in the Central African Republic, in southeastern Cameroon, and of armed conflict between Boko Haram and security forces in the Far North. A significant deployment of security forces in the Far North prevented Boko Haram from taking control of Cameroonian soil. However, security forces at times failed to protect the civilian population from attacks and themselves committed crimes under international law and human rights violations.

## ABUSES BY ARMED GROUPS

Boko Haram committed crimes under international law and human rights abuses, including suicide bomb attacks in civilian areas, summary executions, torture, hostage taking, abductions, the recruitment of child soldiers, looting and destruction of public, private and religious property. These crimes appear to be part of a systematic attack against the civilian population across both northeastern Nigeria and the Far North in Cameroon. According to the UN, 770 civilians were killed and some 600 women and girls abducted by Boko Haram in Cameroon since 2013. Many schools were also targeted, leaving 35,000 children without access to education since 2014.

On 4 February, Boko Haram attacked the village of Fotokol, killing at least 90 civilians and 19 soldiers, and set dozens of buildings alight. On 17 April, it attacked the village of Bia, killing at least 16 civilians, including two children, and burned over 150 houses. In Maroua, between 22 and 25 July, three suicide attacks in crowded civilian areas killed at least 33 people and wounded more than 100. At least 23 suicide bombings carried out between July and December 2015 resulted in the deaths of about 120 civilians. Boko Haram used girls as young as 13 to carry out the attacks.

## ARBITRARY ARRESTS AND DETENTIONS

Security forces arrested at least 1,000 people accused of supporting Boko Haram in the Far North, including in mass cordon and search operations where dozens of men and boys were rounded up and arrested. During such operations, security forces used excessive force and committed human rights violations such as arbitrary arrests, unlawful killings – including of a seven-year-old girl – and destruction of property. Other violations include enforced disappearances, deaths in custody and mistreatment of prisoners.

Eighty-four children were detained without charge for six months in a children's centre in Maroua, following a raid on Qur'anic schools in the town of Guirvidig on 20 December

2014.

Journalists continued to be arrested and detained without charge by security forces, as part of their operation against Boko Haram. Simon Ateba, a Cameroonian journalist, was arrested on 28 August at the Minawao refugee camp and held by Cameroonian officials for four days. He had travelled to Minawao to investigate the living conditions of Nigerian refugees, but was accused of spying on behalf of Boko Haram. Radio France Internationale correspondent Ahmed Abba was arrested in Maroua on 30 July and was held incommunicado for over three months before being charged with "inciting or justifying terrorism".

On 27 April, the UN Working Group on Arbitrary Detention stated that the detention of Franco-Cameroonian lawyer Lydienne Yen Eyoum was arbitrary.

## DEATHS IN CUSTODY AND ENFORCED DISAPPEARANCES

Over 200 men and boys were arrested on 27 December 2014 in a cordon and search operation in the villages of Magdeme and Doublé. At least 25 men died during the night of their arrest in a makeshift cell, while 45 others were taken to Maroua prison the following day. At least 130 people therefore remain unaccounted for and are presumed to be victims of enforced disappearance, with evidence suggesting more may have died in custody. An internal investigation has yet to identify those victims, reveal the location of their bodies, and interview key witnesses.

## PRISON CONDITIONS

Prison conditions remained poor: chronic overcrowding, inadequate food, limited medical care, and deplorable hygiene and sanitation. The wave of arrests of individuals suspected of supporting Boko Haram further aggravated these conditions. Maroua prison houses 1,300 detainees, more than three times its intended capacity (350), and over 40 detainees died between March and May. The population of the central prison in Yaoundé is approximately 4,100, for a maximum capacity of 2,000. The main factors of recent prison overcrowding, in addition to the wave of arrests of Boko Haram suspects, included the large number of detainees held without charge and the ineffective judicial system. In response, the government has provided funding to build more cells at Maroua prison, and committed to building new prisons across the country.

## REFUGEES' AND MIGRANTS' RIGHTS

At least 180,000 refugees from the Central African Republic lived in harsh conditions in crowded camps along bordering areas of southeastern Cameroon. Since the escalation of violence in northeastern Nigeria in 2013, hundreds of thousands of people have fled across the border into Cameroon. The Minawao refugee camp in the Far North hosted over 50,000 refugees as of December, 75% of whom were between eight and 17 years of age. There were concerns that, contrary to the provisions of the 1951 UN Convention relating to the Status of Refugees, the Cameroonian military deported Nigerians who had long resided in Cameroon back to Nigeria, accusing them of supporting Boko Haram.

## RIGHTS OF LESBIAN, GAY, BISEXUAL, TRANSGENDER AND INTERSEX PEOPLE

Discrimination, intimidation, harassment and violence against LGBTI people remained a concern, although the number of arrests and prosecutions reduced from previous years. The continued criminalization of same-sex sexual activity still led to individuals being harassed and blackmailed, including by security forces, because of their suspected sexuality. Two people remain in prison on charges – one of whom is awaiting trial – relating to their sexual identity. A peaceful demonstration organized by an LGBTI organization to commemorate the death of LGBTI activist Eric Lembembe and call for a thorough investigation was held on 14 July.

## HUMAN RIGHTS DEFENDERS

Human rights defenders continued to be victims of intimidation, harassment and threats. In February, following a statement by the Central Africa Human Rights Defenders Network (REDHAC) on the alleged death in custody of more than 50 people in Maroua, executive director Maximilienne Ngo Mbe and president Alice Nkom received death threats on TV and in the press. Ngo Mbe has been the target of repeated threats because of her human rights-related work.

Alhadji Mei Ali, head of human rights organization Os-Civile, was repeatedly threatened by state agents since July. This followed his campaign against the impunity surrounding the killing of a human rights defender who had challenged the appointments of two traditional leaders in 2011.

## FREEDOMS OF EXPRESSION, ASSOCIATION AND ASSEMBLY

Perceived or actual opponents of the government were denied the right to organize peaceful activities and demonstrations. On 15 September, five members of Dynamique Citoyenne, a platform regrouping several civil society organizations, were arrested while holding a seminar on electoral governance and democratic change. They were held in custody for seven days without charge.

Journalists reported practising self-censorship to avoid repercussions for criticizing the government, especially on security matters. The National Communication Council sanctioned more than 20 media outlets during the year and some of its decisions were contested by the Journalism Trade Union. At the end of the year, journalists Rodrigue Tongué, Felix Ebole Bola and Baba Wamé still faced charges in front of a military tribunal for the "non-denunciation" of sources.

# CANADA

Canada
Head of state: Queen Elizabeth II, represented by Governor General David Johnston
Head of government: Justin Trudeau (replaced Stephen Harper in November)

Sweeping reforms to national security laws raised human rights concerns. Following a change of government, the process to develop a long-demanded public inquiry into missing and murdered Indigenous women and girls was launched and commitments were made to address a range of other human rights concerns.

## INDIGENOUS PEOPLES' RIGHTS

In June, the Truth and Reconciliation Commission released its calls to action based on six years of hearing. It included a finding that Canada's residential school system for Aboriginal children constituted "cultural genocide" and set out extensive recommendations to help restore Indigenous communities and prevent further harm to Indigenous children.

In July, construction of the Site C dam in British Columbia began without addressing its impact on the rights of Indigenous Peoples.

In July, the UN Human Rights Committee called on Canada to report back within one year on progress made in addressing violence against Indigenous women and girls and protecting Indigenous land rights.

An appeal against the decision to allow the Northern Gateway Pipeline project to proceed in northern British Columbia, despite opposition from many Indigenous Peoples who depend on lands and waters potentially impacted by the project, was pending at the end of the year.

A Canadian Human Rights Tribunal ruling in a case started in 2008 alleging discrimination in federal government underfunding of child protection in First Nations Indigenous communities had been pending for 14 months at the end of the year.

## WOMEN'S RIGHTS

In March, the CEDAW Committee concluded that the Canadian police and justice system had failed to effectively protect Indigenous women from violence, hold offenders to account and ensure redress for victims.

In December, following the change of government, a process to launch a public inquiry into violence against Indigenous women and girls was initiated; the inquiry was expected to begin in 2016.

## COUNTER-TERROR AND SECURITY

In May, Omar Khadr, a Canadian citizen held at Guantánamo Bay for 10 years beginning when he was 15 years old and repatriated to Canada in 2012 under a prisoner transfer agreement, was released on bail pending an appeal against his conviction in the USA. Also in May, the Supreme Court of Canada ruled that Omar Khadr must be treated as a minor within the Canadian corrections system.

In June the 2015 Anti-terrorism Act became law. It expands the authority of Canadian government agencies to share information about individuals without adequate safeguards and allows the Canadian Security Intelligence Service to take measures to reduce security threats, even if such measures would violate rights. The new law creates a criminal offence of advocating or promoting the commission of "terrorism offences in general" which undermines the right to freedom of expression. A legal challenge to the new law was pending at the end of the year and the new government made a commitment to revise some of its provisions.

A legal challenge to Citizenship Act reforms passed in 2014 allowing dual nationals convicted of terrorism and other offences to be stripped of Canadian citizenship remained pending. The new government promised to repeal the 2014 reforms.

## JUSTICE SYSTEM

In September, the Royal Canadian Mounted Police laid criminal charges for torture against a Syrian military intelligence officer in the case of Canadian citizen Maher Arar who was illegally imprisoned in Syria in 2002-2003 after being subject to rendition from the USA. The charges were the first ever brought in Canada for torture outside the country.

Two lawsuits challenging the widespread use of solitary confinement remained pending.

## REFUGEES AND ASYLUM-SEEKERS

In October, reports emerged that government officials suspended processing Syrian refugee cases for several weeks during the summer and were screening cases to prioritize refugees from ethnic and religious minorities as well as refugees who have run businesses and who speak English or French fluently. In November, the new government announced a plan to resettle 10,000 Syrian refugees by the end of 2015 towards a total of 25,000 by early 2016. At the end of the year, approximately 6,000 Syrian refugees had arrived in Canada.

In July the UN Human Rights Committee called on Canada to report back within a year on a range of human rights concerns facing immigrants and refugees.

In July, the Federal Court overturned the "designated country of origin" list under which refugee claimants from "safe" countries were denied the right to appeal refused refugee claims.

In August, Cameroonian national Michael Mvogo was deported from Canada, 13 months after the UN Working Group on Arbitrary Detention had called for him to be released from indefinite detention.

In November, the new government announced that cuts to the Interim Federal Health Program for refugees and refugee claimants would be reversed and health coverage restored.

## CORPORATE ACCOUNTABILITY

In February, a joint investigation was launched by federal and provincial agencies into whether Imperial Metals breached any laws when the tailings dam at its Mount Polley mine collapsed in 2014. The disaster spilled

24 million cubic metres of mining waste water into fish-bearing waterways.

In May, the fourth annual report to Parliament assessing the human rights effects of the Canada-Colombia Free Trade Agreement was released. It again failed to consider human rights concerns, including serious abuses facing Indigenous Peoples, Afro-descendant communities and others in areas of resource extraction investment in Colombia.

In October, Canada was one of 12 countries to sign the Trans-Pacific Partnership, a major new free trade deal, which did not include human rights safeguards.

By the end of the year, five lawsuits were pending before Canadian courts seeking to establish Canadian parent company liability for human rights harms committed in mining operations in Eritrea and Guatemala.

## LEGAL, CONSTITUTIONAL OR INSTITUTIONAL DEVELOPMENTS

Draft legislation which would have added gender identity as a prohibited ground of discrimination in Canada's Human Rights Act and hate crimes laws did not pass the Senate before Parliament was recessed in advance of federal elections.

Despite repeated calls, the government did not ratify the Arms Trade Treaty or the Optional Protocol to the UN Convention against Torture.

# CENTRAL AFRICAN REPUBLIC

Central African Republic
Head of state: Catherine Samba-Panza
Head of government: Mahamat Kamoun

Crimes under international law, including war crimes and crimes against humanity, were committed by all parties to the conflict. Security operations by international forces and political initiatives such as the National Reconciliation Forum held in the capital, Bangui, in May did not succeed in bringing an end to violations of international humanitarian law and violations and abuses of international human rights law. Many of those suspected of criminal responsibility for crimes under international law, including commanders of the Séléka and anti-Balaka forces, as well as other militias and their allies, were yet to be effectively investigated or brought to justice. The International Criminal Court (ICC) continued to investigate crimes under international law. According to the UN and relief organizations, 2.7 million people remained in need of humanitarian assistance, including more than 460,000 internally displaced people and 452,000 refugees in neighbouring countries.

## BACKGROUND

The conflict that led to the loss of thousands of lives in 2014 continued throughout 2015. Between September and October, a major upsurge in violence, including attacks targeted at civilians, resulted in the deaths of more than 75 people and injuries to hundreds more, in addition to widespread destruction of private and public property. The UN Multidimensional Integrated Stabilization Mission in the Central African Republic (MINUSCA), supported by the French "Sangaris" force, struggled to fully prevent violations of international humanitarian law.

In January, a ceasefire agreement between former Presidents François Bozizé and Michel Djotodia, both under UN and US sanctions, and radical factions of the anti-Balaka and ex-Séléka forces, was signed in Nairobi but was rejected by the transitional authorities and the international community. In May a national reconciliation forum postponed elections originally scheduled for August and ruled out immunity for those suspected of criminal responsibility for crimes under international law. A Disarmament, Demobilization, Rehabilitation and Reintegration accord and an agreement on the demobilization of child soldiers were also signed by 11 armed groups.

In August, the Special Representative of the UN Secretary-General to the Central African Republic resigned following allegations that a 12-year-old girl was raped by a UN peacekeeper during a security operation in Bangui.

On 13 December a new Constitution was approved in a referendum.

## ABUSES BY ARMED GROUPS AND COMMUNAL VIOLENCE

Serious violations of human rights and international humanitarian law, including unlawful killings, torture and other ill-treatment, abductions, sexual assaults, looting and destruction of property, were perpetrated by all armed groups involved in the conflict, including the ex-Séléka and the anti-Balaka whose fighters could operate freely across much of the country, facilitated by the heavy circulation of small arms.

In February, armed ethnic Peulh herders, at times supported by ex-Séléka and anti-Balaka fighters, attacked civilians along a corridor used for the seasonal movement of livestock in the central regions, leading to temporary mass displacement of populations in the towns of Kouango, Kaga Bandoro and Batangafo.

On 26 September, following the killing of a 17-year-old Muslim moto-taxi driver, armed men attacked residents of areas near the Muslim enclave known as PK5, killing dozens of people. Members of Muslim self-defence groups, anti-Balaka militia and a number of their supporters committed widespread abuses, including killings, rapes and destruction of property. More than 75 people were killed and 400 wounded, including civilians. More than 250 houses were set alight in non-Muslim areas and more than 40,000 civilians were forced to flee their homes. Although MINUSCA, supported by French peacekeepers, helped to secure key installations in Bangui, including the airport and government buildings, its intervention was slow and failed to protect civilians from violence.

On 26 October, anti-Balaka fighters attacked a delegation of ex-Séléka who had come to Bangui to meet President Samba-Panza. Two of the four members of the delegation remained unaccounted for. In the ensuing violence houses were burned and people killed during confrontations involving armed Muslim gangs, anti-Balaka and national security forces.

## VIOLATIONS BY UN PEACEKEEPERS

On 10 July, four men were severely beaten after being arrested by MINUSCA peacekeepers in the town of Mambéré in the south-west. One died later of his wounds. Twenty peacekeepers were repatriated on 20 July by MINUSCA for excessive use of force against detainees.

On 2 and 3 August, a failed attempt by MINUSCA peacekeepers to arrest a Muslim self-defence group leader in the PK5 enclave of Bangui resulted in fierce fighting and the death of one peacekeeper. Evidence strongly suggested that a 12-year-old girl was raped by a MINUSCA soldier during the operation, while two civilians were killed after UN soldiers apparently shot indiscriminately down an alleyway.[1] An investigation by the UN International Office for Oversight was under way at the end of the year.

Allegations of sexual violence by French and other peacekeepers against children as young as nine were under investigation at the end of the year.

## FREEDOM OF MOVEMENT AND DISPLACEMENT

In the first months of 2015, internally displaced people from the Peulh community stranded in the town of Yaloké were repeatedly forbidden from leaving the town by local authorities, acting under orders from the interim central government.

The freedom of movement of about 25,000 Muslims living in enclaves in several towns protected by UN peacekeepers was restricted because of risks of attack by members of anti-Balaka and their affiliates.

More than 460,000 people remained internally displaced, including approximately 60,000 in Bangui, living in harsh conditions in makeshift camps. The crisis forced around 200,000 people to flee to Cameroon, Chad, Democratic Republic of the Congo and the Republic of Congo since December 2013, bringing the number of Central African refugees in neighbouring countries to about 452,000.

## FREEDOM OF RELIGION AND BELIEF

Some Muslims returning to ethnically cleansed areas in the west of the country were forced by anti-Balaka to abandon their religion or convert to Christianity. Outside areas in the west of the country where Muslims live under the protection of UN peacekeepers, threats by anti-Balaka meant that Muslims had little freedom to practise their religion in public, wear traditional Muslim clothing or reconstruct destroyed mosques.

## IMPUNITY

The presence and functioning of judicial institutions remained limited, especially outside Bangui. Judicial authorities lacked the capacity to investigate and prosecute suspects of crimes, including human rights violations.

Few of those suspected of criminal responsibility for crimes under international law, including commanders of the Séléka, anti-Balaka, other militias and their allies, were investigated or brought to justice. On 17 January, Rodrigue Ngaïbo, a prominent anti-Balaka leader known as "Andilo", was arrested by MINUSCA in the town of Bouca.

In October, MINUSCA met with Nourredine Adam, an ex-Séléka commander suspected of crimes against humanity and subject to UN sanctions and national and international arrest warrants.

## PRISON CONDITIONS

Prison conditions remained poor and security weak. In August, 17 detainees, including some high-ranking anti-Balaka commanders, escaped from the Ngaragba male prison in Bangui. On 28 September, between 500 and 700 detainees, including anti-Balaka fighters, escaped from the same prison as violence escalated in Bangui. On 4 November, 11 inmates escaped from the detention facility in the town of Bria.

## INTERNATIONAL JUSTICE

On 30 May, the President promulgated a law creating a Special Criminal Court composed of national and international prosecutors and judges, tasked with investigating international crimes committed in the country since January 2003 and to complement the work of the ICC. By the end of year, the Special Criminal Court was yet to be operational, due particularly to lack of funding. ICC investigations, which had begun in September 2013 into crimes committed since August 2012, continued.

## NATURAL RESOURCES

Conflict diamonds smuggled from the Central African Republic were traded on international markets, funding amed groups who controlled mine sites, "taxed" miners and extorted protection money. Two of the biggest diamond buying houses – Badica and Sodiam – purchased diamonds worth several million dollars during the conflict, including from areas where ex-Séléka and anti-Balaka groups were known to operate. While both companies denied buying conflict diamonds, it was believed they purchased diamonds without adequately investigating whether they funded armed groups. The government failed to provide protection to artisanal (small-scale) miners, including children, who often worked in dangerous conditions.

---

1.  Central African Republic: UN troops implicated in rape of a girl and indiscriminate killings must be investigated (News story, 11 August)

# CHAD

**Republic of Chad**
Head of state: **Idriss Déby Itno**
Head of government: **Kalzeubé Payimi Deubet**

The armed group Boko Haram stepped up attacks in the capital, N'Djamena, and around Lake Chad, killing and abducting civilians, and looting and destroying properties. The authorities took several counter-terrorism and security measures, including passing a restrictive anti-terrorism law. The security forces carried out arbitrary arrests and detentions. The authorities continued to restrict the right to freedom of expression by dispersing demonstrations, often using excessive or unnecessary force. Hundreds of thousands of refugees from Nigeria, Central African Republic, Sudan and Libya continued to live in difficult conditions in crowded refugee camps. Former Chadian President Hissène Habré faced trial on charges of crimes against humanity, torture and war crimes at the Extraordinary African Chambers in Senegal.

## ABUSES BY ARMED GROUPS

Boko Haram killed more than 200 civilians during the year, and looted and destroyed private properties and public facilities. Violence led to the displacement of approximately 70,000 people.

In February, Boko Haram killed more than 24 people, including civilians, on the islands of Lake Chad, including in the localities of Kaiga-Kingiria, Kangalom, and Ngouboua. On 3 April Boko Haram ambushed civilians going to market and killed seven with knives and guns in the village of Tchoukou Telia. On 15 June, 38 civilians were killed and more than 100 injured in a twin suicide attack by suspected Boko Haram members in N'Djamena. On 11 July, a suspected Boko Haram suicide bomber wearing a woman's burqa killed at least 15 civilians in a market in N'Djamena and injured more than 80. On 10 October at least 43 civilians were killed in

separate suicide attacks in the market of Bagassola and in an informal settlement of internally displaced people in Kousseri. On 5 December, at least 27 civilians were killed and more than 80 injured in three suicide attacks in different locations in the market of Loulou Fou, in the Lake Chad region.

## COUNTER-TERROR AND SECURITY

On 30 July, the National Assembly adopted an anti-terrorism law that provided for the death penalty and increased the punishments for lesser terrorism offences from the previous maximum of 20 years' imprisonment to life. The maximum period before suspects must be brought before a court was increased from 48 hours to 30 days, renewable twice by the Public Prosecutor. The definition of "terrorism" in the bill is extremely broad, including disruption of public services, and opposition parties and civil society organizations expressed concern that the bill could be used to curtail freedoms of expression and association. The bill became law on 5 August.

Also in July, the authorities imposed a series of counter-terrorism measures affecting the Chadian population and foreign nationals. In addition to an increase in search operations in homes, checkpoints and public places, veils fully covering the face and public begging were banned.

On 9 November, a state of emergency was declared in the Lake Chad region and provided the governor of the region with the authority to ban the movement of people and vehicles, search homes and recover arms.

The security forces were accused of carrying out arbitrary arrests and detentions by both local civil society organizations and international bodies. The UN Office of the High Commissioner for Human Rights reported that more than 400 foreign nationals of 14 nationalities were arrested following spot checks in a two-week period after the 15 June bomb attack in N'Djamena.

## EXCESSIVE USE OF FORCE

The rights to freedom of expression and

association were violated as security forces used excessive or unnecessary force to disperse demonstrations in N'Djamena and other towns such as Kyabé in the south of the country, where at least three people were reportedly killed during a demonstration on 25 April.

On 9 March, in N'Djamena, security forces dispersed a students' demonstration using tear gas, batons and live ammunition. Four students were allegedly killed and many other protesters injured. No one was investigated or charged in relation to these deaths during 2015. Videos also showed that students arrested during the demonstration were subjected to torture and other ill-treatment by members of the Mobile Police Intervention Group. Security forces beat the students and forced them to roll on the ground, to wipe their faces with sand and to pull their own ears.

On 20 May, after a video revealing the identity of the security forces who tortured and otherwise ill-treated the students was broadcast on the internet, the Supreme Court of N'Djamena sentenced eight policemen to six months' imprisonment and a fine of 50,000 CFA francs (US$80) for "unlawful violence, wilfully beating and wounding and complicity". Six other officers were acquitted.

## FREEDOM OF EXPRESSION

On 15 June, Djeralar Miankeo, land rights activist and Director of Association Ngaoubourandi (ASNGA), was arrested and charged with "insulting the judiciary" by the Public Prosecutor of Moundou after questioning the competence of Chadian judicial officials in a radio interview. He was sentenced to two years' imprisonment and a fine by the High Court of Justice of Moundou. On 28 July the Appeal Court of Moundou overturned the verdict, dropped all charges against him and released him.

On 22 June, Mahamat Ramadane, editor of the newspaper *Alwihda*, was arrested and held until the following day for photographing a security operation in N'Djamena where the police were reported to have used excessive force.

On 23 June, Laurent Correau, a journalist with Radio France Internationale, was assaulted alongside an international human rights defender in N'Djamena by state agents. Laurent Correau was forcibly expelled from Chad the same day.

## REFUGEES' AND MIGRANTS' RIGHTS

In addition to approximately 70,000 people internally displaced by Boko Haram attacks, Chad hosted almost 500,000 refugees – the second highest total in Africa – from neighbouring countries including Sudan, Central African Republic, Nigeria and Libya. Many lived in poor conditions in overcrowded refugee camps. The UN Office of the High Commissioner for Human Rights reported that during 2015 Chad forced Nigerian refugees back to their country, contrary to the principle of *non-refoulement*, accusing them of being Boko Haram members.

## INTERNATIONAL JUSTICE

On 20 July, the trial of former Chadian President Hissène Habré opened at the Extraordinary African Chambers in Senegal on charges of crimes against humanity, torture and war crimes, allegedly committed between 1982 and 1990 when he ruled Chad. This was the first time that an African court had prosecuted a former African president under the principle of universal jurisdiction.[1]

On 25 March, 20 former state security agents connected to President Habré's regime were convicted of torture by the N'Djamena Criminal Court. The court acquitted four of the accused and found the Chadian state liable for the defendants' actions. The defendants and the state were ordered to pay compensation of 75 billion CFA francs (US$125 million) to the 7,000 civil parties. In 2014 the Chadian authorities had declined to transfer these suspects to the Extraordinary African Chambers in Senegal, or to allow representatives of the Chambers to interview them in Chad.

## DEATH PENALTY

On 29 August, 10 suspected Boko Haram members were executed by firing squad after being sentenced to death in a trial held behind closed doors the previous day. They were convicted of carrying out the twin attacks that killed 38 people in N'Djamena in June. It was the first execution since 2003. In 2014 Chad had announced that it would abolish the death penalty, but in July 2015 included it in a new anti-terrorism law.

---

1. Chad: Time for justice for victims of Hissène Habré's regime (News story, 20 July)

# CHILE

**Republic of Chile**
Head of state and government: **Michelle Bachelet Jeria**

Cases of police violence continued to be dealt with by military courts. Legal proceedings against those responsible for past human rights violations continued. Abortion remained criminalized in all circumstances.

## BACKGROUND

In October, President Bachelet announced the process that would be followed in order to adopt a new Constitution in 2017. The current Constitution was adopted during the military government of General Pinochet and, for many, is not consistent with a democratic system.

Allegations of political corruption, involving a number of public officials, were investigated throughout the year.

## SECURITY FORCES AND THE MILITARY JUSTICE SYSTEM

Cases of human rights violations involving members of the security forces continued to be dealt with by military courts, despite public commitments by the authorities to reform the relevant legislation. The Supreme Court, however, upheld the right to due process and international human rights obligations in specific cases when deciding to transfer such cases to the jurisdiction of ordinary courts.[1]

In May, the Martial Court (the appeal court in the military justice system) reduced the sentence imposed on a former police officer for fatally shooting 16-year-old Manuel Gutiérrez Reinoso and injuring Carlos Burgos Toledo during a protest in 2011, from three years and 61 days to 461 days. The Martial Court disregarded the military tribunal's finding that methods short of the use of firearms were available to disperse the demonstrators, instead stating that there was no proof of intention to cause injury on the part of the officer.[2] This decision was confirmed by the Supreme Court in December.

Investigation into the death of Iván Vásquez Vásquez in police custody in 2014 in Chile Chico, Aysén region, made some progress. The family requested a third, more comprehensive, autopsy, given the discrepancies between two previous autopsies. In July the Martial Court agreed to conduct this autopsy, which was still pending at the end of the year.

A few cases of police violence were dealt with by the ordinary courts. Among them were the cases of Nelson Quichillao, a mineworker who was shot dead by the security forces during a protest in July in El Salvador, Atacama Region, and that of 28-year-old student Rodrigo Avilés who was seriously injured by police water cannon in May. Investigations into the cases were continuing at the end of the year.

In September, the Special Rapporteur on the rights to freedom of peaceful assembly and of association called on the authorities to end the use of military courts to deal with cases of human rights violations.

## IMPUNITY

Efforts to bring to justice those responsible for past human rights violations continued. According to the President of the Supreme Court, by March there were 1,056 active cases, of which 112 related to allegations of torture. Official data from the Ministry of the Interior Human Rights Programme indicated that 72 of the 122 people who were convicted of human rights violations between 2014 and September 2015 were serving prison sentences.

However, victims' organizations condemned the slow progress in establishing the truth about the thousands of victims of enforced disappearance.

Information and documentation gathered by the Valech Commission on politically motivated torture and imprisonment during the Pinochet era remained classified as confidential, even from the judiciary, and therefore secret for 50 years and unavailable to those seeking justice for the victims.

In October, after a 40-day hunger strike by some victims of torture, a law was passed granting early economic reparation to victims of torture and political imprisonment.

In July, 10 former military officers were charged with the kidnapping and killing of the singer and political activist Víctor Jara in 1973.

Following information received from a military officer, seven former military officers were charged in July for burning 19-year-old Rodrigo Rojas to death and severely injuring 18-year-old Carmen Gloria Quintana in 1986.

No progress was made in overturning the 1978 Amnesty Law.[3]

In September, the Inter-American Court of Human Rights ruled that Chile had denied effective remedy to 12 people sentenced by a military tribunal between 1974 and1975. The case against them had not been quashed, despite evidence that their confessions were extracted under torture, and their allegations of torture had not been investigated.

## SEXUAL AND REPRODUCTIVE RIGHTS
Abortion remained a criminal offence in all circumstances.[4] A bill to decriminalize abortion when the pregnancy poses a threat to the life of the woman or is the result of rape or incest or in cases of serious foetal malformation was pending before Congress at the end of the year.

In July, the UN Committee on Economic, Social and Cultural Rights (CESCR) urged Chile to expedite the adoption of a bill to decriminalize abortion in some circumstances.

## INDIGENOUS PEOPLES' RIGHTS
There were renewed allegations of excessive use of force and arbitrary detention during police operations against Mapuche communities.

In July, the CESCR urged Chile to guarantee constitutional recognition of the rights of Indigenous Peoples, ensuring their right to free, prior and informed consent with regard to decisions that may directly affect their rights.[5]

In October, the Inter-American Commission of Human Rights ordered precautionary measures for Mapuche Indigenous leader Juana Calfunao and members of her family living in the community of Juan Paillalef in southern Chile. The decision followed reports of excessive use of force by the security forces, threats and intimidation against the family in 2014 and 2015 linked to land disputes.

## RIGHTS OF LESBIAN, GAY, BISEXUAL, TRANSGENDER AND INTERSEX PEOPLE
In October, legislation on civil partnerships, including for same-sex couples, came into force.

A bill on the right to gender identity that would allow people to change their name and gender on official documents remained pending before the Senate at the end of the year.

---

1.  Chile: Un avance: Otro caso de violaciones de derechos humanos se traspasa a la justicia ordinaria (AMR 22/1149/2015)

2.  Chile: El uso excesivo e innecesario de la fuerza policial debe investigarse y sancionarse en tribunales ordinarios (AMR 22/1738/2015)

3.  Chile: Amnesty law keeps Pinochet's legacy alive (News story, 11 September)

4.  Chile's failure to protect women and girls: The criminalization of

abortion is a human rights violation (Amnesty International Chile, June 2015)

5. Chile: Submission to the UN Committee on Economic, Social and Cultural Rights: 55th session (AMR 22/1479/2015)

# CHINA

**People's Republic of China**
Head of state: **Xi Jinping**
Head of government: **Li Keqiang**

A series of new laws with a national security focus were drafted or enacted that presented grave dangers to human rights. The government launched a massive nationwide crackdown against human rights lawyers. Other activists and human rights defenders continued to be systematically subjected to harassment and intimidation. Five women's rights activists were detained for planning to mark International Women's Day with a campaign against sexual harassment. Authorities stepped up their controls over the internet, mass media and academia. Televised "confessions" of critics detained for investigation multiplied. Freedom of religion continued to be systematically stifled. The government continued its campaign to demolish churches and take down Christian crosses in Zhejiang province. In the predominantly Muslim Xinjiang Uighur Autonomous Region, the regional government enacted new regulations to more tightly control religious affairs and ban all unauthorized religious practice. The government maintained extensive controls over Tibetan Buddhist monasteries. The UN Committee against Torture regretted that previous recommendations had not been implemented.

## HUMAN RIGHTS DEFENDERS

Human rights defenders, lawyers, journalists and activists faced increased intimidation, harassment, arbitrary arrest, and violence.

The detention of lawyer Wang Yu and her family on 9 July marked the beginning of an unprecedented government crackdown on human rights lawyers and other activists. Over the following weeks, at least 248 lawyers and activists were questioned or detained by state security agents, and many of their offices and homes were raided. At the end of the year, 25 people remained missing or in custody, and at least 12 of them, including prominent human rights lawyers Zhou Shifeng, Sui Muqing, Li Heping and Wang Quanzhang, were held in "residential surveillance in a designated location" on suspicion of involvement in state security crimes.[1] This form of detention allows the police to hold individuals suspected of such crimes for up to six months outside the formal detention system, with suspects denied access to legal counsel and families. Family members were also subject to police surveillance, harassment and restriction of their freedom of movement.

Human rights lawyer Pu Zhiqiang was given a three-year suspended sentence on charges of "picking quarrels and provoking troubles" and "inciting ethnic hatred", primarily on the basis of comments he had made on social media. He was barred from practising law as a result of the conviction.

In April journalist Gao Yu was sentenced to seven years' imprisonment by a court in the capital, Beijing, on the charge of "disclosing state secrets" for sharing an internal Communist Party document in which freedom of the press and "universal values" such as freedom, democracy and human rights came under severe attack. In November, her sentence was reduced to five years and she was released from prison on medical parole. Her release came after her family and friends claimed she did not have access to necessary medical care in detention.[2]

Of the more than 100 people in mainland China detained for supporting Hong Kong protests in 2014, eight had been formally arrested and remained in detention as of December. At least two had reported being tortured in detention.[3]

In March, five women's rights activists – Wei Tingting, Wang Man, Wu Rongrong, Li

Tingting and Zheng Churan – were arrested and detained on the charge of "picking quarrels and provoking troubles" for planning to mark International Women's Day by launching a campaign against sexual harassment. They were released on "bail pending trial" on 13 April after unprecedented international pressure, although they continued to suffer police interrogations, evictions and confiscation of personal items while on bail.

Many former employees and volunteers of Yirenping, a well-known anti-discrimination advocacy organization, were detained and suffered harassment and intimidation. Two former employees – Guo Bin and Yang Zhangqing – were detained on 12 June on suspicion of "illegal business activity"; they were released on bail on 11 July.[4]

In December, at least 33 workers and labour rights activists were targeted by police; seven were detained in Guangdong province, where labour unrest and strikes were on the rise. The detention centres did not allow access to lawyers on the grounds that the cases involved "endangering national security".[5]

## LEGAL, CONSTITUTIONAL OR INSTITUTIONAL DEVELOPMENTS

The government enacted or drafted a series of sweeping laws and regulations under the pretext of enhancing national security. There were fears that they could be used to silence dissent and crack down on human rights defenders through expansive charges such as "inciting subversion", "separatism" and "leaking state secrets". There were concerns that the National Security Law, enacted on 1 July, includes a broad and vague definition of "national security" that comprises areas such as politics, culture, finance and the internet.

The draft Foreign NGO Management Law, if enacted in the form presented for public consultation in May, would severely restrict the rights to freedom of association, peaceful assembly and expression.[6] While the law was ostensibly designed to regulate and even protect the rights of foreign NGOs, it would give the Ministry of Public Security the responsibility to oversee the registration of foreign NGOs, as well as supervising their operations and pre-approving their activities. The wide discretion given to authorities to oversee and manage the work of NGOs raised the risk that the law could be misused to intimidate and prosecute human rights defenders and NGO workers.

The draft Cyber Security Law,[7] which purports to protect internet users' personal data from hacking and theft, would also force companies operating in China to censor content, store users' data in China, and enforce a real-name registration system in a way that runs counter to national and international obligations to safeguard the right to freedom of expression and the right to privacy. The draft law would prohibit individuals or groups from using the internet to "harm national security", "upset social order", or "harm national interests" – vague and imprecise terms that could be used to further restrict freedom of expression.

In December, parliament passed the Anti-Terrorism Law, which had virtually no safeguards to prevent those who peacefully practised their religion or simply criticized government policies from being persecuted on broad charges related to "terrorism" or "extremism".

## FREEDOM OF EXPRESSION – INTERNET AND JOURNALISTS

In January the government announced that the internet would be the main "battlefield" in 2015 in its campaign to "fight pornography, and unlawful [information]". The same month, the government announced it had shut down 50 websites and WeChat accounts – many related to discussion of current events, military affairs or anti-corruption platforms, and 133 accounts that were disseminating information that was "distorting history of the Communist Party and national history". Also in January, the Minister of Education stated that foreign textbooks would be banned in order to stop the spread of "wrong Western values", and he warned against universities being infiltrated by "hostile forces".

In August, according to state media, 197 people were "punished" in a special campaign led by the Ministry of Public Security for allegedly spreading rumours about the stock market, the chemical explosion in the coastal city of Tianjin earlier that month, or other issues.

Later that month, Wang Xiaolu, a reporter with the financial magazine *Caixin*, was detained after the government claimed that an article he wrote about the stock market was "fabricated". He was forced to make a "confession", which was broadcast on national TV and was subsequently placed in "residential surveillance in a designated location". Chinese media observers believed he was used as a scapegoat and as a caution to keep the press from reporting negative news about the downturn in the stock market.

In October, investigative reporter Liu Wei was detained after he exposed a corruption scandal involving government officials. Famed historian Yang Jisheng was forced to resign as editor at the liberal journal *Yanhuang Chunqiu* after the State Administration of Press, Publication, Radio, Film and Television criticized the magazine for publishing dozens of articles that were "against the regulations".

## FREEDOM OF RELIGION AND BELIEF

The campaign to demolish churches and take down crosses in Zhejiang province that was launched in 2013 intensified throughout 2015. According to international media reports, more than 1,200 crosses had been torn down during the campaign, prompting a series of protests. In July, the Zhejiang provincial government passed a regulation restricting the size of an object attached at the top of a building to not exceed one tenth of the total size of the building, which many believed was aimed at legitimizing the removal of crosses.

Zhang Kai, a lawyer who was offering legal assistance to the affected churches, was detained on 25 August on suspicion of state security crimes and "disturbing public order"

and was later placed under "residential surveillance in a designated location".[8] Numerous other pastors and "house church" leaders were also subsequently put under the same form of incommunicado detention.

Falun Gong practitioners continued to be subjected to persecution, arbitrary detention, unfair trials and torture and other ill-treatment.

## DEATH PENALTY

Amendments to the Criminal Law, which came into effect in November, reduced the number of crimes punishable by death from 55 to 46.[9] State media indicated that although the nine crimes were rarely used and would have little impact in reducing the number of executions, their deletion was in line with the government's policy of "kill fewer, kill more cautiously". However, the revised provisions still failed to bring the Criminal Law in line with requirements under international law and standards on the use of the death penalty. Statistics continued to be classified as state secrets.

On 24 April, Li Yan, a victim of domestic violence who had killed her husband in 2010, was given a "suspended" death sentence with a two-year reprieve which is normally converted into a life sentence at the end of that period. The Supreme People's Court, in an unprecedented move in 2014, had overturned her initial death sentence and ordered a retrial. Evidence of the sustained domestic violence had been ignored by judges at the original trial, just as her previous calls for police protection had gone unheeded. In March, the Supreme People's Court and government had issued new guidelines on domestic violence cases, including recommendations on sentencing for victims of domestic violence who commit crimes against their abuser. In December the parliament passed the Domestic Violence Law which for the first time required police to investigate all reports of domestic violence and set up a restraining order system to protect victims.

## TORTURE AND OTHER ILL-TREATMENT

Torture and other ill-treatment remained widespread in detention and during interrogation, largely because of shortcomings in domestic law, systemic problems in the criminal justice system, and difficulties with implementing rules and procedures in the face of entrenched practices. Lawyer Yu Wensheng was tortured during his detention from October 2014 to January 2015 at Daxing Detention Centre in Beijing. He was questioned for 15 to 16 hours every day while seated on a rigid restraint chair, handcuffed for long hours and deprived of sleep.[10]

Detainees with deteriorating health were either denied or were unable to access adequate medical treatment. These included Gao Yu and Su Changlan, the latter a prominent women's rights activist who remained in detention throughout the year after being detained in October 2014 for supporting the pro-democracy protests in Hong Kong.

Zhou Jinjuan, an 84-year-old victim of forced eviction who had sought redress in Beijing by visiting government offices, was detained in August and placed in an unofficial detention facility for more than a week without necessary medical treatment, which contributed to her losing sight in one eye.

On 18 June, when Wang Quanzhang, defence lawyer for several Falun Gong practitioners, was speaking in Dongchangfu District Court in Liaocheng City, Shandong Province, he was interrupted by the judge and expelled from the courtroom for "disrupting court order". Wang Quanzhang said that court police dragged him to another room and beat him.

In December the UN Committee against Torture repeated recommendations on legal safeguards to prevent torture; and reported harassment of lawyers, human rights defenders and petitioners as well as lack of statistical information on torture. It also urged the authorities to stop sanctioning lawyers for taking action in accordance with recognized professional duties, and to repeal legal provisions that allowed de facto incommunicado detention through "residential surveillance in a designated location".

## SEXUAL AND REPRODUCTIVE RIGHTS

In October, the government announced changes to the family planning policy. After many years of incremental changes, the authorities promoted this change as an end to the "one-child policy", and as allowing one couple to have two children. Policies allowing rural households and ethnic minorities under certain circumstances to have additional children would continue. The government also announced that it would take steps to regularize the status of China's 13 million undocumented children born in contravention of the old policy.[11]

## TIBET AUTONOMOUS REGION AND TIBETAN POPULATED AREAS IN OTHER PROVINCES

To mark the 50th anniversary of the establishment of the Tibetan Autonomous Region in September, the Chinese government issued a white paper denouncing the "middle way" approach advocated by the Dalai Lama and the "Dalai Lama group's separatist activities". In a ceremony marking the anniversary, political leader Yu Zhengsheng vowed to fight against separatism and urged the army, police and judicial staff in Tibet to be ready to fight a protracted battle against the "14th Dalai clique".

Ethnic Tibetans continued to face discrimination and restrictions on their rights to freedoms of religious belief, expression, association and peaceful assembly. Several Tibetan monks, writers, protesters and activists were detained, including Tibetan monk Choephel Dawa and Tibetan writer and blogger Druklo.[12] At the end of the year the charges against them and their place of detention were not known.

Tenzin Deleg Rinpoche, a Tibetan religious and community leader who was imprisoned for "inciting separatism" in 2002, died in July while serving a life sentence. Police harassed and detained family members and others who had gathered to demand the return of his body so that customary Buddhist religious rites could be performed.[13] The authorities cremated his body against the family's wishes. There were also reports that the police countered these large-scale protests with excessive and arbitrary use of force, including tear gas and gunshots.

At least seven people set themselves on fire in Tibetan-populated areas during the year in protest against repressive policies by the authorities; at least five died as a result. The number of known self-immolations since February 2009 rose to 143.

## XINJIANG UIGHUR AUTONOMOUS REGION

A "Strike Hard" campaign targeting "violent terrorism and religious extremism", which had originally been a limited one-year-long campaign launched in May 2014, was extended throughout 2015. At the campaign's one-year mark in May, the authorities claimed to have broken up 181 "terror groups". An increasing number of violent incidents and counter-terrorism operations were reported, resulting in many casualties.

On 1 January new "Enforcement of Religious Affairs Regulations" came into effect in the region, with the professed goal of more tightly controlling online communications, and clamping down on the role of religion in "marriage, funerals, culture, the arts, and sports". In effect, this further tightened restrictions on Uighurs, a mainly Muslim Turkic ethnic group, living in the region who have been subjected to extensive discriminatory practices for many years. The same month, the region's capital city, Urumqi, banned the wearing of burqas.

As in previous years numerous counties posted notices on their websites stating that primary and secondary school students and Communist Party members should not be permitted to observe Ramadan.

## FORCED REPATRIATIONS FROM NEIGHBOURING COUNTRIES

After Chinese diplomatic pressure, in July, Thailand deported 109 Uighurs to China, where they were at risk of torture, enforced disappearance and execution.[14] In November, two pro-democracy activists who had been granted refugee status by UNHCR, the UN refugee agency, and had confirmed resettlement destinations, were also repatriated to China. China continued to ignore *non-refoulement* obligations in international law by repatriating North Koreans to North Korea, where they risked detention, imprisonment, torture and other ill-treatment and forced labour.

## HONG KONG SPECIAL ADMINISTRATIVE REGION

Police in Hong Kong formally arrested 955 people during the year who had taken part in the 79-day pro-democracy protests in Hong Kong between September and December 2014, also known as the "Umbrella Movement". A further 48 were summoned. Among those arrested were opposition lawmakers, the three co-founders of the "Occupy Central" civil disobedience campaign, and leaders of two student groups – Alex Chow of the Federation of Students and Joshua Wong of "Scholarism", a youth-led pro-democracy organization. A pattern of long intervals between initial arrests and the decision to prosecute meant that only a small proportion of the protesters who had been arrested were convicted by the end of 2015.

In October, Ken Tsang Kin-Chiu, a pro-democracy activist whose beating by police during the protest in 2014 was caught on camera by a local TV channel, was charged with one count of "assaulting police officers in the due execution of their duties" and four counts of "resisting a police officer in the due execution of his duty". The seven police officers who allegedly carried out the beating were charged with "causing grievous bodily harm with intent" on the same day. In December the officers and Ken Tsang pleaded not guilty.

The Hong Kong University administration was criticized for decisions which raised concerns about academic freedom in Hong

Kong. These included university sanctions, in August against law professor Benny Tai for his handling of anonymous donations related to the protests, which the administration claimed violated university procedures, and in September, the university's governing council rejection of a nomination committee's choice to appoint Johannes Chan Man-mun, professor of law and former Dean of the Faculty of Law, as a pro-vice-chancellor. Media, academics and students claimed these decisions were retaliation for the two academics' support for the 2014 "Umbrella" protests.

In a landmark judgment in February, Law Wan-Tung was found guilty of intimidating, assaulting and causing bodily harm to her employees, Indonesian migrant domestic workers Erwiana Sulistyaningsih and Tutik Lestari Ningsih. She was sentenced to six years in prison.

1. China: Latest information on crackdown against lawyers and activists (Press release, 28 August)
2. China: Authorities show callous disregard for imprisoned journalist by denying appropriate medical care (Press release, 6 August)
3. China: Release supporters of Hong Kong pro-democracy protests (Press release, 28 September)
4. Further information – China: Two activists released in China (ASA 17/2097/2015)
5. China: Activists held in crackdown on labour rights (ASA 17/3015/2015)
6. China: Submission to the NPC Standing Committee's Legislative Affairs Commission on the second draft Foreign Non-Governmental Organizations Management Law (ASA 17/1776/2015)
7. China: Submission to the NPC Standing Committee's Legislative Affairs Commission on the draft "Cyber Security Law" (ASA 17/2206/2015)
8. China: Lawyer supporting churches in China detained (ASA 17/2370/2015)
9. China: Submission to the NPC Standing Committee's Legislative Affairs Commission on the Criminal Law Amendment (9) (Second Draft) (ASA 17/2205/2015)
10. China: Submission to the UN Committee against Torture (ASA 17/2725/2015)
11. China: Reform of one-child policy not enough (News story, 29 October)
12. China: Fears for Tibetan monk detained in China – Choephel Dawa (ASA 17/1551/2015)
13. China: Return the body of prominent Tibetan monk Tenzin Deleg Rinpoche who died in prison (ASA 17/2102/2015)
14. Thailand must not send Uighurs to Chinese torture (News story, 9 July)

# COLOMBIA

Republic of Colombia
Head of state and government: **Juan Manuel Santos Calderón**

Peace talks between the government and the Revolutionary Armed Forces of Colombia (Fuerzas Armadas Revolucionarias de Colombia, FARC) made significant progress. The two sides announced that an agreement had been reached on transitional justice and that a peace deal would be signed in 2016. The agreement appeared to fall short of international law standards on victims' right to truth, justice and reparation.

The FARC's unilateral ceasefire and the government's suspension of aerial bombardments on FARC positions reduced the intensity of hostilities. However, the conflict continued to have a negative impact on the human rights of the civilian population, especially Indigenous Peoples, Afro-descendant and peasant farmer communities, and human rights defenders. The security forces, guerrilla groups and paramilitaries were responsible for crimes under international law.

Congress approved legislation that threatened to exacerbate the already high levels of impunity, especially for members of the security forces implicated in human rights violations, including unlawful killings, torture, enforced disappearances, death threats, forced displacement and rape.

Hundreds of candidates in the October regional elections were threatened and some killed, mainly by paramilitaries, but in fewer numbers than in previous polls.

## PEACE PROCESS
On 23 September, the government and the FARC announced an agreement on transitional justice – made public on 15

December – and that a peace deal would be signed by 23 March 2016. Its central component was a Special Jurisdiction for Peace, which would consist of a tribunal and special courts with jurisdiction over those directly or indirectly involved in the conflict implicated in "serious human rights violations and breaches of international humanitarian law".

Those who deny responsibility for grave crimes, if found guilty, would face up to 20 years in prison. Those who admit responsibility would receive non-custodial sentences of between five and eight years' "effective restriction of freedoms".

By proposing sanctions that do not appear to be proportionate to the severity of crimes under international law, Colombia may be failing to comply with its obligation under international law to prevent and punish such crimes.

An Amnesty Law that would benefit those accused of "political and related crimes" was proposed. Although a definition of what constitutes "related crimes" had yet to be agreed, those convicted of grave crimes would be excluded.

On 4 June, the two sides announced plans for a truth commission, although the courts would not be able to use any information uncovered by the commission. This could undermine the ability of the judiciary to prosecute crimes under international law.

On 17 October, the two sides reached agreement on a mechanism to locate and recover the remains of many of those – both civilians and combatants – still missing as a result of the conflict.

## INTERNAL ARMED CONFLICT

The armed conflict continued to have a significant human rights impact on civilians, especially those living in rural areas.[1] Many communities living in poor urban areas, including Afro-descendants in the Pacific city of Buenaventura, were also affected.[2]

All the parties to the conflict were responsible for crimes under international law, including unlawful killings, forced displacement, enforced disappearances, death threats and crimes of sexual violence. Children continued to be recruited as combatants by guerrilla groups and paramilitaries.

By 1 December, the Victims' Unit had registered 7.8 million victims of the conflict, including almost 6.6 million victims of forced displacement, more than 45,000 enforced disappearances and around 263,000 conflict-related killings; the vast majority of victims were civilians.

According to figures from the Colombian NGO CODHES (Consultoría para los Derechos Humanos y el Desplazamiento), more than 204,000 people were forcibly displaced in 2014, compared to almost 220,000 in the previous year.

The National Indigenous Organization of Colombia recorded 35 killings and 3,481 forced displacements in 2015. The situation of Indigenous communities in Cauca Department, many of which were campaigning for recognition of their territorial rights, was particularly acute.

On 6 February, Gerardo Velasco Escue and Emiliano Silva Oteca of the Toéz Indigenous *resguardo* (reservation) were forcibly disappeared after being stopped by unidentified armed men near the hamlet of La Selva in Caloto Municipality, Cauca Department. Two days later, the community found their bodies bearing signs of torture in the municipality of Guachené. On 5 February, a death threat by the Black Eagles (Águilas Negras) paramilitary group announcing that it was "time for social cleansing in northern Cauca" had been circulated in the area and neighbouring municipalities.

On 2 July, two small explosive devices injured several people in Bogotá. The authorities attributed the attack to the guerrilla group National Liberation Army (ELN). Fifteen people, many of them human rights defenders and student activists belonging to the People's Congress (Congreso de los Pueblos) social movement, were arrested, although only 13 were charged.

Some public officials linked all 13 to the July explosions and the ELN, but only three were eventually charged with "terrorism" and membership of the ELN. The other 10 were charged with weapons-related offences.

There were concerns that these events may have been used to undermine the work of human rights defenders. Some members of the People's Congress have in the past been subjected to death threats and harassment for their work in defence of human rights. In January, one of the leaders of the People's Congress, Carlos Alberto Pedraza Salcedo, was killed in Bogotá.

## SECURITY FORCES

Reports of extrajudicial executions by the security forces, a widespread and systematic practice during the conflict, continued to fall. Such practices included "false positives": unlawful killings by the security forces – in return for benefits such as bonuses, additional leave or promotions – in which the victims, usually poor young men, were falsely presented as combat kills. "False positives" were prevalent during the administration of President Álvaro Uribe (2002-2010).

Although the latest report of the UN High Commissioner for Human Rights, published in January, did not record any "false positives", it did include cases "in which the armed forces attempted to disguise victims of arbitrary killings as enemy combat casualties or rearranged the crime scene to make it appear as self-defence".

Little progress was made in investigating those suspected of criminal responsibility for such crimes, especially high-ranking officers. The Office of the Attorney General registered more than 4,000 reported extrajudicial executions over recent decades.

## GUERRILLA GROUPS

Guerrilla groups were responsible for crimes under international law and human rights abuses, including unlawful killings and indiscriminate attacks that placed civilians at risk. Afro-descendant community leader Genaro García of the Alto Mira y Frontera

Community Council was shot dead by the FARC on 3 August in Tumaco Municipality, Nariño Department. The FARC had threatened in October 2014 that they would kill him if he remained leader of the Council, which had been seeking the restitution of territory since 2012.

According to the NGO País Libre, there were 182 kidnappings in January-November. The ELN accounted for 23 of these, the FARC for seven and paramilitaries for 24. However, most kidnappings (123) were attributed to common delinquency. Landmines, mostly laid by the FARC, continued to kill and maim civilians and members of the security forces.

## PARAMILITARIES

Paramilitary groups, which the government referred to as criminal gangs (bandas criminales, bacrim), continued to commit crimes under international law and serious human rights violations, despite their supposed demobilization in the government-sponsored Justice and Peace process that began in 2005. Paramilitaries – sometimes acting with the support or acquiescence of state actors, including members of the security forces – threatened and killed, among others, human rights defenders.

On 11 January, a pamphlet from the Black Eagles Northern Bloc Atlantic Coast (Bloque Norte Costa Atlántica Águilas Negras) was circulated in Atlántico Department. The death threat named around 40 individuals, including human rights defenders, trade unionists, land claimants, and a state official working on land restitution. Those named in the death threat had been involved in the land restitution process and issues relating to the peace process.

Only 122 of the more than 30,000 paramilitaries who supposedly laid down their arms in the demobilization process had been convicted of human rights-related crimes by the end of the year. Some 120 paramilitaries were released after serving the maximum eight years in prison stipulated in the Justice and Peace process. Legal proceedings against most of them were ongoing. Concerns remained about the security risks the paramilitaries posed to the communities to which they returned after their release. Most paramilitaries, however, did not submit themselves to the Justice and Peace process and received de facto amnesties without any effective investigations to determine their possible role, or that of those who colluded with them, in human rights violations.

## IMPUNITY

The state continued to fail to bring to justice the vast majority of those suspected of individual criminal responsibility for crimes under international law. The government also steered through approval of legislation – such as Legislative Act No 1 amending Article 221 of the Constitution and Law 1765 – that threatened to increase the already high levels of impunity.

The military justice system continued to claim jurisdiction over and subsequently close investigations into alleged human rights violations by members of the security forces, without holding to account those allegedly implicated.

Relatives of victims of human rights violations who campaigned for justice, as well as members of human rights organizations helping them, faced death threats and other serious human rights violations from paramilitaries and members of the security forces.[3]

Some progress was made in bringing to justice some of those implicated in a scandal involving the now-disbanded civilian intelligence service (Departamento Administrativo de Seguridad, DAS). The DAS was implicated in threats and illegal surveillance of human rights defenders, politicians, journalists and judges, mainly during the government of President Uribe. On 28 April, the Supreme Court of Justice sentenced former DAS Director María del Pilar Hurtado to 14 years in prison and President Uribe's former chief of staff, Bernardo Moreno, to eight years' house arrest for their roles in the scandal. On 1 October, former DAS intelligence director Carlos Alberto Arzayús Guerrero was sentenced to six years' imprisonment for the psychological torture of journalist Claudia Julieta Duque.

On 6 November, in a ceremony ordered by the Inter-American Court of Human Rights, President Santos assumed responsibility and asked forgiveness for the state's role in the enforced disappearance of 10 people, the enforced disappearance and extrajudicial execution of an 11th person, and the torture of several other individuals. These crimes occurred after security forces stormed the Palace of Justice in Bogotá in November 1985 where people were being held hostage by the M-19 guerrilla group. Some 100 people died in the assault. Very few of those alleged to have been responsible for these crimes have been held to account.

On 16 December, the Supreme Court overturned the conviction of retired colonel Luis Alfonso Plazas Vega who in 2010 had been sentenced to 30 years in prison for the crime of enforced disappearance in relation to this case.

## LAND RIGHTS

The land restitution process, which began in 2012 with the aim of returning to their rightful occupants some of the millions of hectares of land illegally acquired or forcibly abandoned during the conflict, continued to make slow progress. By the end of 2015, only 58,500 hectares of land claimed by peasant farmers, one 50,000-hectare Indigenous territory and one 71,000-hectare Afro-descendant territory were subject to judicial rulings ordering their return. The main stumbling blocks included the failure to guarantee the security of those wishing to return, and the lack of effective social and economic measures to ensure any returns were sustainable.

Leaders of displaced communities and those seeking the return of their lands were threatened or killed.[4] Members of Indigenous and Afro-descendant communities seeking to defend their territorial rights, including by denouncing the presence of illegal mining or opposing the development of outside mining interests on their collective territories, were also targeted.[5]

There were concerns that Law 1753, approved by Congress on 9 June, could enable mining and other economic sectors to gain control over illegally acquired lands. This could undermine the right of many of these lands' legitimate occupants, especially on Indigenous and Afro-descendant territories, to claim ownership over them.[6]

## HUMAN RIGHTS DEFENDERS

Human rights defenders – including Indigenous, Afro-descendant and peasant farmer community leaders, trade unionists, journalists, land activists and those campaigning for justice – were at risk of attack, mainly by paramilitaries.[7] There were also reports of thefts of sensitive information held by human rights organizations.

Some criminal investigations into human rights defenders continued to raise concerns that the legal system was being misused in an attempt to undermine their work. In September, Indigenous leader Feliciano Valencia was sentenced to 18 years' imprisonment for illegally holding captive a member of the security forces who had infiltrated an Indigenous protest in Cauca Department. Feliciano Valencia, who had long been the target of harassment by civilian and military officials for his defence of Indigenous Peoples' territorial rights, denied the charges.

According to the NGO We Are Defenders (Somos Defensores), 51 human rights defenders were killed in January-September, compared to 45 during the same period in 2014. According to provisional figures from the NGO National Trade Union School (Escuela Nacional Sindical), 18 members of trade unions were killed in 2015, compared to 21 in 2014.

The number of death threats against human rights defenders again increased. An email sent on 9 March by the Black Eagles South Bloc (Águilas Negras Bloque Sur) threatened 14 individuals, including politicians active on human rights and peace-related issues, and two human rights NGOs. The threat read: "Communist guerrillas…

your days are numbered, your blood will be as fertilizer for the fatherland… this message is also for your children and women."

## VIOLENCE AGAINST WOMEN AND GIRLS

All parties to the conflict were responsible for crimes of sexual violence committed mainly against women and girls. Very few of the alleged perpetrators were brought to justice.

In June, the decision by prosecutors to close the case against and release one of the main suspects in the kidnapping and rape of journalist Jineth Bedoya by paramilitaries in 2000 led to a public outcry that forced prosecutors to quickly reverse their decision.

In July, the government promulgated Law 1761, which categorized femicide as a separate crime and increased the punishment for those convicted of this offence to up to 50 years' imprisonment.

Human rights defenders campaigning for justice in sexual violence cases were threatened, and some threats against women activists involved threats of sexual violence.[8]

## US ASSISTANCE

US assistance to Colombia continued to fall. The USA allocated some US$174.1 million for military and US$152.2 million for non-military assistance to Colombia. In September, 25% of the total military assistance for the year was released after the US Secretary of State determined that the Colombian authorities had made progress on human rights.

## INTERNATIONAL SCRUTINY

In his January report, the UN High Commissioner for Human Rights welcomed progress in the peace talks, but expressed concern about impunity and the human rights impact of the conflict, especially on Indigenous and Afro-descendant communities and human rights defenders. Although the report noted that all the warring parties were responsible for human rights abuses and violations, it stated that paramilitaries (referred to as "post-demobilization armed groups linked to organized crime") represented "the main public security challenge".

In August, the CERD Committee noted that the armed conflict continued to have a disproportionate impact on Indigenous Peoples and Afro-descendant communities and criticized the failure to ensure the effective participation of these communities in the peace process.

The UN Committee against Torture expressed concern over "the persistence of grave human rights violations, including extrajudicial killings and enforced disappearances in the State party" and the fact that "it has not received information concerning criminal trials or convictions for the offence of enforced disappearance ".

1. Colombia: Peasant farmer linked to Peace Community killed (AMR 23/2554/2015)
2. Colombia: Human rights defender under surveillance: Berenice Celeita (AMR 23/1945/2015)
3. Colombia: Caller "will kill" missing man's mother (AMR 23/2022/2015)
4. Colombia: Land restitution process sparks more threats (AMR 23/0003/2015)
5. Colombia: Restoring the land, securing the peace: Indigenous and Afro-descendant territorial rights (AMR 23/2615/2015)
6. Colombia: National Development Plan threatens to deny the right to land restitution to victims of the armed conflict and allow mining firms to operate on illegally acquired lands (AMR 23/2077/2015)
7. Colombia: Director of human rights NGO threatened: Iván Madero Vergel (AMR 23/2007/2015)
8. Colombia: Harassed for fighting sexual violence (AMR 23/002/2015)

# CONGO (REPUBLIC OF)

**Republic of Congo**
Head of state and government: **Denis Sassou Nguesso**

Security forces used unnecessary or excessive force, including lethal force, against demonstrators opposing proposed changes to the Constitution. Protesters were arbitrarily arrested and freedom of expression was curtailed. Expulsions of non-nationals resumed, targeting West African citizens, while no investigations were launched into the 2014 "Mbata ya Bakolo" operation, in which more than 179,000 nationals from the Democratic Republic of the Congo (DRC) were expelled. The UN Committee against Torture expressed serious concern that torture and other ill-treatment occurred in most places of detention. Conditions of detention remained harsh. Presidential elections will be held in March 2016.

## BACKGROUND

A referendum to amend the Constitution was held on 25 October. It was both boycotted by the main opposition coalition and the subject of major demonstrations. However, the amendment was passed on 27 October and confirmed by the Constitutional Court on 6 November, allowing the incumbent President to run for a third term in 2016.

## FREEDOMS OF EXPRESSION AND ASSEMBLY

Freedom of expression was curtailed. Members of opposition parties who spoke against the proposed amendment to the Constitution were particularly targeted. From July to October, there was a wave of arrests of political opponents protesting against the constitutional review.

In October, media freedom was arbitrarily restricted when mobile internet, text messaging services and some radio broadcast signals were disrupted in the capital, Brazzaville, ahead of protests organized by the opposition.

On 9 October, six activists from youth movements were arrested following a peaceful protest they had organized against the referendum. They were charged with "participation in an unauthorized protest ".

On 22 October, security forces surrounded the house of opposition leader Guy Brice Parfait Kolélas in Brazzaville. He was kept under de facto house arrest for 12 days together with 25 others. No judicial warrant authorized the action.

On 23 November, Paulin Makaya, president of the political party "Unis pour le Congo" (UPC), who openly opposed the proposed changes to the Constitution, was arrested by police officers while at the office of the Public Prosecutor of the High Court of Brazzaville. He was with his lawyer to report for questioning as part of an investigation. He was kept in detention at the Central Police Station of Brazzaville from 23 November until 1 December without being brought before a court or charged and was questioned on several occasions in the absence of his lawyer. A request for bail submitted by his lawyers on 2 December was not addressed, despite a reminder on 11 December. Paulin Makaya was still in pre-trial detention at the central prison of Brazzaville at the end of the year. On 5 June, protests were organized by students in the cities of Brazzaville, Pointe-Noire and Dolisie following the revocation of the Baccalauréat exam due to massive fraud and serious irregularities. Many students were injured in clashes with the police and several were arrested.

## EXCESSIVE USE OF FORCE

On 17 October, in Pointe-Noire, a plain-clothes police officer fired live ammunition into a crowd demonstrating against the referendum, wounding 13 people.

On 20 October, security forces fired tear gas and live ammunition at protesters in Brazzaville demonstrating against the proposed constitutional changes. Six people were reported to have been killed. On the same day, opposition groups reported that at least 12 protesters and bystanders had been killed by military police and several others wounded in protests organized in Pointe-Noire. No investigations into these incidents had been initiated at the end of the year.

## REFUGEES' AND MIGRANTS' RIGHTS

No investigations were launched into serious human rights violations committed in 2014 by Congolese security forces and others during the first phase of the Mbata Ya Bakolo operation, in which more than 179,000 DRC nationals, including refugees and asylum-seekers, were rounded up, arbitrarily detained and forcibly returned by the police. Government authorities portrayed the security operation as a response to increased criminality, which they believed was being driven by *kuluna* gangs (organized criminal gangs) from the DRC.

On 14 May, the second phase of the operation was launched in Pointe-Noire. It was characterized by arrests, detentions and deportations targeting West African nationals, including Senegalese, Malians, and Ivorians. Police targeted specific neighbourhoods, carrying out cordon and search operations, resulting in arbitrary arrests. Those arrested were placed in retention facilities lacking access to running water, adequate food and bedding as well as washing and sanitary facilities. NGOs were denied access to the retention sites. No official figures were issued concerning the number of people arrested and returned during the operation.

## INTERNATIONAL SCRUTINY

On 7 May, the UN Committee against Torture expressed serious concern about numerous reports of torture and other ill-treatment occurring in most of the country's places of detention. The Committee highlighted the systematic use of pre-trial detention, the failure by authorities to observe statutory limits on its imposition and the failure to ensure detainees' right to legal representation and to have their relatives informed of their detention.

## PRISON CONDITIONS

Detention conditions remained extremely poor, including through chronic overcrowding, inadequate food, lack of drinking water, limited medical care and personnel and sub-standard hygiene and sanitation facilities. In April, three detainees died in detention at the Pointe-Noire Central police station, including one, Batola Régis, who was held in a small, overcrowded cell and died of malnutrition. No investigation had been launched into these deaths by the end of the year.

# CÔTE D'IVOIRE

Republic of Côte d'Ivoire
Head of state: **Alassane Ouattara**
Head of government: **Daniel Kablan Duncan**

Hundreds of detainees still awaited trial in connection with post-electoral violence in 2010 and 2011, and concerns remained about selective accountability for crimes committed during that period. Freedoms of expression and assembly were restricted and there was a wave of arbitrary arrests of political opponents prior to elections. The trial of Laurent Gbagbo and Laurent Blé Goudé at the ICC was scheduled to begin in 2016. Simone Gbagbo was not transferred to the ICC despite an outstanding arrest warrant.

## BACKGROUND

The security situation remained stable despite attacks in early 2015 by armed groups and intercommunal clashes in the west. In June, the mandate of the UN Operation in Côte d'Ivoire (UNOCI) was extended for an additional year. In the same month, the National Assembly adopted a law against terrorism, giving the Prosecutor of the Court of First Instance in Abidjan jurisdiction to qualify crimes as acts of terrorism and to hold suspects in custody for up to eight days.

The 2014 report of the Dialogue, Truth and Reconciliation Commission (CDVR), established to shed light on post-electoral violence, had still not been made public by the end of the year. In March, the National Commission for Reconciliation and Compensation of Victims (CONARIV ) was created to complete the work of the CDVR, in particular to register unidentified victims of the post-electoral violence. In December, President Ouattara committed to pardoning over 3,000 people detained since the electoral crisis, either totally or partially removing their sentences. At the end of the

year, the list of those pardoned had not been made public.

Largely peaceful presidential elections were held in October. President Ouattara was re-elected for another five-year term on a turnout of 53%, with some opposition members boycotting the poll.

## JUSTICE SYSTEM

More than 200 supporters of former President Gbagbo remained in detention on charges including public disorder and genocide linked to the conflict after the 2010 elections. Among them were more than 30 prisoners extradited from Liberia in 2012 and 2014. In August, 20 military officers who had backed President Ouattara, including Chérif Ousmane and Losséný Fofana, were charged with crimes relating to post-electoral violence.

In March, 78 supporters and relatives of Laurent Gbagbo, including Simone and Michel Gbagbo and Geneviève Bro Grebé, were tried in the Abidjan Assize Court. Eighteen people were acquitted, and some of those convicted received suspended prison sentences. Simone Gbagbo was sentenced to 20 years' imprisonment for undermining state security, participation in an insurrectionary movement, and public disorder. Geneviève Bro Grebé was sentenced to 10 years for similar crimes. At the end of the year the implementation of her sentence was suspended pending an appeal.

Amnesty International's trial observer noted that, contrary to the right to have a criminal conviction reviewed by a higher tribunal, Côte d'Ivoire's law restricts appeals to points of law before the Court of Cassation. The right to appeal in this case was further undermined by the Assize Court's failure to provide a full written judgment. He also noted that, although during the trial several of the accused raised allegations that they had been tortured in pre-trial detention, the Court did not appear to consider them.

## ARBITRARY ARRESTS AND DETENTIONS

In May, Sébastien Dano Djédjé, Justin Koua and Hubert Oulaye, high-ranking members of the Ivorian Popular Front (FPI), were arrested.[1] They had organized a ceremony to inaugurate Laurent Gbagbo as FPI President in Mama, his home town. Sébastien Dano Djédjé and Justin Koua were charged with violation of a court order, violence and assault on security forces, rebellion and public disorder. Hubert Oulaye was charged with killing UNOCI soldiers in 2012. Sébastien Dano Djédjé was provisionally released in December. The other two men were detained pending trial. The arresting officers allegedly beat Hubert Oulaye's 15-year-old granddaughter, who was suffering from malaria, at his home. In September, one guard accused of informing the family of Sébastien Dano Djédjé that he was sick was arrested and detained.

Between mid-September and October, more than 50 people, mostly members of the political opposition, were arrested. The majority were held on charges of public disorder after participating in unauthorized peaceful demonstrations.[2] Although some were later released, more than 20 remained detained at the end of the year. Many were ill-treated during arrest and were held in incommunicado detention for several weeks. In September, Samba David's house was ransacked and he was beaten with rifle butts. He was held incommunicado for two days without access to a lawyer or medical treatment. He was charged with public disorder, violation of a court order and complicity in the destruction of property, and sentenced to six months' imprisonment.

## FREEDOMS OF EXPRESSION AND ASSEMBLY

The authorities banned at least 10 protest marches organized by NGOs and the main opposition party. Tear gas and batons were used to disperse protesters. At least 80 people were arrested in different parts of the country and charged with public disorder. At the end of 2015, they were still in detention awaiting trial.

In its March report, the UN Human Rights Committee expressed concern about freedom of the press. In July, Joseph Gnanhoua Titi, director of Aujourd'hui, a daily newspaper, was arrested and charged with publishing false news and insulting the President. An article published earlier that month accused President Ouattara of embezzling foreign aid and money laundering. A week later, the charges against Joseph Gnanhoua Titi were dropped and he was released.

## INTERNATIONAL JUSTICE

Despite the outstanding ICC arrest warrant for Simone Gbagbo for alleged crimes against humanity, President Ouattara stated in April that there would be no more transfers to the ICC. In the same month, the ICC joined the trials of Laurent Gbagbo and Charles Blé Goudé. In May, the ICC rejected Côte d'Ivoire's appeal against the admissibility of Simone Gbagbo's case before the ICC. In October, the ICC also rejected Laurent Gbagbo's request to hold the opening statements of his trial in Abidjan or Arusha. In the same month, it was announced that the trial of Laurent Gbagbo and Charles Blé Goudé would start in January 2016. Laurent Gbagbo's latest request for provisional release was also rejected.

## PRISON CONDITIONS

The UN Human Rights Committee report in March conveyed concerns about prison conditions throughout the country. It noted in particular the large number of pre-trial detainees, the unsanitary conditions and lack of adequate medical facilities, the failure to detain children and adults separately, and the severe overcrowding in the Maison d'Arrêt et de Correction d'Abidjan (MACA) detention centre in Abidjan.

## DEATH PENALTY

In March, Parliament unanimously approved two bills amending the Criminal Code and the Code of Criminal Procedure to exclude the death penalty, which had been abolished in the 2000 Constitution.

1. Côte d'Ivoire. L'arrestation d'opposants à l'approche de la présidentielle envoie un signal préoccupant (News story, 7 May)
2. Côte d'Ivoire: Il faut mettre fin aux arrestations arbitraires d'opposants à l'approche de la présidentielle (Press release, 5 October)

# CROATIA

**Republic of Croatia**
Head of state: **Kolinda Grabar-Kitarović (replaced Ivo Josipović in February)**
Head of government: **Zoran Milanović**

Croatia struggled to provide adequate reception conditions and access to asylum proceedings to the large number of refugees and migrants that arrived in the country. Parliament passed a law providing survivors of war crimes of sexual violence with reparations. Discrimination against Croatian Serbs and Roma continued.

## DISCRIMINATION

The state-wide celebration in August of the 20th anniversary of Operation Storm, which saw 200,000 Serbs flee from Croatia in 1995, brought tensions between Serb and Croat nationalists back.

In August, the town council of Vukovar passed a motion to remove public signs in the Cyrillic (Serb) alphabet, and to require a special request and the payment of a fee for the receipt of official communications in Cyrillic, despite the fact that 34% of the town's population were ethnic Serbs. The Croatian law on minority rights entitles minorities amounting to one third of the municipal population to official usage of their languages and scripts. Discrimination against Croatian Serbs in public sector employment and in the restitution of tenancy rights to social housing vacated during the 1991-1995 war persisted.

Social exclusion of and discrimination against Roma remained widespread, particularly in accessing adequate housing and employment opportunities.

The municipal court in Split acquitted three men standing trial for a homophobic attack against six women in the town in 2012. The victims alleged that the local police had threatened them when they filed their complaint, failed to arrest the suspects on the spot and investigate the crime effectively.

## FREEDOM OF EXPRESSION

In June, the Osijek County Court confirmed the decision of the Zagreb Municipal Court, finding that Zagreb Pride, a lesbian, gay, bisexual, transgender and intersex (LGBTI) organization, violated the honour and dignity of a former employee of the Croatian Radio Television (HRT) by placing her on the annual list of candidates for the most homophobic person of the year 2013. The Court ordered the organization to pay 41,018.91 HRK (€5,414) to the journalist and to publish the verdict on its website.

## INTERNATIONAL JUSTICE

In February, the International Court of Justice cleared Serbia and Croatia of mutual claims of genocide, finding that neither Serbia nor Croatia had established the necessary intent on the part of the other to commit genocide during the conflict in the 1990s.

In May, the Croatian Parliament passed the Law on the rights of victims of sexual violence in war. The Law provides survivors of wartime sexual violence with Croatian citizenship, a lump-sum compensation amounting to €13,000 and a monthly allowance amounting to €328. In addition to the payments, survivors will be entitled to health care, medical rehabilitation and psychological support. The Law entered into force in June with the first allowances due to be paid out in January 2016.

However, Croatia had not yet adopted a comprehensive legislative framework that would regulate the status of, and access to reparation for, all civilian victims of war crimes.

Croatia did not ratify the International Convention against Enforced Disappearances nor did it adopt a law on missing persons. In the absence of these legal instruments, relatives of the 1,600 missing persons in Croatia were denied access to justice and reparations.

## REFUGEES' AND MIGRANTS' RIGHTS
By the end of the year, more than 550,000 refugees and migrants had transited through Croatia towards other EU countries, with the assistance of state authorities providing free transportation.[1] Only a few hundred people made an asylum application and, by October, 37 had been granted international protection. The authorities failed to identify vulnerable individuals, including unaccompanied minors and victims of human trafficking entering the country through its land borders.

---

1. Hundreds of refugees stranded in dire conditions on Croatia/Slovenia border (News story, 19 October)

# CUBA

**Republic of Cuba**
Head of state and government: **Raúl Castro Ruz**

Despite increasingly open diplomatic relations, severe restrictions on freedoms of expression, association and movement continued. Thousands of cases of harassment of government critics and arbitrary arrests and detentions were reported.

## BACKGROUND
The year saw significant changes in Cuba´s diplomatic relations. In April, President Castro met US President Barack Obama during Cuba's first attendance of the Summit of the Americas, the first meeting between leaders of the two countries in nearly 60 years. In May, Cuba was removed from the USA's list of countries designated as state sponsors of international terrorism. Cuba and the USA reopened their respective embassies and announced their intent to re-establish diplomatic relations.

Despite this, in September President Obama renewed the Trading with the Enemy Act, which imposes financial and economic sanctions on Cuba. In October the UN General Assembly adopted, for the 24th consecutive year, a resolution calling on the USA to lift the unilateral embargo.

By the end of the year, Cuba had failed to ratify either the ICCPR or ICESCR, both of which it had signed in February 2008, or the Rome Statute of the International Criminal Court.

## FREEDOMS OF EXPRESSION AND ASSOCIATION
Government critics continued to experience harassment, "acts of repudiation" (demonstrations led by government supporters with participation of state security officials), and politically motivated criminal prosecutions. The judicial system remained under political control.

The government continued to control access to the internet and blocked and filtered websites, limiting access to information and criticism of the state. Activists reported that mobile phones were without service during the Pope's visit in September.

## ARBITRARY ARRESTS AND DETENTIONS
Reports continued of government critics, including journalists and human rights activists, being routinely subjected to arbitrary arrests and short-term detention for exercising their rights to freedom of expression, association, assembly and movement.

The Cuban Commission for Human Rights and National Reconciliation (CCDHRN) documented more than 8,600 politically motivated detentions of government opponents and activists during the year.

Prior to Pope Francis' visit in September, the authorities announced they would release 3,522 prisoners, including people over 60 years of age, prisoners under 20 years of age with no previous criminal record, chronically ill prisoners, and foreign nationals whose countries agreed to repatriate them, according to *Granma*, the official newspaper of the Communist Party.

However, before and during the Pope's visit, human rights activists and journalists reported significant increases in arrests and short periods of detention. In September alone, the CCDHRN registered 882 arbitrary arrests. They included three activists who reportedly approached the Pope to discuss human rights. The three went on hunger strike in detention.

Members and supporters of the Ladies in White, a group of women calling for the release of political prisoners and greater freedoms, and members of the Patriotic Union of Cuba, a dissident group, were regularly arrested and detained for periods of up to 30 hours, according to CCDHRN. The detentions were carried out to prevent the activists from attending their regular Sunday marches and to stop them protesting.

On 10 December, International Human Rights Day, the political police detained activists, including many in their homes, to prevent their peaceful protest. They also stopped journalists from leaving their offices to report the story.

## PRISONERS OF CONSCIENCE

Laws covering "public disorder", "contempt", "disrespect", "dangerousness" and "aggression" were used in politically motivated prosecutions, or threats of prosecution, against government opponents.

In January, the authorities released five prisoners of conscience along with a group of more than 50 people believed to have been imprisoned for political reasons. The USA had requested they be freed as part of an agreement between the two governments to "normalize" relations.

On 7 and 8 January, brothers Vianco, Django and Alexeis Vargas Martín, were released from prison. The three men had been detained since December 2012 and were sentenced in June 2014 to between two-and-a-half and four years' imprisonment for "public disorder". On 8 January, prisoners

of conscience Iván Fernández Depestre and Emilio Planas Robert were apparently released unconditionally. The two men had been sentenced to three and three-and-a-half years' imprisonment respectively, on the charge of "dangerousness".[1]

Prisoner of conscience Ciro Alexis Casanova Pérez was released upon completion of his sentence in June 2015.[2] He had been found guilty in December 2014 of "public disorder" following his one-man demonstration against the government in the streets of his hometown Placetas.

Graffiti artist Danilo Maldonado Machado, known as El Sexto, was arrested by agents of the political police in Havana while travelling in a taxi on 25 December 2014. He was carrying two pigs with "Raúl" and "Fidel" painted on their backs, which he intended to release at an art show on Christmas Day. He was accused of "disrespecting the leaders of the Revolution" but was never brought to court. He was released from detention on 20 October.

## INTERNATIONAL SCRUTINY

Cuba has not granted Amnesty International access to the country since 1990.

1. Cuba: Prisoner releases must lead to new environment for freedoms (Press release, 8 January)
2. Urgent Action: Political dissident must be released (AMR 25/1379/2015)

# CYPRUS

**Republic of Cyprus**
Head of state and government: **Nicos Anastasiades**

Irregular migrants were detained for prolonged periods in inadequate conditions. In November, Parliament recognized the right to same-sex civil unions. Allegations of ill-treatment by law enforcement officials continued.

## BACKGROUND

In May, the Greek Cypriot and Turkish Cypriot leaders resumed negotiations regarding the reunification of the island.

## REFUGEES' AND MIGRANTS' RIGHTS

Certain categories of asylum-seekers and irregular migrants who could not be deported continued to be detained for prolonged periods. Domestic remedies to challenge immigration detention remained ineffective.

In July, the European Court of Human Rights issued three rulings relating to the detention of 17 Syrian Kurds in 2010 and their subsequent deportation despite some of them having asylum proceedings pending before the Supreme Court. The Court ruled that their detention had no legal basis and the procedures available to asylum-seekers and irregular migrants to challenge their detention did not offer an effective remedy.

In September, 14 detainees including several asylum-seekers at the Menoya immigration detention centre started a hunger strike in protest at their prolonged detention and substandard detention conditions.

In September, 115 people were rescued from a vessel off the southern coast and settled in a reception centre for asylum-seekers in Kofinou. Most of the asylum-seekers who arrived in 2015 entered from the north and via the UN Buffer Zone.

In September, the Minister of Interior stated that Cyprus was willing to take up to 300 Syrian refugees under the EU agreed relocation scheme, but would "seek for them to be Christian Orthodox".

In mid-November, Nataliya Konovalova, a Russian national, was extradited to Russia despite pending asylum proceedings.

In December, the Council of Europe Commissioner for Human Rights expressed his concerns about the grave shortcomings of the Cypriot asylum system and urged for improvement of reception conditions for asylum-seekers.

There was an increase in the international protection status recognition rates in comparison to 2014.

## ENFORCED DISAPPEARANCES

Between January and August, the Committee of Missing Persons in Cyprus exhumed the remains of 111 people, bringing the total number of exhumations since 2006 to 1,061. Between August 2006 and January 2015, the remains of 625 missing individuals (476 Greek Cypriots and 149 Turkish Cypriots) had been identified and restituted to their families.

## TORTURE AND OTHER ILL-TREATMENT

Allegations of ill-treatment in pre-trial custody and immigration detention continued. In August, a video was released showing police officers beating an individual in pre-trial custody at the Chrysochous police station in February 2014. The General Prosecutor ordered the Authority Investigating Allegations and Complaints against the Police to bring criminal charges against the police officers involved in the incident.

## RIGHTS OF LESBIAN, GAY, BISEXUAL, TRANSGENDER AND INTERSEX PEOPLE

At the end of November, Parliament recognized the right to same-sex civil unions. However, the new legislation does not include joint adoption rights for same-sex couples and the legal recognition of transgender people.

# CZECH REPUBLIC

Czech Republic
Head of state: **Miloš Zeman**
Head of government: **Bohuslav Sobotka**

**The European Commission continued infringement proceedings against the Czech Republic for discrimination against Roma. The government adopted measures aimed at improving equal access to education. The routine detention of refugees and migrants provoked domestic and international criticism.**

## DISCRIMINATION – ROMA

## Education

The European Commission continued infringement proceedings against the Czech Republic for discrimination against Roma in education, amounting to a violation of the EU Race Equality Directive, on account of the over-representation of Romani children in schools and classes for pupils with mild mental disabilities, where they represent a third of all pupils. In March, Parliament adopted an amendment to the Schools Act introducing measures to support pupils with special educational needs in mainstream schools. The amendment will enter into force on 1 September 2016. In May, the Prime Minister dismissed the Minister of Education following Ministry staff's complaints of bullying by the Minister. On 17 June, a new Minister of Education with a record of engagement in human rights was appointed. On 23 September, the government adopted an amendment to the Schools Act that introduced a compulsory year of pre-school education. In September, the Minister of Education announced that the Ministry was considering abolishing the educational programme for pupils with mild mental disabilities.

## Housing

In October, a government report on the situation of the Roma minority concluded that about half of the 242,000 Roma in the country met the government's definition of social exclusion. The government presented a Conceptual Framework on Social Housing in October with the aim of improving access to affordable housing for those in need. The Framework envisaged the adoption of a new law on social housing in 2016.

## Sexual and reproductive rights

On 1 October, the government rejected a draft law on reparations for Romani women who were forcibly sterilized between 1966 and 2012. The draft, presented by the Minister for Human Rights, aimed to ensure access to remedies for the women, such as monetary compensation, including in cases where they could not access remedies through court proceedings due to the statute of limitations. In a letter to the Prime Minister in October, the Council of Europe Commissioner for Human Rights urged the government to adopt the law. The Prime Minister dismissed the recommendation, arguing that it was not necessary.

## RACISM AND XENOPHOBIA

Between June and September, hundreds of protesters participated in anti-refugee and migrant demonstrations in the capital, Prague, and other cities. Some protests were countered by refugee rights and anti-racism activists.

Groups supporting refugees faced threats from far-right organizations. In September, stickers featuring a noose and "death to traitors" were placed on the display window and door of the community centre Kašpárek, in the town of Pardubice. The incident happened a few days after the centre organized a food drive and other aid for refugees. Police informed the media that they were investigating the case as a misdemeanour.

## REFUGEES' AND MIGRANTS' RIGHTS

The government continued to refuse the relocation of refugees within the EU. In October, the Prime Minister called for the powers of the EU Border Agency, Frontex, to be strengthened, to protect the external borders of the Schengen area. According to opinion polls, 50% of Czech people opposed policies consisting of accepting refugees fleeing armed conflict.

Since the beginning of the year, police routinely checked trains for irregular migrants. Those without valid visas were apprehended and brought to a detention centre while their deportation proceedings were pending. The NGO Organization for Aid to Refugees reported in September that about 700 refugees and migrants, predominantly from Syria, Afghanistan and Iraq, were held in one of the centres, Bělá-Jezová. As the centre only had a capacity of 260 people, a large number of refugees and migrants had to sleep in military tents, a gym and pre-fabricated containers.

In October, the Public Defender of Rights (Ombudsperson) stated that living conditions in the Bělá-Jezová centre amounted to degrading treatment and were worse than in prison. Adults were brought to the premises handcuffed, routinely checked by the police in the evening and accommodated in unhygienic sleeping quarters. Food was distributed by police officers wearing balaclavas and helmets. Refugees and migrants held in the centre were charged for their stay at a rate of €260 per month. In its response on 13 October, the Ministry of Interior ignored these concerns and rejected the Ombudsperson's recommendation to stop placing families with children in the centre. On 22 October, the UN High Commissioner for Human Rights criticized the treatment of migrants and refugees and expressed concern that the government was pursuing detention as a routine policy. The President's spokesperson said the criticism was part of a campaign against the country. On 17 November, the President attended a demonstration in Prague organized by the anti-Islam group Block Against Islam. In his speech he declared that there are half a million foreigners living in the country with whom "there are no problems... Their culture is fully compatible with European values. It is not a culture of assassins, it is not a culture of religious hatred."

## TORTURE AND OTHER ILL-TREATMENT

Patients with mental disabilities continued to be ill-treated in mental health institutions. In March, the European Committee for the Prevention of Torture called for an end to the practice of police officers restraining agitated patients in psychiatric hospitals; expressed concerns over the use of net beds as a protective measure or means of restraint, often for excessive duration; and reiterated its call to withdraw them from psychiatric hospitals and to use more suitable means, such as bordered beds, for patients in need of protective measures.

## RIGHTS OF LESBIAN, GAY, BISEXUAL, TRANSGENDER AND INTERSEX PEOPLE

In November, a district court in Prostějov recognized an adoption order which had been issued for a gay couple by a district court in California in 2007. The Czech-French couple permanently living in the USA applied for the recognition to move to the Czech Republic and continue enjoying the right to family life. The Prostějov court held that recognition of the adoption was in the best interests of the children despite the lack of legislative provision allowing adoption by same-sex couples.

# DEMOCRATIC REPUBLIC OF THE CONGO

Democratic Republic of the Congo
Head of state: **Joseph Kabila**
Head of government: **Augustin Matata Ponyo Mapon**

**Government repression of protests against attempts by President Kabila to run for the presidency beyond the two terms allowed by the Constitution intensified. Violations of the rights to freedoms of expression, association and peaceful assembly increased. Human rights defenders, youth activists and politicians were threatened, harassed, arbitrarily arrested and in some cases convicted for peacefully exercising their rights. In the east of the Democratic Republic of the Congo (DRC), the security situation remained volatile, with numerous armed groups perpetrating serious abuses of human rights and violations of international humanitarian law. The failure of the Congolese army and the UN peacekeeping force MONUSCO (UN Organization Stabilization Mission in the DRC) to protect the civilian population led to a high civilian death toll and mass displacements.**

## BACKGROUND

Speculation on constitutional change and other ways to extend President Kabila's mandate, due to end in December 2016, triggered public protests and widespread criticism.

In February, the government started a decentralization process, dividing the country's 11 provinces into 26 entities. The Independent National Election Commission (CENI) failed to organize local elections planned for 25 October and elections for the governors of the new provinces. On 29 October, the President appointed special commissioners to govern the provinces. In October, both the President and the Vice-President of the CENI resigned, which increased concerns that presidential elections would not be organized within constitutional delays.

In September, the "G7", a platform of parties within the majority, was excluded from the ruling coalition after calling on the President to respect the Constitution.

Nine members of the National Human Rights Commission were appointed.

The government-led military Operation "Sokola 1" ("operation clean-up" in Lingala) against the armed group Allied Democratic Forces (ADF) continued in Beni territory, North Kivu province. In early September, there was an upsurge of attacks by presumed ADF members against civilians, after an absence thereof for nearly four months.

After the expiration of a six-month ultimatum for the Democratic Forces for the Liberation of Rwanda (FDLR) to disarm, the Congolese army implemented Operation "Sokola 2" to neutralize the FDLR, whose military capacity is said to be still largely intact.

Following the appointment of two generals suspected of having committed human rights violations, MONUSCO decided to halt its military collaboration with the Congolese army on "Sokola 2". However, the army's operations against the Front for Patriotic Resistance in Ituri (FRPI) continued with the support of MONUSCO. The overall deteriorating relationship between the army and MONUSCO left them unable to adequately protect civilians and sparked the creation of self-proclaimed "self-defence" groups.

## FREEDOMS OF ASSOCIATION AND ASSEMBLY

Security forces dispersed demonstrations against a bill amending the electoral law, seen as an attempt to extend President Kabila's term, using excessive force. At least 36 people were killed and several hundred arrested between 19 and 21 January. Two opposition leaders, Ernest Kyaviro and Cyrille Dowe, were arrested at the protests and held in incommunicado detention for 86 and 145 days respectively. Jean-Claude Muyambo, who had left the ruling coalition after speaking out publicly against a third term for President Kabila, was arrested on 20 January. His trial on seemingly politically motivated charges was ongoing at the end of the year.

On 15 March, security forces stormed a press conference in the capital Kinshasa, where youth activists were launching a civic education platform, Filimbi. Twenty-seven people were arrested. Two of them, Fred Bauma and Yves Makwambala, remained in detention at the end of the year and faced serious charges, including conspiracy against the head of state.[1] Solidarity protests following the arrests were systematically repressed. Protesters were arbitrarily arrested and subjected to torture and other ill-treatment. On 18 September, four activists from the youth movement Lutte pour le Changement (LUCHA, "struggle for change") were convicted of incitement to civil disobedience in violation of their right to peaceful assembly.

On 15 September, a peaceful opposition rally in Kinshasa was attacked by unidentified assailants. Police failed to protect the protesters.

On 8 October, the Mayor of Lubumbashi issued a ban on all public political protests.

## FREEDOM OF EXPRESSION

Freedom of expression was seriously curtailed during the year.[2] The authorities targeted politicians and activists for peacefully mobilizing against perceived attempts by President Kabila to extend his term and delays in the organization of presidential elections.

Vano Kiboko, a former MP from the ruling coalition, was arrested and convicted after he suggested during a press conference that the coalition should start identifying a successor to President Kabila.

Journalists continued to be victims of harassment, threats and arbitrary arrests; free flow of information was often impeded.

On 16 January, Canal Kin Télévision (CKTV) and Radiotélévision Catholique Elikya (RTCE) had their transmission signals cut after they broadcast the opposition's call for mass protests. RTCE's signal was re-established in June. CKTV remained closed; Radio Télévision Lubumbashi Jua, a station owned by Jean-Claude Muyambo, was closed down when he left the ruling coalition. TV station Canal Futur remained closed throughout the year.

During the January protests, internet and text messaging services were cut by the authorities, supposedly to manage public order. The signal of Radio France Internationale was also temporarily blurred.

Five radio stations which had been closed in November 2014 after they reported attacks by the ADF remained closed throughout the year.

## ARBITRARY ARRESTS AND DETENTIONS

The numbers of arbitrary arrests and detentions remained high. Many of them were carried out by intelligence services. Arbitrary arrests were often followed by prolonged incommunicado detention during which people were detained without charge, access to a lawyer or being presented to a judge.

## ABUSES BY ARMED GROUPS

Armed groups continued to commit abuses against civilians in the east of the country.

The ADF was responsible for a high number of unlawful killings, pillages, kidnappings as well as incidents of rape and sexual slavery. On 2 May, the ADF attacked two locations close to Mavivi, North Kivu province, and killed at least 10 civilians.

Abuses by the FDLR included unlawful killings, looting, rape and other sexual violence as well as forced labour. FDLR fighters forced civilians to work in mines and to transport pillaged goods, weapons and munitions.

The FRPI was responsible for large-scale looting operations, rape and other sexual violence as well as unlawful killings of civilians. Operations against the armed group caused large displacements of civilians.

## VIOLENCE AGAINST WOMEN AND GIRLS

Sexual violence against women and girls remained rampant, both in conflict and non-conflict zones, urban and rural areas. The prosecution of such crimes remained challenging due to a lack of resources. Most perpetrators enjoyed total impunity.

## CHILD SOLDIERS

Armed groups continued to recruit children throughout the year. They were used as combatants, escorts, servants, tax collectors, messengers or cooks. In the first eight months of the year, more children were successfully rescued from armed groups than in the whole of 2014.

## COMMUNAL VIOLENCE

The conflict between the Batwa and Luba communities continued throughout the year and caused a high civilian death toll. On 21 October, a peace deal was signed between the two communities.

## CORPORATE ACCOUNTABILITY

Victims of forced evictions that took place in the Kawama community, Lubumbashi, in 2009, continued to be denied access to justice and their right to remedy by Congolese courts. The evictions were carried out by the police using bulldozers belonging to the mining company Entreprise Générale Malta Forrest – a subsidiary of the Belgian company Groupe Forrest International – with rights to the concession located next to the community. The company continued to deny any responsibility in enabling the evictions. An appeal against the court decision was ongoing in Lubumbashi.

## IMPUNITY

The justice system continued to suffer from a serious lack of capacity to prosecute all crimes under international law. Persisting impunity for past crimes paved the way for ongoing violations and abuses against civilians by armed groups and the army.

The army was allegedly responsible for an attack against the city of Matukaka in February, during which more than 10 civilians were killed. Bernard Byamungu, from the 809th regiment, was arrested in February for a similar attack against civilians in the villages of Tenambo and Mamiki in October 2014. He reportedly remained in military custody at the end of the year.

Cobra Matata, FRPI leader, was arrested in January. He was indicted by the military prosecutor for war crimes and crimes against humanity, including the recruitment of children.

In March, over 400 bodies were reported to have been buried in a mass grave on the outskirts of Kinshasa. Some of the bodies were suspected to be those of victims of extrajudicial executions and enforced disappearances. No credible, independent and effective investigation had taken place at the end of the year.[3]

In September, a trial of 23 members of the Bantu and Batwa communities for genocide and crimes against humanity started before the Court of Appeal in Lubumbashi. It was the first trial for international crimes to take place before civil courts in the country.

In another positive step in the fight against impunity, the National Assembly and the Senate adopted legislation implementing the Rome Statute of the ICC in June and November respectively. The final bill, promulgated into law on 2 January 2016, contains the death penalty for war crimes, crimes against humanity and genocide.

## PRISON CONDITIONS

Prison conditions remained dire. Malnutrition, a lack of basic hygiene, infectious diseases and poor medical care led to the deaths of scores of prisoners. Detention facilities were highly overcrowded and the prison administration was severely underfunded.

## HUMAN RIGHTS DEFENDERS

Human rights defenders and activists continued to be targets for intimidation, threats, arbitrary arrests, ill-treatment as well as incommunicado and secret detention.

Christopher Ngoyi, a human rights defender monitoring the excessive use of force by police during the January protests, was arrested and detained incommunicado for 21 days. He remained in detention at the end of the year, awaiting trial.

Youth movements working on civic education and governance were targeted. Three individuals linked to Filimbi and LUCHA were arbitrarily arrested and held in incommunicado detention before being released without charge.

On 18 September, a final verdict was handed down for the double murder of human rights defender Floribert Chebeya and his driver Fidel Bazana. Police officer Daniel Mukalay, who was found guilty under extenuating circumstances, was sentenced to 15 years in prison while four other officers were acquitted.

## INTERNATIONAL JUSTICE

In April, ADF leader Jamil Mukulu was arrested in Tanzania. He was extradited to Uganda on 10 July and faced charges of murder, terrorism, treason, human rights abuses, kidnapping and recruitment of minors in both Uganda and DRC.

On 2 September, the trial of former Congolese general Bosco Ntaganda started before the ICC. He was being prosecuted for 13 counts of war crimes and five counts of crimes against humanity – including murder, rape and sexual slavery as well as forced recruitment and use of child soldiers – allegedly committed in 2002-2003 in Ituri province.

Two FDLR leaders, Ignace Murwanashyaka and Straton Musoni, were sentenced by a court in Germany in September. Both were convicted of leading a terrorist organization and Ignace Murwanashyaka was found guilty of war crimes.

Despite an ongoing military operation against the FDLR, Sylvestre Mudacumura, the alleged commander of its armed branch, remained at large.

1. DRC: Free human rights activists (News story, 19 March)
2. Treated like criminals: DRC's race to silence dissent (AFR 62/2917/2015)
3. DRC: Authorities should work hand in hand with MONUSCO to ensure thorough and independent investigations into mass grave (AFR 62/1414/2015)

# DENMARK

Kingdom of Denmark
Head of state: **Queen Margrethe II**
Head of government: **Lars Løkke Rasmussen (replaced Helle Thorning-Schmidt in June)**

**Impunity for the majority of rape cases continued. A commission established to investigate actions of Danish soldiers involved in military operations overseas was closed down by the government before it was able to come to any conclusions about possible wrongdoing.**

## VIOLENCE AGAINST WOMEN AND GIRLS

The majority of reported rape cases were closed by the police or the prosecution and never reached trial. Most cases were closed due to "the state of the evidence ".[1] During the year the State Prosecutors released two reports showing that many reported rape cases were being closed by the police before a formal police investigation had even been

started, and in November the Director for Public Prosecutions called for changes to howpolice were handling these cases. The reports, however, did not include the examination of the reason for the disproportionately high attrition rate in prosecuting cases of rape.

## REFUGEES AND ASYLUM-SEEKERS

People awaiting the result of their asylum claim or deportation to their country of origin – including victims of torture, unaccompanied children and persons with mental illness – continued to be held in detention for immigration control purposes. No effective screening of asylum-seekers was put in place to identify people who were unfit to be placed in detention.

In November, a number of potentially harmful amendments to the Aliens Act were introduced in order, according to the government, to respond to the increasing number of people seeking asylum in the country. The amendments included powers to temporarily suspend judicial oversight of decisions made by the police to detain asylum-seekers and migrants, as well as a widening of the grounds on which asylum-seekers can be detained by the police.

## FREEDOM OF ASSEMBLY

In September, the Eastern High Court ruled that the Copenhagen police had unlawfully removed and detained a protester during an official state visit by Chinese officials in 2012. During the hearing, evidence was heard alleging that the police removed demonstrators and confiscated their banners without an adequate legal basis. The Copenhagen police conceded that the evidence "raised doubts" about the police action and referred the case to the Independent Police Complaints Authority.

New evidence subsequently emerged suggesting that police officers acted on orders from superiors, despite denials by senior officers in a parliamentary hearing. The Copenhagen police also informed parliament that they were unable to identify the police officers involved, although a number of officers subsequently claimed that their identity had been known. As a result of this apparent misinformation and the alleged violations of the rights to freedom of expression and peaceful assembly, the Ministry of Justice established a commission to investigate.

## TORTURE AND OTHER ILL-TREATMENT

In June, the government closed down the Iraq-Afghanistan Commission established in 2012 by the previous government to investigate actions of Danish soldiers involved in military operations overseas. In particular, the Commission was tasked to investigate practices regarding the apprehension and detention of Iraqis, whether Danish soldiers had handed over detainees to personnel from other countries and determine Danish liability and responsibility for the detainee under international law. The Commission was closed before it could come to any conclusions, as the government stated that there was no need for such an investigation as no new information would emerge.

---

1. Denmark: Human Rights in Review: 2011-2015 – Amnesty International Submission to the UN Universal Periodic Review, January–February 2016 (EUR 18/2332/2015)

# DOMINICAN REPUBLIC

Dominican Republic
Head of state and government: **Danilo Medina Sánchez**

---

A law to reform the police was not passed. Many people of Haitian descent remained stateless despite the implementation of a law intended to address their situation (Law 169-14). A new Criminal Code removing the total ban on abortion failed to enter into force. Parliament failed to adopt legislation that could have advanced the protection of the rights of women, girls and lesbian, gay, bisexual, transgender and intersex (LGBTI) people.

## BACKGROUND

In June, following an agreement between the ruling and the main opposition parties, Congress adopted an amendment to the Constitution allowing the outgoing President to run for a consecutive term. A few days later, the President announced his intention to run for a second term in the 2016 presidential elections.

A draft regulation governing the internal procedures of the Public Defender's Office, established in 2013, was submitted to Congress in July, but remained pending at the end of the year.

The Ministry of Foreign Affairs led a consultative process with different civil society groups aimed at developing a national human rights plan.

## POLICE AND SECURITY FORCES

The Office of the Prosecutor General reported 152 killings by security forces between January and September. Many killings took place in circumstances suggesting that they may have been unlawful.

Congress continued to debate a draft law on police reform, but had not approved it by the end of the year. As a consequence, the process for a comprehensive reform of the police was further delayed.

There was a 6% fall in the number of murders between January and September compared with the same period in 2014; however, the number remained high. Apart from the publication of progress reports on the national system of response to emergencies, no information was made available on the implementation of the National Security Plan, which had formally been launched in March 2013.

## IMPUNITY

No progress was made in the investigation into the enforced disappearance of three men – Gabriel Sandi Alistar, Juan Almonte Herrera and Randy Vizcaíno González – who were last seen in police custody in July 2009, September 2009 and December 2013, respectively. Their fate and whereabouts remained unknown. In June, the Supreme Court accepted the appeal of six members of the security forces arguing that their 2013 prosecution for the killing of Cecilio Díaz and William Checo in 2009 had been initiated after the expiry of the statute of limitations, and decided to terminate the proceedings against them.

## DEPRIVATION OF NATIONALITY

The authorities continued to implement Law 169-14, which was intended to restore nationality to those who had been arbitrarily and retroactively deprived of their Dominican nationality by a 2013 Constitutional Court judgment. The administrative process for Dominican-born people of foreign descent whose birth had been previously registered in the Dominican Civil Registry (so-called "Group A") to regain their nationality was slow, and many people continued to be arbitrarily deprived of their identity documents. Of the estimated 55,000 Dominican-born people of foreign descent whose birth had never been registered (so-called "Group B"), only 8,755 applied for the naturalization plan provided by the Law within the deadline, set for 1 February. The government failed to publicly acknowledge the existence of a large group of people who could not enrol in the plan and who therefore remained stateless.[1]

Scores of Dominicans of Haitian descent were arbitrarily detained and threatened with expulsion to Haiti as "irregular" migrants. However, in the vast majority of cases the authorities released them upon verification that they were born in the Dominican Republic.

## MIGRANTS' RIGHTS

In February, following an escalation of tensions between the Dominican Republic and Haiti, the body of a Haitian migrant was found hanging from a tree in a park in Santiago. There were fears that he may have been the victim of a xenophobic killing. No one had been brought to justice for the killing by the end of the year. Attacks on Haitian migrants in retaliation for crimes allegedly committed by other Haitians were reported.[2]

On 17 June, the deadline expired for applications to the National Regularization Plan for Foreigners with Irregular Migration Status. The government announced that 288,486 migrants had applied. At the end of September, the government stated that the status of more than 239,000 applicants had been regularized.

The government officially resumed deportations of irregular migrants in mid-August.[3] From mid-June onwards, tens of thousands of Haitian migrants decided to return to Haiti, mainly because of fear of violent expulsion or xenophobic pressures from employers or neighbours. This movement of people led to an escalation of tensions between the Dominican Republic and Haiti. The OAS responded by sending a mission to both countries in July. Following the visit, the Dominican authorities refused the offer of mediation by the OAS Secretary General or to negotiate a protocol for deportations with Haiti. The authorities did not make their own protocol public.

In most deportation cases, the authorities assessed each case individually. However, according to the International Organization for Migration and some Dominican and Haitian civil society organizations, several people who had applied to the National Regularization Plan reported having been deported.

## VIOLENCE AGAINST WOMEN AND GIRLS

According to official statistics, the first semester of the year saw a decrease of 4% in the number of killings of women and girls, compared with the same period in 2014.

Parliament had yet to adopt a comprehensive law to prevent and address violence against women approved by the Senate in 2012.

## SEXUAL AND REPRODUCTIVE RIGHTS

In December 2014, Congress passed

amendments to the Criminal Code decriminalizing abortion where pregnancy posed a risk to the life of the woman or girl; where the foetus would be unable to survive outside the womb; or where the pregnancy was the result of rape or incest. Anti-abortion groups subsequently challenged the constitutionality of the reform. On 2 December, the Constitutional Court declared that the adoption of the Code was unconstitutional due to procedural errors and ordered the previous one, adopted in 1884, to remain in force.[4]

The Ministry of Health, in co-operation with civil society organizations, drafted protocols to implement the decriminalization of abortion in the three circumstances permitted by the Criminal Code.

In July, following pressure from religious groups, the President of the Chamber of Deputies removed a draft law on sexual and reproductive health from the agenda for discussion by Parliament. The law had not been debated by the end of the year.

## RIGHTS OF LESBIAN, GAY, BISEXUAL, TRANSGENDER AND INTERSEX PEOPLE

Civil society organizations reported hate crimes against LGBTI people, including murder and rape.

The commission of the Chamber of Deputies which analyzed the draft law on sexual and reproductive health removed proposed sanctions for discrimination in access to health care on grounds of sexual orientation and gender identity. The law was pending discussion at the end of the year.

---

1. "Without papers, I am no one": Stateless people in the Dominican Republic (AMR 27/2755/2015)

2. Dominican Republic: Authorities must investigate xenophobic violence (AMR 27/1449/2015)

3. Dominican Republic officially resumes deportations amid concerns for Dominicans of Haitian descent (AMR 27/2304/2015)

4. Dominican Republic takes women's rights back to 1884 (News story, 3 December)

# ECUADOR

Republic of Ecuador
Head of state and government: Rafael Vicente Correa Delgado

**Those critical of the authorities, including human rights defenders, faced attacks, fines and unfounded criminal charges. The rights of Indigenous Peoples to free, prior and informed consent over decisions affecting their livelihoods were not fulfilled.**

## BACKGROUND

The National Assembly voted in favour of 15 constitutional amendments proposed by the executive, which included authorizing the use of the military to respond to internal public security situations and enabling the indefinite re-election of the President and other authorities.

Nationwide anti-government protests led by trades unions, Indigenous Peoples' organizations and civil society took place throughout the year. They were marked by clashes between the security forces and protesters and reports of excessive use of force and arbitrary arrests by the security forces. At least 21 people detained during anti-government protests in December in the capital, Quito, were sentenced amid concerns about violations of their right to a fair trial.

In March, the International Court of Justice (ICJ) backed a 2011 Ecuadorian court ruling that granted compensation to Amazon Indigenous communities affected by environmental damage caused by the USA-based energy company Chevron. The ICJ ruled that a previous agreement between Chevron and authorities did not prevent Amazon Indigenous communities from seeking compensation from the company. In a separate court case, also in March, the ICC ruled that it lacked jurisdiction to decide on a complaint filed by Indigenous communities against Chevron's Chief Executive Officer.

## FREEDOMS OF EXPRESSION, ASSOCIATION AND ASSEMBLY

Human rights defenders and others who openly criticized government policies were threatened and harassed. Attempts were made to prevent them from carrying out their work and they faced attacks, fines, harassment and unfounded criminal charges.

In September, using an executive decree granting the authorities wide powers to monitor and dissolve NGOs, the National Communication Secretariat threatened to close down human rights NGO Fundamedios, apparently in reprisal for the organization's denunciations of violations of the rights to freedom of expression and association. At the end of September, the Secretariat issued a "final warning" to Fundamedios to "comply with the prohibition of exercising matters of a political nature, avoiding raising unfounded alerts for the sole purpose of damaging the prestige of Ecuador and its institutions".

Human rights defender Paulina Muñoz Samaniego was subjected to an intimidation campaign which she believed was related to her work with Ecuador Decide, a coalition of civil society organizations which oppose the Free Trade Agreement between Ecuador and the European Union. No investigation had been opened by state prosecutors by the end of the year despite her having filed a complaint.

In February, environmental activist and community leader Darwin Javier Ramírez Piedra was sentenced to 10 months' imprisonment on charges of "rebellion" for his alleged participation in an attack against National Mining Agency delegates. The prosecution did not provide credible evidence against him and his sentence appeared to be an attempt to silence his campaign against the impact of mining activities on the right to water of Junin communities in Intag region, Imbabura province, northern Ecuador. He was released the same day as his sentencing, as he had already served the length of his sentence in pre-trial detention.

Media outlets continued to receive fines under a communication law granting wide-ranging powers to the Information and Communication Superintendent, a public servant elected from a shortlist provided by the President, to limit and regulate the media. There were concerns that the law's application was jeopardizing the right to freedom of expression and creating a climate of self-censorship. In May, La Hora newspaper was fined US$3,540 for not covering an event by the Mayor of Loja which was deemed to be of public interest. The newspaper refused to pay the fine.

In February, the owner of Crudo Ecuador, a Facebook page that published satirical political memos, closed down the page after receiving threats. The threats commenced after the President referred to Crudo Ecuador in his weekly television programme and encouraged his supporters to counteract those who criticized the authorities through social media.

## INDIGENOUS PEOPLES' RIGHTS

The authorities continued to fail to fully implement the 2012 ruling of the Inter-American Court of Human Rights in favour of the Kichwa People of Sarayaku, including the complete removal of explosives left on their land and the issuing of legislation to regulate Indigenous Peoples' right to free, prior and informed consent over laws, policies and measures that affect their livelihoods. In May, personnel authorized by the Ministry of the Environment entered the Sarayaku territory without consent to carry out an environmental impact assessment for future oil extraction on the territory.

## SEXUAL AND REPRODUCTIVE RIGHTS

Women and girls continued to face limited access to modern contraceptives, with the most vulnerable disproportionately affected. In February, the CEDAW Committee raised concerns at the limited access to sexual and reproductive health services, education and information.

Abortion remained illegal in all cases, except where the life of the woman was at risk or in cases of rape when the victim was a woman with a mental disability.

# EGYPT

**Arab Republic of Egypt**
Head of state: **Abdel Fattah al-Sisi**
Head of government: **Sherif Ismail (replaced Ibrahim Mahlab in September)**

The human rights situation continued to deteriorate. The authorities arbitrarily restricted the rights to freedom of expression, association and peaceful assembly, enacted a draconian new anti-terrorism law, and arrested and imprisoned government critics and political opposition leaders and activists, subjecting some to enforced disappearance. The security forces used excessive force against protesters, refugees, asylum-seekers and migrants. Detainees faced torture and other ill-treatment. Courts handed down hundreds of death sentences and lengthy prison sentences after grossly unfair mass trials. There was a critical lack of accountability; most human rights violations were committed with impunity. Women and members of religious minorities were subject to discrimination and inadequately protected against violence. People were arrested and tried on charges of "debauchery" for their perceived sexual orientation or gender identity. The army forcibly evicted communities from their homes along the border with Gaza. Executions were carried out following grossly unfair trials.

## BACKGROUND

Security conditions remained tense, particularly in the Sinai region. The authorities said that the army and other security forces killed hundreds of "terrorists", mostly in North Sinai, where the armed group calling itself Sinai Province, an affiliate of the armed group Islamic State (IS), claimed responsibility for several major attacks.

Egypt closed its border with Gaza, State of Palestine, for much of the year. The Egyptian army destroyed smuggling tunnels under the border, reportedly flooding the area with water.

In February, Egypt carried out air strikes in Libya killing at least seven civilians, after an armed group there beheaded a group of Egyptian Coptic Christians they had abducted.[1]

In March, Egypt joined the Saudi Arabia-led international coalition that engaged in the armed conflict in Yemen. President al-Sisi announced that the Arab League had agreed to form a "joint Arab military force" to combat regional threats.

On 13 September, army and security forces in the Western Desert region attacked and killed 12 people, including eight Mexican tourists, apparently after mistaking them for members of an armed group.

On 23 September, President al-Sisi pardoned 100 men and women, including journalists and scores of activists imprisoned for participating in protests. The pardon did not extend to imprisoned leaders of Egypt's youth movement or Muslim Brotherhood leaders.

Parliamentary elections held between October and December had an officially reported turnout of 28.3%.

## COUNTER-TERROR AND SECURITY

In August the government enacted Law 94 of 2015, a new anti-terrorism law that defines a "terrorist act" vaguely and in overly broad terms. The new law gave the President powers to "take necessary measures to ensure public order and security", equivalent to those granted by a state of emergency; established special courts; and provided for heavy fines for journalists whose reporting on "terrorism" differed from official statements.[2]

## ABUSES BY ARMED GROUPS

Armed groups launched attacks deliberately targeting civilians.

On 29 June, the Prosecutor General was killed by a bomb in the capital, Cairo. It was unclear who was responsible.

The armed group Sinai Province claimed responsibility for several attacks, including one on 29 January that reportedly killed 40 people, including civilians, soldiers and police officers. On 1 July, an assault by Sinai Province on the North Sinai town of Sheikh Zuweid killed 17 members of the army and security forces, according to the Ministry of Defence; at least 100 members of the armed group were also killed in the assault. Sinai Province also claimed responsibility for causing the crash of a civilian Russian airliner on 31 October. All 224 people on board were killed, mostly Russian nationals. Russia's Federal Security Service announced on 17 November that a bomb had brought down the plane.

## FREEDOM OF EXPRESSION

Journalists working for outlets critical of the authorities, or linked to opposition groups, were prosecuted for reporting "false news" and on other politically motivated criminal charges. Courts sentenced some to lengthy prison terms and one was sentenced to death. Individuals continued to face prosecution on criminal charges such as "defaming religion" and offending "public morals" for peacefully exercising their right to freedom of expression. In November, a prominent investigative journalist was briefly detained by military intelligence and prosecutors over an article he wrote about the army.

Photojournalist Mahmoud Abu Zeid, known as Shawkan, was referred to trial in August with 738 co-defendants, who included leaders of the Muslim Brotherhood group and their supporters. Arrested while covering the violent dispersal by security forces of a protest on 14 August 2013, Mahmoud Abu Zeid was detained without charge for almost two years before the Public Prosecution Office referred his case to court. The trial was due to begin in December, but was postponed because the courtroom could not hold the hundreds of defendants.

On 1 January, the Court of Cassation, Egypt's highest court, overturned the convictions of three jailed journalists working for the broadcaster Al Jazeera – Peter Greste, Mohamed Fahmy and Baher Mohamed – and ordered their retrial. The authorities deported Peter Greste on 1 February; Mohamed Fahmy and Baher Mohamed were released on bail on 12 February but sentenced to prison terms of three and three and a half years respectively on 29 August on charges of broadcasting "false news" and operating without authorization. President al-Sisi pardoned the two men on 23 September.

On 11 April a court in Cairo sentenced 14 opposition-linked journalists to 25-year prison terms after convicting them of "broadcasting false news", and sentenced another journalist to death for allegedly forming "media committees" and "leading and funding a banned group". The court tried several defendants in their absence. They were tried as part of a group of 51 alongside leading Muslim Brotherhood figures. Those jailed lodged appeals with the Court of Cassation, which overturned their conviction in December and ordered a retrial.

## FREEDOM OF ASSOCIATION

Human rights organizations were subject to arbitrary restrictions on their activities and funding under the Law on Associations (Law 84 of 2002). Staff of some human rights organizations were arrested and questioned by security officials, and also questioned by an "expert committee" appointed by the authorities as part of an ongoing criminal investigation into the activities and foreign funding of human rights groups. The authorities prevented some human rights and political activists from travelling abroad.[3]

By the end of the year, the government said it had closed more than 480 NGOs because of their alleged links to the Muslim Brotherhood group.

On 21 October, security forces raided the Mada Foundation for Media Development, a Cairo-based journalism NGO. They detained all those present and questioned them for several hours before releasing all but the organization's director, whom they held without charge on suspicion of "international bribery – receiving foreign funding" and belonging to the Muslim Brotherhood.

## EXCESSIVE USE OF FORCE
The authorities arbitrarily restricted the right to freedom of peaceful assembly under the Protest Law (Law 107 of 2013). There were fewer protests than in recent years, but security forces continued to use excessive or unnecessary force to disperse "unauthorized" demonstrations and other public gatherings, resulting in deaths and serious injuries.

Security forces shot and killed protester Shaimaa Al-Sabbagh on 24 January during a demonstration in central Cairo. Widely circulated videos and photographs of her death sparked outrage. At least 27 people died in protest-related violence between 23and 26 January across Egypt, most as a result of excessive force from the security forces. Two members of the security forces also died.

At least 22 fans of the Zamalek football club died in a stampede at a stadium in New Cairo on 8 February, after security forces recklessly fired tear gas to disperse them.

## ARBITRARY ARRESTS AND DETENTIONS
Security forces arrested 11,877 members of "terrorist groups" between January and the end of September, according to the Assistant Minister for Public Security at the Ministry of the Interior. The crackdown was thought to include members and perceived supporters of the Muslim Brotherhood and other government critics. The authorities had previously stated that they had arrested at least 22,000 people on such grounds in 2014.

In some cases, detainees in political cases were held in prolonged detention without charge or trial. By the end of the year, at least 700 people had been held in preventive detention for more than two years without being sentenced by a court, in contravention of the two-year limit on such detention in Egyptian law.

Student Mahmoud Mohamed Ahmed Hussein remained detained without charge or trial, more than 700 days after his arrest in January 2014 for wearing a T-shirt with the slogan "Nation without torture". Prison guards beat him in July, his family said.

## ENFORCED DISAPPEARANCES
Human rights groups reported receiving scores of complaints concerning cases of individuals arrested by the security forces and then detained incommunicado, in conditions that in some cases amounted to enforced disappearance.

Security forces arrested students Israa Al-Taweel, Sohaab Said and Omar Mohamed Ali in Cairo on 1 June and subjected them to enforced disappearance for 15 days, during which Sohaab Said said that he and Omar Mohamed Ali were tortured. Both men faced an unfair trial before a military court. Israa Al-Taweel, who has a disability as a result of being shot during a protest in 2014, was released from prison in December but remained under house arrest.

## TORTURE AND OTHER ILL-TREATMENT
Detainees held by state security forces and military intelligence were tortured, including by being beaten and subjected to electric shocks and stress positions. Security forces frequently beat detainees at the time of their arrest and when transferring them between police stations and prisons. Throughout the year there were reports of deaths in custody as a result of torture and other ill-treatment and lack of access to adequate medical care.[4]

Conditions of detention in prisons and police stations remained extremely poor. Cells were severely overcrowded and unhygienic, and in some cases officials prevented families and lawyers giving food, medicine and other items to prisoners.

## UNFAIR TRIALS
The criminal justice system continued to serve as an instrument of state repression, with courts convicting hundreds of defendants on charges such as "terrorism",

"unauthorized protesting", engaging in political violence and belonging to banned groups, after grossly unfair mass trials in which prosecutors did not establish the individual criminal responsibility of the defendants.[5]

At least 3,000 civilians stood trial before unfair military courts on "terrorism" and other charges alleging political violence. Many, including leaders of the Muslim Brotherhood, were tried in mass trials. Military trials of civilians are fundamentally unfair.

Former President Mohamed Morsi faced five separate trials, alongside hundreds of co-accused, including Muslim Brotherhood leaders. On 21 April a court sentenced him to 20 years in prison for alleged involvement in armed clashes outside Cairo's Presidential Palace in December 2012. On 16 June, he was sentenced to death for allegedly orchestrating a prison escape during the 2011 uprising, and a 25-year prison term on an espionage charge. The trials were fundamentally unfair as they relied on evidence gathered while Mohamed Morsi was subject to enforced disappearance by the army, during the months after he was ousted from power in 2013. Verdicts in other trials against the former President were still pending at the end of the year.

## IMPUNITY

The authorities failed to conduct effective, independent and impartial investigations into most incidents of human rights violations, including the repeated use of excessive force by security forces that resulted in the deaths of hundreds of protesters since July 2013. Investigations by the Public Prosecution into protests and incidents of political violence instead focused on alleged abuses by the authorities' opponents and critics.

Courts held a small number of members of the security forces responsible for unlawful killings, in cases arising from several incidents that had attracted wide national and international condemnation.

On 11 June a court sentenced one member of the security forces to 15 years' imprisonment for fatally wounding protester Shaimaa Al-Sabbagh. However, the authorities also separately prosecuted 17 eyewitnesses to the killing, including human rights defender Azza Soliman, on charges of "unauthorized protesting" and "disturbing public order". Courts acquitted the 17 eyewitnesses on 23 May, and again on 24 October following an appeal by the Public Prosecution Office.

Two members of the security forces were jailed for five years in December on charges of torturing to death a lawyer at Mattareya Police Station in Cairo in February.

Former President Hosni Mubarak and several of his former senior security officials were retried by the Court of Cassation in November on charges of orchestrating a deadly crackdown on protesters during the 2011 "25 January Revolution". The trial was ongoing at the end of the year.

## WOMEN'S RIGHTS

Women and girls continued to face discrimination in law and in practice, and were inadequately protected against sexual and other gender-based violence. Despite announcing a national strategy to combat violence and discrimination against women and girls, the authorities largely failed to implement substantive measures, including amending or repealing discriminatory Personal Status Laws that prevent women from obtaining a divorce from an abusive husband without forfeiting their financial rights.[6]

## DISCRIMINATION – RELIGIOUS MINORITIES

Religious minorities, including Coptic Christians, Shi'a Muslims and Baha'is, continued to face discriminatory restrictions. There were new incidents of sectarian violence against Coptic Christian communities; these communities also faced obstacles to rebuilding churches and other properties damaged in sectarian attacks in 2013.

The Ministry of Endowments closed the al-

Imam al-Hussein Mosque in Cairo from 22 to 24 October to prevent Shi'a Muslims from marking the Day of Ashura there; the Ministry said the closure was to prevent "Shi'a untruths".

## RIGHTS OF LESBIAN, GAY, BISEXUAL, TRANSGENDER AND INTERSEX PEOPLE

Individuals continued to face arrest, detention and trial on "debauchery" charges, under Law 10 of 1961, on the basis of their real or perceived sexual orientation and gender identity.

On 12 January a court acquitted 26 men of "debauchery" charges; they had been arrested at a Cairo bathhouse in December 2014.

## REFUGEES' AND MIGRANTS' RIGHTS

Security forces continued to use excessive force and unnecessary lethal force against refugees, asylum-seekers and migrants who sought to enter or leave Egypt irregularly.[7] At least 20 Sudanese nationals and one Syrian national were killed while trying to leave Egypt irregularly.

## HOUSING RIGHTS – FORCED EVICTIONS

The armed forces continued to forcibly evict communities living along Egypt's border with Gaza, where the authorities sought to create a security "buffer zone".

The government continued to discuss development plans for Cairo that did not include sufficient safeguards to prevent forced evictions.

## DEATH PENALTY

Courts handed down hundreds of death sentences on defendants convicted on "terrorism" and other charges related to the political violence that followed Mohamed Morsi's ousting in July 2013, and for murder and other crimes. Those executed included prisoners sentenced after unfair trials before criminal and military courts.[8]

At least seven men were executed in relation to political violence; one on 7 March after an unfair trial. Six men executed on

17 May had been sentenced after a grossly unfair trial before a military court, despite evidence that security officials tortured them to force them to "confess" to capital offences and falsified their arrest dates in official documents.

1. Libya: Mounting evidence of war crimes in the wake of Egypt's airstrikes (News story, 23 February)
2. Egypt's president to sign draconian counter-terrorism law today (News story, 13 August)
3. Egypt: Renewed crackdown on independent groups: Government investigating human rights workers (MDE 12/1873/2015)
4. Egypt: Spate of detainee deaths points to rampant abuse at Cairo's Mattareya Police Station (News story, 4 March)
5. Generation jail: Egypt's youth go from protest to prison (MDE 12/1853/2015)
6. Circles of hell: Domestic, public and state violence against women in Egypt (MDE 12/004/2015)
7. Syria: Voices in crisis - August 2015 (MDE 24/2352/2015)
8. Egypt: Confirmation of 183 death sentences "outrageous" (News story, 2 February)

# EL SALVADOR

Republic of El Salvador
Head of state and government: **Salvador Sánchez Cerén**

A total legal abortion ban remained in place, violating women's human rights. Human rights defenders of lesbian, gay, bisexual, transgender and intersex (LGBTI) communities and those defending and promoting sexual and reproductive rights faced increasing risks and particularly suffered violence and intimidation from state agents, individuals and private groups. The 1993 Amnesty Law was not repealed, presenting an obstacle for accessing justice and reparations for victims of human rights violations that occurred during the 1980-1992 armed conflict.

## BACKGROUND

Legislative and municipal elections were held in March. A 30% gender quota in the electoral lists was required for the first time. No party reached the required number of representatives to achieve a majority in the Legislative Assembly.

Levels of gang-related violence and organized crime surged and homicide rates soared. According to official records, 4,253 homicides were registered in the first eight months of the year, compared with 3,912 for the whole of 2014. Criminal violence forced many Salvadorians to leave the country, and also led to the internal displacement of thousands of families, according to the Civil Society Roundtable against Forced Displacement Provoked by Violence and Organized Crime.

In September, the Inter-American Commission on Human Rights requested El Salvador to adopt precautionary measures to protect the life and personal integrity of three men who allegedly had been subjected to enforced disappearances, and of their families who had been attacked and threatened after enquiring with the authorities about the whereabouts of their relatives.

In September, amid reports and complaints of increased violence against LGBTI communities, the Legislative Assembly reformed the Criminal Code to increase the penalties for crimes motivated by political opinions, racial hatred or sexual orientation and gender identity.

## WOMEN'S RIGHTS

Between January and October, 475 women were murdered, an increase from 294 in 2014, according to information gathered by the Salvadoran Women's Organization for Peace and official records. Despite the Special Comprehensive Law for a Life Free from Violence for Women, some judges continued to qualify gender-based murders of women and girls as homicide instead of the crime of feminicide as defined in law, according to the Salvadoran Women's Organization for Peace.

In January, the Legislative Assembly granted the request of pardon in favour of "Guadalupe", a woman incarcerated on pregnancy-related grounds. She was released after serving seven years of a 30-year sentence based on charges of "aggravated murder" after suffering a miscarriage. Authorities recognized judicial errors in the original prosecution. More than 15 women remained in jail under similar circumstances.

In March, the UN Human Rights Council adopted the outcome of the UPR of El Salvador. Fourteen recommendations were made relating to sexual and reproductive rights. While El Salvador accepted recommendations to provide access to sexual and reproductive health services, including contraception, it merely "noted" the recommendation to decriminalize abortion and remove the total ban. El Salvador remained silent on a recommendation to immediately and unconditionally release all women imprisoned for having undergone an abortion or suffering a miscarriage.[1]

In November, the Office of the Human Rights Ombudsman issued a resolution on the case of Maria Teresa Rivera, who was sentenced to 40 years in prison after experiencing an obstetric complication and was wrongfully accused of having an abortion. The Ombudsman found violations of due process and the presumption of innocence, and determined that the participation of Maria Teresa Rivera was not demonstrated during trial.

## HUMAN RIGHTS DEFENDERS

The Citizen Group for the Decriminalization of Therapeutic, Ethical and Eugenic Abortion and the Feminist Collective for Local Development – leading organizations in the promotion of sexual and reproductive rights – were harassed and stigmatized by state officials, individuals and private groups because of their work on women's rights. Both organizations were called "unscrupulous groups" and "unpatriotic traitors".

Human rights defenders working for the defence and promotion of sexual and reproductive rights were also particularly stigmatized for the legal assistance provided to women convicted of homicide after suffering obstetric emergencies. Defamatory campaigns against human rights defenders aggravated the risks they faced. The authorities failed to take effective measures to curb their stigmatization and reduce risks.[2]

Human rights defenders from the LGBTI communities also reported violence and intimidation. In May, Francela Méndez, a transgender activist and member of the Salvadoran Women's Network of Human Rights Defenders, was murdered.[3] By the end of 2015, no one had been brought to justice. Organizations reported an increase in cases of harassment and violence against the transgender community by state agents and other individuals.

## IMPUNITY

The 1993 Amnesty Law remained in place, denying access to justice and reparations to victims of the human rights violations committed during the armed conflict (1980-1992). In April, former General and Defence Minister Eugenio Vides Casanova was deported from the USA after an immigration judge in Florida ruled in 2012 that he should be sent back to El Salvador for his role in human rights violations committed by the armed forces during the armed conflict.[4] By the end of the year, there was no public information suggesting that former General Vides was facing any legal proceeding.

In March, the Human Rights Ombudsman called upon the authorities to overcome the prevalent impunity for human rights violations during the armed conflict. The Ombudsman also called on the Legislative Assembly to deprive the Amnesty Law of its legal effects and urged the Attorney General's Office to effectively investigate victims' claims.

In March, more than a year after a ruling by the Constitutional Chamber of the Supreme Court of Justice ordering the Attorney General's Office to thoroughly investigate the 1981 San Francisco Angulo massacre, in which 45 people were killed allegedly by members of the army, the Constitutional Chamber required the Attorney General to

report the status of the investigation. Almost two months later, the Attorney General submitted a report, followed by a second in July after the Constitutional Chamber requested additional details. By the end of the year, no decision had been issued by the Constitutional Chamber.

In July, the Constitutional Chamber established the responsibility of the armed forces in the enforced disappearance of 11 people in the context of the 1982 military "Cleaning Operation". The Constitutional Chamber's ruling required the National Defence Ministry to provide information about the operation and in particular the fate and whereabouts of the victims. The Constitutional Chamber requested the Attorney General's Office to immediately start an investigation.

---

1. Amnesty International calls on El Salvador to decriminalize abortion and immediately release all women imprisoned for pregnancy-related complications (AMR 29/1254/2015)
2. Defenders under attack! Protecting sexual and reproductive rights in the Americas (AMR 01/2775/2015)
3. El Salvador: El Estado debe garantizar justicia en el asesinato de activista transgénero (AMR 29/1855/2015)
4. El Salvador: No amnesty for human rights violations (AMR 29/1431/2015)

# EQUATORIAL GUINEA

**Republic of Equatorial Guinea**
Head of state and government: **Teodoro Obiang Nguema Mbasogo**

---

**Children were among hundreds of people arbitrarily arrested, detained and beaten following disturbances at the African Cup of Nations football tournament. The rights to freedom of expression and assembly were suppressed and police used excessive force to disperse peaceful demonstrations. Political opponents were banished and confined to their home villages.**

## BACKGROUND

In January and February, Equatorial Guinea hosted the African Cup of Nations football tournament. As opposition to the tournament mounted, President Obiang threatened severe measures against those who disrupted or called for a boycott of the games.

In May, President Obiang dissolved the judiciary. For nearly a month there was no functioning judiciary in the country.

## FREEDOM OF EXPRESSION

Criticism of the government was not allowed. In mid-January several people including political activist Celestino Okenve were arbitrarily arrested and detained for up to two weeks for criticizing the hosting of the African Cup of Nations and calling for a boycott of the games. All were later released uncharged.[1]

On 19 February, Luis Nzo Ondo, a member of the political party Republican Democratic Force (FDR), was arbitrarily arrested and banished to his village for campaigning against the unlawful arrest and banishment of FDR leader Guillermo Nguema Ela.[2] They both remained confined to their respective villages at the end of the year.

## CHILDREN'S RIGHTS

On 5 February, dozens of children were among 300 youths arbitrarily arrested and beaten following disturbances during the African Cup of Nations semi-finals in the capital, Malabo. At least 12 of those arrested were under 16, the age of criminal responsibility in Equatorial Guinea, including four children between nine and 11 years of age. The majority were arrested in their homes at night, or in streets far from the football stadium. They were taken to Malabo Central Police Station, where the young detainees reported having received floggings of 20 to 30 lashes each. They were held in appalling conditions in overcrowded and poorly ventilated cells also occupied by adult criminal suspects. Some detainees were released after their families paid bribes to the police. However, on 11 February some 150 detainees appeared before the investigating judge, who ordered the release of those aged nine to 11, but confirmed the detention of the rest and ordered their transfer to Black Beach prison in Malabo. At the prison, child and adult detainees and convicted prisoners were held together. On 13 February, the detainees again appeared in court and all were released without charge.

## FREEDOM OF ASSEMBLY

On 25 and 26 March, police in Bata and Malabo used excessive force and tear gas to disperse peaceful demonstrations by university students protesting over the system for granting scholarships. Scores of students were arrested and beaten in both cities. Those arrested in Bata were released without charge the next day. In Malabo, police carried out arbitrary arrests and beatings of students and others suspected of being students, in the streets and in their homes. A 13-year-old boy was arrested in the street as he used his mobile phone to film police arresting and beating students and forcibly entering their homes. At least 50 students were held for two weeks before being released without charge. However, the 13-year-old boy and five other young people remained in police custody for another week before being released without charge. The police claimed that as they were not students they must have been "troublemakers".

---

1. Equatorial Guinea: African Cup of Nations peaceful protesters must be released (News story, 29 January), Urgent Action: Three detainees should be released (AFR 24/0001/2015), Equatorial Guinea: Three detainees released (AFR 24/0002/2015)
2. Equatorial Guinea: Release human rights defender and opposition leader (Press release, 20 March 2015)

# ERITREA

State of Eritrea
Head of state and government: Isaias Afewerki

**Thousands continued to leave the country to flee the indefinite National Service, a**

nationwide system amounting to forced labour. During the summer, Eritreans constituted the third largest group crossing the Mediterranean, after Syrians and Afghans, and a majority of those who lost their lives in the journey. Rule of law remained non-existent; political opposition was still banned; and independent media or universities were not allowed to operate. Restrictions on freedoms of religion and movement remained. Arbitrary detention without charge or trial continued to be the norm for thousands of prisoners of conscience.

## BACKGROUND

In May, new Civil and Penal Codes, as well as Civil and Penal Procedure Codes, were promulgated to replace the transitional Codes in place since the country's independence.

In September, a joint venture formed of Sunridge Gold Corp, a Canadian company, and the Eritrean National Mining Corporation (ENAMCO) signed an agreement with the Ministry of Energy and Mines for gold, copper and zinc mining operations. Nevsun Resources, a Canadian mining company, faced a lawsuit in Canada over the alleged use of conscripted labour by its sub-contractor, the Eritrean state-owned Segen Construction, at the Bisha mine – also a joint venture with ENAMCO.

## FORCED LABOUR – NATIONAL SERVICE

Mandatory National Service continued to be extended indefinitely in a system that amounts to forced labour. A significant proportion of the population was in open-ended conscription, in some cases for up to 20 years. Conscripts were paid low wages that did not enable them to cover their families' basic needs, and had limited and arbitrarily granted leave allowances which in many cases disrupted their family life. Conscripts served in the defence forces and were assigned to agriculture, construction, teaching, civil service and other roles. There was no provision for conscientious objection.

Children continued to be conscripted into military training under the requirement that all children undergo grade 12 of secondary school at the Sawa National Service training camp. There they faced harsh living conditions, military-style discipline and weapons training. Some children dropped out of school early to avoid this fate. Children were also conscripted into training in round-ups conducted by the military, in search of people evading National Service.

Thousands of people tried to avoid this system, including by attempting to flee the country. Those caught trying to do so, including children, were arbitrarily detained without charge or trial, often in harsh conditions, and lacked access to a lawyer or family members.

A "shoot-to-kill" policy remained in place for anyone evading capture and attempting to cross the border into Ethiopia.

Older people continued to be conscripted into the "People's Army", where they were given a weapon and assigned duties under threat of punitive repercussions. Men of up to 67 years of age were conscripted.

## PRISONERS OF CONSCIENCE

Thousands of prisoners of conscience and political prisoners, including former politicians, journalists and practitioners of unauthorized religions, continued to be detained without charge or trial, and lacked access to a lawyer or family members. Many had been detained for well over a decade.

The government denied it was detaining many of these prisoners and refused to provide families with information on their whereabouts and health, or to confirm any reports of deaths in custody.

## TORTURE AND OTHER ILL-TREATMENT

Detainees, including children, were held in harsh conditions, often in underground cells and shipping containers, with inadequate food, water, bedding, access to sanitation facilities or natural light. In some cases, these conditions amounted to torture. Children were sometimes detained with adults.

## REFUGEES AND ASYLUM-SEEKERS

Eritreans fleeing the country faced multiple dangers on routes through Sudan, Libya and the Mediterranean to reach Europe, including hostage-taking for ransom by armed groups and people smugglers.

Refugees arriving in Europe reported having paid smugglers, many of whom were Eritreans themselves, for each stage of the journey. There were allegations of members of the army being involved in smuggling people out of Eritrea.

High numbers of children left Eritrea alone to avoid conscription, leaving them vulnerable to abuse. Smugglers reportedly offered to take children to Europe for free, holding them hostage once they reached Libya and demanding money from their parents in Eritrea to free them.

In response to the increasing numbers of refugees, some European countries such as the UK tightened their guidance on asylum cases of Eritrean nationals, making untenable claims of improvements in the country of origin as a basis on which to reject cases.

## INTERNATIONAL SCRUTINY

In June, the UN-mandated Commission of Inquiry on Human Rights in Eritrea presented its first report, documenting numerous cases and patterns of human rights violations since the country's independence and stating that the government may be responsible for crimes against humanity.

# ESTONIA

**Republic of Estonia**
Head of state: **Toomas Hendrik Ilves**
Head of government: **Taavi Rõivas**

**Legislation allowing unmarried, including same-sex, couples to register their cohabitation was due to enter into force on 1 January 2016. The authorities took significant steps to reduce statelessness, especially among children, but around 83,000 people remained stateless. The**

number of asylum applications remained low.

## RIGHTS OF LESBIAN, GAY, BISEXUAL, TRANSGENDER AND INTERSEX PEOPLE

The Cohabitation Act, passed in October 2014, allowing unmarried, including same-sex, couples to register their cohabitation, was due to enter into force on 1 January 2016. However, the authorities' failure to undertake all required preparatory work, especially amendments to related laws, was likely to undermine its positive impact for some time.

## DISCRIMINATION – ETHNIC MINORITIES

According to data from the Ministry of Interior, 83,364 people resident in the country remained stateless as of 1 September, over 6% of the population. The vast majority were Russian speakers.

The authorities made significant steps to address statelessness, especially among children. On 21 January parliament approved several amendments to the Citizenship Act, due to enter into force on 1 January 2016. The amendments aimed to facilitate the acquisition of Estonian citizenship, for example by providing for its automatic acquisition by children born to stateless parents.

In February the Estonian language requirements to obtain citizenship were simplified for applicants aged over 65, allowing this group to take only an oral test and not a written exam.

Unemployment remained significant among ethnic minorities, perpetuating concern that Estonian language requirements for all public employees and private sector jobs that interface with the public were placing them at a disadvantage.

## REFUGEES AND ASYLUM-SEEKERS

The number of asylum applications, although still low, increased over 2014, with about 200 received in the first nine months of 2015. While most asylum-seekers gained access to Estonian territory by crossing the country's borders irregularly, concern remained about denial of access to territory and asylum at official border crossings.

In early September, there was an arson attack against the only asylum-seekers' reception centre in the country, in Vao village, Lääne-Viru County. Although no serious injuries were reported, about 50 people, including several children, were sleeping in the centre at the time. Investigations were ongoing at the end of the year.

# ETHIOPIA

Federal Democratic Republic of Ethiopia
Head of state: **Mulatu Teshome Wirtu**
Head of government: **Hailemariam Desalegn**

Members and leaders of opposition parties as well as protesters were extrajudicially executed. General elections took place in May against a backdrop of restrictions on civil society, the media and the political opposition, including excessive use of force against peaceful demonstrators, the disruption of opposition campaigns, and the harassment of election observers from the opposition. The police and the military conducted mass arrests of protesters, journalists and opposition party members as part of a crackdown on protests in the Oromia region.

## BACKGROUND

The ruling political party, the Ethiopian People's Revolutionary Democratic Front, won all the seats in the Federal and Regional Parliaments in the general election.

The opposition Semayawi Party reported that the National Election Board of Ethiopia (NEBE) refused to register over half of its proposed candidates for the House of Peoples' Representatives: of 400 candidates, only 139 were able to stand for election. The opposition Medrek coalition reported that the NEBE only approved 270 of the 303 candidates it had proposed to register.

Famine due to rainfall shortages during the main harvesting season (June to September)

affected more than 8 million people in the north and east.

## ARBITRARY ARRESTS AND DETENTIONS

Police and security officers arrested Omot Agwa Okwoy, Ashinie Astin Titoyk and Jemal Oumar Hojele at Addis Ababa Bole International Airport on 15 March, on their way to a workshop in Nairobi, Kenya. The workshop was organized by the NGO Bread for All with the support of the NGOs Anywaa Survival Organisation and GRAIN. The police held the three men for 161 days without bail at the Maekelawi detention centre, beyond the four months allowed by the Anti-Terrorism Proclamation (ATP), under which they were charged on 7 September.

On 12 May, security officers arrested two campaigners and three supporters of the Semayawi Party who were putting up campaign posters in the capital, Addis Ababa. They were released on bail after four days in detention.

On 19 May, Bekele Gerba and other members of the Oromo Federalist Congress were campaigning in Oromia when police and local security officers beat, arrested and detained them for a couple of hours.

Over 500 members of Medrek were arrested at various polling stations in Oromia region on 24 and 25 May. Security officers beat and injured 46 people during the elections; six people sustained gunshot injuries and two were killed.

## EXTRAJUDICIAL EXECUTIONS

Four members and leaders of opposition parties were killed after the election.

Samuel Aweke, founder of the Semayawi Party, was found dead on 15 June in the city of Debre Markos. A few days before his death he had published an article in his party's newspaper, *Negere Ethiopia,* criticizing the behaviour of local authorities, police and other security officials. The Semayawi Party claimed that Samuel Aweke had received threats from security officials after the article was published.

On 16 June, Medrek member Taddesse

Abreha was accosted on his way home in the Western Tigrai zone by three unknown people who attempted to strangle him. He died shortly after reaching his home.

Medrek member Berhanu Erbu was found dead on 19 June near a river in the Hadiya zone, 24 hours after he was taken from his home by two police officers.

Asrat Haile, election observer on behalf of Medrek in the Adio Kaka unit, Ginbo Woreda district and Kefa zone, died after being repeatedly beaten by police officials on 5 July.

None of these deaths except Samuel Aweke's was investigated. The Semayawi Party said the trial, conviction and sentencing of Samuel Aweke's killer were a "sham", intended to protect the real culprit.

## FREEDOM OF EXPRESSION

In the run-up to the general elections, the government continued to use the ATP to suppress freedom of expression through the continued detention of journalists and protracted trials: it arrested and charged at least 17 journalists under the ATP. Many also fled the country due to intimidation, harassment and politically motivated criminal charges.

Police arrested Habtamu Minale, editor-in-chief of *Kedami* newspaper and reporter for *YeMiliyonoch Dimts* newspaper, on 9 July at his house. He was released on 26 July without charge.

The Public Prosecutor dropped the charges against two members of the Zone 9 bloggers' group. On 16 October, the High Court acquitted five of the Zone 9 bloggers of terrorism charges, after they had spent over 500 days in pre-trial detention.

On 22 October, the High Court convicted and sentenced in his absence Gizaw Taye, Manager of Dadimos Entertainment and Press, to 18 years' imprisonment for terrorism.

## FREEDOM OF ASSEMBLY

On 27 January, police used excessive force to disperse a peaceful demonstration in Addis Ababa that was organized by the Unity for Democracy and Justice opposition party. Police beat demonstrators with batons, sticks and iron rods on the head, face, hands and legs, injuring more than 20 of them.

On 22 April, the government called a rally on Meskel Square to condemn the killing in Libya of Ethiopian migrants by affiliates of the armed group Islamic State (IS). When some demonstrators shouted slogans during the rally, police used excessive force, including tear gas and beatings, to disperse the crowd, which escalated the situation to clashes between protesters and police. A journalist reported that 48 people had been injured and admitted to hospital, and that many others sustained minor injuries. Hundreds were reported to have been arrested. Woyneshet Molla, Daniel Tesfaye, Ermias Tsegaye and Betelehem Akalework were arrested on 22 April and charged with inciting violence during the rally. They were convicted and sentenced to two months in prison, and were kept in custody for more than 10 days after the completion of their prison term, although courts had ordered their release. The police released them on bail on 2 July.

# FIJI

Republic of Fiji
Head of state: Jioji Konousi Konrote (replaced Ratu Epeli Nailatikau in November)
Head of government: Josaia Voreqe Bainimarama

**Fiji became the 100th abolitionist country when it abolished the death penalty for all crimes. A review of a decree which has curtailed workers' rights since 2011 was announced but had not been completed by the end of the year. The prosecution of the 2012 torture case of prisoner Iowane Benedito began. Freedom of expression remained restricted by a range of national laws, including the Media Industry Development Decree 2010.[1]**

## INTERNATIONAL SCRUTINY

In March, following its examination under the

UPR, Fiji accepted numerous recommendations by the UN Human Rights Council, in particular to issue a standing invitation to the UN Special Procedures. At the same session, however, Fiji failed to accept recommendations to amend national legislation to ensure guarantees of the rights to freedom of expression, association and peaceful assembly in line with international human rights law.

## FREEDOM OF EXPRESSION

Freedom of expression remained restricted by a range of national laws, including the Media Industry Development Decree 2010. Despite a small amendment to the Decree in July 2015 which decreased fines on individual journalists for reporting certain news, heavy fines remained in place for publishers and editors. After the amendment no further fines were imposed on publishers and editors during the year.

## WORKERS' RIGHTS

In March the government announced a review of the Essential National Industries (Employment) Decree 2011 which severely restricts collective bargaining rights, the right to strike and the right to form and join trade unions in certain sectors. The proposed amendment to the Decree would need to meet international labour standards, including compliance with ILO treaties ratified by Fiji, as recommended in the review.

Despite protests by union members, the announcement of the review led to the ILO deferring a Commission of Inquiry on the basis that there would be a joint implementation report delivered to the ILO governing body meeting by the government, the Employer's Federation and the Fiji Islands Council of Trade Unions. The joint implementation report was not agreed to by all parties and in November the ILO decided to initiate a mission to Fiji to determine obstacles to progress.

Despite strong opposition the government passed the Employment Relations Amendment Act in July. Trade union organizations and opposition parties claimed that the Act contravened ILO core conventions.

## ARBITRARY ARRESTS AND DETENTIONS

Between July and December, 76 people were arrested on sedition and related charges related to acts in August 2014. Various concerns were raised by the defendants' lawyers regarding the lack of disclosure of information leading to the arrests; prolonged detention periods before bringing them in front of a court; the denial of access to lawyers and family visits; and harsh prison conditions.

## TORTURE AND OTHER ILL-TREATMENT

Extensive immunities under the Constitution continued to make it almost impossible to hold state actors accountable for serious human rights violations such as torture and other ill-treatment. In October court proceedings began in the case of police and military officers accused of torturing escaped prisoner Iowane Benedito in 2012. However, the authorities failed to launch investigations into many past cases of torture and other ill-treatment. Fiji had still not ratified the UN Convention against Torture.

---

1. Fiji: Amnesty International welcomes the government's efforts to recognize economic and social rights, but regrets the rejection of recommendations on freedom of expression, assembly and association (ASA 18/1257/2015)

# FINLAND

**Republic of Finland**
Head of state: **Sauli Niinistö**
Head of government: **Juha Sipilä (replaced Alexander Stubb in May)**

**Reforms to immigration and asylum legislation made some limited improvements to the detention of asylum-seeking and migrant children, but concerns about detention conditions remained.**

Support for victims of gender-based violence remained inadequate and under-resourced.

## REFUGEES' AND MIGRANTS' RIGHTS

In July, amendments to the Aliens Act on detention of asylum-seekers and migrants came into force. The law stated that unaccompanied children under the age of 15 can no longer be detained under any circumstances. However, unaccompanied children aged between 15 and 17 may be detained for up to 72 hours once there is an enforceable decision on their removal from Finland; the period of detention can be extended by 72 hours for extraordinary reasons. Families with children may be detained where no sufficient alternatives exist, and where the child and a social welfare representative's views have been heard.

The legislative amendments included restrictions on visits and broader authorization for trained staff to use force in detention centres.

In August, the European Committee for the Prevention of Torture published its report on Finland, recommending several improvements to legislation on detention and conditions of detention.

## VIOLENCE AGAINST WOMEN AND GIRLS

In April, Finland ratified the Council of Europe Convention on Preventing and Combating Violence against Women and Domestic Violence (Istanbul Convention), which entered into force in Finland in August. Despite ratification, there was neither an action plan nor any dedicated budget for the effective implementation of the Convention. Services for women who have experienced violence remained inadequate and under-resourced. Finland fell short of the shelter requirements and recommendations in the Istanbul Convention, and despite the national shelter network becoming state-funded and co-ordinated, the number of shelters and accessibility for disabled people was insufficient. There were no walk-in services, no long-term support services for survivors of violence, nor a 24/7 helpline for victims of gender-based violence.

In September, the Ministry of Social Affairs and Health prepared a draft decree to create a body to co-ordinate work combating violence against women. The Ministry proposed that the body consist of a network of civil servants working within the limitations of their current offices, but envisioned only a limited role for women's or victim support organizations.

## DISCRIMINATION – TRANSGENDER PEOPLE

Legislation on legal gender recognition continued to violate the rights of transgender individuals. Transgender people can obtain legal gender recognition only if they agree to be sterilized, are diagnosed with a mental disorder, and are aged over 18.

## COUNTER-TERROR AND SECURITY

In June, the new government stated an intention to draft legislation criminalizing travel for terrorism purposes and participation in organizations proscribed as terrorist organizations by the EU and the UN.

## CONSCIENTIOUS OBJECTORS

Conscientious objectors to military service continued to be punished for refusing to undertake alternative civilian service, which remained punitive and discriminatory in length. The duration of alternative civilian service was 347 days, more than double the shortest military service period of 165 days.

# FRANCE

French Republic
Head of state: **François Hollande**
Head of government: **Manuel Valls**

**In January and November, several attacks targeting the population were carried out in and around the capital, Paris, killing over 140 people and injuring hundreds. In January, the government adopted further counter-terrorism measures. On 14**

November, it formally declared a state of emergency that was subsequently extended by Parliament until February 2016.

## COUNTER-TERROR AND SECURITY

In January, violent attacks in Paris on journalists at the satirical weekly *Charlie Hebdo* and at a Jewish supermarket left 17 people dead. In the aftermath of the attacks, the government issued several decrees aimed at implementing some of the provisions of the 2014 anti-terrorism law. In particular, on 14 January, the government issued a decree banning travel abroad for the purposes of committing a terrorist act as defined under French law. According to the Ministry of Interior, 222 individuals were subjected to such a travel ban between January and November.

On 5 February, authorities issued a decree regulating the administrative blockage of websites, including those deemed to incite or justify terrorist acts. According to the Ministry of Interior, 87 websites were blocked from January to November. Moreover, about 700 individuals were prosecuted for inciting or justifying terrorism, on the basis of a new provision ("apology of terrorism") which had been introduced in the 2014 anti-terrorism law. Due to the vague definition of the offence, in many cases authorities prosecuted individuals for statements that did not constitute incitement to violence and fell within the scope of legitimate exercise of freedom of expression.

After a series of eight seemingly co-ordinated armed attacks in and around Paris on 13 November that resulted in 130 deaths and hundreds of injuries, the government declared a state of emergency. On 20 November, Parliament passed a bill that extended the state of emergency until 26 February 2016, amended the 1955 law on the state of emergency, and provided for a range of measures that deviated from the ordinary criminal law regime. The measures included house searches without a warrant, forced residency and the power to dissolve associations or groups broadly described as participating in acts that breach public order. Under the law, pre-judicial authorization for these measures was not required.

In December, the government proposed a bill to include a provision on the state of emergency in the Constitution.

According to the Ministry of Interior, police carried out 2,029 house searches between 14 November and 1 December. In the same period, 296 individuals were subjected to forced residency. Public demonstrations were banned in the Paris region (Ile-de-France) shortly after 13 November. The ban was extended to other regions between 28 and 30 November, when several demonstrations were scheduled to take place in the context of the Paris Climate Conference (the 21$^{st}$ Conference of Parties, known as COP 21).

Several Muslim individuals were targeted for house searches or forced residency on the basis of vague criteria, including religious practices deemed by the authorities to be "radical", and thus constituting a threat to public order or national security. The police also searched mosques and other Muslim prayer spaces, and in some instances shut them down. The authorities imposed forced residency on 26 environmental activists in the context of the COP 21 on the basis of their possible engagement in violent demonstrations.

## SURVEILLANCE

In July, Parliament passed a law that granted the Prime Minister the power to authorize – without independent judicial oversight and only upon consultation with an ad hoc committee – the use of surveillance measures on the national territory for a wide range of goals, including the protection of economic or overarching foreign policy interests. The measures included the power to employ mass surveillance techniques for the purpose of tackling terrorism.

In November, another law was passed, allowing the mass surveillance of all electronic communications sent to – or received from – abroad. The Prime Minister retained the power to authorize such surveillance, without any prior consultation or independent judicial oversight, for the purpose of achieving vaguely defined goals.

## TORTURE AND OTHER ILL-TREATMENT

On 6 February, the French and Moroccan governments signed an additional protocol to their bilateral convention for legal co-operation on criminal matters. The agreement facilitated the transfer to Moroccan authorities of complaints filed in France by Moroccan victims of alleged crimes perpetrated in Morocco.

In April, the Paris Court of Appeal approved a petition to call Geoffrey Miller, former chief of the US detention facility at Guantánamo Bay, Cuba, to give testimony in the cases of two French former Guantánamo detainees, Nizar Sassi and Mourad Benchellali, who had alleged that they were tortured at the detention centre.

On 17 September, the Prime Minister signed an order to extradite Kazakhstani national Mukhtar Ablyazov to Russia, despite the high risk of unfair trial or onward transfer from Russia to Kazakhstan, where he would be at risk of torture or other ill-treatment. An appeal was pending before the Council of State at the end of the year.

## REFUGEES' AND MIGRANTS' RIGHTS

Approximately 5,000 migrants, asylum-seekers and refugees continued to live in harsh conditions in an informal settlement in the northern city of Calais.

On 23 November, the Council of State found that living conditions in the informal settlement in Calais amounted to inhuman treatment, and ordered the immediate installation of water and sanitation services in the settlement.

Both the UN Human Rights Committee and the national Ombudsperson raised concerns over instances of violence, harassment and ill-treatment of migrants, asylum-seekers and refugees by law enforcement agents in Calais. On 2 December, the independent authority overseeing places of detention criticized the abusive use of administrative detention targeting migrants in Calais.

In July, a new asylum law was passed with the aim of strengthening procedural guarantees for asylum-seekers, shortening the waiting time for assessing applications and protecting asylum-seekers' economic and social rights.

Authorities agreed to relocate almost 31,000 asylum-seekers in 2016-2017 and to resettle 2,750 refugees, mainly from Syria.

Unaccompanied children continued to be routinely detained at the Roissy Charles de Gaulle airport's "waiting zone".

## DISCRIMINATION

According to NGOs, almost 4,000 Roma living in 37 informal settlements were forcibly evicted in the first half of the year. Migrants and asylum-seekers were also forcibly evicted from informal settlements throughout the year. In June and July, hundreds of them were repeatedly evicted from several locations in Paris.

In March, the European Court of Human Rights communicated to the government three cases regarding transgender individuals who were denied legal recognition of their female gender because they had refused to comply with medical criteria.

On 17 April, the government adopted an action plan to combat racism and anti-Semitism. Among other measures, it recommended the adoption of an amendment to the Criminal Code to ensure that perpetrating a crime with a racist or anti-Semitic motive constituted an aggravating circumstance.

In August, the UN Human Rights Committee recommended the revision of the 2004 law prohibiting the wearing of religious symbols in schools and of the 2011 law banning face covering. The Committee stated that the laws constituted a violation of the right to freedom of religion and that they had a disproportionate impact on women and girls, as well as on specific religious groups. In November, the European Court of Human Rights found that the refusal of a state employer to extend the contract of a social worker who was wearing the headscarf did not violate her rights to freedoms of expression and religion.

## FREEDOM OF EXPRESSION
On 20 October, the Court of Cassation confirmed the conviction of 14 individuals for incitement to racial discrimination on the basis of the 1881 law on freedom of the press. In 2009 and 2010, they had participated in non-violent initiatives in a supermarket calling for the boycott of Israeli products.

## CORPORATE ACCOUNTABILITY
In November, the Senate rejected a bill aimed at establishing a framework to ensure the respect of human rights by multinational companies, including their subsidiaries, sub-contractors and suppliers. The bill had been approved in March by the National Assembly.

# GAMBIA

Republic of the Gambia
Head of state and government: **Yahya Jammeh**

The December 2014 attempted coup led to arrests and further human rights violations. The authorities continued to repress dissent and display a lack of willingness to co-operate with UN and regional human rights mechanisms or comply with their recommendations.

## BACKGROUND
In April, Gambia rejected 78 of the 171 recommendations at the UPR, including removing restrictions on freedom of expression, ratifying the International Convention against enforced disappearance, and abolishing the death penalty.[1]

The government ignored calls by the international community to conduct a joint independent investigation into the aftermath of the 2014 attempted coup, most notably disregarding the African Commission on Human and Peoples' Rights resolution in

February seeking an invitation to conduct a fact-finding mission.

In June, Gambia expelled the EU's Chargée d'Affaires, asking her to leave within 72 hours with no explanation.

Plans for a Human Rights Commission were developed. In November, President Jammeh announced that female genital mutilation (FGM) would be banned and a bill criminalizing FGM was passed in December by the National Assembly.

## ENFORCED DISAPPEARANCES
In January, dozens of friends and relatives of people accused of involvement in the 2014 attempted coup were detained incommunicado. The authorities refused to acknowledge their detention or to provide information on their whereabouts. Those detained included women, elderly people and a child. They were released in July after six months in detention without charge, in violation of Gambia's Constitution. Some of those detained were tortured at the National Intelligence Agency (NIA) headquarters, including with beatings, electric shocks, waterboarding or being detained in confined holes in the ground.

## FREEDOM OF EXPRESSION – JOURNALISTS AND HUMAN RIGHTS DEFENDERS
Journalists and human rights defenders were arbitrarily arrested and detained and restrictive laws continued to curb the right to freedom of expression.

On 2 July, Alagie Abdoulie Ceesay, director of Teranga FM radio station, was detained and held incommunicado for 12 days. A few days after his release, Alagie Abdoulie Ceesay was again detained, beaten, charged with several counts of sedition and denied bail. He remained in detention; his trial was ongoing at the end of the year.[2]

In June, a well-known rapper, Killa Ace, fled Gambia after receiving death threats following the release of a song accusing the government of repression and extrajudicial executions.

In June, Lamin Cham, a radio show host and music promoter, was arrested in the capital, Banjul, and detained at NIA headquarters and released without charge 20 days later.

Human rights activist Sait Matty Jaw, who was arrested in Banjul in December 2014 and tried over work done on a survey for Gallup on good governance and corruption, was finally discharged in April.

## FREEDOM OF ASSEMBLY

In April, police obstructed a nationwide tour by the opposition United Democratic Party with roadblocks. The tour was granted permission to continue after a four-day stand - off.

In November, police arrested over 40 people during and after a protest by young people and community members in Kartong against sand mining. Witnesses reported excessive use of force by the police with some people injured. Thirty-three were charged with various offences including conspiracy, breach of the peace, riot, causing malicious injuries and riotously interfering with a vehicle. They were unconditionally released eight days later, following a statement by the President ordering their release.[3]

## TORTURE AND OTHER ILL-TREATMENT

The UN Special Rapporteur on torture issued a report in March citing that torture was "prevalent and routine", particularly by the NIA in the early stages of detention. The report expressed concerns over prison conditions and the lack of an effective complaints mechanism to address allegations of torture and other ill-treatment. He noted that "the nature of the torture is brutal and includes very severe beatings with hard objects or electrical wires; electrocution, asphyxiation by placing a plastic bag over the head and filling it with water and burning with hot liquid".[4]

On 25 July, at least 200 prisoners were released by President Jammeh from Mile 2 prison, including several detained for treason and several government officials, such as the former director of the NIA, Lamin Bo Badjie, and former police chief, Ensa Badjie. Despite the releases, other political opponents, journalists and prisoners of conscience remained in detention, including the national treasurer of the opposition United Democratic Party, Amadou Sanneh, as well as party members Alhagie Sambou Fatty and Malang Fatty.[5]

## DEATH PENALTY

On 30 March, a military court at the Fajara barracks in Bakau, near the capital, handed down death sentences on three soldiers and sentenced three others to life imprisonment for their involvement in the 2014 coup. The trial was held in secret, with media and independent observers barred from observing.[6]

## RIGHTS OF LESBIAN, GAY, BISEXUAL, TRANSGENDER AND INTERSEX PEOPLE

Three men suspected of being gay were put on trial for "unnatural acts". Two were acquitted in August while the remaining man was still facing trial at year's end. They had been arrested in November 2014, a month after Gambia introduced life sentences for the offence of "aggravated homosexuality". Many LGBTI people fled the country.

## IMPUNITY

The UN Special Rapporteur on extrajudicial, summary or arbitrary executions issued a report in May, documenting a handful of state investigations into police abuse, none of which resulted in convictions. It stated that citizens were "reluctant to denounce abuses, engage legal services or seek redress, even for the most serious violations, including disappearances, torture or probable executions."

The authorities made no progress towards implementing the judgments of the ECOWAS Court of Justice in the enforced disappearance of journalist Ebrima Manneh (2010), the torture of journalist Musa Saidykhan (2010) and the unlawful killing of Deyda Hydara (2014).

# GEORGIA

**Georgia**
Head of state: **Giorgi Margvelashvili**
Head of government: **Giorgi Kvirikashvili (replaced Irakli Garibashvili in December)**

Legal battles around the pro-opposition TV channel Rustavi 2 raised concerns over freedom of expression. Allegations of political pressure on the judiciary and selective justice persisted, particularly following the rearrest and conviction of a former politician one day after the Constitutional Court ordered his release. In several instances police prevented or limited peaceful gatherings. The investigation of allegations of ill-treatment by law enforcement officials remained slow and ineffective, while a proposal for an independent investigative mechanism was put forward but not yet legislated on.

## BACKGROUND

Towards the end of the year, political tensions rose following incendiary remarks by the then Prime Minister against the opposition party United National Movement (UNM), public screenings of clandestine videos of prison rape dating back to the UNM-led government, and leaked communications between the exiled former President and managers of pro-opposition TV channel Rustavi 2. Several UNM offices across the country were vandalized by mobs in politically motivated attacks.

A 26% devaluation of the national currency against the US dollar affected numerous families who had taken out loans in earlier years, and increased economic vulnerability for many.

Movement in and out of the breakaway territories Abkhazia and South Ossetia remained restricted, while security and humanitarian concerns over the two dormant conflicts persisted. Tensions heightened when, on 10 July, border posts were unilaterally moved several hundred metres outward from South Ossetia. Several civilians were reportedly detained and fined for "illegally" entering into South Ossetia across a largely undemarcated de facto border.

In October, the Prosecutor of the ICC visited Georgia, shortly after requesting that the ICC authorize an investigation into the situation during the Georgian-Russian war in August 2008.

## JUSTICE SYSTEM

Concerns over fairness of judiciary selective justice and politically motivated prosecutions persisted.

On 17 September, the Constitutional Court ruled to release Gigi Ugulava, an opposition activist and former Mayor of the capital, Tbilisi. It deemed his pre-trial detention since 2013 – on charges of misappropriation of public funds and money laundering – illegal as it exceeded the nine-month legal limit. The Court's judges came under heavy criticism from senior government officials for this decision and were threatened with violence by some pro-government groups. On 18 September, Gigi Ugulava was sentenced to four-and-a-half years' imprisonment on account of these charges, and rearrested the same day.

Contrary to widely held expectations, the judge who presided in a controversial 2006 murder trial was reappointed by the High Council of Justice on 25 December at the end of his tenure. He had been criticized for his handling of the case in which, according to the European Court of Human Rights 2011 decision, "the different branches of State power... acted in concert in preventing justice from being done."

## FREEDOM OF EXPRESSION

Concerns over freedom of expression were voiced by local NGOs and political commentators who believed that a lawsuit by a former shareholder of Rustavi 2 against its current owners was prompted by the government to deprive the opposition of its main mouthpiece. On 21 October, the director of Rustavi 2 reported having been blackmailed, claiming that the security services threatened to release intimate footage of him unless he resigned. The Tbilisi City Court found in favour of the former shareholder, and Rustavi 2 managers were forcibly replaced with pro-government caretakers on 5 November, against the Constitutional Court ruling that an appeal had to be heard first.

## FREEDOM OF ASSEMBLY

In several instances police unduly limited or prevented peaceful gatherings, while on a number of occasions they failed to prevent clashes between political opponents.

On 15 March, approximately 50 supporters of the Georgian Dream ruling coalition forcibly entered the local offices of UNM and an affiliated group in Zugdidi, armed with wooden sticks, throwing stones and smashing windows. Nine people were reported injured, including one of the police officers who tried to intervene but were outnumbered by the attackers.

On 12 June, 15 activists attempted to stage a protest at Heydar Aliyev Square in Tbilisi against Azerbaijan's poor human rights record, ahead of the first European Games in Azerbaijan's capital Baku. Ahead of the picket, police officers cordoned off the square and denied access to activists without providing a reason.

## RIGHTS OF LESBIAN, GAY, BISEXUAL, TRANSGENDER AND INTERSEX PEOPLE

The International Day against Homophobia and Transphobia (IDAHOT) proceeded peacefully in Tbilisi in a discreet location on 17 May. The authorities had refused to guarantee the event's safety unless it was held at a specific location without any prior public announcement.

On 12 May, the European Court of Human Rights ruled in *Identoba and Others v. Georgia* that the police's failure to protect participants of the 2012 IDAHOT march constituted discrimination and restricted participants' freedom of assembly.

On 7 August, Tbilisi City Court convicted a man of arson and battery and sentenced him to four years in prison for physically assaulting one transgender woman and burning the flat of another whom he had killed. However, the Court ruled that the killing was an act of self-defence and acquitted him of the relevant charge.

On 23 October, Tbilisi City Court acquitted four men charged with attacking the 2013 IDAHOT rally in Tbilisi due to "insufficient evidence" despite the men reportedly being identifiable on video and photo footage of the event. A fifth man, also identifiable in the footage, had been acquitted earlier. Dozens of men had taken part in the attack but none were convicted.

## TORTURE AND OTHER ILL-TREATMENT

Local human rights organizations reported new cases of ill-treatment by law enforcement officials. The investigation of alleged abuses by members of the General Inspection of the Ministry of Internal Affairs was slow and ineffective.

A draft model of an independent investigative mechanism for the investigation of criminal offences committed by law enforcement officials was jointly proposed by the human rights Ombudsman and some NGOs. However, the law required to establish the mechanism was not considered until the end of the year.

# GERMANY

**Federal Republic of Germany**
Head of state: Joachim Gauck
Head of government: Angela Merkel

Around 1.1 million asylum-seekers entered the country throughout the year. The government unilaterally decided for a period of time not to return Syrian asylum-seekers to their first country of entry in the EU. It expanded the list of safe countries of origin and introduced severe cuts to benefits for certain categories of asylum-seekers. The authorities' failure to effectively investigate alleged human rights violations by police persisted. Hate crimes against refugees, asylum-seekers and migrants increased sharply.

## REFUGEES AND ASYLUM-SEEKERS

The influx of asylum-seekers, mostly from Syria, Iraq and Afghanistan, increased considerably in the second half of the year, from already high levels. By the end of the year Germany had received around 1.1 million asylum-seekers. In August, Prime Minister Angela Merkel highlighted the necessity to address the needs of incoming refugees; invited other European leaders to share responsibility for people seeking protection in Europe; and decided to consider asylum applications submitted by tens of thousands of Syrians arriving in Germany through countries such as Hungary and Austria, rather than seeking their return to the first EU country they entered – a measure that was enforced for about three months. By the end of the year, 476,649 asylum applications had been submitted. Germany contributed to the EU schemes for resettlement and relocation by pledging 1,600 and 27,555 places respectively.

In July, a new law improved the legal status of resettled refugees, including by facilitating family reunification, but increased powers to detain asylum-seekers under the Dublin Regulation and those whose asylum application had been rejected. The amended Asylum Seekers Benefits Act, in force since April, fell short of human rights standards, particularly regarding access to health care. A new law passed in October expanded the list of safe countries of origin to include Kosovo, Albania and Montenegro, thus limiting the opportunity for nationals of these countries to seek protection. The law also introduced severe cuts to benefits set out in the Asylum Seekers Benefits Act for rejected asylum-seekers remaining in Germany in breach of an order to leave the country – or anyway remaining without legal status – and for asylum-seekers who moved to Germany despite having been relocated to another European country.

## TORTURE AND OTHER ILL-TREATMENT

The authorities continued to fail to effectively investigate allegations of ill-treatment by police and did not establish any independent complaints mechanism to investigate those allegations. The obligation for police officers to wear identity badges was not extended beyond the federal states of Berlin, Brandenburg, Rhineland-Palatinate, Bremen, Hessen and Schleswig-Holstein.

The National Agency for the Prevention of Torture, Germany's preventive mechanism under the Optional Protocol to the UN Convention against Torture, remained severely under-resourced. The appointment procedure for the National Agency's members continued to fall short of international standards on independence and transparency, and excluded civil society representatives.

In May, national media reported on the alleged abuse of two Afghan and Moroccan refugees in the holding cells of the federal police at Hannover's main train station in 2014. Investigations against a federal police officer were ongoing at the end of the year.

## DISCRIMINATION

On 27 January, the Constitutional Court found that the prohibition on teachers wearing religious symbols and dress, with the exception of those expressing Christian or Western values, which was in force in North-Rhine Westphalia since 2006, was discriminatory. Similar prohibitions remained in force in other German states.

Opposition to refugees, asylum-seekers and migrants, particularly Muslims, resulted in hundreds of protests being staged across the country. Hate crimes against refugees, asylum-seekers and migrants increased sharply. According to the government, 113 violent attacks against asylum shelters were perpetrated in the first 10 months of the year, compared with 29 in 2014.

The Federal Parliament considered an amendment to Section 46 of the Criminal Code, which, if passed, would require courts to take into account a racist or xenophobic motivation when deciding sentences.

In June, the UN Committee on the Elimination of Racial Discrimination highlighted the authorities' failure to investigate the racial motivation of offences, including in relation to murders perpetrated by the far-right group National Socialist Underground (NSU) against members of ethnic minorities. Moreover, the Committee raised concerns regarding the discriminatory impact of police stop-and-search powers on ethnic minorities.

Several proceedings regarding the alleged discriminatory impact of identity checks carried out by federal police under Section 22(1)(a) of the Federal Police Act were pending at various levels of administrative courts.

## ARMS TRADE

In March, the Federal Security Council released new principles in line with international standards for the sale of small arms and light weapons. In July, the Federal Cabinet passed a policy paper for the introduction of post-shipment controls.

## INTERNATIONAL JUSTICE

On 21 May, the Federal Court of Justice partially overturned the decision of the Frankfurt Higher Regional Court in the case of Rwandan citizen Onesphore Rwabukombe, who was sentenced in 2014 to 14 years' imprisonment for aiding the commission of a massacre at the Kiziguro church compound. It was found on appeal that Rwabukombe was actively involved in the murder of 450 people at the Kiziguro church, and that his previous sentence was too lenient. The case was referred back to a lower court in Frankfurt for retrial.

On 28 September, the Higher Regional Court in Stuttgart sentenced Rwandan leaders of the Democratic Forces for the Liberation of Rwanda (FDLR) Ignace Murwanashyaka and Straton Musoni to 13 and eight years in prison respectively. They were both found guilty of leadership of a foreign terrorist group, while Ignace Murwanashyaka was additionally convicted of aiding in war crimes. It was the first trial based on the 2002 Code of Crimes against International Law.

On 5 December 2014, the Higher Regional Court in Düsseldorf convicted three German citizens, originally from Rwanda, for their support to the FDLR.

# GHANA

**Republic of Ghana**
Head of state and government: **John Dramani Mahama**

**Excessive use of force by police was reported in the context of demonstrations and mass evictions. Torture and other ill-treatment continued to be reported and prison conditions remained a concern. Violence against women remained widespread; there was particular concern about banishment for witchcraft. Lesbian, gay, bisexual, transgender and intersex (LGBTI) people faced discrimination and were targeted for attack. Death sentences continued to be handed down.**

## BACKGROUND

A process to review the Constitution was delayed owing to a court case challenging the legality of the Constitutional Review

Implementation Committee. In October, the Supreme Court dismissed the case.

## FREEDOM OF ASSEMBLY

In September, police fired tear gas and used batons to disperse demonstrators taking part in a peaceful demonstration, after failing to agree on a route for the march. The demonstration was organized by the Let My Vote Count Alliance calling for a new voters' register.

## TORTURE AND OTHER ILL-TREATMENT

In October, the UN Special Rapporteur on torture visited Ghana to follow up on the recommendations he had made following his 2013 visit. While welcoming the fact that some progress had been made, he expressed concern that the police and intelligence services continued to use torture and other ill-treatment.

He also noted the lack of due diligence and urgency shown by oversight mechanisms in investigating allegations of torture or other ill-treatment and the need for the expansion and effective implementation of the Legal Aid Scheme.

He noted no significant lessening of overcrowding in detention centres or improvement in conditions of detention, such as poor sanitation and inadequate nutrition.

## HOUSING RIGHTS

A National Housing Policy was adopted in March, with the overall goal of providing decent and affordable housing that is accessible and sustainable.

On 20-21 June, several thousand people were evicted from Accra's largest slum, Old Fadama. Popularly known as Sodom and Gomorrah, the slum was home to around 50,000 people. Police used tear gas against people demonstrating against the demolition and several people were injured. Amnesty International expressed concern that these evictions did not conform to international human rights standards and that better guidelines are needed.

## VIOLENCE AGAINST WOMEN AND GIRLS

Violence against women and girls remained widespread. In recent years, several hundred women have been accused of witchcraft by members of their communities and banished to live in isolated camps with minimal access to health care, education, sanitation and other services. Although the government, in collaboration with traditional leaders and civil society, shut down the Bonyasi witch camp in December 2014, and announced it would close others, some camps remained open at the end of the year.

## RIGHTS OF LESBIAN, GAY, BISEXUAL, TRANSGENDER AND INTERSEX PEOPLE

Consensual same-sex conduct between men remained a criminal offence and many LGBTI people faced discrimination, violence and police harassment.

In February, some Ghanaian celebrities condemned the beating of a music promoter who was suspected of being gay.

In September, police arrested Sulley Fuiseni, leader of a group called Safety Empire which is accused of attacking LGBTI people in the Nima disctrict of Accra. His trial was continuing at the end of the year.

## DEATH PENALTY

No executions have taken place since 1993. However, Ghana retains the death penalty and courts continued to hand down death sentences. The government took no action during the year in response to the recommendations made in 2014 by the UN Human Rights Committee and the Committee's condemnation of the use of automatic and mandatory death sentences in Ghana.

Proposals made by the Constitutional Review Implementation Committee to abolish the death penalty were stalled as a result of delays in the constitutional review process.

# GREECE

**Hellenic Republic**
Head of state: **Prokopis Pavlopoulos (replaced Karolos Papoulias in March)**
Head of government: **Alexis Tsipras (replaced Vassiliki Thanou Christophilou in September, who served as interim Prime Minister after the resignation of Tsipras in August)**

The dramatic increase in arrivals of asylum-seekers and irregular migrants on the Aegean islands pushed an ineffective first reception system beyond breaking point. Collective expulsions continued at the Greek-Turkish border. Allegations of torture and other ill-treatment and excessive use of force by police persisted. A law extending civil unions to same-sex couples was voted at the end of the year.

## BACKGROUND

At the end of June, the government imposed capital controls on banks while in a July referendum 61.3% of voters rejected a stringent bailout plan by Greece's creditors. Shortly after, following several months of intensive negotiations, the government agreed a new bail-out plan with the European Institutions and the International Monetary Fund.

In October, the UN Committee on Economic, Social and Cultural Rights expressed concern about the severe impact of the financial crisis on the enjoyment of the rights to work, social security and health particularly by certain disadvantaged groups.

The trial of 69 people including the leader, MPs and supporters of Golden Dawn began in April. The defendants had been indicted for running and participating in a criminal organization and a range of other offences, including numerous racist attacks and the murder of anti-fascist singer Pavlos Fyssas in 2013. In September, the party's leader, Nikos Mihaloliakos, acknowledged during a media interview that the party had political responsibility for the murder of Pavlos Fyssas.

During the same month, the party took third place in the parliamentary elections and elected 18 MPs.

## REFUGEES, ASYLUM-SEEKERS AND MIGRANTS

More than 851,319 refugees, asylum-seekers and migrants crossed the sea to arrive in the Aegean islands during the year. In the same period, more than 612 people, including many children, died or were unaccounted for in the crossing when the boats carrying them capsized.

Collective expulsions by police continued at the Greek-Turkish land border; several refugees and asylum-seekers reported instances of violent push-backs. Push-backs also continued at sea. Eleven push-back incidents were reported to have occurred at the Greek-Turkish land and sea borders between November 2014 and the end of August 2015. In October, the Prosecutor of the Thessaloniki Appeals Court ordered the Internal Affairs Directorate of the Police to conduct a criminal investigation into a series of reports by NGOs concerning collective expulsions of refugees and migrants by police in Evros.

In July, new legislation (Law 4332/2015) was adopted setting out requirements for the granting of Greek citizenship to children of migrants.

### Reception conditions

The already ineffective first reception system proved incapable of adequately responding to the dramatic increase in refugees and migrants arriving on the Aegean islands. Poor planning, the ineffective use of EU funds and the deep financial crisis exacerbated the humanitarian crisis on the islands. Local activists, volunteers, NGOs and UNHCR, the UN refugee agency, tried to cover the enormous gaps in humanitarian provision for refugees.[1]

Reception conditions on islands such as Lesvos and Kos were inhuman. Deficiencies included a lack of police and coastguard staff, insufficient tents, lack of food and poor hygiene conditions. The vast majority of new arrivals had no access to the First Reception Service.

In mid-October, the Greek authorities established a pilot scheme for the screening of new arrivals by the EU border agency and the Greek police. The "hotspot" operated at the Moria immigration detention centre on Lesvos. However, reception conditions there remained dire.[2]

There was inadequate accommodation and facilities for refugees and migrants arriving in Athens, the capital, where hundreds of people, including families, stayed for several days and nights in parks and squares of the city. In August, the authorities established a reception centre in the area of Elaionas, in Athens, to provide temporary shelter to new arrivals. Three stadiums in Attika were also used to provide temporary shelter to refugees and migrants when needed.

In November and December, reception conditions at the informal Idomeni refugee camp deteriorated markedly after Macedonian authorities imposed selective border controls on arriving refugees and migrants.[3] The camp was evacuated following a police operation in mid-December. People not allowed to cross the border were transferred to Athens by bus and offered temporary shelter in a stadium.

### Detention of asylum-seekers and migrants
In February, the Ministers for Migration Policy and Citizens' Protection took some steps to reform the policy of systematic and prolonged detention of asylum-seekers and irregular migrants. In particular, the authorities ceased to implement the widely criticized policy of indefinite detention and released a large number of asylum-seekers and irregular migrants held for more than six months.

Unaccompanied children were often held with adults and remained in detention for several weeks under poor conditions. Conditions in immigration detention areas, including police stations, often amounted to inhuman or degrading treatment. At the end of the year, the authorities started detaining

third-country nationals from Maghreb countries for immigration purposes.

Obstacles to accessing asylum procedures remained for both detained and non-detained asylum-seekers.

## TORTURE AND OTHER ILL-TREATMENT
Allegations of torture and other ill-treatment of individuals, including refugees and migrants in immigration detention or during push-back operations, persisted.

In September, lawyers reported that nine individuals, some of them children, were ill-treated by police officers belonging to the DELTA special police unit following their arrest in the neighbourhood of Exarcheia in Athens. A criminal investigation was initiated by the Internal Affairs Directorate of the Police.

In April, the Athens Mixed Jury Court convicted two police officers of the torture in May 2007 of Christos Chronopoulos, who had a mental health disability. The Court handed down sentences of eight years' imprisonment to each officer; the sentences were suspended on appeal.

## EXCESSIVE USE OF FORCE
Allegations of excessive use of force by police continued. In August, more than 2,000 refugees and migrants were locked in inhuman conditions in the local sports stadium on Kos. Reports emerged of police being unable to manage the crowd and dispersing them by spraying them with fire extinguishers. On several occasions between August and October, riot police on Lesvos reportedly used tear gas and beat refugees and migrants waiting to be admitted for screening at the Moria immigration detention centre and those being registered in Mytilene port.

## DISCRIMINATION

### Hate crime
Hate-motivated attacks against refugees and migrants continued. In July, the Piraeus Felony Court of Appeals found a bakery

owner guilty of abducting, robbing and causing serious bodily harm to Egyptian migrant worker Walid Taleb in 2012. The Court sentenced him to 13 years and two months in prison. Three other men were found guilty of abetting and were given prison sentences which were later suspended on appeal.

On 3 September, a group of 15 to 25 men, allegedly members of Golden Dawn, attacked refugees on Kos and threatened activists. Police took no action to stop the group from attacking the refugees, and riot police only intervened after the physical attacks had started.

During the year, the NGO Colour Youth documented in the project "Tell us" 73 incidents of hate-motivated attacks against members of the LGBTI community, compared with 22 incidents documented during the whole of 2014. On 24 September, two men were convicted of an attack against a transgender woman in a bar in Thessaloniki on 19 September and received a sentence of 19 months' imprisonment.

At the end of the year, the investigation of the homophobic and racist attack in August 2014 against Costas, a Greek national, and his partner, had made no progress. The perpetrators had not been found or identified.

### Rights of lesbian, gay, bisexual, transgender and intersex people

On 22 December, Parliament passed a law extending civil unions to same-sex couples. The new law enables same-sex couples to enjoy some of the rights granted to married couples, including emergency medical decisions and inheritance rights, but does not guarantee adoption rights and legal gender recognition for transgender people.

### Roma

Roma children continued to face segregation or exclusion from education in many parts of Greece, including the towns of Aspropirgos, Sofades and Karditsa. Despite the 2013 ruling of the European Court of Human Rights in *Lavida and others v. Greece*, Roma children

remained in a segregated separate school in Sofades, a town in Central Greece.

In April, the UN Special Rapporteur on contemporary forms of racism expressed concerns about the housing conditions at the Roma settlement in Spata, a town near Athens, including the lack of electricity and its implications for the education and health of Roma children.

## WOMEN'S RIGHTS

In October, the UN Committee on Economic, Social and Cultural Rights reiterated its concerns over the high incidence of domestic violence and the low rates of prosecution, as well as the under-representation of women in political and public life.

## CONSCIENTIOUS OBJECTORS

Alternative civilian service remained punitive and discriminatory. Men refusing military conscription who also refused to carry out alternative civilian service continued to face prosecution in the military justice system for insubordination, facing sentences of up to two years' imprisonment and significant fines.

1. Humanitarian crisis mounts as refugee system pushed to breaking point (Press release, 25 June)

2. Urgent Action: Refugees face hellish conditions on Islands (EUR 25/2798/2015)

3. Fear and fences: Europe's approach to keeping refugees at bay (EUR 03/2544/2015)

# GUATEMALA

**Republic of Guatemala**
Head of state and government: **Alejandro Maldonado Aguirre (replaced Otto Pérez Molina in September)**

**In a landmark development, the President and Vice-President resigned and were detained on corruption charges. Important progress towards accountability was made, although justice was still elusive for human rights violations and crimes under international law committed during the**

internal armed conflict. Human rights defenders, including environmental and land rights defenders protesting against hydroelectric and mining projects, and journalists, were threatened, attacked, harassed and intimidated. Violence against women and girls continued to be systemic.

## BACKGROUND

The country was shaken by revelations in April by the International Commission against Impunity in Guatemala and the Guatemalan Public Prosecutor's Office of wide-reaching corruption involving the customs agency. More than a dozen officials were charged and arrested for their alleged participation, including Vice-President Roxana Baldetti. In September, President Pérez Molina resigned, one day after Congress stripped him of his immunity from prosecution. Otto Pérez Molina was the first ever serving president to face criminal charges.

The scandal gained momentum over a period of months during which public protests mounted. Massive anti-corruption demonstrations lasting several months were seen in the streets of a number of cities around the country, bringing together many different groups and sectors of society in an unprecedented fashion. However, the atmosphere of increased social mobilization, demonstrations and civic activity also resulted in threats and intimidation against participants.

In September, Alejandro Maldonado Aguirre, a former Constitutional Court judge, was sworn in as President. Presidential elections, which had been scheduled before the scandal broke, were held in September with a run-off in October. The winner, comedian James Ernesto "Jimmy" Morales Cabrera, was due to take office in January 2016.

## IMPUNITY

Truth, justice and reparations for human rights violations and crimes under international law committed during the country's internal armed conflict between

1960 and 1996 continued to be slow and halting. However, important steps towards accountability were made. In October, a Guatemala City appeals court declared that a 1986 amnesty decree could not be applied to crimes against humanity and genocide. As a result, the case against former President and Commander-in-Chief of the Guatemalan army, José Efraín Ríos Montt, could proceed.

In August, the Guatemalan Court for High Risk ruled that Efraín Ríos Montt should be tried behind closed doors in special criminal proceedings due to begin in January 2016.[1] Ríos Montt will be represented by a third party during the trial and the court is not empowered to hand down a prison sentence, owing to the 89-year-old defendant's poor health. In January, a civilian court in Guatemala City found Pedro García Arredondo, former chief detective of the now-defunct National Police, guilty of orchestrating a fire in the city's Spanish Embassy that killed 37 people in 1980.[2] He was sentenced to 90 years in prison for murder, attempted murder and crimes against humanity.

Civil society organizations continued to push for the approval of Law 3590, which would create a National Commission for the Search for Victims of Enforced Disappearance and Other Forms of Disappearance. The law was first presented before Congress in 2006.

## HUMAN RIGHTS DEFENDERS

Human rights defenders, particularly Indigenous leaders and protesters defending environmental and land rights and opposing hydroelectric and mining megaprojects faced continuous attacks, threats, harassment and intimidation during the year.

The Guatemalan human rights organization UDEFEGUA documented 337 acts of aggression against human rights defenders in the first half of 2015, more than the number recorded in the whole of 2012, the year President Pérez Molina took office. Documented abuses rose by over 166% during his presidency, according to UDEFEGUA.

UDEFEGUA stated that almost 71% of all

documented attacks and intimidation against human rights defenders in the first half of 2015 targeted Indigenous leaders and defenders working on environmental and land rights issues. Leaders of movements opposing hydroelectric projects in Huehuetenango Department were arbitrarily arrested and tried in proceedings that local groups said were characterized by irregularities and violations of due process. According to UDEFEGUA, eight human rights defenders were in prison at the end of the year.

## FREEDOM OF EXPRESSION – JOURNALISTS

In March, *Prensa Libre* correspondent Danilo López and Radio Nuevo Mundo reporter Federico Salazar were shot dead by gunmen while walking in a park in Mazatenango, the capital of Suchitepéquez Department. Danilo López, according to the authorities the probable target of the attack, had frequently received threats for his reporting on local government corruption and was investigating a story on money laundering shortly before his death. The authorities arrested several people they accused of having carried out or planned the crime, including two police officers, but no one was charged with ordering the crime. At the end of the year, it remained unclear who was behind the killings; investigations were ongoing.

## LAND DISPUTES

In July, an appeals court suspended operations of the contested El Tambor gold mine until further community consultations were held. In a separate case in September, a criminal court suspended operations of a palm oil company in Petén Department pending further investigation of its alleged responsibility for the contamination of a local river. In both cases, the activists and human rights defenders involved had been intimidated, threatened and attacked.

## VIOLENCE AGAINST WOMEN AND GIRLS

The National Institute of Forensic Science reported that 766 women were murdered throughout the year, compared with 774 in 2014. The Public Prosecutor's Office stated that violence against women had been the most frequently reported crime in the country in 2013 and 2014.

Guatemala had yet to comply with a 2014 ruling of the Inter-American Court of Human Rights in the case of María Isabel Véliz Franco, who was 15 at the time of her death in 2001. The Court found Guatemala responsible for her gender-based killing and the subsequent failure to investigate, prosecute and punish those responsible. The judgment called on the authorities to carry out an effective investigation, make a public apology, and reinforce state institutions to investigate and prosecute gender-based violence. Compensation for victims, including María Isabel Véliz Franco's mother, had not been paid by the end of the year.

1. Guatemala: Court ruling on Ríos Montt's case highlights flaws in justice system (News story, 25 August)
2. Guatemala: Conviction of ex-police chief finally brings justice for 1980 Spanish embassy attack (News story, 20 January)

# GUINEA

Republic of Guinea
Head of state: **Alpha Condé**
Head of government: **Mohamed Saïd Fofana**

**In the context of the presidential election, authorities banned demonstrations and the security forces regularly used excessive force against demonstrators. Arbitrary arrests continued, including of opposition members. People were arrested because of their perceived sexual orientation. Impunity for human rights violations persisted.**

## BACKGROUND

President Alpha Condé was re-elected in October with 57.84% of the vote. The opposition contested the election results, citing irregularities. Violence between members of opposition parties and clashes with security forces led to at least 20 deaths and hundreds of people injured in incidents linked to the elections throughout the year.

## INTERNATIONAL SCRUTINY

Guinea's human rights record was assessed under the UPR in January. The concerns raised included restrictions on the right to freedom of peaceful assembly, excessive use of force to disperse demonstrators and a culture of impunity within the security forces. Guinea did not accept recommendations to abolish the death penalty or to decriminalize consensual same-sex relations.[1]

## EXCESSIVE USE OF FORCE

At least 20 people died during violence around the election period, at least half of which were killed by security forces.[2] Other people, including children, were injured by live ammunition, misuse of riot equipment, or in accidents with security force vehicles. Three journalists were beaten by the police in Hamdallaye, Boké region, in May.

In June, the National Assembly passed a bill on maintaining public order which defined how and when force can and cannot be used to police protests. The bill could restrict the right to peaceful assembly: it would not allow spontaneous public assembly, while security forces would retain the power to disperse groups of otherwise peaceful protesters if at least one person is believed to have a weapon. Such clauses could be used as grounds for banning or repressing peaceful protests.

## ARBITRARY DETENTIONS

Members of opposition groups, trade unionists and other people who expressed dissent were arbitrarily detained ahead of the elections.[3] Jean Dougo Guilavogui, a union leader and retired member of the armed forces, was arrested in the capital, Conakry, on 19 September and detained without being brought before judicial authorities until his indictment on 25 September. His extended detention is contrary to international law and to Guinean law. Four other members of the

union were arrested in October. All of them were charged with contempt of the head of state and defamation. They were still in detention at the end of the year.[4]

In May, the UN Working Group on Arbitrary Detention found that the detention of General Nouhou Thiam, Adjudant Mohamed Kaba, Lieutenant Mohamed Condé, Colonel Saadou Diallo and Lieutenant Kémo Condé was arbitrary. They were arrested in 2011 following an attack on President Condé's house. The Working Group called on Guinea to release the men. They were still in detention at the end of the year.

## RIGHTS OF LESBIAN, GAY, BISEXUAL, TRANSGENDER AND INTERSEX PEOPLE

Article 325 of the Criminal Code criminalizes consensual same-sex sexual acts. At least three people were arrested because of their perceived sexual orientation. Two men were arrested on 22 April in Conakry. In May, the Tribunal of Mafanco sentenced them to three months' imprisonment.

## IMPUNITY

Investigations continued into the massacre in the Grand Stade de Conakry in 2009, when security forces killed more than 100 peaceful demonstrators and injured at least 1,500 others. Dozens of women were raped and others disappeared. Moussa Dadis Camara, then head of the military junta, was indicted in July. Mamadouba Toto Camara, then Minister of Public Security and Civilian Protection, was indicted in June.

Impunity for other human rights violations committed by members of the security forces persisted. No progress was made towards bringing to trial gendarmes and police officers suspected of criminal responsibility for using excessive force against peaceful demonstrators, leading to death and injuries between 2011 and 2015.

There was no investigation of members of the police, gendarmerie and army who were involved in the systematic pillage and contamination of water sources of Womey, Nzérékoré region, in September 2014.

Security forces had been deployed to the area following the killings of seven members of an Ebola sensitization team and a bystander in Womey. Several people arrested reported being subjected to torture and at least six women were raped as they attempted to return to their village to seek food or valuables. Two men died in detention in December 2014 and May 2015. In April, the Tribunal of Nzérékoré sentenced 11 of the villagers to life imprisonment for murder.

In March the Assize Court of Kankan adjourned the trial of four security force members charged with killing six people during a strike at a mine in Zogota in 2012. The accused officers failed to appear in court.

In June, members of the community of Saoro village, Nzérékoré region, filed a case before ECOWAS Community Court of Justice, claiming that the Guinean authorities made no effort to prosecute security forces accused of arbitrary arrest, torture, rape and unlawful killings of villagers protesting against their forced eviction in 2011.

1. Guinea: The culture of excessive use of force threatens civil and political rights ahead of the presidential elections (AFR 29/1950/2015)
2. Guinea: Preventing the excessive use of force and respecting freedom of peaceful assembly in the run-up to the 2015 elections and beyond – a call to action (AFR 29/2160/2015); "Guinea: Unarmed people shot in the back and beaten to death by the security forces in Conakry" (News story, 22 October)
3. Guinea: Urgent health concern for two detainees (AFR 29/1868/2015); Guinea: Further information: Two detainees released on health grounds (AFR 29/1889/2015)
4. Guinea: Further information: Four more trade unionists detained (AFR 29/2660/2015)

# GUINEA-BISSAU

Republic of Guinea-Bissau
Head of state: **José Mário Vaz**
Head of government: **Carlos Correia (replaced Baciro Djá in September, who replaced Domingos Simões Pereira in August)**

**The human rights situation improved. However, there were reports of torture and other ill-treatment and deaths in police custody. The authorities took no action to improve poor detention conditions.**

## BACKGROUND

In January, Guinea-Bissau's human rights record was assessed under the UPR. The government accepted most recommendations made and noted for further consideration those related to the ratification of the Optional Protocol to the ICESCR, and the Convention on the Non-Applicability of Statutory Limitations to War Crimes and Crimes against Humanity.

August saw the unconstitutional dismissal by President Vaz of Prime Minister Simões Pereira and his government. A week later President Vaz appointed Baciro Djá as Prime Minister, despite opposition from Parliament and widespread protest by civil society which demanded the reinstatement of Domingos Simões Pereira. Lacking parliamentary approval, Baciro Djá was unable to form a government until 10 September, only to be dismissed five days later after the Supreme Court ruled the President's actions unconstitutional. Carlos Correia was then appointed Prime Minister and a new government was formed in mid-October, with Parliament's support.

## TORTURE AND OTHER ILL-TREATMENT

There were several reports of torture and other ill-treatment by police in the northern town of Bissorã, where local residents referred to the police station as a torture centre. Tchutcho Mendonça was arrested on 3 July at his home in Bissorã, following an argument with his father. He was taken to Bissorã police station where he was tortured and died two days later. Those who saw his body reported that it showed signs consistent with torture. Ten police officers were subsequently arrested but none had been tried by the end of the year.

Also in July, police approached and beat Mamadú Djaló in a street in Bissorã, causing injuries to his torso. No investigation was known to have been carried out into the beating by the end of the year.

## PRISON CONDITIONS

In June, the NGO Guinea-Bissau Human Rights League reported that conditions of detention throughout the country were appalling and amounted to cruel and inhuman treatment, particularly the cells of the Criminal Investigation Police and the Second Police Station, both in the capital Bissau, and called for their closure. Conditions in these cells included severe overcrowding, with some inmates having to sleep in the toilets, poor sanitation and ventilation, all of which reportedly led to detainees becoming ill. According to the NGO, the cell at the Criminal Investigation Police had capacity for 35 people but regularly held over 100. The authorities had taken no action to improve conditions by the end of the year.

# GUYANA

**Republic of Guyana**
Head of state and government: **David Arthur Granger**
**(replaced Donald Ramotar in May)**

There were continuing concerns about excessive use of force by the police, violence against women and girls, and discrimination and violence towards lesbian, gay, bisexual, transgender and intersex (LGBTI) people.

## BACKGROUND

Violent crime remained widespread. By November, 133 people had been murdered, compared with 130 during the same period in 2014, according to the Guyana Police Force (GPF).

General elections were held in May and David Granger was elected President. Granger's coalition won over a party which had held power for 23 years.

Prior to elections, during a sensitive electoral contest, a political activist was killed, causing concern about potential limitations on freedom of expression. In January, Guyana's human rights record was examined under the UPR.

## POLICE AND SECURITY FORCES

Allegations of excessive use of force by the GPF during arrests and detention remained a concern. Guyana accepted recommendations made during the UPR to strengthen the independence of the Police Complaints Authority and increase its resources and capacity.

## CHILDREN'S RIGHTS

Corporal punishment continued in schools, in contravention of the UN Convention of the Rights of the Child. While the government conducted consultations with civil society on the use of corporal punishment, the law remained unchanged.

## VIOLENCE AGAINST WOMEN AND GIRLS

High levels of sexual and other physical violence against women and girls continued. According to a Latin American Public Opinion Project survey published in 2014, acceptance of domestic violence was high in Guyana. The GPF had registered 300 reports of rape for 2015 as of November, compared with 238 for the same period last year.

Conviction rates for sexual offences remained alarmingly low. According to women's rights groups, police continued to fail to take reports seriously.

In July, the former Minister of Health was charged with using insulting language towards a women's rights activist who confronted him on issues of maternal health.

He had threatened to "slap" her and have her "stripped" of her clothes.

## RIGHTS OF LESBIAN, GAY, BISEXUAL, TRANSGENDER AND INTERSEX PEOPLE

Violence and discrimination towards LGBTI people remained a serious concern. There continued to be no legal protection against discrimination based on real or perceived sexual orientation and gender identity and expression, and same-sex sexual conduct between men remained criminalized.

In July 2015, days after civil society groups held a candlelight vigil to mark the one-year anniversary of the death of two transgender sex workers, a transgender sex worker known as "Nephi" was killed in Georgetown. A suspect was reportedly charged in August.

The Society Against Sexual Orientation Discrimination (SASOD), a local NGO, continued to receive reports of discrimination based on sexual orientation and gender identity in the workplace. According to SASOD, transgender youth continued to be made homeless due to discrimination from within their home environment and children's homes lacked the capacity to respond to their needs.

In response to recommendations made during the UPR, Guyana agreed "to strengthen the protection of LGBT individuals" and "to continue its effort in eliminating discrimination against LGBTI people starting with the review of its related legislation". Another 14 recommendations on LGBTI issues, including to reform the Criminal Law Offences Act, were rejected by Guyana.

# HAITI

**Republic of Haiti**
Head of state: **Michel Joseph Martelly**
Head of government: **Evans Paul**

Legislative, presidential and municipal elections were held amid violence and controversy. More than 60,000 people made homeless by the January 2010 earthquake remained displaced. Hundreds of Haitian migrants returning or deported from the Dominican Republic settled in makeshift camps with no access to services. Concerns remained over the lack of independence of the justice system.

## BACKGROUND

The failure to hold long-overdue legislative elections rendered Parliament dysfunctional. On 16 January, following an agreement with the political parties, the President confirmed the appointment of Evans Paul as Prime Minister who, two days later, announced the formation of a transitional government including members of opposition parties.

The first round of legislative elections was held on 9 August, and was marked by widespread disruption and violence. The first round of presidential elections as well as the second round of legislative elections and municipal elections were held on 25 October. Although these election rounds saw minimal violence, opposition candidates and national election observers alleged massive frauds. Following mass demonstrations and the refusal of the presidential candidate who had qualified second to participate in the electoral run-off scheduled on 27 December, on 22 December President Martelly established a commission tasked with evaluating the 25 October election. On 21 December, the run-off was postponed.

In October, the UN Security Council renewed the mandate of the UN Stabilization Mission in Haiti (MINUSTAH) for a 12th year and affirmed its intention to consider the possible withdrawal of the mission within a year.

Severe drought in the North-West and South-West departments negatively impacted on food security and nutrition, especially for rural families and those living on the Dominican-Haitian border.

## INTERNALLY DISPLACED PEOPLE

At the end of June, more than 60,000 people made homeless by the January 2010 earthquake were still living in 45 makeshift camps. Living conditions in camps worsened as many humanitarian programmes ended due to a lack of funding. Many displaced people left the camps after being allocated one-year rental subsidies. However, the government failed to implement durable solutions for displaced people.[1]

## REFUGEES' AND MIGRANTS' RIGHTS

Tens of thousands of Haitian migrants and their families returned to Haiti after the Dominican authorities announced that deportations of irregular migrants would resume from 17 June. Many were reportedly deported; others fled following threats or fearing violent expulsion. Hundreds settled in makeshift camps at the border. Haitian and international human rights organizations, as well as the UN Independent Expert on the situation of human rights in Haiti, raised concerns about the lack of access to services for people living in camps in the Anse-à-Pitres municipality.

## RIGHT TO HEALTH – CHOLERA EPIDEMICS

In the first six months, the number of cases and deaths from cholera tripled compared with the same period in 2014. According to official statistics, 9,013 people died of cholera between October 2010 and August 2015. The humanitarian response remained largely underfunded. The UN, which is deemed to have inadvertently triggered the epidemic, continued to refuse to ensure victims' right to remedy and reparations.[2]

## VIOLENCE AGAINST WOMEN AND GIRLS

A bill on preventing, prosecuting and eradicating violence against women, drafted in 2011, and the draft penal code containing progressive provisions on gender-based violence remained stalled because of the dysfunctional Parliament. Convictions in cases of sexual violence against women remained low and the majority of domestic violence cases were not investigated or prosecuted.

## IMPUNITY

The investigation into alleged crimes against humanity committed by former President Jean-Claude Duvalier and his former collaborators made little progress. Following his visit to Haiti in September, the UN Independent Expert on the situation of human rights in Haiti reiterated his recommendation for the creation of "a truth, justice and peace commission to clarify and provide remedy" for the victims of past human rights violations under François and Jean-Claude Duvalier and President Jean-Bertrand Aristide.

## JUSTICE SYSTEM

The appointment of a new President of the High Council of the Judiciary in March helped restore the institution's credibility. It was also strengthened by the appointment of a Director of the Judicial Inspectorate and 10 sitting judges as inspectors. However, delays in the renewal of judges' tenure and in vetting processes negatively impacted on the efficiency of the judiciary.

Concerns remained about the overall lack of independence of the justice system. For example, human rights organizations expressed concern that a decision by the Port-au-Prince criminal court in April to dismiss the case against two alleged gang members was politically motivated.

About 800 detainees in penitentiaries in the Port-au-Prince region benefited from a case review ordered by the Ministry of Justice to deal with prolonged pre-trial detention and prison overcrowding. However, by the end of September, an excessively high number of detainees remained in pre-trial detention.

## RIGHTS OF LESBIAN, GAY, BISEXUAL, TRANSGENDER AND INTERSEX PEOPLE

Cases of verbal and physical attacks against LGBTI people were reported during the year, most of which were not thoroughly investigated. According to LGBTI rights organizations, some presidential and legislative candidates made homophobic statements during the electoral campaign.

Although LGBTI rights organizations were

able to contribute to the training of new police recruits, no similar training was known to have been organized for existing police officers.

---

1. Haiti: "15 Minutes to leave": Denial of the right to adequate housing in post-quake Haiti (AMR 36/001/2015)
2. Haiti: Five years on, no justice for the victims of the cholera epidemic (AMR 36/2652/2015)

# HONDURAS

**Republic of Honduras**
Head of state and government: **Juan Orlando Hernández Alvarado**

---

Amid a general climate of crime and violence, human rights defenders, Indigenous, peasant and Afro-descendant leaders involved in land disputes, lesbian, gay, bisexual, transgender and intersex (LGBTI) activists, justice officials and journalists were targeted with violence and intimidation by state and criminal actors in retaliation for their work. A weak criminal justice system and corruption contributed to a climate of extensive impunity for these abuses.

## BACKGROUND

The Honduran Supreme Court ruled in April to eliminate an article in the Constitution that limits presidential terms to one in office. The change meant that President Hernández would be able to seek re-election in 2017.

Tens of thousands of protesters dubbed "the indignant ones" (*los indignados*) protested for months against corruption after a series of scandals involving the government and political parties, in some of the biggest marches in recent Honduran history. The government resisted the protesters' demand for the formation of an international commission with the power to investigate crimes and corruption by government officials. Instead, it announced in September an initiative in conjunction with the OAS to reform the justice system and strengthen the independence of the judicial branch. The protesters rejected this proposal as insufficient and continued to push for an international commission with investigative powers.

## HUMAN RIGHTS DEFENDERS

Congress approved in April the Protection Law for Human Rights Defenders, Journalists, Social Communicators and Justice Officials. The move was welcomed as an important step to protect these groups, but in August a group of civil society organizations wrote to the government to voice concerns about the vagueness and lack of transparency of the draft implementation regulations, and asked to postpone its approval by several months.

Human rights defenders, particularly women, faced threats and violence – abuses which were rarely investigated. The government failed to implement protection measures ordered by the Inter-American Commission on Human Rights (IACHR) and to investigate a series of abuses in recent years against Indigenous Tolupan leaders, including the killings of two of their members by local hitmen during demonstrations in 2013.[1]

In addition to violence, human rights defenders faced judicial harassment in retaliation for their work. Women's rights defender Gladys Lanza Ochoa was convicted of criminally defaming the director of the Foundation for the Development of Urban and Rural Social Housing (FUNDEVI) and sentenced to a year and a half in prison after her organization supported a woman who had accused him of sexual harassment.[2] She remained free as she appealed against her sentence. Journalist Julio Ernesto Alvarado lost a series of appeals against his conviction on charges of criminal defamation against the dean of the economics school at the Autonomous National University of Honduras (UNAH). His sentence included a 16-month ban on practising journalism.

In August, Honduras said it would comply with 2014 recommendations by the IACHR regarding human rights violations committed by the state against environmental activist Carlos Escaleras Mejía, who was murdered in 1997, and members of his family. The IACHR had established that Honduras was responsible for the violation both of Escaleras' right to life, freedom of association and political rights, and of his family's integrity. The recommendations include accepting international responsibility for the state's failure to carry out an effective investigation into the killing, fully investigating the murder and disciplining the officials who failed in their duty.

## IMPUNITY

Although government statistics showed a decrease in homicide rates, the country continued to suffer from a high rate of violent crime which, together with a deficient criminal justice system, resulted in pervasive impunity for human rights abuses. The Alliance for Peace and Justice, a Honduran NGO, found in a 2014 report that fewer than 4% of murder cases resulted in a conviction.

The ineffective criminal justice system and evidence of corruption and human rights violations by police officers contributed to a lack of trust in law enforcement and justice institutions.

## LAND DISPUTES

Local *campesino* organizations in the Bajo Aguán region faced violent attacks and threats in recent years by private security guards with ties to powerful landowners, and abuses by soldiers during evictions related to long-running land disputes. Local organizations in the Bajo Aguán region claim that 90 *campesinos* were killed between 2008 and 2013. Despite the establishment in April 2014 of a special unit in the Attorney General's Office to investigative these killings, there was little progress in the cases.

In September, a forced eviction of *campesinos* in the department of Cortés resulted in the death of a teenager in unclarified circumstances. Peasant farmers said the boy was shot and killed by a policeman but a police spokesperson said the officers who participated in the eviction never fired their weapons, and that the police would launch an investigation.

## LEGAL DEVELOPMENTS

Local civil society groups warned that proposed changes to the Criminal Code before Congress would eliminate language introduced in 2013 to Article 321, which prohibits discrimination on the basis of sexual orientation and gender identity.

---

1. El Estado hondureño debe garantizar la vida e integridad personal de líderes Indígenas Tolupanes (AMR 37/2193/2015)

2. Honduras: Nadie debe ser criminalizado por defender los derechos humanos y Gladys Lanza no puede ser la excepción (AMR 37/001/2015)

# HUNGARY

**Hungary**
Head of state: **János Áder**
Head of government: **Viktor Orbán**

**Hungary constructed fences along its southern borders, criminalized irregular entry to its territory and expedited the return of asylum-seekers and refugees to Serbia, effectively transforming Hungary into a refugee protection-free zone. Roma continued to be at risk of forced eviction and inadequately protected against hate crimes.**

## BACKGROUND

In March, the NGOs Eötvös Károly Institute, Hungarian Helsinki Committee and Hungarian Civil Liberties Union published a report concluding that the replacement of judges of the Constitutional Court and the 2010 constitutional amendments undermined the Court's independence.

## REFUGEES AND ASYLUM-SEEKERS

In response to a significant increase in the number of refugees and migrants entering the country since January, the government adopted measures aimed at keeping them out of the country. On 15 September, the government declared a "state of crisis due to the situation caused by mass immigration". On the same day, the construction of a fence on the border with Serbia was finished, while amendments to the Criminal Code and Asylum Law entered into force, making it an offence to enter the country through the border fence and establishing "transit zones" at the border. On 17 October, a fence on the border with Croatia was completed. Within two days, the number of refugees and migrants entering Hungary daily dropped from over 6,000 to a few dozen. By the end of the year, over 900 people were prosecuted for "illegal border crossing" and subjected to expulsion proceedings.

Criminalization of irregular entry and the sealing off of the borders complemented legislative measures adopted in the summer that had restricted access to asylum more generally. On 1 August, an amendment to the Asylum Law entered into force, authorizing the government to issue a list of "safe countries of origin" and "safe third countries of transit". As a result, asylum applications by people from "safe countries of origin" could be rejected, and those who transited through "safe third countries" before reaching Hungary could be returned to the transit country. Serbia, Macedonia and EU member states, including Greece, were subsequently deemed "safe" by the authorities. This led to concerns expressed by NGOs that the application of the law could lead to the violation of Hungary's obligation of *non-refoulement*, as Hungary would not assess whether an individual applicant would be at risk of serious human rights violations in the country of origin or transit. In October, the European Commission expressed a number of concerns in response to these measures, including that Hungary is carrying out a "possible quasi-systematic dismissal" of asylum applications submitted at the border with Serbia. In December, the European Commission initiated infringement proceedings against Hungary for breaching the EU asylum law.

## FREEDOM OF ASSOCIATION

NGOs critical of government policies faced harassment and threats of losing their registration. In January, four NGOs responsible for managing and distributing the European Economic Area (EEA)/Norway Grants faced a criminal investigation and were threatened with suspension of their tax registration number. The proceedings initiated to withdraw their registration were suspended by the courts in February and May. On 19 June, following a motion submitted by NGOs, the Administrative and Labour Court of Eger requested the Constitutional Court to clarify whether the attempt to suspend the NGOs' registration was in breach of the Basic Law of Hungary (the Constitution). On 5 October, the Constitutional Court found that the procedure did not violate the Constitution.

One of the affected NGOs, the Ökotárs Foundation, reported in January that the Office of the Public Prosecutor was also investigating the lawfulness of activities of two NGOs that received funding from the Grants. In June, it concluded its investigation into the NGOs and found no criminal wrongdoing. In May, the Norwegian Ministry for European Economic Area and EU Affairs announced the results of an independent audit into NGO programmes funded by the Grants in Hungary and concluded that the programmes were run in line with legal requirements.

A district court in Buda held in January that a police raid carried out on the offices of two NGOs in September 2014 following a criminal complaint by the Government Control Office for misappropriation of assets was unlawful.

## DISCRIMINATION – ROMA

Discrimination against Roma in access to housing and the failure to protect Roma and other minorities from hate crimes continued. In June, the European Commission against Racism and Intolerance noted that racist motivation still doesn't feature as a specific aggravating circumstance for offences in the Criminal Code.

### Hate crimes

In September, the County Court in Eger held that police discriminated against Roma in the town of Gyöngyöspata when it failed to protect them from far-right groups in the spring of 2011. The complaint was submitted by the Hungarian Civil Liberties Union, which alleged that police failed to intervene against various paramilitary groups that held patrols in the Roma neighbourhood in Gyöngyöspata for several weeks.

In October, the European Court of Human Rights found in *Balázs v. Hungary* that Hungary had violated the prohibition of discrimination, resulting from the failure to investigate a racist attack against a Romani man in Szeged in 2012. The man suffered bodily injuries and alleged that they were aggravated by the perpetrator's racist motive. The European Court of Human Rights held that the prosecuting authorities failed to identify the racist motive of the crime despite "powerful hate crime indicators", in breach of the European Convention on Human Rights.

### Access to housing

Around 100 families, mainly Roma, remained at risk of forced eviction in the "Numbered Streets" neighbourhood of Miskolc. Between March and June, roughly 120 families were forcibly evicted. Many had to move in with relatives, to houses requiring renovation, or face homelessness. The vast majority of previously evicted families were not provided with adequate alternative housing or compensation.

On 14 May, Hungary's highest court ruled that the Miskolc municipality violated the country's equal treatment legislation when it forcibly evicted hundreds of Roma from a long-established neighbourhood, as well as their rights to a private and family life and to freedom of movement.

On 5 June, the Office of the Commissioner for Fundamental Rights published a report on the situation in Miskolc, criticizing the municipality's approach to so-called "slum clearance". The report also urged the municipality to prevent evictions, develop a plan for families facing homelessness and devise a holistic approach with the Ministry of Human Capacities to deal with slum eliminations.

In July, the Equal Treatment Authority upheld a discrimination complaint by the Hungarian NGO NEKI against the municipality. The municipality's appeal was pending at the end of the year.

## FREEDOM OF RELIGION

Freedom of religion continued to be restricted. Following the 2011 Church Law that required churches and other religious organizations to re-register and the 2014 European Court of Human Rights judgment in *Magyar Keresztény Mennonita Egyház and others v. Hungary*, which held that the deregistration had violated the right to religious freedom, the government proposed an amendment to the law in September. However, according to the NGO Forum for Religious Freedom, the amendment did not address the arbitrariness of the deregistration procedure that was criticized by the European Court of Human Rights. The Forum further voiced concerns that a number of religious communities would continue to be denied rights they held previously as churches.

# INDIA

**Republic of India**
Head of state: **Pranab Mukherjee**
Head of government: **Narendra Modi**

**Authorities clamped down on civil society organizations critical of official policies, and increased restrictions on foreign funding. Religious tensions intensified, and gender- and caste-based discrimination and violence remained pervasive. Censorship and attacks on freedom of expression by hardline Hindu groups grew. Scores of artists, writers and scientists returned national honours in**

protest against what they said was a climate of growing intolerance. Controversial land acquisition measures were dropped following popular opposition. Abuses by armed groups continued to threaten civilians, but a historic peace framework agreement was reached in Nagaland. The criminal justice system remained flawed, violating fair trial rights and failing to ensure justice for abuses. Extrajudicial executions and torture and other ill-treatment persisted.

## ABUSES BY ARMED GROUPS

In March, three men were tortured and killed in Lohardaga, Jharkhand state, allegedly by Maoist fighters. In May, around 250 villagers were abducted and held hostage for a day in Sukma, Chhattisgarh state, reportedly by Maoist fighters attempting to pressurize the state government to stop work on a bridge. Maoist armed groups were accused of threatening and intimidating Adivasi (Indigenous) people and occupying schools.

In Jammu and Kashmir state, armed groups threatened mobile phone operators and attacked mobile towers and telecom offices in May, June and July, killing two people. In September, unidentified gunmen killed a three-year-old boy and his father in Sopore. The same month, the bodies of four armed group members suspected to have been killed by rival groups were found in the state.

In July, armed group members attacked a police station and bus station in Gurdaspur, Punjab state, killing three civilians.

In August, the government announced a peace agreement with the National Socialist Council of Nagaland (Isak-Muivah faction) armed group, which civil society groups said could improve the human rights situation in Nagaland state and parts of northeast India.

## ARBITRARY ARRESTS AND DETENTIONS

Human rights defenders, journalists and protesters continued to face arbitrary arrests and detentions. Over 3,200 people were being held in January under administrative detention on executive orders without charge or trial. Authorities also continued to use "anti-terror" laws such as the Unlawful Activities (Prevention) Act and other state-specific laws which do not meet international human rights standards.

In April, the state government of Gujarat passed an anti-terror bill containing several provisions which violated international standards. The bill was pending approval by the President in December. Similar laws remained in force in Maharashtra and Karnataka states.

## CASTE-BASED DISCRIMINATION AND VIOLENCE

Incidents of violence against Dalits and Adivasis were reported from states including Uttar Pradesh, Bihar, Karnataka and Tamil Nadu. According to statistics released in August, over 47,000 crimes against members of Scheduled Castes, and over 11,000 crimes against members of Scheduled Tribes, were reported in 2014. In October, two Dalit children were burned to death in an arson attack near Delhi, allegedly by dominant caste men.

In December, Parliament amended the Scheduled Castes and the Scheduled Tribes (Prevention of Atrocities) Act, recognizing several new offences. The amendments also required that special courts be established to try these offences and that victims and witnesses receive protection.

In July, an official census stated that over 180,000 households were engaged in "manual scavenging" – the practice of cleaning human waste carried out mainly by Dalit people. Activists said the figure was an underestimate.

Dominant castes continued to use sexual violence against Dalit and Adivasi women and girls.

## CHILDREN'S RIGHTS

A legal requirement that private schools reserve 25% of places at the entry level for children from disadvantaged families continued to be poorly enforced. Dalit and

Adivasi children continued to face discrimination.

In December, Parliament passed amendments to juvenile justice laws which allowed children aged 16 to 18 to be treated as adults in cases of serious crimes, in violation of India's international legal obligations.

In May, the cabinet approved amendments to child labour laws which prohibited the employment of children under 14. The amendments made an exception for children working in family enterprises or in the entertainment industry, which activists said would encourage child labour and disproportionately affect children from marginalized groups and girls.

## COMMUNAL AND ETHNIC VIOLENCE

Authorities failed to prevent hundreds of incidents of communal violence across the country. Some politicians contributed to religious tensions by making speeches justifying discrimination and violence. At least four Muslim men were killed in attacks by mobs which suspected them of stealing, smuggling or slaughtering cows.

In September, a commission investigating communal violence in Muzaffarnagar, Uttar Pradesh state, in 2013 submitted a report which journalists said blamed members of political parties, police and senior administrative officials.

In February, the government formed a team to reinvestigate closed cases related to the 1984 Sikh massacre and file charges. The team's term was extended for a year in August.

At least eight people were killed in ethnic clashes in Manipur state over demands for regulating the entry of non-domicile people into the region, and the enactment of laws affecting the rights of Indigenous people.

## CORPORATE ACCOUNTABILITY

In February, the government introduced a bill to amend India's land acquisition law which removed requirements related to obtaining consent and conducting impact assessments for a range of industrial projects. Following nationwide opposition from farmers' groups, civil society and political parties, the government said in August that it would not pursue the amendments. Many industries, including public sector coal mines, railways and highways, were still not required to obtain the consent of Indigenous communities or conduct social impact assessments.

Vulnerable communities in resource-rich areas remained at risk of forced evictions. The Environment Ministry sought to abolish a requirement for consent from village assemblies for certain infrastructure projects.

In April, the Environment Ministry rejected an offer from the UN Environment Programme to assess the spread of toxic wastes at the site of the 1984 Bhopal gas leak disaster. In August, the Madhya Pradesh state government incinerated 10 tonnes of the waste in Pithampur, 250km from Bhopal, which activists said had violated Supreme Court orders and endangered the health of local residents.

## DEATH PENALTY

In August, two MPs introduced bills seeking abolition of the death penalty. The State Assembly of Tripura passed a unanimous resolution urging the central government to abolish capital punishment for murder.

In August, the Law Commission of India submitted a report to the government favouring speedy abolition of the death penalty. The Commission said that the death penalty in India is "an irreversible punishment in an imperfect, fragile and fallible system" but recommended that it be retained for terrorism-related offences and "waging war against the state".

## EXTRAJUDICIAL EXECUTIONS

In March, a Delhi court acquitted 16 policemen accused of killing 42 Muslim men in Hashimpura, Uttar Pradesh, in 1987. The court stated it could not convict anyone because of the "scanty, unreliable and faulty investigation".

In April, Andhra Pradesh police and forest

officials shot dead 20 suspected smugglers in an alleged extrajudicial execution. The same month, police killed five pre-trial detainees in Telangana who were being taken to court, claiming they had attempted to overpower them. Police investigations into both incidents were ongoing at the end of the year.

A Central Bureau of Investigation Court discharged several police officials suspected of involvement in an extrajudicial execution in Gujarat in 2005. In June, the UN Special Rapporteur on extrajudicial executions noted in a follow-up report on India that guidelines by courts and the National Human Rights Commission often "remained on paper with little or no implementation on the ground".

In July, the Supreme Court ordered the central government, Manipur state government and National Human Rights Commission to file a report on over 1,500 cases of alleged extrajudicial executions in Manipur.

## FREEDOM OF ASSOCIATION

Authorities took several measures to repress civil society organizations, including using the Foreign Contribution (Regulation) Act (FCRA) – which restricted organizations from receiving foreign funding – to harass NGOs and activists.

The government took a series of actions against Greenpeace India, including preventing one of its campaigners from travelling to the UK in January, ordering the organization's bank accounts to be frozen in April and cancelling its FCRA registration in September. High Courts ruled that some of these steps were illegal.

The Ministry of Home Affairs cancelled the FCRA registration of thousands of NGOs for violating provisions of the law. In April, the Ministry ordered that it would have to approve foreign funds from certain identified donor organizations.

In July, the Central Bureau of Investigation registered a case against human rights activists Teesta Setalvad and Javed Anand for allegedly violating provisions of the FCRA. In September, authorities suspended the registration of an NGO run by the activists to receive foreign funding.

## FREEDOM OF EXPRESSION

Laws which did not meet international standards on freedom of expression were used to persecute human rights defenders and others. In January, two activists were arrested in Kerala for possessing "pro-Maoist" literature. In October, a Dalit folk singer was arrested in Tamil Nadu for writing songs criticizing the state government and Chief Minister.

In March, the Supreme Court struck down Section 66A of the Information Technology Act as being vague and overly broad. The law had been used to prosecute people for legitimately exercising their right to free speech online.

In August, the Maharashtra state government issued a circular on how India's sedition law must be applied, suggesting that criticism of a government representative would amount to sedition. It withdrew the circular in October. In December, an MP introduced a bill in Parliament seeking revision of the sedition law.

There were several instances of intimidation and attacks against journalists, authors, artists and human rights defenders by religious and caste-based groups. Two rationalist writers were killed in attacks thought to be related to their criticism of religious intolerance and idolatry.

In July, the government argued before the Supreme Court that privacy was not a fundamental right under the Constitution. In September, authorities proposed – and withdrew after facing opposition – a draft encryption policy which would have threatened free expression and privacy.

Authorities restricted access to internet services on several occasions, including in Gujarat and Jammu and Kashmir states, on grounds of public order.

## IMPUNITY – SECURITY FORCES

Impunity for violations by security forces persisted. Legislation providing virtual immunity from prosecution such as the Armed Forces Special Powers Act (AFSPA) remained in force in Jammu and Kashmir state and parts of northeast India.

In February, the Ministry of Home Affairs officially rejected the report of a committee set up in 2004 to review the AFSPA, which recommended the repeal of the law. In June, the state of Tripura withdrew the AFSPA 18 years after it was introduced "in view of the decrease of militancy-related incidents". In July, a committee appointed to evaluate the status of women recommended the repeal of the AFSPA. In November, the Meghalaya High Court directed the central government to consider enforcing the AFSPA in one region to maintain law and order.

In September, the Indian Army confirmed life sentences for six of its personnel found guilty by a military court of killing three men in Machil, Jammu and Kashmir in an extrajudicial execution in 2010.

## PROLONGED PRE-TRIAL DETENTION

Prolonged pre-trial detention and overcrowding in jails remained widespread. As of January, over 282,000 prisoners – 68% of the total prison population – were pre-trial detainees. Dalits, Adivasis and Muslims continued to be disproportionately represented.

A 2014 Supreme Court order directing district judges to release pre-trial detainees who had been held for over half of the term they would have served if convicted was poorly implemented.

In September, the central information commission, responding to an Amnesty International India application, said that state governments were obligated to periodically provide information to authorities and prisoners about detainees' eligibility for release.

## RIGHTS OF LESBIAN, GAY, BISEXUAL, TRANSGENDER AND INTERSEX PEOPLE

In April, the upper house of Parliament passed a bill to protect the rights of transgender people, including their rights to education and health care. Attacks on transgender people continued.

Section 377 of the Penal Code continued to be used to criminalize same-sex relations between consenting adults. Senior government officials made contradictory statements about whether the law should be retained. In December, the introduction of a bill to decriminalize same-sex relations was defeated in the lower house of Parliament.

In August, the state government of Delhi proposed a draft bill on women's rights which specified equality before the law for every woman "irrespective of her sexual orientation", the first time a state government had recognized discrimination on the basis of sexual orientation in law.

## TORTURE AND OTHER ILL-TREATMENT

Torture and other ill-treatment in police and judicial custody were reported. In July, the Supreme Court directed state governments to install closed-circuit television cameras in all prisons within two years to prevent torture and other violations of prisoners' rights, and to consider installing them in all police stations. Also in July, the Ministry of Home Affairs stated that the government was considering amending the Penal Code to specifically recognize torture as a crime. In November, the Chhattisgarh police began investigating allegations that security force personnel had raped two women and a girl the previous month.

NGOs continued to report deaths from torture of prisoners while in police custody. Statistics released in August showed that 93 cases of deaths and 197 cases of rapes in police custody were reported in 2014. In August the National Human Rights Commission recorded 1,327 deaths in judicial custody between April 2014 and January 2015.

## VIOLENCE AGAINST WOMEN AND GIRLS

Although nearly 322,000 crimes against women, including over 37,000 cases of rape, were reported in 2014, stigma and discrimination from police officials and authorities continued to deter women from reporting sexual violence. A majority of states continued to lack standard operating procedures for the police to deal with cases of violence against women.

In over 86% of reported rape cases, the survivors knew the alleged offenders. Statistics released in August showed that nearly 123,000 cases of cruelty by husbands or relatives were reported in 2014. In March, the central government announced that it was considering allowing for the withdrawal of a complaint of cruelty if a compromise is reached between the parties.

In July, a committee appointed to evaluate the status of women made key recommendations on prevention, protection and access to justice for women and girls facing violence. Among other recommendations, it urged the government to make rape within marriage a criminal offence, introduce a special law on honour crimes, and not dilute laws relating to cruelty by husbands.

In December, the government stated in Parliament that it intended to amend the Penal Code to criminalize marital rape.

Caste-based village bodies continued to order sexually violent punishments for perceived social transgressions. Discrimination and violence against women from marginalized communities remained widespread, but reporting and conviction rates were low.

# INDONESIA

**Republic of Indonesia**
Head of state and government: **Joko Widodo**

**Security forces faced allegations of human rights violations, including the use of unnecessary or excessive force. Arbitrary arrests of peaceful protesters, especially in Papua, occurred throughout the year. The government restricted activities marking the 50th anniversary of the serious human rights violations of 1965-1966.**

**Harassment, intimidation and attacks against religious minorities occurred throughout the country. A new Acehnese Islamic Criminal Code came into force in October, expanding the use of corporal punishment to include consensual sexual relations. There were 14 executions.**

## BACKGROUND

Despite commitments made during his election campaign in 2014, President Joko Widodo failed to address past human rights violations. Freedom of expression was further restricted and the use of the death penalty for drug-related offences increased.

## POLICE AND SECURITY FORCES

Reports continued of human rights violations by police and military, including unlawful killings, unnecessary and excessive use of force, torture and other cruel, inhuman or degrading treatment or punishment.

In March, members of the Police Mobile Brigade (Brimob) attacked residents in Morekau village, Seram Bagian Barat District, Maluku province, after they had complained to Brimob officers who had entered the village that they were disturbing a religious ceremony. Thirteen people were seriously injured. Despite promises of an investigation by the head of the regional police, no charges were brought.

In August, off-duty military personnel shot dead two people after opening fire in front of a church in Timika, Papua province. Also in Timika, police shot two unarmed high school students during a "security operation" in September, killing one.

In Jakarta, the provincial police force used unnecessary force against protesters at a peaceful labour rally in October. Police arrested and beat 23 protesters, as well as two legal aid activists who reported injuries to the head, face and stomach. Police blamed the protesters for the violence. All were released after being charged with threatening public officials and refusal to disperse.

## IMPUNITY

More than 10 years after the murder of prominent human rights defender Munir Said Thalib, the authorities had failed to bring all the perpetrators to justice.

September marked the 50th anniversary of the serious human rights violations of 1965-66. Human rights organizations have documented a range of human rights violations in the context of the abortive 1965 coup, including unlawful killings, torture including rape, enforced disappearances, sexual slavery and other crimes of sexual violence, slavery, arbitrary arrest and detention, forced displacement and forced labour. An estimated 500,000 to one million people were killed during that time and hundreds of thousands were held without charge or trial for periods ranging from a few days to more than 14 years. Although no legal impediments to full citizenship remained for victims of these crimes, a culture of impunity continued to exist for perpetrators.

In May, the Attorney General announced that the government would establish a non-judicial mechanism to resolve past human rights violations through a "reconciliation committee". It was seen by human rights groups as a small but positive step following decades of impunity for past human rights violations and abuses that occurred during the rule of former President Suharto (1965-1998). However, victims and NGOs remained concerned that this process would prioritize reconciliation and undermine efforts at truth and justice.

In 2015, the people of Aceh commemorated the 10th anniversary of the 2005 Helsinki Peace Agreement between the government and the armed pro-independence Free Aceh Movement. The agreement ended a 29-year conflict during which between 10,000 and 30,000 people were killed, many of them civilians. In November, the Aceh House of People's Representatives appointed a team charged with appointing commissioners for the Aceh Truth and Reconciliation Commission, a body set up to examine abuses that occurred during the conflict. Some provisions in the by-law under which the Commission was created fell short of international law and standards. Its mandate was limited to genocide, crimes against humanity and war crimes and did not include other crimes under international law including torture, extrajudicial executions and enforced disappearances.[1]

Investigations into shootings, torture and other ill-treatment by police and the military continued to stagnate. Despite promises from President Widodo for a thorough investigation into the December 2014 incident in which security forces shot dead four students in Paniai, no one had been brought to justice by the end of the year.[2]

## FREEDOM OF EXPRESSION

Prisoner of conscience Filep Karma was released on 19 November after spending more than a decade in prison for his peaceful political expression. This was the latest in a positive but limited step by the authorities to increase freedom in Papua and West Papua provinces. In May, the President granted clemency to five political activists in Papua province imprisoned for breaking into a military compound, and pledged to grant clemency or an amnesty to other political activists.

Prisoners of conscience, including Johan Teterissa in Maluku, remained imprisoned for peaceful demonstrations under articles of the Indonesian Criminal Code relating to *makar* (rebellion).[3] At least 27 prisoners in Papua also remained imprisoned under these articles, and 29 prisoners of conscience from Maluku remained imprisoned.

The arrest and detention of peaceful activists also continued in Papua and West Papua provinces. In May, authorities arrested 264 peaceful activists who had planned peaceful protests marking the 52nd anniversary of the handover of Papua to the Indonesian government by the UN.[4] A further 216 members of the West Papua National Committee (KNPB) were arbitrarily detained for participating in peaceful demonstrations in support of Papua's application to join the

Melanesian Spearhead Group – a sub-Pacific intergovernmental organization. While most were later released, 12 were charged for participating in the protest, including under the "rebellion" laws.[5]

President Widodo announced in May that restrictions on foreign journalists applying to visit Papua were to be lifted; this had not been implemented fully by the end of the year. In early October, three Papuan male activists who had accompanied a French journalist to Pegunungan Bintang District in Papua to cover the activities of the KNPB were arrested and interrogated by the local immigration officer about the activities of the journalist. They were held for 10 hours before being released without charge.

Convictions continued to be documented throughout the year of people peacefully expressing their views under laws concerning criminal defamation, blasphemy and "hate speech".

In March, the Bandung District Court sentenced a woman to five months' imprisonment after she had written a "private" message to a friend on Facebook accusing her husband of abusing her. He reported her to the police after finding the accusation when he accessed her account and she was charged under Article 27(1) of the Electronic Information and Transaction Law (Law No.11/2008) with "transmitting electronic content that violated decency".[6] A further three people were convicted of criminal defamation under the law in Yogyakarta, South Sulawesi and Central Java during the year.

The government continued to restrict activities relating to the serious human rights violations of 1965-1966. In October, police in Salatiga, Central Java, confiscated and burned hundreds of copies of *Lentera* magazine, run by the Satya Wacana University's Faculty of Social and Communication Studies in Salatiga, because it featured an in-depth report and front cover commemorating the 50th anniversary of the violations. That same month, the Ubud Writers and Readers Festival removed three panel sessions related to these human rights violations after authorities threatened to revoke their permit.[7]

At least six people remain detained or imprisoned under blasphemy laws. In January, six members of Gafatar, a national cultural movement that was criticized by Islamic organizations who believed it promoted "deviant" beliefs, were arrested in Banda Aceh in Aceh Province and charged under Article 156 of the Criminal Code for insulting religion. In June the head of the group was sentenced to four years' imprisonment.

In October, police passed a new national regulation (Surat Edaran No. SE/6/X/2015) on hate speech. Although the regulation refers to expression "aimed to inflict hatred or hostility [against] individuals", civil society activists were concerned that they may be used to charge individuals accused of criminal and religious defamation.

## FREEDOM OF RELIGION AND BELIEF

Harassment, intimidation and attacks against religious minorities persisted, fuelled by discriminatory laws and regulations at both national and local levels.

In July, members of the Christian Evangelical Church (Gereja Injil di Indonesia, GIDI) burned down a Muslim place of worship in Karubaga, Tolikara District, Papua province, where Muslims were celebrating Eid al-Fitr. Members of GIDI originally had gathered to complain that the noise from the place of worship was interrupting a church event. Security officials from both the military and police shot into the crowd, killing one man. GIDI youths then destroyed the Muslim place of worship and several shops in the vicinity. Two men were arrested for inciting violence.

In October, Christian churches were attacked by a group of at least 200 people in Aceh Singkil District after the local government ordered the destruction of 10 churches in the district, citing provincial and district level by-laws limiting houses of worship. The attackers burned down one church and attempted to attack another but were stopped by local security forces. One assailant was killed during the violence and approximately 4,000 Christians fled to neighbouring North Sumatra Province immediately afterwards. Ten people were arrested. The Aceh Singkil government went ahead with its plans to destroy the remaining churches.[8]

In November, a place of worship of a local Indigenous beliefs community in Rembang, Central Java, was burned down by a mob during the process of renovation. Before the attack, the community leader had received a threat by a local Islamic organization and was also asked by the Rembang District head of government to stop the renovation. At the end of 2015 no one had been held accountable for the attack.

The situation of a number of religious minority communities who had been subject to harassment, violence and forced eviction remained uncertain. Three years after local authorities evicted a community of Shi'a Muslims in Sampang, East Java, after an anti-Shi'a mob threatened violence, 300 members remained displaced from their homes.[9]

Members of the Presbyterian Yasmin Church and the Filadelfia Church continued to hold congregations outside the presidential palace in Jakarta in response to their churches remaining sealed off in Bogor and Bekasi respectively. Although the Supreme Court overturned the Bogor administration's revocation of the Yasmin Church's building permit in 2011, the Bogor city government continued to refuse to allow the church to reopen.

## CRUEL, INHUMAN OR DEGRADING PUNISHMENT

At least 108 people were caned in Aceh under Shari'a law for gambling, drinking alcohol or "adultery" during the year. In October, the Acehnese Islamic Criminal Code came into force, expanding the use of corporal punishment for same-sex sexual relations and intimacy between unmarried individuals, with punishment of up to 100 and

30 lashes respectively. The by-law makes it difficult for victims of rape to seek justice, as the victims themselves now need to provide evidence of rape. False accusations of rape or adultery were also punishable by caning.[10]

## DEATH PENALTY

Fourteen prisoners were executed in January and April, 12 of whom were foreign nationals. All of these related to drug-trafficking offences, for which President Widodo had previously stated he would refuse to consider any clemency applications.[11] The government allocated funding to conduct further executions in 2016. At least 131 people remained under sentence of death.

---

1. Indonesia: Appointment of Aceh Truth Commission selection team a step closer to truth and reparation for victims (ASA 21/2976/2015)
2. Indonesia: Paniai shootings – make investigation findings public and bring perpetrators to justice (ASA 21/0001/2015)
3. Indonesia: Release Johan Teterissa and other prisoners of conscience (ASA 21/1972/2015)
4. Indonesia: End attacks on freedom of expression in Papua (ASA 21/1606/2015)
5. Indonesia: End mass arbitrary arrests of peaceful protesters in Papua (ASA 21/1851/2015)
6. Indonesia: Two women convicted under internet law for social media posts (ASA 21/1381/2015)
7. Indonesia: Stop silencing public discussions on 1965 violations (ASA 21/2785/2015)
8. Indonesia: Christian minority in Aceh under threat (ASA 21/2756/2015)
9. Indonesia: Three years later, forcibly evicted Sampang Shi'a community still wanting to go home (ASA 21/2335/2015)
10. Indonesia: Repeal or revise all provisions in the new Aceh Islamic Criminal Code that violate human rights (ASA 21/2726/2015)
11. Flawed justice: Unfair trials and the death penalty in Indonesia (ASA 21/2434/2015)

# IRAN

**Islamic Republic of Iran**
Head of state: **Ayatollah Sayed 'Ali Khamenei (Leader of the Islamic Republic of Iran)**
Head of government: **Hassan Rouhani (President)**

The authorities severely curtailed the rights to freedom of expression, association and assembly, arresting and imprisoning journalists, human rights defenders, trade unionists and others who voiced dissent, on vague and overly broad charges. Torture and other ill-treatment of detainees remained common and was committed with impunity; prison conditions were harsh. Unfair trials continued, in some cases resulting in death sentences. Women and members of ethnic and religious minorities faced pervasive discrimination in law and in practice. The authorities carried out cruel punishments, including blinding, amputation and floggings. Courts imposed death sentences for a range of crimes; many prisoners, including at least four juvenile offenders, were executed.

## BACKGROUND

Negotiations between Iran and the five permanent member states of the UN Security Council, plus Germany, resulted with Iran agreeing in July to restrict its nuclear development programme in return for the lifting of international sanctions.

In March, the UN Human Rights Council renewed the mandate of the UN Special Rapporteur on the situation of human rights in Iran; the Iranian authorities continued to deny him entry to Iran and to prevent access by other UN experts. The Human Rights Council also formally adopted the outcome of its second UPR of Iran. Iran accepted 130 recommendations, partially accepted 59 others, and rejected 102. Those rejected included recommendations that Iran ratify the UN Convention against Torture and CEDAW, and cease using the death penalty against those aged under 18 at the time of the alleged crime.

## FREEDOMS OF EXPRESSION, ASSOCIATION AND ASSEMBLY

The authorities continued to severely restrict freedoms of expression, association and assembly. They blocked Facebook, Twitter and other social media websites, closed or suspended media outlets including the *Zanan* monthly women's magazine, jammed foreign satellite television stations, arrested and imprisoned journalists and online and other critics, and suppressed peaceful protests.

In August, the Ministry of Communications and Information Technology announced the second phase of "intelligent filtering" of websites deemed to have socially harmful consequences, with the support of a foreign company. The authorities continued efforts to create a "national internet" that could be used to further impede access to information via the internet, and arrested and prosecuted those who used social media to express dissent.[1] In June, a spokesperson for the judiciary said that the authorities had arrested five people for "anti-revolutionary" activities using social media, and five others for "acts against decency in cyber-space".

Opposition leaders Mir Hossein Mousavi, Zahra Rahnavard and Mehdi Karoubi remained under house arrest without charge or trial. Scores of prisoners of conscience continued to be detained or were serving prison sentences for peacefully exercising their human rights. They included journalists, artists, writers, lawyers, trade unionists, students, women's and minority rights activists, human rights defenders and others.

Under the 2013 Islamic Penal Code, individuals convicted of multiple charges must serve only the lengthiest single sentence, but judges are required to impose sentences that exceed the statutory maximum for any single offence when they convict defendants of more than three crimes. This has resulted in the authorities bringing multiple spurious charges against some peaceful critics as a means to ensure a lengthy prison term.[2]

The authorities continued to suppress peaceful protests. On 22 July, police temporarily arrested scores and dispersed thousands of teachers who gathered outside Parliament in the capital, Tehran, to protest against the authorities' harassment of teachers engaged in trade union activities and related protests, and demand the release of prominent trade unionists, including Ismail Abdi, who remained in detention.[3]

## TORTURE AND OTHER ILL-TREATMENT

Detainees and prisoners continued to report acts of torture and other ill-treatment, particularly during primary investigations mainly to force "confessions" or gather other incriminatory evidence.

A new Code of Criminal Procedures, which entered into force in June, introduced some safeguards including central electronic registers of detainees held in each province. However, the new Code did not provide adequate protection against torture and failed to bring Iranian law into conformity with international law and standards. The Code failed to guarantee individuals adequate access to an independent lawyer from the time of arrest, a legal requirement for protection against torture and other ill-treatment. No specific crime of torture is defined in Iranian law and the new Code failed to establish detailed procedures for investigating torture allegations. Moreover, while the Code excludes statements obtained through torture as admissible evidence, it does so only in general terms, without providing detailed provisions.

Detainees and sentenced prisoners were denied adequate medical care; in some cases, the authorities withheld prescribed medications to punish prisoners, or failed to comply with medical doctors' recommendations that prisoners should be hospitalized for treatment.[4] The authorities also frequently subjected detainees and prisoners to prolonged solitary confinement amounting to torture or other ill-treatment.

Prisoners were kept in severely overcrowded and insanitary conditions with inadequate food and exposed to extreme temperatures. This included prisoners in Dizel Abad Prison in Kermanshah, Adel Abad Prison in Shiraz, Gharchak Prison in Varamin, and Vakilabad Prison in Mashhad. According to some former detainees, in Tabriz Central Prison, some 700 to 800 prisoners were held in three poorly ventilated, insanitary cells with access to only 10 toilets. The authorities often disregarded prison regulations which required that different categories of detainees and prisoners be held in separate prison sections, prompting hunger strikes by some political prisoners, including prisoners of conscience. The death of at least one prisoner of conscience, Shahrokh Zamani, was reported, possibly attributable to poor prison conditions and inconsistent medical care.

### Cruel, inhuman or degrading punishment

Courts continued to impose, and the authorities continued to carry out, punishments that violate the prohibition of torture and other cruel, inhuman or degrading punishment. These were sometimes carried out in public and included flogging, blinding and amputations. On 3 March the authorities in Karaj deliberately blinded a man in his left eye after a court sentenced him to "retribution-in-kind" (*qesas*) for throwing acid into the face of another man. He also faced blinding of his right eye. The authorities postponed punishment of another prisoner scheduled for 3 March; he was sentenced to blinding and being made deaf.[5]

On 28 June, authorities at the Central Prison in Mashhad, Khorasan Province, amputated four fingers from the right hands of two men sentenced for theft, apparently without anaesthetic.[6]

Sentences of flogging were also carried out. In June, a Deputy Prosecutor General in Shiraz announced that 500 people had been arrested and 480 of them had been tried and convicted within 24 hours for publicly breaking their fast during Ramadan. Most received flogging sentences administered by the Office for Implementation of Sentences. Some floggings were reportedly carried out in public.

## UNFAIR TRIALS

Many trials, including some that resulted in death sentences, were grossly unfair. Prior to trial, the accused were frequently detained for weeks or months during which they had little or no access to lawyers or their families, and were coerced into writing or signing . "confessions" that were then used as the main evidence against them in unfair proceedings. Judges routinely dismissed defendants' allegations of torture and other ill-treatment in pre-trial detention without ordering investigations.

After years of deliberation, the new Code of Criminal Procedures took effect in June. It brought about some improvements, including stricter regulation of interrogations and the requirement that detainees be informed of their rights, but it was seriously weakened by amendments approved only days before its entry into force. These included an amendment that restricted the right of detainees in national security cases to be represented by lawyers of their own choosing during the often lengthy investigation phase; instead, they can only choose a lawyer approved by the Head of the Judiciary. The Code applied the same restriction to suspects in cases of organized crime, which can result in sentences of death, life imprisonment or amputation.[7] Responding to criticism of the amendments, a senior judiciary official said, "the issue is that there are individuals among lawyers who could be trouble makers". In some cases, it appeared that courts had extended the restriction on defendants' right to a lawyer of their own choosing to the trial phase.

Special courts, including the Special Court for the Clergy which was effectively established outside the law, and the Revolutionary Courts, continued to function without observing international fair trial standards. The judiciary was not independent and courts remained susceptible to pressure from security authorities, such as the Ministry of Intelligence and Revolutionary Guards, to convict defendants and impose harsh penalties.[8]

## FREEDOM OF RELIGION AND BELIEF

Members of religious minorities, including Baha'is, Sufis, Yaresan (Ahl-e Haq), Christian converts from Islam, Sunni Muslims, and Shi'a Muslims who became Sunni, faced discrimination in employment and restrictions on their access to education and freedom to practise their faith. There were reports of arrest and imprisonment of dozens of Baha'is, Christian converts and members of other religious minorities, including for providing education for Baha'i students who are denied access to higher education.

The authorities continued to destroy sacred sites of Baha'is, Sunnis and Sufis including their cemeteries and places of worship.

In August, a Revolutionary Court in Tehran convicted Mohammad Ali Taheri of "spreading corruption on earth" for establishing a spiritual doctrine and group called Erfan-e Halgheh, and sentenced him to death. He had previously received a five-year prison term and been sentenced to 74 lashes and a fine in 2011 for allegedly "insulting Islamic sanctities".[9] Prison sentences were also issued against several of his followers. In December, the Supreme Court overturned his sentence due to "incomplete investigations" and remanded the case to the Court of First Instance.

## DISCRIMINATION – ETHNIC MINORITIES

Iran's disadvantaged ethnic groups, including Ahwazi Arabs, Azerbaijani Turks, Baluchis, Kurds and Turkmen, continued to report that the state authorities systematically discriminated against them, particularly in employment, housing, access to political office, and the exercise of cultural, civil and political rights. They remained unable to use their own language as a medium of instruction for primary education. Those who called for greater cultural and linguistic rights faced arrest, imprisonment, and in some cases the death penalty.

Security forces disproportionately repressed

protests by ethnic minorities including Ahwazi Arabs, Azerbaijani Turks and Kurds. Between March and April, the authorities were reported to have carried out many arrests in the Arab-populated Khuzestan province, including after a football match in March where Ahwazi Arab young men displayed a banner in solidarity with Younes Asakereh, an Ahwazi Arab street vendor who died on 22 March after setting himself alight in a protest against the city authorities. He was apparently left without emergency medical treatment due to lack of funds. The arrests took place in the lead-up to the 10th anniversary of mass anti-government demonstrations in Khuzestan in April 2005 following the publication of a letter that referred to government plans to implement policies that would reduce the population of Arabs in Khuzestan. During the protest, police were reported to have particularly targeted men wearing traditional Arab clothing for arrest and beatings.[10]

In November, several individuals belonging to the Azerbaijani Turk ethnic group were reported to have been arrested, after largely peaceful demonstrations erupted in several cities in protest against a television programme that members of the Azerbaijani Turk community considered offensive.

On 7 May, riot police were reported to have used excessive or unnecessary force to disperse demonstrators in Mahabad, a city in West Azerbaijan province largely populated by members of the Kurdish minority, who were protesting after a Kurdish woman fell to her death in unclear circumstances.

## WOMEN'S RIGHTS
Women remained subject to discrimination under the law, particularly criminal and family law, and in practice. Women and girls also faced new challenges to their sexual and reproductive health and rights. Parliament debated several draft laws that would further erode women's rights, including the Bill to Increase Fertility Rates and Prevent Population Decline, which would block access to information about contraception

and outlaw voluntary sterilization. The general principles of another draft law, the Comprehensive Population and Exaltation of Family Bill, were passed in Parliament on 2 November. If enacted, the law would require all private and public entities to prioritize, in sequence, men with children, married men without children and married women with children when recruiting staff. The law also risks further entrenching domestic violence as a private "family matter".

In practice, women continued to have reduced access to affordable modern contraception as the authorities failed to restore the budget of the state family planning programme cut in 2012.

Women and girls remained inadequately protected against sexual and other violence, including early and forced marriage. The authorities failed to adopt laws criminalizing these and other abuses, such as marital rape and domestic violence. Compulsory "veiling" (hijab) laws also continued to empower police and paramilitary forces to target women for harassment, violence and imprisonment.

The authorities came under local and international pressure to allow women access as spectators to international men's volleyball matches in Tehran's Azadi Stadium but continued to exclude them in the face of opposition from ultra-conservative groups, such as Ansar Hezbollah.

## DEATH PENALTY
The authorities continued to use the death penalty extensively, and carried out numerous executions, including of juvenile offenders. Some executions were conducted in public.

The courts imposed numerous death sentences, often after unfair trials and for offences such as drugs offences that did not meet the threshold of most serious crimes under international law. The majority of those executed during the year were sentenced on drugs charges; others were executed for murder or after being convicted on vague charges such as "enmity against God".

Many detainees accused of capital offences

were denied access to legal counsel during the investigative phase when they were held in detention. The new Code of Criminal Procedures repealed Article 32 of the 2011 Anti-Narcotics Law, which had denied prisoners sentenced to death on drugs charges a right of appeal. It remained unclear, however, whether those sentenced before the Code took effect would be eligible to appeal.

Scores of juvenile offenders remained on death row. Several juvenile offenders were re-sentenced to death after receiving a retrial pursuant to the new juvenile sentencing guidelines of the 2013 Islamic Penal Code. Amnesty International was able to confirm the execution of at least three juvenile offenders: Javad Saberi, hanged on 15 April, Samad Zahabi, hanged on 5 October, and Fatemeh Salbehi, hanged on 13 October. Human rights groups reported that another juvenile offender, Vazir Amroddin, an Afghan national, was hanged in June or July. In February, the authorities transferred Saman Naseem, sentenced in 2013 for a crime that was committed when he was aged 17, to an undisclosed location prompting fears and wide international concern that he was about to be executed. He was subjected to enforced disappearance for five months; the authorities ultimately permitted him to phone his family in July, and confirmed to his lawyer that the Supreme Court had ordered his retrial in April.[11]

The Islamic Penal Code continued to provide for stoning as a method of execution; at least two stoning sentences were issued but no executions by stoning were reported during the year.

1. Iran: Film producer given jail term after unfair trial: Mostafa Azizi (MDE 13/2272/2015); Iran: Couple sentenced to jail on security charges (MDE 13/2520/2015)

2. Iran: Harsh prison sentences for two female activists highlight rampant injustice (News story, 2 June)

3. Iran: Prominent trade unionist unlawfully detained: Ismail Abdi (MDE 13/2208/2015)

4. Iran: Death of trade unionist must trigger action to tackle appalling prison conditions (MDE 13/2508/2015)

5. Iran: Man forcibly blinded in one eye in "unspeakably cruel" retribution punishment (News story, 5 March)

6. Iran amputates fingers of two men in shocking act of cruelty (MDE 13/1998/2015)

7. Iran: Draconian amendment further erodes fair trial rights (MDE 13/1943/2015)

8. Iran: Activists tortured for alleged "flag-burning" (MDE 13/2110/2015)

9. Iran: Mohammad Ali Taheri sentenced to death (MDE 13/2245/2015)

10. Iran: Sweeping arrests of Ahwazi Arab activists (News story, 28 April)

11. Iran: Whereabouts of juvenile offender on death row emerge five months after scheduled execution (News story, 13 July)

# IRAQ

Republic of Iraq
Head of state: **Fuad Masum**
Head of government: **Haider al-Abadi**

**The human rights situation continued to deteriorate. Government security forces, government-allied militias and the armed group Islamic State (IS) committed war crimes and human rights abuses. Government forces carried out indiscriminate attacks on areas under IS control, and committed extrajudicial executions. IS forces carried out mass execution-style killings and abductions, including abductions of women and girls for sexual slavery. Government authorities held thousands of detainees without trial; torture and other ill-treatment of detainees remained rife. Many trials did not meet international standards of fairness. Women and girls faced discrimination and sexual and other violence. Journalists operated in hazardous conditions. Courts continued to impose death sentences, mostly on terrorism charges; dozens of executions were carried out.**

## BACKGROUND

The armed conflict continued between government security forces and IS forces; the latter controlled predominantly Sunni areas north and east of the capital, Baghdad, including the city of Mosul. Government forces were supported by Popular Mobilization Units (PMUs) composed mainly of Shi'a militias. In May, IS forces captured Ramadi, capital of Anbar province, causing thousands to flee to Baghdad and other cities, and massacred captive members of the security forces. In response to the IS advance, Prime Minister al-Abadi agreed to the deployment of PMUs to support a counter-offensive by government forces, despite the PMU's record of committing serious human rights violations against Sunni Muslims. At the end of the year, Mosul remained under IS control while Ramadi was recaptured by Iraqi security forces in December. Kurdish Peshmerga forces discovered mass graves in Sinjar after they recaptured the town from IS in November.

The conflict caused the deaths of some 6,520 civilians between January and October, according to the UN, and the forcible displacement of nearly 3.2 million people since January 2014, exacerbating the existing humanitarian crisis. Many of those displaced sought refuge in the semi-autonomous Kurdistan region in northern Iraq.

All parties to the conflict committed war crimes, other violations of international humanitarian law and human rights abuses. Both PMUs and IS reportedly used child soldiers.

Parliament created a Human Rights Advisory board for NGOs in January to facilitate consultation with civil society groups over revising legislation to comply with human rights; however, no significant legal reforms had been made by the end of the year.

In August, an official investigation into the capture of Mosul by IS forces in June 2014 blamed former Prime Minister Nuri al-Maliki and his officials for the security forces' abandonment of the city.

In September, President Masum ratified Law 36 of 2015, prohibiting political parties from having military wings or affiliating with armed groups, but a proposed amnesty law and draft laws on accountability and justice had not been enacted at the end of the year.

Prime Minister al-Abadi pledged to dismiss corrupt military officers. A draft National Guard Law to regulate armed militias and support greater local control of the security forces and police to reduce the marginalization of Sunnis and Kurds within the security forces proved particularly controversial; some members of Parliament said it threatened national security.

Several UN human rights bodies that conducted reviews of Iraq in 2015, including the Committee on the Rights of the Child, the Committee against Torture and the Human Rights Committee, expressed concern about the deteriorating human rights situation.

## INTERNAL ARMED CONFLICT

Government forces and PMUs committed war crimes, other violations of international humanitarian law and human rights violations, mostly against Sunni communities in areas under IS control. In Anbar, Ninevah and Salah al-Din provinces, indiscriminate air strikes by government forces killed and injured civilians and hit mosques and hospitals.

In areas they recaptured from IS, government security forces and allied militias carried out reprisal killings of local Sunnis suspected of supporting IS and burned homes and mosques. In one such case in January, security forces and allied Shi'a militias extrajudicially executed at least 56 Sunni Muslims in Barwana village, Diyalah province, after rounding up local men ostensibly to check their identities. The victims were shot, mostly while handcuffed.

Also in January, members of a Yezidi militia attacked Jiri and Sibaya, two predominantly Sunni Arab villages in the northwestern Sinjar region. The militia carried out execution-style killings of 21 civilians, including children and elderly men and women, and abducted other civilians. Residents said that Kurdish Peshmerga and Asayish forces were present when the killings were perpetrated. The homes of Sunni Arabs were also looted and burned by Yezidi militias after Peshmerga forces recaptured Sinjar from IS in November.

US, UK, French and other foreign military forces carried out air strikes against IS in support of the Iraqi government; some of these attacks reportedly killed and injured civilians in areas controlled or contested by IS.

## ABUSES BY ARMED GROUPS

Armed groups killed and injured civilians throughout Iraq in suicide and car bomb attacks that were either indiscriminate or deliberately targeted civilians. IS fighters killed civilians in indiscriminate shelling and continued to abduct and kill civilians in areas where they gained control, including civilians who opposed their control. In March and November, media reported that IS forces used chlorine gas in bomb attacks. Some 500 people, including civilians, died during the fighting for control of Ramadi in May. IS forces that seized control of the city killed civilians and members of the security forces, throwing some bodies in the Euphrates River. The armed group also summarily killed some of its own fighters for fleeing.

IS enforced strict rules on dress, behaviour and movement on the inhabitants who remained in the areas they controlled, and severely punished infractions. Its fighters carried out execution-style public killings and other punishments, including after its "courts" condemned people for transgressing its rules or its interpretation of Islamic law. IS also summarily killed dozens of men they perceived to be gay, often throwing them to their deaths from high-rise buildings. In Mosul, IS forces controlled all movement into and out of the city and prevented people leaving to obtain medical care elsewhere unless they provided guarantors of their return; IS reportedly beheaded some guarantors when people they had allowed to leave failed to return.

IS fighters burned or destroyed Shi'a, Yezidi and other religious shrines and cultural artefacts, as well as homes vacated by government officials and members of the security forces.

## VIOLENCE AGAINST WOMEN AND GIRLS

Women and girls faced discrimination in law and in practice, and were inadequately protected against sexual and other violence. They were subjected to acute abuses in IS-controlled areas, where women and girls were reportedly sold as slaves, forced to become wives of IS fighters or killed for refusing. In March, IS forces reportedly killed at least nine Shi'a women belonging to the Turkmen minority for refusing to marry IS fighters after IS forces killed their husbands.

## ARBITRARY ARRESTS AND DETENTIONS

Security forces carried out arrests without judicial warrants and without informing those they arrested or their families of any charges. Detainees, particularly terrorism suspects, were held incommunicado for weeks or months following arrest, often in conditions amounting to enforced disappearance and in secret prisons controlled by the Ministries of the Interior and Defence that were not open to inspection by the Office of the Public Prosecution or any monitoring bodies. In May, the Minister of the Interior denied that his ministry operated secret detention facilities, in response to complaints of enforced disappearances by detainees' families. Many detainees were released without charge but thousands of others continued to be held in harsh conditions, including at Nassiriyah Prison, south of Baghdad, which was mostly used to hold Sunni men convicted of or facing trial on terrorism charges, and where prisoners were reportedly abused.

## TORTURE AND OTHER ILL-TREATMENT

Torture and other ill-treatment remained common and widespread in prisons and detention centres and was committed with impunity. Interrogators tortured detainees to extract information and "confessions" for use against them at trial; some detainees reportedly died as a result of torture. In April, a member of the parliamentary Human Rights Committee said that detainees continued to face torture and the use of forced confessions. The UN Committee against

Torture criticized the government's failure to investigate torture allegations and called for increased safeguards against torture.

## UNFAIR TRIALS

The criminal justice system remained critically flawed and the judiciary lacked independence. Trials, particularly of defendants facing terrorism charges and possible death sentences, were systematically unfair with courts often admitting torture-tainted "confessions" as evidence, including "confessions" broadcast by state-controlled television channels before suspects were referred to trial.

Lawyers representing terrorism suspects faced threats and intimidation by security officials and were physically attacked by members of militias. Judges, lawyers and court officials continued to be attacked and killed by IS and other armed groups.

In July, the Central Criminal Court of Iraq in Baghdad sentenced 24 alleged IS members to death after it convicted them of unlawfully killing at least 1,700 military cadets from the "Speicher" Military Camp, near Tikrit in Salah al-Din governorate, in June 2014. Four other men were acquitted. The trial, which was completed in a few hours, was based mainly on "confessions", which the defendants said they had been forced to make under torture in pre-trial detention, and video footage of the massacre previously circulated by IS. The defendants all denied involvement in the killings, with some denying that they had been present in Tikrit at the time of the crime. None of the defendants had legal counsel of their own choosing but were represented by court-appointed lawyers, who requested leniency but did not dispute the evidence or the admissibility of the "confessions".

## FREEDOMS OF EXPRESSION AND ASSEMBLY

The authorities restricted the right to freedom of expression, including media freedom. In June the government introduced a new law to regulate media networks; the official Independent High Commission for Human Rights said it was overly restrictive.

In July and August, thousands of people took to the streets in Baghdad, Basra and other cities to protest against official corruption, electricity cuts, water shortages and the authorities' failure to provide other basic services. At least five people were killed when the security forces used unnecessary force to disperse the protests. In the weeks that followed, several protest leaders were killed by unidentified assailants in Baghdad, Nassiriyah and Basra. The Minister of the Interior claimed that the killings were unconnected to the protests but it was unclear to what extent they were investigated by the authorities.

The situation for journalists remained hazardous. They were subject to threats and violence by the security forces and abduction and killing by IS and other armed groups. In April, the Minister of the Interior claimed that negative media reporting about the security forces was hampering the fight against IS.

In February, several journalists were assaulted by a senior security official's bodyguards at a press conference in Baghdad. In April, Reuters news agency's Baghdad bureau chief, Ned Parker, left Iraq because of threats he received from Shi'a militia. The threats came after he reported that PMUs had committed abuses and looting after they recaptured Tikrit from IS.

In May, Raed al-Juburi, an outspoken journalist at al-Rasheed television channel and columnist for *Azzaman* newspaper, was found dead at his home in Baghdad with bullet wounds to his chest. The outcome of the investigation into his death remained undisclosed at the end of the year.

## REFUGEES AND INTERNALLY DISPLACED PEOPLE

Iraq continued to host some 244,527 refugees from Syria. Fighting between government forces and IS caused nearly 3.2 million people, mostly from Anbar, Ninevah and Salah al-Din provinces, to flee their homes and become internally displaced. Many fled to the Kurdistan region or other governorates. Some were forcibly displaced more than once. Some 500,000 people fled Anbar province in May when IS forces captured Ramadi; many were denied entry to Baghdad by the authorities. Humanitarian conditions for internally displaced people remained harsh; they often lacked access to basic services and some were reportedly attacked and injured by local residents in the Kurdish city of Sulaimaniyah. Others who fled to the Kurdistan region were arrested for suspected links to IS.

## KURDISTAN REGION OF IRAQ

Political tensions rose in the semi-autonomous Kurdistan region, amid efforts by the Kurdistan Democratic Party (KDP) to extend KDP leader Massoud Barzani's term of office as President of the Kurdistan Regional Government (KRG); a move that other political parties opposed. In October, hundreds of public sector employees protested in Sulaimaniyah and other eastern cities to demand payment of overdue salaries. In October, KDP militia forces fired at protesters in Qaladze and Kalar, killing at least five and injuring others. The KDP said investigations were opened into the burning of its headquarters but did not specify that the investigations would cover killings by its militias.

The KRG authorities arrested and detained people suspected of supporting or having links to IS but did not disclose their number.

## DEATH PENALTY

The authorities continued to impose the death penalty extensively and carried out dozens of executions. Most of those sentenced to death were Sunni men convicted under the 2005 Anti-Terrorism Law. In June, the Cabinet agreed to amend the Code of Criminal Procedures to allow the Minister of Justice to ratify execution orders if the President fails to act on them within 30 days. The following month, President Masum ratified at least 21 death sentences.

In September, a court in Baghdad sentenced three brothers – Ali, Shakir and Abdel-Wehab Mahmoud Hameed al-'Akla – to death on terrorism charges for beheading a man in 2010. All three alleged that security officials tortured them during months of incommunicado detention and forced them to "confess" to killing people unknown to them.

In August, the KRG authorities hanged Farhad Jaafar Mahmood and his wives Berivan Haider Karim and Khuncha Hassan Ismaeil, ending a seven-year hiatus on executions in the region. A court in Dohuk had sentenced the three to death in April 2014 after convicting them on abduction and murder charges.

# IRELAND

Republic of Ireland
Head of state: **Michael D. Higgins**
Head of government: **Enda Kenny**

**Access to and information about abortion remained severely restricted and criminalized. Equal access to civil marriage for same-sex couples was introduced. Legal gender recognition legislation was enacted.**

## SEXUAL AND REPRODUCTIVE RIGHTS

In July the UN Committee on Economic, Social and Cultural Rights (CESCR) criticized Ireland's "highly restrictive legislation on abortion and its strict interpretation thereof", and its "criminalization of abortion, including in the cases of rape and incest and of risk to the health of a pregnant woman". It recommended that Ireland take all necessary steps, including a referendum on abortion, to revise its legislation on abortion. Concerns were raised at the impact on women and girls of the law on access to and information about abortion, and how the constitutional protection afforded to the foetus also impacted on maternity care.[1] Abortion is constitutionally permitted only when a woman's or girl's life is at "real and substantial risk", and carries a possible 14-year prison sentence in all other circumstances.

## VIOLENCE AGAINST WOMEN AND GIRLS

In November, Ireland signed the Council of Europe Convention on preventing and combating violence against women and domestic violence.

The CESCR expressed concern at the government's responses to domestic violence. It criticized the lack of a prompt, thorough and independent investigation into the allegations of past abuses in the religious-run "Magdalene Laundries", and that survivors were not provided with adequate remedies.

## DISCRIMINATION

In May, a popular referendum was passed ensuring constitutional provision for equal access to civil marriage for same-sex couples. Legislation was enacted in October.

Legislation providing for legal gender recognition was enacted and came into force in September, substantially meeting human rights standards.

There were renewed concerns at the institutionalization of people with disabilities and the poor living conditions for people with disabilities in residential centres. Concerns were also raised at possible neglect and abuse in some centres.

## LEGAL, CONSTITUTIONAL OR INSTITUTIONAL DEVELOPMENTS

The CESCR was critical of the limited statutory definition of human rights provided in respect of some of the functions of the Human Rights and Equality Commission.[2] It concluded that this limitation, together with the lack of recognition of economic, social and cultural rights in domestic law, are "major factors" preventing the Commission from exercising its mandate and applying the full range of rights. It recommended that the government review the 2014 legislation.

By the end of the year the government had still not responded to the February 2014 recommendation by the government-established Constitutional Convention that the Constitution be amended to incorporate economic, social and cultural rights. Several other Convention recommendations for

constitutional reform in areas including equality for women and blasphemy remained outstanding.

## TORTURE AND OTHER ILL-TREATMENT

In November, the European Committee for the Prevention of Torture published the findings of its 2014 visit. The Committee noted improvements in the prison system, but expressed concern at interprisoner violence, continuing lack of in-cell sanitation in some prisons, conditions akin to solitary confinement as punishment, deficiencies in health care (including mental health care), and the placement of immigration detainees with remand and convicted prisoners. The Committee noted receiving some reports of ill-treatment by the police, and recommended improved health care services in police stations as a safeguard against ill-treatment.

There were concerns at delays by the government in ratifying the Optional Protocol to the UN Convention against Torture and establishing the required National Preventive Mechanism.

## REFUGEES AND ASYLUM-SEEKERS

In September, the government announced that it would accept up to 4,000 people in need of international protection, including both those requiring relocation from within the EU, and the 520 Syrian refugees then being resettled in Ireland directly from the Middle East.

Concerns remained about the poor living conditions in "direct provision" centres and the lengthy stay (around 51 months) by asylum-seekers. A report was issued in June by a working group established by the government to identify possible improvements to direct provision. The government established a task force in July to further consider whether and how to implement the group's recommendations.

Legislation providing for a single procedure to deal with both claims for refugee status and claims for other forms of protection was enacted in December.

# ISRAEL AND THE OCCUPIED PALESTINIAN TERRITORIES

**State of Israel**
Head of state: **Reuven Rivlin**
Head of government: **Benjamin Netanyahu**

In the West Bank, including East Jerusalem, Israeli forces committed unlawful killings of Palestinian civilians, including children, and detained thousands of Palestinians who protested against or otherwise opposed Israel's continuing military occupation, holding hundreds in administrative detention. Torture and other ill-treatment remained rife and were committed with impunity. The authorities continued to promote illegal settlements in the West Bank, and severely restricted Palestinians' freedom of movement, further tightening restrictions amid an escalation of violence from October, which included attacks on Israeli civilians by Palestinians and apparent extrajudicial executions by Israeli forces. Israeli settlers in the West Bank attacked Palestinians and their property with virtual impunity. The Gaza Strip remained under an Israeli military blockade that imposed collective punishment on its inhabitants. The authorities continued to demolish Palestinian homes in the West Bank and inside Israel, particularly in Bedouin villages in the Negev/Naqab region, forcibly evicting their residents. They also detained and deported thousands of African asylum-seekers, and imprisoned Israeli conscientious objectors.

## BACKGROUND

Israeli-Palestinian relations remained tense throughout the year. In January, after Palestine applied to join the ICC and accepted its jurisdiction over crimes committed in the Occupied Palestinian Territories (OPT) since June 2014, Israel temporarily ceased paying monthly tax revenues due to the Palestinian authorities. Later in January, the ICC Prosecutor opened a preliminary examination into alleged crimes under international law by Israel and by Palestinian armed groups; Israel condemned the move, but began limited engagement with the ICC Prosecutor in July.

International efforts failed to restart Israeli-Palestinian negotiations. The Israeli government continued to support the promotion and expansion of illegal settlements in the West Bank, including East Jerusalem, and took steps to authorize several West Bank settlement outposts that had been established without government permission.

From October there was a significant upsurge in violence in which Palestinians, mostly individuals not affiliated with armed groups, carried out stabbings, shootings, car-ramming and other attacks against Israeli forces and civilians in both Israel and the West Bank, and increased protests against Israel's military occupation. Israeli forces responded to attacks and protests with lethal force. Twenty-one Israeli civilians and one US national were killed by Palestinians during the year, all but four between October and December. Israeli forces killed more than 130 Palestinians between October and December.

Palestinian armed groups in Gaza sporadically fired indiscriminate rockets into southern Israel; no deaths were reported. Israel responded with air strikes on Gaza; one strike in October killed two civilians. Israel also carried out several air strikes and other attacks on sites in Syria.

## FREEDOM OF MOVEMENT – GAZA BLOCKADE AND WEST BANK RESTRICTIONS

Israeli forces maintained their land, sea and air blockade of Gaza, in force since 2007, imposing collective punishment on the territory's 1.8 million inhabitants. Israeli controls on the movement of people and goods into and from Gaza, particularly on essential construction materials, combined with Egypt's closure of the Rafah border crossing and destruction of cross-border tunnels, severely hindered post-conflict reconstruction and essential services and exacerbated poverty and unemployment.

Israeli forces continued to impose a "buffer zone" inside Gaza's border with Israel and used live fire against Palestinians who entered or approached it. They also fired at Palestinian fishermen within or near an "exclusion zone" that Israel maintained along Gaza's coast, killing one and injuring others.

In the West Bank, Israel severely restricted the movement of Palestinians, who were excluded from large areas that had either been designated as military firing zones, or were near the fence/wall constructed by Israel or within illegal settlements, and maintained an array of military checkpoints and bypass roads that restricted Palestinian travel while allowing free movement for Israeli settlers. Israeli forces established new checkpoints and barriers, particularly in East Jerusalem and the Hebron governorate, amid the upsurge in violence from October, subjecting hundreds of thousands of Palestinians to restrictions amounting to collective punishment.

## ARBITRARY ARRESTS AND DETENTIONS

The authorities detained thousands of Palestinians from the OPT; most were held in prisons inside Israel, in violation of international law. Hundreds were held without charge or trial under renewable administrative detention orders, based on information withheld from them and their lawyers; some engaged in prolonged hunger strikes in protest. Mohammed Allan, a lawyer, went on hunger strike for 65 days to protest against his administrative detention; he was released in November without charge.

The Israeli authorities launched a new clampdown on protests by Palestinians in the OPT amid the escalation in violence from October, arresting more than 2,500 Palestinians, including hundreds of children, and significantly increasing their use of administrative detention. More than 580 Palestinian administrative detainees were held by the end of the year, including at least five children. In addition, several Israeli Jews suspected of planning attacks on Palestinians were held in administrative detention.

Palestinians from the OPT who were charged faced unfair trials in military courts. In December, Palestinian parliamentarian Khalida Jarrar was sentenced to 15 months' imprisonment and a fine following a plea bargain made after months of unfair military court proceedings.[1]

## TORTURE AND OTHER ILL-TREATMENT

Israeli military and police forces, as well as Israel Security Agency (ISA) personnel, tortured and otherwise ill-treated Palestinian detainees, including children, particularly during arrest and interrogation. Reports of torture increased amid the mass arrests of Palestinians that began in October. Methods included beating with batons, slapping, throttling, prolonged shackling, stress positions, sleep deprivation and threats. Jewish suspects detained in connection with attacks on Palestinians also alleged torture. Impunity for torture was rife. The authorities had received almost 1,000 complaints of torture at the hands of ISA since 2001 but had yet to open any criminal investigations.

In July, Israel's parliament, the Knesset, extended legislation exempting the police and ISA from recording interrogations of Palestinian "security suspects", with government endorsement, contravening a 2013 recommendation of the Turkel Commission (see below). The same month the Knesset approved legislation allowing the authorities to subject detainees on hunger strike to forced feeding, despite opposition from human rights groups and the UN.

## UNLAWFUL KILLINGS

Israeli soldiers and police killed at least 124 Palestinians from the OPT in the West Bank, including East Jerusalem, 22 in the Gaza Strip, and 10 inside Israel during the year. Many of those killed, including children, appeared to be victims of unlawful killings. They included Muhammad Kasba, aged 17, and 15-year-old Laith al-Khalidi, who were shot in the back on 3 and 31 July respectively after throwing stones or petrol bombs at Israeli military checkpoints or vehicles, and Falah Abu Maria, who was shot in the chest on 23 July when Israeli forces raided his home.

Many of the deaths occurred in the last quarter of the year when Israeli police and military forces fatally shot Palestinians who carried out stabbings or other attacks on Israelis, including civilians, or were suspected of intending such attacks, in circumstances where they were not posing an imminent threat to life and could have been apprehended, making the killings unlawful. In some cases, Israeli forces shot dead Palestinians as they lay wounded, or failed to provide timely medical assistance to injured Palestinians.

### Extrajudicial executions

Some Palestinians appeared to be victims of extrajudicial executions, including Fadi Alloun, whom Israeli forces shot dead on 4 October in Jerusalem; Dania Ershied, 17, and Sa'ad al-Atrash, whom Israeli forces shot dead in Hebron on 25 and 26 October; and Abdallah Shalaldah, whom Israeli undercover forces killed on 12 November in al-Ahli Hospital in Hebron.

## EXCESSIVE USE OF FORCE

Israeli forces, including undercover units, used excessive and lethal force against protesters in both the West Bank and the Gaza Strip, killing dozens, including 43 in the last quarter of the year, and injuring thousands with rubber-coated metal bullets and live ammunition. While many protesters threw rocks or other projectiles, they generally posed no threat to the lives of well-protected Israeli soldiers when they were shot. In September, Israel's security cabinet authorized police to use live ammunition in East Jerusalem. On 9 and 10 October, Israeli forces used live ammunition and rubber-coated metal bullets against Palestinian protesters in border areas of the Gaza Strip, killing nine, including a child, and injuring scores.

## FREEDOMS OF EXPRESSION, ASSOCIATION AND ASSEMBLY

Israeli military orders prohibiting unauthorized demonstrations in the West Bank were used to repress protests by Palestinians and jail activists, including human rights defender Murad Shtewi, who was released in January after serving a nine-and-a-half-month sentence under Military Order 101. On numerous occasions, journalists covering protests and other developments in the West Bank were assaulted or shot by Israeli police and military forces.

The authorities also increased restrictions on Palestinian citizens inside Israel, banning the northern branch of the Islamic Movement and closing 17 NGOs associated with it in November, and arresting more than 250 demonstrators and protest organizers between October and December.

In September, Israeli whistle-blower Mordechai Vanunu was sentenced to one week's house arrest following an interview with Israel's Channel 2. He continued to be banned from travelling abroad and communicating electronically with foreign nationals throughout the year.

## HOUSING RIGHTS – FORCED EVICTIONS AND DEMOLITIONS

In the West Bank, including East Jerusalem, Israeli forces demolished at least 510 Palestinian homes and other structures built without Israeli permits, which are virtually impossible to obtain, forcibly evicting more than 610 people. They also forcibly evicted more than 120 people by demolishing or making uninhabitable 19 family homes of Palestinians who carried out attacks on Israelis. In Area C of the West Bank, under full Israeli control, dozens of Bedouin and herding communities continued to face forcible relocation.

The authorities also demolished scores of Palestinian homes inside Israel that they said were built without permits, mostly in Bedouin villages in the Negev/Naqab region. Many of the villages were officially "unrecognized". In May, the Supreme Court approved the planned demolition of the "unrecognized" village of Um al-Heiran and the eviction of its Bedouin residents to construct a new Jewish town. In November the government approved the establishment of five new Jewish communities in the region, including two on the sites of existing Bedouin villages.

## SETTLER VIOLENCE

Israelis living in illegal settlements in the occupied West Bank frequently attacked Palestinian civilians and their property, sometimes in the presence of Israeli soldiers and police who failed to intervene. A settler arson attack on the Dawabsheh family home in the village of Duma, near Nablus, on 31 July killed 18-month-old Ali and his parents Sa'ad and Riham, and critically injured his four-year-old brother Ahmad. The incident highlighted an increase in settler attacks inside Palestinian communities, leaving many Palestinians feeling unsafe in their homes. Suspects were subsequently arrested, and several remained in detention at the end of the year.

An Israeli civilian shot and killed Fadel al-Qawasmeh in close proximity to Israeli soldiers in the Old City of Hebron on 17 October; the Israeli man was not arrested at the scene and there were no indications he would be prosecuted.

Although two of the three Israelis charged with the July 2014 abduction and killing of Palestinian teenager Muhammad Abu Khdeir were convicted in November and due to be

sentenced in January 2016, in most cases the Israeli police failed to investigate alleged crimes by settlers effectively and prosecute suspects, leading to continued impunity for settler violence.

## IMPUNITY

In June the UN Independent Commission of Inquiry on the 2014 Gaza Conflict published its report, documenting war crimes by Israeli forces and Palestinian armed groups during the 50-day conflict and calling for accountability. Israel rejected the UN findings and continued its military investigations, but they were not independent and failed to deliver justice. Israeli military authorities opened investigations into deaths of Palestinians killed by Israeli forces in the West Bank, but these investigations were similarly flawed, and only one case from 2013 led to an indictment for "negligent use of a firearm", following lengthy delays and an appeal to Israel's High Court.

In September, a government committee released its review of the Turkel Commission's recommendations of 2013 on Israel's investigation systems and their compliance with international law. It side-stepped some recommendations, such as making war crimes offences under national law, and failed to define practical steps or budgets necessary to implement others.

## VIOLENCE AGAINST WOMEN AND GIRLS

There were new reports of violence against women, particularly within Palestinian communities in Israel. According to activists, at least 18 women were murdered in Israel, mostly by partners or family members; some were killed after seeking police protection.

## REFUGEES AND ASYLUM-SEEKERS

The authorities continued to deny asylum-seekers, over 90% of whom were from Eritrea and Sudan, access to a fair refugee status determination process. More than 4,200 were held at the Holot detention facility and Saharonim Prison in the Negev/Naqab desert at the end of the year.

In August, the High Court of Justice ruled that provisions of a December 2014 amendment to the Prevention of Infiltration Law allowing the authorities to detain asylum-seekers at Holot for 20 months were disproportionate, and ordered the government to revise the law and release those who had been held at the facility for more than a year. Around 1,200 out of approximately 1,800 asylum-seekers were subsequently released from Holot, but they were arbitrarily banned from the cities of Tel Aviv and Eilat. Thousands of others were summoned to Holot under expanded detention criteria, and the numbers detained at the facility reached an all-time high. In November the government introduced a new draft amendment under which asylum-seekers would be detained at Holot for a year, extendable by an additional six months.

Only a handful of the thousands of Eritrean and Sudanese nationals who had applied for asylum by the end of the year were granted asylum, and the authorities continued to pressure many, including detainees at Holot, to leave Israel "voluntarily". By the end of November, more than 2,900 asylum-seekers had accepted such "voluntary return". In November, a district court upheld a government decision announced in March to deport some of the 45,000 asylum-seekers still in the country without their consent to Rwanda and Uganda or detain them indefinitely at Saharonim prison. The government refused to release details on reported agreements with Rwanda and Uganda, or any guarantees that those deported, "voluntarily" or otherwise, would not subsequently be transferred to their home countries, violating the prohibition of *refoulement*.

## CONSCIENTIOUS OBJECTORS

At least four conscientious objectors were imprisoned. They included Edo Ramon, imprisoned repeatedly from March for refusing to serve in the Israeli military.

1. Israel/Occupied Palestinian Territories: Palestinian parliamentarian sentenced: Khalida Jarrar (MDE 15/3031/2015)

# ITALY

**Republic of Italy**
Head of state: **Sergio Mattarella (replaced Giorgio Napolitano in February)**
Head of government: **Matteo Renzi**

**A spiralling death toll among refugees and migrants trying to reach Italy by boat from North Africa was recorded between January and April. The number of deaths decreased after European governments deployed naval resources to save lives on the high seas. The implementation of an EU-agreed system to screen arrivals – the "hotspot approach" – raised concerns. Discrimination against Roma continued, with thousands segregated in mono-ethnic camps. Italy failed to introduce the crime of torture into domestic legislation, to establish an independent national human rights institution and to provide legal recognition to same-sex couples.**

## REFUGEES' AND MIGRANTS' RIGHTS

Over 153,000 refugees and migrants arrived in Italy after crossing the central Mediterranean on unseaworthy and overcrowded boats. The overwhelming majority departed from North Africa and were rescued at sea by the Italian coastguard and Navy, other countries' vessels, or by NGOs' or merchant vessels.

About 2,900 refugees and migrants died or disappeared at sea while attempting the crossing during the year. The death rate considerably increased in the first four months, when about 1,700 deaths were reported, including over 1,200 caused by two major shipwrecks in April alone. This was linked to the reduction in resources for proactive patrolling enforced at the end of 2014, with Operation Mare Nostrum being replaced with the smaller, border control-focused Operation Triton by Frontex, the EU border management agency.

At the end of April, European governments decided to reinstate patrolling of the central Mediterranean, through improvements to the Triton operation, the launch of independent life-saving operations by individual governments and the establishment of the EU military operation in the southern Central Mediterranean (EUNAVFOR MED, later relabelled Operation Sophia), to tackle human smuggling. Such measures, coupled with increased efforts by NGOs, led to a drastic reduction of the death rate in the following months. However, due to the high number of people travelling – pushed by the deteriorating situation in countries of origin and transit – and the absence of safe and legal alternatives to seek protection in Europe, loss of life at sea continued to be recorded during the remainder of the year.

Italian authorities struggled to ensure adequate reception conditions for the tens of thousands of people disembarked in the country. The government enforced a plan to distribute them in reception centres across the country, in some cases encountering fierce resistance from local authorities and population, including violent attacks. In July, in Quinto di Treviso, Northeast Italy, residents and far-right militants broke into flats destined to receive asylum-seekers, took the furniture outside and set it on fire, leading the authorities to move the asylum-seekers to another location.

In August, new legislation was adopted to transpose EU directives on asylum, restructuring the reception system. Concern was raised in relation to a planned increase in the use of detention in Identification and Expulsion Centres (CIEs).

In September, Italy started applying the so-called "hotspot approach", under which asylum-seekers of certain nationalities would be identified to benefit from relocation to other EU member states where they could seek asylum. The relocation programme led to the transfer of 184 people by the end of the year. There were concerns that asylum-seekers and migrants may be subjected to arbitrary detention and forced fingerprinting in centres designated as "hotspots". In Sicily, authorities issued expulsion orders to individuals upon arrival, raising concern that people ineligible for relocation may be expelled without being previously granted an opportunity to seek asylum or receive information regarding their rights.

In September, the European Court of Human Rights condemned Italy, in the Khlaifia case, for the arbitrary detention, ill-treatment and collective expulsion of a group of Tunisians in 2011. The case concerned their detention in the Lampedusa reception centre and on military vessels, and their summary repatriation to Tunisia, without taking into account their individual circumstances.

"Irregular entry and stay" in the territory remained a crime. The government failed to adopt decrees to abolish it, although instructions to do so had been passed by Parliament in April 2014.

## DISCRIMINATION

### Roma

Thousands of Romani families continued to live in segregated camps and shelters, often in poor conditions, as highlighted by the UN Committee on Economic, Social and Cultural Rights in October. The government's failure to effectively implement the National Strategy for Roma Inclusion (NSRI) meant that, three years after its adoption, no significant progress had been achieved towards offering adequate alternative housing to Romani families unable to provide for themselves. Roma living in camps continued to have little chance to access social housing, particularly in the capital, Rome. Forced evictions of Roma were reported across the country. In February, about 200 people, including children and pregnant women, were evicted from the Lungo Stura Lazio camp in Turin. The European Commission against Racism and Intolerance criticized evictions, often executed without providing procedural safeguards and alternative accommodation. It also reiterated recommendations to strengthen the independence and powers of the National Office against Racial Discrimination (UNAR), co-ordinating the implementation of the NSRI. However, the government reduced the UNAR's resources and interfered with its activities.

In May, the Rome Civil Court recognized in a landmark ruling that the assignment of housing to Roma in the mono-ethnic camp of La Barbuta, near Ciampino airport, in an area deemed unsuitable for human habitation, constituted discriminatory conduct and had to be discontinued. The authorities had not taken any concrete action to enforce the ruling by the end of the year.

### Rights of lesbian, gay, bisexual, transgender and intersex people

In July, the European Court of Human Rights held in the Oliari case that Italy had violated the applicants' right to a private and family life, because of the lack of legal framework to protect the rights of same-sex couples. Nonetheless, Parliament failed to approve pending legislation to address this gap. In December, the Court of Appeal of Rome confirmed the right of a woman to formally adopt the child born by her female partner as a result of artificial insemination.

In July, the Court of Cassation ruled that transgender individuals must be able to obtain legal recognition of their gender without the requirement to undergo any medical treatment.

At the end of the year, Parliament had not yet approved legislative amendments to extend to homophobic and transphobic crimes the application of penalties against hate crimes based on other grounds.

### TORTURE AND OTHER ILL-TREATMENT

A bill to incorporate the crime of torture into national legislation initially passed one branch of Parliament in April, but failed to pass in the end. Similarly, the government failed to introduce identification tags on the uniforms of law enforcement officers that would facilitate accountability for abuse.

In April, the European Court of Human Rights found in the Cestaro case that police storming the Diaz school, Genoa, during the G8 summit in 2001, had committed torture against demonstrators sheltered therein. The Court underscored how no official had been convicted for such treatment, linked to the absence of the crime of torture within the domestic legislation, to the application of the statute of limitations, and to the lack of police co-operation.

A national ombudsperson for the rights of detainees was still due to become operational at the end of the year.

### DEATHS IN CUSTODY

Concerns remained about the lack of accountability for deaths in custody, despite slow progress in a few cases.

In June, a trial for manslaughter started against four police officers and three Italian Red Cross volunteers, in the case of Riccardo Magherini, who died during his arrest in a street in Florence in March 2014. Shortcomings in the investigations had been reported in previous months.

New evidence, including witness statements, emerged in the case of Stefano Cucchi, who died a week after his arrest in the prison wing of a Rome hospital in 2009, reinforcing the presumption that he may have died as a result of beatings. In September, fresh investigations were launched by prosecutors against police officials involved in his arrest. In December, the Court of Cassation ordered a new trial for five doctors who had been acquitted on appeal of charges of manslaughter.

### COUNTER-TERROR AND SECURITY

The European Court of Human Rights convened a public hearing in June in the Nasr and Ghali case. Lawyers for Usama Mostafa Hassan Nasr (known as Abu Omar) and his wife Nabila Ghali argued that Italian police and intelligence operatives were responsible for colluding with the CIA in Abu Omar's kidnapping in February 2003 and ill-treatment in Milan, his subsequent illegal rendition to Egypt, and his torture and other ill-treatment in secret detention in Cairo. The case remained pending at the European Court of Human Rights. In December, President Mattarella granted a pardon to a CIA agent and a partial pardon to another one; both agents had previously been convicted in their absence by Italian courts for their role in the kidnapping and rendition.

In February, new counter-terrorism laws were adopted that increased prison sentences for "persons who are recruited by others to commit acts of terrorism", and provided penalties for persons who organize, finance, or promote travel "for the purpose of performing acts of terrorism". The laws also made it a crime for a person to participate in a conflict on a foreign territory "in support of a terrorist organization", and granted the government the authority to keep a list of websites used for recruitment and to instruct Internet service providers to block such sites.

## LEGAL, CONSTITUTIONAL OR INSTITUTIONAL DEVELOPMENTS
Despite the government's promises, Italy again failed to establish a national human rights institution in accordance with the Principles relating to the Status of National Institutions (Paris Principles).

# JAMAICA

Jamaica
Head of state: **Queen Elizabeth II, represented by Patrick Linton Allen**
Head of government: **Portia Simpson Miller**

**Excessive use of force by the police and extrajudicial executions continued. A Commission of Enquiry into alleged human rights violations during the 2010 state of emergency was under way. Violence and discrimination against lesbian, gay, bisexual, transgender and intersex (LGBTI) people continued. In August Jamaica held its first gay pride march.**

## BACKGROUND
Jamaica continued to have one of the highest homicide rates per capita in the world. Violent crime remained a key concern for the public. Between January and June, police recorded 1,486 reports of serious and violent crimes, classified as murders, shootings, rapes and aggravated assaults. According to media reports, there were more than 1,100 murders during the year, an increase of approximately 20% compared with 2014.

The Dangerous Drugs (Amendment) Act 2015 came into force in April, removing powers of arrest and detention for possession or use of small quantities of cannabis and allowing members of the Rastafarian faith to use the drug for religious purposes.

In May, Jamaica was examined under the UPR. Jamaica accepted 23 of the 177 recommendations made.

The government took steps to establish a National Human Rights Institution.

## POLICE AND SECURITY FORCES
Human rights organizations continued to highlight concerns around arbitrary arrests and ill-treatment in police custody.

After years of rising numbers of police killings (over 200 per year from 2011 to 2013), the numbers began to decline in 2014 and 2015. The Independent Commission of Investigation (INDECOM), an independent police oversight agency, reported 50 killings involving the police in the first half of 2015, fewer than for the same period of 2014.

A long-overdue Commission of Enquiry into human rights violations committed during the 2010 state of emergency began in December 2014 and was scheduled to be completed in early 2016. During the state of emergency, 76 civilians were killed by security forces, including 44 who were alleged to have been extrajudicially executed.

## JUSTICE SYSTEM
Major backlogs in the judiciary led to continued delays and hampered access to justice. In particular, investigations into police killings remained slow. With a high number of

new cases and few resources, the capacity of the Coroner's Court to help resolve the backlog also remained limited.

## CHILDREN'S RIGHTS

According to the Jamaica Constabulary Force, 29 children were murdered between January and June, suggesting a failure by the state to protect children from extreme violence and abuse. Conditions of detention and treatment of juvenile offenders were poor. The NGO Jamaicans for Justice (JFJ) documented high levels of attempted suicide among children and young people in juvenile prisons, raising serious concerns about the psychosocial health and well-being of juveniles in state institutions. JFJ also reported that juvenile offenders were not presented promptly before a judge, exceeding the constitutional period to assess the legality of detention and contravening the UN Convention on the Rights of the Child.

## VIOLENCE AGAINST WOMEN AND GIRLS

High levels of gender-based violence and domestic violence continued with high numbers of women killed by their spouse or partner. Lesbian, bisexual and transgender women were at risk of sexual violence due to their real or perceived sexual orientation and gender expression.

The government was finalizing a National Strategic Plan of Action to Eliminate Gender-based Violence in Jamaica. A Joint Select Committee of Parliament was under way to review the Sexual Offences Act 2009. Civil society organizations made recommendations during the review, which included widening the definition of rape, decriminalizing sex work, and using gender-neutral language throughout the Act.

## RIGHTS OF LESBIAN, GAY, BISEXUAL, TRANSGENDER AND INTERSEX PEOPLE

There remained no legal protection against discrimination based on real or perceived sexual orientation or gender identity. Consensual sex between men remained criminalized. Between January and July, the Jamaica Forum of Lesbians, All-Sexuals and Gays (J-FLAG) received 47 reports of human rights violations against LGBTI people. Homelessness and displacement of LGBTI youths remained a concern. Young people pushed out of their homes because of their sexual orientation or gender identity continued to live in storm drains and abandoned buildings. Local NGOs supported homeless LGBTI youths, while the state did little to help. By mid-year, J-FLAG had provided social and crisis services to 329 LGBTI people and continued to receive requests for advice from LGBTI Jamaicans planning to seek asylum in other countries.

In August, a gay pride celebration was held in Jamaica for the first time. The Minister of Justice called for tolerance during the celebration and expressed his support for the rights of LGBTI people to express themselves peacefully.

# JAPAN

Japan
Head of government: **Shinzo Abe**

**Despite the post-World War II Constitution that renounced the "use of force as means of settling international disputes", in July Prime Minister Shinzo Abe pushed through the House of Representatives new legislation that would allow Japan's self-defence forces to join collective military actions overseas. Negative public reaction opposing the legislation included one of the largest demonstrations in decades. The Japanese and South Korean governments reached a settlement on the military sexual slavery system before and during World War II; the outcome was severely criticized by survivors. Executions of people on death row continued.**

## DISCRIMINATION – ETHNIC MINORITIES

Despite a 2014 recommendation by the CERD Committee , the ruling coalition opposed legislation prohibiting racial discrimination. A group of national lawmakers nonetheless submitted a bill to the Parliament that would require the government to create anti-discrimination programmes. Discussion of the bill began in August. With the increase of demonstrations targeting ethnic Koreans, some municipal governments, including Osaka, proposed ordinances to curb hate speech against foreigners and minorities.

## REFUGEES AND ASYLUM-SEEKERS

Concerns around the refugee application process continued. The Ministry of Justice granted refugee status to only 11 people out of more than 5,000 applicants in 2014. In June the Ministry unveiled plans to introduce a pre-screening procedure to exclude "ineligible" applicants from entering the process, claiming that people seeking job opportunities accounted for the increased numbers of applications for asylum. Criteria for qualification were not clearly specified. In August, a man from Sri Lanka filed another lawsuit against the Ministry, which continued to refuse him refugee status despite an Osaka District Court ruling in his favour. This was the first time that a government refusal to follow a court decision on refugee status resulted in a second lawsuit.

## MIGRANT WORKERS' RIGHTS

The government maintained tight restrictions on immigration and announced plans to expand further the existing Technical Intern Training Program to bring in more foreign workers. The Program was subject to abuse by employers, resulting in forced labour, lack of effective oversight or protection for workers, and other human rights abuses. As of June, some 180,000 foreigners worked under the Program.

## RIGHTS OF LESBIAN, GAY, BISEXUAL, TRANSGENDER AND INTERSEX PEOPLE

In April, the Shibuya ward in Tokyo became the first municipality in Japan to pass an ordinance that would acknowledge same-sex unions as equivalent to marriage. Registered same-sex partners would be offered non-legally binding certification, and have visitation rights in hospitals and the ability to co-sign tenancy agreements. The Setagaya ward in Tokyo adopted similar guidelines in July, while cities outside Tokyo announced possible future arrangements for same-sex partnerships.

## VIOLENCE AGAINST WOMEN AND GIRLS

On the 70th anniversary of the end of World War II, Prime Minister Abe expressed grief, but only referred to apologies made by former heads of government. The government reached an agreement with South Korea in December and acknowledged Japan's deep responsibility for the military sexual slavery system before and during the war, which resulted in women and girls being forced into sexual slavery by the Japanese Imperial Army. The outcome was criticized as the agreement did not take into account the views and needs of survivors and they were not involved in the negotiations.

## FREEDOM OF EXPRESSION

The Act on the Protection of Specially Designated Secrets, which came into effect in December 2014, contained provisions that could violate the right to access information held by public authorities. Critics of the Act stressed that the government could withhold information without clear designation criteria, that parliamentary committees overseeing the designation of secrets were too weak, and that journalists risked imprisonment for soliciting and reporting information designated as secrets. At the end of the year the government had yet to set up an independent oversight mechanism that would include whistleblower provisions and could effectively prevent abuse of the Act.

## JUSTICE SYSTEM

A bill revising the criminal procedure law to require video or audio recording of interrogations by police or prosecutors in their entirety was passed at the House of Representatives in August, but had not been discussed at the House of Councillors by the end of the year. The proposed law was applicable only to "serious crimes" to be tried under the lay judge system, approximately 2% of all criminal cases. It also failed to abolish or reform the *daiyo kangoku* system, which allows the police to detain suspects for up to 23 days prior to charge, facilitating torture and other ill-treatment in order to extract confessions during interrogation.

# JORDAN

Hashemite Kingdom of Jordan
Head of state: **King Abdullah II bin al-Hussein**
Head of government: **Abdullah Ensour**

**The authorities restricted freedoms of expression, association and assembly, and prosecuted and imprisoned government critics. Torture and other ill-treatment continued in detention centres and prisons, and the State Security Court continued to conduct unfair trials. Women were discriminated against in law and in practice and inadequately protected against sexual and other violence. Courts passed death sentences and executions were carried out. Jordan hosted more than 641,800 refugees from Syria.**

## BACKGROUND

Jordan continued to be affected by the armed conflict in neighbouring Syria, hosting refugees and suffering civilian casualties in cross-border firing from Syria. In February, Jordanian warplanes launched further attacks on areas in Syria controlled by the armed group Islamic State (IS), after IS issued a video showing its fighters burning to death the captured Jordanian fighter pilot Muath al-Kasasbeh.

Around 12 people reportedly died during violent clashes with security forces who raided several homes in Ma'an in southwest Jordan in May and June. In May, following the events in Ma'an and the death in custody of Abdullah Zu'bi (see below), the Interior Minister resigned and the heads of the Public

Security Directorate (PSD), which runs the police and prisons, and the gendarmerie, were prematurely retired. The Prime Minister announced that this was due to a "lack of co-ordination between security organizations".

## COUNTER-TERROR AND SECURITY

Alleged supporters of IS and other armed groups were prosecuted under anti-terrorism laws and other legislation by the State Security Court (SSC), a quasi-military court whose procedures failed to meet international fair trial standards.

## TORTURE AND OTHER ILL-TREATMENT

In August, the National Centre for Human Rights (NCHR) said it had received 87 complaints of torture and other ill-treatment during 2014. In response, Prime Minister Ensour announced the appointment of a ministerial committee including officials from the General Intelligence Department (GID) and Public Security Directorate (PSD), and chaired by the government's co-ordinator on human rights, to examine the NCHR's findings. In December, the UN Committee against Torture expressed concern at "consistent reports of widespread use of torture and ill-treatment of suspects by security and law enforcement officials" highlighting GID and Criminal Investigation Department (CID) detention facilities.

Amer Jubran, a Palestinian-Jordanian activist, said he was tortured and otherwise ill-treated during two months in GID detention and forced to sign a "confession", which the SSC panel of military judges accepted as evidence against him when they sentenced him in July to 10 years' imprisonment on charges that included possessing arms and explosives and belonging to Hizbullah. In November, the Court of Cassation confirmed his conviction. His co-defendants, some of whom also alleged that they were tortured by the GID, received sentences of two to three years' imprisonment.

## DEATHS IN CUSTODY

In May, Abdullah Zu'bi died in custody in

Irbid following his arrest for alleged drugs offences. Three police officers were charged with forcing a "confession" and beating Abdullah Zu'bi to death; two others faced charges of negligence and disobeying orders. An official autopsy, conducted after a video of Abdullah Zu'bi's bruised body was shared on the internet, attributed his death to a beating inflicted in custody. At the end of the year it remained unclear whether the accused police officers had been tried. In another case, an official autopsy concluded that Omar al-Naser died due to being beaten in CID custody in September; the case was referred to the police Public Prosecutor. Police officers accused of such crimes in Jordan are prosecuted before a special police court that is neither independent nor transparent.

## ADMINISTRATIVE DETENTION

During the year, thousands of people were detained under the 1954 Crime Prevention Law, which empowers regional governors to authorize the detention of criminal suspects for up to one year without charge, trial or any means of legal remedy.

## FREEDOMS OF EXPRESSION, ASSOCIATION AND ASSEMBLY

The authorities restricted the rights to freedom of expression, association and assembly using laws that criminalize peaceful protest and other peaceful expression. Tens of journalists and activists were arrested and detained, including under provisions of the Penal Code, which bans criticism of the King and government institutions, and the anti-terrorism law as amended in 2014, which criminalizes criticism of foreign leaders or states that is deemed to harm Jordan's relations with those states. Those prosecuted included journalists, pro-reformists and members of the Muslim Brotherhood, some of whom were tried before the SSC.

The Ministry of Justice proposed comprehensive amendments to the Penal Code, which were pending at the end of the year, including a proposal to prohibit and criminalize strikes by workers in "vital sectors".

## WOMEN'S RIGHTS

Women suffered discrimination in law and practice, and were inadequately protected against violence, including so-called "honour" crimes. The Citizenship Law continued to bar almost 89,000 Jordanian women with foreign spouses from passing their nationality to their children or spouses, denying them access to state services. In January, however, the government enabled the children of women with foreign spouses to apply for identity cards if they have resided in Jordan for at least five years, thus increasing their access to medical care, education, work permits, property ownership and a driving licence.

Tadamun, the Jordanian Women's Solidarity Association, reported in September that it had documented 10 possible "honour" killings of women and girls between January and August, based on media reports. In May, the cabinet approved amendments cancelling provisions of the Penal Code under which rapists could escape prosecution by marrying their victim. This did not apply to cases where the rape victim was between 15 and 18 years old, on the grounds that marriage to the perpetrator could protect her from being killed by family members in the name of "honour".

## REFUGEES AND ASYLUM-SEEKERS

Jordan hosted more than 641,800 refugees from Syria, including some 13,800 Palestinians, as well as a growing number of refugees from Iraq. The authorities maintained strict controls at official and informal border crossings and denied entry to Palestinians, single unaccompanied men unable to prove family ties in Jordan, and people without identity documents. In March, Prime Minister Ensour told the Third International Humanitarian Pledging Conference that refugee numbers already exceeded Jordan's capacity. Yet international humanitarian funding and resettlement allocations for Syria's refugees in Jordan remained inadequate.

Jordan forcibly returned scores of refugees to Syria. In violation of international law it denied entry to over 12,000 refugees from Syria who remained in dire conditions in the desert area on the Jordanian side of the border with Syria; and, in December, deported more than 500 Sudanese refugees and asylum-seekers to Sudan, where they were at risk of human rights violations.

## DEATH PENALTY

Courts continued to impose death sentences and executions were carried out. In February, Sajida al-Rishawi and Ziad al-Karbouli, two Iraqi nationals linked to al-Qa'ida, were hanged. It appeared from the timing of the executions that they were a response to the killing by IS of a Jordanian pilot. In 2006, Sajida al-Rishawi had told the UN Special Rapporteur on torture that she had been tortured in pre-trial detention.

# KAZAKHSTAN

Republic of Kazakhstan
Head of state: Nursultan Nazarbayev
Head of government: Karim Massimov

Impunity for torture and other ill-treatment remained largely unchallenged, and there was still no independent and full investigation into reports of torture following the suppression of the Zhanaozen protests in 2011. Freedoms of expression, association and peaceful assembly continued to be restricted.

## BACKGROUND

A new Criminal Code, Criminal Procedure Code and Code of Administrative Offences came into force at the beginning of the year. Early presidential elections were held unexpectedly in April. President Nazarbayev was re-elected to a fifth term in office, winning 97.7% of the vote. OSCE election monitors reported that the elections lacked "credible opposition".

Falling oil prices led to an economic downturn. The national currency was devalued in August.

## TORTURE AND OTHER ILL-TREATMENT

The new Criminal Code and Criminal Procedure Code included positive amendments. The changes included a provision that allegations of torture should be automatically registered and investigated as criminal offences by a different agency from the one whose officers were accused of abuse, bypassing the prior internal screening which had resulted in the dismissal of most complaints. The statute of limitations in relation to cases of torture was abolished, and those charged or convicted of torture were excluded from potential amnesties. The maximum penalty for torture was increased to 12 years' imprisonment. However, lawyers reported that, while complaints of torture and other ill-treatment were registered as crimes, they were still not properly investigated. In May, Iskander Tugelbaev was beaten in prison; he was in a coma for three days, which left him unable to speak or walk unaided, according to his lawyer. At the end of the year, he was still waiting to hear whether the case would proceed to prosecution.

From 1 January to 30 November, 119 complaints of torture were registered and 465 cases of torture were terminated. Eleven cases reached court and five people were found guilty, of whom only one was given a prison sentence. These numbers did not reveal the real scale of the problem, as many victims were too afraid to register a complaint of torture.

Public Monitoring Commissions and the National Preventive Mechanism (NPM) had the right to visit prisons and most places of detention, but had limited capacity and resources to do so, and faced bureaucratic restrictions. The NPM could only undertake unannounced visits with the Ombudsman's permission.

# FREEDOM OF EXPRESSION

The operating climate for the media remained restricted, and media outlets were forcibly closed or prevented from operating on administrative grounds or because they were accused of being a threat to national security. Journalists continued to face harassment and intimidation. Independent media outlets had difficulty generating advertising revenue, as businesses feared reprisals from the authorities if they placed advertisements in these publications.

In February, an appeal against the closure of the newspaper *Adam Bol* was rejected. *Adam Bol* had been closed down on national security grounds in December 2014, after it published an interview with a member of the opposition who was based in Ukraine. Later in the year, the Almaty city authorities attempted to close down its successor publication, *Adam,* on administrative grounds. In September, a three-month ban came into force, on the grounds that *Adam* was registered to publish in Russian and Kazakh, but was only publishing in Russian. In October, *Adam* was ordered by a court to close down upon the request of the Office of the Prosecutor General, on the grounds that it was illegally continuing to publish content via its Facebook page.

Amendments to the Communications Law adopted in 2014 gave the Office of the Prosecutor General the power to force internet providers to block access to internet content without a court order, should that content be deemed as "extremist" and a security threat. These powers were used to block access intermittently or permanently to Kazakhstan-based news outlets and to individual articles on international news sites.

The Criminal Code retained criminal sanctions for defamation and for vaguely worded offences of inciting social and other "discord". At least four people faced criminal investigation for inciting national discord for their posts on social media sites.

A proposed Law on Protection of Children from Information Harming their Health and Development included administrative sanctions for "propaganda of non-traditional sexual orientation" among minors.[1] It was rejected by the Constitutional Council in May for technical reasons, but was expected to be revised and sent back to Parliament.

# FREEDOM OF ASSOCIATION

Clauses in the Criminal and Administrative Offences Codes made it a criminal offence to lead or participate in an unregistered organization. "Leaders" of associations became a separate category of offenders, providing for harsher penalties; the definition of "leader" was very broad, potentially including any active member of an NGO or other civic association. In practice, many NGOs were denied registration for minor infringements.

In October, legal amendments affecting NGOs' access to funding were passed by Parliament, and were signed into law in December. These will lead to the creation of a central "operator" to administer and distribute all state and non-state grants to NGOs, including foreign funding, for projects and activities that comply with a vaguely worded list of issues approved by the government. Failure to supply accurate information for the operator's centralized database could lead to fines or a temporary ban on activities. Civil society activists were concerned that this new law would limit NGOs' access to foreign funding and constrain their activities.

# FREEDOM OF ASSEMBLY

Freedom of peaceful assembly remained heavily restricted. Permission from local authorities was needed to hold any kind of street protest and this was often refused, or permission was given to hold the event in a non-central location. Penalties of up to 75 days' administrative detention were introduced for violations of the rules on holding assemblies; "promotion" of a protest, including via social media, was effectively criminalized.

Authorities used "preventive" detention to stop peaceful protests from going ahead. In January, journalists were arrested on their way to a protest in Almaty in support of *Adam Bol*; they were taken to local police stations to "acquaint them with the law", and released shortly after.

The UN Special Rapporteur on the rights to freedom of peaceful assembly and of association, who visited Kazakhstan in January and August, called on the authorities to allow an international investigation into the use of lethal force against protesters in Zhanaozen in 2011, and into reports of torture and other ill-treatment of those detained following the protests. He also expressed concern that the criminalization of "incitement of discord" in the Criminal Code could be used to criminalize the activities of political parties and trade unions.

---

1.  Urgent action: Kazakhstan: Stop LGBTI "propaganda" legislation (EUR 57/1298/2015)

# KENYA

**Republic of Kenya**
Head of state and government: **Uhuru Muigai Kenyatta**

---

**Continued attacks in Kenya carried out by al-Shabaab, the Somali-based armed group, led Kenya to step up its counter-terrorism operations, which resulted in an increase of extrajudicial executions, enforced disappearances and other human rights violations. Human rights organizations reporting on violations by security agencies during these operations were increasingly harassed. Some civil society organizations were shut down or threatened with closure through judicial or administrative measures.**

## BACKGROUND

In the context of counter-terrorism operations and the prevailing security situation, hundreds of individuals were forcibly disappeared or extrajudicially executed. Civil society organizations, especially those documenting human rights violations in the context of security operations, were accused

of not complying with tax and regulatory norms or accused of providing support to terrorists. NGOs were threatened with deregistration by the NGOs Co-ordination Board (NGO Board), which was challenged in court.

Kenya continued to ask the ICC to drop the case involving Deputy President William Ruto, arguing that the Office of the Prosecutor, through local civil society organizations, had procured some of the witnesses. In the build-up to the Assembly of State Parties, MPs affiliated with the ruling coalition ratcheted up calls for the case to be dropped. No measures were put in place to ensure justice and reparations for victims of the 2007-2008 post-electoral violence. The President announced during his State of the Nation address on 26 June that Kenya would set up a reparation fund to compensate victims, but that it would not be limited to victims of the 2007-2008 post-electoral violence.

## POLICE AND SECURITY FORCES

On 2 April, gunmen attacked Garissa University College in northeastern Kenya, near the Somali border. The attackers killed 147 students and injured 79 before detonating suicide vests when cornered by security forces. Al-Shabaab claimed responsibility for the attack. The government made publicly available their list of the most wanted suspected members of al-Shabaab and appealed to the public to provide information leading to their arrest.

On 14 June, 11 people believed to be al-Shabaab members and two Kenyan military officers were killed in an attack on a military base in Lamu, a town near the Kenya-Somalia border. The attack occurred on the first anniversary of a similar attack in Mpeketoni town, in which suspected members of al-Shabaab killed at least 60 people.

## REFUGEES AND ASYLUM-SEEKERS

Politicians and community leaders blamed Somali refugees for the attack on Garissa University College. They publicly claimed that the Daadab refugee camp, in Garissa, was the breeding ground for terrorism. Daadab hosts at least 600,000 refugees and asylum-seekers, most of whom are Somali.

The Deputy President called for the closure of Dadaab refugee camp within three months from April.[1] At a UNHCR, the UN refugee agency, meeting in Geneva on 4 October, Kenya's Interior Minister expressed concern "about the alleged involvement or complacency of some UNHCR personnel, who facilitate terrorist activities" in the country.

Around 350,000 Somali refugees were at risk of being forcibly returned to Somalia, which would amount to a violation of Kenya's obligations under international law and put hundreds of thousands of lives at risk. There were also at least 250,000 refugees from other countries. Forcibly returning them would have put them at risk of human rights abuses, such as rape and killings. Kenya is a party to the UN Refugee Convention and the African Union Convention Governing the Specific Aspects of Refugee Problems in Africa, both of which include the principle of *non-refoulement* that prohibits states from forcibly returning people to a place where they would be at real risk of human rights violations.

## FREEDOM OF EXPRESSION

On 19 December 2014, the President approved the Security Laws (Amendment) Act (SLAA). Two of the sections contain provisions restricting freedom of speech and media freedom. As soon as the amendment was adopted and signed into law, a coalition including opposition parties filed a petition before the High Court challenging many provisions of the SLAA on the grounds that they were contrary to the right to freedom of expression.

On 23 February, the Constitutional and Human Rights Division of the High Court ruled on the constitutionality of the SLAA, holding that eight clauses of the law were unconstitutional. In its ruling, the High Court struck down Section 12 of the law for "violating the freedom of expression and the

media guaranteed under Articles 33 and 34 of the Constitution". The section penalized media coverage "likely to cause public alarm, incitement to violence, or disturb public peace" or that "undermines investigations or security operations by the National Police Service or the Kenya Defence Forces." The maximum sentence for offenders was three years in prison, a fine of 5 million shillings (US$55,000) or both.

On 25 October, the Parliamentary Powers and Privileges Bill 2014 was passed, criminalizing, among other things, any publication deemed by the Speaker of Parliament or parliamentary committee chairs to amount to false or scandalous libel of Parliament. The bill also prescribed a 500,000-shilling fine or two-year jail term, or both, for journalists found guilty of contravening the provision. Journalists reporting on issues such as bribery or corruption scandals were at risk for exercising their right to freedom of expression. On 10November , John Ngirachu, a *Daily Nation* parliamentary editor, was arrested by Criminal Investigation Department officers at Parliament for allegedly breaching confidentiality over a story highlighting questionable spending within the Interior Ministry.

On 7 July, Gatundu South MP Moses Kuria made a statement encouraging residents in his constituency to slash with machetes critics of the National Youth Service project in the constituency. On 8 July, the National Cohesion and Integration Commission (NCIC) called for the Inspector General of the Police to arrest and prosecute the legislator over incitement. Kuria was detained at Kilimani Police Station after the Director of Public Prosecutions (DPP) Keriako Tobiko ordered his prosecution for inciting his constituents. Other politicians also faced charges for incitement, including Nairobi Orange Democratic Movement chair George Aladwa, who appeared in court on 27 October. On 15 December, the DPP lodged an appeal with the High Court to have Kuria and Aladwa detained.

## CRACKDOWN ON CIVIL SOCIETY ORGANIZATIONS

A week after the attack on Garissa University, 85 companies and NGOs, including Muslims for Human Rights (MUHURI) and Haki Africa, were designated as "specified entities" by the Inspector General of the Police (IGP) in a Gazette notice, a step before being classified as a terrorist organization under the Prevention of Terrorism Act.

On 20 and 21 April, the Kenya Revenue Authority raided the offices of MUHURI and Haki Africa, disabling their servers, confiscating computer hard drives and other documents to determine whether the two organizations were tax compliant. Their hard drives were returned on 23 December. The Mombasa High Court ruled on 12 June that the organizations had no links to terrorism, but fell short of giving an explicit order to unfreeze their bank accounts. The two organizations appealed the ruling and on 12 November, the High Court found that the Inspector General of the Police's action to freeze their accounts was unconstitutional and therefore null and void. The judge ordered the immediate unfreezing of the accounts.

On 15 May, a task force created in 2014 by the Cabinet Secretary for Devolution and Planning to consult stakeholders on amendments to the Public Benefit Organizations Act 2013 released its report. Among its key recommendations, the report asked to monitor donors and beneficiaries, as well as Public Benefit Organizations (PBOs), for transparency and accountability. The report also recommended that PBOs be obliged to disclose the sources of their funding and declare how they intend those funds to be utilized. Civil society organizations opposed the recommendations of the report, arguing that many of them never came up during the 2014 public hearings.

On 28 October, the NGO Board notified 957 NGOs, through its executive officer, of their requirement to submit their audited bank accounts within two weeks or be deregistered. The NGO Board accused the NGOs of misappropriation of funds, funding of terrorism, money laundering, diversion of donor money and failing to file their audited books of accounts as required by law. On 30 October, the Cabinet Secretary for Devolution and National Planning ordered the revocation of the decision to issue the notice of deregistration. The NGO Kenya Human Rights Commission instituted a suit against the NGO Board's illegal and irregular actions.

## FREEDOM OF ASSEMBLY

On 19 January, the police used tear gas against schoolchildren of Langata Primary School who were peacefully protesting against a politician's alleged move to seize their playground and turn it into a car park. Five pupils and a police officer were injured during the protest. The officer in charge of the operation was suspended.

## FORCED EVICTIONS

During the night of 17 May, a bulldozer accompanied by armed police woke up residents of Jomvu in Mombasa County.[2] The bulldozer demolished shops and homes that had been marked with yellow crosses for demolition, to pave way for the expansion of the Mombasa-Mariakani Highway. The authorities had not adequately engaged residents of Jomvu in prior genuine consultations on the evictions and alternatives to them. Over 100 people were made homeless overnight. Approximately 3,000 residents of Deep Sea, an informal settlement in the capital, Nairobi, were threatened with evictions multiple times to make way for the EU-funded "Missing Link" road construction project.[3] The community had challenged the eviction in court and raised concerns around due process and adequate compensation. On 8 July, the Kenya Urban Roads Authority told residents that unless they withdrew their court action challenging the eviction, authorities would not engage with them.

On 21 August, more than 300 homes were destroyed and an estimated 500 people were forcibly evicted in a government operation in Nairobi's informal settlement of Mathare. No warnings were given and no alternative housing was provided.

## RIGHTS OF LESBIAN, GAY, BISEXUAL, TRANSGENDER AND INTERSEX PEOPLE

On 24 April, the High Court ruled that members of an LGBTI rights organization could formally register their organization. The Court rendered its decision following a petition filed by the National Gay and Lesbian Human Rights Commission to register under the NGO Board Act. The NGO Board had rejected the group's request to register in March 2013. The three-judge High Court ruled that the NGO Board's decision violated Article 36 of Kenya's Constitution and was contrary to the right of freedom of association.

1. Crisis looms for Somali refugees as Kenya orders closure of Dadaab refugee camp (News story, 16 April)
2. Kenya: Driven out for development; forced evictions in Mombasa, Kenya (AFR 32/2467/2015)
3. Kenya: Deep Sea residents at risk of forced eviction (AFR 32/2054/2015)

# KOREA (DEMOCRATIC PEOPLE'S REPUBLIC OF)

Democratic People's Republic of Korea
Head of state: **Kim Jong-un**
Head of government: **Pak Pong-ju**

North Koreans continued to suffer denial and violations of almost every aspect of their human rights. Authorities continued to arbitrarily arrest and detain individuals without fair trial or access to lawyers and family, including nationals of the Republic of Korea (South Korea). Households, particularly those with members suspected of having fled the country or trying to access outside information, remained under systematic surveillance. The government arranged for more than 50,000 people to work in other countries, collecting their wages directly from employers and keeping a significant portion for its own revenue. Little progress was made in addressing cases of abductions and enforced disappearances of foreign nationals.

## BACKGROUND

In the fourth year of Kim Jong-un's rule, international media continued to report executions of senior officials. The Head of State did not attend celebrations marking the anniversary of the end of World War II in China and Russia. Inter-Korean relations remained tense. Explosions of North Korean landmines in the demilitarized zone between North and South Korea in early August caused severe injuries to two South Korean soldiers. South Korean broadcasts across the border to seek an apology resulted in the military on both sides exchanging artillery fire later that month. The tension was resolved after a 43-hour high-level dialogue; North Korea expressed regret over the explosions, and a mutual agreement was reached to continue the reunions of separated families. Natural disasters including a severe summer drought and floods killed at least 40 people, and affected more than 10,000 others, according to state media.

## FREEDOM OF EXPRESSION

The authorities continued to impose severe restrictions on freedom of expression, including the right to seek, receive and impart information regardless of national borders. Although there were three million domestic mobile service subscribers among the population of 25 million, virtually all nationals were barred from international mobile telephone services and access to the internet. Only tourists and foreign residents were allowed to purchase special SIM cards to make calls outside the country or access the internet using smart phones. The existing computer network remained available, providing access to domestic websites and domestic email services only, but even this was not yet widely accessible.

North Koreans who lived close to the Chinese border undertook significant risks in using smuggled mobile phones that were connected to Chinese networks in order to make contact with individuals outside the country. People who did not own one of these phones needed to pay an exorbitant fee and go through a broker. While calling outside North Korea was not a criminal offence in itself, the use of smuggled mobile phones to connect to Chinese mobile networks exposed all individuals involved to the risk of surveillance, as well as arrest and detention on various charges, including espionage.

The government continued to restrict access to various outside sources of information despite the absence of any domestic independent newspapers, media or civil society organizations. Authorities used radio waves to obstruct the reception of foreign television or radio broadcasts, while also making foreign channels unreceivable on legally available appliances. Individuals keeping, watching or copying and sharing foreign audiovisual materials risked arrest, if the material was deemed to be "hostile broadcasting or enemy propaganda" under the criminal law.

## RIGHT TO PRIVACY
North Koreans who made calls using smuggled mobile phones reported that they experienced frequent jamming of lines and wiretapping of conversations, among other forms of infringement on the right to privacy. A special unit of the State Security Department for covert intelligence and digital operations used sophisticated, imported monitoring devices to detect mobile phone users who tried to make calls out of the country. Individuals whose conversations were overheard could be arrested if they were found calling someone in South Korea, or if they requested money to be sent to them.

Person-to-person systems of surveillance also remained a threat to privacy. Neighbourhood groups set up by the government for such purposes as ideological education were authorized to conduct home visits at any time, and report on people's activities. Group leaders, together with another dedicated unit of the State Security Department, monitored people's radio and television habits. Households that were suspected of watching foreign audiovisual materials, or receiving money from a family member who had fled the country, were subject to heightened surveillance.

## ARBITRARY ARRESTS AND DETENTIONS
North Koreans who fled the country reported that arrests had increased, as border controls of both people and goods had tightened under Kim Jong-un's rule. These arrests were arbitrary, as they often took place as a punishment for exercising human rights, as a crackdown on the private market economy, or for extorting bribes.

Hundreds of thousands of people remained detained in political prison camps and other detention facilities, where they were subjected to systematic, widespread and gross human rights violations such as torture and other ill-treatment, and forced labour. Many of those held in these camps had not been convicted of any internationally recognizable criminal offence, but were detained through "guilt-by-association", only for being related to individuals deemed threatening to the state.

In May and June, three South Korean men, Kim Jung-wook, Kim Kuk-gi and Choe Chun-gil, were given life sentences after being convicted of espionage, among other charges, through judicial procedures that fell short of international fair trial standards. A South Korean student, Joo Won-moon, who had been arrested for illegally entering the country in April, was released in October after more than five months of detention without access to his lawyer or family.[1]

## MIGRANT WORKERS' RIGHTS
The government dispatched at least 50,000 people to countries such as Libya, Mongolia, Nigeria, Qatar and Russia to work in various sectors including medicine, construction,

forestry and catering. Workers were often subjected to excessively long hours, poor safety conditions, deprivation of information about labour laws and lack of access to any government agencies monitoring compliance. Workers did not receive wages directly from employers, but through the North Korean government after significant deductions. Workers remained under surveillance in the host countries as they would be in North Korea, and contact with the local population was heavily restricted.

## FREEDOM OF MOVEMENT

In the first 10 months of 2015, the South Korean Ministry of Unification reported the arrival of 978 North Koreans, among them a teenage soldier who walked across the inter-Korean border on 15 June. According to South Korea media, the North Korean military planted extra landmines in 2015 to prevent its soldiers from fleeing to South Korea. The numbers of arrivals were in line with the 1,397 people reported to have arrived in 2014, and similar figures for 2013 and 2012. These figures remained low compared with previous years, due to tight border controls.

North Koreans forcibly returned from China or other countries continued to be at risk of detention, imprisonment, forced labour and torture and other ill-treatment. China ignored non-refoulement obligations in international law by sending back North Koreans and seemingly continued this practice through a 1986 agreement with North Korean authorities. Russia was reported to be formalizing a similar agreement.

## RIGHT TO FOOD

The UN Food and Agriculture Organization reported in September that, after increases in three consecutive years, food production had been stagnant in 2014, while the drought of 2015 had reduced the production of rice and other cereals by more than 10%. Possibly as a result, the government reduced the daily food rations for households in July and August from 410g to 250g per person, well below the amount distributed during the same months in 2013 and 2014. The public distribution system was the main channel of providing food to at least 18 million people – three quarters of the population. With the reduction in rations, the right to adequate food of most individuals was severely threatened.

## INTERNATIONAL SCRUTINY

Following intensified international scrutiny after the publication in 2014 of a report by the UN Commission of Inquiry on Human Rights in the Democratic People's Republic of Korea, and related discussion at the UN Security Council later that year, the UN High Commissioner for Human Rights opened a field office in Seoul, the capital of South Korea, on 23 June. The new office had been among the recommendations of the report, and was tasked with monitoring and documenting the human rights situation in North Korea, as steps towards accountability. Its opening was met with severe criticism from the North Korean government. The UN Security Council held another discussion of human rights in North Korea on 10 December.

Other UN bodies made efforts to address international abductions and enforced disappearances, but yielded minimal tangible progress. The North Korean government wrote to the UN Working Group on Enforced or Involuntary Disappearances in August with regard to 27 outstanding cases; the Working Group noted in its report that the information provided was insufficient for clarification of the cases.

---

1. Further information: Student released by North Korea (ASA 24/2609/2015)

# KOREA (REPUBLIC OF)

Republic of Korea
Head of state: **Park Geun-hye**
Head of government: **Hwang Kyo-ahn (replaced Chung Hong-won in June)**

The authorities continued to restrict the rights to freedom of expression, association and peaceful assembly. Police used unnecessary force during a vigil walk in memory of the victims of the Sewol ferry accident, and a protester was seriously injured in a demonstration where police used water cannons. Although the right of conscientious objectors to be exempted from military service continued to be denied, lower courts made a number of decisions in favour of recognizing conscientious objection. Migrant agricultural workers faced trafficking for exploitation.

## BACKGROUND

The outbreak of the Middle East Respiratory Syndrome (Mers) resulted in 38 deaths, restrictions to daily life and a severe blow to the economy of the Republic of Korea. The government was criticized by the public and international actors for inadequate preparation and delay in the response to the virus. The selection of the new Chairperson of the National Human Rights Commission of Korea lacked transparency and there was insufficient consultation with civil society groups and other relevant stakeholders.[1] The annual Pride Parade took place peacefully in June although police initially rejected the application, citing clashes between lesbian, gay, bisexual, transgender and intersex participants and conservative protesters in 2014.

## FREEDOM OF EXPRESSION

Detentions and prosecutions under the National Security Law (NSL) were used to intimidate and imprison people exercising their right to freedom of expression. The government broadened the application of the NSL to include new categories and additional groups of individuals such as politicians, serving parliamentarians and foreign nationals.

In January, the Supreme Court upheld an earlier Seoul High Court decision which found Lee Seok-ki and six other members of the opposition Unified Progressive Party (UPP) guilty of charges under the NSL, shortly after the Constitutional Court decision in late 2014 that dissolved the UPP because it had violated the country's "basic democratic order".

Also in January, US national Shin Eun-mi was deported for allegedly speaking positively about the Democratic People's Republic of Korea (North Korea). Hwang Seon, a national of South Korea, was arrested the same month, charged in February under the NSL with "causing social confusion" through a speaking tour allegedly praising the North Korea regime, and was released on bail in June.[2]

## CONSCIENTIOUS OBJECTORS

No effective steps were taken to recognize the right of conscientious objectors to be exempted from military service.[3] More than 600 conscientious objectors remained in prison, facing economic and social disadvantages beyond their jail terms due to their criminal records.

However, a number of decisions recognizing conscientious objection have been made by lower courts, including three in 2015. While the Constitutional Court was still examining the legality of conscientious objection, in May the Gwangju District Court acquitted three conscientious objectors accused of breaking the law by refusing military duty. District courts in Suwon and Gwangju further acquitted three other conscientious objectors in August.

The revision of the Military Service Act and the Enforcement Decree of the Military Service Act came into force on 1 July. Based on this revision, information on individuals refusing to perform military service without "justifiable" reasons was liable to be made public on the internet, potentially leading to violations of the rights to freedom of thought, conscience and religion, to privacy and to freedom from discrimination.[4]

## FREEDOM OF ASSOCIATION

In May, the Constitutional Court upheld the constitutionality of Article 2 of the Teachers' Union Act, which provided the government with the legal basis to strip the Korean Teachers and Education Workers Union of its official status. At the end of the year the original case challenging the government's action was still pending at the Seoul High Court.

The Supreme Court ruled in June that irregular migrant workers had the same rights to form and join a union as other South Korean workers, but the authorities continued to delay registering the Seoul-Gyeonggi-Incheon Migrants' Trade Union (MTU). The Seoul Regional Labour Office demanded that the MTU change its rules and regulations before finally granting registration in August.

## FREEDOM OF ASSEMBLY

The Sewol ferry accident in April 2014, which resulted in the deaths of more than 300 people, many of them students, generated a series of overwhelmingly peaceful demonstrations expressing discontent about the government's response. Police blockaded street rallies marking the one-year anniversary and used unnecessary force against participants on a vigil walk in memory of the victims, near Gwanghwamun in central Seoul on 16 April.[5]

In July, two prominent human rights defenders, Park Rae-goon and Kim Hye-jin, were detained by police for organizing demonstrations to seek additional action from the government in response to the accident.[6] The two were members of the standing committee for the group "April 16 Alliance" calling for an investigation into the accident. They had been under investigation for three months on charges which included violation of the Assembly and Demonstration Act and obstructing police in relation to the rallies. The police claimed that some of these protests were illegal, even though the protesters said they were lawfully exercising their rights to freedom of expression and peaceful assembly.

## MIGRANT WORKERS' RIGHTS

Migrant agricultural workers continued to be trafficked for exploitation, including forced labour. Many were compelled to work in conditions they had not agreed to – including excessive working hours and underpayment – under the threat of punishment such as dismissal and violence. Under the terms of the Employment Permit System, it was extremely difficult for migrant workers to seek and secure alternative employment if they were subject to exploitation or other abuse by their employer.

## DEATH PENALTY

In July, lawmaker Yu In-tae of the New Politics Alliance for Democracy submitted a bill to the National Assembly that would abolish the death penalty. This was the seventh time that such a bill had been introduced but none were brought to a vote before the full Assembly.

---

1. South Korea: Secrecy of Chair appointment undermines independence of National Human Rights Commission of Korea (ASA 25/2161/2015)
2. South Korea: National Security Law continues to restrict freedom of expression (ASA 25/001/2015)
3. South Korea: Sentenced to life – conscientious objectors in South Korea (ASA 25/1512/2015)
4. South Korea: Amnesty International's submission to the UN Human Rights Committee, 115th Session (19 October - 6 November 2015) (ASA 25/2372/2015)
5. South Korea: Clampdown against Sewol ferry anniversary protest an insult to the victims (Press Release, 17 April)
6. South Korea: Arrest of two human rights defenders for organizing demonstrations (ASA 25/2129/2015)

# KUWAIT

**State of Kuwait**
Head of state: **Sheikh Sabah al-Ahmad al-Jaber al-Sabah**
Head of government: **Sheikh Jaber al-Mubarak al-Hamad al-Sabah**

The authorities tightened restrictions on freedom of expression, including by adopting a new cybercrime law, and prosecuting opposition and online critics. The government also adopted a law requiring all citizens and residents to provide DNA samples on anti-terrorism grounds. Members of the Bidun minority faced discrimination and were denied citizenship rights. Migrant workers faced inadequate protection against exploitation and abuse. Courts continued to hand down death sentences; no executions were reported.

## BACKGROUND

On 26 June a suicide bomber attacked the Imam Sadiq Mosque, a Shi'a mosque in Kuwait City, killing 27 people and wounding more than 220 others. It was Kuwait's most devastating suicide attack to date.

In March, Kuwait joined the Saudi Arabia-led international coalition that engaged in the armed conflict in Yemen (see Yemen entry).

In June, the government accepted 179 recommendations made during the UPR of Kuwait, including nine relating to freedom of expression. It rejected 71 others, including recommendations on the rights of Bidun and advocating abolition of the death penalty.

## FREEDOMS OF EXPRESSION AND ASSEMBLY

The authorities continued to restrict the right to freedom of expression, prosecuting and imprisoning government critics and online activists under penal code provisions that criminalize comments deemed offensive to the Emir, the judiciary and foreign leaders. In June, Parliament adopted a new cybercrime law criminalizing and further restricting online expression, due to come into force in January 2016, and extended prohibitions in existing legislation to include online expression, including social media and blogs.

There were prosecutions for insulting Arab leaders on social media, including the late King Abdullah of Saudi Arabia.

In January, a court sentenced Bidun rights activist Abdulhakim al-Fadhli to one year's imprisonment followed by deportation on charges arising from his participation in a February 2014 gathering that marked the third anniversary of a demonstration calling for Bidun people to be granted Kuwaiti citizenship. His sentence was upheld on appeal in December. He also received a separate five-year prison term and a deportation order after a court convicted him on charges of insulting the Emir, damaging a police vehicle and taking part in an illegal demonstration.

In March, police arrested and beat human rights activist Nawaf al-Hendal as he monitored a peaceful opposition demonstration. He was detained for two days before being charged with "illegal gathering".

Musallam al-Barrak, a prominent government critic and former MP, began serving a two-year prison term in June. He had been sentenced in April 2013 to five years' imprisonment for a speech criticizing the government; the sentence was reduced on appeal. More than 60 others who protested against his arrest by publicizing or reciting extracts from his speech also faced prosecution; two people were sentenced to prison terms and 21 others received suspended sentences.

In July, prosecutors questioned 13 people over discussions on the social media site WhatsApp about video footage taken in 2014 that appeared to show leading members of the government advocating the Emir's removal from power. The 13, who included members of the ruling family, were freed on bail and banned from leaving Kuwait; their trial was ongoing.

## COUNTER-TERROR AND SECURITY

The authorities increased security measures following the June suicide bombing at the Imam Sadiq Mosque. They tried 29 Kuwaitis and foreign nationals, five in their absence, on charges linked to the attack. Fifteen were convicted and, of these, seven were sentenced to death. In December, the Appeal Court confirmed one of the death sentences and commuted another to 15 years' imprisonment; it had not ruled on the other defendants' appeals by the end of the year.

The authorities also prosecuted people accused of supporting extreme jihadist armed groups in Iraq and Syria. In July, the Criminal Court sentenced six men to prison terms ranging from five to 20 years, followed by deportation, after convicting them of "hostile acts" against Iraq and Syria, endangering Kuwait's relations with those countries, and joining the banned organization Daesh (another name for the armed group Islamic State, or IS). Another two defendants were acquitted. All eight defendants alleged in court that security officials had beaten them in pre-trial detention to coerce them to confess. The court failed to investigate their allegations.

In July, Parliament approved a new law requiring all citizens and residents in Kuwait to provide samples of their DNA, citing anti-terrorism as the justification. Refusal to comply with the law became punishable by up to one year's imprisonment and a fine. Press reports in July indicated that the government planned to implement an emergency decree to extend the length of time that a suspect can be held in detention without charge; however, no such provision had been enacted by the end of the year.

In September, further torture allegations emerged after 25 Kuwaitis and an Iranian went on trial before the Criminal Court accused of espionage and terrorism-related charges. The defendants said officials had tortured them with electric shocks, hanging by the legs and beatings to force them to "confess". The Court was due to deliver its verdict in January 2016.

## DEPRIVATION OF NATIONALITY

In April, the authorities arrested Sa'ad al-'Ajmi, a political activist and adviser to former MP Musallam al-Barrak (see above), and deported him to Saudi Arabia, claiming that he held Saudi citizenship, which he denied.

In May, the Administrative Appeal Court ordered the government to restore the Kuwaiti citizenship of Abdullah Hashr al-Barghash, a former MP whose nationality the authorities revoked in July 2014. The government appealed against the ruling. In November the Administrative Appeal Court ruled that the case fell outside its jurisdiction.

## DISCRIMINATION – BIDUN

The government continued to withhold Kuwaiti citizenship from over 100,000 Bidun, or stateless residents of Kuwait, whom they considered to be illegal residents. Bidun rights activists faced arrest and prosecution. Two days after the June mosque bombing, for which 13 Bidun were among those arrested, the authorities stopped issuing Bidun with travel documents except for those seeking medical treatment abroad.

In an August memorandum to Parliament, the government's Central System to Resolve Illegal Residents' Status, which administers Bidun affairs in Kuwait, said that it was not mandatory that 31,189 Bidun listed in the 1965 census, used by the government as the basis for determining citizenship, should be naturalized. The Central System said that other considerations, such as security, should be taken into account when considering their right to Kuwaiti nationality. This determination adds a further obstacle for Bidun to be granted Kuwaiti nationality.

## WOMEN'S RIGHTS

Kuwaiti women had the right to vote and stand as candidates in elections, but continued to face discrimination in law and in practice. In particular, the law accorded women fewer rights than men in family matters, such as divorce, child custody and inheritance.

## MIGRANT WORKERS' RIGHTS

Migrant workers, including those in the domestic, construction and other sectors, faced exploitation and abuse. Parliament passed a law in June that for the first time gave migrant domestic workers, predominantly women, labour rights including one day of rest per week, 30 days' annual paid leave and an end-of-service payment equivalent to one month's salary for each year worked.

## DEATH PENALTY

At least 15 people were sentenced to death, including five in their absence. No executions were reported.

# KYRGYZSTAN

Kyrgyz Republic
Head of state: **Almaz Atambaev**
Head of government: **Temir Sariev (replaced Dzhoomart Otorbaev in May)**

No impartial and effective investigation took place into human rights violations, including crimes against humanity, committed during the June 2010 violence and its aftermath. The authorities failed to take effective measures to end torture and other ill-treatment and bring perpetrators to justice. The space for civil society continued to shrink, against the background of growing intolerance towards ethnic, sexual and other minorities. Legislation restricting freedoms of expression and association was introduced and later withdrawn "for consultation". Prisoner of conscience Azimjan Askarov remained in detention while the homes of lawyers and the NGO who worked on his and other ethnic Uzbeks' cases were raided by security officials.

## TORTURE AND OTHER ILL-TREATMENT

Torture and other ill-treatment, and impunity for these violations, remained commonplace despite the introduction, in late 2014, of a programme of monitoring of places of detention under the National Preventive Mechanism and instructions on how to document torture issued by the Ministry of Health to medical personnel based on the UN Manual on the Effective Investigation and Documentation of Torture and Other Cruel, Inhuman or Degrading Treatment or Punishment (Istanbul Protocol).

On 16 June 2015, the European Court of Human Rights issued a judgment on *Khamrakulov v. Russia*, stating that forcible return of ethnic Uzbek applicants from Russia to Kyrgyzstan would expose them to risk of torture and other ill-treatment.

Kyrgyzstan accepted the recommendations of the UPR of Kyrgyzstan in June, aimed at combating torture and other ill-treatment. These concerned the investigation of allegations, particularly those by members of ethnic minorities, relating to the June 2010 violence and ensuring that the National Centre for the Prevention of Torture be adequately resourced and remained independent.

## IMPUNITY

Only a minority of alleged torture and of gender-based violence cases led to an effective investigation, and still fewer resulted in the prosecution of perpetrators.

The NGO Coalition against Torture in Kyrgyzstan documented 79 cases of torture and other ill-treatment in the first half of 2015. A specialist investigation unit created by the Prosecutor General's Office in June started criminal investigations into three cases of torture. By October, 35 criminal cases in relation to over 80 law enforcement officers accused of acts of torture were under consideration by the courts. However, only in four cases dating back to 2011 did courts hand down a guilty verdict.

The authorities made no genuine effort to effectively investigate the June 2010 ethnic violence in Osh and Jalal-Abad, where serious crimes were committed by members of both ethnic Kyrgyz and Uzbek communities, but the latter sustained most deaths, injuries and damage. Since then, ethnic Uzbeks have been targeted disproportionately for prosecution. Nonetheless, Kyrgyzstan rejected the UPR recommendations to redress the lack of ethnic representation in the police and security forces, and adopt comprehensive anti-discrimination legislation. Lawyers defending ethnic Uzbeks detained in the context of the violence have continued to face harassment in connection with their work.

On 21 May, the Sokolukski District Court sentenced three staff members of a local court in the Talas region to eight years each for gang-raping a woman, Kalia Arabekova, in December 2013. However, the judge refused to order the arrest of the men pending their appeal hearing, despite the victim's repeated complaints about the threats she was receiving. On the night of 21 July, she was assaulted, threatened and raped at her place of residence by two masked men, one of whom she was able to recognize as her initial assailant.

## PRISONERS OF CONSCIENCE
Azimjan Askarov, an ethnic Uzbek human rights defender and a prisoner of conscience who was sentenced to life in prison for purportedly participating in the 2010 ethnic violence, remained in prison. His award by the US State Department of the Human Rights Defenders Award in July prompted an angry response from senior Kyrgyz officials. The President denounced the award as a provocation aimed at inciting separatism and the government rescinded a 1993 co-operation agreement with the USA.

## FREEDOMS OF EXPRESSION AND ASSOCIATION
In a climate of growing intolerance and discrimination against members of the lesbian, gay, bisexual, transgender and intersex (LGBTI) community, a draft homophobic law introduced in Parliament in 2014 was adopted in its second reading in June by an overwhelming majority of MPs. It proposed amendments to the Criminal Code and other legislation which criminalized

"fostering positive attitude" towards "non-traditional sexual relations", and envisaged sanctions ranging from fines to one-year imprisonment. The draft law was withdrawn before it could be voted in the third and final reading, "for additional consultation", and is expected to be returned to Parliament again.

Human rights defenders and other civil society activists faced increasing harassment and pressure from the authorities in connection with their work, and complained of a growing climate of insecurity.

A draft law was reintroduced in Parliament that would force NGOs receiving foreign aid and engaging in any form of vaguely defined "political activities" to adopt and publicly use the stigmatizing label of "foreign agents". The President and senior political figures spoke strongly in support of this initiative, modelled on similar legislation adopted in Russia in 2012. The draft law was withdrawn "for further discussion" in June, but was expected to be back before Parliament for further consideration and adoption.

On 27 March members of the State Committee of National Security (GKNB) in Osh searched the office of human rights NGO Bir Duino ("one world") and the homes of two lawyers working for it, Valerian Vakhitov and Khusanbai Saliev. During these raids, GKNB officers seized documents relating to the cases the lawyers were working on, as well as computers and digital memory devices. The lawyers' complaint about the searches and the local court's decision authorizing them was heard at Osh Regional Court and the Supreme Court on 30 April and 24 June respectively, both of which ruled that the searches constituted illegal interference in the lawyers' work. Bir Duino has, among other things, provided legal assistance to ethnic Uzbeks who faced prosecution following the June 2010 violence in Osh, including Azimjan Askarov.

# LAOS

Lao People's Democratic Republic
Head of state: **Choummaly Sayasone**
Head of government: **Thongsing Thammavong**

**Severe restrictions on freedom of expression, association and peaceful assembly continued and authorities prepared to further tighten control of civil society groups. Two prisoners of conscience arrested in 1999 for attempting a peaceful protest remained imprisoned. One activist was imprisoned for online criticism of the government. Restrictions on practising Christianity were reported, including arrests and prosecutions. No progress was recorded in the case of a prominent civil society member, three years after his enforced disappearance.**

## BACKGROUND

In June, Laos accepted 116 of 196 recommendations received during the second UPR of Laos. While Laos did not reject outright any recommendations, it indicated disagreement with the remaining 80 recommendations which were noted. Several of these pertained to freedom of expression, association and peaceful assembly, and to human rights defenders.

Ahead of Laos chairing the ASEAN in 2016, civil society groups in the region called for their annual gathering, the ASEAN People's Forum, to be held outside the country on the grounds that free discussion of key regional rights issues will be impossible in Laos.

A concession for the construction of a controversial hydropower dam on the Mekong River at Don Sahong was approved by Parliament, despite objections from downstream countries as to the dam's expected ecological and social impact. Construction of the US$3.5 billion Xayaburi Dam entered its final stage. Plans for scores more dams throughout the country were either under development or under construction, including eight mainstream Mekong River dams potentially impacting livelihoods in neighbouring countries.

## FREEDOM OF EXPRESSION

After the enactment of the Prime Ministerial Decree on management of information through the internet in 2014, at least two individuals were arrested in relation to information posted online.

A Natural Resources and Environmental Department staff member was arrested in June for posting a "confidential document" on Facebook regarding a land concession granted by the Luang Prabang local authorities to Chinese investors. She was released in August. Another woman, Phout Mitane, was detained for two months after a photograph she took showing police allegedly extorting money from her brother was posted online.

In October Bounthanh Thammavong, a Polish national of Lao descent, was convicted of criticizing the ruling party in a Facebook posting and sentenced to four-and-a-half years' imprisonment. A diplomatic official complained that Bounthanh Thammavong was denied access to a lawyer during his trial.

## FREEDOM OF ASSOCIATION

A new Decree on Associations and Foundations, severely limiting the right to freedom of association in violation of international law, was still pending in December. In May, the UN Special Rapporteurs on freedom of expression, on freedom of peaceful assembly and association, and on the situation of human rights defenders, expressed serious concerns about numerous provisions of the Decree. It requires associations and foundations to "operate in accordance with the [ruling] Party's policy, government's socio-economic development plan, State's laws and its regulations".

## ENFORCED DISAPPEARANCES

Sombath Somphone, a prominent civil society member who was abducted outside a police post in the capital, Vientiane, in December

2012, remained disappeared with no progress in his case. In March, a former military general heading a non-profit organization – widely believed to be a government proxy – made a failed attempt to have Sombath Somphone's name removed from the agenda of the ASEAN People's Forum event. No progress was made in the case of Sompawn Khantisouk, an entrepreneur who was active on conservation issues. He remained disappeared since being abducted by men believed to be police in 2007. Laos accepted some, but not all, UPR recommendations calling for an impartial investigation into Sombath Somphone's enforced disappearance and for Laos' ratification of the International Convention for the Protection of All Persons from Enforced Disappearance.

## DEATH PENALTY

Approximately 20 people were reported to have been sentenced to death in 2015, mainly for drug-related offences. While Laos is not known to have carried out executions since 1989, it failed to accept more than a dozen UPR recommendations calling for an official moratorium on the death penalty.

# LATVIA

**Republic of Latvia**
Head of state: **Raimonds Vējonis (succeeded Andris Bērziņš in July)**
Head of government: **Laimdota Straujuma**

**Parliament passed amendments to the Education Law which discriminated against lesbian, gay, bisexual, transgender and intersex (LGBTI) people. Protection for LGBTI people against hate crimes remained inadequate. Over 262,000 people remained stateless. Appeals against negative asylum decisions had no suspensive effect, leaving people at risk of being returned to countries where their rights could be violated.**

## RIGHTS OF LESBIAN, GAY, BISEXUAL, TRANSGENDER AND INTERSEX PEOPLE

In June, Parliament passed amendments to the Education Law requiring schools to provide "morality" education based on constitutional values, which include a definition of marriage as the union between a man and a woman. The new legislation risked placing Latvia in breach of its international obligations to respect freedom of expression and the requirement of non-discrimination with regard to LGBTI people's relationships and families. There was also concern that it would restrict children's access to sex and sexuality education with potentially negative impacts on their right to health.

Concerns remained about the lack of express protection in criminal law against incitement to hatred and violence on grounds of sexual orientation and gender identity. In the first nine months of 2015, Latvian NGO Mozaika recorded 14 attacks against LGBTI people. None resulted in serious injuries. Victims told Mozaika they did not report the attacks to the police for fear that they would not be taken seriously.

In June, EuroPride, an international gathering in support of LGBTI people's rights, took place in Riga, the capital, without major incidents. About 5,000 people participated, including three Latvian MPs. The authorities allowed the parade to pass through the main street of Riga and to cover 2.2km, a route four times longer than in the past. The police offered effective protection to participants.

## DISCRIMINATION – STATELESS PERSONS

There continued to be a high number of stateless people – over 262,000 at the beginning of 2015, according to figures of UNHCR, the UN refugee agency. Stateless people, the vast majority ethnic Russians, were excluded from the enjoyment of political rights.

## REFUGEES AND ASYLUM-SEEKERS

The number of asylum applications remained low, with about 200 received in the first eight months of the year. Recognition rates also remained very low. However, in September Latvia agreed to relocate 531 asylum-seekers from other European countries. Concerns remained about the excessive use of detention for asylum-seekers and the non-suspensive effect of appeals against negative decisions under the accelerated asylum procedure. The latter increased the risk of individuals being returned to countries where they could face serious human rights abuses.

# LEBANON

Lebanese Republic
Head of state: **vacant since May 2014, when Michel Suleiman's term ended**
Head of government: **Tammam Salam**

Security forces used excessive force to disperse some demonstrations and to quell a protest by prisoners. Women continued to be discriminated against in law and in practice. Migrant workers faced exploitation and abuse. The authorities took no steps to investigate the fate of thousands of people who disappeared or went missing during the civil war of 1975 to 1990. Palestinian refugees long-resident in Lebanon continued to suffer discrimination. Lebanon hosted over 1.2 million refugees from Syria but closed its border and enforced new entry requirements from January, and barred the entry of Palestinians fleeing from Syria. Courts handed down at least 28 death sentences; there were no executions.

## BACKGROUND

Political disagreements between the main political parties prevented the election of a successor to President Suleiman, who left office in May 2014. In June 2015, thousands of people took to the streets of the capital, Beirut, to protest against the government's failure to provide basic services amid an escalating waste-management crisis, accusing the authorities of corruption and a lack of accountability and transparency.

The armed conflict in Syria had huge repercussions for Lebanon. Cross-border firing and the participation of Hizbullah fighters in the conflict in support of the Syrian government threatened Lebanon's security. Some 1.2 million Syrians had claimed refugee status in Lebanon by the end of the year. In January, Lebanon ended its open-border policy, preventing refugees without entry visas from entering the country.

In August, fighting between rival factions at Ain el-Helweh, Lebanon's largest Palestinian refugee camp, caused three deaths. Security conditions in Tripoli remained fragile due to tensions related to the Syrian conflict. In Syria, the armed group Islamic State (IS) continued to hold Lebanese soldiers and members of security forces whom they abducted in 2014, while Jabhat al-Nusra freed the ones it held.

## EXCESSIVE USE OF FORCE

There were several incidents of excessive use of force, particularly by the Internal Security Forces (ISF). In August, ISF officers and army soldiers used excessive force against people demonstrating in Beirut as part of the "You Stink" protests against the lack of rubbish clearance and other public services. Officers fired live ammunition, rubber bullets, tear gas canisters and water cannon, reportedly injuring over 300 people. The Minister for the Interior said eight members of the ISF would face disciplinary action over the incident.

## TORTURE AND OTHER ILL-TREATMENT

In June, five officers were charged with using violence against prisoners at Roumieh Prison after two videos were posted on social media showing ISF officers beating inmates.

Despite ratifying the Optional Protocol to the UN Convention against Torture in 2000, by the end of the year Lebanon had yet to establish a national monitoring body on torture, as the Optional Protocol requires.

## REFUGEES AND ASYLUM-SEEKERS

Lebanon hosted around 300,000 Palestinian refugees and 1.2 million Syrian refugees. Palestinian refugees, many of whom entered

Lebanon decades ago, remained subject to discriminatory laws and regulations that deny them the right to inherit property or access free public education and prevent them from working in 20 professions. At least 3,000 Palestinians who did not hold official identity documents also faced restrictions in registering births, marriages and deaths.

In January the government overturned its open-border policy and began restricting entry for Syrian refugees. Lebanon also continued to bar the entry of Palestinians fleeing the Syrian conflict. In May, Lebanon instructed UNHCR, the UN refugee agency, to provisionally suspend all new registrations of Syrian refugees. Refugees from Syria who entered Lebanon before January faced problems in renewing residency permits. Those who could not afford to renew annual residency permits, which they required to remain in Lebanon legally, became irregular in status and liable to arrest, detention and deportation.

The international community failed to provide adequate support to help Lebanon cope with the Syrian refugee crisis. Humanitarian assistance remained underfunded and there were few resettlement places offered by third countries to the most vulnerable refugees.

## WOMEN'S RIGHTS

Women continued to face discrimination in law and in practice, particularly in relation to family matters including divorce, child custody and inheritance. Lebanese women married to foreign nationals remain barred from passing on their nationality to their children. The same restriction did not apply to Lebanese men married to foreign nationals. The authorities failed to criminalize marital rape or gender-based violence outside the home.

## MIGRANT WORKERS' RIGHTS

Migrant workers were excluded from the protections provided under national labour laws, exposing them to exploitation and abuse by employers. Migrant domestic workers,

predominantly women, were especially vulnerable as they were employed under the *kafala* sponsorship system that ties the worker to their employer. In January, the Minister for Labour refused to recognize the trade union formed by migrant workers.

## INTERNATIONAL JUSTICE

### Special Tribunal for Lebanon

The Netherlands-based Special Tribunal for Lebanon (STL) continued to try five men in their absence for alleged complicity in the killing of former Prime Minister Rafic Hariri and others in a car bombing in Beirut in 2005. In September, the STL acquitted Lebanese journalist Karma Khayat and her employer Al Jadeed TV of obstructing justice but convicted her of contempt of court for ignoring a court order to remove information related to confidential witnesses, sentencing her to a fine of €10,000.

## IMPUNITY

The fate of thousands of people who were abducted, forcibly disappeared or who went missing during and after the civil war of 1975-1990 remained undisclosed. The authorities failed to establish an independent national body to investigate the fate of those disappeared and missing.

## DEATH PENALTY

Courts imposed at least 28 death sentences for murder and terrorism-related crimes, including some in cases where the defendants were tried in their absence. No executions have been carried out since 2004.

# LESOTHO

Kingdom of Lesotho
Head of state : **King Letsie III**
Head of government: **Pakalitha Mosisili (replaced Thomas Motsoahae Thabane in March)**

**Political instability persisted following an attempted coup in 2014. Tension within the**

armed forces resulted in the killing of the former Lesotho Defence Force (LDF) commander, Lieutenant-General Maaparankoe Mahao, in June. At least 23 soldiers were arrested in May, accused of leading a mutiny. They remained in detention and were allegedly tortured.

## BACKGROUND

More than half the population live below the poverty line and persistent droughts, flooding and early frosts have led to low agricultural productivity in recent years. Lesotho's economy is largely dependent on textile manufacturing, income from the Southern African Customs Union (SACU), diamond mining, and remittances from miners in South Africa. The country faces food insecurity exacerbated by weather-related shocks, widespread chronic malnutrition and the second highest rate of HIV and AIDS in the world. The worsening food deficit, as well as the growing retrenchment of Lesotho nationals working in countries such as South Africa, exacerbated household poverty in Lesotho.

General elections on 28 February failed to produce a clear winner. A coalition government was formed by Prime Minister Pakalitha Mosisili's Democratic Congress and six other political parties. The Southern African Development Community (SADC) continued to mediate between the country's political rivals in order to de-escalate tension between the military and the police, tension that had its roots in the politicization of the security sector.

## EXTRAJUDICIAL EXECUTIONS

On 25 June, former LDF head Lieutenant-General Maaparankoe Mahao was shot dead in Maseru by soldiers seeking to arrest him for allegedly plotting to lead a rebellion in the army. Maaparankoe Mahao had been dismissed from the LDF on 21 May. He challenged his dismissal in court in June, shortly before his killing, arguing that it was illegal. The government claimed that Maaparankoe Mahao had resisted arrest, but

his family disputed this, insisting his killing was a carefully planned assassination by former army colleagues.

A 10-member SADC Commission of Inquiry led by Justice Mpaphi Phumaphi of Botswana was set up on 3 July to investigate security-related issues facing Lesotho, including the killing of Maaparankoe Mahao. The Commission concluded its work prematurely on 23 October due to the lack of co-operation by the government and the LDF.

## TORTURE AND OTHER ILL-TREATMENT

Some LDF members fled to South Africa after being harassed and threatened because of their perceived loyalty to the former army chief.

At least 23 soldiers thought to be loyal to Maaparankoe Mahao were detained at Maseru Maximum Security Prison in May. They were charged with sedition and mutiny, charges that carry the death penalty. They appeared before a court-martial on 5 October, but the court-martial was then suspended to allow the SADC Commission to carry out its work. The 23 remained in detention and were allegedly tortured.

The soldiers challenged their detention and the composition of the court-martial in the Maseru High Court. On 5 October, the High Court ordered the release of the 23 soldiers on "open arrest", a form of military bail, to enable them to participate in the SADC Commission of Inquiry. The LDF failed to comply with the court order to release all the soldiers. Only five soldiers were released by early December on "open arrest", with their movements being monitored. The court-martial resumed on 1 December but it was later adjourned until 1 February 2016.

## POLICE AND SECURITY FORCES

Members of the armed forces obstructed police investigations into a number of high profile criminal cases from 2014 and 2015 linked to politicized divisions within the armed forces. These included attacks on the homes of senior politicians, political killings and abductions.

On 17 August, former police commissioner Khothatso Tšooana was compelled by the government to take early retirement. He was accused of incompetence, and of polarizing and politicizing the Lesotho Mounted Police Service.

## FREEDOM OF EXPRESSION
Members of political elites and the army continued to interfere with the broadcast media. Journalists were subjected to harassment and intimidation by political and security authorities. There was no progress in the case of Lloyd Mutungamiri, editor of the *Lesotho Times*, who was charged with criminal defamation in September 2014 for reporting on police corruption.

## DEATH PENALTY
Lesotho retained the death penalty under Statutory Law as a form of punishment. The country achieved 20 years without carrying out any executions.

## INTERNATIONAL SCRUTINY
In January Lesotho's human rights record was examined under the UPR. Plans to set up a Human Rights Commission, as recommended during the UPR, progressed during 2015.

# LIBYA

State of Libya
Head of state: **Disputed**
Head of government: **Fayez Serraj became Prime Minister designate of the Government of National Accord on 17 December. He replaced Abdallah al-Thinni of the interim government and Khalifa Ghweil of the National Salvation Government.**

**The armed conflict continued. Forces affiliated to two rival governments, as well as armed groups, committed war crimes and other violations of international humanitarian law and human rights abuses with impunity. Rights to freedom of expression, association and assembly were severely restricted. Detention without trial persisted; torture and other ill-treatment was common. Women, migrants and refugees faced discrimination and abuses. The death penalty remained in force; several former senior officials were sentenced to death after a deeply flawed trial.**

## BACKGROUND
Two rival governments and parliaments claimed legitimacy and fought for control, each supported by loose coalitions of armed groups and forces over which they did not exercise effective control; armed groups exploited the absence of central authority to consolidate their power. Operation Dignity, comprising Libyan National Army battalions, tribal militias and volunteers, supported the government and House of Representatives (HOR) based in Tobruk and al-Bayda. The Tobruk and al-Bayda-based administration was the internationally recognized government until the adoption of the Libyan Political Agreement in December (see below). Libya Dawn, a coalition of militias from cities and towns in western Libya, backed the Tripoli-based self-declared National Salvation Government (NSG) and General National Congress (GNC). Military blocks fragmented throughout the year contributing to the chaotic situation.

In October, the HOR extended its mandate by amending the constitutional declaration. Both parliaments adopted new laws but it remained unclear to what extent they were enforced.

Most fighting between Libya Dawn and Operation Dignity forces occurred along Libya's western coast and in the Nafousa Mountains. Local ceasefires contributed to reduced fighting, prisoner exchanges and releases in western Libya. In the east, fighting between Operation Dignity and the Shura Council of Benghazi Revolutionaries, a coalition of Islamist armed groups including Ansar al-Shari'a, caused civilian casualties and extensive damage in Benghazi, and trapped civilians without access to humanitarian aid.

Elsewhere, armed groups pursuing their own ideological, regional, tribal, economic and ethnic agendas fought for control. In August, the armed group Islamic State (IS) consolidated its control of the city of Sirte and surrounding coastal areas. IS forces were also present in the cities of Benghazi, Sabratha and Derna, although they lost control of Derna in June after clashes with the Shura Council of Mujahidin in Derna, an apparently al-Qa'ida-affiliated coalition of armed groups.

In December, following 14 months of negotiations facilitated by the United Nations Support Mission in Libya (UNSMIL), members of the political dialogue including members of rival parliaments signed the Libyan Political Agreement to end the violence and form a "Government of National Accord" consisting of a Presidency Council and Cabinet. Despite being unanimously endorsed by the UN Security Council, the agreement did not cease hostilities and was opposed by the heads of rival parliaments who sought to reach a separate deal, highlighting rifts within the political blocks.

In October, the Constitution Drafting Assembly issued the first draft of a new Constitution which included key human rights provisions but failed to comply with Libya's international human rights obligations relating to freedom of expression, non-discrimination and the right to life.

In February, the HOR repealed Law 13/2013 on Political and Administrative Isolation that had barred officials from the previous administration of Mu'ammar al-Gaddafi from holding positions of responsibility within public institutions.

The lack of rule of law saw rising criminality, with increasing abductions of foreign nationals and others for ransom.

## INTERNAL ARMED CONFLICT

Civilians continued to bear the brunt of the conflict. According to the UN Office for the Coordination of Humanitarian Affairs, by October some 2.44 million people needed humanitarian assistance and protection. The number of civilian casualties remained unknown, but some 20,000 were injured between May 2014 and May 2015, the UN estimated. At least 600 civilians were killed in 2015 according to the ICC Prosecutor.

Violence impeded civilian access to food, health care, water, sanitation and education. Many health facilities were closed, damaged or inaccessible due to fighting; those still functioning were overcrowded and lacked essential supplies. Around 20% of children were unable to attend school.

All sides committed serious violations of international humanitarian law, including war crimes, and human rights abuses. They carried out reprisal abductions and detained civilians including humanitarian workers and medical staff because of their perceived political affiliation or origin, often holding them as hostages to secure prisoner exchanges or ransoms. They tortured and otherwise ill-treated detainees and carried out summary killings. The warring parties also launched indiscriminate and disproportionate attacks and direct attacks on civilians and civilian objects.

In May and June, Libya Dawn-affiliated armed groups abducted scores of Tunisians, including consular staff, in the capital, Tripoli, apparently in retaliation after Tunisian authorities arrested a Libya Dawn commander. They were released weeks later.

IS forces committed scores of summary killings of captured fighters and abducted civilians, including foreign nationals, suspected informants and opponents, and men accused of engaging in same-sex sexual relations or practising "black magic". In Sirte and Derna, IS enforced its own interpretation of Islamic law, carrying out public execution-style killings in front of crowds containing children, and leaving victims' corpses on public display. They also carried out public floggings and amputations, and publicized some crimes, including their beheading and shooting dead of at least 49 Egyptian and Ethiopian Coptic Christians, in videos posted on the internet.[1]

IS forces carried out indiscriminate suicide attacks and direct attacks on civilians, such as the January shooting and bombing of a Tripoli hotel that killed at least eight people. In August, following an attempt to oust IS forces from Sirte, IS forces indiscriminately shelled a residential neighbourhood forcing civilians to flee, and destroyed homes of civilians they perceived as opponents.

Libya Dawn and the Libyan Air Force launched air strikes, some of which killed and injured civilians. Evidence of use of internationally banned cluster bombs was found in at least two locations; Operation Dignity forces appeared to be responsible.

Operation Dignity forces also attacked and burned the homes of suspected supporters of the Shura Council of Benghazi Revolutionaries and others, and reportedly abducted, detained, tortured and otherwise ill-treated civilians. They also reportedly committed summary killings of civilians and captured fighters.

In the south, fighting along ethnic and tribal lines often in urban areas, between Tebu and Tuareg militias in Obari and Sabha, as well as between Tebu and Zway militias in Kufra, caused hundreds of civilian casualties in addition to mass displacement and damage to civilian objects.

Allies of Libya's internationally recognized government, including the USA, carried out air strikes against IS and other armed groups they accused of "terrorism". In February, at least one air strike by Egypt appeared to be disproportionate; it hit a residential area killing seven civilians and injuring others.[2]

## IMPUNITY

In March, the UN Human Rights Council asked the UN High Commissioner for Human Rights to investigate violations and abuses of human rights committed in Libya since the beginning of 2014. Also in March, UN Security Council resolution 2213 called for an immediate, unconditional ceasefire; the release of arbitrarily held detainees and the transfer of others to state custody; and accountability, including targeted sanctions against perpetrators. The Security Council also called on the authorities to co-operate

with the ICC; despite this the authorities failed to transfer Saif al-Islam al-Gaddafi to the ICC to face prosecution on charges of crimes against humanity. He remained in militia detention.

The ICC Prosecutor expressed concern about IS crimes and alleged international humanitarian law violations by Libya Dawn and Operation Dignity forces but failed to initiate new investigations, citing insufficient resources and Libya's instability, and called on state parties to the Rome Statute of the ICC to provide funding. The Prosecutor did not seek judicial review of a 2013 admissibility decision allowing a Libyan court to try former al-Gaddafi era Military Intelligence chief Abdallah al-Senussi; he was among nine defendants sentenced to death in July.

In July, the HOR adopted a law granting amnesty for some crimes committed since a similar law was adopted in 2012. It excluded terrorism; torture, including rape; and other serious crimes, but not forced displacement.

In December, UN Security Council resolution 2259 called on the new Government of National Accord to hold to account perpetrators of violations of international humanitarian law and human rights abuses.

## INTERNAL DISPLACEMENT

There were some 435,000 internally displaced persons in Libya; many were displaced more than once. Over 100,000 internally displaced persons resided in makeshift camps, schools and warehouses.

Under UNSMIL sponsorship, representatives of Tawargha and Misratah signed a document setting out principles and measures to allow the safe, voluntary return of 40,000 people forcibly displaced from Tawargha in 2011 as well as plans for reparations and accountability for human rights abuses.

## JUSTICE SYSTEM

The criminal justice system remained dysfunctional and ineffective. Courts in Sirte,

Derna and Benghazi remained closed for security reasons.

Judges, prosecutors and lawyers faced attacks, abduction and threats. The body of Mohamed Salem al-Namli, an appeal court judge in al-Khoms, was found near Sirte in August, 10 days after his abduction by IS.

Several GNC decisions further undermined the independence of the judiciary. The GNC appointed the President of the Supreme Court in May, and appointed 36 judges to the Supreme Court in October.

In Tripoli, judges suspended work in June in response to alleged interference by executive and legislative authorities, and called for protection for the courts and prosecutors.

Misratah authorities released scores of detainees that they had held without trial since the 2011 armed conflict, including people displaced from Tawargha. Thousands of other detainees remained held without charge or trial across the country.

## UNFAIR TRIALS

Although the criminal justice system largely failed to function, the Tripoli Court of Assize tried 37 former officials from the administration of Mu'ammar al-Gaddafi for allegedly committing war crimes and other offences during the 2011 armed conflict. The trial was marked by serious violations of due process, in particular defence rights and the court's failure to duly investigate allegations of torture and other ill-treatment of defendants. The defendants included Saif al-Islam al-Gaddafi, a son of Mu'ammar al-Gaddafi, who was tried in his absence as he continued to be held at an undisclosed location in Zintan. On 28 July, the court sentenced him along with Abdallah al-Senussi and seven other defendants to death and imposed prison sentences ranging from five years to life imprisonment on 23 other defendants.[3] A review of the convictions before the Supreme Court was still pending at the end of the year.

## FREEDOMS OF EXPRESSION,

## ASSOCIATION AND ASSEMBLY

Armed groups and unknown perpetrators targeted media and NGO workers and human rights defenders with assassinations, abductions and threats.

In January, unknown assailants fired rocket-propelled grenades at al-Nabaa television station in Tripoli, a station perceived to hold pro-Libya Dawn views.

In February, armed men abducted two members of the National Commission for Human Rights, a local human rights NGO, in Tripoli; they were released a few weeks later. Also in February, Intissar Husseiri, a civil society activist, and her aunt were found dead in a car in Tripoli; both had been shot in the head. The General Prosecution opened an investigation but did not disclose its findings.

In April, armed men killed journalist Muftah al-Qatrani at his Benghazi office. The bodies of five members of a crew from Barqa television station, missing since August 2014, were found near al-Bayda. The fate of Tunisian media professionals Sofiane Chourabi and Nadhir Ktari and Libyan political activist Abdel Moez Banoun, all missing since 2014, remained undisclosed.

The Tripoli-based NSG intermittently blocked access to online media outlets including Bawabat al-Wasat, perceived to be critical of the NSG's actions. In November, the Ministry of Culture of the NSG issued a statement urging civil society organizations not to attend any meetings abroad without prior notification, while the Minister of Culture of the internationally recognized government urged security agencies to ban any media or civil society organizations funded by foreign entities.

The NGO Reporters Without Borders recorded more than 30 militia attacks against journalists between January and November.

## TORTURE AND OTHER ILL-TREATMENT

Torture and other ill-treatment remained common in prisons and detention centres throughout Libya, under both the internationally recognized government and the Tripoli authorities, as well as militias, and led in some cases to death.

In August, a video circulated on social media apparently showed officials torturing As-Saadi al-Gaddafi and other detainees at al-Hadba Prison in Tripoli. Later videos showed officials threatening to torture As-Saadi al-Gaddafi.[4] The prison director said he had suspended those responsible but it was unclear whether an investigation by the General Prosecutor resulted in prosecutions. The authorities informed UNSMIL that arrests had been carried out without providing further details. There were reports that those responsible went into hiding.

## WOMEN'S RIGHTS

Women remained subject to discrimination in law and in practice, and were inadequately protected against gender-based violence.

Armed groups intimidated and threatened women activists and human rights defenders to deter them from engaging in public affairs and advocating for women's rights and disarmament.

Child marriage appeared to be increasing. Girls as young as 12 years old were reportedly married to IS fighters in Derna to protect their families.

In October, the Tripoli-based GNC amended the 1984 Law on marriage, divorce and inheritance, introducing more discriminatory provisions against women and girls, and increasing the potential for child marriage. The amendments allowed men to divorce their wives unilaterally without obtaining court approval and prohibited women from acting as witnesses to marriage.

Women faced arbitrary restrictions on their freedom of movement. Those travelling without a male companion were harassed by militias, and in some cases prevented from travelling abroad, in accordance with a 2012 fatwa by Libya's Grand Mufti.

## REFUGEES' AND MIGRANTS' RIGHTS

In September, the UN estimated that there were around 250,000 refugees, asylum-seekers and migrants in Libya in need of protection or assistance. Many faced serious abuses, discrimination and labour exploitation. Members of religious minorities, especially Christians, were particularly targeted by armed groups seeking to enforce their own interpretation of Islamic law. Foreign nationals who entered Libya irregularly were subject to extortion, torture, abduction and sometimes sexual violence by criminal gangs engaged in smuggling and people trafficking.

The Tripoli-based Department of Combating Irregular Migration continued to hold between 2,500 and 4,000 undocumented foreign nationals in indefinite detention at 15 centres across the country, where many faced torture, following their detention or interception at sea.

Amid violence and abuses, thousands sought to leave Libya and cross the Mediterranean Sea to Europe in unseaworthy vessels. By 5 December, some 153,000 refugees and migrants had reached Italy by sea, most after departing from Libya; about 2,900 drowned while attempting the journey, according to the International Organization for Migration.

The internationally recognized government prohibited the regular entry into Libya of Syrian, Palestinian, Bangladeshi and Sudanese nationals in January, and extended the ban to include nationals of Yemen, Iran and Pakistan in September.

## DEATH PENALTY

The death penalty remained in force for a wide range of crimes. Former al-Gaddafi era officials and perceived supporters of his rule were sentenced to death. No judicial executions were reported.

---

1. Cold-blooded murder of Copts in Libya a war crime (MDE 19/0002/2015)

2. Libya: Mounting evidence of war crimes in the wake of Egypt's air strikes, (News story, 23 February)

3. Libya: Flawed trial of al-Gaddafi officials leads to appalling death sentences (News story, 28 July)

4. Libya: Allegations of torture of As-Saadi al-Gaddafi and two others

# LITHUANIA

**Republic of Lithuania**
Head of state: **Dalia Grybauskaitė**
Head of government: **Algirdas Butkevičius**

An investigation continued at the national level into allegations that Lithuania hosted a secret site for the CIA where detainees were tortured. A decision on a related case was pending at the European Court of Human Rights. Legal gender recognition remained unavailable to transgender people.

## COUNTER-TERROR AND SECURITY

Arvydas Anušauskas, a Member of Parliament and former head of a parliamentary committee that had investigated allegations that Lithuania hosted a CIA secret detention facility, publicly stated that a December 2014 report by a US Senate committee "makes a convincing case that prisoners were indeed held at the Lithuanian site". In January 2015, the NGO Reprieve published a dossier, including new evidence sourced by Reprieve and information from the US Senate report, which concluded "beyond reasonable doubt" that detainees were held in secret CIA detention in Lithuania in 2005 and 2006.

In April, a closed investigation into the secret site allegations was reopened and merged with an ongoing investigation into claims by Saudi Arabian national Mustafa al-Hawsawi that he had been held in secret detention in Lithuania and tortured at some point between 2004 and 2006. The investigation was ongoing at the end of 2015.

In September, final submissions were filed against Lithuania at the European Court of Human Rights in a case brought by Abu Zubaydah, who alleged that he had been held in secret CIA detention in Lithuania between February 2005 and March 2006. The Lithuanian Prosecutor General had refused to investigate the illegal transfer, secret detention and torture of Abu Zubaydah, who remained detained at the US detention facility Guantánamo Bay in Cuba. A final decision by the European Court was pending at the end of the year.

## RIGHTS OF LESBIAN, GAY, BISEXUAL, TRANSGENDER AND INTERSEX PEOPLE

Transgender people continued to be denied legal gender recognition because of legislative gaps. At the end of the year, a bill aimed at prohibiting gender reassignment was pending before Parliament.

Several bills on registered partnerships were considered by Parliament. In October, a proposal introduced by the Ministry of Justice on registered partnerships for different-sex couples was rejected by Parliament. The Minister of Justice explicitly opposed registered partnerships for same-sex couples.

At the end of the year, a proposal aimed at banning civil partnerships for all couples and a second proposal to establish civil partnerships for all couples were pending. Several bills aimed at restricting the rights of LGBTI people were under consideration by Parliament.

# MACEDONIA

**The former Yugoslav Republic of Macedonia**
Head of state: **Gjorge Ivanov**
Head of government: **Nikola Gruevski**

The publication of audio recordings not only revealed evidence of government corruption, but demonstrated widespread covert surveillance. The authorities failed to respect the rights of refugees and migrants, including by the use of unlawful detention and the excessive use of force.

## BACKGROUND

A political crisis followed the publication of audio recordings of conversations between ministers, members of the ruling party (Internal Macedonian Revolutionary Organization – Democratic Party for

Macedonian National Unity) and public officials.

The recordings, made public by Zoran Zaev, leader of the opposition Social Democratic Union of Macedonia (SDSM) revealed government corruption, abuse of office, electoral fraud and a lack of respect for human rights and the rule of law, including interference in the independence of the judiciary.

Zoran Zaev was indicted, with others, for crimes including espionage; the government claimed that the recordings were fabricated by foreign intelligence services. In May, mass demonstrations called on the Prime Minister to resign following his suggested complicity in covering up responsibility for the killing of a young man at a demonstration in 2011. The Minister of Interior and the Director of Security and Counter-Intelligence resigned in May.

Following an EU-brokered agreement in June, the opposition ended their boycott of Parliament in September. After further EU intervention, the SDSM took up ministerial posts in an interim government in November, and deputy prosecutors were appointed to investigate the alleged criminal offences revealed in the surveillance recordings. A package of electoral reforms required before elections in April 2016 was not in place at the end of the year.

## FREEDOM OF EXPRESSION

Over 2,000 journalists were estimated to be under surveillance by the government. Published recordings indicated the indirect financing of pro-government media, and political influence over the appointment of journalists and news content.

Attacks on independent journalists continued: in April, critical journalist Borjan Jovanovski received death threats and in July Sashe Ivanovski was punched by a deputy Prime Minister. Investigative journalist Tomislav Kezarovski was released in January from house arrest following appeal, and international condemnation of his imprisonment under a sentence imposed in 2013 for defamation.

## EXCESSIVE USE OF FORCE

On 9 May, special police units launched an armed operation in Kumanovo, with the alleged aim of preventing attacks against state and civilian targets. In heavy exchanges of fire, 14 ethnic Albanians and eight police officers were killed. Thirty ethnic Albanians, including former members of the Kosovo Liberation Army, were arrested; some alleged that they were beaten in detention. The Ministry of Interior ignored calls for an independent inquiry into the operation.

## REFUGEES AND ASYLUM-SEEKERS

At least 600,000 migrants and refugees, predominantly from Syria, travelled through Macedonia, aiming to seek asylum in the EU.

Before June, refugees and migrants were routinely pushed back to Greece, at the border and from within the country, ill-treated by border police and subjected to arbitrary detention, and were vulnerable to exploitation by smugglers and attacks by armed gangs.[1] In August, UNHCR, the UN refugee agency, reported that the asylum system was unable to provide effective protection.

After 19 June, following an amendment to the Law on Asylum, 388,233 refugees registered their interest in claiming asylum at the border. However, most travelled by train to the Serbian border. According to Ministry of Interior statistics, only 86 asylum applications were submitted after 19 June.

At the time, up to 7,000 people a day were entering the country from Greece. On 19 August, the government declared a crisis on the border and deployed paramilitary police and the army, which used stun grenades and baton rounds to push refugees back or prevent them from crossing into the country. Police again used excessive force against refugees at the end of August, and arbitrarily beat refugees in September. From 19 November, only Afghan, Iraqi and Syrian nationals were allowed to enter the country; police initially used excessive force to deny access to other nationalities arbitrarily identified as economic migrants.

Over 1,000 mainly Syrian refugees and migrants, including children, were unlawfully detained in inhuman and degrading conditions at the Reception Centre for Foreigners in Gazi Baba, Skopje. Many alleged they were ill-treated by Ministry of Interior guards. The centre closed during July following international pressure, including from the UN Committee against Torture. However, the unlawful detention of refugees and migrants resumed after the November border closure; around 55 people, predominantly Iranian and Moroccan nationals, were detained in December.

Some 10,210 Macedonians, many of them Roma, fled discrimination and poverty to apply for asylum in EU countries; few were successful.

## RIGHTS OF LESBIAN, GAY, BISEXUAL, TRANSGENDER AND INTERSEX PEOPLE

During Pride week in June, activists protested against the authorities' failure to investigate attacks on the lives of LGBTI individuals and their organizations' premises. In January, Parliament voted to amend the Constitution to define marriage as solely between a man and a woman.

## COUNTER-TERROR AND SECURITY

In February, the government finally submitted an action plan to the Council of Europe in the case of German national Khaled el-Masri, as required by the 2012 judgment of the European Court of Human Rights, although it failed to provide for an effective criminal investigation into his allegations. The Court had ruled Macedonia liable for Khaled el-Masri's incommunicado detention, enforced disappearance, torture and other ill-treatment in 2003, and subsequent handover to the US CIA, which transferred him out of Macedonia to a secret detention site in Afghanistan.

1. Europe's borderlands: Violations of the rights of refugees and migrants in Macedonia, Serbia and Hungary (EUR 70/1579/2015)

# MADAGASCAR

Republic of Madagascar
Head of state: **Hery Rajaonarimampianina**
Head of government: **Jean Ravelonarivo (replaced Roger Kolo in January)**

Extrajudicial executions by security forces in the south, in the context of action to combat cattle theft, continued with almost total impunity. Journalists, students, environmental activists and others were harassed and intimidated. Some were sentenced to terms of imprisonment.

## BACKGROUND

Fifty-five years after independence, Madagascar remained the fifth poorest maritime country in the world with an estimated 92% of Malagasy living on less than US$2 per day. It was ranked bottom of its tier in the Human Development Index.

Political instability continued, putting national reconciliation and economic development at risk. On 26 May, opposition members in the National Assembly voted overwhelmingly in favour of removing President Rajaonarimampianina from office. The President challenged the legitimacy of the vote and rejected the outcome. On 13 June, the High Constitutional Court ruled in favour of the President.

Ongoing high levels of poverty among the majority of the population undermined access to economic and social rights including food, water and education, and fuelled social tensions. An outbreak of plague in August led to at least 10 deaths. Severe flooding between January and March left tens of thousands of people displaced and at least 19 dead.

Cattle theft remained a serious problem, leading to violent clashes between villagers and cattle rustlers, in which dozens of people died.

## POLICE AND SECURITY FORCES

Widespread killings of suspected cattle rustlers continued. A military operation,

Fahalemana 2015, launched in mid-August to combat cattle theft, led to a number of violent clashes between cattle rustlers and security forces, with killings by both sides. Several suspected cattle rustlers were extrajudicially executed by the military. Local people were injured and some were killed. The killings were not investigated and no-one was held to account.

On 26 August, eight soldiers and 15 suspected cattle rustlers died following a clash at Ankazoabo-Sud. Witnesses reported indiscriminate assaults by state security forces on villagers presumed to be cattle rustlers. In September, at least 18 people, including at least one police officer, three villagers and 14 suspected cattle rustlers, were killed during violent clashes in Ivahona commune. According to witness testimonies, military officers later summarily executed the suspects.

On 2 September, the extrajudicial executions of three people were reported after security forces entered Tsarazaza Maevatanana village to make documentation checks.

## FREEDOM OF EXPRESSION – ENVIRONMENTAL ACTIVISTS
Environmental activists were at risk of imprisonment for criticizing activities by extractive industries, in particular illegal logging of rosewood.

On 22 May, environmental activist Armand Marozafy was sentenced to six months' imprisonment and ordered to pay 12 million ariary (US$3,650) after his personal email reporting that two local tour operators were involved in illegal rosewood trafficking was leaked on social media. The court in Maroantsetra found him guilty of defamation under a controversial cyber criminality law.

## EXCESSIVE USE OF FORCE
On 31 August, the gendarmerie used excessive force to break up a demonstration by students at Ankatso University in the capital, Antananarivo. Student leader Jean-Pierre Randrianamboarina was beaten and

suffered multiple injuries. He was given a six-month suspended sentence in September after being convicted on charges including incitement to disturb public order and to overthrow the government.

## CHILDREN'S RIGHTS
In March, UNICEF reported that 47% of children under five suffered chronic malnutrition, and that their living conditions were adversely affected by factors including homelessness, poor nutrition and lack of access to basic health care.

## PRISON CONDITIONS
Prisons were overcrowded with more than half of all detainees in pre-trial detention. Food rations allocated to prisoners were cut by more than half in 2015, according to the ICRC, posing serious threats to health.

# MALAWI

**Republic of Malawi**
Head of state and government: **Arthur Peter Mutharika**

Attacks against people with albinism increased sharply. In May, Malawi's human rights record was assessed under the UPR. The government adopted 154 out of 199 recommendations, mainly rejecting those concerning abolition of the death penalty and repealing sections of the Penal Code criminalizing same-sex sexual conduct between consenting adults.

## DISCRIMINATION – PEOPLE WITH ALBINISM
There was a sharp increase in attacks on people with albinism by individuals and gangs seeking body parts to sell for use in witchcraft. People with albinism and their families lived in fear of attacks and in some instances children with albinism stopped going to school. The Association of People Living with Albinism in Malawi recorded at least 19 cases of killings, attempted abductions or disappearances. Fifteen of

those cases involved children, 10 of them girls.

On 19 March, the President issued a statement condemning attacks on people with albinism, and called on security agencies to arrest perpetrators and provide protection to people at risk of attack. The Minister of Internal Security reported that eight suspects had been arrested in connection with some of the attacks.

In May, police reported that they had arrested four men for abducting and killing Symon Mukota, a man with albinism, in December 2014. The men were caught with the deceased's bones after failing to find a buyer.

In September, a primary schoolteacher, Philip Ngulube, pleaded guilty before the Principal Magistrate in Mzuzu of attempting to sell a woman with albinism to a foreign national, who reported the matter to the police. In December four people appeared in court after being arrested in Mchinji district in connection with the alleged murder of Pepuzan Prescote, a man with albinism who had disappeared in August. The four were remanded in custody at Lilongwe Maximum Prison.

## RIGHTS OF LESBIAN, GAY, BISEXUAL, TRANSGENDER AND INTERSEX PEOPLE

During the UPR the government accepted a recommendation to take measures to protect LGBTI people against violence and to prosecute the perpetrators. The authorities also agreed to guarantee that LGBTI people have effective access to health services, including treatment for HIV/AIDS. The government rejected recommendations to repeal provisions in the Penal Code criminalizing consensual same-sex sexual conduct between adults.

## REFUGEES' AND MIGRANTS' RIGHTS

Concerns remained about unregistered migrants kept in detention beyond expiry of their custodial sentences, with limited prospect of being released or deported. At least 500 such detainees, mostly from Ethiopia, were held in overcrowded prisons after being charged with illegal entry and fined US$35 or imprisoned for between two and nine months. However, in November the International Organization for Migration in collaboration with the Ethiopian government facilitated the return of 223 Ethiopians. Earlier in the year at least 164 of the most vulnerable cases, including minors and elderly people, were also returned to Ethiopia. At the end of the year, 20% of the total prison population were awaiting trial with some having been on remand for years without appearing before a court.

## DEATH PENALTY

After years of delay, in February the process was begun to re-sentence death row prisoners following the 2007 High Court ruling declaring mandatory death sentencing unconstitutional. Forty-six prisoners were released immediately and five were sentenced to terms of imprisonment.

# MALAYSIA

Malaysia
Head of state: **King Abdul Halim Mu'adzam Shah**
Head of government: **Najib Tun Razak**

**The crackdown on freedom of expression and other civil and political rights intensified. The Sedition Act was amended and a new Prevention of Terrorism Act was passed. Police used unnecessary or excessive force when arresting opposition party leaders and activists.**

## BACKGROUND

In February, the Federal Court upheld the conviction and five-year prison sentence of opposition leader and prisoner of conscience Anwar Ibrahim on sodomy charges dating to 2008. The charges were seen as politically motivated and an attempt to silence government critics.[1] In December, a National Security Council bill was passed by Parliament, effectively granting expansive powers to an appointed Council and the security forces.

## FREEDOM OF EXPRESSION

The Sedition Act was amended in April resulting in a further erosion of freedom of expression.[2] The scope of offences was amended to cover electronic media, including harsher penalties such as mandatory and increased prison sentences. It was used to silence government critics. At least 15 people were charged under the Act, including political cartoonist Zulkiflee Anwar Haque ("Zunar").[3] All cases were ongoing at the end of 2015. On 6 October, five Federal Court judges unanimously dismissed a case brought by law lecturer Azmi Sharom, challenging the constitutionality of the Sedition Act.

In March, three journalists were arrested by police and officers from the Malaysian Communication and Multimedia Commission for publishing a report concerning the Kelantan state Hudud Bill, which criminalizes certain acts, purportedly according to Islamic principles. The amended Bill as proposed allows corporal and capital punishment for a number of acts, including "adultery".

The authorities continued to use the Printing Presses and Publications Act to set restrictions on and suspend media outlets and publishing houses, and ban materials critical of the government. Licences for print publications, revocable by the Home Minister and difficult for independent outlets to obtain, remained a stringent requirement.

## FREEDOM OF ASSEMBLY AND ASSOCIATION

Various laws were used against organizers and participants of peaceful protests throughout the year. The Peaceful Assembly Act, Sedition Act, and Sections 120, 141, 124b, 124c and 143 of the Penal Code, were used alone or in combination against individuals involved in a street demonstration in February, the #KitaLawan rally in March, and the 1 May Workers Day rally. Peaceful protesters were often charged under Section

124 of the Penal Code for acts "detrimental to parliamentary democracy".

The government imposed travel bans on some opposition members. On 29-30 August, the Bersih 4 rallies, which demanded free and fair elections, among other things, were held in Kuala Lumpur, Kuching and Kota Kinabalu despite being declared illegal by the government.

## ARBITRARY ARRESTS AND DETENTIONS

The Prevention of Terrorism Act, passed on 7 April, allowed for the detention of terrorist suspects without charge or trial for up to two years, renewable without judicial review of the reasons for detention. The Act established a Prevention of Terrorism Board which will have powers to make detention or restriction orders "in the interest of the security of Malaysia" on the advice of inquiry officers who may obtain evidence in any form, including evidence that would not be admissible in court. The Bar Council and human rights groups were concerned that the Act could lead to torture of detainees, and could facilitate repression of legitimate dissent and freedom of expression.

The Security Offences (Special Measures) Act continued to be used to arbitrarily arrest and detain people alleged to have committed security offences. It allowed for indefinite, so-called preventive, detention without charge or trial and undermined fair trial rights.

## POLICE AND SECURITY FORCES

Unnecessary or excessive use of force and allegations of torture and other ill-treatment of detainees by the police continued to be reported. Caning continued to be used as a form of punishment. There were 11 recorded deaths in custody as a result of alleged torture or other ill-treatment. The government continued to reject calls to establish an Independent Police Complaints and Misconduct Commission as recommended by a Royal Commission in 2005.

## REFUGEES AND ASYLUM-SEEKERS

Malaysia faced international criticism as thousands of refugees and migrants from

Myanmar and Bangladesh attempted to land on Langkawi Island, Kedah state, in May. Malaysia and Indonesia eventually agreed to provide humanitarian assistance and temporary shelter for up to 7,000 refugees and migrants for up to one year.[4]

The discovery in May and August of more than 100 mass graves on the Thai-Malaysian border raised renewed concerns about human trafficking.

## DEATH PENALTY

The death penalty continued to be retained as the mandatory punishment for drug trafficking, murder and discharge of firearms with intent to kill or harm in certain circumstances. In November the government announced that legislative reforms to review the mandatory death penalty laws would be introduced in Parliament in early 2016. Official figures indicated that 33 executions were carried out between 1998 and 2015, but no further details on executions were made publicly available.

---

1. Malaysia: Anwar verdict will have chilling effect on freedom of expression (News story, 10 February)
2. Malaysia: Human rights "black hole" expanding (ASA 28/1356/2015)
3. Malaysia: Stop politically motivated arrests under the Sedition Act (ASA 28/1235/2015)
4. Indonesia/Malaysia/Thailand: Further information: Ensure the safety of refugees and migrants (ASA 01/1786/2015)

# MALDIVES

**Republic of Maldives**
Head of state and government: **Abdulla Yameen Abdul Gayoom**

---

Judicial overreach included curtailing the independence of the Human Rights Commission of Maldives, which the government failed to defend. Judicial impartiality was a serious concern. Leading political opponents of the government were sentenced to long-term imprisonment after grossly unfair trials. Hundreds of opposition activists were detained and later released after being charged with criminal offences. The government stated that flogging would not be removed from Maldivian law.

## BACKGROUND

The Supreme Court increasingly assumed the role of a legislature by unilaterally issuing rulings that had the force of law, some of which undermined human rights. One such ruling reduced the period for launching an appeal from 90 to 10 days, making it extremely difficult for prisoners to prepare their appeal. Another severely undermined the constitutional independence of the Human Rights Commission of the Maldives (HRCM) when the Supreme Court declared that it should "work like a ministry or an extension of the government instead of an independent body". The government failed to ensure the Commission's independence.

Maldives' human rights record was assessed under the UPR in May. It focused on a range of human rights concerns, including flaws within the judicial system that had not been addressed since the previous UPR.

The new Penal Code finally came into force in July. There were reports that some people had been charged and tried under the new Code. They included two women sentenced by a Hithadhoo court to 100 lashes and several months house arrest, each for giving birth to a child years ago without being married.

## UNFAIR TRIALS

Constitutional safeguards for the right to a fair trial were increasingly eroded. Although the government maintained that due process was followed, severe irregularities were revealed during a series of trials leading to the long-term imprisonment of the government's political opponents. They included the trials of former President Mohamed Nasheed, sentenced in March to 13 years for allegedly ordering the detention of a judge during his presidency; former Defence Minister Mohamed Nazim, sentenced in March to 11 years for allegedly keeping an unlicensed weapon; and former Deputy Speaker of Parliament Ahmed Nazim, sentenced in March to 25 years for alleged corruption.[1]

In these cases, the lawyers for the accused were not given adequate time to prepare their defence and the right of the defence to call and examine witnesses was either denied or severely limited. Impartiality was a serious concern. In Mohamed Nasheed's trial, two of the three judges who tried and convicted him had themselves acted as witness to the alleged offence by signing a witness statement as part of the initial complaint. In the former Defence Minister's trial, some of the documents provided by the prosecution and used as evidence at the trial were never shown to the defence.

The UN Working Group on Arbitrary Detention concluded in October that the detention of Mohamed Nasheed was politically motivated and his trial unfair. The Working Group stated that "the adequate remedy would be to release Mr Nasheed immediately and accord him an enforceable right to compensation". The government rejected the Working Group's opinion.

## JUSTICE SYSTEM
Judicial impartiality remained a serious concern which the government failed to address. The authorities frequently claimed that they would not address any complaints against the judiciary because courts were independent. At the same time, the government failed to strengthen the Judicial Services Commission to enable it to address impartiality and other issues related to the judiciary.

## FREEDOM OF ASSEMBLY
Hundreds of political opponents of the government taking part in peaceful demonstrations were arrested, detained for days or weeks, and released only after having conditions imposed preventing them from taking part in future demonstrations for a certain period. Journalists, human rights defenders and opposition politicians received death threats, and police failed to carry out effective investigations and bring the perpetrators to justice. Political rallies were attacked by gangs suspected of working in collaboration with the police. None of the attackers, even those allegedly known to the police, had been brought to justice by the end of the year.

## CRUEL, INHUMAN OR DEGRADING PUNISHMENT
Courts continued to sentence people, the vast majority of them women, to flogging, most commonly for fornication.[2] The sentences were carried out. Despite flogging constituting cruel, inhuman and degrading punishment, and concerns voiced by the CEDAW Committee in February, the government stated that they would not remove the punishment from Maldivian law.

## DEATH PENALTY
No executions have been carried out for more than 60 years, but the government continued to declare that people sentenced to death would be executed.

---

1. Maldives: Assault on civil and political rights (ASA 29/1501/2015)
2. 60th session of the Committee on the Elimination of Discrimination against Women: The Republic of Maldives - review of the combined fourth and fifth periodic report (ASA 29/002/2015)

# MALI

---

**Republic of Mali**
Head of state: **Ibrahim Boubacar Keïta**
Head of government: **Modibo Keïta (replaced Moussa Mara in January)**

---

**The internal armed conflict perpetuated a climate of insecurity, particularly in the north, despite the signing of a peace agreement. Crimes under international law and abuses by armed groups persisted in different parts of the country.**

## BACKGROUND

Violent clashes and insecurity threatened different parts of the country with attacks against government forces and the UN Multidimensional Integrated Stabilization Mission in Mali (MINUSMA). In June, the government and the Co-ordination of the Movement of Azawad (CMA) signed a peace agreement in Algiers, Algeria, that included initiatives for further decentralization and the establishment of an international Commission of Inquiry to investigate crimes under international law, including war crimes, crimes against humanity, genocide and crimes of sexual violence. The peace agreement also provided that there would be no amnesty for those suspected of criminal responsibility for the named crimes. In order to remove any obstacle to the CMA signing the peace agreement, arrest warrants were lifted against 15 of its members who faced charges including sedition and terrorism, and others were later released from detention in the capital, Bamako. In the same month, the MINUSMA mandate was extended by one year. At the end of the year, armed groups still controlled Kidal, one of the largest northern cities. In November, a nationwide state of emergency was declared following an attack on the Radisson Hotel in Bamako; it was extended to the end of March 2016.

Clashes between armed groups, MINUSMA and government forces continued, leading to over 250 casualties – including over 60 civilians.

In August, a former minister and member of the political opposition, Ousmane Oumarou Sidibé, was made president of the Truth and Reconciliation Commission (CVJR).

More than 130,000 Malian refugees were still in neighbouring countries, and over 60,000 people remained internally displaced.

## ABUSES BY ARMED GROUPS

In March, a masked gunman opened fire in a bar-restaurant in Bamako, killing three Malians and two foreign nationals. The armed group Al-Mourabitoun claimed responsibility for the attack.

In July, members of the armed group al-Qa'ida in the Islamic Maghreb (AQIM) attacked MINUSMA soldiers on the road between Goundam and Timbuktu, killing six MINUSMA soldiers and injuring five. In August, an armed group attacked a residency for UN subcontractors in Sévaré, killing over 10 people, including foreign nationals.

In October, six civilians were killed and two injured after armed men used landmines and rocket launchers to attack a convoy of vehicles between Gossi and Gao in the north. Vehicles belonging to MINUSMA subcontractors were the main targets.

In November, armed groups killed 19 civilians during a siege at the Radisson Hotel in Bamako in which more than 150 people were taken hostage. Both Al-Mourabitoun and the Massina Liberation Front claimed responsibility.

At the end of the year Stephen McGowan and John Gustafsson, kidnapped by members of AQIM in northern Mali in 2011, were still being held hostage.

## EXCESSIVE USE OF FORCE

In January, MINUSMA soldiers fired live bullets at civilians outside a UN base in Gao, killing three and injuring four others during a violent demonstration against the UN plan to create a buffer zone in the northern town of Tabankort. In March, the victims' families filed complaints against MINUSMA for murder; a UN investigation recognized MINUSMA officers as responsible for the deaths and said that the police unit had used unauthorized and excessive force. The full report of the investigation was not made public.

## ARBITRARY ARRESTS AND DETENTIONS

In August, around 200 people peacefully protested against heavy taxation in the western town of Yélimané, in the Kayes region. One day later, the police arrested 17 members of the Yélimané Dagkane association; they were later charged with inciting revolt, opposing legitimate authority and participation in an unauthorized protest.[1]

Two other members, Bakary Diambou and Daman Konte, were also arrested in Bamako and charged with inciting rebellion. All were provisionally released in November.

## IMPUNITY

In Bamako in March, seven human rights organizations filed complaints on behalf of 33 victims, against 15 people, for war crimes and crimes against humanity committed in 2012. In June, the authorities lifted arrest warrants issued against 15 CMA officials suspected of committing crimes under international law.

In October, the UN Independent Expert on the situation of human rights in Mali expressed deep concern about the time taken to investigate and bring to trial cases of war crimes and human rights violations committed during the 2012 conflict. In the same month, eight supporters of General Amadou Sanogo, leader of the military junta that ruled Mali for part of 2012, escaped from prison. They were facing trial for the murder and kidnapping of "red beret" soldiers who had opposed the 2012 military coup. At the end of the year, General Sanogo and 29 others, including General Ibrahim Dahirou Dembélé, were still in detention and awaiting trial for murder and complicity in kidnapping of the "red berets".

## INTERNATIONAL JUSTICE

In September, Ahmed Al Faqi Al Mahdi, member of armed opposition group Ansardine and allegedly head of the Manners Brigade (also known as Hesbah), which occupied northern Mali in 2012, was surrendered to the ICC by Niger, following the issuance of a warrant of arrest against him. He is suspected of war crimes over the destruction of nine mausoleums and a mosque in Timbuktu in 2012. The preliminary hearings were due to be held in January 2016.

---

1. Mali must release 17 prisoners of conscience detained for two months (AFR 37/2675/2015)

# MALTA

**Republic of Malta**
Head of state: **Marie-Louise Coleiro Preca**
Head of government: **Joseph Muscat**

---

**There was a further reduction in the number of refugees and migrants entering Malta irregularly by boat or disembarked there after search and rescue operations. Authorities continued to automatically detain them, but introduced a review process to assess the reasons for detention in each case, leading to a shortening of detention periods. New legislation was approved to advance transgender and intersex people's rights. Abortion remained prohibited in all circumstances.**

## REFUGEES AND ASYLUM-SEEKERS

Malta participated under the Frontex Triton operation in the rescue of refugees and migrants crossing the central Mediterranean irregularly on overcrowded and unseaworthy vessels. However, authorities maintained a restrictive interpretation of search and rescue obligations at sea. By the end of the year, 104 people had arrived on Malta irregularly by boat. This was a reduction over previous numbers as most people rescued at sea were disembarked in Italy.

In January, a boat carrying about 122 people from sub-Saharan Africa drifted in the central Mediterranean for about eight days. When it eventually reached Maltese territorial waters, about 35 people had either died or disappeared at sea. Maltese authorities rescued the 87 men found alive on board and disembarked them in Malta, where they were placed in precautionary quarantine due to fears they could carry diseases. The asylum-seekers remained held there even after the quarantine was lifted.

The authorities continued to automatically detain asylum-seekers and migrants arriving irregularly, in breach of international law obligations. However, a review process to assess the grounds for detention in each individual case was introduced in practice, and then codified through subsidiary legislation adopted in December. The introduction of such a review process, combined with the reduced number of arrivals, led to most people being released within three months, a significant reduction in the length of detention. In December, the government adopted a new policy aiming at the abolition of automatic detention, to align with EU legislation and previous judgments of the European Court of Human Rights.

In January, the Minister of Interior told Parliament that no records had been kept between 2004 and 2012 of allegations of excessive use of force by officers of the detention services against refugees and migrants in detention, nor of any related investigation or disciplinary proceedings. Serious abuses against detainees had been described within the findings of the inquiry, published in December 2014, on the death in custody of Malian national Mamadou Kamara in 2012.

In May, the UN Special Rapporteur on the human rights of migrants published his report on his December 2014 visit to Malta. His recommendations included that detention of migrants should not be automatic but decided on a case-by-case basis, and that all detainees should have full access to justice, including a more accountable system for lodging complaints within detention and reception centres.

As of the end of November, Malta had received 1,561 asylum applications. The vast majority were submitted by individuals who had been able to travel regularly to Malta or who had been living in the country already before the reason for their asylum application materialized, particularly Libyan nationals.

In June, the government initiated consultations aimed at the adoption of a National Migrant Integration Strategy to facilitate non-EU nationals' integration within Maltese society.

At the end of the year, the government was still refusing to disclose detailed information about the search and rescue operation of a trawler carrying over 400 people which sank in October 2013, resulting in about 200 deaths. According to testimonies from survivors and other evidence, failures by Italian and Maltese authorities delayed the rescue operation.

## RIGHTS OF LESBIAN, GAY, BISEXUAL, TRANSGENDER AND INTERSEX PEOPLE

In April, Parliament approved unanimously the Gender Identity, Gender Expression and Sex Characteristics (GIGESC) Act. Welcomed by LGBTI organizations internationally, the Act includes ground-breaking provisions for the advancement of transgender and intersex people's rights. It prohibits discrimination on grounds of gender identity and provides for a simplified procedure allowing transgender individuals to obtain legal recognition of their gender without the requirement to undergo any medical treatment or psychological assessment. The Act also outlaws any sex assignment treatment or surgical intervention on the sex characteristics of an intersex minor, if these can be deferred until the person can provide informed consent. At the end of the year, over 40 people were reported as having obtained legal recognition of their gender on the basis of the new legislation, doubling the total number recorded in the previous 15 years.

In January, for the first time the Maltese Refugee Commissioner granted international protection to a transgender person on grounds of gender identity. The parliament had amended the Constitution in 2014 to protect individuals against discrimination on grounds of sexual orientation or gender identity.

## SEXUAL AND REPRODUCTIVE RIGHTS

Women continued to be denied access to abortion, which remained prohibited in all circumstances, including when the woman's life is at risk.

# MAURITANIA

Islamic Republic of Mauritania
Head of state: **Mohamed Ould Abdel Aziz**
Head of government: **Yahya Ould Hademine**

Three anti-slavery activists were imprisoned and a blogger received a death sentence for apostasy, as restrictions on freedoms of expression and assembly increased; a new law on civil society associations further threatened these freedoms. Conditions of detention remained harsh, while the practice of torture and other ill-treatment was widespread, with long periods of police custody allowed by anti-terrorist legislation. New laws defined torture and slavery as crimes against humanity and strengthened measures to combat them.

## BACKGROUND

In November, Mauritania's human rights record was investigated under the UPR.[1] Mauritania adopted more than 136 recommendations, including the establishment of a national mechanism to combat torture. It rejected 58 recommendations, including the abolition of the death penalty and removing the crime of apostasy from legislation.

## FREEDOMS OF EXPRESSION, ASSEMBLY AND ASSOCIATION

Freedoms of expression and assembly were curtailed, which led to the detention of prisoners of conscience.

In December 2014, Mohamed Mkhaïtir, a blogger who was held in pre-trial detention for almost a year, was sentenced to death for apostasy at the Nouadhibou Court in northwest Mauritania. He had written a blog criticizing the use of religion to marginalize certain groups in society, and was still in detention at the end of 2015.[2]

In January, the Rosso Court in southern Mauritania sentenced Brahim Bilal Ramdane, Djiby Sow and Biram Dah Abeid, a former presidential candidate and president of the Initiative for the Resurgence of the Abolitionist Movement in Mauritania, to two years in prison for belonging to an unrecognized organization, participating in an unauthorized assembly and assaulting security officers. The three activists were arrested in November 2014 with other protesters while campaigning against slavery and raising awareness among the local population of the land rights of people of slave descent. Their sentences were upheld by the Appeal Court of Aleg in August 2015.[3]

In August, the UN Special Rapporteur on the rights to freedom of peaceful assembly and association called on the National Assembly to reject a draft law on civil society associations that had been approved by the Council of Ministers without public consultation.

In November, retired colonel Oumar Ould Beibacar was arrested at a political rally in the capital Nouakchott, during which he spoke of the extrajudicial execution of military officers in the 1990s. He was detained at the Nouakchott Directorate for National Security and released six days later but remained under judicial supervision.

## TORTURE AND OTHER ILL-TREATMENT

Prisoners suspected of belonging to al-Qa'ida in the Islamic Maghreb (AQIM) and the armed group Islamic State (IS), as well as women and children, were subjected to torture and other ill-treatment. These practices were routinely used to extract "confessions" and punish and humiliate suspects. The use of torture and other ill-treatment was also facilitated by the 2010 anti-terrorist law, which allowed for detainees suspected of terrorist acts to be held in police custody for up to 45 days. This limit was regularly exceeded, including by more than a year in one case.

One prisoner in the Nouakchott civil prison, arrested in April 2015 and accused of belonging to IS, was allegedly tortured while in pre-trial detention. His eyes were blindfolded, and he was handcuffed, punched, and beaten with batons. After seven days he said he was forced to sign a "confession". He alleged torture at his hearing in June 2015, but was ignored and convicted. There has been no investigation into his allegations.

One woman was allegedly tortured in pre-trial detention, where she said officers tore her clothes and slapped her to force a confession. After her trial, she was taken out of prison and brought to a police station where she was again beaten. The prison authorities saw the bruising on her body upon her return and the case was brought to the attention of the public prosecutor.

Children were also beaten in both pre-trial detention and in prison, where they shared a courtyard with adults. One of them reported being handcuffed and beaten for four days so he would confess. Other reported torture methods included being whipped with cables, suspended from the ceiling and having water poured into the nostrils.

Prisoners in the Salahdine prison reported that they were never allowed to practise any exercise in the courtyard and that the water given to them was dirty, making some of them ill.

In August, new laws defined torture as a crime against humanity, prohibited secret detention and created a national body with a mandate to investigate detention centres at any time.

## ENFORCED DISAPPEARANCES

In February, Khadim Ould Semen, Mohamed Ould Cbih and Mohamed Khaled Ould Ahmed, three prisoners sentenced to death for a shooting at Tourine, were victims of enforced disappearance. They were part of a sit-in organized in prison after a prisoner was not released on the due date. Prison authorities reported that violence occurred during the sit-in. The prison guards fired tear gas canisters and beat the prisoners with batons before taking the three men away, who have not been seen since. In July, the Minister of Justice said that he was unable to clarify their whereabouts and that a delegation would be allowed to visit them in

October, after the adoption of the law on torture. They remained disappeared at the end of the year.

The authorities have still not opened an investigation into the cases of 14 men convicted of terrorism-related offences, who were victims of enforced disappearance in 2011. They were held in harsh conditions in Salahdine prison, where one of them died in May 2014; the remaining 13 were transferred to Nouakchott central prison in May and July 2014.

## SLAVERY

In August, a new law was adopted against slavery (amending the 2007 law), defining slavery as a crime against humanity, doubling the prison term for offenders and defining 10 types of slavery, including forced marriage.

In December, two people were placed in detention and charged with acts of slavery.

## DEATH PENALTY

Although no executions were carried out in over 20 years and in spite of a de facto moratorium, death sentences continued to be imposed. In July, two men were sentenced to death after being convicted of the rape of a young girl. In December, one person who had been sentenced to death for terrorist acts escaped from the Nouakchott central prison.

---

1.  Mauritania: Actions speak louder than words: Amnesty International submission to the Universal Periodic Review, November 2015 (AFR 38/1813/2015)

2.  Mauritania must immediately release Mohamed Mkhaïtir, blogger sentenced to death for apostasy (AFR 38/0002/2015)

3.  Mauritania must immediately release jailed anti-slavery activists and human rights defenders (AFR 38/0001/2015); Mauritania: Anti-slavery activist's harsh sentence upheld on appeal (News story, 20 August)

# MEXICO

**United Mexican States**
Head of state and government: **Enrique Peña Nieto**

Impunity persisted for grave human rights violations including torture and other ill-treatment, enforced disappearances and extrajudicial executions. More than 27,000 people remained missing or disappeared. Human rights defenders and journalists continued to be threatened, harassed or killed. The number of detentions, deportations and complaints of abuse of irregular migrants by the authorities increased significantly. Violence against women continued to be widespread. Large-scale development and resource exploitation projects were carried out without a legal framework regarding the free, prior and informed consent of Indigenous communities they affected. The Supreme Court upheld same-sex couples' rights to marry and adopt children.

## BACKGROUND

President Peña Nieto reached the middle of his six-year administration term. The ruling Institutional Revolutionary Party retained a majority in elections to renew the lower house of the National Congress; several states elected governors and other local officials.

A new General Transparency Law enacted in May strengthened protections on the right to access information.

The government defended its education reforms against mass protests from teacher unions and social movements. It prosecuted members of teacher unions in cases that appeared to be politically motivated and transferred four defendants to a maximum security prison in October.

A 10-point security plan, announced in November 2014 by President Peña Nieto after mass demonstrations against the enforced disappearance of 43 students, resulted in a number of state governments taking control over municipal police, as well

as a bill before Congress to create special economic zones in the impoverished south. Other measures announced in the package such as new laws on torture and disappearances had yet to be implemented.

The share of people living in poverty rose from 45.5% to 46.2% between 2012 and 2014, according to official data released in July. The share of those living in extreme poverty decreased from 9.8% to 9.5% in the same period.

In April, the Supreme Court ruled that 40 days of pre-charge detention (*arraigo*) is constitutional for serious offences, a practice that has been condemned by several treaty bodies.

## POLICE AND SECURITY FORCES

Violence related to organized crime remained a serious concern. Despite official figures reporting a slight increase in homicides from 35,930 in 2014 to 36,126 in 2015, the figures combined manslaughters and murders, omitting the fact that the monthly average number of murders increased by 7%. While fewer soldiers were deployed in law enforcement operations, numerous human rights violations were still attributed to armed forces. There were plans to increase the presence of marines in law enforcement tasks.

Human rights violations at the hands of armed forces and police remained common, especially in the states of Tamaulipas, Michoacán and Guerrero, where major security operations were carried out.

In April, the Inter-American Court of Human Rights deemed that the 2014 reform to the Code of Military Justice did not fully comply with several of the Court's previous rulings, since it failed to exclude from military jurisdiction human rights violations committed against members of the armed forces. Congress failed to further reform the Code to comply with the Court's rulings.

## EXTRAJUDICIAL EXECUTIONS

Perpetrators of extrajudicial executions continued to enjoy almost absolute impunity.

For the second consecutive year, the authorities published no statistics on the number of people killed or wounded in clashes with the police and military forces, as part of the fight against organized crime.

Journalists alleged that 16 unarmed people were killed by federal police officers and other security forces in Apatzingán, Michoacán, in January. The National Human Rights Commission ordered an investigation into the killings. More than 40 people were killed in May during a police operation in Tanhuato, Michoacán. Investigations into the crimes were not made public and no one had been prosecuted at the end of the year.

In June, the NGO Centro Prodh uncovered that a military order "to take down criminals" (meant as "to kill" in this context) was the basis for operations carried out in 2014 in Tlatlaya, state of Mexico, when soldiers killed 22 people who allegedly belonged to a gang. The authorities claimed that the event was a shootout with gunmen, but the National Human Rights Commission and a special congressional commission of inquiry separately concluded that a majority of people were shot when they no longer posed a threat. Seven soldiers were arrested, but only three remained in jail pending trial at the end of the year. The Federal Attorney General's Office did not investigate any military officers or others with command responsibility who failed to prevent or stop these crimes.

## TORTURE AND OTHER ILL-TREATMENT

Torture and other ill-treatment remained widespread among law enforcement and investigative officials and little progress was made to eradicate it. Authorities denied the magnitude of the problem, while torture complaints at both federal and state levels persisted. The government was unable to provide information on any charges laid or sentences handed down at a federal level. In April, three police officers were charged with torture in Baja California state; the charges were rejected by a judge and appealed by the prosecutor.

Legislative and policy developments to tackle torture were announced, including internal investigation guidelines on torture from the Federal Attorney General's Office. On 10 December, President Peña Nieto presented a bill to Congress for a General Law on Torture, resulting from a constitutional reform that enabled Congress to legislate on torture and disappearances at federal and state levels.

As in previous years, the special medical examination procedure of the Federal Attorney General's Office for cases of alleged torture was not applied in most cases, with a backlog of more than 1,600 requests on file.[1] Officials generally failed to apply the procedure in compliance with the principles of the Istanbul Protocol. In many cases, investigations into torture and other ill-treatment did not advance without the presence of an official examination. Independent medical experts continued to face obstacles to carry out their work and have their examinations accepted as evidence in criminal trials.

In September, in its first ruling on the country, the UN Committee against Torture found that the torture by soldiers of four men in 2009 who had been charged with crimes including kidnapping breached the UN Convention against Torture. Following the ruling, the four men were acquitted of all charges; however, the soldiers had not been charged at the end of the year.

## ENFORCED DISAPPEARANCES

Enforced disappearances with the involvement of the state and disappearances committed by non-state actors continued to be widespread. By the end of the year, the government reported that 27,638 people (20,203 men and 7,435 women) were missing but did not specify how many were subjected to enforced disappearance. The few criminal investigations that took place into these cases were generally flawed, with authorities failing to search for the victims. Impunity for these crimes remained almost absolute. In October, the Attorney General created a Special Prosecutor's Office to handle cases of disappeared or missing people.

Groups of victims and their families as well as human rights organizations engaged in a national debate and produced a series of requirements for the General Law on Disappearances. On 10 December, President Peña Nieto sent a bill to Congress which fell short of international standards.

In January, the Federal Attorney General again stated that 43 students from a teacher training college in Ayotzinapa, Guerrero, who were forcibly disappeared in September 2014 and remained missing, were killed, burned and dumped in a river. The remains of one student were identified, but the whereabouts of the other 42 remained undisclosed. In September, an Interdisciplinary Group of Independent Experts (GIEI) appointed by the Inter-American Commission on Human Rights determined that the investigation was seriously flawed and concluded that the conditions of the site made it impossible to burn the bodies in the way described by the authorities. The GIEI confirmed that military intelligence agents in plain clothes followed and watched the students during the attacks and detentions, and that municipal, state and federal authorities were aware of the attacks. By the end of the year, approximately 100 people had been arrested and were on trial, but none had been charged with enforced disappearance.

## HUMAN RIGHTS DEFENDERS AND JOURNALISTS

Human rights defenders and journalists continued to be threatened, harassed, attacked or killed. Those defending the environment and land rights continued to be at particular risk. A number of journalists working on issues related to the state of Veracruz were killed. The federal Mechanism for the Protection of Human Rights Defenders and Journalists lacked resources and co-ordination, which left human rights defenders and journalists inadequately protected. The Prevention, Monitoring and Analysis Unit was installed three years after the Mechanism was established. The number of requests for protection under the Mechanism remained steady and approximately 90% of requests were admitted. Impunity for threats and acts of aggression remained.

In June, Mayan journalist Pedro Canche was released after spending nine months in pre-trial detention under unsubstantiated charges of sabotage brought against him as a reprisal for peacefully exercising his right to freedom of expression. Other journalists continued to be harassed by authorities, some of whom fled their hometown or suspended their work for fear of reprisals. In July, photojournalist Rubén Espinosa Becerril, activist Nadia Dominique Vera Pérez and three other women were found dead in an apartment in Mexico City. Both Rubén Espinosa and Nadia Vera had left the state of Veracruz months earlier due to threats.

## FREEDOM OF ASSEMBLY

The Supreme Court continued to analyze a legal challenge to Mexico City's 2014 Law on Mobility. The law threatens freedom of peaceful assembly, including through a prior authorization regime for demonstrations, a lack of provisions on spontaneous demonstrations and government powers to ban protests in specific places. Amnesty International and other international organizations submitted a joint *amicus* brief to the Court, arguing that certain provisions in the law violate international law standards.

## VIOLENCE AGAINST WOMEN AND GIRLS

Violence against women and girls remained endemic, including killings, abductions and sexual violence. The National System for the Prevention, Sanction and Eradication of Violence against Women announced for the first time the activation of a "Gender Alert" mechanism in the state of Morelos and parts of the state of Mexico. The "Gender Alert" is designed to mobilize authorities to combat widespread gender-based violence and elicit an effective, official response to cases of violence.

In July, five men were handed multiple life

sentences for the abduction, sexual exploitation and killing of 11 women in the US border town Ciudad Juárez, whose remains were found in the desert surrounding the town in 2012. The court's ruling recognized the endemic nature of gender-based violence in the area, and ordered new investigations for other perpetrators involved.

## REFUGEES' AND MIGRANTS' RIGHTS

Migrants and asylum-seekers passing through Mexico continued to be subjected to mass abductions, extortion, disappearances and other abuses committed by organized crime groups, often working in collusion with state agents. A majority of reported abductions took place in the state of Tamaulipas. Mass attacks against migrants by criminal groups persisted throughout the country, with no proper investigations nor access to justice and reparations for victims. In June, armed men attacked a group of approximately 120 Central American migrants in Sonora state; no investigation had been carried out at the end of the year. An expert forensic commission formed in 2013 to identify remains of migrants massacred in San Fernando, Tamaulipas, and nearby municipalities reported on the identification of victims to relatives in Central America. Authorities continued to obstruct the Commission's work by withholding information and complicating the delivery of remains to families.

The flow of refugees and migrants from Central America continued to increase, many of them leaving their country due to violence.

The implementation of the Southern Border Plan led to increased numbers of deportations and detentions of migrants entering the country. As of November, 178,254 irregular migrants had been apprehended and detained by the National Institute of Migration, compared with 127,149 in 2014; however, this was not reflected by a commensurate increase in the number of asylum claims granted. The number of deportations of Central American migrants by Mexico overtook those by the USA. Complaints of heavy-handed joint operations

by migration authorities, police and the military were registered along Mexico's southern border.

## INDIGENOUS PEOPLES' RIGHTS

The country still lacked a legal framework on the right of Indigenous Peoples to free, prior and informed consent regarding development projects affecting their lands and traditional way of life. Two Indigenous Yaqui leaders who had been imprisoned for protesting against the construction of an aqueduct were released because of a lack of evidence against them. The aqueduct's operation, however, continued even after a national anthropology authority found that it threatened the survival of the Indigenous community.

## INTERNATIONAL SCRUTINY

The government reacted harshly to international criticism of its human rights record. In March, the UN Special Rapporteur on torture was publicly questioned after he published a report describing torture as widespread in the country. A report on Mexico by the UN Committee on Enforced Disappearances was described by the government as "not contributing additional elements" to address the problem.

In May, the Supreme Court decided that the country was not bound to comply with judgments of the Inter-American Court of Human Rights that relate to restrictions on human rights contained in the Constitution. The decision contradicted international law and risks perpetuating human rights violations such as *arraigo*.

For the first time since 1996, the Inter-American Commission on Human Rights visited Mexico in September to assess the human rights situation. In its preliminary observations the Commission highlighted, among others, the issues of torture, enforced disappearances, violence against women and extrajudicial executions, and expressed concern about the impunity for such crimes. The UN High Commissioner for Human Rights visited the country for a similar purpose and stated that "there is broad consensus nationally, regionally and internationally on the gravity of the human rights situation in Mexico today".

---

1. Paper promises, daily impunity: Mexico's torture epidemic continues (AMR 41/2676/2015)

# MOLDOVA

**Republic of Moldova**
Head of state: **Nicolae Timofti**
Head of government: **Gheorghe Brega (replaced Valeriu Streleţ in October as acting Prime Minister, who replaced Chiril Gaburici in July, who replaced Iurie Leancă in February)**

Corruption scandals and economic deterioration prompted a series of anti-government protests. The number of registered complaints of torture and other ill-treatment slightly decreased, while impunity for torture persisted. The Chişinău Pride march took place under police protection but hate crimes on the basis of sexual orientation or gender identity were not effectively addressed.

## BACKGROUND

In May, it transpired that US$1 billion had disappeared from three Moldovan banks through questionable transactions in November 2014. On 6 September, tens of thousands of people attended a peaceful demonstration in the capital, Chişinău, demanding the resignation of the President and the government, and hundreds of protesters camped in tents in the city centre. Eight activists from a left-wing party tried to forcibly enter the Prosecutor General's Office and were detained; their leader, Grigore Petrenco, and six others were repeatedly remanded and accused of trying to incite mass disturbances. A handful of protesters were still camping in central Chişinău at the end of the year.

Political and media revelations led to several high-profile resignations, including of three successive Prime Ministers in the course of the year.

Leader of the Liberal Democratic Party of Moldova and former Prime Minister Vladimir Filat was stripped of his parliamentary immunity by an unexpected vote in Parliament on 15 October, and remanded as a suspect in a corruption case.

## TORTURE AND OTHER ILL-TREATMENT

Torture and other ill-treatment of detainees by the police persisted, in spite of ongoing reform of the Ministry of Interior. The Prosecutor General's Office registered 319 complaints during the first half of the year, a negligible reduction from the same period in 2014. Impunity remained a concern, with criminal investigations initiated in 53 cases, and only six reported convictions resulting in imprisonment for the perpetrators.

The persistent issue of inhuman and degrading conditions in pre-trial detention gained new prominence in connection with public awareness of the detention of Vladimir Filat and of members of the "Grigore Petrenco group".

On 30 June, the Supreme Court of Justice reviewed the four-year sentence of former Minister of Interior Gheorghe Papuc, who had been convicted of negligence during events on 7 April 2009 that had resulted in the death of Valeriu Boboc and dozens of injured street protesters. The Court issued him with a fine of MDL20,000 (US$1,000) instead and acquitted Vladimir Botnari, former police commissioner of Chişinău, who had previously been given a two-year conditional sentence.

In March the Chişinău Court of Appeal found a former police officer guilty of "abuse of power and intentional infliction of serious bodily or health injury" in connection with the death of Valeriu Boboc, and sentenced him to 10 years' imprisonment. The officer had fled Moldova and was sentenced in his absence.

## FREEDOM OF EXPRESSION

Television viewers across the country

complained of unexplained broadcast interruptions by Jurnal TV in early September, prompting speculation that the disruption had been caused by national telecommunications operator Moldtelecom to limit the coverage of the 6 September mass protest in Chişinău. Some cable television providers reportedly took Jurnal TV off air at the same time, citing technical issues.

## RIGHTS OF LESBIAN, GAY, BISEXUAL, TRANSGENDER AND INTERSEX PEOPLE

An LGBTI march took place on 17 May in Chişinău, under police protection. Counter-demonstrators, including Orthodox Christian activists, attempted to disrupt the event and pelted eggs and firecrackers at the participants. Five attackers were arrested by the police but it is unknown whether they were charged with any offence.

## DISCRIMINATION

Hate crimes, which are not a distinct crime under the Criminal Code, remained under-reported and poorly investigated, instead being qualified as hooliganism or robbery.

LGBTI organization GenderDoc-M registered at least four instances of hate crimes and 19 hate-motivated incidents.

In September, the Supreme Court of Justice overturned the decision of the lower court and acquitted Bishop Marchel of the Moldovan Orthodox Church of hate speech, incitement to discrimination and spreading false information. The Bishop had called for LGBTI individuals to be barred from working in educational, catering and medical institutions because, he claimed, "92% of them have HIV".

# MONGOLIA

Mongolia
Head of state: Tsakhia Elbegdorj
Head of government: Chimediin Saikhanbileg

In December, a new Criminal Code was passed, fully abolishing the death penalty once it goes into effect in September 2016. Impunity for torture and other ill-treatment, particularly by law enforcement officials during interrogations to obtain "confessions", remained widespread. Residents of urban areas continued to be at risk of forced eviction. Discrimination and harassment against lesbian, gay, bisexual, transgender and intersex (LGBTI) people remained of concern. Journalists often practised self-censorship for fear of prosecution. Human rights defenders and journalists continued to raise increased difficulties in carrying out human rights work.

## TORTURE AND OTHER ILL-TREATMENT

Impunity persisted for many allegations of torture and other ill-treatment committed by law enforcement officials. Since the closure in 2014 of the Special Investigation Unit, complaints of torture against law enforcement officers were investigated by police themselves and not an independent body, raising concerns regarding impartiality. Only certain officials tasked with investigation within the justice system were considered liable under Article 251 of the Criminal Code, thereby potentially allowing others suspected of extracting forced testimonies to escape accountability. Complaints of mental torture were dropped more often than those of physical ill-treatment because of alleged difficulties in establishing the facts.

## UNFAIR TRIALS

Regular instances of denial of pre-trial rights continued to be reported, such as the right to freedom from torture and other ill-treatment, as well as the rights to access health care, families and lawyers. Instances were reported of police and prosecutors using deception and intimidation against suspects and their family members.

## HOUSING RIGHTS – FORCED EVICTIONS

Residents of *ger* districts (areas without adequate access to essential services) of the capital, Ulaanbaatar, claimed that they were under constant fear of forcible eviction from their homes. Problems were exacerbated by the lack of transparency in city development plans and lack of clear prohibition against forced evictions in law or policy. Some residents of Bayanzurkh district in Ulaanbaatar claimed they were harassed and threatened into signing development plans and contracts to turn over their land.

## RIGHTS OF LESBIAN, GAY, BISEXUAL, TRANSGENDER AND INTERSEX PEOPLE

LGBTI people continued to face widespread discrimination. According to an LGBTI rights organization, police officers were often reluctant to intervene. Their responses to LGBTI people alleging discrimination revealed deeply discriminatory attitudes, and they often became abusers themselves by further harassing individuals.

## FREEDOM OF EXPRESSION – JOURNALISTS

Defamation laws, as outlined in Mongolia's criminal and civil laws, were used against journalists reporting content deemed offensive, including corruption and the activities of legislators. Many journalists and independent publications practised a degree of self-censorship due to fear of legal reprisals.

## DEATH PENALTY

In December a new Criminal Code removing the death penalty for all crimes was adopted by the State Great Hural (Parliament). At least two individuals were sentenced to death, including one who was reported to have been 17 years old when the crime was committed. One of the sentences was commuted to 25 years' imprisonment on appeal.[1]

---

1. Mongolia: Open letter on the death penalty (ASA 30/2490/2015)

# MONTENEGRO

Montenegro
Head of state: **Filip Vujanović**
Head of government: **Milo Djukanović**

---

Threats and attacks against independent media and journalists continued; few perpetrators were brought to justice. Police used excessive force during mass protests organized by opposition parties against the government's failure to address poverty, crime and corruption.

## CRIMES UNDER INTERNATIONAL LAW

In October the Supreme Court rejected a request to review the legality of the final judgment in the "Deportations Case" which had acquitted nine former police officials of the enforced disappearance in 1992 of 60 Bosnian refugees. Amnesty International had considered the verdict to be inconsistent with domestic law and international humanitarian law.

In September the UN Committee on Enforced Disappearances expressed concerns about shortcomings in war crimes proceedings, which may have led to impunity, urged the authorities to recognize the relatives of the disappeared as victims, and called on the new Commission on Missing Persons to establish the whereabouts of 61 people missing since the armed conflicts of the 1990s.

## FREEDOM OF EXPRESSION

In May a Commission established to investigate historical attacks on journalists requested access to relevant classified documents; the request was rejected without legal reasoning by the agency responsible for protection of personal data.

A witness to the 2004 murder of *Dan* newspaper editor Duško Jovanović was promised protection before testifying. In August, his widow left the country after her car was vandalized. Damir Mandić's conviction for complicity in the murder was confirmed in October.

In November, on the eve of International Day to End Impunity for Crimes against Journalists, the prosecutor closed the investigation into the beating in 2007 of journalist Tufik Softić, despite the arrest and detention of two suspects in 2014.

Journalists and human rights defenders were vilified in pro-government media. In January, TV Pink called for the imprisonment of Tea Prelević, director of the NGO Human Rights Action, following her advocacy on behalf of a trafficked woman.

In April, Podgorica Court found that the security services' surveillance since 2010 of the NGO MANS, which conducts investigations into corruption and organized crime, had been unlawful, and awarded compensation to MANS employees.

## EXCESSIVE USE OF FORCE

Hundreds of riot police used excessive force and tear gas on 17 October to remove a camp outside Parliament, established during mass demonstrations that commenced on 27 September. Opposition leaders and Members of Parliament were injured. Two journalists were detained. On 24 October, members of the Democratic Front opposition party attempted to force their way into Parliament after being denied entry, injuring 20 police officers. Police reacted with tear gas, shock-grenades and rubber bullets, injuring 27 protesters, including those who had not used violence. The Council for Civil Control of the Police, which subsequently reviewed three incidents, found police officers responsible for ill-treatment and abuse of authority. In November, two members of the Special Anti-Terrorist Unit were detained on suspicion of the ill-treatment of Miodrag Martinović.

## TORTURE AND OTHER ILL-TREATMENT

In April the European Court of Human Rights ruled that Montenegro should pay compensation to Dalibor Nikezić and Igor Milić, who were ill-treated at Spuž prison in 2009, finding that the state prosecutor had discontinued criminal proceedings without adequately assessing the available evidence.

## RIGHTS OF LESBIAN, GAY, BISEXUAL, TRANSGENDER AND INTERSEX PEOPLE

Proposed Pride marches in Nikšić were prohibited on three occasions on security grounds; the Podgorica Pride took place without incident in December.

In May, three men were each sentenced to three months' imprisonment for a verbal attack in April on Stevan Milivojević, director of the NGO LGBT Forum Progres.

## REFUGEES' AND MIGRANTS' RIGHTS

Some 1,107 Roma, Egyptians and Ashkali people displaced from Kosovo in 1999 had been granted legal status in Montenegro. However, 595 others remained at risk of statelessness, pending approval of their applications; most of the 700 who had not applied were believed to have left the country. According to UNHCR, the UN refugee agency, 144 Roma, Ashkali and Egyptians were assisted to return to Kosovo. In December, 48 Kosovo Roma and Egyptian families who had lived at Konik camp since 1999 were finally resettled into new apartments.

Over 4,000 Montenegrins sought asylum in the EU, 3,233 of them in Germany.

Montenegro remained a transit country for migrants and refugees, mainly Syrian nationals. By the end of November, out of 1,570 applicants, 14 had been granted refugee status, and two subsidiary protection.

# MOROCCO / WESTERN SAHARA

Kingdom of Morocco
Head of state: **King Mohamed VI**
Head of government: **Abdelilah Benkirane**

**The authorities restricted rights to freedom of expression, association and assembly, arresting and prosecuting critics, harassing human rights groups and forcibly dispersing**

protests. **Torture and other ill-treatment and unfair trials were reported. Women continued to face discrimination. Migrants and asylum-seekers were arbitrarily arrested and subjected to unnecessary and excessive use of force. Courts continued to impose death sentences; there were no executions.**

## BACKGROUND

In March, Morocco joined the Saudi Arabia-led coalition of states that engaged in the armed conflict in Yemen (see Yemen entry).

In April, the government published a draft bill to amend the Penal Code, part of broader plans to reform the justice system. Human rights groups said the draft failed to rectify existing deficiencies in the Code. Other draft laws to amend the Code of Criminal Procedure and the Statute of Judges, and to establish a Higher Judicial Council, remained under consideration.

## FREEDOM OF EXPRESSION

The authorities prosecuted journalists deemed to have insulted public figures, state institutions and the government's human rights record, and convicted some on apparently trumped-up, common-law charges. They continued to crack down on human rights advocates, activists and artists, subjecting some to prosecutions and restrictions on movement.

In March, a court in the capital Rabat sentenced journalist Hicham Mansouri to 10 months' imprisonment after convicting him of adultery in an unfair trial brought on apparently politically motivated charges.[1] In July, a court in Kenitra convicted caricaturist Khalid Gueddar of public drunkenness and causing "offence to a public institution ", imposing a three-month prison sentence.

Several independent journalists were convicted on charges of false reporting, defamation and insult, and given heavy fines.[2] In August, the Court of First Instance in Meknes convicted Hamid Elmahdaouy, editorial director of the online news website Badil.info, of reporting false news and publishing an unregistered newspaper, after

the website reported on the explosion of a car. The court fined him and suspended Badil.info for three months. In November, the Court of First Instance in Casablanca convicted Taoufik Bouachrine, editorial director of Akhbar Al Yaoum newspaper, of defamation after the newspaper published a story based on leaked diplomatic cables. The court sentenced him to a two-month suspended prison term and a fine of 1.6 million Moroccan dirhams (about US$150,000).

The authorities prevented several human rights activists from leaving Morocco to attend events abroad and subjected them to interrogations. In November, seven Moroccan civil society activists, including Maati Monjib, an historian and co-founder of the NGO Freedom Now, were prosecuted on various charges including harming internal state security after training people to use a citizen journalism smartphone application. They faced penalties of up to five years in prison if convicted.

The authorities also banned cultural events, including the public performance of a play about African migrants in Morocco.

## FREEDOM OF ASSOCIATION

Groups that criticized the government's human rights record were harassed by the authorities, who prevented them from carrying out legitimate public events and internal meetings, often informally through verbal warnings or by using the security forces to block access to venues. They restricted research activities by international human rights groups, including Amnesty International, Human Rights Watch and NOVACT International Institute for Nonviolent Action.

In June the authorities expelled two Amnesty International staff members who were visiting Morocco to investigate conditions for migrants and refugees at the country's border with Spain.[3] The authorities said they had not given permission for the visit, despite previously informing Amnesty International that no such permission was required.

The authorities continued to bar the legal registration of several human rights organizations. At the end of the year, 41 of the 97 local branches of the Moroccan Association for Human Rights (AMDH), Morocco's largest human rights group, remained unregistered and in legal limbo because local officials refused to accept their registration applications or provide receipts for those deposited. In June the administrative tribunal of Fes ruled that authorities in Tahla could not refuse to accept the registration documents filed by the local AMDH branch and should issue a receipt.

## FREEDOM OF ASSEMBLY

The security forces dispersed protests by human rights defenders, political activists, unemployed graduates and students, sometimes by force. Some protesters were arrested, fined and imprisoned.

In January, a court in Ouarzazate sentenced Mustafa Faska and Omar Hourane to three years' imprisonment after convicting them on charges that included robbery, violence and forming a criminal gang after they participated in protests against a silver mine in Imider, where a peaceful sit-in protest has continued since 2011.

In July the authorities prevented three members of the al-'Adl Wal Ihsane (Justice and Spirituality) organization from leaving Morocco for failing to pay fines imposed for "holding an unauthorized meeting" in a private home. They had previously told a court that they would go to prison rather than pay the fines.

In September, security forces arrested 80 members and supporters of the Annahj Addimocrati (Democratic Path) party as they sought to participate in marches and distribute flyers calling for a boycott of communal and regional elections. None faced charges. Some accused the mostly plain-clothes security officers of using excessive force.

## REPRESSION OF DISSENT – SAHRAWI ACTIVISTS

The authorities targeted Sahrawi activists who advocated for the self-determination of Western Sahara and reported human rights abuses. They forcibly dispersed gatherings, often using excessive force, and prosecuted protesters. Some Sahrawi prisoners went on hunger strike to protest against torture and other ill-treatment. The authorities also restricted access to Western Sahara for foreign journalists, activists and human rights defenders, barring entry to some and expelling others.

More than two years after his arrest, Mbarek Daoudi, a former soldier and advocate of Sahrawi self-determination, received a five-year prison sentence on what appeared to be politically motivated charges of possessing ammunition without a licence and attempting to make a weapon. He alleged that interrogators forced him to sign an incriminating statement under torture following his arrest in September 2013. In December, Hamza Ljoumai was sentenced to a two-year prison term after taking part in a protest for self-determination in 2013. He said that police officers tortured him in custody and forced him to sign an interrogation report he was not allowed to read.

In March, the NGO Sahrawi Association of Victims of Grave Human Rights Violations Committed by the Moroccan State obtained official registration 10 years after it first submitted its application to the authorities, although its activities remained restricted. Other Sahrawi rights associations, such as the Collective of Sahrawi Human Rights Defenders, continued to be denied official registration, which they require to operate legally.

In April the UN Security Council extended the mandate of the UN Mission for the Referendum in Western Sahara (MINURSO) for another year, again without including any human rights monitoring component.

## TORTURE AND OTHER ILL-TREATMENT

The authorities failed to ensure that detainees and prisoners were adequately protected against torture and other ill-treatment. In particular, the authorities failed to promptly investigate allegations or ensure accountability.

In September, the Moroccan authorities closed the investigation into the torture allegations of Ali Aarrass, which they had opened in May 2014 following a decision by the UN Committee against Torture. Ali Aarrass, who received a 12-year prison sentence on terrorism charges in 2012 after Spanish authorities forcibly returned him to Morocco, remained imprisoned despite calls for his immediate release by the UN Working Group on Arbitrary Detention and had yet to receive a response by the Court of Cassation nearly three years after his appeal.

Some prisoners launched hunger strikes in protest against alleged ill-treatment by prison staff and harsh prison conditions, including overcrowding, poor hygiene and lack of access to medical care.

The authorities responded to allegations of torture against Moroccan officials, filed in French courts and submitted to UN bodies, by prosecuting the complainants on defamation and other charges. Those prosecuted included Zakaria Moumni, who said he was tortured in detention in 2010, ACAT-France, a French anti-torture NGO, and two torture complainants who were assisted by ACAT-France.[4] In July, France and Morocco adopted an amendment to a judicial co-operation agreement between the two countries. The amendment decreed that all complaints alleging violations on Moroccan territory, including by French nationals, are to be transferred to Moroccan courts, thus denying victims of torture or other serious abuses in Morocco any means of obtaining remedy through French courts.

In June a court in Fes sentenced two prison officials to five-year prison terms for causing the death of an inmate at Ain Kadou Prison in Fes in 2008. The victim's family appealed against the apparent leniency of the sentences.

## COUNTER-TERROR AND SECURITY

The authorities detained Younous Chekkouri, a former detainee of the US detention facility at Guantánamo Bay, immediately upon his return to Morocco in September and investigated him on terrorism-related charges.

In May the government passed a new law making it a crime for Moroccans to join a terrorist group abroad, punishable by up to 10 years in prison. The amendment compounded problematic aspects in existing anti-terrorism legislation including the provision for 12 days' pre-charge detention with delayed access to legal counsel, and the vague concept of "advocacy of terrorism", punishable by up to 10 years' imprisonment.

## IMPUNITY

Victims of serious human rights violations committed between 1956 and 1999 continued to be denied justice.[5] The authorities failed to implement recommendations made by the Equity and Reconciliation Commission, which examined human rights violations between 1956 and 1999, including a national strategy to combat impunity.

## WOMEN'S RIGHTS

Women faced discrimination in law and in practice, and were inadequately protected against sexual and other violence.

In March the King asked the government to revise Morocco's restrictive abortion laws. In May the authorities said that access to abortion would be extended to women whose health was at risk due to foetal impairment or who were pregnant as a result of rape or incest; the authorities had not published draft legislation by the end of the year.

In July the authorities charged two women with public indecency, apparently for wearing short skirts. The charges were dropped following a national and international public outcry.

The government failed to move forward on a draft law, announced in 2013, criminalizing violence against women and children.

## RIGHTS OF LESBIAN, GAY, BISEXUAL, TRANSGENDER AND INTERSEX PEOPLE

Consensual same-sex sexual relations remained a crime. In May and June, courts in Oujda and Rabat convicted five men on charges that included indecency and engaging in homosexual acts, and sentenced them to prison terms of up to three years, reduced to five months on appeal.

## REFUGEES' AND MIGRANTS' RIGHTS

Migrants and asylum-seekers from countries in sub-Saharan Africa faced arrest and alleged that Moroccan and Spanish border authorities used unnecessary and excessive force to prevent them gaining entry to Spain. Moroccan authorities allowed the summary return of some migrants who did gain irregular entry to Spain (see Spain entry).

In February the authorities arrested over 1,000 migrants and asylum-seekers in raids in and around the northeastern port city of Nador. They transported them to cities in southern Morocco and detained them for several days before releasing them. In May, the government announced that it would build a wall along Morocco's border with Algeria. In November, two migrants allegedly died of asphyxiation after the authorities lit a fire outside a cave they had taken refuge in during a raid near the northern city of Fnideq.

## POLISARIO CAMPS

The Polisario Front again failed to take any steps to hold to account those responsible for human rights abuses committed in the 1970s and 1980s in camps under its control.

## DEATH PENALTY

Courts handed down death sentences; there have been no executions since 1993.

---

1. Morocco: Further information: Jail term of press freedom advocate upheld: Hicham Mansouri (MDE 29/1754/2015)

2. Morocco: Court orders suspension of news website, editors fined for "false news" and "defamation" (MDE 29/2260/2015)

3. Amnesty International staff members expelled from Morocco (Press release, 11 June)

4. Shadow of impunity: Torture in Morocco and Western Sahara (MDE 29/001/2015)

5. Morocco/Western Sahara: Time for truth 50 years after enforced disappearance of opposition leader Mehdi Ben Barka (MDE 29/2747/2015)

# MOZAMBIQUE

Republic of Mozambique
Head of state and government: Filipe Jacinto Nyussi

**No one was held responsible for the murder of a constitutional law expert who stated that a proposal by the opposition party on provincial autonomy was constitutional. The Public Prosecutor charged two men with a crime against the security of the state for criticizing former President Armando Guebuza. A new Penal Code came into force. Draft laws impacting on the rights of women and girls were passed into law.**

## BACKGROUND

Filipe Nyussi of the Mozambique Liberation Front (FRELIMO), the ruling party, was sworn in as President on 15 January, after winning 57% of the votes cast in October 2014.

Afonso Dhlakama, leader of the Mozambican National Resistance (RENAMO), the main opposition party, rejected the election outcome and boycotted the opening of Parliament in January. Throughout the year, RENAMO campaigned for provincial autonomy in the central and northern regions, where the party claimed it had taken the majority of votes. In April, Parliament rejected a bill put forward by RENAMO that aimed to formalize regional autonomy.

In September, clashes between national armed forces and RENAMO's militia resumed following several months of post-electoral tension. On 13 September, Afonso Dhlakama's convoy was hit by gunfire while he was campaigning in Manica province. The result of an investigation into the incident was still pending at the end of the year.

A stagnation of the country's poverty level in the past decade contributed to fuelling social clashes.

## LEGAL DEVELOPMENTS

In October, the Council of Ministers approved the Regulation of the Access to Information Law, which had come into force in December 2014. The law established the responsibility of governmental authorities and private entities with regard to the release and dissemination of information that is in the public interest; deadlines for providing the information; and a legal mechanism whenever a request for information is denied.

A new Penal Code came into force in July. It includes a number of positive revisions such as the decriminalization of abortion, the option of non-custodial sentences as an alternative to prison, and the criminalization of actions that are destructive to the environment.

Under the new Code, abortion is legal when the pregnancy poses a risk to the mother's or the foetus' health, when it is the result of rape or incest, or when the abortion is undertaken during the first 12 weeks of pregnancy by a qualified health professional at an official health centre.

The need to approve the Regulation on the decriminalization of abortion and the fact that the Criminal Procedure Code has not been revised constitute an obstacle for the implementation of the new legislation.

## FREEDOM OF EXPRESSION

On 19 June, the Public Prosecutor formally charged Carlos Nuno Castel-Branco with a crime against the security of the state for defaming former President Armando Guebuza. The accusation was based on an open letter published on Carlos Nuno Castel-Branco's Facebook page in November 2013, which criticized Armando Guebuza's governance record.

The Facebook post was later published in *Mediafax*, a newspaper. Fernando Mbanze, editor of *Mediafax*, was charged with "abusing freedom of the press" and

breaching the State Security Law.

On 16 September, the Kampfumo Municipal District Court acquitted both men on the grounds that publishing a letter did not qualify as a crime under Mozambican law. The Public Prosecutor appealed against the Court's decision. The Court had not yet decided on the appeal at the end of the year.

On 3 March, Gilles Cistac, a constitutional law expert, was shot dead by four gunmen in Maputo, the capital. A prominent academic, he had publicly stated that RENAMO's proposal on provincial autonomy was constitutional, drawing criticism from FRELIMO. Hundreds of human rights activists and students marched in Maputo on 7 March, calling for justice for his murder. The police publicly launched an investigation into his killing but those responsible had not been identified by the end of the year.

## ARBITRARY DETENTIONS

For the third year running, no action was taken to hold anyone to account for the arbitrary and unlawful detention of José Capitine Cossa. He was detained without charge or trial in Machava Maximum Security Prison and released in 2012.

# MYANMAR

**Republic of the Union of Myanmar**
Head of state and government: **Thein Sein**

Authorities failed to address rising religious intolerance and incitement to discrimination and violence against Muslims, allowing hardline Buddhist nationalist groups to grow in power and influence ahead of the November general elections. The situation of the persecuted Rohingya deteriorated still further. The government intensified a clampdown on freedoms of expression, association and peaceful assembly. Reports of abuses of international human rights and humanitarian law in areas of internal armed conflict persisted. Security forces suspected of human rights violations continued to enjoy near-total impunity.

## BACKGROUND

On 8 November, Myanmar held much anticipated general elections, which saw the opposition National League for Democracy claim the majority of seats in Parliament. A new government was scheduled to be in place by the end of March 2016. Although widely praised as being credible and transparent, the elections were otherwise marred by the disenfranchisement of minority groups and ongoing restrictions on freedom of expression.

In June, the military blocked an attempt to amend the 2008 Constitution to remove its legislative veto over constitutional amendments and a clause which bars opposition leader Aung San Suu Kyi from being elected President by Parliament.

In July Myanmar ratified the Chemical Weapons Convention and signed the ICESCR.

## DISCRIMINATION

There was an alarming rise in religious intolerance, and in particular anti-Muslim sentiment, with hardline Buddhist nationalist groups growing in influence. The authorities failed to address incitement to discrimination and violence based on national, racial and religious hatred.

Between May and August Parliament adopted four laws aimed at "protecting race and religion", originally proposed by hardline Buddhist nationalist groups. The laws – the Religious Conversion Law, the Buddhist Women's Special Marriage Law, the Population Control Healthcare Law and the Monogamy Law – were passed despite containing provisions that violate human rights, including by discriminating on religious and gender grounds. There were fears that they would entrench widespread discrimination and fuel further violence against minority groups.[1]

People who spoke out against discrimination and rising religious intolerance faced retaliation from state and non-state actors. On 2 June, writer Htin Lin Oo was sentenced to two years in prison with hard labour for "insulting religion" in an October 2014 speech criticizing the use of Buddhism to promote discrimination and prejudice. Women's rights activists and other human rights defenders who spoke out against the four "protecting race and religion" laws were subjected to harassment and intimidation, including sexually abusive threats.

### The Rohingya minority

The situation of the Rohingya minority continued to deteriorate. Most remained effectively deprived of citizenship rights under the 1982 Citizenship Law, and continued to face severe restrictions on their right to freedom of movement, limited access to life-saving health care, and denial of their rights to education and equal employment opportunities. There were ongoing reports of arbitrary arrests and torture and other ill-treatment of Rohingya in detention, as well as deaths in custody at the hands of security forces. Access to Rakhine State for international observers remained severely restricted.

In February, the President announced the revocation of all Temporary Registration Cards (TRCs) – also known as "white cards" – leaving many Rohingya without any form of identity document. The move effectively barred Rohingya – and other former TRC holders – from being able to vote in the November elections. The exclusion of the Rohingya was further cemented by the disqualification of almost all Rohingya who applied to contest the elections as candidates. Many other Muslims were also disqualified on discriminatory grounds.

The deteriorating situation of the Rohingya led increasing numbers to leave Myanmar. According to UNHCR, the UN refugee agency, 33,000 people – Rohingya as well as Bangladeshi nationals – left the Bay of Bengal by boat during the year. In May, a crackdown on trafficking in neighbouring Thailand saw thousands of people – many Rohingya fleeing Myanmar – stranded at sea on overcrowded boats controlled by traffickers and people smugglers. Many were beaten and held hostage for ransom.[2]

## PRISONERS OF CONSCIENCE

Authorities continued to arrest and imprison people for peacefully exercising their rights, including student protesters, political activists, media workers and human rights defenders, in particular land and labour activists.[3] By the end of the year at least 114 prisoners of conscience were behind bars while hundreds of others released on bail were facing charges – and prison – solely for the peaceful exercise of their rights.

In March the police violently dispersed a largely peaceful student protest against the new National Education Law in the town of Letpadan in Bago Region. Over 100 student protesters, leaders and their supporters were subsequently charged with a range of criminal offences for their participation in the protests. Among them was student leader Phyoe Phyoe Aung, who was facing over nine years' imprisonment if convicted for her peaceful activities. In the subsequent days and weeks, authorities subjected students and their supporters to surveillance and other forms of harassment in a blatant attempt to intimidate and punish those connected with the student protests.[4]

In October, one month ahead of the general elections, authorities detained several people for social media posts mocking the military. Among those detained was ethnic Kachin peace activist Patrick Kum Jaa Lee, whose repeated requests for bail were rejected, despite him suffering from ill-health in detention. These people were charged under the 2013 Telecommunications Act, raising alarm that authorities may be moving their repression to the digital sphere.

A prisoner amnesty on 30 July saw the release of 11 prisoners of conscience among the 6,966 prisoners released. Prisoner of conscience Tun Aung was released in January following a Presidential pardon.

On 5 January, President Thein Sein reconstituted a committee established in 2013 to scrutinize cases of remaining prisoners of conscience. According to state media, the new Prisoners of Conscience Affairs Committee would be "promptly carrying out prisoners of conscience affairs at the grassroots level". However, by the end of the year, there was no information regarding its mandate, resources or activities and it was unclear whether it was operational.[5]

## FREEDOMS OF EXPRESSION, ASSOCIATION AND PEACEFUL ASSEMBLY

Broad and vaguely worded laws were used to stifle dissent and restrict the rights to freedom of expression, association and peaceful assembly. They included the Peaceful Assembly and Peaceful Procession Law, Penal Code provisions criminalizing "unlawful assemblies", "insulting religion" and "incitement", and the Unlawful Associations Act among others. There were no attempts to review or amend laws which restricted these rights.

Authorities intimidated and monitored human rights defenders and peaceful activists, subjecting them to multiple forms of harassment and surveillance – including being followed; having their photo taken when attending events and meetings; searches in their offices and homes; and harassment and intimidation of their family members, colleagues or friends.

Journalists remained subjected to harassment, arrest, prosecution and imprisonment solely for carrying out their activities peacefully, leading some to self-censor.[6]

## INTERNAL ARMED CONFLICT

On 15 October, the government and eight ethnic armed groups signed the Nationwide Ceasefire Agreement, aimed at putting an end to decades of armed conflicts between the military and the many armed ethnic groups. However, the authorities' decision to exclude some armed ethnic groups from the accord meant that the seven other groups invited to sign the agreement – including all those in active conflict with the Army – chose not to do so.

Fighting intensified in Kachin and Shan states, with ongoing reports of killings, enforced disappearances, rape and other crimes of sexual violence and forced labour.[7] The government continued to deny full and sustained access for humanitarian workers to displaced communities.

In February thousands were displaced, with reports of killings when renewed fighting broke out between the Myanmar Army and the armed group the Myanmar National Democratic Alliance Army in the Kokang Self-Administered Zone. The President imposed Martial Law in the region on 17 February, lifting it nine months later on 17 November. In October, new military offensives in central Shan State led to the displacement of around 6,000 people. Up to 4,000 were still displaced by the end of the year.

In September, the government signed the Optional Protocol to the UN Convention on the Rights of the Child on the involvement of children in armed conflict. The Army was reported to have discharged 146 children and young adults from its forces. There were continued reports that child soldiers were being recruited by state and non-state actors.

## CORPORATE ACCOUNTABILITY

The legal framework remained inadequate to prevent businesses from causing or contributing to human rights abuses. There was no legislation prohibiting forced evictions, nor adequate environmental safeguards ensuring that people were protected against negative human rights impacts of water, air or soil pollution caused by extractive and manufacturing industries.

Thousands of people were at risk of being forcibly evicted from their homes and farms to make way for the controversial Letpadaung copper mine in central Myanmar. The wider Monywa mining project, of which Letpadaung forms part, has a long history of human rights abuses, including forced evictions, violent repression of protests by the authorities, and environmental impacts posing a threat to local people's health and access to clean water. None of the companies involved had been

held to account for any human rights abuses by the end of the year.[8]

## REFUGEES AND INTERNALLY DISPLACED PEOPLE

According to the UN Office for the Coordination of Humanitarian Affairs (OCHA), there were over 230,000 internally displaced people in Myanmar. These included over 100,000 people displaced by fighting in Kachin and Northern Shan states and 130,000 people, mostly Rohingya, in Rakhine State displaced since violence erupted there in 2012. In July, 1.7 million people were temporarily displaced by massive floods across the country.

Some 110,000 refugees and others from Myanmar lived in nine camps on the Thailand-Myanmar border, uncertain of their future. Many expressed concerns about returning to Myanmar, pointing to ongoing militarization, persistent impunity, the continued presence of landmines, and limited education and employment opportunities as barriers to voluntary returns.

## IMPUNITY

Members of the security forces continued to violate human rights with near-total impunity. Investigations into human rights violations by the security forces were rare, and when they did occur they lacked transparency and independence. Perpetrators were seldom held to account. Victims and their families continued to be denied their rights to justice, truth and reparation.[9]

In May, the Myanmar National Human Rights Commission (MNHRC) announced that it had been made aware that a military court had acquitted two army officials of charges relating to the death of journalist Aung Kyaw Naing (also known as Par Gyi), who was shot dead in military custody in October 2014. The court-martial was held despite a police investigation and court inquest already being underway. Aung Kyaw Naing's family was unaware of the court-martial until the MNHRC announcement. No one had been brought to justice for the killing by the end of the year.

State officials, including members of the security forces, remained protected from prosecution for past human rights violations by immunity provisions in the 2008 Constitution. In December, a bill was submitted to Parliament which would guarantee former Presidents lifetime immunity from prosecution for "actions" – which could include human rights violations, crimes against humanity and war crimes – taken while they were in office. The bill had not been adopted by the end of the year.

## DEATH PENALTY

No executions were carried out. At least 17 new death sentences were imposed during the year.

## INTERNATIONAL SCRUTINY

In November, Myanmar's human rights record was assessed under the UPR.[10] Myanmar rejected key recommendations to review specific laws which restrict the rights to freedom of expression, association and peaceful assembly and refused to acknowledge the systemic discrimination facing the Rohingya minority.

The UN Special Rapporteur on the situation of human rights in Myanmar made two official visits to the country during the year, yet she was hampered in carrying out her mandate. In August, she was only given permission to travel for five days, had difficulties meeting with government interlocutors, and was denied access to Rakhine State. She also reported surveillance and harassment of civil society members who met with her. By the end of the year, there was still no agreement to establish an Office of the UN High Commissioner for Human Rights (OHCHR) in Myanmar. While OHCHR staff were able to operate in Myanmar, they did not have full and sustained access to the country, impeding their ability to undertake their work.

1. Amnesty International and the International Commission of Jurists

(ICJ): Parliament must reject discriminatory "race and religion" laws (ASA 16/1107/2015)

2. Deadly journeys: The refugee and trafficking crisis in Southeast Asia (ASA 21/2574/2015)

3. "Going back to the old ways": A new generation of prisoners of conscience in Myanmar (ASA 165/2457/2015)

4. Myanmar: End clampdown on student protesters and supporters (ASA 16/1511/2015)

5. Amnesty International and Human Rights Watch: Open letter on the establishment of the Prisoners of Conscience Affairs Committee (ASA 16/0007/2015)

6. Caught between state censorship and self-censorship: Prosecution and intimidation of media workers in Myanmar (ASA 16/1743/2015)

7. Myanmar: Investigate alleged rape and killing of two Kachin women (ASA 16/0006/2015)

8. Open for business? Corporate crime and abuses at Myanmar copper mine (ASA 16/0003/2015)

9. Myanmar: Four years on, impunity is the Kachin conflict's hallmark (ASA 16/1832/2015)

10. Myanmar: Stalled reforms: Impunity, discrimination and ongoing human rights abuses: Amnesty International submission to the Universal Periodic Review (ASA 16/2276/2015)

# NAMIBIA

**Republic of Namibia**
Head of state and government: **Hage Gottfried Geingob**

The long-running Caprivi detainees' treason trial concluded. Violations of the right to freedom of expression continued. Cases of women being killed as a result of domestic violence were reported. A journalist was assaulted and briefly detained by police for taking a photograph of police arresting a criminal suspect.

## CAPRIVI DETAINEES' TRIAL

The Caprivi detainees' trial concluded on 7 September. Judge Elton Hoff found 30 of the 65 accused guilty of charges of high treason, nine charges of murder, and 90 counts of attempted murder. Thirty-two people were acquitted and released, and a further three were found guilty of other charges. The detainees were originally arrested and charged in 1999 for allegedly attempting to secede the then Caprivi region from the rest of the country. They had spent more than 14 years in remand prison. The majority of them suffered health problems linked to age and prolonged detention and many of their relatives had no means of visiting them. Many of the Caprivi detainees were possible prisoners of conscience because they were arrested solely on the basis of their actual or perceived political views, ethnicity or membership of certain organizations. The length of their pre-trial detention violated the rights of the accused to a fair trial. Ten of the accused died in police custody before the High Court trial commenced in Grootfontein, Otjozondjupa Region, in 2003, while another 12 who went on trial died before its end.

Most of the detainees reported being tortured or otherwise ill-treated at the time of their arrest.

In passing his verdict, Judge Hoff upheld a 2001 Supreme Court decision, making confessions extracted under coercion inadmissible and also dismissed testimonies secured by torture or illegal police behaviour.

## FREEDOM OF EXPRESSION

The right to freedom of expression continued to be violated.

On 5 December, *New Era* journalist Nuusita Ashipala was physically assaulted by a police officer in Oshakati, Oshana Region, and was locked up in a police van for about 30 minutes for taking pictures of police officers arresting a criminal suspect at the Game shopping complex. She was ordered to delete the pictures from her camera before being released without charge.

## VIOLENCE AGAINST WOMEN AND GIRLS

Violence against women, in particular so-called passion killings, remained a concern.

On 21 April, the police reported the death of a 26-year-old mother of two from the Oneshila informal settlement in Oshakati East. She had been murdered in full view of her children by her male partner.

On 20 June, Martha Iyambo died after being stabbed by her ex-boyfriend at Oyovu village in the Omuntele constituency,

Oshikoto Region. In the same month, Justine Shiweda, a 50-year-old teacher at Onalulago Primary School in Oniipa constituency, was shot dead by her husband. In 2014, UNAIDS, the joint UN Programme on HIV/AIDS, and Victims 2 Survivors, a Namibian NGO, called for gender-based violence to be declared a national disaster.

# NAURU

Republic of Nauru
Head of state and government: **Baron Waqa**

**There were ongoing concerns about independence of the judiciary and restrictions on freedom of expression. Asylum-seekers continued to be housed at the Australian-run immigration processing centre on Nauru amid reports of sexual and other physical abuse, including of children.**

## FREEDOM OF EXPRESSION

In April the government blocked access to Facebook for several weeks, claiming it needed to stop the sexual exploitation of children. On 12 May, new criminal laws imposed seven-year prison sentences for publishing statements which coerced, intimidated or caused emotional distress. These laws failed to comply with international human rights law and standards on the right to freedom of expression and imposed excessive penalties.

Court cases continued against five opposition MPs who were suspended from Parliament in 2014 after being accused of criticizing the government in international media. All five had their passports cancelled. In June three of the MPs were also detained, two without bail for one month, after participating in protests criticizing the government.

## FAIR TRIALS

Concerns remained about the independence of the judiciary and unreasonable delays after judicial officers were effectively dismissed in early 2014, jeopardizing the right to a fair trial.

## REFUGEES AND ASYLUM-SEEKERS

By 30 November, 543 people, including 70 children, remained in the Australian-run centre on Nauru. Approximately 621 refugees were living on temporary visas in the community. The reopening of Australia's immigration processing centre on Nauru in 2012 led to numerous human rights abuses. In March, an independent report released by the Australian government made recommendations to address ongoing concerns about the safety of women and children in the centre (see Australia entry). The Nauru government stated it was deeply concerned by the findings and would make all resources available to help Australia implement the changes. However, in August a report by the Australian Senate into the abuse allegations stated that the current conditions and circumstances were not adequate, appropriate or safe. Despite key recommendations, Nauru had yet to implement a child protection framework.

In October the Nauru government announced that the centre would be an "open" facility, with those housed there free to come and go. It also announced that the remaining 600 asylum claims would be processed "within a week". By the end of December processing had still not been completed.

Ongoing reports of violence against refugees in the community raised concerns that Nauru remained ill-equipped to provide the necessary safeguards to protect asylum-seekers and to meet the needs of refugees who were settled.

A ban on foreign journalists visiting the island was made explicit in a statement from the Nauru government in October.

## INTERNATIONAL SCRUTINY

In May, the UN Subcommittee on Prevention of Torture inspected Nauru's police station and prison, as well as the Immigration Detention Centre. The government committed to establishing a National Preventive Mechanism to monitor places of detention at the earliest opportunity.

In November, Nauru's human rights record was assessed for the second time under the UN UPR. The government agreed to ensure judicial independence, introduce specific laws against family violence, and to improve measures to safeguard the rights of refugees and asylum-seekers.

# NEPAL

Federal Democratic Republic of Nepal
Head of state: **Bidhya Devi Bhandari (replaced Ram Baran Yadav in October)**
Head of government: **Khadga Prasad Sharma Oli (replaced Sushil Koirala in October)**

**A new Constitution was rushed through in the aftermath of the devastating earthquake of 25 April. Adopted in September, it was marked by human rights shortcomings and a federalist structure rejected by ethnic groups in the Terai. Violent clashes between protesters and police led to more than 50 deaths. Discriminatory relief distribution after the earthquake impacted marginalized groups, and reconstruction efforts were delayed in all affected areas. Discrimination, including on the basis of gender, caste, class, ethnic origin and religion, remained rife.**

## BACKGROUND

On 25 April, a magnitude 7.8 earthquake struck Nepal, followed by hundreds of aftershocks. By October, the Home Ministry had reported 8,856 deaths and 22,309 people injured in the original earthquake. A total of 602,257 homes were recorded as having been completely destroyed and a further 285,099 partially destroyed. Over 100,000 displaced people were forced to live in camps for months. Access to basic health services was challenging or non-existent for many and food security was fragile.

The Constituent Assembly failed to adopt a

new Constitution by the 22 January deadline but, following the earthquakes, rushed to an agreement on a text that was adopted in September. Madhesi and Tharu groups organized often violent protests in response to the proposed federal structure, and security forces resorted to the use of force. Starting from the third week of September, obstructions at the various entry/exit points at the India-Nepal border prevented trucks carrying fuel, food and medicine from entering from India, causing severe shortages.

## LEGAL, CONSTITUTIONAL OR INSTITUTIONAL DEVELOPMENTS

The draft Constitution presented for public consultation in July raised major human rights concerns, with the rights of women, and marginalized communities such as Dalits, inadequately protected. There were serious concerns around the citizenship provisions which discriminated against single women and same-sex couples, and around provisions including freedoms of religion and expression, access to justice, preventative detention, sexual and reproductive rights and child rights. During the public consultation, approximately 40,000 recommendations from human rights organizations and the public were received by the Constituent Assembly, but it failed to make necessary changes and key concerns remained unaddressed in the final text, adopted on 20 September.

On 8 August, four major political parties brokered an agreement to define Nepal as a federal republic in the new Constitution and to split it into seven federally administered states. Ethnic groups in south and mid-west Nepal protested against the new structure which they saw as denying them political representation. This resulted in a surge of often violent protests in the Tarai region. Security forces resorted to excessive, disproportionate or unnecessary force in several clashes with protesters. By October, at least 47 civilians and 10 police had been killed in clashes.

## IMPUNITY

On 26 February, the Supreme Court ruled against provisions that recommend amnesties for crimes under international law in the Truth and Reconciliation Commission (TRC) Act, passed by the Constituent Assembly in April 2014. The government rejected the Supreme Court's decision and filed a review petition. The TRC and a Commission on Enforced Disappearances, established under the Act, began operating despite the amnesty provisions, risking further impunity for perpetrators of international crimes committed during the armed conflict.

Accountability for human rights abuses continued to be seriously undermined by police failures to register First Information Reports, conduct investigations and follow court orders. These included cases of alleged extrajudicial executions, gender-based violence, torture and other ill-treatment, and trafficking of women and children.

## MIGRANT WORKERS' RIGHTS

Just over 500,000 Nepalese migrated through official channels for work, largely in low-skilled sectors such as construction, manufacturing and domestic work. Many continued to be trafficked for exploitation and forced labour by recruitment agencies and brokers. Recruiters deceived migrant workers about their pay and conditions, and charged fees despite the government's "free visa" policy which allowed migrant workers to travel abroad without cost. Women aged under 30 were banned from migrating for work to Gulf States. While this was intended to protect women, it meant many were forced to use informal channels, thus increasing their risk of exploitation and abuse. Following the April earthquakes, migrant workers in the Gulf, Malaysia and other countries also encountered problems with returning to their families in Nepal.

## TORTURE AND OTHER ILL-TREATMENT

Torture and other ill-treatment by police continued, particularly during pre-trial detention, to extract confessions and intimidate individuals. Following the Constitution-related violence in the Tarai, reports of pre-trial detention spiked.

By the end of 2015 the Constituent Assembly had failed to pass legislation defining and providing criminal penalties for torture, or to reform the Penal Code and Criminal Procedure Code in line with international law and standards. A bill criminalizing torture was before the Assembly. This did not meet international standards as it recognizes torture and other ill-treatment as taking place only in police custody, limits punishments for perpetrators and compensation for victims, and places a 90-day limitation for registering complaints.

## HUMAN RIGHTS PROTECTION POST-EARTHQUAKE

There were serious concerns that relief efforts failed to ensure that the needs of all earthquake-affected populations were met, particularly those from marginalized groups. Reports from survivors indicated numerous incidents of discrimination based on caste, socioeconomic status and gender in relief distribution.

In June the government refused to waive costly and time-consuming customs duties and procedures for aid deliveries. These decisions worsened the already serious risk of leaving affected populations without access to desperately needed aid. By October, the government had not set up the National Reconstruction Authority or spent the US$4.1 billion pledged at a donor conference on 25 June for earthquake reconstruction.

At the end of 2015, the rights of affected populations to basic needs such as adequate housing, recognition under law, food, water and sanitation, and to freedom of movement, including protection against forced relocation of displaced persons, remained at risk.

## DISCRIMINATION

Discrimination, including on the basis of gender, caste, class, ethnic origin and religion, persisted. The Caste-based Discrimination and Untouchability Act of

2011 was applied in only a handful of criminal cases due to a lack of awareness about the Act and victims' fears of reporting attacks.

Women from marginalized groups, including Dalits and impoverished women, continued to face particular hardship because of discrimination. Laws criminalizing rape continued to be inadequate and to reflect discriminatory attitudes towards women. Gender-based discrimination also limited the ability of women and girls to control their sexuality and make choices related to reproduction, including use of contraception; to challenge early marriages; to ensure adequate antenatal and maternal health care; and to access sufficient nutritious food. It also put them at risk of domestic violence, including marital rape. One consequence was that women and girls continued to be at high risk of developing uterine prolapse, often at an early age.

# NETHERLANDS

**Kingdom of the Netherlands**
Head of state: **King Willem-Alexander**
Head of government: **Mark Rutte**

Solitary confinement continued to be used in immigration centres. The government failed to introduce measures to prevent ethnic profiling by the police.

## REFUGEES' AND MIGRANTS' RIGHTS

### Immigration detention

Solitary confinement continued to be used in immigration detention centres, both as a means of control and as a punitive measure.[1] In March, body scan equipment was introduced in detention centres, making strip searches of detained migrants largely unnecessary.

In September the government tabled a draft law regulating immigration detention. The law mentions the need to consider alternatives to detention. However, it includes provisions that would, in practice, likely lead to harsher conditions for detained irregular migrants and asylum-seekers.[2] The law also fails to establish an effective mechanism to prevent the detention of vulnerable groups, and the authorities' power to use solitary confinement remain unchanged.

### Economic, social and cultural rights
The government failed to implement the recommendation by the European Committee of Social Rights that all people, including irregular migrants, should unconditionally have access to shelter and basic necessities. In April, the government put forward a proposal to establish shelters in a limited number of municipalities, but make accommodation there dependent on the willingness of the irregular migrant to co-operate in their deportation.

#### Refoulement
The government continued its attempts to deport rejected asylum-seekers to southern and central Somalia, including – under certain circumstances – to al-Shabaab-controlled areas, against guidelines issued by UNHCR, the UN refugee agency. In August, the government decided to temporarily halt forced returns of Uighurs to China, in anticipation of a new guidance report.

In May, Mathieu Ngudjolo, a former Congolese militia leader, was returned to the Democratic Republic of the Congo despite alleged fears for his safety, after the Council of State rejected his request for asylum. Mathieu Ngudjolo was acquitted by the ICC of war crimes and crimes against humanity, a decision confirmed on appeal on 27 February.

### DISCRIMINATION – POLICING
In response to concerns about ethnic profiling by the police, the government committed to undertaking measures focused on awareness raising and training of police officers. However, it still did not introduce clear guidelines to limit widespread stop-and-search powers that increase the risk of ethnic profiling, or institute systematic monitoring of stop-and-search operations.

### RIGHT TO PRIVACY
In July the government published proposals to amend the powers of the intelligence and security services, including provisions which in effect would legalize indiscriminate bulk collection of telecoms data. The proposals also failed to include necessary safeguards, such as prior judicial approval of decisions to intercept personal communication or hack electronic devices.

### TORTURE AND OTHER ILL-TREATMENT
The government refused to take steps to evaluate or amend the current operation of the Dutch National Prevention Mechanism, established under the Optional Protocol to the Convention against Torture, despite ongoing criticism of its independence and efficacy.

---

1. Netherlands: Isolation in detention (Press release, 3 March)
2. Netherlands: Submission to the UN Committee against Torture (EUR 35/2104/2015)

# NEW ZEALAND

New Zealand
Head of state: **Queen Elizabeth II, represented by Jerry Mateparae**
Head of government: **John Key**

---

Economic, social and cultural rights lacked sufficient legal protection. Māori (Indigenous people) continued to be over-represented in the criminal justice system. Family violence was widespread and levels of child poverty remained high. Asylum-seekers were detained alongside remand prisoners.

### LEGAL, CONSTITUTIONAL OR INSTITUTIONAL DEVELOPMENTS
The government did not give a formal response to the recommendations made by the Constitutional Advisory Panel in 2013 to

improve the Bill of Rights Act 1990.

Economic, social and cultural rights continued to lack full protection in domestic legislation.

## JUSTICE SYSTEM

Both the UN Committee against Torture and the UN Working Group on Arbitrary Detention expressed concern at the disproportionate representation of Māori in the criminal justice system. Māori, who are 15% of the general population, make up 51% of the total prison population and 65% of the female prison population.

The High Court in July held that a blanket ban on prisoners' right to vote was inconsistent with the Bill of Rights Act.

## VIOLENCE AGAINST WOMEN

Acknowledging that the level of family violence was "horrific", the Ministry of Justice in August initiated a consultation, including on the need for a review of existing legislation. In the document, the Ministry acknowledged that "gender is a significant risk factor for victimization and harm across all forms of family violence" and that the substantial majority of intimate partner violence involving coercive control occurs against women. Young women were identified as particularly vulnerable, and at increasing risk when they have children.

## CHILDREN'S RIGHTS

New Zealand retained three reservations to the UN Convention on the Rights of the Child.

The 2015 Technical Report on Child Poverty found that up to 29% of New Zealand children lived in relative poverty and 9% were living in severe poverty, impacting on their access to adequate housing, health care, food and education.

## RIGHT TO PRIVACY

The extent of surveillance powers and the sharing of that information with foreign intelligence partners remained unclear. Leaked National Security Agency documents revealed the Government Communications

Security Bureau's (GCSB) "full-take collection" of data on the Pacific region. The Inspector-General of Intelligence and Security opened an inquiry into the way the GCSB undertakes its foreign intelligence activities.

## REFUGEES AND ASYLUM-SEEKERS

The UN Working Group on Arbitrary Detention expressed concern that New Zealand was using the prison system to detain some asylum-seekers alongside remand detainees.

# NICARAGUA

Republic of Nicaragua
Head of state and government: **Daniel Ortega Saavedra**

**Human rights defenders as well as Indigenous and Afro-descendant groups were threatened and intimidated in retaliation for their work, particularly in the context of public protests. News outlets and civil society organizations faced harassment. Several people were killed and hundreds displaced as a result of an intensifying land conflict in the North Caribbean Coast. Violence against women continued; a total ban on abortion remained in place.**

## BACKGROUND

The Sandinista National Liberation Front party continued to excercise significant control over all branches of government. In November, the government formally approved an environmental impact study that would allow the construction of a major infrastructure project known as the Gran Canal Interoceánico, a channel connecting the Atlantic Ocean and the Pacific Ocean, to go forward. Its fate was uncertain due to financial constraints.

## LAND DISPUTES AND INDIGENOUS PEOPLES' RIGHTS

The Inter-American Commission on Human Rights (IACHR) ordered Nicaragua to provide protection measures to the Miskito people, after the ongoing conflict between the Indigenous community and *colonos* (settlers) attempting to take over the community's ancestral land escalated in September. The Center for Justice and Human Rights of the Atlantic Coast of Nicaragua reported that between 2013 and 2015, 24 Miskitos had been killed, 30 attacked and hundreds more displaced.

Indigenous, Afro-descendant and other groups protesting against the Gran Canal Interoceánico were intimidated, attacked and arbitrarily detained, according to the Nicaraguan Center for Human Rights (CENIDH). In October, police officers created a roadblock to stop thousands of *campesinos* (peasant farmers) from protesting against the canal; several protesters were attacked by pro-government groups, according to the human rights organization Popol Na Foundation. Protesters accused the government of granting the licence for the canal without the free, prior and informed consent of the Indigenous Peoples who could be displaced by its construction.

Activists protesting against mining projects in Nicaragua were also intimidated and harassed, according to the CENIDH.

## FREEDOMS OF EXPRESSION, ASSOCIATION AND ASSEMBLY

Government officials and supporters sought to repress and stigmatize the work of civil society organizations and media outlets that had been critical of the ruling party. In May, two members of the Center for Justice and International Law, a regional human rights organization, were denied entry into the country and deported when they arrived at the airport in the capital, Managua, to attend a human rights event. No official reason was given.[1]

## WOMEN'S RIGHTS

In a hearing in October before the IACHR, Nicaraguan and regional human rights organizations discussed their concerns about human rights abuses against women and girls, including the total ban on abortion and access to justice for women and girls suffering from acts of violence or abuse. The Nicaraguan Network of Women Against Violence reported that 35 women and girls were murdered (classified as "femicide" in the Criminal Code) in the first half of the year, down from 47 in the same period in 2014. However, the NGOs expressed concern about reforms passed in 2013 that weakened the Comprehensive Law against Violence against Women (Law 779), by offering women mediation with their abusive partners in some cases of domestic violence.

---

1. Nicaragua: Defensores de derechos humanos deportados arbitrariamente (AMR 43/1687/2015)

# NIGER

**Republic of Niger**
Head of state: **Mahamadou Issoufou**
Head of government: **Brigi Rafini**

---

**The armed group Boko Haram committed crimes under international law, escalating the conflict and leading to an increase in the number of people displaced. The authorities introduced a state of emergency in Diffa region. Human rights defenders were arbitrarily arrested. The government restricted freedom of expression. Thousands of refugees were deported back to Nigeria.**

## BACKGROUND

Boko Haram (which changed its name in April to Western African Province of the Organisation of the Islamic State) intensified its attacks against civilians, mainly in the southeastern Diffa region bordering Nigeria and Lake Chad. The resulting displacement and destruction, in addition to measures taken by the government in response, had a major impact on the economy of the region, causing severe food shortages. Following an attempted coup in December, nine soldiers were arrested and will be tried before a military tribunal.

## ARMED CONFLICT

Boko Haram carried out more than 20 attacks against civilian objects and army positions in Diffa region killing at least 190 civilians and 60 security force members.

In April, Boko Haram members attacked the Isle de Karamga, surrounding the island with boats at night and shooting dead 28 civilians and 46 soldiers. There were further attacks in Diffa region between June and December, including suicide bombings.

The security forces carried out reprisal attacks and arrested more than 1,000 people. In February, the Nigerien army bombed a convoy of trucks carrying smoked fish to Nigeria, a trade banned under the state of emergency as it is believed to be a source of food and revenue for Boko Haram.

In February, at least 36 civilians were killed in the village of Abadam-Niger, on the Nigerian border, when an unidentified military plane bombed a funeral party.

In September, the Office of the High Commissioner for Human Rights (OHCHR) expressed concerns about attacks on civilians by both Boko Haram and the Nigerien army.

## SECURITY AND HUMAN RIGHTS

The impact of abuses committed by armed groups was exacerbated by the state's response, notably forced displacement and restrictions on freedom of movement.

In February, the government decreed a state of emergency in the entire Diffa region. It was extended for three months in May and reinstated in October. The state of emergency prohibited the circulation of vehicles with two wheels, or registered in Nigeria, as well as sales of pepper and fish. In July, after suicide attacks involving women wearing burqas, the authorities prohibited veils covering the cheeks. In July, an imam who protested

against this measure was detained without charge for two days.

According to OHCHR, the Ministries of Interior and Defence interfered in the judicial process, leading to the rearrest of Boko Haram suspects acquitted for lack of evidence. The same ministries refused to investigate allegations of torture and other ill-treatment by the army, claiming that this could demoralize troops.

OHCHR also expressed concern about the arrest in July of 40 children in Diffa region and their detention in Koutoukale and Kollo prisons before they were transferred to the juvenile section in Niamey prison.

## FREEDOM OF EXPRESSION

Freedom of expression was severely restricted, sometimes in the name of national security.

In June, two newspapers, *L'Actualité* and *L'Opinion*, were banned from publishing for one month for "violating the journalists' charter". The Superior Council for Communication gave no further explanation.

In May, Moussa Tchangari, Secretary General of Alternative Citizens' Spaces, was arrested while taking food to eight village chiefs in Diffa region who had been arrested for "failure to cooperate with the authorities in the fight against Boko Haram". His organization had criticized the government's failure to protect human rights in view of Boko Haram attacks. He was provisionally released after 10 days.[1]

Nouhou Azirka, President of the Movement for the Promotion of Responsible Citizenship, was detained in police custody for "endangering national defence" in May. He had stated in a television interview that soldiers in Diffa region had complained of poor working conditions. He was provisionally released after four days.[2]

In November, five journalists were arrested, including Souleymane Salha, journalist of the weekly *Le Courrier*. He was released without charge after 10 days.

## INTERNALLY DISPLACED PEOPLE AND REFUGEES

The number of refugees and displaced people rose significantly, exacerbating the humanitarian situation, particularly in the south. By the end of the year, Niger was host to more than 115,000 people displaced by conflict in Nigeria, Libya and Mali, and to more than 100,000 internally displaced people and returnees.

In April, the Governor of Diffa ordered the evacuation of islands on Lake Chad, following a Boko Haram attack. At least 14 people died from hunger, thirst and heat during the long march to the camp of N'guigmi. Soldiers reportedly prevented them from being transported to the camp by local carriers and essential resources such as water and food were lacking when they arrived.

In January and May, the army forced thousands of refugees back to Nigeria, accusing them of bringing Boko Haram attacks to the area.

## PRISON CONDITIONS

Prisons remained very overcrowded. Civil society groups reported that at the end of 2014, 1,000 people were held in Niamey civilian prison, which has a capacity of 350.

<hr>

1. Niger: The fight against Boko Haram must not serve as an excuse to violate freedom of expression (News story, 19 May); Urgent Action, Human rights defenders held without charge (AFR 43/1716/2015)
2. Urgent Action: Human rights defenders held without charge (AFR 43/1716/2015)

# NIGERIA

Federal Republic of Nigeria
Head of state and government: **Muhammadu Buhari (replaced Goodluck Ebele Jonathan in May)**

<hr>

**The conflict between the military and the armed group Boko Haram continued, resulting in the deaths of thousands of civilians and over 2 million internally displaced people (IDPs) at the end of the** year. **Torture and other ill-treatment by the police and security forces were widespread. Demolitions of informal settlements led to the forced eviction of thousands of people. Death sentences continued to be imposed; no executions were reported.**

## BACKGROUND

The general election took place on 28 March to elect the President and members to the Senate and the House of Representatives; the governorship and state assembly election was held on 11 April. The candidate from the opposition All Progressives Congress (APC) party, Muhammadu Buhari, won the presidential election. The new cabinet members were sworn in on 11 November.

In July, President Buhari retired the military service chiefs appointed by former President Goodluck Jonathan – including two military officials whom the authorities failed to investigate for their potential responsibility for crimes under international law – and replaced them.

Protests for an independent state of Biafra took place in the south and southeast. On 14 October, Nnamdi Kanu, leader of the Indigenous People of Biafra (IPOB) and director of Radio Biafra, was arrested and charged with criminal conspiracy, managing and belonging to an unlawful society and intimidation. On 17 December, the Federal High Court in the capital Abuja ordered his unconditional release from the custody of the Department of State Services. However, he was not released and was charged with treason on 18 December; he remained in detention at the end of the year.

In November, the report of an investigative committee established by the President on the procurement of arms and equipment in the security sector found, among other things, fictitious contracts amounting to several billion US dollars. The President ordered the arrest of all those implicated in the report, including Sambo Dasuki, the National Security Adviser for 2012-2015. He remained in detention at the end of the year.

# ARMED CONFLICT

## Boko Haram

Boko Haram continued to commit war crimes and crimes against humanity in northeastern Nigeria, killing thousands of civilians.[1] In January, the group expanded the territory under its control by seizing the towns of Baga and Monguno in Borno state. Boko Haram fighters deliberately killed civilians, particularly men of fighting age, detained others and destroyed buildings. In the attack on Baga, Boko Haram killed hundreds of civilians in what may be its deadliest attack to date. Satellite images revealed that more than 3,700 buildings had been damaged or destroyed in the attack.

Thousands of civilians lived under Boko Haram's violent rule, either in the captured towns or after being abducted and taken to camps. Many women and girls were raped and forced into marriage.

From March, a sustained offensive by the military, with assistance from the armed forces of Cameroon, Chad and Niger, forced Boko Haram out of major towns in northeastern Nigeria. However, Boko Haram continued to kill civilians through raids on smaller towns and villages as well as bomb attacks.[2]

Bomb attacks targeted markets, transport hubs, bars, restaurants and places of worship in cities across the northeast, as well as Abuja and the towns of Jos, Kano and Zaria.[3] Boko Haram used young women and girls as suicide bombers in many of the incidents.

The military announced the recovery of more than 1,400 people from Boko Haram-controlled territory, mostly women and children. The fate of 219 schoolgirls abducted from the town of Chibok, Borno state, on 14 April 2014 remained unknown.

## Security forces

The military committed war crimes and possible crimes against humanity in its response to Boko Haram between 2011 and 2015.[4] President Buhari promised to investigate evidence of several instances of war crimes by the military between June and December. However, no further action was taken to initiate independent and impartial investigations. In its November report on preliminary examinations, the Office of the Prosecutor of the ICC identified eight potential cases involving the commission of crimes against humanity and war crimes by Boko Haram (in six cases) and the security forces (two cases).

Extrajudicial executions by the military of people suspected of being members of Boko Haram continued.

The military arrested people during "screening operations", where members of the public were lined up in front of informants, or arrested at their homes. Others were arbitrarily arrested as they attempted to flee attacks by Boko Haram or areas controlled by the group. In many cases the arrests were made without reasonable suspicion or without adequate investigation.

Suspects detained by the military had no access to their families or lawyers and were not brought before a court. They were mostly young men, although women, children and older men were also detained.

Muhammad Mari Abba, a doctor and consultant for the WHO who was arrested in 2012 in Yobe state, had not been charged and remained in incommunicado detention at the end of the year.

Alhaji Bukar Yaganami, a businessman who was arrested in Maiduguri, Borno state, in 2013, remained in military detention at the end of the year, in spite of a July 2014 court order for his release on bail.

Conditions in some military detention centres seemingly improved. Detainees were given three meals a day, access to washing facilities and to medical assistance. However, suspects continued to die in detention. Routine torture and other ill-treatment led to deaths in detention centres, as suspects continued to be held incommunicado.

Small numbers of suspects were released throughout the year; the military announced the release of 310 suspects in July and September, following the completion of investigations. Many had been detained for over a year. Some detainees received 10,000 naira (approximately US$50) or clothes upon their release, while others received nothing.

On 21 December, the Federal High Court in Abuja discharged five police officers of the alleged murder of Boko Haram leader Mohammed Yusuf in 2009.

### Internally displaced people
In September, the International Organization for Migration estimated that over 2.1 million people were internally displaced in northern Nigeria; 92% of them lived in host communities, while the remainder lived in camps. The camps in Maiduguri were overcrowded, with inadequate access to food and sanitation. The government established a committee to investigate allegations of human trafficking and sexual abuse of IDPs, with the complicity of security and camp officials. The results of the investigation had not been made public by the end of the year.

## EXCESSIVE USE OF FORCE
On 12-13 December, the military reportedly killed hundreds of members of the Shi'a Islamic Movement of Nigeria in Zaria, Kaduna state. The group's leader, Ibraheem Zakzaky, was arrested at his residence and remained in incommunicado detention at the end of the year. Hundreds of others were also arrested.

On 17 December, the military killed five people when they opened fire on members of the IPOB who were demonstrating in Onitsha, Anambra state, in celebration of the initial announcement of Nnamdi Kanu's release.

## COMMUNAL VIOLENCE
Violence between ethnic groups continued to claim lives. In Riyom and Barikin Ladi, local government areas in Plateau state, communities clashed over allegations of cattle rustling and land disputes. Perpetrators of violence were rarely investigated and prosecuted.

## JUSTICE SYSTEM
In May, the Administration of Criminal Justice

Act was passed into law. The Act adopted new provisions which improved the criminal justice system. Key provisions included compensation to victims of crime, non-custodial sentences and electronic records of proceedings.

However, prisons remained overcrowded and court processes slow; frequent strikes by court employees, such as court clerks, over pay and the consequent closure of courts led to delays in trials and the supervision of pre-trial detention.

## TORTURE AND OTHER ILL-TREATMENT
Torture and other ill-treatment by police and military remained pervasive. Extrajudicial executions, extortion, and arbitrary and prolonged detention were rife.

In July, the police announced they were reviewing the Force Orders, including Force Order 237, which allows police officers to shoot suspects and detainees who attempt to avoid arrest or escape – whether or not they pose a threat to life. The Inspector General of Police also announced that over the past three years, almost 1 billion naira (US$5 million) had been paid out as compensation to victims of human rights violations by the police.

Many police divisions, including the Special Anti-Robbery Squad (SARS) and the Force Criminal Investigation Division, kept rooms where suspects were tortured while being interrogated. In November, the Inspector General of Police announced the creation of a Complaints Response Unit and a reform initiative for the SARS, in response to public concerns about alleged violations by police officers across the country.

The Anti-Torture Bill – intended to prohibit and criminalize the use of torture – was passed by Parliament in June. It had not been signed into law by the end of the year.

## DEATH PENALTY
The authorities continued to sentence people to death. No executions were known to have been carried out.

In December, the death sentences

imposed on 66 soldiers by a court martial in 2014 were commuted to 10 years' imprisonment each.

On 28 May, Moses Akatugba was pardoned after 10 years on death row.

On 25 June, the Upper Sharia Court in Kano sentenced Islamic scholar Abdulaziz Dauda, also known as Abdul Inyass, and eight of his followers to death for blasphemy.

In September, the Governor of Cross River state signed into law a bill making the death penalty mandatory for kidnapping.

## HOUSING RIGHTS

Mass forced evictions continued.

The new governments of the states of Lagos and Kaduna rendered thousands of people homeless and vulnerable to other human rights violations when they conducted mass forced evictions without consultation, compensation and the provision of alternative accommodation.

In August, hundreds of residents of the Bayan Alhudahuda community in Zaria were given a demolition notice of 28 days, ordering them to demolish their own houses or risk being charged a fee for the authorities to do so. Ninety-two homes, with between 10 and 40 residents each, were demolished. Two weeks later, the affected residents were still sleeping in the classrooms of a nearby school, mosques and marketplaces.

In September, around 10,200 residents of the Badia-East community, Lagos, were forcibly evicted from their homes less than 24 hours after being notified that the *Ojora* (traditional ruler of the community) had been granted the right to take possession of them. Many of the residents continued to sleep on the demolition site for up to three weeks afterwards and remained homeless.

In July, 10 residents of Bundu Ama in the city of Port Harcourt received 6.5 million naira (approximately US$30,000) as part of the payment of 11 million naira awarded by the ECOWAS Court against the federal government. This was compensation for unlawful shootings during a peaceful protest against the planned demolition of their houses in 2009.

## RIGHTS OF LESBIAN, GAY, BISEXUAL, TRANSGENDER AND INTERSEX PEOPLE

The rights of LGBTI people continued to be curtailed. Human rights defenders reported a significant increase in the number of arrests of LGBTI people and of police extortion.

The Coalition for the Defense of Sexual Rights, a coalition of NGOs working on the rights of LGBTI people in Nigeria, cited over 200 cases across the country where people perceived to be LGBTI were beaten by mobs and handed over to the police.

## WOMEN'S RIGHTS

In May, former President Jonathan signed the Violence Against Persons (Prohibition) Act into law. The law criminalizes female genital mutilation and "subjecting a widow to harmful traditional practices". However, the Act's definition of rape falls short of international standards in that it does not sufficiently cover all forms of coercion. The law could also be strengthened by explicitly prohibiting marital rape.

## FREEDOM OF EXPRESSION

Section 38 of the Cyber Crime Act, which became law in May, requires internet service providers to keep all traffic and other data of subscribers for two years and make that data available to law enforcement agencies upon request, without a court order, thus violating the rights to privacy and freedom of expression.

In March, two Al Jazeera journalists covering the conflict in northeastern Nigeria were detained by the military in Maiduguri. They were released after 13 days.

## CORPORATE ACCOUNTABILITY

Twenty years after the execution of environmental activist Ken Saro-Wiwa and eight others, oil pollution continued to cause devastation to the Niger Delta region, harming the livelihoods and health of its inhabitants. There were hundreds of new spills during the year, and oil companies failed to clean up the contamination of previous spills, some of which occurred decades ago.[5]

The government continued to fail to hold oil companies operating in the Niger Delta to account. It did not provide the oversight needed to ensure that companies do more to prevent spills from happening, or to respond to them in a timely and adequate manner. Companies' response to spills was frequently slow and clean-up was inadequate.

Oil companies continued to blame the vast majority of spills on sabotage and theft, a claim which was based on a flawed oil spill investigation process led by the oil companies rather than the government watchdog, the National Oil Spill Detection and Response Agency (NOSDRA).

NOSDRA published details and a map of investigations into spills online, but it did not release information about the response to spills and clean-up.

In August, President Buhari announced that his government would begin the clean-up and restoration of the oil-damaged Ogoniland region, in line with the recommendations of the UN Environment Programme.

A sum of £55 million (US$83 million) paid out by the oil company Shell was distributed to the Bodo community, following the settlement of a court case in the UK in 2014. However, Shell had yet to clean up the damage caused by two massive spills at Bodo in 2008.

---

1. "Our job is to shoot, slaughter and kill": Boko Haram's reign of terror in north east Nigeria (AFR 44/1360/2015)

2. Boko Haram: Civilians continue to be at risk of human rights abuses by Boko Haram and human rights violations by state security forces (AFR 44/2428/2015)

3. Nigeria: Boko Haram: Bombing campaign sees civilian deaths spiral (AFR 44/2498/2015)

4. Nigeria: Stars on their shoulders, blood on their hands – war crimes committed by the Nigerian military (AFR 44/1657/2015)

5. Nigeria: Clean it up: Shell's false claims about oil spill response in the Niger Delta (AFR 44/2746/2015)

# NORWAY

Kingdom of Norway
Head of state: King Harald V
Head of government: Erna Solberg

A new, independent national human rights institution was established. The Ministry of Health proposed legislation to improve access to legal gender recognition for transgender people. Serious concerns remained about rape and other violence against women.

## LEGAL, CONSTITUTIONAL OR INSTITUTIONAL DEVELOPMENTS

On 1 July the National Institution for Human Rights was re-established as an independent body reporting to Parliament. Prior to this, since its establishment in 2002, it had been part of the Norwegian Centre for Human Rights based in the Law Faculty at the University of Oslo.

## INTERNATIONAL JUSTICE

On 19 January, the Court of Appeal dismissed an appeal by a Rwandan national against his 2013 conviction by the Oslo District Court for murder during the 1994 genocide in Rwanda. The Court of Appeal confirmed his sentence of 21 years' imprisonment for premeditated complicity in the murder of 2,000 people in two massacres, and of seven people in a separate incident. He appealed against the decision to the Supreme Court. He was not charged with genocide, as the article defining genocide only entered into force in 2008 and does not have retroactive effect.

## DISCRIMINATION – TRANSGENDER PEOPLE

In June, the Ministry of Health proposed legislation granting transgender people access to legal gender recognition from the age of 16 on the basis of self-identification. Children aged between seven and 16 will have access to legal gender recognition with the consent of parents or guardians. The proposed law is expected to be presented to Parliament and put to a vote during 2016.[1]

Despite this positive development, violence motivated by discriminatory attitudes towards transgender people was still not criminalized as hate crime.

## VIOLENCE AGAINST WOMEN

Serious concerns remained about rape and violence against women, in particular around the legal definition of rape in the Penal Code, low conviction rates and inadequate access for rape survivors to reparation and rehabilitation. In January the National Police Directorate published an evaluation which concluded that police investigations were unsatisfactory in 40% of sexual violence cases reported to the police.

## REFUGEES AND ASYLUM-SEEKERS

According to government statistics, 31,145 people claimed asylum in Norway during the year, a three-fold increase on 2014.

In April, the government announced that children of asylum-seekers whose applications had been rejected and who had been returned to their countries of origin between 1 July 2014 and 18 March 2015, after spending four and a half years or more in Norway, could seek to have their cases reopened. The move followed strong criticism of the immigration authorities' previously narrow interpretation of the principle of the best interests of the child in asylum and removal proceedings.

On 25 November the Ministry of Justice issued an instruction which denied access to the asylum procedure in Norway for any person who applied for protection after having lived in or transited through Russia. Third-country nationals, including those without any regular legal status in Russia, faced being returned to Russia. This caused particular concern for Syrian asylum-seekers. The decision followed Parliament's adoption of amendments to section 32 of the Immigration Act 2008, earlier in November, removing any requirement for Norwegian authorities to consider whether asylum-seekers had had an application for protection examined in another country en route to Norway.

## CORPORATE ACCOUNTABILITY

In October, after two years' delay, the government launched a national action plan to implement the UN Guiding Principles on business and human rights. The action plan lacked clarity on due diligence and the extent to which the guiding principles ought to apply to Norwegian companies operating in the country and those operating abroad.

---

1. Norway: High hopes for a watershed moment on transgender rights (News story, 10 April)

# OMAN

Sultanate of Oman
Head of state and government: **Sultan Qaboos bin Said Al Said**

---

The authorities restricted freedom of expression and increased arrests and harassment of political and human rights activists and government critics. Women continued to face discrimination in law and in practice. The death penalty remained in force; no executions were reported.

## BACKGROUND

Oman's human rights record was examined under the UPR in November. Oman said it would consider all 233 recommendations and was due to respond by 31 March 2016.

## FREEDOM OF EXPRESSION

The authorities continued to restrict freedom of expression, arresting and prosecuting online journalists, bloggers and others on public order charges or under vaguely worded penal code provisions that criminalize insulting the Sultan. The authorities also harassed activists by confiscating their identification papers and banning them from foreign travel.

In March, the authorities detained online

activist Talib al-Saeedi for three weeks and released him without charge. The same month, a court in the southern city of Salalah sentenced blogger Saeed al-Daroodi, arrested in October 2014, to one year in prison and a fine; he was convicted of "trying to overthrow the government" and "spreading hate".

In April, an appeal court in Salalah released human rights activist Saeed Jaddad after he appealed against his one-year prison sentence and a fine following his conviction under the Cyber Crimes Law. In November his sentence was upheld and he was arrested to serve his prison sentence. In a separate case, in September, the Appeal Court in Muscat upheld his three-year prison sentence and a fine on charges of "undermining the prestige of the state", "incitement to protest" and "using social media to disseminate information that infringed the sanctity of public order".

The authorities arrested at least eight men in July and August following comments they had made on social media websites and their alleged links to Mohammad al-Fazari, a human rights activist and founder and editor of the *Citizen* online journal, who fled Oman in July.

Former Shura Council member Dr Talib al-Ma'mari and city councillor Saqr al-Balushi remained in prison serving four-year and one-year terms respectively, after an unfair trial in 2014. The UN Working Group on Arbitrary Detention had in December 2014 stated that Dr Talib al-Ma'mari was arbitrarily detained and that the government should release and compensate him.

In April, the UN Special Rapporteur on the rights to freedom of peaceful assembly and of association reported on his 2014 visit to Oman. Among other findings, he described "the legal environment for the exercise of the rights to freedom of peaceful assembly and association", including online expression, as "problematic" He urged Oman to ratify key international human rights treaties and withdraw its reservations to other treaties to which it is a party. The government criticized the Special Rapporteur's visit and rejected his findings.

## WOMEN'S RIGHTS

Women were not accorded equal rights with men in criminal law, which attached less weight to the evidence of a woman than to the evidence of a man, and under personal status law, which accorded men greater rights in relation to divorce, child custody, inheritance and conferral of nationality.

## DEATH PENALTY

Oman retained the death penalty for a range of crimes; no executions were reported.

# PAKISTAN

Islamic Republic of Pakistan
Head of state: **Mamnoon Hussain**
Head of government: **Muhammad Nawaz Sharif**

Executions resumed following the Pakistani Taliban-led attack on the Army Public School in Peshawar in December 2014. Adding to concerns over fair trials, newly established military courts were authorized to try all those accused of terrorism-related offences, including civilians. A new National Human Rights Commission was established with a mandate to promote and protect human rights, but was restricted from investigating allegations of human rights abuses against the intelligence agencies. Religious minorities continued to face discrimination, persecution and targeted attacks. Human rights activists experienced harassment and abuse. In March, Baloch activists were barred from leaving the country to speak at a conference in the USA about human rights violations in Balochistan and Sindh. A new policy for international NGOs was passed in October, giving the government the power to monitor their funds and operations and to close them down on the basis of activities considered to be against the interests of Pakistan. In November, the government restored a separate Ministry of Human Rights, which it had merged with the Ministry of Law and Justice in 2013.

## BACKGROUND

Following the attack on the Army Public School in Peshawar on 16 December 2014 in which 149 people were killed, including 132 children, the political and military leadership announced a 20-point National Action Plan (NAP) to counter terrorism. Its implementation started with the immediate resumption of executions for prisoners convicted of terrorism-related offences. In January, the President signed the 21st Constitutional Amendment Bill of 2015 and the Pakistan Army (Amendment) Act 1952, giving military courts jurisdiction for two years to try civilians for terrorism-related offences. Under the NAP the government also pledged to curb hate through speech and literature, protect minorities, and prevent terrorism. By October, up to 9,400 people had been arrested according to government figures on allegations of inflaming sectarian hate; some booksellers and publishers claimed they were unfairly targeted by police who were under pressure to make arrests. Major floods for the fifth year in a row displaced hundreds of thousands and killed more than 200 people. In October, an earthquake in the Hindu Kush range of Afghanistan killed at least 28 people in Pakistan.

## DEATH PENALTY

The Prime Minister announced the resumption of executions of people convicted of terrorism-related offences following the Peshawar school attack in December 2014. In March the moratorium on the death penalty was lifted for all 28 offences for which the death penalty is provided, including non-lethal crimes. In November, a parliamentary panel approved the punishment of life imprisonment or the death penalty for the rape of girls aged 13 or under.

More than 300 executions were recorded during the year, most for murder and others for rape, attempted assassination, kidnapping, and terrorism-related charges. Faisal Mehmood and Aftab Bahadur were among those executed despite claims and supporting evidence submitted by their lawyers that they were juveniles at the time of the offences for which they were convicted. In October, the Supreme Court upheld the death sentence of Mumtaz Qadri for killing the Punjab governor in 2011.

Military courts sentenced at least 27 people to death and four to life imprisonment. Details of the allegations and trial proceedings remained unknown. Death sentences imposed on at least two people were challenged in the Peshawar High Court (PHC), including by Haider Ali, whose parents claimed he was a juvenile when arrested in 2009, and Qari Zahir Gul, whose parents claimed he did not have a fair trial. The PHC upheld both death sentences in October during in-camera proceedings.

## DISCRIMINATION – RELIGIOUS MINORITIES

Religious minorities, both Muslim and non-Muslim, continued to face laws and practices that resulted in discrimination and persecution. In February, Tehreek-e-Taliban Pakistan (TTP) claimed responsibility for an attack on a Shiite mosque in Peshawar that killed at least 20 worshippers and injured 60. In March, a suicide attack on two churches in Lahore claimed by Jamaat ul Ahrar, a splinter group of the TTP, killed at least 22 people. Following the attack, a group of Christians in the same neighbourhood killed two Muslim men. In May, 45 Ismailis on a bus in Karachi were attacked and killed; and various groups, including TTP, Jundullah and the armed group Islamic State (IS), claimed responsibility. At least three Hindu temples in Sindh province were attacked; there were no reports of deaths or injuries.

Blasphemy laws remained in force, mostly in Punjab province; they applied to people of all religions but were disproportionately used against religious minorities. An appeal against the death sentence of Asia Noreen (also known as Asia Bibi) in October 2014 was admitted in the Supreme Court but a hearing date was not confirmed at the end of the year. An appeal against Sawan Masih's conviction and death sentence for blasphemy allegations that sparked a mob attack against residents of Lahore's Joseph Colony in 2013 remained pending in the Lahore High Court. In its judgment against Mumtaz Qadri, the Supreme Court noted that criticism of the blasphemy law did not amount to blasphemy.

It remained a criminal offence for members of the Ahmadiyya faith to propagate, profess or practise their religion openly.

Forced conversions and marriages of Hindu girls to Muslim men continued, particularly in Sindh.

## ABUSES BY ARMED GROUPS

Armed groups continued to carry out targeted attacks against civilians, including health workers and civilians affiliated with the government.

At least eight members of polio vaccination teams – six men and two women – were killed by armed groups in Khyber Pakhtunkhwa (KPK) province, the Federally Administered Tribal Areas (FATA) and Balochistan province.

Armed groups continued to target civilians affiliated with the government or government-run projects. In April, 20 construction workers from Sindh and Punjab were killed in Kech district, Balochistan; the Balochistan Liberation Front claimed responsibility. In August, several armed groups, including Lashkar-e-Jhangvi, claimed responsibility following a suicide attack that killed 18 people, including the Punjab Home Minister.

## POLICE AND SECURITY FORCES

Enforced disappearances continued with impunity, particularly in Balochistan, KPK and Sindh. Bodies were later found bearing apparent bullet wounds and torture marks. Raja Dahir, affiliated with the banned Sindhi nationalist party Jeay Sindh Mutihida Muhaz, was subjected to enforced disappearance after a raid on his home by security forces in Sindh in June. His body was recovered a month later in Jamshoro district.

The NGO, Human Rights Commission of Pakistan, documented a rise in killings of suspects in Karachi during paramilitary security operations, as 255 people were killed in the first half of 2015. The political party Muttahida Qaumi Movement claimed that some of its members were abducted and unlawfully killed.

In November, an amendment to the Pakistan Army Act gave retrospective legal cover to arrests by the armed forces and law enforcement agencies. Lawyers for Qari Zahir Gul and Haider Ali, who were tried in the newly established military courts, claimed they were subjected to enforced disappearance and unlawful detention prior to their trials.

## INTERNAL ARMED CONFLICT

The civilian population in FATA continued to be affected by internal armed conflict. The Pakistan Army continued its military operations, started in 2014, against non-state armed groups in North Waziristan and Khyber tribal agency. The Army claimed that over 3,400 militants were killed and at least 21,193 arrested during these operations. Due to the lack of transparency of the operations and independent media coverage, and previous concerns of disproportionate use of force in similar operations, serious concerns remained about the circumstances surrounding the killings, and the treatment in detention and fair trials of those arrested.

More than one million people remained displaced as a result of the current and past armed conflict in the northwest.

US drone strikes reduced in number and were carried out mainly in North Waziristan. Information about the impact on civilians was scarce. Two foreign aid workers – US national Warren Weinstein and Italian national Giovanni Lo Porto – who had been held as hostages by al-Qa'ida were among those killed in a US drone strike in January, highlighting again the wider concerns that drone strikes lead to the unlawful killing of civilians.

The Pakistan Army launched its first drone strike on 7 September, claiming it killed three leaders of armed groups in North Waziristan.

Armed conflict continued in areas of North Waziristan, with allegations by human rights groups that civilians were killed and injured as result of indiscriminate military operations.

## FREEDOM OF EXPRESSION

Some journalists and media channels exercised self-censorship for fear of reprisals from the Pakistan Army and armed groups. Following coverage of Pakistan's response to the intervention of Saudi Arabia in Yemen in May, and the stampede in September at the annual Hajj pilgrimage to Mecca where more than 2,000 pilgrims died, the state-run Pakistan Electronic Media Regulatory Authority (PEMRA) issued warnings to the media against airing reports deemed critical of Saudi Arabia. In both instances PEMRA invoked Article 19 of the Constitution, which provides for exemptions to the right to freedom of expression in cases of criticism of the military, judiciary and Pakistan's relations with "friendly countries".

At least two media workers were killed and six injured in connection with their work. Zaman Mehsud was killed on 3 November in Tank. The TTP claimed responsibility for the attack saying it was for his writings against them. TTP factions threatened journalists with severe consequences if they did not provide them with coverage. The Prime Minister's promise of March 2014 to appoint Special Prosecutors to try cases involving attacks on journalists had not been fulfilled by the end of the year.

In April, human rights activist Sabeen Mahmud was killed after hosting a discussion on Balochistan at her cafe in Karachi. Her driver, a key witness, subsequently was shot dead, despite the Sindh Witness Protection Act 2013 that was passed to protect witnesses.

Three Baloch activists, including Abdul Qadeer Baloch, Vice Chairman of the organization Voice for Baloch Missing Persons, were banned from travelling to the USA in March to attend a conference organized by Sindhi and Baloch activists. They were detained at Karachi airport for a few hours, accused of engaging in terrorism and anti-state activities. No charges were brought against them.

In October, a new policy was announced requiring all international NGOs to register and obtain permission from the Ministry of Interior for carrying out activities. The policy also empowered the government to monitor their funds and operations and to close them down on the basis of activities considered to be against the interests of Pakistan.

In September, the National Assembly Standing Committee on Information Technology and Telecommunication approved the proposed Prevention of Electronic Crimes Bill which allows the government to censor online content and access internet users' data. Activists raised concerns about provisions which threatened privacy and freedom of expression and imposed heavy punishments. The Bill was awaiting final approval by the National Assembly at the end of the year.

## VIOLENCE AGAINST WOMEN AND GIRLS

Women and girls continued to face violence and threats. At least 4,308 cases of violence against women and girls were reported for the first six months of 2015. The figure included 709 cases of murder; 596 of rape and gang rape; 36 of sexual assault; 186 of so-called "honour" crimes; and 1,020 of kidnapping. Despite the enactment of the Acid Control and Acid Crime Prevention Act in 2011, at least 40 acid attack cases were recorded between January and June.

In Sahiwal a number of knife attacks were reported against women seen outside their homes without a male companion. Up to six cases were reported in one week in September.

Tabassum Adnan, the founder of Khwendo Jirga, Pakistan's first all-women *jirga* (informal judicial court), received the US State Department's 2015 International Women of Courage Award in KPK. Following the publicity received through the award, she faced anonymous threats via phone and text messages that forced her to relocate to another city.

Despite efforts in recent years to enact legislation protecting women from violence, laws remained in force under which female rape victims can be convicted for adultery. Women continued to be denied equality and protection in law, a situation exacerbated by factors including the absence of legislation against incest and a gender-insensitive criminal justice system.

# PALESTINE (STATE OF)

**State of Palestine**
Head of state: **Mahmoud Abbas**
Head of government: **Rami Hamdallah**

The Palestinian authorities in the West Bank and the Hamas de facto administration in the Gaza Strip both restricted freedom of expression, including by arresting and detaining critics and political opponents. They also restricted the right to peaceful assembly and used excessive force to disperse some protests. Torture and other ill-treatment of detainees remained common in both Gaza and the West Bank. Unfair trials of civilians before military courts continued in Gaza; detainees were held without charge or trial in the West Bank. Women and girls faced discrimination and violence; some were victims of so-called "honour" killings by male relatives. Courts in both Gaza and the West Bank imposed death sentences; no executions were reported. Neither the Palestinian authorities in the West Bank nor the Hamas authorities in Gaza took steps to investigate and ensure accountability for war crimes and other serious abuses, including summary killings, committed during the 2014 conflict with Israel and previous conflicts.

## BACKGROUND

Negotiations between Israel and the Palestinian government and institutions under Mahmoud Abbas remained stalled throughout the year. Continuing tensions between Fatah and Hamas undermined the Palestinian national unity government formed in June 2014. Hamas continued to exercise de facto authority in Gaza, where it announced a new security force in July after President Abbas made changes to the cabinet of the unity government. Reports that Hamas engaged in indirect negotiations with Israel regarding a possible ceasefire and lifting of Israel's air, sea and land blockade of Gaza further heightened tensions between Fatah and Hamas. In January, the State of Palestine applied to join the ICC; Israel opposed Palestine's application and withheld tax revenue payments due to the Palestinian authorities until April. Palestine formally joined the ICC in April. In September, President Abbas told the UN General Assembly that the Palestine Liberation Organization would no longer abide by commitments it made under the Oslo Accords, the 1990s peace agreements it signed with Israel, while the Israeli authorities continued to violate them; however, security co-operation between Palestinian security forces in the West Bank and Israel continued.

Gaza remained under an Israeli air, sea and land blockade, in force continuously since June 2007. The continuing restrictions on imports of construction materials under the blockade contributed to severe delays in reconstruction of homes and other infrastructure damaged or destroyed in recent armed conflicts and widespread impoverishment among Gaza's 1.8 million inhabitants. The Egyptian authorities tightly restricted movement through Gaza's only other access to the outside world, closing the Rafah Crossing for almost the entire year, and destroying hundreds of tunnels used for smuggling between Gaza and Egypt. Within Gaza, there were sporadic clashes between Hamas forces and supporters of Salafist and other Palestinian armed groups, some of whom occasionally fired indiscriminate rockets towards and into Israel from Gaza.

The West Bank saw rising tension between Palestinians and Israelis, particularly from September, when Israel further curtailed Palestinian access to the Al-Aqsa Mosque in Jerusalem, heightening protests and clashes between Palestinian demonstrators and Israeli forces. The last three months of the year saw a surge in Palestinian protests against the Israeli occupation and in attacks by Palestinians on Israeli forces and civilians, to which Israeli troops and police responded with lethal force. Seventeen Israeli civilians were killed by Palestinian attackers during this period, mostly acting alone and not affiliated with armed groups, while Israeli forces killed more than 130 Palestinians in the West Bank, Gaza Strip, and inside Israel.

## ARBITRARY ARRESTS AND DETENTIONS

Security authorities in the West Bank, including Preventative Security and General Intelligence, and those in Gaza, particularly Internal Security, arbitrarily arrested and detained their critics, including supporters of rival political organizations.

## UNFAIR TRIALS

In both the West Bank and Gaza, political and judicial authorities failed to ensure adherence to basic due process rights, such as prompt access to legal counsel and to charge or release. Palestinian security forces in the West Bank held detainees for long periods without trial on orders of regional governors, and delayed or failed to comply with court orders for the release of detainees in dozens of cases. In Gaza, Hamas military courts continued to convict defendants in unfair trials, sentencing some to death.

## TORTURE AND OTHER ILL-TREATMENT

Torture and other ill-treatment of detainees remained common and was committed with impunity by Palestinian police and other security forces in the West Bank, and Hamas police and other security forces in Gaza. In both areas, the victims included children. The Independent Commission for Human Rights, Palestine's national human rights institution, reported receiving a total of 613 allegations of torture and other ill-treatment of detainees between January and November, 179 from the West Bank and 434 from Gaza, with the majority of complaints in both areas against police. Neither the Palestine national unity government nor the Hamas de facto administration in Gaza independently investigated torture allegations or held perpetrators to account.

## FREEDOMS OF EXPRESSION, ASSOCIATION AND ASSEMBLY

The national unity government and Hamas severely curtailed the rights to freedom of expression, association and peaceful assembly in the West Bank and Gaza respectively. In both areas, security forces arrested and detained critics or supporters of rival political organizations; in the West Bank, security forces detained Hamas supporters, while in Gaza, Hamas security forces detained supporters of Fatah. Security forces in both areas dispersed opposition protests, sometimes using excessive force, and assaulted journalists reporting on protests, damaged their equipment and harassed them and social media activists, including by repeatedly summoning them for questioning.

In the West Bank, Preventative Security officers detained Birzeit University student Bara' al-Qadi for 13 days after arresting him in January for criticizing a government official in comments he posted on the website Facebook. Preventative Security officers also detained and questioned other student activists, some of whom filed complaints alleging ill-treatment, after a Hamas-affiliated student group won Birzeit University's student council elections in April.

## EXCESSIVE USE OF FORCE

Security forces were accused of using excessive force to disperse protests and when attempting to make arrests in both the West Bank and Gaza.

In the West Bank in March, police and

other security agents used force to break up a peaceful sit-in protest in Ramallah by relatives of political detainees held by the authorities, kicking protesters and hitting them with gun butts. In June, police raids on homes in Balata, the West Bank's largest refugee camp, sparked violent confrontations. At least one camp resident was wounded by gunfire. Some camp residents who were arrested and later released said they had been tortured in detention.

In Gaza, police beat demonstrators in Khuza'a, near the city of Khan Younis, who were protesting against recurrent power cuts in March; several protesters were injured and some were arrested. In September, police forcibly dispersed renewed protests against power shortages in the city of Rafah, beating demonstrators and seizing film and equipment from journalists covering the protests.

On 2 June, Gaza security forces killed Yunis Sa'id al-Hunnar, an Islamist activist and Hamas opponent, during a raid on his home in the Sheikh Redwan area of Gaza City. The Gaza Ministry of the Interior said security forces shot him dead after he refused to surrender and opened fire on them; however, the authorities failed to conduct an independent investigation. On 8 July, Gaza police officers killed one man and wounded two other people during a disturbance following a funeral.

## ABUSES BY ARMED GROUPS

Palestinian armed groups in Gaza occasionally fired indiscriminate rockets into Israel; no deaths resulted. While the Hamas authorities prevented rocket firing much of the time, they failed to prosecute those responsible.

While most of the Palestinian attackers responsible for stabbing, shooting and carrying out other attacks on Israelis in the West Bank and Israel, which killed 21 Israeli civilians and a US national during the year, were not members of Palestinian armed groups, these groups frequently praised the attacks.

## IMPUNITY

A climate of impunity continued to prevail. The authorities again failed to investigate unlawful killings, including summary executions, and the firing of indiscriminate weapons and other alleged war crimes committed by the military wing of Hamas and other Palestinian armed groups during armed conflicts with Israel in 2014 and previously. Nor did they conduct independent investigations or hold to account officials responsible for torturing and ill-treating detainees or using excessive force against protesters.

## WOMEN'S RIGHTS

Women and girls continued to face discrimination in law and in practice, and were inadequately protected against sexual and other violence, including so-called "honour" killings. At least 18 women and girls were reported to be victims of such killings during the year.

## DEATH PENALTY

The death penalty remained in force for murder and other crimes. Courts in the West Bank handed down three death sentences; courts in Gaza issued at least 10. There were no executions.

# PANAMA

Republic of Panama
Head of state and government: **Juan Carlos Varela**

**The trial of former President Manuel Noriega relating to the enforced disappearance in 1970 of Heliodoro Portugal was suspended. An Indigenous community held protests against a hydroelectricity project that they said had not received their free, prior and informed consent. Civil society organizations denounced poor conditions at a naval prison.**

## BACKGROUND

The Supreme Court approved new investigations against former President Ricardo Martinelli (2009-2014) for corruption and the illegal wiretapping and electronic surveillance of political opponents, journalists, union leaders and other prominent members of society. Ricardo Martinelli, who left the country, denied the allegations against him and said he was the victim of political persecution.

## INDIGENOUS PEOPLES' RIGHTS

In February, Panama's National Environmental Authority temporarily suspended the construction of the Barro Blanco hydroelectric dam, which had been at the centre of a land dispute with the Ngöbe-Buglé Indigenous community, for failings in its environmental impact assessment. However, the government later said that construction of the nearly completed dam will continue. The Ngöbe-Buglé community had protested against the dam for several years, saying they were not properly consulted beforehand and that the dam will flood their land.

## IMPUNITY

The trial of former President Manuel Noriega for the enforced disappearance of union leader and activist Heliodoro Portugal in 1970 was suspended shortly before it was due to begin in May. The suspension came after Manuel Noriega's lawyer appealed, arguing that the trial would violate the terms of his extradition from France in 2011. It was unclear when the court would rule on the appeal or if the trial would proceed.

The Inter-American Court of Human Rights had ruled in 2008 that Panama was responsible for Heliodoro Portugal's enforced disappearance as well as the failure to investigate the crime. The Inter-American Court ruled that the government must carry out an effective investigation and ensure the perpetrators are punished, as well as make reparations to the family.

Although Panama ratified the International Convention against enforced disappearance in 2011, it had not recognized the competence of the Committee on Enforced Disappearances to receive and consider communications from or on behalf of victims or from other states parties.

In June, Ecuadoran national Jesús Vélez Loor travelled to Panama to appear before a prosecutor and answer questions about his detention and torture by Panamanian authorities between 2002 and 2003. The Inter-American Court held a hearing in February with representatives of the government to discuss Panama's failure to fully comply with a 2010 judgment regarding his case, which ruled that Panama must investigate the human rights violations committed against him and improve treatment towards migrants.

## PRISON CONDITIONS

Local civil society organizations, the UN Special Rapporteur on torture and the head of the UN Working Group on Arbitrary Detention called on the authorities to halt the transfer of prisoners to a maximum security prison located at the naval base on Punta Coco Island. The UN experts said the prison operated outside of the official penitentiary system, had unsanitary conditions, and prisoners were being moved there without proper notification to their lawyers and families. The director of the penitentiary system, Gabriel Pinzón, denied that the prisoners' human rights were being violated but said the government would establish a sub-commission to investigate.

# PAPUA NEW GUINEA

Independent State of Papua New Guinea
Head of state: **Queen Elizabeth II, represented by Governor General Michael Ogio**
Head of government: **Peter Charles Paire O'Neill**

**The government took little action to address violence against women or sorcery-related violence.**

**Reports of unnecessary or excessive use of force by police and military persisted. Hundreds of men remained in detention at the Australia-run immigration detention centre on Manus Island.**

## VIOLENCE AGAINST WOMEN AND GIRLS

Sexual and gender-based violence remained pervasive. Legal reforms in recent years, including the repeal of the Sorcery Act and introduction of the 2013 Family Protection Act, were not followed up by effective action, such as improving social services, access to health care, counselling and women's shelters. The police force remained understaffed and under-resourced to deal with the high volume of family violence reports, preventing many women from accessing justice. Lack of government services in remote areas disproportionately affected women in rural locations from accessing health care and other services.

Reports continued of women and children being subjected to violence, sometimes resulting in death, following accusations of sorcery. In May a woman was hacked to death by a group of men after being accused of sorcery. A video showing four women being tortured as suspected sorcerers surfaced in October. Although it had not been verified independently by the end of the year, there remained concerns about the continued high level of incidents of sorcery-related violence.

A climate of intimidation and threats by police and non-state actors continued against human rights defenders who sought justice on issues such as sexual and gender-based violence.

## EXCESSIVE USE OF FORCE

Many incidents of excessive use of force by police were reported throughout the year. In January police in the capital, Port Moresby, fired indiscriminately into a market after a dispute between vendors and local council officials, killing two vendors. No arrests had been made by the end of the year.

In November, two policemen in Papua New Guinea's East New Britain were charged with murder over the death of a man in a police cell.

Another officer was suspended pending an investigation into the sexual assault of a female inmate in a Kokopo police cell after she was arrested over the death of her husband.

In Enga province police and Papua New Guinea Defence Force soldiers reportedly pointed guns at two shop owners and allowed people to steal their goods.

In December the Papua New Guinea Police Commissioner said he will review the Royal PNG Constabulary rules of engagement to ensure that officers used firearms responsibly.

## LACK OF ACCOUNTABILITY

While some attempts were made to improve accountability in individual cases, many police abuses such as torture including rape, and unlawful detention, went unpunished. Marginalized groups, including sex workers and LGBTI people, were particularly vulnerable to abuses by the police while in custody.

## DEATH PENALTY

The death penalty was retained in law; the last execution was carried out in 1954. In May, the Prime Minister announced that the government would review its 2013 decision to resume executions following a global outcry against the implementation of death sentences in Indonesia. Thirteen prisoners are reported to remain on death row. Officials in the Attorney General's Office confirmed in October that the government was considering a different approach and that an official announcement would be made at a later date.

## REFUGEES AND ASYLUM-SEEKERS

As of 30 November, 926 adult men were detained at the Australia-run immigration detention centre on Manus Island. Despite some improvements to conditions at the centre, concerns remained about prolonged and arbitrary detention, as well as safety and security following an attack on the centre in February 2014. Plans regarding long-term resettlement were uncertain. A number of human rights restrictions applied to those who were moved to a more "open" facility in Lorengau. Concerns remained around *refoulement*.

A two-week hunger strike involving more than 700 detainees took place in January. Concerns were raised about how the security services dealt with this incident and its aftermath.[1]

In October, the Australian and Papua New Guinean governments announced that decisions regarding refugee status would finally be made for remaining detainees and that successful applicants would be resettled across Papua New Guinea by the end of 2015. While around 40 men had previously been released into alternative accommodation on Manus Island, their movements and right to work were severely restricted. Refugees were granted only a one-year temporary visa, as the necessary political and legislative processes to create a new visa class for refugees had not been completed.

The trial of those charged with the killing of Manus Island detainee Reza Berati in February 2014 began in March 2015. Three other suspects, including nationals of New Zealand and Australia, were also being sought.

---

1. Australian and PNG authorities must respect asylum-seekers' right to protest (News story, 19 January)

# PARAGUAY

**Republic of Paraguay**
Head of state and government: **Horacio Manuel Cartes Jara**

Indigenous Peoples continued to be denied access to their traditional lands. Sexual and reproductive rights were not guaranteed and abortion continued to be criminalized in most cases.

## BACKGROUND

In October, the Special Rapporteur on the right of everyone to the enjoyment of the highest attainable standard of physical and mental health highlighted that the criminalization of abortion contributes to high rates of early pregnancy and unsafe abortions, and that widespread discrimination and deep inequalities threaten the right to health.

No progress was made in passing legislation on non-discrimination. A bill had been rejected by the Senate at the end of 2014 due to a lack of agreement to include all prohibited grounds. In November, two new draft bills to tackle discrimination were introduced to the Congress.

## INDIGENOUS PEOPLES' RIGHTS

Indigenous Peoples faced delays in acquiring titles and access to their ancestral lands.

In June, a second attempt by a landowner to nullify the 2014 expropriation law – passed to return their land to the Sawhoyamaxa community – was rejected by the Supreme Court. A resolution to a complaint filed by the community against the occupation of their land by the landowner's employees was still pending at the end of the year.

The Yakye Axa community was still unable to resettle on their land – despite an agreement between the authorities and the landowne having been finalized in January 2012 – due to incomplete road works. No government funds were made available for the Xákmok Kásek community to buy their land back from the company owning it, in spite of a 2014 agreement.

The Ayoreo Totobiegosode community denounced the invasion and deforestation of their traditional territory by cattle companies, and the risks to those living in voluntary isolation.[1]

The Ayoreo Atetadiegosode community denounced the deforestation, attacks by private security guards and delay in the regularization of their traditional territory.[2]

## IMPUNITY AND JUSTICE SYSTEM

Judicial proceedings against 13 *campesinos* (peasant farmers) continued for their alleged involvement in the killings of six police officers and other related crimes in the context of a 2012 land dispute in the Curuguaty district. No one was charged for the deaths of 11 peasant farmers who also died during the clashes, raising concerns over the investigation's impartiality.[3]

In July, 12 of the 13 accused *campesinos* requested to change their lawyers. The legal representatives faced an administrative measure started in 2014 for allegedly delaying the process. The procedure was still ongoing at the end of the year.

In October, the *campesinos'* trial was suspended for the ninth time, after the defence sought a recusal of the magistrate court, arguing lack of impartiality. The defence's allegations were dismissed and the trial continued at the end of the year.

In July, the appeal court confirmed that there was insufficient evidence to prove Lucía Sandoval's involvement in the killing of her husband in 2011. She filed a complaint for the abuse she suffered at the hands of her husband before his death. By the end of the year she had not yet recovered the custody of her children.

## TORTURE AND OTHER ILL-TREATMENT

Investigations into allegations of torture of *campesinos* during the 2012 clashes in the Curuguaty district were ongoing. The defence denounced delays and a lack of investigative measures from the Prosecutor's Office.

The trial of three suspects in the deaths of two adolescents in April 2014 at the Itauguá Educational Centre juvenile detention facility was announced in June.

## WOMEN'S AND GIRLS' RIGHTS

Legislation that was submitted in March to the Deputy Chamber to prevent and punish violence against women was still being discussed at the end of the year. In June, a public hearing in which civil society organizations commented on the project took place. In May, a bill to prevent and punish sexual violence and establish integral support for victims of sexual abuse was presented to the Deputy Chamber, and was still under debate at the end of the year.

Abortion was only permitted when the life of the woman or girl was at grave risk, and remained criminalized in all other circumstances, including when the pregnancy was the result of rape or incest, or when the foetus would be unable to survive outside the womb.[4]

National and international outrage was generated by the case of a 10-year-old girl who was pregnant after being raped – allegedly by her stepfather – and was denied the possibility of having an abortion in April.[5] A year earlier, the mother had reported the sexual abuse to the Prosecutor's Office, but the case was dismissed. The pregnancy went undetected after visits to several public health centres. After the girl gave birth in August, her family denounced the lack of medical, educational and financial support that had been promised by the authorities. Investigations into the supposed responsibility of the imprisoned stepfather were ongoing at the end of the year. The mother also faced an investigation for breaching her duty of care; the charges were dismissed in November.

## HUMAN RIGHTS DEFENDERS

Lawyers who represented the rights of Indigenous communities and *campesinos* faced administrative measures in carrying out their work.[6]

In December, a lawyer representing the

Sawhoyamaxa and Yakye Axa Indigenous communities was given a warning by the Supreme Court following an administrative investigation for criticizing a judge's ruling on an expropriation law that benefited the community. An appeal to the warning was pending at the end of the year.

1. Indigenous group in voluntary isolation at risk (AMR 45/2041/2015)
2. Paraguay: Security guards threatening Indigenous group (AMR 45/2700/2015)
3. Paraguay: Continúa la impunidad a tres años de las muertes en Curuguaty, 15 June 2015 (News story, 15 June)
4. Submission to the UN Universal Periodic Review, June 2015 (AMR 45/2142/2015)
5. Paraguay: Life of a pregnant 10-year-old girl at risk (AMR 45/1554/2015); Paraguay: Raped 10-year-old must be allowed an abortion (Press release, 29 April)
6. Administrative inquiry against human rights defender in Paraguay is disproportionate (AMR 45/1476/2015)

# PERU

**Republic of Peru**
Head of state and government: **Ollanta Moisés Humala Tasso**

Government critics were attacked. Excessive force by security personnel was reported. Indigenous Peoples continued to be denied their full rights. There was some progress in tackling impunity. Sexual and reproductive rights were not guaranteed.

## BACKGROUND

In December, the President ratified a national mechanism for the prevention of torture, approved by Congress in 2014. A draft law to search for those who disappeared during the internal armed conflict had not been submitted to Congress despite agreement between the authorities and victims' relatives in 2014. Challapalca prison, situated over 4,600m above sea level in Tacna region, remained open amid concerns that conditions constituted cruel, inhuman and degrading treatment. In June, the state of emergency in

Alto Huallaga, San Martín region, declared 30 years previously due to actions by the armed opposition group Shining Path, was lifted.

## FREEDOMS OF EXPRESSION AND ASSEMBLY

Critics of extractive industry projects were subjected to intimidation, excessive use of force and arbitrary arrests by the security forces.

Máxima Acuña Atalaya and her family, subsistence farmers in a longstanding land dispute with the Yanacocha mining company, continued to face harassment by the security forces in attempts to drive them from where they lived in Tragadero Grande, Cajamarca region. In February, police demolished a structure she was building to make her house weatherproof.

In May, Ramón Colque was shot dead when police opened fire against residents attempting to block the Southern Pan-American Highway during protests against the planned Tía María copper mining project in the Tambo Valley, Islay province, Arequipa department. They claimed the project would affect their access to clean water. Three other men were killed, including a police officer, and scores were ill-treated and arbitrarily arrested. At the end of the year all detainees had been released but many were still facing charges. Community leaders were intimidated.[1]

In September, four civilians died and scores of people were injured, including police officers, during protests against the copper mining project in Las Bambas and Apurímac regions. A state of emergency was declared in Apurímac and Cusco regions for four weeks at the end of September.

## INDIGENOUS PEOPLES' RIGHTS

Indigenous Peoples continued to be denied their right to free, prior and informed consent in relation to proposals affecting their livelihoods.

In May, the authorities passed legislation which allowed expropriation of land and reduced the requirement to approve environmental impact assessments for major development projects, amid concerns that the law could affect Indigenous Peoples' rights and territories.

At the end of the year, the trial was still ongoing of 53 people, including Indigenous people and some of their leaders, who stood accused of killing 12 police officers during clashes with security forces in a 2009 operation to disperse a road blockade led by Indigenous people in Bagua, Amazon region. A total of 33 people died in the clashes, including 23 police officers, and over 200 people were injured. No security personnel have been held accountable.

## IMPUNITY

### Internal armed conflict
Some progress was made in the investigation of human rights violations during the internal armed conflict (1980-2000).

In March, 10 military personnel were charged with crimes against humanity for sexual violence, including rape, inflicted on scores of women from Manta and Vilca, Huancavelica province. This was the first case to have reached the courts of sexual violence committed during the internal armed conflict. According to the register of victims established in 2005, over 4,400 women and girls reported being raped or sexually abused by the military during that period.

In May, retired Lieutenant-Colonel José Luis Israel Chávez Velásquez was arrested in connection with the disappearance of seven people in Huancapi, Ayacucho region, in 1991. The arrest warrant was issued 11 years before his arrest.

In September, the Inter-American Court of Human Rights ruled that Peru was responsible for the forced disappearance of 15 people, including seven children, from the peasant community of Santa Bárbara, in Huancavelica, in 1991, and ordered Peru to prosecute those responsible, offer reparation to the relatives and exhume and identify the remains of the victims.

### Excessive use of force
The vast majority of deaths during protests as a result of excessive use of force by security forces remained unresolved.

In April, the Public Prosecutor's Office said that only two investigations had been opened into deaths allegedly caused by excessive use of force by police during protests. At least 50 cases had been documented by human rights organizations since 2012.

## SEXUAL AND REPRODUCTIVE RIGHTS
Women and girls continued to have limited access to contraception. Free distribution of emergency contraceptives, including in cases of sexual abuse, continued to be banned. According to figures from the National Statistics Institute in July, teenage pregnancy increased to nearly 15% of girls and women aged between 15 and 19 in 2014.

In November, the Congress' Constitutional Commission rejected a draft law to legalize abortion for victims of rape.

In May, the Public Prosecutor's Office reopened and extended the investigation into the case of over 2,000 Indigenous and women farmers who were allegedly forcibly sterilized. Over 200,000 women were sterilized in the 1990s under a family planning programme, many without their consent.

In November, a decree law establishing a register of victims of forced sterilization was issued as a first step to guarantee the right to justice and adequate reparation.

## RIGHTS OF LESBIAN, GAY, BISEXUAL, TRANSGENDER AND INTERSEX PEOPLE
In March, the Commission of Justice and Human Rights rejected a law granting equal rights to same-sex couples.

---

1. Peru: Urgently investigate two deaths amid anti-mining protests (News story, 6 May)

# PHILIPPINES

**Republic of the Philippines**
Head of state and government: **Benigno S. Aquino III**

Torture and other ill-treatment by police continued in a climate of impunity for human rights violations. There were no convictions under laws criminalizing torture and enforced disappearances. Journalists, judges, lawyers and Indigenous Peoples were targeted and killed by unidentified gunmen and suspected militia. Progress towards realizing women's sexual and reproductive rights was halting. Tens of thousands of victims of past human rights violations sought redress.

## BACKGROUND

Despite the 2014 peace accord between the government and the armed group Moro Islamic Liberation Front, an encounter between police forces and rebel groups in Maguindanao in January resulted in the deaths of 44 elite police officers and 23 rebels. This stalled efforts to pass a landmark law creating an autonomous Bangsamoro region in the southern Philippines.

The Human Rights Victims' Claims Board received 75,000 applications for compensation from victims of Martial Law, in force from 1972 to 1981 under the rule of President Ferdinand Marcos. In July, the UN Special Rapporteur on the human rights of displaced persons raised a range of concerns following his visit, including on Indigenous Peoples displaced due to economic development activities.

## TORTURE AND OTHER ILL-TREATMENT

The Senate conducted its first hearing on police torture in January and a second in December;[1] the inquiry into the issue had been opened in December 2014.

Reports of torture continued, mostly citing police officers as perpetrators. Despite the criminalization of torture under the 2009 Anti-Torture Act, no perpetrators had been convicted under the Act by the end of 2015. Several criminal investigations and prosecutions were ongoing.

The national Commission on Human Rights recorded 51 cases of torture in 2014, involving 59 individuals. From January to September, it recorded 47 more cases involving 65 victims.

In May, the chief of police of Carmona, Cavite province, appeared in a video hitting a male detainee suspected of theft with a thick piece of wood. The incident was shown on national television, prompting the Philippine National Police (PNP) to dismiss him from his post.

After a year-long administrative investigation, the PNP found two police officers liable for the torture of Alfreda Disbarro in 2013 and demoted them by one rank.

The PNP initiated administrative investigations against police officers accused of torturing Jerryme Corre in 2012. There were continuing criminal prosecutions for torture in his case, as well as that of Darius Evangelista, tortured in 2010.

Cases arising from the 2014 discovery of a secret detention facility in Laguna province, in which police officers apparently used a "roulette wheel" to decide which torture method to use on detainees, remained at the preliminary investigation stage by the end of the year.

## ENFORCED DISAPPEARANCES

Three years after the enactment of the Anti-Enforced or Involuntary Disappearance Law in December 2012, there have been no convictions under the law.

Hearings continued in the trial of retired army General Jovito Palparan, charged with kidnapping and illegally detaining two women university students in 2006. General Palparan was arrested in 2014 and remanded in custody. In October, his attempt to temporarily leave his detention cell to register and run for the Senate was denied by the court.

## IMPUNITY

Hearings continued in the case of the 2009 Maguindanao massacre, in which 58 people, including 32 media workers, were killed by state-armed militias allegedly led by government officials. It was feared that the trial would not conclude before the end of President Aquino's term in June 2016. The case continued, despite efforts by the Supreme Court to expedite proceedings. Witnesses and their relatives remained at risk of being killed or intimidated, although 175 witnesses had testified and more than 100 of the 200 suspects had been arrested. At least eight witnesses and their family members were killed since November 2009, but no one was held accountable.

In August, assailants killed four men accused of raping and killing a 14-year-old girl in Marawi City. The suspects had been arrested but were released after no charges were filed. A local government official was quoted as saying the families of the suspects and of the victims agreed to the execution-style killing in order to avoid *rido,* or a family feud.

In September and November, three judges were shot dead in broad daylight. Erwin Alaba was killed outside his courtroom in Aurora while Wilfredo Nieves was killed inside his car in Bulacan on the way home. Reynaldo Espinar was killed in a cockpit in Northern Samar. Three lawyers were also shot dead in the second half of the year. Amelie Ocanada-Alegre was killed in August in Mandaue City while Ramon Eduardo Elesteria was shot in Bayawan City. Another lawyer, Pepito Suello, was killed in Bukidnon in October on his way to a hearing.

According to the International Association of People's Lawyers, at least 25 judges and more than 80 lawyers have been murdered since 1999. While investigations have been conducted, no charges were reported to have been brought.

## FREEDOM OF EXPRESSION

Seven journalists were killed in 2015. Newspaper reporter Nerlita Ledesma was shot near her house in Balanga City in January. In February, radio anchor Maurito Lim was shot outside a radio station in Tagbilaran City and newspaper reporter Melinda Magsino was shot in the head near her apartment in Batangas City in April.

In August, three journalists were killed in two weeks. Newspaper publisher Gregorio Ybanez was shot in front of his house in Tagum City. Radio anchor Teodoro Escanilla was also shot in front of his house in Sorsogon. Radio presenter Cosme Maestrado was shot by four gunmen in Ozamiz City. In October, another radio reporter, Jose Bernardo, was shot at close range by two unidentified gunmen.

According to the Center for Media Freedom and Responsibility, if the killings were found to be work-related, this would bring to 150 the number of journalists killed in the line of duty since 1986, when restrictions on freedom of expression were lifted after the end of the former President Marcos regime. Only 15 people had been convicted in connection with the killings of journalists by the end of 2015.

In September, the primary suspects in the 2011 killing of broadcaster and environmental advocate Gerardo Ortega were arrested in Thailand and extradited to the Philippines.

## ABUSES BY ARMED MILITIAS

In September, three leaders of the Lumad, a group of Indigenous Peoples in southern Philippines, were killed in Surigao del Sur. Dionel Campos and his cousin Aurelio Sinzo were shot; Emerito Samarca, a school director, was hogtied and stabbed to death.

According to the Indigenous people's party KATRIBU, 13 Lumads were killed and 4,000 evacuated in 2015 due to armed attacks by suspected militia, including the three killed in Surigao del Sur. The group recorded a total of 53 extrajudicial killings of Lumads during President Aquino's administration since 2010. Human rights groups accused an armed militia allegedly trained by the military of being behind the killings.

UN Special Rapporteurs on the rights of

indigenous peoples and on the situation of human rights defenders condemned the killings. Charges were filed against several suspects following an investigation by the Department of Justice.

## SEXUAL AND REPRODUCTIVE RIGHTS

Authorities implemented the Reproductive Health Law in November, three years after it was passed into law. However, a year after the Supreme Court upheld the constitutionality of the Reproductive Health Law, which provides certain sexual/reproductive rights to women, it issued in June a temporary restraining order stopping the Department of Health from procuring, distributing and promoting contraceptive implants.

In May, the UN Committee on the Elimination of Discrimination against Women found that the Philippines violated women's human rights by denying them access to a full range of reproductive health services, including universal and affordable contraceptives.

---

1.  Philippines: Senate hearing should be first step to tackling endemic torture (News story, 12 January)

# POLAND

**Republic of Poland**
Head of state: **Andrzej Duda (replaced Bronislaw Komorowski in August)**
Head of government: **Beata Szydło (replaced Ewa Kopacz in November)**

---

**Parliament failed to reform hate crime legislation. The government committed to relocate 5,000 refugees from Italy and Greece, amid a climate of intolerance and discriminatory speech, fuelled by some public officials. The domestic criminal investigation into the co-operation with the CIA and the hosting of a secret detention site was still pending.**

## LEGAL, CONSTITUTIONAL OR INSTITUTIONAL DEVELOPMENTS

As of November, the Polish Ombudsman, national NGOs, the National Council of the Judiciary and other authorities expressed concerns regarding respect for the rule of law. They referred to the President's refusal to swear in five constitutional judges who had been elected by the previous Parliament (*Sejm*) and to the amendments of the Law on the Constitutional Court adopted by the newly elected Parliament. In December, the Constitutional Court confirmed the election of three out of five replacement judges. President Duda continued to uphold his position that the replacement judges were elected "illegally". President Duda also signed into law the constitutional tribunal bill, which said the court must approve rulings with a two-thirds majority, rather than the previous simple majority, and required 13 of the court's 15 judges to be present for the most contentious cases, instead of the previous nine. A new law on media giving the government direct control over management positions in public service broadcasters was widely criticized. A number of laws were rapidly adopted by Parliament without public consultation and debate.

## DISCRIMINATION

### Hate crimes

In March, the European Commission against Racism and Intolerance recommended extending the scope of provisions on racist and xenophobic crimes to crimes perpetrated with a homophobic or transphobic motive.

Parliament continued to discuss three joint bills aimed at providing protection against hate crime perpetrated on grounds such as sexual orientation, gender identity or disability. However, it failed to pass them before parliamentary elections in October.

### Rights of lesbian, gay, bisexual, transgender and intersex people

On 26 May and 5 August, Parliament rejected two bills on civil partnerships, including for same-sex couples, without initiating a debate on the bills.

In September, Parliament approved the Gender Accordance Act, which established a framework for legal gender recognition of transgender people. On 2 October, President Duda vetoed the Act. Parliament failed to hold a vote on the presidential veto before parliamentary elections.

### Roma

On 22 July, 10 Romani women, men and children were forcibly evicted from an informal settlement in the city of Wrocław. They were given no notice by municipal authorities and their houses and belongings were destroyed while they were at work.

## COUNTER-TERROR AND SECURITY

After the December 2014 release of a US Senate report documenting the torture of detainees secretly held by the US CIA from 2002-2006, former President Aleksander Kwasniewski and former Prime Minister Leszek Miller acknowledged their co-operation with the CIA and agreement to host a secret site.

The former President subsequently stated publicly that he took steps to end the activity at the site, amid pressure from other Polish officials who were concerned that coerced interrogations were being conducted there. The Polish criminal investigation into the secret site allegations, launched in 2008, continued and was criticized for severe delays.

In February, the European Court of Human Rights confirmed as final the July 2014 decisions in the cases of Zayn al-Abidin Muhammed Husayn (Abu Zubaydah) and Abd al-Rahim al-Nashiri. The Court had ruled against the Polish government for co-operating with the CIA in the enforced disappearance of the two men, their illegal transfer, secret detention and torture. Poland submitted an action plan to the Council of Europe in August detailing the measures it had taken or would take to implement the final judgments in the men's

cases. These included earlier actions in May, paying compensation, and the submission to US authorities of a diplomatic note requesting that the death penalty not be imposed or applied to Abd al-Rahim al-Nashiri in military commissions proceedings at the US detention facility in Guantánamo Bay, Cuba.

## REFUGEES' AND MIGRANTS' RIGHTS

The debates regarding relocation and resettlement of refugees took place in a climate of mounting discriminatory speech, fuelled by some public officials throughout the year.

In July, the government announced the resettlement of 900 Syrian refugees from Lebanon and 1,100 refugees currently in Italy and Greece within its relocation programme. In September, the government supported the EU plan to relocate 120,000 refugees from other European countries. On the basis of the agreed quotas, about 5,000 refugees would be relocated from Greece and Italy to Poland in the next two years. Following the parliamentary elections, the new government backtracked from the commitments under the EU resettlement and relocation scheme.

At the end of the year, integration measures remained insufficient and the authorities did not adopt a comprehensive integration strategy.

Authorities continued to use detention disproportionately for migrants and asylum-seekers. In September, the European Court of Human Rights communicated the case *Bistieva v. Poland* to the government. The applicant argued that the authorities' decision to detain her and her three children, while waiting for the decision regarding their asylum claims, had violated their rights to private life and to liberty and security.

## WOMEN'S RIGHTS

In April, Poland ratified the Council of Europe Convention on preventing and combating violence against women and domestic violence. However, at the end of the year, authorities had not yet adopted a comprehensive plan to implement the Convention.

### Sexual and reproductive rights
In September, Parliament rejected a draft bill which aimed at banning abortion in all instances and removing any reference to prenatal diagnosis as well as the woman's right to information and testing.

On 7 October, the Constitutional Court ruled that the legal duty imposed on objecting doctors to refer women to an alternative facility or practitioners, in order for them to access legal abortion, was unconstitutional. This was in spite of the European Court of Human Rights' earlier ruling that the right of conscientious objections must not result in barriers for women to access legal abortion services in Poland.

### FREEDOM OF EXPRESSION
In October the Constitutional Court ruled that the provision which criminalizes "offending religious feelings" was constitutional.

# PORTUGAL

Portuguese Republic
Head of state: **Aníbal António Cavaco Silva**
Head of government: **António Costa (replaced Pedro Manuel Mamede PassosCoelho in November)**

**Roma and people of African descent continued to face discrimination. There were further reports of excessive use of force by police and prison conditions remained inadequate.**

### BACKGROUND
Following a visit in January, the UN Special Rapporteur on the independence of judges and lawyers expressed concern that rising court and legal fees were obstructing access to justice for more people living in poverty as a result of the economic crisis. The Constitutional Court ruled that some austerity measures affecting economic and social rights were unconstitutional.

### TORTURE AND OTHER ILL-TREATMENT
There were reports of unnecessary or excessive use of force by police and prison conditions remained inadequate.

In May, a police officer was filmed beating a man in front of his two children and father outside the Guimarães football stadium. The footage shows a police officer pushing a seemingly peaceful football fan to the ground and hitting him several times with a baton while his children are restrained. The same officer can also be seen punching the man's father in the face twice as he intervenes to stop the beating. According to the Ministry of Internal Affairs, the officer was given a 90-day suspension from duty, pending disciplinary proceedings.

### REFUGEES AND ASYLUM-SEEKERS
Only 39 of the 44 refugees previously selected for resettlement in Portugal in 2014, and none of those selected for resettlement in 2015, had arrived in the country by the end of the year. Portugal further committed to receive 4,574 asylum-seekers to be relocated from Italy and Greece under the EU relocation programme within the following two years. However, only 24 people had been relocated by the end of the year.

According to the Portuguese Refugee Council, the reception centre for refugees in the capital Lisbon remained overcrowded.

### DISCRIMINATION

#### Roma
Discrimination against Roma continued to be reported in several municipalities.

In July, the Mayor of Estremoz barred Roma living in the Quintinhas neighbourhood from using municipal swimming pools following reported acts of vandalism by a number of its residents. The decision was challenged by the Commission for Equality and against Racial Discrimination and a ruling was pending at the end of the year.

#### People of African descent
Racially motivated abuse and unnecessary

use of force by police against people of African descent continued to be reported.

In February, five young men of African descent reported having been beaten and subjected to racist comments by police officers in the Alfragide police station, after complaining about excessive use of force during an arrest in the Alto da Cova da Moura neighbourhood earlier the same day. They received medical treatment for injuries sustained and were charged with resistance and coercion of an officer. Investigations into their allegations of ill-treatment were ongoing at the end of the year.

## RIGHTS OF LESBIAN, GAY, BISEXUAL, TRANSGENDER AND INTERSEX PEOPLE
In December, new legislation was adopted giving same-sex couples the right to adopt children.

## VIOLENCE AGAINST WOMEN AND GIRLS
According to data provided by the NGO UMAR, as of 20 November, 27 women had been killed, and there were also 33 attempted murders, particularly by people with whom the women maintained intimate relationships.

In July, a study by the New University of Lisbon estimated that 1,830 girls residing in Portugal had been subjected to, or were at risk of, female genital mutilation (FGM). New legislation entered into force in September, introducing FGM as a specific crime in the Penal Code.

# PUERTO RICO

Commonwealth of Puerto Rico
Head of state: **Barack Obama**
Head of government: **Alejandro García Padilla**

The right of same-sex couples to marry legally was recognized. However, lesbian, gay, bisexual, transgender and intersex (LGBTI) people continued to face discrimination. The 2013 reform of the police had limited impact and incidents of excessive use of force by law enforcement officials continued.

## BACKGROUND
In May, the Governor submitted a draft law to Congress to create the office of human rights Ombudsman and unify several functions currently carried out by different authorities.

The government proposed austerity measures in September, raising concerns about their potentially negative impact on the most marginalized and disadvantaged groups and on labour rights.

## RIGHTS OF LESBIAN, GAY, BISEXUAL, TRANSGENDER AND INTERSEX PEOPLE
Transgender people continued to face difficulties in accessing gender reassignment treatment because of a lack of adequate protocols and legal gender recognition, and health insurance providers' refusal to cover treatment costs. Although in August the Governor issued instructions allowing for gender to be changed on driving licences, there were no provisions for changing gender in other identity documents.

In June, the Governor issued instructions to comply within 15 days with the landmark US federal Supreme Court's decision affirming the right of same-sex couples to marry legally.

In July, the Secretary of the Family issued a directive instructing officials to ensure equal treatment for LGBTI couples wishing to adopt a child and to use the "best interest of the child" as the only criterion in deciding on adoptions. In December, a court authorized the first adoption of a child by a same-sex couple.

## POLICE AND SECURITY FORCES
Puerto Rican human rights organizations continued to report incidents of excessive use of force, discrimination by the police towards Afro-descendants and Dominican communities and a failure to investigate reports of gender-based violence. In its June periodic report, the technical advisor monitoring the implementation of police reforms reported allegations of human rights

violations by the police in the context of counter-narcotic operations.

Reforms of the Puerto Rico Police Force, agreed between the government of Puerto Rico and the US Department of Justice in 2013, had limited impact. They focused primarily on acquiring new equipment and amending internal policies and regulations. Civil society organizations provided comments and suggestions to the policy reviews, including on the use of force and the investigation of domestic violence, but it was unclear to what extent their comments were taken into account.

A bill submitted to the Senate by the Puerto Rican branch of the American Civil Liberties Union proposing the creation of an independent board to oversee the work of the police was rejected in May on the grounds that police oversight was already carried out by the Federal Department of Justice.

# QATAR

**State of Qatar**
Head of state: **Sheikh Tamim bin Hamad bin Khalifa Al Thani**
Head of government: **Sheikh Abdullah bin Nasser bin Khalifa Al Thani**

The authorities arbitrarily restricted the rights to freedom of expression, association and peaceful assembly. A prisoner of conscience was serving a lengthy sentence for writing and reciting poems. Migrant workers, including domestic workers and those employed in high-profile construction projects, continued to face exploitation and abuse. Discrimination against women remained entrenched in both law and practice. The death penalty remained in force; no executions were reported.

## BACKGROUND
In March, Qatar joined the Saudi Arabia-led international coalition that engaged in the armed conflict in Yemen (see Yemen entry).

## FREEDOM OF EXPRESSION
The authorities continued to restrict freedom of expression. Qatari poet Mohammed al-Ajami (also known as Ibn-Dheeb) remained a prisoner of conscience. He had received a 15-year prison sentence in 2012 for writing and reciting poems deemed by the authorities to be offensive to the Emir and the state. In February, the Minister for Foreign Affairs denied that Mohammed al-Ajami was jailed for his peaceful opinions.[1]

In May, security authorities detained four media workers, including British journalist Mark Lobel, although they had official authorization to visit Qatar to report on conditions of migrant workers. They were released without charge after two days and were allowed to remain in Qatar.

## JUSTICE SYSTEM
In March, the UN Special Rapporteur on the independence of judges and lawyers reported on her 2014 visit to Qatar. She concluded that there were serious shortcomings that negatively affected the enjoyment of human rights in Qatar and the independence and impartiality of those working in the justice system.

The Court of Appeal in the capital Doha confirmed the conviction of Filipino national Ronaldo Lopez Ulep, who received a sentence of life imprisonment in 2014 for espionage. His conviction was largely based on a pre-trial "confession" that he said security officers had forced him to make under torture. The Court of Appeal reduced his sentence to 15 years' imprisonment, while also confirming the convictions and reducing the sentences of two other Filipinos tried alongside Ronaldo Ulep.

## MIGRANT WORKERS' RIGHTS
Migrant workers, who numbered more than 1.6 million according to the authorities and made up more than 90% of Qatar's workforce, continued to face exploitation and abuse. The Emir and the Minister for Foreign Affairs both committed to addressing exploitation of migrant workers in the

recruitment chain during official visits to India and Nepal respectively, from where many of Qatar's migrant workers originate. In October the Emir approved changes to the *kafala* sponsorship system, creating a new system for migrant workers to appeal a sponsor's decision to refuse them an exit permit to leave the country and increasing the state's oversight of the process by which workers seek to change jobs or leave Qatar. However, migrant workers were still required to obtain their sponsor's approval to change jobs or leave the country. The new regime would not be enforceable until at least the end of 2016. In February the Emir approved the introduction of an electronic Wage Protection System that sought to regularize the payment of salaries by requiring all businesses to pay workers by bank transfer.

Migrant workers commonly had their passports confiscated by their employers, in breach of Qatari law, exposing them to forced labour and other abuses. Thousands of workers in construction and related industries continued to live in dirty, overcrowded and often unsafe conditions. The government said it would build new facilities to house up to 258,000 workers by the end of 2016, and announced in August that it had completed the construction of housing for 50,000 workers.

Thousands of domestic workers, most of whom were women, and other migrant workers employed by small companies or in informal work arrangements continued to face the greatest risk of abuse, including forced labour and human trafficking. Workers employed by large companies also complained of chronic labour abuse such as inadequate housing, low pay and late payment of wages, poor working conditions, and of being prevented from changing jobs or leaving the country under the *kafala* system.

Following the devastating earthquakes in Nepal in April and May, many Nepalese migrant workers complained that employers denied them exit permits to leave Qatar or refused to pay their return airfares, a legal requirement for those whose contracts had ended. Without this support, few could afford to return. Of those who did return to Nepal, many complained that their employers in Qatar withheld pay due to them.

## WOMEN'S RIGHTS
Women faced discrimination in law and in practice, and were inadequately protected against violence within the family. Personal status laws continued to discriminate against women in relation to marriage, divorce, inheritance, child custody, nationality and freedom of movement.

## DEATH PENALTY
The Court of Appeal confirmed at least one death sentence. No executions were reported.

---

1.   Qatar: Release the poet, Mohammed al-Ajami (MDE 22/2760/2015)

# ROMANIA

Romania
Head of state: **Klaus Iohannis**
Head of government: **Dacian Cioloş (replaced Victor Ponta in November)**

Roma continued to experience discrimination, forced evictions and other human rights violations. Following the release of the US Senate report on the CIA secret detention programme, a new investigation into Romania's co-operation was opened. In April, the UN Committee against Torture reviewed Romania for the first time in 18 years.

## BACKGROUND
In November, Prime Minister Ponta resigned following protests across the country that were prompted by the deaths of 63 people in a nightclub in the capital Bucharest on 30 October. A technocratic government headed by Dacian Cioloş was appointed until the December 2016 parliamentary elections.

## DISCRIMINATION – ROMA

Roma continued to face systemic discrimination and were targeted with hate crimes, including excessive use of force by law enforcement officials. Anti-Roma sentiment continued to be frequently expressed in public and political discourse. A report by the Superior Council of Magistracy on access to justice for Roma and other vulnerable groups concluded that the judiciary was insufficiently sensitive to discrimination and that legal aid rules failed to ensure the affordability of legal representation to vulnerable groups, particularly Roma. The UN Special Rapporteur on extreme poverty and human rights highlighted the "official state of denial" regarding anti-Roma discrimination and raised concerns over a pattern of housing rights violations against Roma, following his visit to the country in November. A new Strategy for the Inclusion of the Romanian Citizens of Roma Ethnicity for 2015-2020 was adopted in January.

### Housing rights – forced evictions

In April, a demolition order issued by the municipality of Cluj-Napoca against 300 Roma living in the centre of the city in December 2010 was ruled unlawful by the Cluj-Napoca District Court. The residents were forcibly evicted within 24 hours and resettled near a waste dump. The Court ruled that the order was insufficiently reasoned, and was executed without prior consultation with affected residents and the offer of adequate alternative accommodation. It also failed to allow sufficient time for its legality to be verified by the Prefect.

About 30 Roma, half of them children, living in the town of Eforie Sud, in Constanţa county, remained at risk of forced eviction at the end of the year. They had been ordered to vacate the publicly owned property they had been occupying since October 2013 following their earlier forced eviction from a long-standing informal settlement.[1]

In July, 22 Roma, including five children, were forcibly evicted by local authorities from the Pirita settlement in Baia Mare. Local authorities stated that the demolition was carried out under a policy to identify and demolish buildings that were illegally constructed on public land in Craica, Pirita, Ferneziu and Gării – all informal settlements inhabited mainly by Roma.

### Police and security forces

In May, the UN Committee against Torture expressed concern over persistent reports of racist crimes against Roma, including the excessive use of force by police resulting in deaths in custody. In January, the European Court of Human Rights ruled that the authorities violated the right to life and the right not to be subjected to inhuman treatment and to discrimination of the Romani community of Apalina, in Mureş county, during a law enforcement operation in 2006 which resulted in 21 people suffering injuries, including gunshot wounds.

## COUNTER-TERROR AND SECURITY

After the release in December 2014 of the US Senate report on the CIA detention and interrogation programme, Ioan Talpeş, former national security adviser to then President Ion Iliescu, admitted that Romania allowed the CIA to operate "one or two" secret sites in the country. Talpeş stated that people were "probably" detained and ill-treated in Romania in 2003-2006, and that he had informed the then president of the CIA activities.[2] The Prosecutor General claimed in January 2015 that an investigation into the allegations had been initiated.

The case of Abd al-Rahim al-Nashiri, a Saudi Arabian national currently detained at the US detention facility at Guantánamo Bay, Cuba, remains pending at the European Court of Human Rights. He lodged a complaint against Romania, alleging that he had been held and tortured in a secret site in Bucharest between 2004 and 2006.

In September, a European Parliament delegation called on the government to conduct an effective investigation into reports of a secret site on its territory, after being denied access to a building in Bucharest that allegedly hosted such a site.

## TORTURE AND OTHER ILL-TREATMENT

In May, the UN Committee against Torture criticized the treatment and living conditions of people with mental disabilities in psychiatric facilities, and the lack of investigation into thousands of deaths in these institutions over the last decade. There are still around 25,000 children in 717 institutions across the country, despite long-standing commitments to reduce the number of people with mental and physical disabilities in psychiatric institutions.

The Committee also expressed concern over the inadequacy of police detention facilities, the low number of prosecutions and convictions in cases of ill-treatment and torture and the lack of an independent complaints mechanism for violations by law enforcement officials.

## REFUGEES AND ASYLUM-SEEKERS

Asylum-seekers continued to face obstacles in accessing asylum proceedings. Rejected asylum seekers and Dublin returnees – asylum-seekers due to be transferred from one EU state to another, under the Dublin III regulation – continued to be detained unnecessarily. Recognized refugees faced obstacles in accessing education, housing and health care.

Around 900 people applied for asylum between January and September 2015, compared to around 1,150 people in the same period in 2014. Romania opposed the mandatory quotas for the relocation of people in need of international protection from Greece, Italy and other EU member states. Following the adoption of the scheme in September, Romania was earmarked to receive 6,351 refugees over a period of two years.

---

1.  Romania: Eforie municipality threatens to evict Roma families third time in two years (EUR 39/1560/2015)
2.  Europe: Complicit governments must act in wake of US Senate torture

report (News story, 20 January); Europe: Breaking the conspiracy of silence: USA's European "partners in crime" must act after Senate torture report (EUR 01/002/2015); USA: Crimes and impunity: Full Senate Committee report on CIA secret detentions must be released, and accountability for crimes under international law ensured (AMR 51/1432/2015)

# RUSSIAN FEDERATION

**Russian Federation**
Head of state: **Vladimir Putin**
Head of government: **Dmitry Medvedev**

**Freedoms of expression and peaceful assembly remained severely restricted. The authorities dominated the print and broadcast media, and further extended their control over the internet. NGOs faced further harassment and reprisals under the "foreign agents" law, while their access to foreign funding was further restricted by a new law banning "undesirable" organizations. Growing numbers of individuals were arrested and criminally charged for criticizing state policy and publicly displaying or possessing materials deemed extremist or otherwise unlawful under vague national security legislation. Four people faced prosecution under the 2014 law that made repeated violations of the law on public assemblies a criminal offence. Deep flaws in the judicial system were further exposed through several high-profile cases; a new law gave the Constitutional Court the authority to overrule decisions by the European Court of Human Rights. Refugees faced numerous obstacles in accessing international protection. Serious human rights violations continued in the North Caucasus, and human rights defenders reporting from the region faced harassment.**

## BACKGROUND

In the face of Russia's growing international isolation and mounting economic problems, the authorities sought to consolidate public opinion around the notions of unity and patriotism, "traditional values" and fear of the country's purported enemies abroad and within. Opinion polls showed a consistently high level of support for President Putin's leadership. Government critics were smeared as "unpatriotic" and "anti-Russian state" in the mainstream media, and were occasionally assaulted. On 27 February, one of Russia's most prominent opposition activists, Boris Nemtsov, was shot dead within sight of the Kremlin. Mourners wishing to commemorate him at the site of his death were harassed by city authorities and pro-government supporters.

The government continued to dismiss mounting evidence of Russia's military involvement in Ukraine, while President Putin decreed in May that human losses among the military during "special operations" in peacetime were a state secret.[1]

The authorities estimated that as of November, 2,700 Russian citizens had joined the armed group Islamic State (IS) in Syria and Iraq, the majority of them from the North Caucasus. Independent experts gave higher estimates.

On 30 September, Russia began air strikes in Syria with the stated aim of targeting IS, but also frequently targeted other groups opposed to Syrian President Bashar al-Assad. Numerous civilian casualties were reported, which Russia denied. On 24 November, Turkey shot down a Russian military jet for allegedly entering its airspace, leading to mutual recriminations and a diplomatic stand-off between the two countries.

## FREEDOM OF EXPRESSION

Media freedom remained severely restricted, through direct state control and self-censorship. The editorial policy of most media outlets faithfully reproduced official views on key domestic and international events.

The authorities extended their control over the internet. Thousands of websites and pages were blocked by internet providers on orders from the media regulator Roskomnadzor. Those targeted in violation of the right to freedom of expression included political satire, information shared by lesbian, gay, bisexual, transgender and intersex (LGBTI) activists, information on public protests and religious texts. A growing, but still small, number of individuals faced criminal prosecution for online postings, usually on charges under anti-extremism legislation; most of them received fines.

Yekaterina Vologzheninova, a shop assistant from Yekaterinburg, was put on trial on 27 October for her satirical posts on social media in 2014 which criticized Russia's annexation of Crimea and its military involvement in eastern Ukraine. The prosecution alleged that she had incited violence and "promoted hatred and enmity towards the Russian government officials, Russian volunteers fighting in eastern Ukraine and the specific ethnic group, the Russians". Her trial was ongoing at the end of the year.[2]

Harassment of independent media outlets and journalists continued. Past incidents of violence against independent journalists were rarely effectively investigated. Two men were arrested in connection with the beating of journalist Oleg Kashin in November 2010, and a third put on a wanted list. One suspect claimed he had proof that the beating had been ordered by the Governor of Pskov region, which tallied with Kashin's suspicions, but the authorities declined to investigate the allegation further.

Elena Milashina, a journalist from the independent newspaper *Novaya Gazeta*, reported that a 17-year-old Chechen girl was being forcibly married to a senior police officer three times her age and reportedly already married. The story was widely reported and caused a public outcry. Chechen leader Ramzan Kadyrov publicly supported the senior police officer and accused Milashina of lying and interfering in the private lives of the Chechen people. On 19 May, the Chechen government-owned online news agency Grozny-Inform published an article containing thinly veiled death threats against Milashina.

The clampdown on freedom of expression extended beyond journalists and bloggers. Natalya Sharina, director of the state-run Library of Ukrainian Literature in the capital Moscow, was detained on 28 October under extremism-related charges. The investigators claimed that works by Ukrainian nationalist Dmitry Korchinsky had been found at the library, in a pile of literature that had not yet been catalogued. She was detained at a police station without bedding, food or drink until 30 October when she was placed under house arrest, pending possible charges.[3]

On 15 September, Rafis Kashapov, an activist from Naberezhnye Chelny, Republic of Tatarstan, was convicted of inciting inter-ethnic hatred and threatening the territorial integrity of the Russian Federation; he was sentenced to three years' imprisonment. He had been under arrest since 28 December 2014 in connection with posts on social media that criticized Russia's role in the conflict in eastern Ukraine and the treatment of Crimean Tatars in Russian-occupied Crimea.

On 10 November, the Kirsanovski District Court ruled that the environmentalist Yevgeny Vitishko should be released. He had served over half of his sentence following his conviction on trumped-up charges in the run-up to the 2014 Sochi Winter Olympic Games. However, on 20 November, a day before the court's decision came into force, the Prosecutor's Office appealed against the decision; Vitishko was finally released on 22 December after an appeal hearing.

## FREEDOM OF ASSEMBLY

The right to freedom of peaceful assembly remained severely curtailed. Protests were infrequent, their number having declined following restrictions introduced in earlier years. Organizers were regularly refused permission to hold street rallies or only allowed to hold them in non-central locations. Those who defied the ban or the rules were penalized through fines and detention.

Monstration, a humorous annual street event in Novosibirsk mocking the pomposity of the May Day march, was disallowed for the first time since 2005. Its organizer, Artem Loskutov, was arrested and sentenced to 10 days' detention for violating the law on assemblies after he and several other "monstrators" joined the official May Day march instead.

For the first time, a peaceful street protester was convicted under the 2014 law which criminalized repeated participation in unauthorized assemblies.

On 7 December, a Moscow court sentenced Ildar Dadin to three years in a prison colony for his repeated participation in "unauthorized" assemblies between August and December 2014. He had been placed under house arrest on 30 January, after serving a 15-day detention for joining a peaceful protest in Moscow against the politically motivated conviction of Oleg Navalny, the brother of anti-graft campaigner and opposition leader Alex Navalny.

Two other peaceful protesters from Moscow, Mark Galperin and Irina Kalmykova, also faced criminal prosecution under the same law at the end of the year.

Prisoners of conscience Stepan Zimin, Aleksei Polikhovich and Denis Lutskevich, who had been detained in 2012 in connection with the Bolotnaya Square protests, were released during the year, having completed their prison sentences. Another prisoner of conscience, Sergey Krivov, remained in prison; the authorities brought criminal proceedings against at least two further individuals in connection with the Bolotnaya protests.

## FREEDOM OF ASSOCIATION

Freedom of association was further restricted. By the end of the year, the Ministry of Justice's register of NGOs considered "foreign agents" contained 111 entries, requiring the NGOs concerned to put this stigmatizing label on all their publications and observe onerous reporting requirements. NGOs that defied these requirements faced hefty fines. Not a single NGO succeeded in challenging their inclusion on the register in court. Seven were struck off the register after giving up all foreign funding, and a further 14 NGOs included on the register chose to close down.

The Human Rights Centre (HRC) Memorial was fined Rub 600,000 (US$8,800) in September after its sister organization, the Historical and Educational Centre Memorial – which was not on the register – did not mark its publications with the label "foreign agent". The HRC Memorial lost its court appeal against the decision. Following a regular inspection of the HRC Memorial in November, the Ministry of Justice concluded that criticism by its members of the Bolotnaya Square trials and of Russian policies in Ukraine "undermined the foundations of the constitutional system" and amounted to "calls for the overthrow of the current government and change of the political regime". The Ministry submitted its "findings" to the Prosecutor's Office for further investigation.

In May, a law was passed authorizing the Prosecutor's Office to designate any foreign organization as "undesirable" on the grounds of posing a "threat to the country's constitutional order, defence or state security", with the immediate effect of rendering its presence, and any activity on its behalf, unlawful. In July, the US-based National Endowment for Democracy was declared "undesirable". Three more donor organizations, the Open Society Foundation, the Open Society Institute Assistance Foundation and the US Russia Foundation for Economic Advancement and the Rule of Law, were declared "undesirable" in November and December.

## RIGHTS OF LESBIAN, GAY, BISEXUAL, TRANSGENDER AND INTERSEX PEOPLE

LGBTI activists continued to operate in an extremely hostile environment. Discrimination against LGBTI individuals continued to be widely reported.

On 25 March, a court in St Petersburg ruled that the Children-404 group – an online community set up by journalist Elena Klimova to support LGBTI teenagers – be blocked. In July, a court in Nizhny Tagil, Sverdlovsk region, fined Klimova Rub 50,000 (US$830) for "propaganda of non-traditional sexual relations among minors". On 2 October, a court in St Petersburg ruled that the page should be unblocked.

The authorities continued to violate LGBTI individuals' right to peaceful assembly. In May, LGBTI activist Nikolay Alekseev attempted to hold an unauthorized Pride march in Moscow. It resulted in clashes with anti-LGBTI protesters and 10 days' detention for three LGBTI activists, including Nikolay Alekseev. In St Petersburg, LGBTI activists were able to conduct some public activities without interference from police.

## JUSTICE SYSTEM

Several high-profile trials exposed deep-rooted and widespread flaws in Russia's criminal justice system, including the lack of equality of arms, the use of torture and other ill-treatment in the course of investigations as well as the failure to exclude torture-tainted evidence in court, the use of secret witnesses and other secret evidence which the defence could not challenge, and the denial of the right to be represented by a lawyer of one's choice. Less than 0.5% of trials resulted in acquittals.

Svetlana Davydova was one of the growing number of cases of alleged high treason and espionage, under vague offences introduced in 2012. She was arrested on 21 January for a phone call she had made to the Ukrainian Embassy eight months earlier, to share her suspicions that soldiers from her town Vyazma, Smolensk region, were being sent to fight in eastern Ukraine. Her state-appointed lawyer told the media that she had "confessed to everything" and declined to appeal against her detention because "all these hearings and the fuss in the media [create] unnecessary psychological trauma for her children". On 1 February, two new lawyers took up her case. She complained that her initial lawyer had convinced her to plead guilty to reduce her likely sentence from 20 to 12 years. On 3 February, she was released; on 13 March, in marked contrast to all other treason cases, criminal proceedings against her were terminated.

In September, the trial of Nadezhda Savchenko, a Ukrainian citizen and member of the Aidar volunteer battalion, began. She was accused of deliberately directing artillery fire to kill two Russian journalists during the conflict in Ukraine in June 2014. She insisted that the case against her was fabricated and the testimonies against her, including by several secret witnesses, were false. Her trial was marred by myriad procedural flaws.

On 15 December, President Putin signed a new law under which the Constitutional Court can pronounce the European Court of Human Rights' and other international courts' decisions "unimplementable" if they "violate" the Russian Constitution's "supremacy".

## REFUGEES' AND MIGRANTS' RIGHTS

According to official figures, in the first nine months of the year, 130,297 people were given temporary asylum, 129,506 of them from Ukraine and 482 from Syria. Only 96 of the 1,079 applications for permanent refugee status were granted, none of them to Syrian nationals. NGOs reported numerous obstacles, including corruption and deliberate misinformation, intended to discourage those seeking international protection from applying for permanent or temporary asylum.

A family of six refugees from Syria, including four children, were stranded in the international transit zone of Moscow's Sheremetyevo airport for over two months. On 10 September, border officials denied them entry claiming their travel documents were fake. On 19 November, Khimki City Court fined them Rub 10,000 (US$150) for trying to enter the country under forged documents; the following day, they were registered as asylum-seekers and relocated to Tver region, with help from the NGO Civic Assistance Committee.

There were regular reports of forcible return of individuals to Uzbekistan and other Central Asian countries, where they risked being subjected to torture and other serious human rights violations.

## NORTH CAUCASUS

Fewer attacks by armed groups were reported in the North Caucasus than in previous years.

Law enforcement agencies continued to rely on security operations as their preferred method of combating armed groups, and continued to be suspected of resorting to enforced disappearances, unlawful detention, as well as torture and other ill-treatment of detainees.

Human rights reporting from the region visibly declined, due to a severe clampdown on human rights defenders and independent journalists, who regularly faced harassment, threats and violence, including from law enforcement officials and pro-government groups.

On 3 June, an aggressive mob surrounded the office building of the human rights group Joint Mobile Group in Chechnya's capital Grozny. Masked men forced their way into the office, destroying its contents and forcing staff to evacuate.[4] No suspects had been identified by the end of the year.

On 6 November, the office and residence in the Republic of Ingushetia of human rights defender Magomed Mutsolgov were searched by armed law enforcement officers, who seized documents and IT equipment. According to Mutsolgov, the warrant authorizing the search stated that he was "acting in the interests of the USA, Georgia, Ukraine and the Syrian opposition".

---

1. Russian Federation: Making troop deaths a secret "attacks freedom of expression" (News story, 28 May)

2. Russian Federation: Prosecuted for criticizing government: Yekaterina Vologzheninova (EUR 46/2682/2015)

3. Russian Federation: Natalya Sharina. Librarian detained for holding "extremist books" (EUR/2900/2015)

4. Russian Federation: Joint Mobile Group office ransacked by mob (EUR 46/1802/2015)

# RWANDA

**Republic of Rwanda**
Head of state: **Paul Kagame**
Head of government: **Anastase Murekezi**

While economic progress and development continued, freedom of expression was further restricted. Journalists, human rights defenders and members of the opposition faced a repressive environment. Rwanda's human rights record was examined under the UPR mechanism in November.

## BACKGROUND

Political debate was dominated by discussion of planned amendments to presidential term limits in the Constitution. More than 3.7 million people petitioned Parliament to lift the two-term presidential term limit to allow President Kagame to stand for a third term in 2017, although there were reports of pressure to sign the petition. On 8 October, the Supreme Court rejected a petition brought by the Democratic Green Party of Rwanda challenging the legality of amending the Constitution. The Chamber of Deputies and the Senate voted in favour of reducing the presidential term from a seven to five-year term renewable once, as well as a provision that would allow the President in place at the time of the amendment to stand for an additional seven-year term. The revised Constitution was adopted in a referendum on 18 December, and Paul Kagame confirmed that he would seek re-election in 2017.

## HUMAN RIGHTS DEFENDERS

Human rights defenders worked in an increasingly challenging environment, facing intimidation and administrative interference.

In January, two former police officers were sentenced by Rubavu High Court to 20 years in prison for the murder of Gustave Makonene, Transparency International's Rubavu co-ordinator, who was killed in 2013.

The Rwandan League for the Promotion and Defense of Human Rights (LIPRODHOR), an NGO, continued to face difficulties. LIPRODHOR members were electing a new executive committee on 5 September when police arrived and interrupted the meeting. On 21 November, a different new executive committee was elected.

On 12 October, the executive secretary of the regional NGO Human Rights League of the Great Lakes Region, headquartered in Rwanda, was taken in for questioning by the immigration services. Seven members of the newly elected executive council and oversight committee were also taken for questioning by police the next day. This took place in the context of a dispute over leadership of the organization.

## POLITICAL PRISONERS

Former prisoner of conscience Charles Ntakirutinka, who was released in March 2012 after 10 years in detention, continued to wait for a response to his request for a passport submitted in April 2012. Other former political prisoners and opposition political figures also continued to report difficulties obtaining travel documents.

## FREEDOM OF ASSOCIATION

The Secretary-General of the opposition political party United Democratic Forces , Sylvain Sibomana, and another party member, Anselme Mutuyimana, remained in detention for inciting insurrection or trouble among the population after organizing a meeting in September 2012. The party complained about conditions of detention, reporting that Sylvain Sibomana was denied his medically prescribed diet from August and that party president Victoire Ingabire was temporarily refused access to her lawyer. The party vice-president Boniface Twagirimana was arrested on 4 December, and released the next day.

There was no progress in the case of Jean Damascène Munyeshyaka, national organizing secretary of the Democratic Green Party of Rwanda, who went missing on 27 June 2014.

## FREEDOM OF EXPRESSION

Journalists continued to work in a difficult environment, with some employing self-censorship to avoid harassment.

On 29 May, the BBC Kinyarwanda services were indefinitely suspended by the Rwanda Utilities Regulatory Authority following the recommendation of a committee of inquiry led by the former Prosecutor-General, Martin Ngoga. BBC services were originally suspended in Rwanda in October 2014 in response to the broadcast of the documentary *Rwanda's Untold Story*, on the grounds that it violated Rwandan laws on genocide denial, revisionism, inciting hatred and divisionism.

Fred Muvunyi, chair of the Rwanda Media Commission, the media's self-regulatory body, resigned in May and left the country, reportedly following a dispute over the handling of the BBC case, as well as criticisms contained in the Commission's (unpublished) report on the state of the media in Rwanda.

## UNFAIR TRIALS

The singer Kizito Mihigo was found guilty on 27 February of plotting against the government, forming a criminal group and conspiracy to commit an assassination. Evidence presented by the prosecution included WhatsApp and Skype messages. Having previously pleaded guilty and asked for pardon, Kizito Mihigo was sentenced to 10 years in prison. His co-accused Cassien Ntamuhanga, a journalist, and Jean Paul Dukuzumuremyi, a demobilized soldier, were sentenced to 25 and 30 years respectively. Agnes Niyibizi, an accountant, accused of being a treasurer for the Rwanda National Congress (a group of political dissidents in exile), was acquitted.

The military court trial of Colonel Tom Byabagamba, retired General Frank Rusagara and retired Sergeant François Kabayiza accused, among other charges, of inciting insurrection or trouble among the population and illegal possession of firearms, continued throughout the year. François Kabayiza claimed in court that he was tortured in detention. Tom Byabagamba and Frank Rusagara were relatives of David Himbara, a former presidential adviser now in exile. Retired captain David Kabuye, who was arrested by Rwandan military intelligence in August 2014, completed a six-month jail term in March 2015 for illegal possession of firearms. He was rearrested and later acquitted on new charges of inciting insurrection or trouble among the population and defamation. Just days before his acquittal, David Kabuye appeared as a prosecution witness in the case against Frank Rusagara. The trials were believed to be politically motivated.

## INTERNATIONAL JUSTICE

Trials of individuals suspected of involvement in the 1994 genocide continued in courts outside Rwanda. The International Criminal Tribunal for Rwanda (ICTR) officially closed on 31 December.

Rwanda's intelligence chief, General Emmanuel Karenzi Karake, was arrested in the UK in June, on a warrant issued by the Spanish authorities in connection with the 2008 war crimes indictment brought against 40 Rwandan officials by Judge Andreu Merelles, under the principle of universal jurisdiction. A UK court dismissed the extradition request in August, and the Spanish Supreme Court ruled on 10 September to revoke the arrest warrants and close the case.

After hearings in April, the ICTR Appeal Chamber ruled in *Nyiramasuhuko et al* on 14 December that the six appellants' right to be tried without undue delay had been violated, and reduced the length of their sentences. This was the last appeal judgment before the ICTR. The six accused were variously convicted in 2011 of crimes of genocide, conspiracy to commit genocide, incitement to commit genocide, crimes against humanity and war crimes. Pauline Nyiramasuhuko was the former Minister of Family and Women's Development.

Jean Uwinkindi, whose case was the first to be transferred from the ICTR to a national jurisdiction, was sentenced to life imprisonment by the Rwandan High Court on 30 December. ICTR indictee Ladislas Ntaganzwa was arrested on 9 December in the Democratic Republic of the Congo. The Prosecutor of the UN Mechanism for International Criminal Tribunals urged his swift transfer for trial in Rwanda.

In September, a Swedish court started trial proceedings against Claver Berinkindi, accused of being one of the leaders of attacks on a municipal building and school in Muyira during the genocide. He faces charges of murder, incitement to murder, attempted murder and abduction, and was previously found guilty in his absence by a Rwandan court.

A French court controversially dropped the case against genocide suspect Wenceslas Munyeshyaka in October, citing a lack of evidence. Wenceslas Munyeshyaka was a priest in the capital Kigali and was accused of taking part in killings and rapes during the genocide, as well as helping the Interahamwe militia to identify Tutsi to be killed and raped.

## REFUGEES

In April, President Kagame confirmed to media that Rwanda was in discussion with Israel to finalize a deal to receive failed Eritrean and Sudanese asylum-seekers who "voluntarily leave" Israel. The NGO International Refugee Rights Initiative reported in September that those sent to Rwanda had their travel documents taken away and were given the option of being "transferred" to Uganda within days of arriving or remaining in Rwanda undocumented. They were not given the opportunity to claim asylum in Rwanda.

At the end of the year, over 70,000 refugees were living in Rwanda after fleeing the crisis in neighbouring Burundi.

# SAUDI ARABIA

Kingdom of Saudi Arabia
Head of state and government: King Salman bin Abdul Aziz Al Saud (replaced King Abdullah bin Abdul Aziz Al Saud in January)

The government continued to severely restrict freedoms of expression, association and assembly. The authorities arrested, prosecuted and imprisoned human rights defenders and government critics, including under the 2014 anti-terror law, often after unfair trials. Some of those detained were prisoners of conscience. Torture and other ill-treatment of detainees remained common. Unfair trials continued before the Specialized Criminal Court (SCC), a special court for hearing terrorism-related cases, with some trials resulting in death sentences. Discrimination against the Shi'a minority remained entrenched; some Shi'a activists were on death row awaiting execution. Women faced discrimination in law and in practice and were inadequately protected against sexual and other violence. Thousands of migrants were summarily expelled, many to countries where they were at risk of serious human rights violations. The authorities used the death penalty extensively and carried out more than 150 executions.

## BACKGROUND

Crown Prince Salman became King on 23 January, following the death of King Abdullah. He appointed his nephew, Minister of the Interior Prince Mohamed bin Nayef, as Crown Prince, and his son, Prince Mohamed bin Salman, as Minister of Defence and second in line to the throne.

On 29 January, King Salman issued a royal pardon which the authorities said resulted in an unprecedented number of prisoner releases. It excluded those held for "crimes related to state security", although these are not defined or codified under Saudi Arabian law. No prisoners of conscience were among those pardoned.

In January, the flogging of blogger Raif Badawi provoked strong international condemnation and strained relations between Saudi Arabia and several European states. Sweden announced that it would not renew a deal to supply arms; in response, the government temporarily withdrew Saudi Arabia's ambassador to Sweden and ceased issuing business visas to Swedes.

The government faced further international criticism in September following news that the Supreme Court had upheld the death sentences of Ali Mohammed Baqir al-Nimr, nephew of a prominent Saudi Arabian Shi'a cleric who was also on death row, and two other activists, Dawood Hussein al-Marhoon and Abdullah Hasan al-Zaher. All three men were under 18 when they were arrested; they said they were tortured into "confessing".

Militants affiliated to the armed group Islamic State (IS) carried out bomb attacks that mostly targeted the minority Shi'a community. The deadliest attacks hit Shi'a mosques in the towns of al-Qudaih and al-Dammam on 22 and 29 May, killing at least 25 people and injuring several others.

In December, the Deputy Crown Prince announced that Saudi Arabia had formed an "Islamic anti-terror coalition", comprising 34 Muslim states but excluding others including Iran and Iraq, to combat "terrorist organizations".

## ARMED CONFLICT IN YEMEN

On 25 March, a Saudi Arabian-led coalition of nine states began a campaign of air strikes against the Huthi armed group which had gained control of large areas of Yemen, including the capital Sana'a, ousting the government, which relocated to Saudi Arabia. In the subsequent months, coalition aircraft and other forces carried out numerous attacks, killing and injuring thousands, many of them civilians. Some coalition air strikes violated international humanitarian law, possibly amounting to war crimes. The coalition also deployed ground troops in Yemen and mounted an air, land and sea

blockade that caused worsening humanitarian conditions for Yemen's civilians.

The US, UK and French governments signed agreements to supply arms worth billions of dollars to Saudi Arabia despite mounting evidence that the Saudi Arabia-led coalition had used arms of a similar nature to commit war crimes and other serious violations of international law in Yemen.

Huthi forces and their allies also committed violations of international humanitarian law, including possible war crimes, by repeatedly carrying out indiscriminate shelling into Najran and other civilian-populated areas of Saudi Arabia near its southern border with Yemen.

## FREEDOMS OF EXPRESSION, ASSOCIATION AND ASSEMBLY

The authorities continued to arrest, prosecute and imprison government critics, including bloggers and other online commentators, political activists, members of the Shi'a minority, and human rights activists and defenders, including women's rights defenders.

Blogger and prisoner of conscience Raif Badawi continued to serve a 10-year prison sentence following his conviction in 2014 for "insulting Islam" and violating the cybercrime law, including through the creation and management of the Free Saudi Liberal Network website. He was also sentenced to be flogged (see below).

Writer and government critic Dr Zuhair Kutbi was taken from his home in Mecca on 15 July by security officials, who beat him with rifle butts and detained him at three different locations before taking him to Mecca's General Prison. Three weeks before his arrest, Zuhair Kutbi had appeared on the *Fi al-Samim* TV talk show, where he criticized political repression in Saudi Arabia and called for reforms. The authorities ordered *Fi al-Samim* to be cancelled. In December, the SCC convicted him of "inciting public opinion", "sowing discord" and "reducing people's respect of the law" through his writings and talks, and sentenced him to four years in prison, followed by a five-year foreign travel ban. He was also fined and banned from writing for publication for 15 years.

The government did not permit the existence of political parties, trade unions or independent human rights groups, and the authorities continued to arrest, prosecute and imprison those who set up or participated in unlicensed organizations. In November, however, the cabinet approved a law of associations based partly on a draft approved by the Shura Council years earlier, but the government did not indicate when it will take effect. The authorities also continued to deny Amnesty International access to Saudi Arabia and took punitive measures against activists and family members of victims who contacted Amnesty International.

All public gatherings, including peaceful demonstrations, remained prohibited under an order issued by the Ministry of the Interior in 2011. Those who sought to defy the ban faced arrest, prosecution and imprisonment on charges such as "inciting people against the authorities". In March, the government warned that it would arrest and prosecute anyone who publicly criticized Saudi Arabia's military actions in Yemen; in November, the Ministry of Justice was reported to have said it would sue anyone who compared Saudi Arabia's justice system to that operated by IS.

## HUMAN RIGHTS DEFENDERS

The authorities continued to imprison human rights defenders, arresting and prosecuting them under anti-terrorism legislation and other laws. Those detained, on trial or serving prison sentences included members and activists of the Saudi Civil and Political Rights Association (ACPRA), a group founded in 2009, which the authorities never licensed and then banned in 2013. At the end of the year, seven members of ACPRA, which campaigned for the release or fair trial of long-term political detainees, were serving prison sentences of up to 15 years imposed on vague, overly broad charges. Two were free pending the outcome of their trial, one was still detained without any charge or trial,

and one had served his sentence but was yet to be released.

In January, the SCC appeal court in the capital Riyadh confirmed the 15-year prison sentence imposed on prominent lawyer and human rights defender Waleed Abu al-Khai, with the judge ordering that he serve the full 15-year term for refusing to apologize for his "offences". The court that first sentenced him had said he should serve only 10 years of his 15-year sentence.

In October, the SCC sentenced Dr Abdulrahman al-Hamid and Dr Abdulkareem al-Khoder, both founding members of ACPRA, to eight and 10-year prison terms respectively, followed by foreign travel bans, after convicting them on terrorism-related charges. A criminal court had previously sentenced Dr al-Khoder to eight years in prison, which an appeal court overturned before his case was referred to the SCC.

## COUNTER-TERROR AND SECURITY

The authorities used the 2014 anti-terrorism law to arrest and prosecute peaceful activists and human rights defenders, as well as people accused of violent opposition to the government. Waleed Abu al-Khair was the first human rights defender to receive a prison sentence under the law and to have it confirmed on appeal. Women's rights activists Loujain al-Hathloul and Maysaa al-Amoudi were charged with offences regulated by the law after they were arrested in late 2014 for defying the ban on women driving cars. They were detained for several weeks before their release on 12 February. It was unclear whether their trial would go ahead.

The authorities publicly deterred citizens from joining or contributing funds or other support to militant Sunni armed groups in Syria and Iraq, and arrested suspected members of armed groups. On 18 July, the Ministry of the Interior said that during "the past few weeks", the authorities had arrested 431 people suspected of belonging to IS but provided few details about any specific charges or offences or under what law they were detained.

## ARBITRARY ARRESTS AND DETENTIONS

Security authorities carried out arbitrary arrests and continued to hold detainees without charge or trial for long periods, with scores of people held for more than six months without being referred to a competent court, in breach of Saudi Arabia's Law of Criminal Procedures and its obligations under international law. Detainees were frequently held incommunicado during interrogation and denied access to lawyers, in violation of international fair trial standards.

## TORTURE AND OTHER ILL-TREATMENT

Torture and other ill-treatment remained common and widespread, according to former detainees, trial defendants and others. There was impunity for past cases. In a number of cases, courts did not exclude statements elicited by torture, ill-treatment or coercion and convicted defendants solely on the basis of pre-trial "confessions" without investigating their allegations that the confessions had been obtained through torture, in some cases sentencing the defendants to death.

Some prisoners sentenced on political grounds in previous years were reportedly ill-treated in prison. Imprisoned ACPRA activist Issa al-Nukheifi, sentenced to a three-year prison term in 2013, accused prison authorities of verbally abusing and subjecting him to frequent strip-searches, and of provoking and/or coercing other inmates to threaten and attack him.

In April, prisoner of conscience Waleed Abu al-Khair was assaulted in Riyadh's al-Ha'ir Prison by another inmate after he complained to prison authorities about poor conditions, including corruption and inadequate food within the prison. He lodged a formal complaint about the assault, after which guards raided his prison cell, damaging some of his belongings.

## DISCRIMINATION – SHI'A MINORITY

The Shi'a minority, who mostly live in Saudi Arabia's oil-rich Eastern Province, faced entrenched discrimination that limited their access to state services and employment. Shi'a leaders and activists faced arrest, imprisonment and in some cases the death penalty, following unfair trials.

In January, the SCC appeal court confirmed an eight-year prison term and subsequent 10-year foreign travel ban imposed in August 2014 on prominent Shi'a cleric Sheikh Tawfiq Jaber Ibrahim al-'Amr for delivering religious sermons and speeches deemed to incite sectarianism, defame the ruling system, ridicule religious leaders, show disobedience to the ruler, and advocate change.

In September, families of Ali Mohammed Baqir al-Nimr, Dawood Hussein al-Marhoon and Abdullah Hasan al-Zaher learned that both the SCC appeal court and the Supreme Court had upheld their death sentences. The three men were convicted of committing offences that included demonstrating against the government, possessing weapons and attacking the security forces, when they were under 18 years of age. They denied the charges and alleged that interrogators forced them to "confess" under torture; however, the trial court failed to investigate their allegations. Ali al-Nimr's uncle, Sheikh Nimr Baqir al-Nimr, a Shi'a cleric from al-Qatif and vocal critic of the government, and three other Shi'a activists, were also on death row.

The SCC continued to try other Shi'a activists for their alleged participation in protests in 2011 and 2012.

## WOMEN'S RIGHTS

Women and girls remained subject to discrimination in law and in practice. Women had subordinate status to men under the law, particularly in relation to family matters such as marriage, divorce, child custody and inheritance, and they were inadequately protected against sexual and other violence. Domestic violence remained endemic, despite a government awareness-raising campaign launched in 2013. A law criminalizing domestic violence which was adopted in 2013 remained unimplemented in practice.

In December, women were allowed to vote and to stand as candidates in municipal elections for the first time, although not to publicly campaign with male voters. Women were elected to 21 of the 2,106 directly elected municipal council seats.

## MIGRANTS' RIGHTS

The authorities continued to crack down on irregular migrants, arresting, detaining and deporting hundreds of thousands of foreign workers. In March, the authorities announced that they had arrested and deported 300,000 irregular migrants in the previous five months.

The authorities deported thousands of migrants to Somalia and other states where they were at risk of human rights violations, in contravention of the principle of *non-refoulement*, but ceased deportations to Yemen in March due to the armed conflict. Many migrants reported that prior to deportation they were packed into severely overcrowded makeshift detention facilities where they received little food and water and were abused by guards.

## CRUEL, INHUMAN OR DEGRADING PUNISHMENT

Courts continued to impose cruel and inhuman punishments, such as flogging, as discretionary additional punishments for many offences, including slander, insult and sexual harassment.

Blogger Raif Badawi received a 50-lash public flogging in Jeddah on 9 January, provoking an international outcry. In 2014 he had received a sentence of 1,000 lashes; the authorities did not subject him to further floggings in 2015.

In November, an appeal court confirmed the 2014 conviction of human rights defender Mikhlif bin Daham al-Shammari on charges that included "stirring public opinion by sitting with the Shi'a" and "violating instructions by the rulers by holding a private gathering and tweeting". The court confirmed his sentence of two years' imprisonment and a flogging of 200 lashes.

## DEATH PENALTY

Courts continued to impose death sentences for a range of crimes, including non-violent drugs offences, often after unfair trials in which they failed to adequately investigate defendants' claims that interrogators tortured, coerced or misled them into making false confessions in pre-trial detention.

In November, the General Court in Abha sentenced Palestinian artist and poet Ashraf Fayadh to death after convicting him of apostasy. Earlier, an appeal court had overturned his original sentence of four years' imprisonment and 800 lashes, imposed after he was convicted of breaching Article 6 of the cybercrime law.

The surge in executions that began in August 2014 continued throughout 2015. By the end of June, Saudi Arabia had executed at least 102 people, more than in the whole of 2014, and by the end of the year the total had risen to more than 150. Many executions were carried out for offences that did not meet the threshold of "most serious crimes" and should therefore not incur the death penalty according to international law. Many executions were carried out publicly by beheading.

# SENEGAL

**Republic of Senegal**
Head of state: **Macky Sall**
Head of government: **Mohammed Dionne**

**The authorities continued to restrict freedom of peaceful assembly and to use excessive force against protesters. Men and women faced arrest because of their real or perceived sexual orientation. Senegal came under international scrutiny for the unfair trial of Karim Wade. The conflict in Casamance continued at low intensity. Impunity was endemic for human rights violations committed by security forces. The trial of former Chadian President Hissène Habré opened at the Extraordinary African Chambers in Dakar, the capital, in July.**

## BACKGROUND

In April, the African Commission on Human and Peoples' Rights reviewed the human rights situation in Senegal. The Commission raised concerns, including on the authorities' failure to protect freedom of expression and on arbitrary arrests and detentions.[1]

Security forces arrested at least seven people, including two male imams and two women, on terrorism-related charges.

## EXCESSIVE USE OF FORCE

Security forces continued to use excessive force.

In July, Matar Ndiaye died after being shot in the leg during a police operation in Dakar. A policeman allegedly fired without warning at a group of men he was pursuing, and Matar Ndiaye was caught in the line of fire. The Criminal Investigation Division of the National Police was in charge of the subsequent investigation, raising concerns about its independence and impartiality.

## FREEDOM OF ASSEMBLY

Authorities continued to ban demonstrations organized by political parties and human rights defenders, and to prosecute peaceful demonstrators.

In September, the Regional Tribunal of Kolda sentenced 12 men to 21 days' imprisonment for taking part in an unauthorized assembly. About 100 people demonstrated peacefully in the commune of Diana Malary on 27 August to call on the authorities to supply electricity. The demonstration was dispersed with tear gas and shots in the air, leading to clashes between demonstrators and the gendarmerie.

## UNFAIR TRIALS

In March, the Court for the Repression of Illicit Acquisition of Wealth (CREI) sentenced Karim Wade, a former minister and son of former President Abdoulaye Wade, to six years' imprisonment and a fine of 138,239,086,396 CFA francs (€210,744,000) for illicit acquisition of wealth. Seven co-defendants were also found guilty of complicity for the same crime. The CREI provides no right to appeal, contrary to regional or international standards. In April, the UN Working Group on Arbitrary Detention found the pre-trial detention of Karim Wade to be arbitrary, including because of delays in court proceedings and differential treatment. In August, the Supreme Court upheld the convictions.

In February, the Dakar Assize Court sentenced two men to 20 years of forced labour in relation to the death of a young auxiliary police officer, Fodé Ndiaye, despite their statements being obtained under torture.

## INTERNAL ARMED CONFLICT

In April, the army exchanged fire with the Movement of Democratic Forces in the Casamance (MFDC) in the department of Oussouye, with the media reporting casualties on both sides. In July, an unidentified armed group abducted 12 men in the region of Sédhiou and released them after four days, in exchange for a ransom.

Civilians continued to suffer from the impact of ongoing conflict. At least one man was killed by a landmine close to the Basse Casamance National Park.

## IMPUNITY

Although the authorities claimed they were investigating killings by law enforcement officers in the context of demonstrations, or torture and other ill-treatment, few investigations were completed or alleged perpetrators tried. Of the 27 cases of torture documented by Amnesty International since 2007, only six led to prosecutions resulting in a sentence, with light sentences being handed down each time. Of the seven cases of people killed by law enforcement agencies during demonstrations, none led to successful prosecutions.

In January, the Regional Tribunal of Kolda found two policemen guilty of acts of violence and assault on Dominique Lopy, who died in custody in 2007. The tribunal handed down a sentence of six months' imprisonment and ordered the policemen to pay 100,000 CFA francs (€152) in damages to his family.

## RIGHTS OF LESBIAN, GAY, BISEXUAL, TRANSGENDER AND INTERSEX PEOPLE

At least 22 people, including three women, were arrested in relation to their perceived sexual orientation. In August, the Tribunal of Dakar convicted seven men of committing "acts against nature" and sentenced them to six months' imprisonment and 18-month suspended sentences. They were arrested in July after the police raided an apartment without presenting a warrant. Several newspapers revealed the men's identities and published homophobic and defamatory remarks. Six of them were transferred to a prison in Diourbel, far from their families and their support networks providing them with food and medicine.

In July, in a separate case, another man was sentenced to six months' imprisonment using the same law. Three women were also arrested in Grand Yoff on 25 November.

On 24 December, the police arrested 11 men in Kaolack, who were detained for five days and subjected to ill-treatment, including insults and beatings, before being released.

## INTERNATIONAL JUSTICE

The trial against former Chadian President Hissène Habré opened in July. He was charged with crimes against humanity, torture and war crimes committed during his tenure between 1982 and 1990. This was the first time a court in an African state had tried the former leader of another state (see Chad entry).

---

1. Senegal: Failing to live up to its promises : Recommendations on the eve of the African Commission on Human and People's Rights' Review of Senegal (AFR 49/1464/2015)

# SERBIA

Republic of Serbia, including Kosovo
Head of state: Tomislav Nikolić
Head of government: Aleksandar Vučić

---

Over 600,000 refugees and migrants travelled through Serbia on their way to the EU. Prosecutions of war crimes continued to be slow. In Kosovo, opposition parties delayed the establishment of a Special War Crimes Court and the implementation of an EU-brokered agreement with Serbia.

## BACKGROUND

Although Serbia's formal recognition of Kosovo was not explicitly required by the European Commission for accession to the EU, the opening of negotiations was delayed by slow progress in the implementation of the EU-facilitated "normalization agreement" between Serbia and Kosovo. Accession talks formally opened in December with chapter 35, on the formalization of relations with Kosovo.

## CRIMES UNDER INTERNATIONAL LAW

Few proceedings were concluded at the Special War Crimes Court in Belgrade, the capital. Seven defendants were acquitted of rape as a war crime in Bijelina (one defendant) and Skočić (six defendants), in Bosnia and Herzegovina, following appeals. The Office of the War Crimes Prosecutor issued only three indictments; in September, eight former Bosnian Serb police officers were indicted for war crimes (rather than genocide) for their part in the murder of over 1,000 Bosniak civilians in Kravica, Srebrenica, in July 1995. Another 23 cases – involving over 200 suspects – remained under investigation. A draft war crimes strategy to address the backlog of cases was published in December.

On 16 December, proceedings were reopened against former Serbian state security officers Jovica Stanišić and Franko Simatović, after the Appeals Chamber of the International Criminal Tribunal for the former

Yugoslavia had overturned their 2013 acquittal. They were both accused of being part of a criminal enterprise which aimed to forcibly and permanently remove non-Serbs from areas of Croatia and Bosnia and Herzegovina in 1991-1995.

## ENFORCED DISAPPEARANCES

In February, the UN Committee on Enforced Disappearances urged Serbia to bring to justice all those – including senior officials – suspected of criminal responsibility for enforced disappearances during the 1990s armed conflicts, and to guarantee reparation and legal status to relatives of the disappeared. In November, a proposed bill on the rights of war veterans and civilian victims of war failed to recognize the right to reparation for victims of enforced disappearance and war crimes of sexual violence; a December amendment was not made public.

In March, five suspects were indicted for the abduction of 20 passengers from a train at Štrpci station in 1993; proceedings against 10 other suspects continued in Bosnia and Herzegovina. Those suspected of the disappearance of the Bytyqi brothers in 1999 remained at large, despite promises made to their relatives by the War Crimes Prosecutor and the Prime Minister.

## REFUGEES, ASYLUM-SEEKERS AND MIGRANTS

Over 600,000 refugees and migrants travelled through Serbia, the majority of whom aimed to seek asylum in the EU. Despite some improvements in implementing the Asylum Law, the authorities failed to provide effective access to international protection. Of 485,169 registrations, only 656 applications for asylum were submitted, and mostly discontinued; of 81 refugees interviewed by the end of November, 16 were granted refugee status and 14 subsidiary protection. In July, as thousands of refugees entered the country daily, a registration centre was opened at Preševo, near the Macedonian border. Reception conditions were inadequate for the numbers arriving, and insufficient care was provided to vulnerable individuals. Most refugees travelled directly to the Hungarian border until September, when Hungary introduced restrictions on asylum for those entering from Serbia, which it considered a safe country of transit. Refugees then headed for the EU through Croatia. Police continued to ill-treat and financially exploit refugees and migrants. In November, the authorities allowed only Afghan, Iraqi and Syrian nationals to enter the country; others arbitrarily identified as economic migrants were denied entry.

## FREEDOM OF EXPRESSION

Thirty-four independent journalists were attacked or received threats which were not effectively investigated. The government interfered in media freedom through selective media subsidies and advertising. In November, the Prime Minister accused three investigative media outlets of working for foreign governments to destabilize the country.

Proceedings continued against Radomir Marković, former head of state security, and three former security service officers for the murder in April 1999 of journalist Slavko Ćuruvija.

Ljubiša Diković, Chief of Military Staff, sued Natasa Kandić, former executive director of the NGO Humanitarian Law Center, for defamation after the NGO published evidence in 2012 of war crimes in Kosovo, allegedly committed by personnel under Ljubiša Diković's command.

## FREEDOM OF ASSEMBLY

A new Law on Public Gatherings had not been adopted by October, when an April decision by the Constitutional Court that the previous Law was unconstitutional entered into force. Consequently, assemblies could not take place, nor could they be prohibited.

## DISCRIMINATION – ROMA

In July, the forced eviction of Roma from the Grmeč settlement in Belgrade was stopped after an application for interim measures was made to the European Court of Human Rights. A draft law prohibiting forced evictions from informal settlements, which broadly met international standards, was proposed in November.

Roma households that were forcibly evicted from Belvil and other informal settlements in 2012 were resettled in new apartments in January, July and September. Twenty-seven apartments were funded by the European Commission and 50 by the European Investment Bank; one resettlement location was racially segregated. Two families were resettled to village houses. Concerns remained about access to employment. No housing solutions were identified for the resettlement of 51 families, who mostly continued to live in containers.

In July, the German government announced plans for the deportation of 90,000 Serbian people whose asylum application had been rejected or who had an irregular status, 90% of whom were Roma.

## RIGHTS OF LESBIAN, GAY, BISEXUAL, TRANSGENDER AND INTERSEX PEOPLE

The Belgrade Pride took place without incident in September; the first Trans Pride was held on the same day. A week later, three members of a lesbian football team and a campaigner against homophobia in sport were violently assaulted by men believed to be football fans. Hate crimes against LGBTI people were seldom effectively investigated, and legislation on hate crime was not implemented.

## KOSOVO

EU-brokered talks between Isa Mustafa, Prime Minister of Kosovo, and the Serbian Prime Minister concluded in August with agreements, including on the creation of an Association of Serbian Municipalities, providing some autonomy for Kosovo Serbs. After vociferous opposition led by the Vetëvendosje party, including the discharge of tear gas in the Assembly, the government suspended the agreement in October.

Following a request by Kosovo President Atifete Jahjag , the Constitutional Court ruled in December that the agreement was constitutional. In the interim, opposition MPs continued to disrupt the Assembly. Mass protests followed the first arrest of an opposition MP for using tear gas. In November, at least 50 activists were injured when Kosovo police used excessive force upon entering the Vetëvendosje offices to arrest party leader Albin Kurti.

Inter-ethnic tensions were also heightened by Kosovo's unsuccessful application for UNESCO membership (and thus the custody of Serbian cultural monuments).

A Stabilization and Association Agreement signed with the European Commission in October paved the way for Kosovo's EU membership, but Kosovo was again denied visa liberalization.

### Crimes under international law

Measures to establish a special court to prosecute former members of the Kosovo Liberation Army (KLA) were repeatedly delayed in the Kosovo Assembly. The measures followed an EU-led investigation into the abduction and transfer of Kosovo Serbs and other prisoners to Albania in 1999, where they were subsequently tortured and murdered. Under international pressure, legislation establishing the special court was finally approved in August. Kosovo as well as the host country, the Netherlands, had yet to complete the remaining agreements for the practical establishment of the court.

In May, two former members of the KLA "Drenica group" were convicted of war crimes against the civilian population, including murder and torture respectively. Three other members were convicted of torture, and six of beating prisoners at the Likovc/Likovac detention centre in 1998-1999.

Proceedings continued against a Kosovo Serb politician, Oliver Ivanović, indicted for ordering the murder of ethnic Albanians in Mitrovica/Mitrovicë in April 1999 and inciting unrest in February 2000, when 10 Albanians were killed.

The National Council for Survivors of Wartime Sexual Violence, led by President Jahjaga, made progress towards establishing a verification commission to process reparation claims. In November, an action plan to ensure their access to justice was finalized; in December, a regulation on victims of sexual violence in conflict was adopted.

**Enforced disappearances**

1,650 people remained missing in the aftermath of the armed conflict; no further grave sites were identified in Serbia or Kosovo despite exhumations at potential mass graves. In Krushe e Vogel, where 68 men were missing, the EU Rule of Law Mission in Kosovo exhumed bodies – believed to have been misidentified – from the cemetery, without adequately notifying the men's relatives.

The UN Interim Administration Mission in Kosovo (UNMIK) failed to provide reparation to the families of missing Kosovo Serbs, whose abductions had not been effectively investigated by UNMIK police. The EU-led police and justice mission, having failed to investigate these and other cases, proposed to transfer them to the Kosovo authorities.

**Inter-ethnic violence**

In January, 80 people, including 50 police officers, were injured in protests calling for the dismissal of Aleksandar Jablanović, Minister of Labour and Social Welfare. He had called ethnic Albanians "savages" for stopping a bus carrying Kosovo Serbs to a monastery on Orthodox Christmas.

Kosovo Serbs were subject to threats, robberies and attacks, including attempted arson, in Goraždevac/Gorazhdec and Klina/Klinë in May and in July, when the vehicles of Serbian families were shot at. In December, the property of two families in Goraždevac/Gorazhdec was damaged by gunfire.

**Refugees and internally displaced people**

Between January and March, at least 48,900

Kosovo citizens applied for asylum in the EU. In Hungary, over 99% of applicants were refused asylum in accelerated procedures and deported. In 29,801 asylum decisions in Germany, which deemed Kosovo a safe country of origin, only 0.4% of Kosovo citizens were granted asylum. Reintegration measures for those deported to Kosovo remained grossly inadequate.

By the end of November, 16,867 people – predominantly Albanians and Kosovo Serbs – remained displaced after the armed conflict, and only 741 members of minority communities had voluntarily returned to Kosovo.

**Discrimination**

Roma, Ashkali and Egyptians continued to suffer institutional discrimination, including in access to social and economic rights. An estimated 7,500-10,000 Roma, Ashkali and Egyptians made up a disproportionate share of those who left Kosovo to seek asylum in the EU. The authorities failed to investigate hate crimes, including physical attacks against LGBTI individuals.

**Freedom of expression**

Government interference in freedom of the media continued. By September, 22 journalists had been threatened or attacked. The Association of Journalists of Kosovo, supported by the OSCE, established a confidential free hotline for journalists to report attacks.

# SIERRA LEONE

Republic of Sierra Leone
Head of state and government: **Ernest Bai Koroma**

**At least 3,955 people died during the Ebola epidemic, during which exploitation and violence against women and girls increased. State of emergency powers were used to curtail the right to peaceful assembly of political opponents. Police accountability was limited. Visibly pregnant girls were**

discriminated against and prevented from attending school and taking their exams. Criminal libel and other laws were used to stifle freedom of expression.

## BACKGROUND

An Ebola epidemic began in May 2014 and was declared over on 7 November 2015. A review of Sierra Leone's Constitution was launched on 30 July 2013 and is still ongoing, with progress delayed due to the Ebola crisis.

## EBOLA OUTBREAK

Sierra Leone was severely affected by the Ebola epidemic that spread across West Africa starting in March 2014, with at least 14,122 confirmed cases. More than 300 health workers were infected and the epidemic weakened an already fragile health care system, particularly for provision of maternal care. Concerns were raised about the lack of safe equipment and the working conditions for health workers. The state of emergency was extended in August 2015 for a year; some restrictions, such as the ban on public gatherings, were lifted. At the end of the outbreak, the President stated he would discuss ending the state of emergency with Parliament.

## ARBITRARY DETENTIONS

Numerous people were arbitrarily detained and prosecuted under the Public Emergency Regulations 2014 and by-laws, such as for public gathering or trading after hours. Pre-trial detention regularly exceeded constitutional time limits and a high number of people remained in pre-trial detention, including juveniles.

On 21 April, 11 men were charged under the Public Order Act 1965 and Public Emergency Regulations 2014, in connection with a riot about a suspected Ebola patient. Six of the men were arrested in October 2014, and the remaining five in February and March 2015, under an executive order issued by President Koroma. The detainees had no warrants or documentation supporting their detention; they were discharged and released in December.[1]

On 6 August, 13 members of the armed forces were acquitted after a two-year detention, including eight months incommunicado, for plotting to mutiny at the Tekoh barracks in Makeni.

## POLICE AND SECURITY FORCES

Police accountability remained weak. Despite the recommendations of three independent inquiries into allegations of unlawful killings since 2007, no police officer was prosecuted. There was minimal investigation into two other allegations of unlawful killings by the police in Kono in 2014. There were also allegations of unlawful killings in the capital, Freetown, in 2015, where in one case police officers were dismissed following an internal disciplinary proceeding and charged with manslaughter. In October, an Independent Police Complaints Board was launched.

## WOMEN'S AND GIRLS' RIGHTS

Exploitation and violence against women and girls increased during the Ebola outbreak. The Sexual Offences Act 2012 was still not implemented properly by the police. There was limited access to legal aid, shelter and rehabilitation services for victims of sexual and domestic violence. Health care services for victims of sexual violence were also inaccessible due to legal and cost barriers.

The Gender Equality Bill, which provides for a minimum 30% representation of women in Parliament and local councils and ministries, departments and agencies, was still not enacted.

In July 2015, Sierra Leone ratified the Protocol to the African Charter on Human and Peoples' Rights on the Rights of Women in Africa. Steps need to be taken to domesticate its provisions.

In December, Parliament passed the Safe Abortion Act. However, the President sent it back to Parliament in January 2016 after concerns by religious leaders.

## Education

In March, the Ministry of Education banned pregnant girls from attending school and sitting exams, in violation of their rights to education and non-discrimination. The policy seemed to be based on discriminatory views and negative stereotypes of pregnant girls and stigmatized an estimated 10,000 girls. The ban was enforced in some schools through humiliating and degrading treatment of girls.[2]

## FREEDOMS OF EXPRESSION AND ASSEMBLY

In February 2015, Mamoud Tim Kargbo was charged with five counts of defamatory libel under the Public Order Act 1965 for forwarding a WhatsApp message he received, said to be defamatory to the President. He was detained for 52 days, released on bail during the trial, and eventually discharged on 28 July.

There were disproportionate restrictions on freedoms of expression and assembly during the state of emergency. Following the removal of former Vice President Samuel Sam-Sumana on 18 March 2015, there was an increase in arrests of opposition members, bans on peaceful protests and a crackdown on dissent.[3]

On 27 April, 15 members of Sierra Leone People's Party (SLPP), the main opposition party, and a senior officer from the Human Rights Commission were arrested in the town of Kenema following a protest at the SLPP office. They are currently on trial. There are concerns about excessive use of force during arrests by the police.

In August, *Monologue*, a radio programme hosted by journalist David Tam Baryoh, was suspended by the Independent Media Commission (IMC) due to allegations that the show infringed national security, and incited violence and public disorder. In October, he was fined 500,000 SLL (around US$100), and is challenging the decision in court.

In December, Jonathan Leigh, managing editor of the *Independent Observer*, was arrested on accusations of publishing false information about reports of political violence

ahead of a by-election. He was granted bail after four days in detention; his trial was ongoing at the end of the year.

---

1. Sierra Leone must release eight people arbitrarily detained after Ebola riot (Press release, 29 January); Two women released, 11 men charged (AFR 51/1603/2015)

2. Shamed and blamed: Pregnant girls' rights at risk in Sierra Leone (AFR 51/2695/2015)

3. Sierra Leone: Ebola regulations and other laws must not be used to curtail freedom of expression and assembly (News story, 4 May)

# SINGAPORE

**Republic of Singapore**
Head of state: **Tony Tan Keng Yam**
Head of government: **Lee Hsien Loong**

---

The People's Action Party, whose founder, former Prime Minister Lee Kuan Yew, died in March, continued to penalize government critics for exercising their right to freedom of expression. The media and human rights defenders were tightly controlled through revocation of licences and criminal charges. Judicial caning and the death penalty were retained.

## FREEDOM OF EXPRESSION

Amos Yee, a 16-year-old blogger, was sentenced to four weeks' imprisonment for "uttering words with deliberate intent to wound the religious or racial feelings of any person" and "transmitting obscene materials", after he uploaded a video and cartoon criticizing Lee Kuan Yew online.[1] The UN Office of the High Commissioner for Human Rights urged Singapore to consider the case in light of its obligations under the UN Convention on the Rights of the Child.

In May, the Media Development Authority suspended the licences permitting editors Yang Kaiheng and Ai Takagi to operate the news website, social media accounts and mobile applications of *The Real Singapore* newspaper after it published articles that allegedly "sought to incite anti-foreigner sentiments in Singapore". The two faced seven counts of sedition and a charge under the Penal Code for failure to produce documents required by the police.

Human rights lawyer M Ravi, who handled cases involving the death penalty; freedom of expression; lesbian, gay, bisexual, transgender and intersex (LGBTI) workers' rights; and the rights of foreign workers facing deportation, was temporarily suspended from his practice in February, ostensibly on health grounds. There were concerns this may have been politically motivated.

## DEATH PENALTY

Death sentences continued to be imposed, including as mandatory punishment for murder and drug trafficking. Muhammad bin Kadar was executed at Changi Prison Complex in April. He had been found guilty of "intentional murder", which continues to carry a mandatory death sentence. Reports indicated that a further two people were executed during the year, but there was no official announcement. In November, Malaysian national Kho Jabing, convicted of murder, was granted a stay of execution pending a review of his case. At least 26 people remained on death row at the end of the year.[2]

## CRUEL, INHUMAN OR DEGRADING PUNISHMENT

Caning continued to be used as punishment for a range of crimes by males aged 16 to 50. It remained mandatory for cases such as drug trafficking and immigration offences. The Supreme Court in March ruled that caning was not unconstitutional.

## COUNTER-TERROR AND SECURITY

M Arifl Azim Putra Norja'i and an unnamed 17-year-old, both deemed to have "self-radicalized", were arrested on terrorism-related charges under the Internal Security Act. M Arifil Azim Putra Norja'i was detained administratively for planning to join the armed group Islamic State (IS) abroad. The 17-year-old was arrested and detained in early May,

but was released from custody in June with a two-year Restriction Order.

1. Singapore: Amos Yee sentence a dark day for freedom of expression (News story, 6 July)
2. Singapore: Submission to the UN Universal Periodic Review 24th session, January-February 2016 (ASA 36/2664/2015)

# SLOVAKIA

Slovak Republic
Head of state: **Andrej Kiska**
Head of government: **Robert Fico**

**Discrimination against Roma remained widespread. The European Commission initiated infringement proceedings against Slovakia for the discrimination against Romani pupils in education. Anti-immigration rallies were held across the country, and Slovakia voted against mandatory relocation quotas of refugees from other EU member states.**

## DISCRIMINATION – ROMA

### Police and security forces

Slovak NGOs reported new cases of excessive use of force by police against Roma, and raised concerns over the lack of effective investigation in past cases. In September, the UN Committee against Torture criticized the absence of an independent mechanism to investigate such reports as the existing body – the Department of Control and Inspection Service (SKIS) – remained subordinate to the Ministry of Interior.

The investigation by the SKIS into the alleged excessive use of force by police during an operation in the Roma settlement of Vrbnica on 2 April was still pending.[1] Nineteen Romani residents reported injuries and damages to their houses, and 17 criminal complaints were filed against police. No police misconduct was acknowledged by the authorities. The Public Defender of Rights criticized the police operation and called on the Public Prosecutor and the Ministry of Interior to ensure that the allegations were adequately investigated, including by unearthing any potential racial motivation.

The UN Committee against Torture noted that no charges were brought against the police officers who participated in an operation in the Roma settlement of Moldava nad Bodvou on 19 June 2013 that resulted in injuries to over 30 individuals, including children.

The Committee also expressed concerns over the decision of the District Court to acquit 10 policemen accused of ill-treatment of six Roma boys at a police station in 2009 in Košice. The Public Prosecutor appealed against the acquittal; the case remained pending at the end of the year.[2]

### Right to education
Romani children continued to be over-represented in "special" schools and classes for children with mild mental disabilities, and placed in ethnically segregated mainstream schools and classes. The segregation of Romani children was reinforced by the continued investment in so-called "container schools" in Romani settlements, instead of ensuring the integration of Romani students in ethnically mixed mainstream schools.[3] In its Annual Report, the Public Defender of Rights criticized the diagnostic procedures for placements in "special" schools and classes, calling them discriminatory.

In April, the European Commission initiated infringement proceedings against Slovakia for breaching the prohibition of discrimination set out in the EU Racial Equality Directive in relation to the access to education of Roma.[4] The authorities justified the disproportionate number of Roma in "special" schools and classes by alleging there is a higher prevalence of genetically determined disorders among Slovak Roma due to inbreeding.[5] The government presented new measures to the European Commission in August, aimed at reducing discriminatory bias in diagnostic procedures.

In June, Parliament adopted an

amendment to the Schools Act that contains provisions on the education of children from socially disadvantaged backgrounds. While the amendment prioritizes integration in mainstream schools and provides financial incentives for schools educating pupils from disadvantaged backgrounds, it does not contain any provisions for eliminating ethnic discrimination against Roma.

### Enforced sterilization of Romani women
The UN Committee against Torture called for an independent and effective investigation into all cases of forced sterilization of Romani women and girls performed in the early 2000s, and for the introduction of an adequate compensation scheme for those harmed.

## RIGHTS OF LESBIAN, GAY, BISEXUAL, TRANSGENDER AND INTERSEX PEOPLE
In February, Slovakia held a referendum on a proposal to define marriage exclusively as a union between a man and a woman, to ban adoption by same-sex couples and to require parental consent for the participation of children in classes on sexual education and euthanasia.[6] The referendum was void as it did not meet the 50% turnout requirement. Slovakia does not legally recognize same-sex partnerships and the Constitution already defines marriage exclusively as a union between a man and a woman.

## COUNTER-TERROR
In June, riot police units raided the apartment of a Tunisian national and former detainee at Guantánamo Bay who resettled to Slovakia in November 2014. The SKIS reportedly feared for his life as he had not been seen or heard of for two days. Following the intervention with rubber bullets, he required medical attention for injuries which left him unable to work for seven days. The SKIS dismissed his complaint on the grounds that the raid was lawful and the coercive measures proportionate, and alleged that he had reacted aggressively.

In December, Parliament rushed through

the adoption of new anti-terrorism measures, including the extension of the maximum period of pre-charge detention to 96 hours for individuals suspected of terrorism-related offences.

## REFUGEES AND ASYLUM-SEEKERS

Anti-immigration rallies were held across Slovakia. In June, at least 140 people were arrested after police clashed with demonstrators reportedly throwing stones and smoke bombs at a rally in Bratislava. The rally was attended by thousands of people protesting against mandatory EU quotas for the relocation of refugees from other EU member states.

In August, the Minister of Interior announced that the country would admit 200 Syrian refugees, on condition that they be Christians. Slovakia voted against mandatory relocation quotas at a meeting of EU Interior Ministers in September, but was obliged to receive 802 refugees over a period of two years following the proposal's adoption by qualified majority.

1. Slovakia must urgently investigate allegations of arbitrary use of force by police against Roma in the village of Vrbnica (EUR 72/1403/2015)
2. Slovakia: Justice still pending for Romani boys abused at police station in 2009 (EUR 72/1158/2015)
3. Slovakia's "container schools" worsen segregation of Roma children from society (News story, 13 March)
4. Slovakia is the second member state to be subjected to an infringement procedure for breach of EU Anti-Discrimination Law (EUR 72/1777/2015)
5. Slovakia: Racist stereotyping should not determine education policy – International NGOs criticize Slovak Government (EUR 72/1834/2015)
6. Slovakia: Referendum on marriage panders to homophobic discrimination (News story, 2 February)

# SLOVENIA

**Republic of Slovenia**
Head of state: **Borut Pahor**
Head of government: **Miro Cerar**

**Slovenia struggled to provide adequate reception conditions to the large number of refugees and migrants that arrived in the country. The authorities failed to restore the status of the "erased" or provide adequate redress, perpetuating the long-standing violations of their rights. Discrimination against Roma remained widespread.**

## REFUGEES AND ASYLUM-SEEKERS

More than 375,000 refugees and migrants arrived in Slovenia through the Western Balkans route, a 250-fold increase on the previous year. From September, hundreds of people were detained for entering the country irregularly, among them refugees from Syria. Others were transported to reception and accommodation centres, some of which did not provide adequate shelter and care. The overwhelming majority were able to transit through the country and exit towards Austria; 141 people submitted an asylum application. At least 20 refugees and migrants were expelled to Croatia, which refused the attempted return of hundreds of others.

## DISCRIMINATION

Slovenia's anti-discrimination framework remained flawed as institutions created to combat discrimination and consider complaints – such as the Human Rights Ombudsman and the Advocate of the Principle of Equality – continued to be undermined by weak mandates and inadequate resources.

### The "erased"

The authorities failed to provide redress for the human rights violations committed against former permanent residents of Slovenia originating from other former Yugoslav republics, known as the "erased", whose legal status was unlawfully revoked in 1992.

No new options had been offered to the remaining "erased" to restore their legal status and related rights since the expiry of the Legal Status Act in 2013. Less than half of the 25,671 "erased" persons had their status restored.

In June, the Constitutional Court ruled that compensation claims made by "erased" persons should not be subject to a statute of limitations, and courts should take into account the claimants' special status.

### Roma

The majority of Slovenia's 10,000 Roma continued to face discrimination and social exclusion. Many lived in isolated, segregated settlements, lacking security of tenure and access to basic services such as water, electricity, sanitation and public transport. Discrimination prevented Roma families from accessing housing outside Roma-populated areas.

Over 200 Roma living in the Dobruška vas settlement in the Škocjan Municipality remained without security of tenure. Following the relocation of two Roma families in 2014, no new proposals were presented to residents at risk of forced eviction as a result of redevelopment plans. In December, one individual took the proceeding regarding his house to the Administrative court. Residents of the informal settlements in Loke and Rimš in the neighbouring Municipality of Krško faced similar risks in the face of redevelopment plans that failed to put in place safeguards against forced eviction or provide adequate alternative housing.

The government announced in August that it would prepare changes to the Roma Community Act. However, a draft submitted by the opposition was rejected by Parliament in November without an alternative proposal.

### RIGHTS OF LESBIAN, GAY, BISEXUAL, TRANSGENDER AND INTERSEX PEOPLE

The law on marriage and family relations was amended in March in order to legalize same-sex marriage and ensure equal rights to married couples, including to adoption. A referendum challenging the amendments was called by opponents and subsequently referred to the Constitutional Court, preventing the amendments from entering into force. The Constitutional Court ruled in October that the referendum could be held. On 20 December, 36% of the voting-age population cast their vote and rejected the marriage equality law by majority, perpetuating the unequal treatment of same-sex couples.

### FREEDOM OF EXPRESSION – JOURNALISTS

In April, the prosecution withdrew charges against journalist Anuška Delić, who had been indicted for publishing classified information of public interest, although it maintained that she acted wrongfully. Three other journalists remained under investigation for similar alleged crimes but proceedings were halted before charges were filed. The Criminal Code was amended in July to add a public interest defence for the publication of state secrets.

# SOMALIA

**Federal Republic of Somalia**
Head of state: **Hassan Sheikh Mohamud**
Head of government: **Omar Abdirashid Ali Sharmarke (replaced Abdiweli Sheikh Ahmed in December 2014)**
Head of Somaliland Republic: **Ahmed Mohamed Mahamoud Silyano**

**Armed conflict continued between Somali Federal Government (SFG) forces, African Union Mission in Somalia (AMISOM) peacekeepers and the armed group al-Shabaab in central and southern Somalia. SFG and AMISOM forces expanded the areas under their control by pushing al-Shabaab out of key towns in the South-West and Jubbaland regions. Over 500 people were killed or injured by armed conflict and generalized violence, and at least 50,000 people were displaced. All parties to the**

conflict were responsible for crimes under international law and human rights violations, which remained unpunished. Armed groups continued to conscript children, and abduct, torture and unlawfully kill civilians. Rape and other forms of sexual violence were widespread. Continued conflict, insecurity and restrictions imposed by the warring parties hampered aid agencies' access to some regions. Three journalists were killed; others were attacked, harassed or fined heavy penalties in courts.

## BACKGROUND

The SFG and AMISOM remained in control of Mogadishu, the capital, and expanded areas under their control by establishing federal administrations in the Galmudug, South-West and Jubbaland States. A joint offensive by AMISOM and the Somali National Armed Forces (SNAF) pushed al-Shabaab out of towns in the Hiraan, Bay, Bakool, Gedo and Lower Shabelle regions, although the armed group maintained control of many rural areas. The offensive displaced more people, while armed clashes and al-Shabaab attacks against civilians continued, particularly in villages with changing control.

International support for government security forces, allied militias and AMISOM continued. The humanitarian situation remained dire: by 9 October, over 3.2 million people were in need of assistance, and over 855,000 were food insecure. Among the most vulnerable were internally displaced persons (IDPs), who comprised 76% of those facing food insecurity.

In August, the country faced a political crisis after MPs submitted a motion of no confidence in President Hassan Sheikh Mohamud. In July, the Speaker of the Federal Parliament, Mohamed Osman Jawari, announced that the 2016 elections would not be held by universal suffrage, although this had been enshrined in the New Deal Compact for Somalia. Opposition MPs protested the decision as a ploy to extend the President's term. The human rights monitoring and reporting mandate within the

UN Assistance Mission in Somalia (UNSOM) was extended by the UN Security Council until 30 March 2016.

Al-Shabaab faced internal fissures over whether to remain aligned with al-Qa'ida or to align with the armed group Islamic State (IS). The situation remained tense in the town of Jilib, 97km north of Kismayo, after al-Shabaab deputy leader Mahad Karate pressured the leader, Abu Ubaidah, to switch allegiance to IS. In October, al-Shabaab leaders leaning towards al-Qa'ida arrested 30 people in Jubbaland who were presumed to be aligned with IS.

## ABUSES BY GOVERNMENT FORCES AND ARMED GROUPS

### Indiscriminate attacks

Civilians continued to be indiscriminately killed and wounded in crossfire during armed clashes, whether by suicide attacks, improvised explosive devices (IEDs) or grenade attacks. Al-Shabaab retained the ability to stage lethal attacks in the most heavily guarded parts of Mogadishu and other towns, killing or injuring hundreds of civilians. High-profile targets remained vulnerable to such attacks. In September, a car explosion at the gate of the presidential palace killed at least six people. In February, al-Shabaab carried out a mortar attack on the presidential palace. In July, a suicide attack at the Jazeera Hotel, which houses several embassies, killed at least 10 people. The number of civilians killed in various attacks was difficult to establish due to the absence of a reliable civilian casualty tracking system. The government and AMISOM offensive resulted in abuses by all parties to the conflict.

### Direct targeting of civilians

Civilians remained at risk of being directly targeted in attacks. In July, reports indicated that AMISOM had directly targeted civilians and killed at least 10 people in Marka. In August, AMISOM revised the figure to seven people, issued an apology and announced that three soldiers had been charged with the killings. Extrajudicial killings, extortion, arbitrary arrests, rape and other forms of gender-based violence continued to be carried out by government forces and aligned militia, partly as a result of poor discipline and weak command control. On 20 August, a SNAF soldier shot and wounded a mentally ill person in the town of Baidoa, after an argument. In September, Jubbaland soldiers executed at least four people, including a woman, near the town of Doolow, Gedo, suspecting that they were al-Shabaab militants. Al-Shabaab continued to torture and extrajudicially kill people they accused of spying or of not conforming to their interpretation of Islamic law. The group carried out public killings and punishments such as stoning to death, amputations and floggings, particularly in areas where AMISOM had withdrawn. On 23 April, al-Shabaab killed a man by firing squad in the town of Jamame, Lower Juba, for "insulting" the Prophet Muhammad. On 25 July, al-Shabaab killed MP Abdulahi Hussein Mohamud and his guard in Mogadishu by spraying their car with gunfire. On 6 September, al-Shabaab beheaded a man in Qahira village, near the Toosweyne settlement, Bay, after accusing him of spying for Ethiopian peacekeepers. On 1 October, al-Shabaab militants shot and killed several people in the village of Kunyabarow, near the town of Barawe in Lower Shabelle, for refusing to obey their orders.

## CHILD SOLDIERS

Children continued to suffer abuses by all parties to the armed conflict. As of 5 June, the UN documented 819 cases of recruitment and use of child soldiers by al-Shabaab, the national army and allied militia, Ahla Sunna W'Jama'a, and other armed groups. Somalia ratified the UN Convention on the Rights of the Child on 1 October, with the reservation that it did not consider itself bound by Articles 14, 20, 21 of the Convention and any other of its provisions that are contrary to the general principles of Islamic Sharia. The federal government did not implement the two Action Plans it signed in 2012 to end the recruitment and use of child soldiers, as well as the killing and maiming of children.

## INTERNALLY DISPLACED PEOPLE, REFUGEES AND ASYLUM-SEEKERS

More than 1.3 million Somalis were internally displaced in 2015. The SNAF and AMISOM offensive disrupted trade routes. Similarly, al-Shabaab blocked supply routes after being pushed out of towns by AMISOM, disrupting humanitarian access. Continued conflict and El Niño rains starting in October threatened to further negatively impact the humanitarian situation.

In January and February, state security forces evicted over 25,700 people without due process from public and private land in Mogadishu. They evicted an additional 21,000 in March. The majority of those who were evicted moved to the outskirts of Mogadishu, particularly to the Sarakusta and Tabelaha areas, in deplorable living conditions. Forced evictions by the interim Jubbaland administration also occurred in the towns of Kismayu and Luuq following an attack on a police post near an IDP settlement. By the end of the year, the federal government had not yet adopted an IDP policy, although a draft framework was prepared in April 2014.

Over 1.1 million Somali refugees remained in neighbouring countries and the diaspora. In April, UNHCR, the UN refugee agency, and the governments of Kenya and Somalia formed a commission to supervise the voluntary repatriation of Somali refugees from Kenya, as agreed in the September 2013 Tripartite Agreement. On 20 September, the UNHCR announced it had repatriated 4,108 Somali refugees from the Dadaab refugee camp in northeast Kenya to Somalia. In January, there were 237,271 Somali refugees in Yemen. By August, however, over 28,000 Somalis had returned to Somalia to escape the escalating armed conflict in Yemen. Meanwhile, other states hosting Somali asylum-seekers and refugees, including Saudi

Arabia, Sweden, the Netherlands, Norway, the UK and Denmark, continued to pressurize Somalis to return to Somalia, alleging that security there had improved.

## FREEDOMS OF EXPRESSION AND ASSEMBLY

Journalists and media workers continued to be intimidated, harassed, attacked and killed. In May, journalist Daud Ali Omar and his wife Hawo Abdi Aden were shot dead by gunmen who broke into their house in the Bardaale neighbourhood of Baidoa. On 26 July, journalists Abdihakin Mohamed Omar of the Somali Broadcasting Corporation and Abdikarim Moallim Adam of Universal TV were killed in a suicide car bomb attack on a hotel in Mogadishu, in which 13 people died. Salman Jamal, a reporter for Universal TV, was seriously injured in the attack.

Media freedom continued to be curtailed, journalists were arrested and media houses closed down. In May, the government ordered all Somali media houses to use the acronym UGUS ("the group that massacres Somali people") when referring to al-Shabaab. The Somali Independent Media Houses Association (SIMHA) called the order a threat to journalists' work. On 2 October, the National Intelligence and Security Agency (NISA) arrested Awil Dahir Salad and Abdilahi Hirsi Kulmiye, two journalists working for Universal TV, and held them for six days without charge in Mogadishu. NISA officers also raided and shut down the broadcaster's offices on the same day. Al-Shabaab continued to suppress the media and retained a ban on the internet in areas under its control.

In Somaliland, the government curtailed the freedom of expression of those who criticized its policies. Somaliland does not have a media law to protect journalists. Guleid Ahmed Jama, a prominent human rights lawyer, was arrested after he questioned the execution of six prisoners on death row in an interview with the BBC Somali Service. Other human rights activists, Otto Bihi and Suldaan Mohamed Muuse Cune, were also arrested

for opposing the postponement of presidential elections to March 2017. Bihi was released and Cune spent 12 days in custody without charge. The government also restricted the opposition's freedom of assembly. On 11 May, security forces denied the main opposition party, WADANI, permission to hold a peaceful demonstration against the extension of the President's term by 22 months. The party's leaders were arrested and held for several hours after police violently broke up peaceful marches in the cities of Hargeisa, Berbera and Burao, and the party's offices were temporarily taken over by government security forces.

## DEATH PENALTY

Somalia continued to use the death penalty despite its support for the UN General Assembly resolution on a moratorium on the death penalty. Members of Somali armed opposition groups such as al-Shabaab, government soldiers and people convicted of murder were executed by firing squad. Military Court processes fell short of international fair trial standards, while executions were often carried out in haste. In September, seven soldiers were executed in the city of Kismayo, Jubbaland, after they were convicted by a military court of killing civilians. In April, a military tribunal in Mogadishu sentenced to death two men accused of killing two members of the Federal Parliament and three intelligence officers.

In Somaliland, civilian courts sentenced people to death – at least 70 people were on death row in February. In July, a civilian court in Sool sentenced a mentally ill man to death after he was convicted of killing his friend. The government announced in February its decision to resume executions after a nine-year moratorium. In April, six prisoners who were on death row at the Mandera maximum-security complex were executed by firing squad.

# SOUTH AFRICA

**Republic of South Africa**
Head of state and government: **Jacob G. Zuma**

Torture and other ill-treatment and excessive use of force by police continued, although some measure of accountability was obtained. Targeted violence against refugees and asylum-seekers resulting in deaths, displacement and property destruction also continued. Access to medical treatment for people living with HIV continued to expand but was marred by shortages in many areas. Progress was made in addressing hate crimes based on people's real or perceived sexual orientation or gender identity. Human rights defenders faced intimidation and threats from ruling party and state officials.

## BACKGROUND

The government came under increasing pressure from opposition political parties, civil society and communities over alleged corruption and poor service delivery, among other issues. Parliamentary processes were undermined by irregular responses to repeated challenges to the ruling African National Congress (ANC) party by opposition parties. Frustration with the slow pace of reform to address the legacy of apartheid resulted in protests across the country in different sectors, including tertiary education institutions. Continuing high levels of inequality led to widespread protests about service delivery in multiple communities across the country.

Criminal justice institutions, including the police oversight body and the prosecuting authority, were destabilized by scandals and internal tensions, affecting their credibility. Tension between the government and the judiciary increased.

In January, South Africa ratified the ICESCR.

## EXCESSIVE USE OF FORCE

On 25 June, President Zuma released the report and recommendations of the Marikana Commission of Inquiry into the deaths of 44 people at the Lonmin Marikana mine in North West Province in August 2012. The Commission found that the "decisive cause" of events on 16 August was the unlawful decision by senior police officials the night before to disarm and disperse strikers, forcibly if necessary, by the end of the next day. The Commission found all officials present at the meeting responsible for the decision, and found that they had obstructed and delayed the Commission by attempting to conceal evidence and fabricating a version of events to justify the deaths.

The Commission also found that at the first scene, where police shot dead 17 people, there was no objective evidence that the dispersing strikers intended to attack the police, and that deaths and injuries could have been avoided if the police had deployed minimum force methods more effectively. The Commission concluded that some of the officers might have exceeded the bounds of reasonable self or private defence.

The Commission found that the police presented no plausible justification for the fatal shooting of 17 other strikers at the second scene and that there was a complete loss of command and control. It recommended the establishment of an expert team, under the authority of the Director of Public Prosecutions, to conduct a criminal investigation into the killings. It also recommended an investigation into the conduct of a senior police officer who failed to deploy medical units under his control to the first scene, which led to the deaths of injured strikers. Preliminary steps had been taken to implement these recommendations by the end of the year.

The President did respond to other recommendations of the Commission, including the establishment of a Board of Inquiry into the fitness of the national commissioner of police, General Riah Phiyega, to hold office, and ordered her suspension. The prosecution service also reinstituted criminal charges against some of the workers involved in the strike in connection with the deaths of two Lonmin security guards and three non-striking workers.

## EXTRAJUDICIAL EXECUTIONS

The Independent Police Investigative Directorate (IPID) reported 396 deaths as a result of police action in 2014/2015, six more than the previous year.

In the Durban High Court, the trial of 27 police officers, the majority of them members of the now disbanded Cato Manor Organized Crime Unit, on 28 counts of murder and other charges, was further delayed until February 2016. The officers were facing criminal charges in connection with the death of, among others, Bongani Mkhize, a taxi company owner who was killed in February 2009, three months after he obtained a High Court order constraining the police from killing him.

In November, four police officers from Krugersdorp near Johannesburg were arrested and appeared in court in connection with the fatal shooting of a crime suspect, Khulekani Mpanza, on 19 October. They were charged with murder and defeating the ends of justice. The arrests followed the media's publication of CCTV footage of the incident. The acting National Commissioner of Police ordered the suspension of the Krugersdorp police station commander.

Sipho Ndovela, a witness to the murder of one of the victims of the ongoing violence at Durban's Glebelands hostel, was shot dead on 18 May in the precinct of Umlazi Magistrate's Court. He was due to provide testimony identifying and implicating a key figure behind the violence at the hostel complex. From March 2014 more than 50 people had died in targeted killings. Official investigations were undermined by the authorities' failure to protect individuals at risk and prevent violations of the rights of suspects detained for questioning by police.

## TORTURE AND OTHER ILL-TREATMENT AND DEATHS IN CUSTODY

IPID reported 244 deaths in custody in 2014-2015. They also reported 145 cases of torture, 34 cases of rape and 3,711 cases of assault by police officers in the same period.

In August, IPID referred the case of Zinakile Fica to the Director of Public Prosecutions for a decision on prosecution following their investigation into his death in police custody in March 2014. He had been arrested at Glebelands hostel along with others and died during interrogation at Prospecton police station. The results of an independent post mortem examination and witness testimony indicated that he had died from suffocation torture during police interrogation.

On 11 November, eight police officers were each sentenced to 15 years' imprisonment after being convicted in August of the murder of Mido Macia in February 2013. The police had shackled the arrested man to the back of their vehicle, dragging him behind it for about 200m before unlawfully detaining him in a police station cell. The High Court in Pretoria also found that seven of the accused had assaulted Mido Macia in the cell where he died.

## INTERNATIONAL JUSTICE

In June, the Southern African Litigation Centre took the government to court in an attempt to force it to implement an ICC arrest warrant for Sudan's President Omar al-Bashir, who was in South Africa for an AU summit. The North Gauteng High Court issued an interim order on 14 June preventing President Bashir from leaving the country pending the finalization of the matter. On 15 June, North Gauteng High Court ordered the state respondents, who included the Ministers of Justice and Police, to arrest and detain President Bashir for his subsequent transfer to the ICC.

On 15 June, South African authorities allowed President Bashir to leave South Africa in direct contravention of the interim court order. The North Gauteng High Court requested that the state submit an affidavit explaining how President Bashir was allowed to leave the country. The state submitted its explanatory affidavit and filed for leave to appeal against the High Court judgment. On 16 September, the North Gauteng High Court denied the state leave to appeal, indicating that the issue was moot, and that there were no prospects of success on appeal. The state petitioned the Supreme Court of Appeal in October. Subsequently, South Africa stated it was considering withdrawing from the ICC.

## CORPORATE ACCOUNTABILITY

In October, attorneys on behalf of 56 representative applicants petitioned the South Gauteng High Court, in *Nkala and others v. Harmony Gold and others,* to certify their case as a class action. The applicants were seeking compensation from 32 gold mining companies on behalf of thousands of mineworkers, former mineworkers and the dependants of deceased mineworkers, for what they allege was a failure to adequately prevent specific illnesses, namely silicosis and tuberculosis, caused by exposure to silica dust underground. Judgment was reserved in the matter.

The Marikana Commission of Inquiry made several findings against Lonmin Plc in its report. The Commission concluded that Lonmin did not use its best endeavours to resolve the labour disputes that led to the killings in August 2012 and that it failed to employ sufficient safeguards to ensure employee safety. The Commission also found Lonmin deficient in its undertakings with regard to its social and labour plans, particularly in relation to its housing obligations. The Commission dismissed Lonmin's argument that it could not afford to implement its housing obligations and found that its failure to comply created an unsafe environment.

## REFUGEES' AND MIGRANTS' RIGHTS

During the year there were numerous incidents involving violence against refugees, asylum-seekers and migrants.

In January, local residents looted 440 small businesses run by refugees and migrants in 15 different areas in Soweto, Gauteng Province. Four people died, including locals caught up in the violence. Nearly 1,400 refugees and migrants were displaced.

In April, a new wave of attacks, primarily in the greater Durban area, led to at least four deaths, many others seriously injured, and looting. At least 5,000 refugees and migrants fled their homes and small businesses to three temporary official camps, or to informal shelters.

The scale of the violence in the Durban area had little precedent and appeared to have been triggered by the widely reported statement by traditional leader King Goodwill Zwelithini that government must ensure all "foreigners" leave South Africa. A preliminary finding of an inquiry by the South African Human Rights Commission into these alleged comments noted the harmful nature of his remarks but absolved the King of inciting violence. The government condemned the violence and established an inter-ministerial committee to co-ordinate responses nationally. In KwaZulu-Natal Province, the provincial government appointed the former UN High Commissioner for Human Rights, Navi Pillay, to lead an inquiry into the violence. It had not been completed by the end of the year.

In October, in Grahamstown, Eastern Cape Province, a verified 138 out of a possible 300 refugee- and migrant-run shops were attacked. The police later acknowledged their failure to act on earlier warnings from civil society organizations and conducted nearly 90 arrests of suspected perpetrators of the violence, who appeared in court in late October.

Hundreds of refugees and asylum-seekers were detained unlawfully and risked deportation during an apparent national-level anti-crime initiative, Operation Fiela, launched on 27 April. The police, backed by the military, conducted raids and arrests in inner city areas, including Johannesburg. After raids and large-scale arrests on 8 May at the

Central Methodist Church and a nearby residential building, police and immigration officials blocked legal access over four days to as many as 400 refugees and asylum-seekers held at Johannesburg Central Police Station, despite emergency court orders for access. On 12 May, the High Court ruled that officials must provide the court with a full list of all detainees and prohibited the authorities from deporting any for two weeks, pending proper legal consultations, which were allowed to proceed.

In March, the Supreme Court of Appeal ordered the Department of Home Affairs (DHA) to re-open the Port Elizabeth Refugee Reception Office. The Constitutional Court dismissed the DHA appeal against the March ruling. However, non-discriminatory access to asylum determination procedures came under a new threat from sweeping government-proposed amendments to the Refugee Act, including restrictions on access to livelihood for asylum-seekers. The draft legislation was still under consideration at the end of the year.

## WOMEN'S RIGHTS

HIV remained the main cause of maternal deaths. Nearly one third of pregnant women were living with HIV but improved access to free anti-retroviral treatment for pregnant women since 2011 had contributed to the significant decline, by almost a quarter, in the institutional maternal mortality ratio (related only to deaths taking place in health facilities). Despite this progress, shortages of doctors and nurses, the lack of appropriately resourced health facilities and shortages of emergency transport continued to hamper efforts to reduce the high rate of maternal deaths. Poor management of the Department of Health at the provincial level was emphasized by both the South African Human Rights Commission and by a civil society-led People's Commission of Inquiry into the Free State Healthcare System.

The expansion of free anti-retroviral drugs through the public health system continued but persistent stock shortages of essential medicines across the country risked undermining progress. The country continued to battle an increased incidence of tuberculosis (TB) and multi-drug-resistant TB cases, a serious health risk for people living with HIV and AIDS.

Medical research reports continued to indicate that young women, aged between 15 and 24, bear the burden of new HIV infections. Women in this age group were up to eight times more at risk of HIV infection due to both biological and social factors. Data collated from health districts reflected high pregnancy rates among girls under 18, accounting for "one in 14 deliveries in the country" in 2014-2015. The report noted with concern that birth rates in this age group were highest in the poorest districts and that the gap between the poorest and wealthiest socioeconomic quintiles was increasing.

Significant progress for adolescent sexual and reproductive rights was ensured with the passing of the Sexual Offences Amendment Act (Act no. 5) of 2015, which gave effect to the Constitutional Court's judgment in the case of *Teddy Bear Clinic for Abused Children v. the Minister of Justice and Constitutional Development and Others* (2013) to protect the rights to dignity and privacy and the best interest of the child principle. The revised Act decriminalized consensual sexual activity between adolescents aged 12-16.

## RIGHTS OF LESBIAN, GAY, BISEXUAL, TRANSGENDER AND INTERSEX PEOPLE

Progress was made in addressing hate crimes based on people's real or perceived sexual orientation or gender identity with the extension of government-led processes from national to provincial level. Provincial Task Teams were established in at least five provinces to ensure a more effective flow of information to the National Task Team, which comprised civil society and government officials.

The Rapid Response Team continued to make progress with the resolution of previously unresolved cases of targeted violence against LGBTI people. In May, the Potchefstroom High Court convicted a man of the August 2014 rape and murder of a lesbian woman, Disebo Gift Makau, and sentenced him to two life terms and 15 years for robbery. The judge acknowledged that the victim was targeted because of her sexual orientation. In July, the Pretoria North High Court convicted a man for the September 2014 rape and murder of a lesbian woman, Thembelihle Sokhela, sentencing him to 22 years in prison. The judge in the case did not take the victim's sexual orientation into account in his ruling.

Civil society monitors continued to express concern at limitations in the police investigation into the murder of David Olyn, a gay man, who was beaten and burned to death in March 2014 in Western Cape Province. A trial began in October.

## HUMAN RIGHTS DEFENDERS

Harassment of human rights defenders and organizations and undermining of oversight bodies by ruling party and state officials remained a major concern.

ANC members in Free State Province targeted activists from the health rights group Treatment Action Campaign (TAC), because of their campaign to improve health services in that province. In February, the ANC Youth League used inflammatory language to mobilize a march against TAC offices in Bloemfontein and in July ANC members interrupted a public meeting of TAC.

The Regulation of Gatherings Act continued to be used by the authorities to limit the right to protest. In October, 94 community health workers and TAC activists who had been arrested during a peaceful vigil at the offices of the Free State Department of Health in July 2014 were found guilty of attending a gathering for which no notice was given. The ruling by the Bloemfontein Magistrate's Court implied that any gathering of more than 15 people without notification to the police was a "prohibited" gathering and therefore unlawful and subject to a prison sentence. The defendants were planning to appeal to the High Court.

Surveillance by crime intelligence or state security officers against human rights defenders, including journalists and community activists, continued to be reported.

There was some measure of support for the office of the Public Protector in the courts. In October, in response to her investigation into the chief operating officer of the state broadcaster, the Supreme Court of Appeal ruled that the Public Protector's rulings, findings and remedial actions could not be ignored without a legal review.

The trial of a police officer for the October 2013 shooting and killing of 17-year-old housing rights activist Nqobile Nzuza during a protest in Cato Crest, Durban, was postponed to February 2016. In March, two ruling party councillors were arrested with another co-accused for the September 2013 murder of housing rights activist Thulisile Ndlovu in KwaNdengezi, Durban. The case was continuing.

# SOUTH SUDAN

**Republic of South Sudan**
Head of state and government: **Salva Kiir Mayardit**

In August, after more than 20 months of intermittent negotiations, South Sudan's warring parties finally agreed to the terms of a wide-ranging peace agreement. However, despite the peace agreement and a subsequent ceasefire declaration, conflict continued in several parts of the country, although at a lower intensity than previously. All parties flouted international human rights and international humanitarian law during the fighting, but no one was held accountable for crimes under international law committed in the context of the internal armed conflict. About 1.6 million people continued to be displaced from their homes within the country, and some 600,000 sought refuge in neighbouring countries. At least 4 million people faced food shortages. The government failed to take steps to realize the right to health. Security agents repressed independent and critical voices from the opposition, media and civil society.

## BACKGROUND

The armed conflict, which erupted in December 2013, pitted forces loyal to President Salva Kiir against those loyal to former Vice-President Riek Machar. Armed militia groups allied to each side participated in the fighting, which continued throughout 2015, but was more sporadic than previously.

The Intergovernmental Authority on Development (IGAD), an eight-country East African organization, began mediating between the government of South Sudan and the Sudan People's Liberation Army/Movement in Opposition (SPLA/M-IO) in January 2014. Despite numerous ceasefire agreements, fighting continued throughout 2014 and into 2015.

On 3 March, the UN Security Council established a sanctions regime of travel bans and asset freezes against South Sudan, targeting individuals suspected of committing crimes under international law and human rights abuses or threatening the peace, security or stability of the country.

On 12 March, IGAD unveiled a new mechanism to exert more concerted pressure on the warring parties to resolve the conflict. It included the three IGAD mediators, plus five AU representatives (Algeria, Chad, Nigeria, Rwanda and South Africa), the UN, the EU, China, the IGAD Partners Forum and the Troika (Norway, the UK and the USA).

On 27 August, President Kiir signed a peace agreement that had been signed 10 days earlier by opposition leader and former Vice-President Riek Machar. The peace agreement provided a framework for parties to end hostilities and addressed a wide range of issues including power sharing, security arrangements, humanitarian assistance, economic arrangements, justice and reconciliation and the parameters of a permanent Constitution.[1]

The Uganda People's Defence Force, who were fighting alongside South Sudan's government, started withdrawing their troops in October in accordance with the peace agreement.

On 3 November, the government and the SPLA/M-IO signed an agreement on a permanent ceasefire and transitional security arrangements that committed both sides to demilitarizing the capital city, Juba, and other key towns. In December the SPLA/M-IO sent a delegation of members to Juba as part of the advance team to prepare for the implementation of the peace agreement.

The mandate of the UN Mission in South Sudan (UNMISS) was renewed in December to include protection of civilians, monitoring and investigating human rights, ensuring the delivery of humanitarian aid and supporting the implementation of the peace agreement.

## INTERNAL ARMED CONFLICT

Conflict was concentrated in the northeast of the country in parts of Jonglei, Unity and Upper Nile states. It was marked by periods of calm and others of intense violence. Both sides continued to engage in clashes despite the August peace agreement, the permanent ceasefire declarations and the November security arrangements agreement. More than 20 different armed forces were involved, including government forces backed by Ugandan soldiers on one side and a range of rebel factions on the other. Armed youth clashed regularly with government forces in parts of Western Equatoria state.

Both government and opposition forces disregarded international human rights and international humanitarian law. Both sides deliberately attacked civilians, often based on their ethnicity or assumed political affiliations. They attacked civilians sheltering in hospitals and places of worship; executed captured fighters; abducted and arbitrarily detained civilians; burned down homes; damaged and destroyed medical facilities; looted public and private property as well as food stores and humanitarian aid; and recruited children to serve in their armed forces. Parties to the conflict also regularly attacked, detained, harassed and threatened humanitarian aid workers and UNMISS staff.

Violence in Unity state, which had subsided, escalated from April. Government and allied youth groups led an offensive in 28 villages in Rubkona, Guit, Leer and Koch counties of Unity state in late April and early May. They set entire villages on fire, beat and killed civilians, looted livestock and other property, burned people alive, committed acts of sexual violence and abducted women and children. In October, clashes in southern and central Unity state intensified with grave consequences for civilians. Thousands of people were forced to flee in search of safety, protection and assistance, of whom about 6,000 arrived in the UNMISS Protection of Civilians site in Bentiu. Other people fled to Nyal and Ganyiel in southern Unity state, taking shelter in swamps and forests.

Although 1,755 child soldiers were released by the Cobra Faction armed group in the Greater Pibor Administrative Area in March, abductions of children continued throughout the year. For example, scores of children, some as young as 13, were abducted from Malakal in February and hundreds were reportedly seized from the northern villages of Kodok and Wau Shilluk in early June. The UN Children's Fund (UNICEF) estimated in November that as many as 16,000 children were associated with armed forces or groups.

Conflict-related sexual and gender-based violence was widespread. This included cases of sexual slavery and incidents of gang rape of girls as young as eight years old. There were also cases of men and boys being castrated.

## JUSTICE SYSTEM

The criminal justice system was grossly under-resourced and lacked capacity in critical areas such as investigations and forensics. It was further hampered by interference or lack of co-operation on the part of security organs and the executive branch. Cases involving human rights abuses

were also hindered by the absence of victim support and witness protection programmes.

The justice system failed to guarantee due process and fair trial rights. Common violations included arbitrary arrest and detention, torture and other ill-treatment, prolonged pre-trial detention and denial of the right to legal counsel.

The internal armed conflict exacerbated pre-existing challenges in the justice system, particularly in Jonglei, Unity and Upper Nile states. Militarization and the defection of many police officers severely undermined law enforcement capacities.

## LACK OF ACCOUNTABILITY

The authorities failed to hold anyone to account for crimes under international law committed during the armed conflict or to conduct thorough and impartial investigations into these crimes.

The August peace agreement provided for the establishment of three mechanisms: a Commission on Truth, Reconciliation and Healing; a Compensation and Reparations Authority; and a Hybrid Court for South Sudan. The Commission on Truth, Reconciliation and Healing mandate covers the peace-building process, and includes gender-based crimes and sexual violence. The Compensation and Reparations Authority mandate is to compensate for property losses incurred during the conflict. The Hybrid Court would have jurisdiction over crimes under international law and crimes established by relevant laws of South Sudan.

In 2014, the AU Peace and Security Council (PSC) set up an AU Commission of Inquiry on South Sudan (AUCISS), chaired by former Nigerian President Olusegun Obasanjo, to investigate human rights violations and abuses committed during the armed conflict in South Sudan. Its mandate included recommending measures to ensure accountability and reconciliation. Amnesty International was among organizations which campaigned throughout 2015 for the PSC to publish the inquiry report.[2]

On 27 October, the PSC published the

report. It found evidence of systematic violations of human rights and crimes under international law by both warring parties, often committed with extreme brutality. The report found compelling evidence of extrajudicial killings, including ethnically motivated killings. Testimonies to the AUCISS consistently indicated that some 15,000 to 20,000 ethnic Nuer were killed during the first three days of conflict (15-18 December 2013). The report also found evidence of torture and mutilation of bodies; abductions; enforced disappearances; looting and pillaging; forcing victims to engage in cannibalistic acts; and forcing victims to jump into fires. Strong evidence was found supporting allegations of systematic sexual violence, which was a common feature of the atrocities committed by both sides. The AUCISS concluded that there was a high likelihood that rape was used as a weapon of war.

The AUCISS recommended that those with the greatest responsibility for atrocities be prosecuted and that the needs of victims, including reparations, be addressed. It called for the establishment of an ad hoc African legal mechanism under the leadership of the AU and other mechanisms for transitional justice similar to the provisions of the August peace agreement. It also recommended the reform of civil and criminal and military justice systems so as to contribute towards ensuring accountability.

## RIGHT TO HEALTH – MENTAL HEALTH
The massive abuses of human rights suffered and witnessed in South Sudan have had severe repercussions on the mental health of many people, as has the widespread incidence of forced displacement, bereavement, destruction or loss of livelihood, loss of family and community and inadequate food and shelter. Recent studies found extremely high levels of post-traumatic stress disorder and depression among South Sudanese populations. Despite this overwhelming need, mental health services are almost non-existent.

During the year, only one public hospital in the country provided psychiatric care, with its inpatient ward having only 12 beds. People with serious mental health issues were routinely incarcerated in prisons. With little or no medical care, mentally ill inmates were often held chained, naked or in solitary confinement.

## FREEDOM OF EXPRESSION
The space for journalists, human rights defenders and civil society to do their work without intimidation continued to shrink, as it had since the start of the conflict. The authorities, especially the National Security Service (NSS), harassed and intimidated journalists, summoning them for questioning and arbitrarily arresting and detaining them.

Reporter Peter Julius Moi was shot dead in Juba on 19 August, days after President Kiir threatened to kill reporters working against the country, a statement that was later said to have been quoted out of context. Two other journalists were killed in the course of their work, one in May and one in December. George Livio, a journalist with Radio Miraya, was held in detention without charge or trial throughout the year; he had been arrested in August 2014, accused of collaborating with rebels.

The print version of the *Nation Mirror* was closed down in January 2015 after a photo of former Vice-President Machar was placed above one of President Kiir. In August, the NSS closed down *The Citizen*, a daily English language paper, and the Arabic daily newspaper *Al Rai*. Several newspapers had issues seized, some held temporarily, some confiscated entirely. The NSS also closed down two radio stations.

A senior lecturer at the University of Juba had to leave the country because of security concerns after hosting and moderating a discussion about a controversial presidential decree issued in October establishing 28 states.

The security forces continued to carry out enforced disappearances, arbitrary arrests and prolonged detentions, and torture and other ill-treatment. Since the start of the conflict, the NSS, Military Intelligence and members of the police force have cracked down on perceived political dissidents, many of whom were detained in violation of international law.

## LEGAL DEVELOPMENTS

In April, South Sudan became a party to the UN Convention against Torture and its Optional Protocol; the UN Convention on the Rights of the Child and its Optional Protocol on the sale of children, child prostitution and child pornography; and CEDAW and its Optional Protocol. By the end of the year, South Sudan had still not deposited instruments of ratification for the African Charter on Human and Peoples' Rights and the AU Convention Governing the Specific Aspects of Refugee Problems in Africa, even though Parliament voted for their ratification in 2014.

In March, the Minister for Justice announced that the National Security Service Bill had become law as the President had exceeded the 30-day time period set out in the Constitution to assent to or return the legislation following Parliament's approval of it in October 2014. There was domestic and international opposition to the passage of this law, and the President did not sign it. The law granted the NSS sweeping powers, including powers of arrest, detention and seizure, without adequate independent oversight or safeguards against abuse.

President Kiir returned the Non-Governmental Organizations Bill back to Parliament, after it received Parliament's approval in late May. The version of the Bill passed by Parliament contained a number of restrictive provisions. It would make registration compulsory and criminalize voluntary work without a registration certificate.

1. South Sudan: Warring parties must fully commit to ensuring accountability for atrocities (News story, 26 August)
2. South Sudan: Release of AU Inquiry Report a vital step for resolution

of crisis (News story, 23 July)

# SPAIN

Kingdom of Spain
Head of State: King Felipe VI de Borbón
Head of government : Mariano Rajoy

**Freedom of assembly was curtailed by new legislation. New cases of ill-treatment and excessive use of force by police officials were reported. Security forces also carried out collective expulsions and used excessive force against individuals who attempted to enter irregularly from Morocco into the Spanish enclaves of Ceuta and Melilla. Impunity remained a serious concern.**

## BACKGROUND

In December, national elections led to a fragmented parliament. The Popular Party, led by the incumbent Prime Minister Mariano Rajoy, came first but without sufficient seats to form a new government on its own.

There were fewer demonstrations against the government's austerity measures than in previous years, although the measures continued, having a detrimental effect on human rights.

## FREEDOMS OF EXPRESSION AND ASSEMBLY

Reforms to the Law on Public Security and the Criminal Code entered into force in July. Both provide for offences which may disproportionately limit the legitimate exercise of the rights to freedom of expression and peaceful assembly. The Law on Public Security imposed limitations on where and when demonstrations could take place, providing for additional penalties on those holding spontaneous demonstrations in front of certain public buildings. Police officers were given broad discretion to fine people who show a "lack of respect" towards them. The Law on Public Security included an offence of disseminating images of police officers in certain cases. Concern at the impact of such legislation was expressed in July by the UN Human Rights Committee.

## TORTURE AND OTHER ILL-TREATMENT

In May, the UN Committee against Torture expressed concern over the continuation of the incommunicado detention regime. It recommended that Spain amend the definition of torture in its domestic law, and conduct effective investigations into all allegations of torture and other ill-treatment.

Cases of ill-treatment by law enforcement officials were reported at the border and in places of detention. Concerns arose regarding delays and the effectiveness of relevant investigations. Many cases had been closed without prosecutions taking place, including some where it was impossible to identify police officers involved due to the lack of identification tags on their uniforms.

A criminal trial against two law enforcement officers for causing serious bodily harm to Ester Quintana, who lost an eye as a result of being hit by a rubber projectile fired by police during a November 2012 protest in Barcelona, had not commenced by the end of the year. In September, the Catalonian government agreed to pay €260,000 as an out-of-court settlement to Ester Quintana.

## REFUGEES' AND MIGRANTS' RIGHTS

On 3 February, six individuals from sub-Saharan Africa were summarily returned from Ceuta to Morocco. Similar collective expulsions, in which Civil Guard officers forcibly returned to Morocco groups of individuals who were within their control, without any individualized assessment of their situation and without affording them an opportunity to claim asylum, had been frequently reported in previous years, particularly in Melilla.

In March, the Aliens Law was amended to legalize the automatic and collective expulsion of migrants and refugees from the borders of the Spanish enclaves of Ceuta and Melilla. This provision paved the way for further collective expulsions, which are prohibited by international law. However, attempts to cross the fences separating Melilla from Morocco decreased after February, when several makeshift camps in the north of Morocco were dismantled by Moroccan authorities.

In May, the UN Committee against Torture expressed concern at the "practice of 'hot expulsion' from the autonomous cities of Ceuta and Melilla, where rejections at the border prevented access to asylum procedures.

In July, the UN Human Rights Committee called on Spain to comply with the principle of *non-refoulement* and provide access to effective asylum procedures.

In August, investigations in Melilla into the beating by Civil Guard officers of a migrant who had tried to cross the border between Morocco and Melilla and had been summarily returned to Morocco in October 2014 were closed. The court could not gather witness statements from other migrants, as they too had been collectively expelled in the course of the same police operation. The man was beaten by Civil Guards and then carried unconscious to the Moroccan side of the border. In spite of film evidence, the Ministry of Interior alleged that it was impossible to identify the officers involved. An appeal against the decision to close the investigation was pending at the end of the year.

In October, the investigation into the excessive use of force by the Civil Guard at the Tarajal beach in February 2014 was closed without bringing any charges. Civil Guard officers had used rubber projectiles and smoke canisters to stop around 200 people trying to swim from the Moroccan to the Spanish side of the beach; 23 people were unlawfully pushed back to Morocco and at least 14 people died at sea.

Restriction on asylum-seekers' freedom of movement continued as asylum-seekers in Ceuta and Melilla were still required to obtain police authorization to leave the enclaves for the mainland. This breaches Spain's national laws and had been ruled unlawful by several courts in Spain.

The Centre for the Temporary

Accommodation of Migrants in Melilla was severely overcrowded. Asylum-seekers usually waited at least two months in Melilla, or even several months in some cases, before being transferred to the mainland. The waiting period in Ceuta was longer.

As of the end of November, 12,500 asylum applications were filed in Spain. In October, Spain agreed to relocate 14,931 asylum-seekers by 2016 under the European relocation scheme. It offered only 130 resettlement places in 2015.

Almost 750,000 undocumented migrants were living in Spain without adequate access to health care. Several UN bodies recommended that Spain guarantee universal access to health care.

## COUNTER-TERROR AND SECURITY

In October, amendments to the Procedural Criminal Law failed to remove the use of incommunicado detention, despite the concerns of international human rights bodies that such detention violated Spain's international obligations. Improvements were limited to excluding the application of incommunicado detention to children under 16.

In July, the Human Rights Committee recommended again that Spain provide Ali Aarrass with an effective remedy for the torture and ill-treatment he suffered in Morocco. Ali Aarrass was extradited by Spain to Morocco in 2010, despite fears that he would be at risk of torture there and despite interim measures requested by the Committee that he not be expelled while they examined the case.

In July, sections of the Criminal Code related to terrorist acts were amended, including a broad definition of what constitutes an act of terrorism. The UN Special Rapporteur on freedom of expression noted that the amendments could criminalize behaviours that would not otherwise constitute terrorism and could result in disproportionate restrictions on the lawful exercise of freedom of expression, among other limitations.

## DISCRIMINATION

The new Law on Public Security stipulated that identity checks should be carried out by police without discriminating on ethnic and other grounds.

In May, an Observatory on discrimination for reasons of gender or sexual orientation was established by the government. The Observatory was created to receive complaints from victims and witnesses and provide a rapid response to acts of discrimination on these grounds.

## VIOLENCE AGAINST WOMEN

According to the Ministry of Health, Social Policy and Equality, 56 women were killed by their partners or former partners as of mid-December.

In July, the CEDAW Committee urged Spain to ensure that women victims of gender-based violence have access to redress and protection, that officials dealing with them are adequately trained, and that perpetrators are prosecuted.

At the end of the year, the government was still refusing to provide reparation to Ángela González Carreño. She had been a victim of gender-based violence and her daughter had been killed by her ex-partner in 2003, having received no adequate protection despite reporting previous instances of domestic violence.

## IMPUNITY

The definitions of enforced disappearance and torture in Spanish legislation continued to be inconsistent with international human rights law. Restrictions on the exercise of universal jurisdiction led to the closure of major international cases. In particular, the Audiencia Nacional Court decided in July to halt its investigation into torture and other ill-treatment at the US detention centre in Guantánamo Bay, Cuba. This was despite the submission in May of documents indicating that Spanish agents had been implicated in interrogations of detainees at the detention facility. An appeal was pending at the end of the year.

Also in July, a military court closed investigations into the torture of two prisoners committed by five Spanish soldiers at a Spanish military base in Iraq in 2004, on the basis that it had not been able to identify either the perpetrators or the victims. Questions remained on the thoroughness of the investigation by the military court.

The rights to truth, justice and reparation continued to be denied to victims of crimes committed during the Civil War and the Franco era (1936-1975), as Spanish authorities failed to adequately co-operate with the Argentine judiciary investigating such crimes. In March, the government rejected a request by the Argentine courts for the extradition of 17 people. Subsequently, a group of UN experts urged Spain to comply with its obligations to extradite or prosecute those responsible for grave human rights violations.

## SEXUAL AND REPRODUCTIVE RIGHTS

Legislation adopted in September required girls under 18 and women with mental disabilities to obtain parental or guardian consent before they can access safe and legal abortion services. Both the CEDAW Committee and the UN Working Group on the issue of discrimination against women in law and in practice called on Spain to refrain from restricting women's and girls' access to safe and legal abortion. The UN Human Rights Committee also recommended Spain to ensure that no legal barriers force women to resort to clandestine abortion, putting their lives and health at risk.

## HOUSING RIGHTS

According to statistics published in March by the General Council of the Judiciary, 578,546 foreclosure procedures were initiated in Spain between 2008 and 2014. In the first nine months of 2015, 52,350 new foreclosure procedures were initiated.

Measures adopted by the government in previous years to improve the situation for people at risk of losing their home were failing to ensure an effective remedy for those whose right to housing may have been infringed.

In June, the UN Committee on Economic, Social and Cultural Rights asked Spain to ensure access to legal remedies for people who face foreclosure proceedings.

# SRI LANKA

**Democratic Socialist Republic of Sri Lanka**
Head of state and government: **Maithripala Sirisena**
**(replaced Mahinda Rajapaksa in January)**

**A new government in January brought constitutional reforms and promises of improved human rights protection. Many human rights challenges remained, including persistent use of arbitrary arrest and detention, torture and other ill-treatment, enforced disappearances and deaths in custody, and a long-standing climate of impunity for these and other violations.**

## BACKGROUND

An investigation by the UN Office of the High Commissioner for Human Rights into alleged abuses during the final seven years of the armed conflict and its immediate aftermath concluded in September that enforced disappearances, unlawful killings, torture and other ill-treatment, sexual violence, forced recruitment and child recruitment, direct military attacks on civilians, denial of humanitarian relief and systematic deprivation of liberty of displaced people on the basis of ethnicity could amount to war crimes and/or crimes against humanity. It recommended legal and procedural reforms to address ongoing violations, and the establishment of a hybrid special court, integrating international investigators, judges, prosecutors and lawyers to try those accused of alleged war crimes and crimes against humanity. The government signalled its agreement with the conclusions by co-sponsoring a UN Human Rights Council resolution in September calling for implementation of the report's recommendations, including ensuring effective witness protection and consulting with victims and families in the design of truth and justice mechanisms.

## ARBITRARY ARRESTS AND DETENTIONS

Tamils suspected of links to the Liberation Tigers of Tamil Eelam (LTTE) were arrested and detained under the Prevention of Terrorism Act (PTA) which permits extended administrative detention, and shifts the burden of proof onto a detainee alleging torture or other ill-treatment. In September the government pledged to repeal the PTA and replace it with anti-terrorism legislation that complied with international standards. It also pledged to review detention records and claimed to have released at least 45 detainees after "rehabilitation". Some detainees were held for many years while waiting for charges to be filed or cases to conclude. Opposition leader Rajavarothiam Sampanthan told Parliament in December that 217 people remained detained under the PTA; most had not been tried. The number did not include those sent for "rehabilitation", another form of arbitrary detention.

## TORTURE AND OTHER ILL-TREATMENT

Torture and other ill-treatment of detainees – including sexual violence – continued to be reported and impunity persisted for earlier cases. In October, the Inspector General of Police ordered an inquiry into the alleged abuse of a 17-year-old boy and a man who were arrested in September in connection with the rape and murder of a five-year-old girl in Kotadeniyawa. Their lawyer said the two were beaten, stripped naked and photographed by police in order to obtain false confessions. Both were released without charge. Shortly before the incidents the government had promised the UN Human Rights Council that it would issue clear instructions to all branches of the security forces that torture and other ill-treatment, including sexual violence, and other human rights violations are prohibited, and that those

responsible would be investigated and punished.

## EXCESSIVE USE OF FORCE

Complaints of excessive force in the policing of demonstrations persisted, and impunity remained for past incidents. Findings of military investigations into the army's killing of unarmed demonstrators demanding clean water in August 2013 were not made public and no one had been prosecuted by the end of 2015. A magisterial inquiry was ongoing.

## DEATHS IN CUSTODY

Suspicious deaths in police custody continued to be reported. Detainees died of injuries consistent with torture and other ill-treatment, including beatings or asphyxiation. Police claimed suspects committed suicide or in one case drowned while trying to escape.

## ENFORCED DISAPPEARANCES

Court testimony by a Criminal Investigation Department (CID) official in connection with habeas corpus petitions by families of five youths who disappeared in 2008 from a suburb of the capital, Colombo, confirmed earlier reports by a former detainee that the Navy had operated secret detention camps in Colombo and Trincomalee where detainees were allegedly tortured and killed.

The Presidential Commission to Investigate into Complaints Regarding Missing Persons received 18,586 reports of missing civilians, but made little progress in clarifying their fate or whereabouts or bringing perpetrators of enforced disappearance to justice. In October the government, noting a widespread lack of confidence in the Commission, announced that they were replacing it with another body. In December, it signed and promised to ratify the International Convention for the Protection of All Persons from Enforced Disappearance and to criminalize enforced disappearances.

## IMPUNITY

Impunity persisted for alleged crimes under international law committed during the armed conflict, including enforced disappearances, extrajudicial executions and the intentional shelling of civilians and protected areas such as hospitals. Impunity also remained for many other human rights violations, including: the January 2006 extrajudicial executions of five students in Trincomalee by security personnel; the killing of 17 aid workers with Action contre la Faim in Muttur in August 2006; the January 2009 murder of newspaper editor Lasantha Wickrematunge; and the disappearances of political activists Lalith Weeraraj and Kugan Muruganandan in Jaffna in 2011. Army personnel and affiliates were questioned about the 2010 disappearance of dissident cartoonist Prageeth Eknaligoda. The investigation was ongoing at the end of the year.

The report of a 2006 Commission of Inquiry that investigated the Trincomalee and Muttur killings was finally released in October. It criticized original police investigations as lacking professionalism. The report of an investigation into civilian deaths during the armed conflict, also released in October, called for new legislation recognizing command responsibility and an independent judicial inquiry into credible allegations that members of the armed forces may have committed war crimes.

## HUMAN RIGHTS DEFENDERS

In January, severed heads of dogs were left outside the homes of Brito Fernando and Prasanga Fernando of the human rights organization Right to Life. They and colleague Phillip Dissanayake also received anonymous threatening phone calls alluding to their activism against police allegedly involved in enforced disappearances.

Human rights defenders in the north and east continued to report police and military surveillance and questioning around their participation in local NGOs and political meetings, demonstrations, campaigns for human rights accountability and key international events such as the UN Human Rights Council sessions. Activists from eastern Sri Lanka reportedly received anonymous phone calls asking for details of meetings they participated in, as well as anonymous threats after signing a statement calling for an independent international investigation into alleged war crimes.

Balendran Jeyakumari, an activist against enforced disappearances, was released on bail in March after nearly a year in detention without charge under the PTA. She was rearrested and detained for several days in September. On 30 June, the Colombo Magistrate's Court lifted a travel restriction on Ruki Fernando which had been imposed in March 2014 on the request of the Terrorist Investigation Division (TID) after he and a Catholic priest, Praveen Mahesan, were arrested under the PTA following their attempts to investigate the arrest of Balendran Jeyakumari. Ruki Fernando remained banned from speaking about the ongoing TID investigation and his confiscated electronic equipment was not returned.

## FREEDOMS OF EXPRESSION, ASSEMBLY AND ASSOCIATION

President Sirisena declared 19 May, the anniversary of the end of Sri Lanka's long armed conflict, to be Remembrance Day, and stressed that it was a day to commemorate all war dead. This move suggested that earlier restrictions on public commemorations by northern Tamils would be lifted. Although memorial events were permitted in most areas, a heavy police presence was reported at such gatherings in the north and east, and ceremonies were reportedly prohibited by the security forces in Mullaitivu, the site of the final offensive.

Complaints persisted of harassment and surveillance by security forces of people attending gatherings and engaged in activism, particularly in the north and east.

## JUSTICE SYSTEM

The new government reinstated Chief Justice Shirani Bandaranayake, who was impeached in 2013 for political reasons. She immediately announced her retirement and was succeeded by Kanagasabapathy Sripavan.

The new government enacted the 19th amendment to the Constitution which placed checks on the powers of the executive presidency, including ending direct presidential appointment and dismissal of senior judges and members of key institutions, including the Judicial Service Commission, and transferring those powers to a Constitutional Council.

## DISCRIMINATION – RELIGIOUS MINORITIES

Muslims and Christians continued to report incidents of harassment by police, members of the public and politicians, particularly in the context of political campaigning by hardline Buddhist political parties in the lead-up to parliamentary elections in August. Earlier incidents of violence and intimidation against religious minorities were not investigated. Deaths, injuries and property loss sustained by Muslim residents of Aluthgama Dharga Town and Beruwala in riots in June 2014 went unpunished.

## VIOLENCE AGAINST WOMEN AND GIRLS

In May, the rape and murder of 17-year-old Sivayoganathan Vidhya on the island of Pungudutivu prompted large demonstrations demanding justice for cases of violence against women and girls. Local police were criticized for refusing to search for the missing teenager, reportedly telling her family that she probably ran off with a lover. In September, the rape and murder of a five-year-old girl in Kotadeniyawa led to calls for the death penalty to be reinstated, even after it became known that police had tortured two suspects in an attempt to force false confessions.

Evidence continued to mount that sexual violence may have been used systematically against Tamils (detainees, surrendered LTTE members and civilians) during and in the immediate aftermath of the conflict, strengthening calls for a justice mechanism to address war crimes. The 7 October conviction of four soldiers for the 2010 gang-rape of a woman in a Kilinochchi resettlement camp

was widely seen as a small victory against the pervasive climate of impunity.

# SUDAN

**Republic of the Sudan**
Head of state and government : **Omar Hassan Ahmed al-Bashir**

**The authorities repressed the media, civil society organizations and opposition political parties, severely curtailing freedoms of expression, association and assembly. Armed conflict in Darfur, South Kordofan and Blue Nile states continued to cause mass displacement and civilian casualties; human rights abuses were perpetrated by all parties to these conflicts. Government forces destroyed civilian buildings, including schools, hospitals and clinics in conflict areas, and obstructed humanitarian access to civilians needing support because of the ongoing hostilities.**

## BACKGROUND

Parliament approved controversial amendments to the 2005 National Interim Constitution in January 2015. These increased the powers of the National Intelligence and Security Service (NISS) and granted the President greater powers to appoint and remove senior officials, including state governors and other senior constitutional, judicial, military, police and security posts. The constitutional amendment to Article 151 transformed the NISS from an intelligence agency focused on information gathering, analysis and advice to a fully fledged security agency exercising functions usually carried out by the armed forces or law enforcement agencies.

In April, presidential and parliamentary elections took place. President Omar al-Bashir was re-elected for five years amid reports of low voter turnout, fraud and vote-rigging. The main political opposition parties boycotted the elections. In the run-up to April's presidential election, the government restricted freedoms of expression, association and peaceful assembly and arrested dozens of political opponents.[1]

The climate of impunity fostered by lack of accountability for crimes under international law and other serious human rights violations remained prevalent in conflict areas. The UN High Commissioner for Human Rights reported in August that, during 2014, there had been at least 411 violent incidents in Darfur in which 980 individuals had been injured or killed. These included abductions, physical assaults and armed attacks against civilians, particularly the internally displaced. Few of these cases were investigated or resulted in arrests. In South Kordofan and Blue Nile states, the conflicts continued with devastating impacts on civilians and limited prospects of peaceful solutions.[2] Fighting began in mid-2011 and the last direct peace talks between the government of Sudan and the Sudan People's Liberation Movement-North (SPLM-N), under the auspices of the AU High-Level Implementation Panel (AUHIP), were suspended in November 2015.

## FREEDOM OF EXPRESSION

The NISS intensified its harassment and censorship of newspapers which regularly faced arbitrary confiscation of their publications. At least 21 different newspapers had editions confiscated by the NISS on 56 different occasions. Newspapers also faced arbitrary requirements imposed by the NISS. For example, they were forbidden from reporting critically on the conduct of the security services, the armed forces, the police and the President. Further, they were banned from reporting corruption cases, human rights violations and the situation in conflict areas.

Al Midan newspaper, affiliated with the Sudanese Communist Party, was prevented from publishing in January and February. Its editor, Madeeha Abdallah , faced several charges under the 1991 Criminal Act including undermining the constitutional order, which carries the death penalty.

On 16 February, NISS agents confiscated the entire print run of 14 newspapers from the printers, without explanation. Some of the newspapers were directly or indirectly funded and supported by the ruling political party, the National Congress Party (NCP). On 25 May, NISS agents confiscated the entire print run of nine newspapers in Khartoum.

## FREEDOM OF ASSOCIATION

The suppression of civil society increased during the year. In January, the NISS shut down three civil society organizations on the basis that they were violating their registration licences. They were the Mahmoud Mohamed Taha Cultural Centre, the National Civic Forum and the Sudanese Writers' Union. In June, the Sudanese Consumer Protection Society was shut down and two of its members were arrested and interrogated by the NISS. They were released without charge after seven days. The Confederation of Sudanese Civil Society Organizations reported in July that, since the beginning of 2015, more than 40 registered organizations had failed to renew their licence due to cumbersome legal procedures or obstruction by the government's regulatory body, the Humanitarian Aid Commission.

## FREEDOM OF ASSEMBLY

The police and NISS agents repeatedly repressed freedom of assembly before and during the elections held from 13-17 April.

Opposition political parties were repeatedly prevented from organizing public events during the pre-election campaign period from 24 February to 10 April. On 28 February, the police forcibly dispersed a meeting of opposition political parties in Dongola, capital of Northern state, seriously injuring many participants . On 12 March, the police in North Kordofan forcibly prevented members of the National Umma Party from organizing a public event. Police arrested 50 party members and closed the party's office. On 2 April, local authorities in Al Nihoud in West Kordofan state prohibited a public event arranged by the Sudanese Congress Party to publicize its boycott of the election.

In August, the NISS prohibited a political symposium of the Sudanese Congress Party (SCP) and arrested three senior members. Also in August, the Minister of Justice dissolved one of the oldest trade unions in the country, the Sudanese Farmers' Union, which had been in existence since 1954. On 5 September, the authorities shut down the Republican Party's offices in Omdurman.

## ARBITRARY ARRESTS, TORTURE AND OTHER ILL-TREATMENT

The NISS carried out arbitrary arrests and detentions, a number of which were politically motivated. Some detainees were released without charge. None appear to have received compensation and no security officers appeared to have been held to account.

Farouk Abu Issa, leader of the opposition alliance National Consensus Forces (NCF), Dr Amin Maki Madani, head of the Alliance of Sudanese Civil Society Organizations, and Farah Al-Aggar, former senior member of the NCP in Blue Nile state, were released on 9 April, after spending 124 days in detention. They had been arrested in December 2014.[3] They were arrested after signing a document calling for democratic transformation, dismantling of the de facto one-party state and an end to conflict in Sudan. Both Dr Amin Maki Madani and Farouk Abu Issa had been charged with capital offences under the 1991 Penal Code including "undermining the constitutional system".

In total, at least 30 political activists were arrested across the country during the election period. In North Darfur, students at Al Fasher University organized peaceful protests on 14 April calling for a boycott of the presidential elections and a change of government. The police and NISS arrested 20 students and charged them with various offences under the Criminal Act, including establishing a "criminal and terrorist organization", rioting and causing a public nuisance. They were subjected to torture and other ill-treatment while in detention. They were all released pending trial.

On 6 July, a court in Khartoum tried and convicted three members of the opposition SCP including its political secretary, Mastour Ahmed Mohamed. They were convicted of disturbing the public peace and each subjected to 20 lashes.

## ARMED CONFLICT

Armed conflicts persisted in Darfur, Blue Nile and South Kordofan, with devastating impacts on civilians across Sudan, ranging from loss of life to denial of humanitarian assistance and lack of access to basic social services such as education and health care. The UN Office for the Coordination of Humanitarian Affairs was targeting support to an estimated 5.4 million people affected by conflict in Sudan in 2015.

### South Kordofan and Blue Nile

Government forces continued to attack rebel-held areas of the Nuba Mountains in South Kordofan and Blue Nile using ground troops and indiscriminate aerial attacks.

Amnesty International visited South Kordofan in early May and documented serious violations of international humanitarian law and human rights, including aerial and ground attacks targeted against civilians and civilian objects and the denial of humanitarian access. Lack of humanitarian access perpetuated other human rights violations, including violations of the rights to health, education, food, safe water and adequate housing. Amnesty International concluded that the Sudanese government was committing war crimes in South Kordofan.[4]

Amnesty International obtained evidence suggesting that government aircraft deliberately bombed hospitals and other humanitarian facilities, and dropped cluster bombs on civilian areas of South Kordofan's Nuba Mountains in February, March and June 2015. Between January and April, the air force dropped 374 bombs in 60 locations across South Kordofan. Since 2011, the air force has bombed 26 health facilities (hospitals, clinics and health units). By 2015 there were only two hospitals operating to serve a population of 1.2 million people.

A Médecins Sans Frontières (MSF) hospital was bombed in January: a Sudan Air Force fighter jet dropped 13 bombs, of which two landed inside the hospital compound and the others just outside the hospital fence.

The aerial bombardments also had a debilitating impact on the right to education in South Kordofan. There were six secondary schools in SPLM-N-controlled areas when the conflict began, of which only three were still operational in 2015. The number of children in secondary schools in SPLM-N-controlled areas fell from 3,000 to about 300-500, while 30 primary schools were closed with enrolment numbers dropping by 23,000 since 2011.

The use of aerial bombardment and flights over civilian villages and communities has been a consistent practice of the Sudan Air Force since 2011 and had a profound psychological impact over the course of the conflict. Aerial bombardments in May and June 2015 disrupted cultivation activities before the rainy season.

Fighting continued intermittently in Blue Nile state between SPLM-N and government armed forces, resulting in the displacement of an estimated 60,000 civilians. In May, armed clashes in Blue Nile led to the deaths of 22 civilians and the displacement of 19,000.

## Darfur

The armed conflict in Darfur entered its 12th year. Although large-scale fighting between the government and armed groups had subsided, there were sporadic clashes, acts of banditry and incidents of intercommunal violence. Restrictions on freedom of movement and political liberties persisted throughout Darfur. An estimated 223,000 people were displaced from their homes by conflict during the year, bringing the total number of internally displaced persons in Darfur to 2.5 million.

In December 2014, the government re-launched Operation Decisive Summer, attacking villages in Jebel Marra and East Jebel Marra by air and land. In its January 2015 report, the UN Panel of Experts on Sudan characterized the government strategy in Darfur as one of "collective punishment of villages and communities from which the armed opposition groups are believed to come or operate" and "induced or forced displacement of those communities", with "direct engagement, including aerial bombardment, of [armed rebel] groups when their location can be identified".

Gender-based and sexual violence remained widespread in Darfur. After her visit to Sudan in May, the UN Special Rapporteur on violence against women urged the government to set up a Commission of Inquiry to investigate allegations of mass rape, including allegations that more than 200 women and girls were raped in late 2014 in the village of Thabit.

1. Sudan: Entrenched repression: Freedom of expression and association under unprecedented attack (AFR 54/1364/2015)
2. Sudan: Don't we matter? Four years of unrelenting attacks against civilians in Sudan's South Kordofan state (AFR 54/2162/2015)
3. Health fears for detained opposition leaders (AFR 54/002/2015)
4. Sudan: Don't we matter? Four years of unrelenting attacks against civilians in Sudan's South Kordofan state (AFR 54/2162/2015)

# SWAZILAND

Kingdom of Swaziland
Head of state: **King Mswati III**
Head of government : **Barnabas Sibusiso Dlamini**

**Some prisoners of conscience and political prisoners were released but repressive legislation continued to be used to suppress dissent. Freedoms of expression, association and peaceful assembly continued to be restricted.**

## BACKGROUND

The USA ended Swaziland's preferential trade agreement under the African Growth and Opportunity Act (AGOA) in January, citing the country's failure to implement promised human rights reforms. The loss of preferential access to the US market for textiles led to factory closures and job losses. Following international pressure, the government responded by releasing a number of prisoners, including prisoners of conscience.

The government flagrantly violated the basic constitutional rights of unions and their leaders, teachers, political parties and civil society, but largely escaped sustained criticism in international media. This was partly because, on the surface, Swazi society appeared close-knit and relatively homogenous.

## LEGAL DEVELOPMENTS

A rule of law crisis that started in 2011 persisted and took a new turn in April with the arrest of several judicial officers. It resulted in the suspension and subsequent dismissal of Chief Justice Michael Ramodibedi, a Lesotho national, for "serious misbehaviour".

On 17 April, the High Court issued an arrest warrant against Chief Justice Ramodibedi and High Court Judge Mpendulo Simelane on 23 charges brought by the Anti-Corruption Commission, including defeating the ends of justice and abuse of power. The Chief Justice evaded arrest by refusing to leave his home. On 7 May, the government suspended Chief Justice Ramodibedi, replacing him with an acting Chief Justice, Bheki Maphalala. Following an inquiry by the Judicial Services Commission into three charges of abuse of office, King Mswati III dismissed Michael Ramodibedi on 17 June.

On 20 April, Judge Mpendulo Simelane and the Minister of Justice, Sibusiso Shongwe, were arrested on charges including abuse of power and defeating the course of justice. High Court Judge Jacobus Annandale and High Court Registrar Fikile Nhlabatsi were also arrested on charges of defeating the ends of justice after they tried to overturn the arrest warrant against Chief Justice Ramodibedi. They were all later released on bail. Sibusiso Shongwe was dismissed as Minister of Justice by King Mswati III on 21 April. Charges against Jacobus Annandale and Fikile Nhlabatsi were dropped. The two

were assisting the prosecution in the case against Sibusiso Shongwe, who was arrested for a second time, in August, on further charges of corruption. He was again released on bail.

The suspension and dismissal of the Chief Justice meant that the Supreme Court postponed hearing appeals from May to July. A number of Swazi judicial officers were appointed to the Supreme Court in late June, fulfilling requirements under the 2006 Constitution.

## UNFAIR TRIALS

Politically motivated trials and laws that violate the principle of legality continued to be used to suppress dissent. There were some signs of improvement with the release of prisoners of conscience and political prisoners, but these gains remained fragile without fundamental legislative reform and full commitment to human rights standards.

Editor Bheki Makhubu and human rights lawyer Thulani Maseko were released on 30 June following an appeal hearing before the Supreme Court. The Crown Prosecutor conceded that the state had no case against them. The two men had been arrested in March 2014 and convicted of contempt of court after a blatantly unfair trial. They were arrested after publishing articles in *The Nation* magazine, questioning judicial independence and political accountability in Swaziland. The fine imposed on the magazine was also overturned.

The authorities continued to use the 2008 Suppression of Terrorism Act and the 1938 Sedition and Subversive Activities Act to limit freedoms of expression, association and peaceful assembly by arresting or threatening to arrest human rights defenders and political activists exercising their rights. Pre-trial proceedings continued in five separate cases of 13 people charged under these laws after arrests dating back to 2009. All the accused were out on bail but appeared in court on remand. Ten were charged under both laws for acts such as shouting slogans in support of the proscribed opposition party, the

People's United Democratic Movement (PUDEMO), possessing PUDEMO leaflets, wearing PUDEMO t-shirts or calling for a boycott of elections in 2013. All trials were postponed pending the outcome of a constitutional challenge to the two laws. The High Court began hearing the application in September but postponed the matter to February 2016.

Among those charged were several people involved in PUDEMO, including Secretary General Mlungisi Makhanya, president Mario Masuku and youth leader Maxwell Dlamini. Mario Masuku and Maxwell Dlamini were arrested on 1 May 2014 and remanded in custody in connection with slogans they allegedly shouted at a Workers' Day rally. They were released on bail on 14 July 2015 by the Supreme Court. They had unsuccessfully applied for bail twice in 2014, and had appealed the High Court's refusal to release them to the Supreme Court.

## FREEDOM OF ASSOCIATION

Police prevented members of the Trade Union Congress of Swaziland (TUCOSWA) from meeting in February and March. The Secretary General of the Swaziland National Association of Teachers (SNAT), Muzi Mhlanga, was assaulted by police during an attempt by TUCOSWA to hold a meeting at the SNAT offices in Manzini on 14 March.

After effectively being banned for over three years, TUCOSWA was finally registered by the Swaziland Ministry of Labour and Social Security on 12 May.

## FREEDOM OF EXPRESSION

Human rights defenders, political activists, religious leaders and trade union officials were threatened with violence by police, arrest or other forms of pressure as a consequence of their advocacy of human rights, respect for the rule of law or political reforms.

## DEATHS IN CUSTODY

Deaths in police custody under suspicious circumstances remained a concern. On 12

June, a Mozambican national, Luciano Reginaldo Zavale, died in police custody after being arrested for possession of a stolen laptop. Independent forensic evidence indicated that he did not die of natural causes. An inquest into his death started in September.

## TORTURE AND OTHER ILL-TREATMENT

Torture in police custody also persisted. In March, while in custody at Big Bend Prison, lawyer Thulani Maseko was held in solitary confinement for three weeks as punishment for an alleged breach of prison rules. He had no access to legal counsel during the disciplinary proceedings and the length of his confinement can be regarded as a form of torture and other ill-treatment.[1]

PUDEMO president Mario Masuku was denied access to adequate and independent medical care for complications relating to diabetes throughout his 14 months in pre-trial detention at Zakhele Remand Centre and Matsapha Central Prison.

## WOMEN'S RIGHTS

Despite high levels of gender-based violence, the Sexual Offences and Domestic Violence Bill had not been enacted by the end of the year. The Bill had been under discussion by Parliament since 2006. The original progressive draft has been diluted and the Bill now contains a narrow definition of rape and excludes marital rape, among other concerns.

## DEATH PENALTY

One person remained under sentence of death. No death sentences were imposed during the year. Two death sentences were commuted to life imprisonment by the King.

---

1. Swaziland: Amnesty International condemns repression of fundamental freedoms (AFR 55/1345/2015).

# SWEDEN

**Kingdom of Sweden**
**Head of state: King Carl XVI Gustaf**
**Head of government: Stefan Löfven**

A police database of Romani individuals received strong criticism from the Parliamentary Ombudsman. The work of a commission tasked with reviewing and recommending improvements to the criminal justice system's investigation and prosecution of rape remained ongoing.

## DISCRIMINATION

On 17 March, the Parliamentary Ombudsman issued a decision strongly criticizing the maintenance of a database of Romani individuals by the Skåne police department, which had come to light following a September 2013 investigatory journalism exposé.[1] The database registered the names of more than 4,000 people, the majority of whom had no recorded criminal convictions. The Ombudsman placed ultimate responsibility on the Skåne County Police Commissioner, but also apportioned responsibility to the Chief of the Criminal Intelligence Unit and police staff working on the database. The Ombudsman's report – unlike earlier reviews by the Commission on Security and Integrity Protection and a prosecutor – found that, in practice, the database ended up being based on ethnicity, in this case of an already marginalized ethnic group.

## VIOLENCE AGAINST WOMEN AND GIRLS

The work of a parliamentary commission established by the government in 2014 to examine how rape investigations and prosecutions are dealt with by the criminal justice system remained ongoing. The commission, set up following an initiative by the Parliamentary Committee on Justice, was tasked with analyzing high rates of attrition in investigating and prosecuting reported rapes, recommending improvements to the legal process in rape cases, and reviewing the penal provisions relating to the offence of rape, including by considering a requirement for genuine consent to the sexual act.

In October, the current affairs television programme *Kalla Fakta* (Hard Facts) broadcast an investigation which showed doctors in three private clinics offering to perform "virginity tests" on teenage girls, against the girls' will and at the request of parents or older relatives. The programme alleged that doctors engaged in the practice were failing to report such cases to social welfare authorities. All three clinics were reported to the Health and Social Care Inspectorate (IVO). The investigations of the IVO, a government agency for overseeing health care and social services, were ongoing at the end of the year. The National Board of Health and Welfare was assessing the need to improve awareness of or issue further guidance on consent and forced or intrusive physical examinations in the health care system.

## TORTURE AND OTHER ILL-TREATMENT

In August, a senior judge tasked by the government to assist the Ministry of Justice issued a memorandum proposing that torture be defined and specified as a crime in domestic law. This was in response to longstanding criticism by human rights organizations and the UN Committee against Torture, including in its concluding observations of December 2014 on Sweden's periodic report.

1. Sweden: Sharp criticism by Parliamentary Ombudsman of Skåne police database of Romanis (EUR 42/1249/2015)

# SWITZERLAND

**Swiss Confederation**
**Head of state and government: Simonetta Sommaruga**

Sweeping new surveillance legislation was passed. Concerns remained about excessive use of force by police, including during deportations, and inadequate police accountability mechanisms. Victims of trafficking in human beings and foreign nationals who were victims of domestic violence faced obstacles to accessing protection.

## LEGAL, CONSTITUTIONAL OR INSTITUTIONAL DEVELOPMENTS

In March, the Swiss People's Party, which ended the year as the largest single party in the Federal Assembly, launched a popular initiative seeking to place the Swiss constitution above any international law obligations. The so-called "self-determination initiative would require a public referendum in order to be passed; the surrounding debate, however, contributed to a climate of hostility towards international human rights treaties including the European Convention on Human Rights.

## TORTURE AND OTHER ILL-TREATMENT

In August, the UN Committee against Torture criticized Switzerland's ongoing failure to incorporate the crime of torture into the Penal Code. The Committee expressed concerns about inadequate resourcing of the National Commission for the Prevention of Torture (NCPT), the national preventive mechanism.

The Committee also called on the Swiss authorities to establish an effective independent police complaints mechanism; to amend legislation and improve training of judiciary and law enforcement officials to increase the rate of prosecutions for violence against women; and to integrate the Istanbul Protocol into training for law enforcement officials.

## POLICE AND SECURITY FORCES

In July, the NCPT issued a report raising concerns about the inappropriate use of restraints by police and security forces during deportation. The report documented cases of the total immobilization of vulnerable people and the use of restraints against people who offered no resistance to deportation. The

NCPT also reiterated concerns about a lack of uniformity in deportation practices by police forces in different cantons (administrative regions).

## REFUGEES' AND MIGRANTS' RIGHTS

### Administrative detention

Civil society organizations and the UN Committee against Torture expressed concern about the excessive use of detention for irregular migrants in some cantons, particularly in relation to the return of asylum-seekers to EU countries under the Dublin regulation. The Committee criticized Switzerland for permitting the detention for up to one year of asylum-seeking children aged between 15 and 18.

### Trafficking in human beings

Civil society organizations criticized a federal directive issued to cantons in July concerning victims of trafficking. The new measures made victims' access to humanitarian protection contingent on being willing to testify in criminal proceedings against traffickers. Victims of trafficking already in an asylum procedure were excluded from humanitarian protection measures.

### Domestic violence

In August, the UN Committee against Torture criticized the authorities for maintaining a "severity" threshold to assess domestic violence suffered by foreign nationals. Under the Foreigners Law, violence must meet a certain threshold in order for survivors to be able to separate from their violent partner without fear of losing their residence permits.

## RIGHT TO PRIVACY

In September, Parliament adopted a new surveillance law which granted sweeping powers to the Federal Intelligence Service including the interception of data on internet cables entering or leaving Switzerland, to access metadata, internet histories and content of emails, and to use government spyware (Trojans).

# SYRIA

**Syrian Arab Republic**
Head of state: **Bashar al-Assad**
Head of government: **Wael Nader al-Halqi**

Government forces and non-state armed groups committed war crimes, other violations of international humanitarian law and gross human rights abuses with impunity in the internal armed conflict. Government forces carried out indiscriminate attacks and attacks that directly targeted civilians, including bombardment of civilian residential areas and medical facilities with artillery, mortars, barrel bombs and, reportedly, chemical agents, unlawfully killing civilians. Government forces also enforced lengthy sieges, trapping civilians and depriving them of food, medical care and other necessities. Security forces arbitrarily arrested and continued to detain thousands, including peaceful activists, human rights defenders, media and humanitarian workers, and children. Some were subjected to enforced disappearance and others to prolonged detention or unfair trials. Security forces systematically tortured and otherwise ill-treated detainees with impunity; thousands of detainees died as a result of torture and other ill-treatment between 2011 and 2015. Non-state armed groups that controlled some areas and contested others indiscriminately shelled and besieged predominantly civilian areas. The armed group Islamic State (IS) besieged civilians in government-controlled areas, carried out direct attacks on civilians and indiscriminate attacks including suicide bombings, alleged chemical attacks and other bombardment of civilian areas, and perpetrated numerous unlawful killings, including of captives. US-led forces carried out air strikes on IS and other targets, in which scores of civilians were killed. In September, Russia commenced air strikes and sea-launched cruise missile attacks on areas controlled by armed opposition groups and on IS targets, in which hundreds of civilians were killed. By the end of the year, the UN estimated that the conflict had caused the deaths of 250,000 people, forced 7.6 million people to become internally displaced and led 4.6 million people to become refugees abroad.

## BACKGROUND

Syria's internal armed conflict, which began after anti-government protests in 2011, raged throughout the year. Government forces and their allies, including Lebanese Hizbullah and Iranian fighters, controlled the centre of the capital Damascus and much of western Syria, while an array of non-state armed groups controlled or contested other areas, sometimes fighting each other. They included groups primarily fighting government forces, such as those affiliated to the Free Syrian Army and others including Ahrar al-Sham; Jabhat al-Nusra, the Syrian branch of al-Qa'ida; IS; and forces of the Autonomous Administration established in predominantly Kurdish enclaves of northern Syria.

Divisions within the UN Security Council impeded efforts to pursue peace, but the Council adopted several resolutions on Syria. In February, Resolution 2199 called on states to prevent the transfer of arms and funds to IS and Jabhat al-Nusra. In March, Resolution 2209 condemned the use of chlorine as a weapon of war and said that those responsible for its use should be held accountable, while supporting the use of military action, economic sanctions or other means against those who did not comply. In August, Resolution 2235 called for a Joint Investigative Mechanism to determine responsibility for the use of chemical weapons in Syria.

Efforts by the UN to broker peace, incrementally via a ceasefire in Aleppo or through other multi-party talks, were unsuccessful. International negotiations known as the "Vienna Process" were set to lead to direct talks between the Syrian government and opposition forces in January 2016.

The independent international Commission of Inquiry on the Syrian Arab Republic, established by the UN Human Rights Council in 2011, continued to monitor and report on violations of international law committed by the parties to the conflict, although it remained barred by the government from entering Syria.

A US-led international coalition of states continued to carry out air strikes against IS and certain other armed groups in northern and eastern Syria. The attacks, which began in September 2014, reportedly killed scores of civilians. Russia began air strikes in support of the Syrian government on 30 September, nominally against IS but mostly attacking armed groups fighting both the government and IS and in October fired cruise missiles at targets in Syria. The Russian attacks reportedly killed hundreds of civilians.

Several suspected attacks by Israel inside Syria targeted Hizbullah, Syrian government positions and other fighters.

## INTERNAL ARMED CONFLICT – VIOLATIONS BY GOVERNMENT FORCES

### Indiscriminate and direct attacks on civilians

Government and allied forces continued to commit war crimes and other serious violations of international law, including direct attacks on civilians and indiscriminate attacks. Government forces repeatedly attacked areas controlled or contested by armed opposition groups, killing and injuring civilians and damaging civilian objects in unlawful attacks. They carried out indiscriminate attacks and direct attacks on civilian residential areas, including artillery shelling and air strikes, often using unguided, high-explosive barrel bombs dropped from helicopters. The attacks caused numerous civilian deaths and injuries, including of children. For example, a barrel bomb attack on Baideen, Aleppo governorate, on 5 February killed at least 24 civilians and injured 80. An air strike on the Sahat al-Ghanem market in Duma on 16 August killed around 100 civilians and wounded hundreds. Aerial bombing accounted for half of all civilian fatalities, according to the Violations Documentation Center, a Syrian NGO.

Government forces also carried out dozens of suspected chlorine gas attacks in areas controlled by non-state armed groups, particularly in Idleb governorate, causing civilian casualties. In one attack on 16 March, government helicopters reportedly dropped barrels containing chlorine on and around Sermin, Idleb governorate, killing a family of five and injuring around 100 civilians.

### Sieges and denial of humanitarian access

Government forces maintained prolonged sieges of predominantly civilian areas in and around Damascus, including Eastern Ghouta, Daraya and Yarmouk, exposing the residents to starvation and denying them access to medical care and other basic services, while subjecting them to repeated air strikes, artillery shelling and other attacks.

Government forces, including Lebanese Hizbullah fighters, began besieging Zabadani and nearby towns and villages in southwestern Syria in July, forcibly displacing thousands of civilians to Madaya, which government forces also besieged and bombarded indiscriminately, causing civilian casualties.

### Attacks on medical facilities and workers

Government forces continued to target health facilities and medical workers in areas controlled by armed opposition groups. They repeatedly bombed hospitals and other medical facilities, barred or restricted the inclusion of medical supplies in humanitarian aid deliveries to besieged and hard-to-reach areas, and disrupted or prevented health care provision in these areas by detaining medical workers and volunteers. The NGO Physicians for Human Rights accused government forces of systematically attacking the health care system in areas controlled by armed opposition groups and of responsibility for the deaths of the vast majority of the 697 medical workers killed in Syria between April 2011 and November 2015.

## INTERNAL ARMED CONFLICT – ABUSES BY ARMED GROUPS

Non-state armed groups committed war crimes, other violations of international humanitarian law and serious human rights abuses.

### Use of indiscriminate weapons and direct attacks on civilians

IS forces carried out direct attacks on civilians as well as indiscriminate attacks. IS reportedly also launched chemical attacks using chlorine and mustard agents. The Syrian American Medical Society said that its staff treated more than 50 civilians with symptoms indicating exposure to chemicals after IS forces fired mortar and artillery shells into Marea, a town in Aleppo governorate, on 21 August. One baby died from the exposure.

IS forces repeatedly attacked Kurdish-controlled areas. At least 262 civilians were killed in direct attacks by IS on civilians in the town of Kobani on 25 June.

IS and other armed groups used imprecise explosive weapons including mortars and artillery shells in attacks on residential areas, killing and injuring civilians. In August, armed groups reportedly fired hundreds of mortar shells into Fu'ah and Kefraya, two predominantly Shi'a villages, and killed 18 civilians in indiscriminate attacks on Deraa city.

### Unlawful killings

IS forces summarily killed captured government soldiers, members of rival armed groups, and media workers and other captured civilians. In areas of al-Raqqa, Deyr al-Zur and eastern Aleppo which it controlled, IS enforced its strict interpretation of Islamic law, carrying out frequent public execution-style killings, including of people they accused of apostasy, adultery or theft, or because of their real or perceived sexual orientation.

On 30 January, IS decapitated abducted

Japanese journalist Kenji Goto and four days later burned to death captured Jordanian Air Force pilot Muath al-Kasasbeh. On 3 March, IS members reportedly threw a man from a tower in Tabqa, al-Raqqa governorate, and then stoned him to death because of his real or perceived sexual orientation

On 5 July in al-Raqqa, IS summarily killed Faisal Hussein al-Habib and Bashir Abd al-Ladhim al-Salem, two peaceful activists who had reportedly documented IS abuses.

On 5 July, IS released a video that showed some of its child soldiers apparently shooting dead captured government soldiers in front of a crowd in an amphitheatre in Palmyra. IS forces deliberately destroyed ancient temples and other cultural artefacts at Palmyra, a UNESCO World Heritage site, after capturing it in May. In August, IS decapitated Khaled al-Asaad, the head of antiquities at Palmyra, having detained him since May.

Other armed groups also committed unlawful killings. In June, Jabhat al-Nusra reportedly shot dead 20 civilians of the Druze faith at Kalb Loze, Idleb. Jaysh al-Islam summarily killed alleged IS members they had captured, according to images released from 25 June. In September, Jaysh al-Fateh fighters led by Jabhat al-Nusra summarily killed 56 captured government soldiers after seizing the Abu al-Dhuhr Air Base in Idleb on 9 September.

### Sieges and denial of humanitarian access

IS forces besieged some 228,000 people in government-controlled western neighbourhoods of Deyr al-Zur city. Local activists said five civilians died in July from lack of food and medical care. IS closed health facilities and reportedly barred women medical workers from working in areas it controlled, curtailing civilians' access to medical care.

For most of the year non-state armed groups also besieged some 26,000 people in Zahraa and Nobel, northwest of Aleppo.

### Abductions

Several non-state armed groups including IS

engaged in abductions and hostage-taking.

On 23 February, IS forces abducted some 253 civilians from mostly Assyrian villages along the Khabur river in al-Hasakeh. Some 48 were later released but there were fears for the fate of those still missing, particularly after IS released a video about the abductees in October showing three unidentified bodies.

There was no news of the fate or whereabouts of human rights defender Razan Zaitouneh, her husband Wa'el Hamada, Nazem Hamadi or Samira Khalil. The four were abducted by unidentified armed men on 9 December 2013. They were taken from the office of the Violations Documentation Center and Local Development and Small Projects Support Office in Duma, an area controlled by Jaysh al-Islam and other armed groups.

## INTERNAL ARMED CONFLICT – ABUSES BY THE PYD-LED AUTONOMOUS ADMINISTRATION

In northern Syria, an Autonomous Administration led by the Democratic Union Party (PYD) controlled the predominantly Kurdish Afrin, Kobani (also known as Ayn al-Arab) and Jazeera enclaves. The Administration's security forces and police forcibly displaced people from 10 villages and towns, including Husseiniya in February, and prevented displaced residents from returning to their homes in Suluk, a town in al-Raqqa governorate, in July after forcing IS to withdraw from the area. They also carried out arbitrary arrests, detentions and unfair trials of suspected supporters of armed groups and others. The Administration's security forces reportedly used child soldiers.

## ATTACKS BY INTERNATIONAL COALITION FORCES

The US-led international coalition continued its air strikes against IS and certain other armed groups in northern and eastern Syria, which it had begun in September 2014. Some attacks resulted in civilian casualties. The Syrian Observatory for Human Rights reported that 243 civilians were killed in coalition attacks in Syria during the year. On

30 April, coalition air strikes on suspected IS targets in Bir Mahli, Aleppo governorate, reportedly killed 64 civilians.

## ATTACKS BY RUSSIAN FORCES

Russia intervened in the conflict in support of the Syrian government, beginning a campaign of air strikes on 30 September primarily against armed opposition groups. The same day, Russian air strikes on Talbiseh, Zafraneh and Rastan in Homs governorate reportedly killed at least 43 civilians.

On 7 October, Russian forces fired cruise missiles into Syria from ships in the Caspian Sea. One missile strike killed five civilians and destroyed at least 12 homes in Darat Izza, Aleppo governorate. On 20 October, two suspected Russian air strikes hit the immediate vicinity of Sermin field hospital in Idleb governorate, killing 13 civilians and putting the hospital out of action. On 29 November, a suspected Russian war plane fired three missiles into a busy market in Ariha, Idleb governorate, killing 49 civilians.

Altogether, the Russian attacks reportedly killed at least 600 civilians and struck at least 12 medical facilities in areas controlled or contested by non-state armed groups.

## REFUGEES AND INTERNALLY DISPLACED PEOPLE

The continuing conflict caused massive population displacement. Some 4.6 million people fled Syria between 2011 and the end of 2015, including 1 million who became refugees during 2015, according to UNHCR, the UN refugee agency. Some 7.6 million, according to the UN Office for the Coordination of Humanitarian Affairs, were internally displaced within Syria. Half of those displaced were children. Turkey, Lebanon and Jordan, the countries hosting the most refugees from Syria, restricted access to refugees fleeing the continuing conflict, exposing them to further attacks and deprivation in Syria. Lebanon and Jordan continued to block the entry of Palestinian refugees from Syria, rendering them especially vulnerable. At least 500,000 Syrian refugees crossed by water or land into Europe but many European countries and other countries in the region failed to accommodate a fair share of those fleeing.

## ENFORCED DISAPPEARANCES

Government forces held thousands of detainees without trial, often in conditions that amounted to enforced disappearance. Tens of thousands of people remained subjected to enforced disappearance, some since the outbreak of the conflict in 2011. They included peaceful critics and opponents of the government as well as family members detained in place of relatives wanted by the authorities.

Those who remained forcibly disappeared since 2012 included Abd al-Aziz al-Khayyir, Iyad Ayash and Maher Tahan, members of the National Co-ordination Body for Democratic Change, who were arrested at an Air Force Intelligence checkpoint on 20 September 2012.

## TORTURE AND OTHER ILL-TREATMENT

Torture and other ill-treatment of detainees by government security and intelligence agencies and in state prisons remained systematic and widespread. Torture and other ill-treatment continued to result in a high incidence of detainee deaths.

Salaheddin al-Tabbaa, a 22-year-old student and Syrian Arab Red Crescent volunteer, died in detention in April according to a death certificate the authorities gave to his family in July. The certificate said he died of a heart attack. He was in good health when government security forces detained him in September 2014. The authorities did not return his body to his family, saying it had been buried.

## ARBITRARY ARRESTS AND DETENTIONS

Tens of thousands of civilians, including peaceful activists, were detained by government security forces. Many were held in prolonged pre-trial detention, where they were tortured and otherwise ill-treated. Others received unfair trials before the Anti-Terrorism

Court or Military Field Courts.

Bassel Khartabil, a peaceful online freedom of expression activist, remained arbitrarily detained since his arrest in March 2012. He was taken before a Military Field Court very briefly in late 2012 but was not told the outcome of the hearing. On 3 October 2015 he was moved from Adra Prison to an undisclosed location.

The authorities released human rights defender Mazen Darwish, head of the Syrian Centre for Media and Freedom of Expression, on 10 August, and Hani al-Zitani and Hussein Gharir, two members of the Centre, in July. All three had been held since February 2012 and were on trial before the Anti-Terrorism Court. The charges against them were later dropped.

## DEATH PENALTY

The death penalty remained in force for many offences but few details emerged of death sentences passed, and there was no information on executions.

The Anti-Terrorism Court reportedly sentenced to death 20 detainees held at Hama central prison for engaging in peaceful protests after grossly unfair trials in May and June.

# TAIWAN

Taiwan
Head of state: **Ma Ying-jeou**
Head of government: **Mao Chi-kuo**

**Freedom of peaceful assembly continued to be curtailed. Executions were carried out and death sentences imposed.**

## FREEDOM OF ASSEMBLY

On 10 February, the Taipei District Prosecutors Office indicted 119 people in connection with a protest movement against the adoption of a trade and services deal with China. The so-called "Sunflower Movement" had organized protests that took place from 18 March to 10 April 2014 at the Legislative

Yuan (Parliament), as well as the occupation of the Executive Yuan (Cabinet) and other similar protests that year. The charges included instigating others to commit a crime, trespassing, obstruction of officers discharging their duty and violating the Assembly and Parade Act. On 5 May, a further 39 people were indicted on the charge of trespassing, in relation to the occupation of the Executive Yuan. Of the 39 people indicted, 24 had filed private criminal lawsuits against former Premier Jiang Yi-huah and other high-ranking officials, seeking justice and accountability for injuries sustained in the clearing of the Executive Yuan complex.

Courts continued to reject the private criminal lawsuits against the former Premier and other high-ranking officials, but in August lawyer Lin Ming-hui won NT$300,000 (approximately US$9,200) in an administrative lawsuit seeking state compensation for a head injury sustained in the Executive Yuan incident. The Taipei City government chose not to appeal. Another 30 people subsequently filed lawsuits seeking state compensation.

By the end of the year no thorough, independent and impartial investigation had taken place into the police use of excessive force during the removal of protesters from the Executive Yuan and surrounding areas on 23/24 March 2014, or into actions of the authorities during the "Sunflower Movement" protests as a whole.

On 23 July, three journalists who were covering a demonstration at the Ministry of Education were arrested on charges of trespassing when they followed a splinter group of protesters who had climbed over a fence and entered the Ministry building. After the journalists refused to pay bail, they were released without charge. On the following day the Mayor of Taipei apologized for the "violation of freedom of reporting" that had occurred.

## DEATH PENALTY

Amid public anger at the murder of an eight-year-old girl in Taipei, the authorities carried out unrelated executions even though in some instances the appeals process had not been exhausted. The Minister of Justice denied that the executions were carried out to assuage public sentiment and stated they had been planned well in advance.

The High Court rejected a motion for a retrial in the case of Chiou Ho-shun, the longest-serving death row inmate in Taiwan, who had been sentenced to death in 1989 for robbery, kidnapping and murder. Chiou Ho-shun's lawyers had requested a retrial after two police officers said they were willing to testify that Chiou Ho-shun had told them at the time that he had been tortured and forced to "confess".

In September, the High Court overturned the conviction of Hsu Tzu-chiang, who had been on death row for 20 years for kidnapping and murder. Hsu Tzu-chiang was found not guilty due to discrepancies in the testimony of witnesses against him, and lack of forensic evidence. In the same month the High Prosecutors Office appealed the decision to the Supreme Court, which was pending at the end of the year.

# TAJIKISTAN

Republic of Tajikistan
Head of state: **Emomali Rahmon**
Head of government: **Qokhir Rasulzoda**

**Authorities continued to impose sweeping restrictions on freedom of expression. Several prominent human rights NGOs were targeted for "inspections" by various authorities, and some were "advised" to close down. Members of opposition groups faced increasing harassment, violence and even death, both in Tajikistan and in exile. Some political opposition activists and those accused of religious extremism were abducted and forcibly returned from several former Soviet countries. Lawyers representing opposition activists or those charged with anti-state offences were themselves at risk of harassment,**

intimidation and punitive arrest. Torture and other ill-treatment remained widespread, and lawyers were repeatedly denied access to their clients.

## BACKGROUND

The country faced increasing economic difficulties. Due to the recession in Russia and other traditional destinations for labour migrants, foreign remittances (the equivalent of half the country's GDP) fell by 40-60% in US dollar terms according to different estimates, and many of the labour migrants – reportedly over a million in Russia alone – were expected to start returning to Tajikistan.

Parliamentary elections were held on 1 March in an atmosphere of increasing reprisals against any political dissent, with only pro-government parties gaining seats in the newly elected legislature.

The government reported attacks by armed groups against police on 4 September in and near Dushanbe, the capital, with at least 26 people killed, including nine police officers. Little independent information on the incident emerged, due to the government's control of the media. The authorities blamed the violence on former Deputy Minister of Defence Abdukhalim Nazarzoda, who escaped the scene but was killed in a security operation on 16 September.

## FREEDOM OF EXPRESSION

Freedom of expression remained severely restricted and access to information was increasingly controlled by the authorities. Independent media outlets and journalists who were critical of the authorities faced intimidation and harassment, including personal attacks in pro-government media, particularly ahead of the parliamentary elections. Regulations were introduced in June requiring state agencies to submit all public communications to Khovar, the state information agency, and mandating media outlets to report on official events exclusively based on information vetted by Khovar.

The government's Communications Service denied that it had ordered internet service providers to block access to certain news or social media sites, but evidence to the contrary continued to emerge. Various media and social media sites were blocked in May, after a video was posted by a former high-ranking police official announcing that he had joined the armed group Islamic State (IS) in Syria.

## FREEDOM OF ASSOCIATION

Amendments to the Law on Public Associations, enacted in August, oblige NGOs registered as public associations with the Ministry of Justice to notify it about any foreign funding they receive. In June, the Ministry proposed a new law requiring that all non-profit organizations, including NGOs, register with it. NGOs in Tajikistan feared that, if passed, the law would give the government the means to deny them registration and thus prevent them from operating legally.

Several prominent NGOs were subjected to "inspections" by various government bodies, including the Ministry of Justice, the Tax Committee, the Prosecutor General's Office, and the State Committee on National Security, under the pretext of "national security considerations". Some NGOs were informally "advised" to close down. In June, the Tax Committee initiated liquidation proceedings against the public foundation Nota Bene. In August, the Bureau on Human Rights and Rule of Law was issued a fine of TJS 42,639 (over US$6,000) for purported tax violations that were never explained.

## REPRESSION OF DISSENT

Members of opposition groups, including Group 24 (banned by the Supreme Court as "extremist" in October 2014) and the Islamic Renaissance Party of Tajikistan (IRPT), faced increasing harassment and violence.

The leader of the political movement Youth for Tajikistan Revival, Maksud Ibragimov, who held Russian citizenship and lived in Moscow, Russia, where he survived an assassination attempt in November 2014, was put on Tajikistan's list of wanted individuals in October 2014. According to his family, on

20 January five men claiming to be Russian immigration officials took him from his flat to an unknown location. On 30 January, Tajikistani authorities reported that Maksud Ibragimov was in pre-trial detention in Dushanbe on charges of "extremism". In June, he was sentenced to 17 years' imprisonment.

On 5 March, Umarali Kuvvatov, an exiled founding member of Group 24, was shot dead by unknown men in Istanbul, Turkey.[1] He had earlier expressed concerns that the authorities had ordered his assassination.

Following months of harassment of its members, the IRPT lost its two remaining seats in Parliament in the March elections. On 28 August, the Ministry of Justice ordered the IRPT to cease its activities by 7 September, claiming it lacked sufficient popular support to qualify as a registered party. In September, 13 high-ranking members of the IRPT were arrested on charges of involvement in "criminal groups" and linking them to the violence on 4 September, which the party's exiled leader, Mukhiddin Kabiri, refuted. On 29 September, the IRPT was designated a "terrorist organization" by the Prosecutor General, on the grounds that several of its members had been involved in groups promoting "extremism", and that the party had used its newspaper, *Salvation*, and other media to spread "extremist ideas" and promote religious hatred.[2] The designation was later confirmed by the Supreme Court.

On 13 January, human rights lawyer Shukhrat Kudratov was sentenced to nine years in prison on charges of fraud and bribery. He claimed the charges were politically motivated and linked to his work for the defence of opposition activist and former Minister of Energy and Industry Zaid Saidov (sentenced in 2013 to 26 years in prison). On 28 September, police arrested Buzurgmekhr Yorov, a lawyer representing detained IRPT members, on unrelated charges of fraud and forgery, and seized documents relating to the IRPT cases in violation of Tajikistan's own laws.

## TORTURE AND OTHER ILL-TREATMENT

Torture and other ill-treatment remained widespread despite the adoption in 2013 of an Action Plan to implement recommendations by the UN Committee against Torture. By mid-August, the NGO Coalition against Torture registered 25 new cases of torture. In most cases, relatives and victims declined to file complaints for fear of reprisals, and many more cases of torture were likely to have gone unreported. Criminal prosecutions against law enforcement officials suspected of torture were rare, and frequently terminated or suspended before completion.

Lawyers were repeatedly denied access to their clients in detention, often for several days at a time. Individuals perceived to be threats to national security, including members of religious movements and Islamist groups or parties, were at particular risk of arbitrary arrests, incommunicado detention, torture and other ill-treatment. Shortly before his own arrest, lawyer Buzurgmekhr Yorov told the media that Umarali Khisainov (also known as Saidumar Khusaini), one of his IRPT clients who was arrested on 13 September, had complained about beatings and other ill-treatment in police custody.

On 9 April, Shamsiddin Zaydulloev was arrested without a warrant at his family's flat in Dushanbe, and taken to the Drug Control Agency building. His mother was able to see him in detention the same day, where he confirmed that he had been beaten. After subsequently being denied access to Shamsiddin Zaydulloev, his mother hired a lawyer who was not allowed to visit his client without the written permission of the investigator in charge of the case. On 13 April, his parents learned that he had died in police custody and noticed multiple bruises on his body in the morgue. They took photographs, hired a new lawyer and demanded a forensic medical examination, which concluded that Shamsiddin Zaydulloev had died of pneumonia. The family contested the findings and the Prosecutor General's Office ordered a second forensic examination, which found on 3 August that Shamsiddin Zaydulloev had suffered serious injuries, including five broken ribs and a fractured skull, which may have caused his death. An additional forensic examination was ordered to finally establish the cause of his death, and its outcome was still pending at the end of the year.

1. Tajikistani dissenters at grave risk after an opposition leader shot dead in Turkey (Press release,6 March)
2. Opposition party leaders arrested, risk torture (EUR 60/2465/2015); Opposition members' lawyer at risk of torture (EUR 60/2567/2015)

# TANZANIA

United Republic of Tanzania
Head of state: **John Magufuli (replaced Jakaya Mrisho Kikwete in November)**
Head of government: **Kassim Majaliwa (replaced Mizengo Peter Pinda in November)**
Head of Zanzibar government: **Ali Mohamed Shein**

**The year was taken up by preparations for the presidential and parliamentary elections, which took place in October. Inefficiencies were reported in the biometric voter registration process, leading to concerns that citizens would be prevented from voting. Legislative restrictions on freedom of expression were introduced. Human rights violations, including killing and torture, against marginalized and minority populations continued with impunity.**

## BACKGROUND

In April, the long-promised referendum on the new Constitution was delayed indefinitely, following delays in voter registration. A new referendum date has not yet been clarified.

Presidential and parliamentary elections took place in October. President Kikwete was constitutionally unable to run for a third term. In July, John Magufuli was chosen as the ruling Chama Cha Mapinduzi (CCM) party's presidential nominee. Also in July, former Prime Minister Edward Lowassa defected from CCM and joined Ukwana, the opposition coalition, as its presidential nominee. Both parties allowed public assemblies to take place, although widespread concern was raised about the efficacy of the new biometric voter registration system, with reports that large constituencies had been unable to register.

## DISCRIMINATION

Over 50 people were killed on the basis of witchcraft beliefs between January and June, while over 350 were killed in documented incidents of mob violence. There have been no meaningful investigations into these killings. Reports indicated the particular vulnerability of older women in rural areas, as well as of children.

There was one report of a young child with albinism being killed for body parts in February 2015 in the Geita region. A further three cases were reported across the country in the first half of the year, involving abduction, mutilation and dismemberment of bodies. The government failed to institute adequate safety measures for people living with albinism.

## FREEDOM OF EXPRESSION

In January, the regional *East African* newspaper was banned from circulation in Tanzania. Through the first half of 2015, several journalists were arrested, harassed, beaten and intimidated on the basis of their work.

In 2015, four bills were introduced to Parliament that collectively codified unwarranted and disproportionate restrictions on the right to freedom of expression. The bills were introduced under a "certificate of urgency", limiting normally available channels for public consultation. With some laws not being published, there was considerable confusion about their status and contents throughout the year.

Of particular concern, the Cyber Crimes Act 2015 (adopted in April) contains overly vague provisions, which purport to criminalize the sharing of "false or misleading" information online. The Statistics Act 2015, passed by Parliament in March, criminalizes and introduces disproportionate custodial sentences for the publication of "false or misleading" statistics.

# THAILAND

**Kingdom of Thailand**
Head of state: **King Bhumibol Adulyadej**
Head of government: **Prayuth Chan-ocha**

**Military authorities extended their powers to excessively restrict rights and silence dissent in the name of security. Political transition plans were delayed and repression deepened. The numbers of people harassed, prosecuted, imprisoned and arbitrarily detained solely for the peaceful exercise of their rights escalated sharply. Arrests and prosecutions under the lese-majesty law continued to increase. Internal armed conflict continued.**

## BACKGROUND

In January, authorities impeached former Prime Minister Shinawatra and filed charges against her for dereliction of duty related to her government's rice subsidy scheme for farmers.

In March, the European Parliament announced it would impose a ban on fish imports from Thailand to the EU unless the government took sufficient measures to address human trafficking and forced labour of migrant workers in the fishing industry. In June, Thailand remained on Tier 3 of the US Department of State Annual Report on Trafficking in Persons for failing to adequately address persistent and widespread trafficking of individuals for forced labour and sexual exploitation. In October, the European Parliament issued a non-binding resolution raising concerns about ongoing repression of rights.

Despite international calls for the lifting of restrictions – announced as temporary measures after the May 2014 coup –

authorities continued to enjoy wide-ranging powers and impunity for violations under Article 44 of the Interim Constitution and further expanded military involvement in the administration of justice. At the same time as lifting martial law in most areas of the country on 1 April, authorities issued a series of orders, including National Council for Peace and Order (NCPO) Order 3/2015, which retained and expanded restrictive excessive powers previously granted by martial law. These included limiting redress for individuals whose rights were violated. The government further delayed implementation of its roadmap to elections following the National Reform Council's rejection in September of the draft Constitution.

The ongoing implementation of other NCPO decrees, including orders on forest conservation, led to violations such as forced evictions and crop destruction.

A bomb attack in August targeting worshippers and visitors at the Erawan Shrine in the capital, Bangkok, killed 20 people and injured 125 others.

## INTERNAL ARMED CONFLICT

Armed conflict continued in the southern provinces of Pattani, Yala, Narathiwat and parts of Songkhla. Civilians were also targets of attacks which were suspected to have been carried out by armed groups.

Two paramilitary rangers charged with the killings of three boys in Bacho, Narathiwat, in February 2014 were acquitted in January. Impunity prevailed for grave human rights violations.

## TORTURE AND OTHER ILL-TREATMENT

A draft bill criminalizing torture and enforced disappearance was put before Parliament but had made no further progress by the end of the year.

Reports of torture and other ill-treatment by police and armed forces continued throughout the year.[1] Individuals held by the army in incommunicado detention without safeguards in unofficial places of detention were at greater risk of torture. In September, a temporary military detention facility was opened for civilian detainees; two detainees died in custody there in October and November.

Those seeking redress for torture continued to face obstacles. In March, Bangkok Remand Prison officials denied a National Human Rights Commissioner access to document injuries inflicted on political activist Sansern Sriounren. He said that he was tortured during incommunicado military detention, including through beatings and more than 40 electric shocks.

In several cases of deaths in custody as a result of torture, limited steps were taken towards accountability. However, impunity for perpetrators of these and other instances of torture prevailed.

## REPRESSION OF DISSENT

Peaceful critics of the authorities were at risk of arbitrary detention[2] and imprisonment. Many faced arrest, charges and prosecution throughout the year for a range of activities including staging plays, posting Facebook comments and displaying graffiti.[3]

In violation of the right to fair trial, civilians were brought before military courts and charged with offences against "internal security", "the security of the monarchy" and infringements of NCPO orders. Detainees were denied the right to judicial appeal against judgments for acts committed during martial law. The Bangkok Military Court summarily dismissed a number of legal petitions questioning its jurisdiction over civilians and seeking a ruling on the incompatibility of the use of military courts with Thailand's international human rights obligations.

NCPO Order 3/2015 authorized military officers to arbitrarily detain individuals and censor a variety of media, and criminalized public political meetings of more than five people.[4] Legislation requiring prior notification for assemblies and criminalizing unapproved exercise of the right to peaceful assembly and protests near government buildings came into force in August. Legislation providing for increased authority for a committee to take cyber security measures that could result in the military's excessive discretion to conduct cyber surveillance activities and restrict freedom of expression remained in draft form at the end of the year.

Throughout the year, authorities made public comments intimidating the media and calling on them to actively censor "negative" commentary. Military officers actively conducted surveillance on and harassed public commentators, including academics and members of the media; they blocked websites and enforced bans on media and online criticism.[5]

Dozens of individuals were charged and prosecuted under Article 116 of the Penal Code relating to sedition for peaceful acts of dissent, including pro-democracy protests expressing peaceful opposition to military rule. The authorities charged and detained 14 members of the New Democracy Movement, and several activists from the Resistant Citizen group, who carried out separate peaceful public protests in February, March, May and June. Supporters of both groups were charged, including Baramee Chairat, an NGO chairperson and Amnesty International board member; and a retired teacher who handed flowers to Resistant Citizen activists during their protest.[6]

The authorities prioritized enforcement of Article 112 of the Penal Code – the lese-majesty law – and continued to treat criticism of the monarchy as a security offence.[7] The judicial process for such offences was marked by secrecy, closed trials and denial of the right to bail. Military courts handed down more and longer sentences than in previous years, including up to 60 years' imprisonment. Military courts also increased sentences handed down for lese-majesty offences by ordering prison terms for separate offences to be served consecutively.

Dozens of former parliamentarians, journalists, academics and activists were detained by the military under powers granted by NCPO Order 3/2015 to detain people without charge or trial in unofficial places of detention for up to one week without any safeguards such as access to lawyers or families. The government justified these detentions as a means to control freedom of expression and prevent or punish public criticism.

Hundreds of people who had been arbitrarily detained since the coup continued to be subject to restrictions on their rights imposed as conditions for release. Some were subjected to surveillance, intimidation and repeated short-term arrests.

## HUMAN RIGHTS DEFENDERS

An unidentified gunman shot and killed land rights activist Chai Bunthonglek of the Southern Peasants Federation of Thailand in Chaiburi, Surat Thani Province, in February. Other members of the group reported ongoing harassment and intimidation in connection with their support for a community involved in a land dispute with an oil palm company.

Court proceedings were initiated in October against at least one military officer for a violent attack in May 2014 on activists of the Khon Rak Ban Ked group in Loei Province in the northeast. The group continued to report acts of harassment and intimidation by the military. One member, Surapan Rujichaiwat, was on trial on defamation charges for a social media post calling for an investigation into the activities of the mining company Tung Khum.

Two journalists from the online news site Phuketwan were acquitted of defamation charges for reproducing a Reuters article exposing official involvement in human trafficking. The Supreme Court also issued an order not to prosecute the NGO Cross Cultural Foundation and its director, after an army officer had pressed charges against the NGO for raising public concern about allegations of torture. The Court dismissed charges of criminal defamation against Andy Hall, a UK national, but he still faced prosecution and a civil suit and possibly million-dollar fines for reporting on labour abuses by a pineapple wholesaler.

## REFUGEES' AND MIGRANTS' RIGHTS

In May, the Prime Minister ordered a 10-day crackdown on human trafficking and smuggling camps following the discovery of shallow graves at sites on the Thai-Malay border, believed to be abandoned camps used by traffickers. The senior police investigator into the crimes sought political asylum in Australia, citing fears for his life and official interference in the investigation. A human rights and humanitarian crisis developed as smugglers responded to the crackdown by abandoning overcrowded boats at sea. Thai authorities prevented abandoned Muslim Rohingya from Myanmar and Bangladeshi passengers from landing in Thailand and were slow to set up search and rescue operations for boats in distress.

In the absence of legal protection of the right to asylum, refugees and asylum-seekers remained vulnerable to harassment, detention and *refoulement*. In August and November, authorities deported 109 people of Turkic origin to China, where they were at risk of violations,[8] as well as two people with UNHCR-recognized refugee status.[9] Authorities arrested and detained scores of asylum-seekers throughout the year, including from Pakistan and Somalia.

## DEATH PENALTY

Death sentences were handed down during the year. No executions were reported. Legislation was enacted expanding the scope of crimes for which the death penalty is applicable. Following a ruling by the Supreme Administrative Court in July, prisoners on death row may be held in shackles permanently.

---

1. Thailand: Martial law detainees at risk of torture (ASA 39/1266/2015)
2. Thailand: Post-coup violations continue: is a "temporary situation" becoming chronic? (ASA 39/1042/2015)
3. Thailand: Military's shutdown of event highlights free speech crackdown (News story, 4 June)
4. Thailand: Post-coup violations concerns abide one year on and a "temporary situation" is becoming permanent (ASA 39/1811/2015)
5. Thailand: Inter-Parliamentary Union must urge Thailand to stop

persecution of dissenting former parliamentarians (ASA 39/2666/2015)

6. Thailand: Students charged for peaceful protest (ASA 39/1977/2015)

7. Thailand: Lese-majesty convictions assault on freedom (News story, 23 February)

8. Thailand must not send Uighurs to Chinese torture (News story, 9 July)

9. Thailand/China: Shameful collusion between China and Thailand in targeting freedom of expression and ignoring refugee rights must end (ASA 39/2914/2015)

# TIMOR-LESTE

Democratic Republic of Timor-Leste
Head of state: **Taur Matan Ruak**
Head of government: **Rui Maria de Araújo (replaced Kay Rala Xanana Gusmão in February)**

Impunity persisted for gross human rights violations committed during the Indonesian occupation (1975-1999). Security forces were accused of arbitrary arrests and unnecessary or excessive use of force during security operations in Baucau district. Levels of domestic violence remained high.

## BACKGROUND

In February, Rui Maria de Araújo, leader of the Revolutionary Front for an Independent East Timor (FRETILIN) was sworn in as Prime Minister. The new government included a coalition of most political parties, including Xanana Gusmão's National Congress for Timorese Reconstruction. In September, Timor-Leste was reviewed by the UN Committee on the Rights of the Child.

## IMPUNITY

Little progress was made in addressing crimes against humanity and other human rights violations committed by Indonesian security forces and their auxiliaries from 1975 to 1999. Many suspected perpetrators remained at large in Indonesia.

No progress by the authorities was reported in implementing recommendations addressing impunity from the Commission for Reception, Truth and Reconciliation (CAVR) and the bilateral Indonesia-Timor-Leste Commission of Truth and Friendship (CTF). In September, a follow-up report by the UN Working Group on Enforced or Involuntary Disappearances noted regret that Timor-Leste had yet to debate a draft law on the establishment of a Public Memory Institute, intended to implement the CAVR and CTF recommendations.

## JUSTICE SYSTEM

Torture and other ill-treatment and unnecessary or excessive use of force by security forces continued to be reported. Accountability mechanisms remained weak.

Dozens of individuals were arbitrarily arrested and tortured or otherwise ill-treated by security forces as part of joint security operations in Baucau district between March and August. These operations were launched in response to attacks allegedly carried out by Mauk Moruk (Paulino Gama) and his banned Maubere Revolutionary Council (KRM) against police in Laga and Baguia subdistricts. Local human rights organizations documented dozens of cases of beatings by security officials who also destroyed property of suspected KRM members.[1] In August, Mauk Moruk was shot and killed. The findings of investigations by the Provedor (Ombudsman for Human Rights and Justice) were issued in November.

The justice system remained hampered by a lack of access to courts and due process. The expulsion of all international judicial officers employed as judges, lawyers and investigators in October 2014 continued to throw into question pending trials, including those addressing crimes against humanity.

## WOMEN'S RIGHTS

The 2010 Law mandating compulsory prosecution in domestic violence cases continued to be used although challenges remained. NGOs raised concerns on access to justice, limited protection for witnesses and victims, and a backlog of cases causing few women to actively file reports.

In November, the CEDAW Committee recommended that Timor-Leste adopt laws to ensure comprehensive reparation for survivors of rape and other forms of sexual violence that occurred during the Indonesian occupation and 1999 referendum, and that there would be no impunity for sexual violence committed during the occupation.

---

1. Dozens arrested and tortured in Timor-Leste (ASA 57/1639/2015)

# TOGO

**Togolese Republic**
Head of state: **Faure Gnassingbé**
Head of government: **Komi Sélom Klassou (replaced Kwesi Ahoomey-Zunu in June)**

---

**The authorities continued to restrict the freedom of peaceful assembly by banning demonstrations. The security forces used excessive force against peaceful demonstrators. Restrictions on the right to freedom of expression and arbitrary arrests and detentions persisted. A new Criminal Code was enacted. It criminalized torture but maintained homophobic provisions and introduced the charge of publishing, disseminating or reproducng false news which could be used to target journalists, human rights defenders and anyone expressing dissent.**

## BACKGROUND

President Gnassingbé was re-elected for a third term in April with 58.8% of the vote. The opposition contested the results of the election.

In July, the National Assembly adopted laws to ratify the Second Optional Protocol to the ICCPR, aiming at the abolition of the death penalty, and the Arms Trade Treaty.

## EXCESSIVE USE OF FORCE

The security forces killed seven people and wounded at least 117 others, including pregnant women and children, in Mango in northern Togo, during demonstrations against the creation of a nature reserve in the area in

November. One policeman was killed on 26 November in clashes with protesters who resorted to violence after security forces opened fire on peaceful demonstrators.[1] Gendarmes and the military fired live bullets at protesters on 25 March at a rally in the city of Glei, 160km north of Lomé, the capital. At least 30 people, including a woman and a child, were wounded. Gendarmes and soldiers charged at a crowd of 100 students, shooting real bullets and hitting them with batons. Students had gathered spontaneously to protest against exams being held despite the academic curriculum having been disrupted by social movements throughout the year. The gendarmes and soldiers who used excessive force have not been brought to justice.

## FREEDOM OF ASSEMBLY

The government continued to restrict freedom of peaceful assembly by arbitrarily banning demonstrations and detaining peaceful demonstrators. On 20 August, in Lomé, the security forces used tear gas to disperse a peaceful demonstration of 100 people protesting against the rise of the cost of living. The gendarmerie arbitrarily arrested the three protest organizers, including Kao Atcholi, a human rights defender leading the Association of Victims of Torture in Togo. They were detained for a day and released without charge.

## FREEDOM OF EXPRESSION

On 29 July, the Criminal Court of Lomé found French national Sébastian Alzerreca guilty of disrupting public order on the basis of "misleading publications" he posted on social media commenting on the results of the presidential elections. He received a two-year suspended prison sentence and was banned from Togo for five years. The cultural centre Mytro Nunya, which he founded, was shut down. Sébastian Alzerreca left Togo in August.

Zeus Aziadouvo, a journalist who produced a documentary on prison conditions in Lomé, and Luc Abaki, director of private TV station

La Chaîne du Futur which broadcast the documentary, were repeatedly summoned for questioning and asked to reveal their sources, including at the headquarters of the Research and Investigation Services and at the High Authority for Audiovisual and Communications on 18 and 26 August respectively.

Local media organizations reported websites, including social media sites, being blocked by internet providers in Togo shortly before and after the publication of the results of the presidential election.

## ARBITRARY ARRESTS AND DETENTIONS

On 25 April, the Community Court of Justice of ECOWAS ruled that Togo subjected Pascal Bodjona, a Togolese politician and former member of the government, to arbitrary detention. It ordered Togo to try Pascal Bodjona in a court of law and to pay him a compensation of 18 million CFA franc (approximately €27,440). Pascal Bodjona was arrested on 1 September 2012 and charged with fraud and complicity in fraud. He was released on bail on 9 April 2013, rearrested on 21 August 2014 on the same charges and has been in detention without trial since then.

Seven out of 10 men convicted in September 2011 of participating in a 2009 coup plot, including Kpatcha Gnassingbé, half-brother of the President, remained in detention throughout 2015. In November 2014, the UN Working Group on Arbitrary Detention stated that their detention was arbitrary and requested their immediate release.

## IMPUNITY

The climate of impunity for human rights violations persisted. Ten years after nearly 500 people died in political violence during the presidential election of 24 April 2005, the authorities have taken no steps to identify those responsible for the deaths. Of the 72 complaints filed by the victims' families with the Atakpamé, Amlamé and Lomé courts, none are known to have been fully investigated.[2]

## LEGAL, CONSTITUTIONAL OR INSTITUTIONAL DEVELOPMENTS

On 2 November, the National Assembly adopted a new Criminal Code. While the Code contains a number of positive human rights developments, including the criminalization of torture in line with international standards, certain provisions undermine freedoms of expression and assembly. The Code maintains homophobic provisions criminalizing sexual relations between consenting adults of the same sex. It criminalizes defamation and publishing false news, with these offences carrying prison terms. It reverses the requirement for peaceful assemblies from prior notification to prior authorization.

1.  Togo: Les forces de sécurité ont tiré à bout portant sur des manifestants non armés à Mango (News story, 11 December)
2.  Togo: One decade of impunity: Five steps to end impunity (AFR 15/1508/2015)

# TRINIDAD AND TOBAGO

Republic of Trinidad and Tobago
Head of state: **Anthony Thomas Aquinas Carmona**
Head of government: **Keith Rowley (replaced Kamla Persad-Bissessar in September)**

**Violence and discrimination continued towards lesbian, gay, bisexual, transgender and intersex (LGBTI) people, and women and girls. Abuse of children was a concern. Trinidad retained the mandatory death penalty for murder.**

## BACKGROUND

General elections took place in September resulting in a new administration. Violent crimes remained a key concern with 329 murders reported by the police between January and September 2015, a similar rate to the same period in 2014.

## EXCESSIVE USE OF FORCE

Serious concerns remained about excessive use of force by the police. The Police Complaints Authority lacked staff and sufficient powers to effectively investigate all alleged misconduct by police officers.

## CHILDREN'S RIGHTS

High levels of sexual and other physical abuse of children remained a serious concern. A new Children's Act came into force in May, increasing penalties for abuse of children and raising the age of consent for sexual relations to 18. A Children's Authority was established and received 1,500 reports of child abuse within its first three months. Despite progress in this area, civil society groups reported that insufficient action had been taken by the authorities to prevent child abuse and cases were still poorly investigated and handled.

Activists raised concern that the Children's Act decriminalized sex between children of the opposite sex (unless exploitative), yet criminalized consensual same-sex sexual activity for those aged under 21 with a potential penalty of life imprisonment, in contravention of the rights of the child.

## RIGHTS OF LESBIAN, GAY, BISEXUAL, TRANSGENDER AND INTERSEX PEOPLE

Consensual same-sex sexual activity remained a crime. Local civil society groups continued to receive reports of violence and discrimination towards LGBTI people. Some LGBTI people did not report these crimes or seek access to justice, for fear of further victimization from law enforcement officials or exposure of their sexual orientation or gender identity. Some youths reported being pushed out of their homes or experiencing domestic violence due to discrimination based on their sexual orientation or gender identity. Social services and shelters were not equipped to respond to the needs of homeless LGBTI people, according to local NGOs.

Parliament failed to act on a 2014 recommendation from the Equal Opportunities Commission that "sexual orientation" be included as a protected ground in the Equal Opportunities Act.

A transgender woman ran as an independent candidate in the elections – the first known transgender candidate to run for public office.

## VIOLENCE AGAINST WOMEN AND GIRLS

High levels of gender-based violence, including domestic violence, continued.

## DEATH PENALTY

Mandatory death sentences continued to be imposed for murder. The Judicial Committee of the Privy Council substituted a conviction for murder with one for manslaughter in the case of a man with a mental disability, and reduced his death sentence to a term of imprisonment.

# TUNISIA

Republic of Tunisia
Head of state: **Beji Caid Essebsi**
Head of government: **Habib Essid (replaced Mehdi Jomaa in January)**

**The authorities tightened restrictions on freedoms of expression and assembly, including by banning demonstrations in some instances. There were new reports of torture and other ill-treatment. Women, girls, and lesbian, gay, bisexual, transgender and intersex (LGBTI) people faced discrimination in law and in practice. Courts continued to pass death sentences; there were no executions.**

## BACKGROUND

Militants apparently affiliated to armed Islamist groups carried out gun attacks at the Bardo Museum in the capital Tunis in March and at a Sousse beach resort in June, killing 61 people, mostly foreign tourists, and injuring many more. In November, an attack in central Tunis on a Presidential Guard bus killed 12 people. Clashes between the security forces and armed militants occurred along Tunisia's borders with Algeria and Libya.

The government declared a nationwide state of emergency in early July, following the Sousse attack, renewing it at the end of July and lifting it in early October. On 24 November, following the second Tunis attack, the authorities again declared a state of emergency that remained in force at the end of the year, imposed a curfew in Greater Tunis until 12 December, and closed Tunisia's border with Libya for two weeks.

The Truth and Dignity Commission, created to address political, social and economic crimes and investigate human rights violations committed since 1 July 1955, began hearing testimonies in May; in December it said it had received more than 22,600 cases and extended the deadline for the submission of cases by six months. However, its work was overshadowed by the resignations of some of its members, allegations of corruption against its head, and media criticism. In July, President Essebsi announced a new draft law on special provisions for reconciliation in the economic and financial sectors. This would offer an amnesty and immunity from further prosecution to officials and business executives accused of corruption and embezzlement under the former administration of President Ben Ali, if they returned the stolen funds. If enacted, the draft law would hamper future investigations by the Truth and Dignity Commission. The proposal sparked protests across the country by the Manich Msamah ("I will not forgive") movement, several of which the security forces dispersed using excessive force. The draft law was awaiting enactment at the end of the year.

In May, a new law was passed to create a Supreme Judicial Council (SJC) to oversee the judicial system and increase its independence from the executive. Although an improvement, the law contained serious flaws relating to the composition of the SJC. In June, the temporary constitutional court ruled the new law unconstitutional and in December ruled a revised version of the law unconstitutional as well.

In October, the Tunisian National Dialogue Quartet, a coalition of trade union, human rights and other civil society groups formed in 2013 to promote peace, democracy and human rights in Tunisia's transition, was awarded the Nobel Peace Prize.

## COUNTER-TERROR AND SECURITY

The government proposed a new law on Repression of Attacks against Armed Forces in March, following the Bardo Museum killings and attacks on the security forces by armed groups. If enacted, it would put journalists, human rights defenders and others who criticize the security forces and army at risk of criminal prosecution and would give security forces excessive powers to use lethal force. The draft law had not been enacted by the end of the year.

Parliament adopted a new counter-terrorism law in July, following the Sousse killings and what the authorities said was a foiled terrorist attack in Gafsa. The new law, which replaced a 2003 law used by the Ben Ali government to repress political opposition, further eroded basic rights. It defined terrorism in vague and broad terms, gave security forces wide monitoring and surveillance powers, and extended the period during which security forces can hold terrorism suspects incommunicado for interrogation from six to 15 days, increasing the risk of torture and other ill-treatment. It also imposed the death penalty for rape and for terrorist acts resulting in death, weakened fair trial guarantees by allowing courts to conduct closed trials and withhold the identity of witnesses, and criminalized expression deemed to be "praising terrorism". By December, the government said the courts had handed down 28 sentences in trials on terrorism charges, including one in which three defendants received death sentences.

In July, the authorities said they had arrested over 1,000 terrorism suspects since the Bardo Museum attack in March and banned 15,000 other suspects from leaving

Tunisia. The government also announced its intention to construct a security wall along Tunisia's border with Libya. Following the November attack in Tunis, the authorities carried out thousands of raids, hundreds of arrests and placed at least 138 people under house arrest, amid reports of security officials' harassment of families of terrorist suspects.

## TORTURE AND OTHER ILL-TREATMENT

There were new reports of torture and other ill-treatment of detainees, mostly during interrogation in the first days after arrest.

Five men arrested as terrorist suspects on 27 July alleged that interrogators beat and tortured them by waterboarding. They filed formal complaints after they were released on 4 August. Counter-terrorism police rearrested them the same day and returned them to their previous place of detention. On 5 August, they were taken for forensic medical examinations. They were provisionally released on 10 August. A special parliamentary committee was appointed to investigate their torture allegations but no findings had been made public by the end of the year.

Thousands of torture cases dating from the Ben Ali administration were registered with the Truth and Dignity Commission. While in most cases those bringing the allegations were men, a number of women spoke of being beaten, tortured and sexually assaulted in detention. It remained unclear how the Commission would refer cases to prosecution and whether such referrals would be to specialized chambers or to the Public Prosecutor.

The National Body for the Prevention of Torture, created under a 2013 law, remained inoperative as its members had still to be appointed.

## FREEDOMS OF EXPRESSION AND ASSEMBLY

The authorities curtailed freedom of expression using laws enacted during the Ben Ali administration, including the 2003 anti-terrorism law and Penal Code articles criminalizing defamation of public figures.

The state of emergency in force from 4 July to 2 October gave the government powers to suspend all strikes and demonstrations, ban and disperse all gatherings deemed to threaten public order, and control and censor print, broadcast and other media and publications. In some instances, security forces used excessive force to disperse and detain peaceful protesters who defied the ban. On 8 September, the Minister of the Interior declared that even peaceful protests were contrary to the emergency law and banned a demonstration planned for 12 September.

Police arrested teacher Abdelfattah Said in July after he posted a video on the Facebook website accusing security officials of being behind the attack that killed 38 people in Sousse. He was charged with complicity in terrorism under the 2003 anti-terrorism law. He was also charged with defaming a public servant and broadcasting false news under Articles 128 and 306 of the Penal Code for posting a caricature of Prime Minister Essid. In November, the terrorism charges were dropped and he was fined and sentenced to a one-year prison term on the false news charge; he was cleared of defamation.

## WOMEN'S RIGHTS

Women and girls continued to face discrimination in law and in practice, and were inadequately protected against sexual and other violence. Survivors of sexual and gender-based violence continued to suffer from a lack of proper access to health and support services and to judicial remedies. Penal Code articles criminalized sexual violence as an assault on personal decency rather than a violation of the victim's bodily integrity. The Penal Code also allowed men accused of raping a girl or woman aged between 15 and 20 to escape prosecution by marrying their victim.

A comprehensive draft law to combat violence against women, which contained provisions increasing protection to survivors of sexual and gender-based violence and which had been leaked in December 2014, remained under consideration at the end of the year. In August, the Council of Ministers approved a draft law which would remove existing discrimination between men and women in giving to or withdrawing from their children travel documents and authorization to travel. The law was approved by Parliament in November.

## RIGHTS OF LESBIAN, GAY, BISEXUAL, TRANSGENDER AND INTERSEX PEOPLE

LGBTI people faced discrimination in law and in practice, and were inadequately protected against violence based on their sexual orientation or gender identity. Article 230 of the Penal Code criminalized consensual same-sex sexual relations, punishing "sodomy and lesbianism" with up to three years' imprisonment. Transgender individuals were at particular risk of arrest and prosecution on the charge of offending public morals. The authorities failed to conduct meaningful investigations into homophobic and transphobic crimes.

A lesbian woman sought asylum abroad after she was subjected to four separate assaults during the year by men who attacked her on the street, beating her with their hands and feet and with broken bottles and on one occasion cutting her neck with a knife. She had been subjected to at least eight homophobic assaults over a period of nine years. She reported the latest assaults to police but they failed to identify and arrest her attackers and warned her that, as a lesbian woman, she could face prosecution and imprisonment.

A male student was sentenced to one year in prison in September for engaging in "sodomy". At the court's request, he was subjected to an anal examination, in violation of the prohibition of torture and other ill-treatment. The examination was conducted by the forensics department in Farhat Hached Hospital in Sousse, supposedly to establish "proof" of anal sex. The student had initially been questioned by the police about his relationship to a murdered man. He said

he admitted that he had had sex with the man after police officers slapped him and threatened to rape him and press murder charges if he did not "confess". He was released on bail in November and his sentence was reduced to two months on appeal in December, which he had already served.

In December, six students received maximum three-year prison terms after a court in Kairouan convicted them on charges of "sodomy". The six, who were subjected to anal examinations after their arrest, were also sentenced to be banished from Kairouan for five years after they complete their prison sentences.

## REFUGEES' AND MIGRANTS' RIGHTS

The authorities generally allowed Libyan nationals fleeing armed conflict in Libya to enter Tunisia. Other foreign nationals, including refugees and migrants, were only allowed entry if they possessed valid entry documents, and were required to depart from Tunisia after a short transit stay.

The navy and coastguard rescued hundreds of refugees, asylum-seekers and migrants from boats in distress in the Mediterranean, including many that had departed from Zuwara in Libya. The authorities took most of those they rescued to the southern governorate of Medenine where they were housed in temporary shelters. There, some returned to their home countries while others remained in a situation of uncertainty.

Although signatory to the UN Refugee Convention and its Protocol, Tunisia did not have a comprehensive asylum law, which contributed to the vulnerability of refugees, asylum-seekers and migrants.

In August, the authorities arrested 10 Sudanese, Nigerian, Kenyan and Liberian nationals who mounted a protest in Tunis asking for resettlement, took them to the Ouardia refugee detention centre and sought to force them to cross the border from Tunisia to Algeria, before eventually allowing them back into Tunisia and eventually releasing them. UNHCR, the UN refugee agency, had rejected the refugee applications of the 10 individuals in 2012 but they had remained in the Choucha camp established by UNHCR, despite its official closure in 2013. The individuals had all worked in Libya prior to the conflict there.

## DEATH PENALTY
The death penalty remained in force for murder and other crimes; the new anti-terrorism law provided for the death penalty for some offences. Courts handed down 11 death sentences; no executions have been carried out since 1991.

# TURKEY

**Republic of Turkey**
Head of state: **Recep Tayyip Erdoğan**
Head of government: **Ahmet Davutoğlu**

The human rights situation deteriorated markedly following parliamentary elections in June and the outbreak of violence between the Kurdistan Workers' Party (PKK) and the Turkish armed forces in July. The media faced unprecedented pressure from the government; free expression online and offline suffered significantly. The right to freedom of peaceful assembly continued to be violated. Cases of excessive use of force by police and ill-treatment in detention increased. Impunity for human rights abuses persisted. The independence of the judiciary was further eroded. Separate suicide bombings attributed to the armed group Islamic State (IS) targeting left-wing and pro-Kurdish activists and demonstrators killed 139 people. An estimated 2.5 million refugees and asylum-seekers were accommodated in Turkey but individuals increasingly faced arbitrary detention and deportation as the government negotiated a migration deal with the EU.

## BACKGROUND
Politically motivated appointments and transfers of judges and prosecutors continued throughout the year, wreaking havoc on a judiciary already lacking independence and impartiality. Criminal Courts of Peace – with jurisdiction over the conduct of criminal investigations, such as pre-charge detention and pre-trial detention decisions, seizure of property and appeals against these decisions – came under increasing government control.

In April, commemorations were held to mark the 100th anniversary of the 1915 massacres of Armenians in Ottoman Turkey with peaceful demonstrations across the country. No progress was made towards fully recognizing the crimes committed.

At the general election in June, the ruling Justice and Development Party (AK Party), in power since 2002, failed to secure an overall parliamentary majority. It regained its majority after a rerun of the elections in November, securing nearly 50% of the vote.

A fragile peace process in place since 2013 between the PKK and the state disintegrated in July. State forces launched attacks on PKK bases in Turkey and northern Iraq, while the PKK launched deadly attacks on police and army targets. Armed clashes between the youth wing of the PKK (YDG-H) and the police and army in urban centres took a particularly heavy toll on the lives of ordinary residents. The mass deployment of security forces to the southeastern provinces in mid-December resulted in an intensification of clashes and, according to local lawyers and activists, the killings of scores of unarmed residents. The Minister of the Interior stated that over 3,000 "terrorists" had been killed since the end of the ceasefire.

Following deadly PKK attacks in September, nationalist mob attacks swept Turkey, mainly targeting Kurds and their property as well as offices of the Kurdish-rooted, left-wing Peoples' Democratic Party (HDP). The Ministry of the Interior reported on the deaths of two members of the public, injuries to 51, and damage to 69 political party buildings and 30 homes and businesses. The HDP reported that over 400 attacks had taken place, including 126 attacks on their offices.

Mass prosecutions under vague and broad anti-terrorism laws continued. In March, all 236 military officers accused of the "Sledgehammer" coup plot to overthrow the AK Party government were acquitted after a retrial. Proceedings continued on appeal in the "Ergenekon" case of civilians accused of plotting to overthrow the government. Prosecutions targeting Kurdish political activists for alleged membership of the PKK-linked Kurdistan Communities Union remained pending, following the 2014 abolition of the anti-terrorism and organized crime courts with special powers. Waves of detentions took place after the eruption of violence between the PKK and state forces in July. By late August it was estimated that more than 2,000 people had been detained for alleged links to the PKK, while over 260 were remanded in pre-trial detention. Prosecutions were commenced of individuals accused of membership of the "Fethullah Gülen Terrorist Organization", including US-based cleric and former AK Party ally Fethullah Gülen.

## FREEDOM OF EXPRESSION

Respect for freedom of expression deteriorated. Countless unfair criminal prosecutions, including under criminal defamation and anti-terrorism laws, targeted political activists, journalists and others critical of public officials or government policy. Ordinary citizens were frequently brought before the courts for social media posts.

The government exerted immense pressure on the media, targeting media companies and digital distribution networks, and singling out critical journalists, who were then threatened and physically attacked by often unidentified assailants. Mainstream journalists were fired after criticizing the government. News websites, including large swathes of the Kurdish press, were blocked on unclear grounds by administrative orders aided by a compliant judiciary. Journalists were harassed and assaulted by police while covering stories

in the predominantly Kurdish southeast.

In March, *Taraf* newspaper journalist Mehmet Baransu was remanded in pre-trial detention, charged with obtaining secret state documents which he wrote about in 2010 and then passed to prosecutors, forming the basis of the "Sledgehammer" coup plot prosecution. He remained in pre-trial detention at the end of the year.

In the six months to March, the Minister of Justice gave permission for 105 criminal prosecutions for insulting President Erdoğan under Article 299 of the Penal Code. Eight people were remanded in pre-trial detention. Prosecutions under the provision, which carries a sentence of up to four years' imprisonment, continued throughout the year. In September, a 17-year-old student was convicted of "insult" for calling the President "the thieving owner of the illegal palace". He received a suspended sentence of 11 months and 20 days by a children's court in the central Anatolian city of Konya.

In November, the first hearing took place in the trial of *Cumhuriyet* newspaper journalist Canan Cöşkun, accused of insulting 10 state prosecutors when she alleged they obtained discounted property because of their status as prosecutors. She faced up to 23 years and four months in prison. In November, the newspaper's editor-in-chief Can Dündar and its Ankara representative, Erdem Gül, were charged with espionage, revealing state secrets and assisting a terrorist organization after a story in the newspaper alleged that the intelligence services had transferred weapons to an armed group in Syria in 2014. The then Prime Minister Recep Tayyip Erdoğan had previously claimed that the trucks were delivering humanitarian aid. The two men were remanded in pre-trial detention and remained there at the end of the year. They faced up to life imprisonment if convicted.

Diyarbakır-based Dutch journalist Frederike Geerdink was acquitted of "making propaganda for the PKK" in April, but detained and deported after covering a story in the southeastern province of Yüksekova in September. In August, three Vice News journalists were questioned by police after covering clashes between the PKK and security forces, then charged with "assisting a terrorist organization" and remanded in pre-trial detention. British citizens Jake Hanrahan and Philip Pendlebury were released and deported after eight days; Mohammed Rasool, an Iraqi Kurdish journalist, remained in pre-trial detention at the end of the year.

Unprecedented steps were taken to silence media linked to investigations of the "Fethullah Gülen Terrorist Organization". In October, Digiturk, a private digital platform, removed seven channels from its service. Four days ahead of the 1 November election, police accompanied a court-appointed government trustee and forcibly entered the head offices of the Koza İpek conglomerate, cutting live broadcasts by two news channels, Bugün and Kanaltürk, and blocking the printing of the *Millet* and *Bugün* newspapers. The fiercely opposition news outlets were re-opened as staunchly pro-government. In November, the state-owned Turkish Satellite Communications Company (Türksat) removed 13 television and radio channels owned by the Samanyolu Broadcasting Group. Hidayet Karaca, the head of the group, remained in pre-trial detention during the entire year.

In November, the head of the Diyarbakır Bar Association and renowned human rights defender Tahir Elçi was shot dead after making a press statement in Diyarbakır. The perpetrator remained unidentified by the end of the year amid concerns over the impartiality and effectiveness of the investigation. He had faced death threats after being charged the previous month with "making propaganda for a terrorist organization", for saying on live national television that the PKK was "not a terrorist organization but an armed political movement with considerable support". He faced over seven years' imprisonment. The news channel CNN Türk was also fined 700,000 liras (€230,000) for broadcasting the remarks.

## FREEDOM OF ASSEMBLY

The right to peaceful assembly continued to be limited in law and denied in practice, depending on the issue being protested and participants' profiles. The practice of arbitrary detentions at assemblies was given legal basis by legislative amendments in March in the Domestic Security Package, providing police with powers to detain without judicial supervision. Peaceful demonstrators continued to be prosecuted and convicted.

Traditional May Day demonstrations in Taksim Square in Istanbul were denied permission to proceed for the third year running. The same grounds of an unspecified security threat and disruption to traffic and tourism were offered by the authorities, who instead proposed locations outside of the city centre. Tens of thousands of police closed off the entire Taksim district and surrounding areas to demonstrators, traffic and tourists alike.

For the first time in its 12-year history, the authorities violently broke up the annual national Pride march in Istanbul in June, citing a lack of formal notification and information about counter-demonstrators. Discussions between representatives of the Pride and the authorities leading up to the event offered no indication that it would be banned. Police used excessive force including tear gas, water cannon and pepper-ball projectiles against marchers during the day and Pride partygoers in the evening. In November, the Governor of Istanbul denied permission for a criminal investigation into the conduct of the police at the Pride march to be opened.

Prosecutions on trumped-up charges against Gezi Park protesters continued. In April, an Istanbul court acquitted members of Taksim Solidarity, an umbrella organization opposing the redevelopment of Taksim Square and Gezi Park, including five who had been accused of "founding a criminal organization". Most trials ended in acquittal but 244 were convicted at a trial of 255 people in Istanbul, on various charges including under the Law on Meetings and

Demonstrations. Two doctors were convicted of "denigrating a place of worship" after giving emergency treatment to injured demonstrators in a mosque. A further case against 94 people for participating in Gezi Park protests in Izmir was opened in September.

## EXCESSIVE USE OF FORCE

Allegations of excessive use of force at demonstrations dramatically increased. Lethal force was used by security forces during anti-terrorism operations, many involving armed clashes with the YDG-H. In many cases, conflicting accounts and the absence of effective investigations prevented the facts from being established. In March, legislative amendments in the Domestic Security Package conflicted with international standards on the use of force.

In January, 12-year-old Nihat Kazanhan was shot dead by a police officer in the southeastern city of Cizre. The authorities first denied the involvement of police, but video evidence emerged showing Nihat Kazanhan and other children throwing stones at police officers and, in separate footage, showing a police officer firing a rifle towards the children. Nihat Kazanhan was killed by a single bullet to the head. The trial of five police officers continued.

Local authorities imposed extended round-the-clock curfews during police operations targeting the YDG-H in cities in the southeast. During the curfews, a total ban on residents leaving their homes was imposed, water, electricity and communications were cut and outside observers banned from entering. Curfews imposed on Sur on 11 December, as well as Cizre and Silopi on 14 December, were still in place at the end of the year.

## TORTURE AND OTHER ILL-TREATMENT

Reported cases of ill-treatment in detention and other inhuman or degrading treatment in the context of police or military operations against the PKK increased.

Four men accused of murdering two policemen in the southeastern city of Ceylanpınar said they had been severely beaten in police custody in July and August, first when they were being transferred to Osmaniye No. 1 T-type prison in Adana province and then at the prison itself. They remained in pre-trial detention at the end of the year.

Images circulated on the internet, apparently taken by special operations police officers, appearing to show the naked and disfigured body of female PKK member Kevser Eltürk (Ekin Wan) being paraded in the streets of Varto in the eastern province of Muş, after clashes with state forces in August. Another photograph showed the body of Hacı Lokman Birlik being dragged behind an armoured police vehicle in the southeastern province of Şırnak in October. The reported autopsy indicated that the man had been shot 28 times. The authorities said that investigations into both incidents were continuing.

## IMPUNITY

Impunity persisted for human rights abuses committed by public officials. Investigations were hampered by police withholding crucial evidence, such as lists of officers on duty and CCTV footage, and the passivity of prosecutors faced with this obstructiveness. Without a long-promised Independent Police Complaints Commission, there was little prospect of improvement. Where they took place, prosecutions were often flawed.

There was a resounding failure to secure accountability for police abuses during the 2013 Gezi Park protests. In January, police officers and civilians were convicted for their part in the beating to death of protester Ali Ismail Korkmaz in the city of Eskişehir. In June, an Istanbul court convicted a police officer who used pepper spray on a peaceful demonstrator, known as "the woman in red". A trial of a police officer for the killing of Abdullah Cömert and a retrial for the killing of Ethem Sarısülük, both protesters, continued.

No prosecution was brought for the killing of 14-year-old Berkin Elvan or in hundreds of other cases where people were injured by police. These included the case of Hakan Yaman, who was filmed being beaten, burned and left for dead by police officers in Istanbul. He lost an eye but survived the attack. Two and a half years on, the police officers in the video had not been identified.

Two prosecutions were brought following Kobani protests in southeastern Turkey in October 2014, which left over 40 people dead. One, in March, was against allegedly pro-PKK youths, for the killing of four people in Diyarbakır. The other, in June, was against 10 private security guards and family members of the AK Party mayor for the fatal shooting of three protesters in Kurtalan, Siirt province. However, investigations in many other cases had not progressed, including in cases of individuals who were believed to have been shot dead by police officers using excessive force during police operations in the southeast. The lack of ballistic reports, crime scene investigations and the taking of witness statements by prosecutors offered little hope that the circumstances of the deaths would be revealed.

In November, all eight defendants, including former district Gendarmerie commander Cemal Temizöz, were acquitted in the landmark case brought for the disappearances and killings of 21 people in Cizre between 1993 and 1995, following a deeply flawed trial.

## ABUSES BY ARMED GROUPS
Three suicide bomb attacks blamed on IS caused major casualties. In June, four people were killed when explosions targeted an HDP rally days before the June elections. In July, a bomb killed 33 young activists in the southeastern city of Suruç as they made a press statement about their mission to deliver humanitarian aid to the neighbouring, predominantly Kurdish city of Kobani in Syria. In October, twin explosions in the capital Ankara targeting a peace rally organized by trade unions, civil society organizations and left-wing parties killed 102 people.

In March, Istanbul Prosecutor Mehmet Selim Kiraz was killed after being taken hostage by the armed group Revolutionary People's Liberation Party-Front (DHKP-C). The two hostage-takers were killed in a police operation at the courthouse.

PKK attacks resulted in the deaths of civilians, including physician Abdullah Biroğul when his car was shot at in the southeastern province of Diyarbakır.

## REFUGEES AND ASYLUM-SEEKERS
Around 2.3 million registered Syrian refugees and 250,000 refugees and asylum-seekers from other countries including Afghanistan and Iraq were accommodated in Turkey. Some 260,000 Syrian refugees were accommodated in well-resourced, government-run camps, but most refugees and asylum-seekers outside camps received little or no assistance and were not granted the right to work. In many cases they struggled to survive, getting by through exploitative and underpaid irregular work and the charity of neighbours. Asylum applications for non-Syrians were rarely processed in practice. The government signed an agreement with the EU in October, aimed at preventing irregular migration from Turkey to the EU.

In September, at least 200 refugees – mostly Syrian – attempting to travel irregularly to Greece were kept in incommunicado or even secret detention at various locations in Turkey. Many were pressured into agreeing to "voluntarily" return to Syria and Iraq, in a flagrant breach of international law.

# TURKMENISTAN

Turkmenistan
Head of state and government: **Gurbanguly Berdimuhamedov**

No improvement in the human rights situation was visible in 2015, and the country remained closed to independent human rights monitors. In January, the government announced plans to introduce a human rights Ombudsman. It remained impossible for independent civil society organizations to operate freely. Freedoms of expression and association were heavily restricted, and many people faced limits on their freedom of movement. Forced evictions were reported. Sex between men remained a criminal offence.

## FREEDOM OF EXPRESSION

Although the principles of media independence and prohibition of state interference in media activities were enshrined in law in 2013, in practice the media remained subject to extensive state censorship and no independent newspapers or other media outlets were able to operate. The authorities continued to use harassment, intimidation and, in at least one case, imprisonment to attempt to silence journalists. Freelance journalist Saparmamed Nepeskuliev, who had reported on corruption for Radio Free Europe/Radio Liberty (RFE/RL) and the Alternative Turkmenistan News service, was detained on 7 July and held incommunicado for over a month. Although unofficial sources told his family he was sentenced to three years' imprisonment on drug-related offences on 31 August, it was widely believed he was targeted for his journalism work.[1] Correspondents for RFE/RL continued to be denied accreditation; they were frequently harassed, intimidated and even threatened with imprisonment.

Access to foreign media and other information sources outside the country was further restricted. During the first half of the year, residents in the capital, Ashgabat, and in other towns and cities were forced by local housing authorities as part of an official campaign to remove and destroy privately installed satellite dishes, blocking their access to foreign media outlets. Access to the internet was monitored and restricted, with social networking sites frequently blocked.

People who attempted to protest against forced evictions near Ashgabat were intimidated, threatened and, in some cases, detained.

## FREEDOM OF RELIGION

Religious practices were tightly controlled, particularly those of religious minorities such as the Armenian Apostolic Christians, Catholics, Protestants and Jehovah's Witnesses. Under the Code of Administrative Offences, religious groups must register with the state, and if refused registration they must publicize that they are banned. Forum 18, a Norwegian human rights organization that monitors freedom of religion, thought, conscience and belief, reported that a Jehovah's Witness had been convicted of "inciting religious hatred" and sentenced to four years in prison. He was arrested during a meeting for worship that he had organized in his home.

## TORTURE AND OTHER ILL-TREATMENT

Ongoing reports indicated that people were still being tortured or otherwise ill-treated by members of law enforcement agencies to extract "confessions" and incriminate others. Activist Mansur Mingelov remained in prison, following his conviction in an unfair trial for drug offences. He had publicized information that members of the Baloch ethnic community were tortured and ill-treated in Mary province in 2012.

## ENFORCED DISAPPEARANCES

The whereabouts of prisoners who were subjected to enforced disappearance after an alleged assassination attempt against then President Saparmurat Niyazov in 2002 remained unknown. The authorities did not respond to a request made in June during the EU-Turkmenistan Human Rights Dialogue to provide relevant information. For 13 years, the families of those detained have not received any information about their whereabouts or wellbeing.

## FREEDOM OF MOVEMENT

The requirement for citizens to obtain "exit visas" to leave the country was abolished in 2006, but arbitrary restrictions on the right to travel abroad still remained in practice. In numerous cases, individuals discovered they were subject to a travel ban at the point when they tried to leave the country. In July, the daughter of exiled parliamentarian Pirimkuli Tanrykuliev was prevented from travelling to Turkey with her two children; passport control officials stamped their passports with a statement saying they were banned from leaving the country.

After numerous attempts over several years, former prisoner Geldy Kyarizov was allowed to travel to Russia for specialist medical treatment and to join his wife, as were other members of his family. Since his release from prison in 2007, Geldy Kyarizov had been repeatedly prevented from doing so. Members of his family accompanying him on these occasions were subject to intimidation and physical violence, including a suspicious car accident in August – similar to a previous incident involving his daughter in early 2014 – which authorities refused to investigate.

## HOUSING RIGHTS – FORCED EVICTIONS

Thousands of people lost their homes in forced evictions and demolitions in and around Ashgabat. Houses were demolished, reportedly to make way for building works linked to the forthcoming 5th Asian Indoor and Martial Arts Games, due to take place in 2017, and as part of wider city redevelopment programmes.[2]

Estimates indicated that around 50,000 people were forcibly evicted in the worst affected area, Choganly neighbourhood, north of Ashgabat. Analysis of high-resolution satellite imagery confirmed that nearly half of the 10,000 houses and other residential structures in Choganly had been demolished by 28 April; later reports indicated that by September the entire neighbourhood had been demolished. Residents were neither consulted about alternatives to eviction nor provided with different or temporary accommodation. The government claimed that because some houses in Choganly were intended as holiday homes (dachas) and other houses were built illegally, their owners or occupiers were not entitled to compensation, alternative accommodation or land.[3]

1. Turkmenistan: Freelance journalist's whereabouts unknown: Saparmamed Nepeskuliev (EUR 61/2229/2015)
2. Turkmenistan: Hundreds of families facing forced evictions (EUR 61/1521/2015)
3. Deprived of homes, deprived of rights: Uncovering evidence of mass forced evictions and house demolitions in Turkmenistan (EUR 61/2693/2015)

# UGANDA

**Republic of Uganda**
Head of state and government: **Yoweri Kaguta Museveni**

**Police brutality and restrictions of the right to freedom of peaceful assembly increased. Attacks against activists, journalists and other media workers continued with impunity. Opposition politicians seeking to participate in the national elections scheduled for early 2016 were arrested and detained, along with their supporters.**

## BACKGROUND

The year was dominated politically by preparations for the national elections, scheduled for early 2016. High-level splits within the ruling National Resistance Movement (NRM) resulted in former Prime Minister Amama Mbabazi announcing his intention to run for presidential office as an independent candidate. Police brutality, arbitrary arrests, torture and the unlawful disruption of numerous public assemblies all subsequently increased. Opposition political parties and their supporters were harassed, arrested and detained.

Discrimination, harassment and violence against lesbian, gay, bisexual, transgender and intersex (LGBTI) people continued with impunity. The authorities' hostility towards civil society organizations and human rights defenders continued. Parliamentary debates took place around the new Non-

Governmental Organizations Bill, which was passed by Parliament in November.

## POLICE AND SECURITY FORCES

The government oversaw the recruitment and training of many thousands of "Crime Preventers", a militarized network of community policing volunteers, believed to be linked to serious human rights violations across the country.

## TORTURE AND OTHER ILL-TREATMENT

On 16 July, Vincent Kaggwa, a 25-year-old spokesperson of the NRM "Poor Youth" was arrested at his home in Wandegeya, Kampala, by security officers. He was detained for four days, during which he was tortured and questioned about his political support for former Prime Minister Amama Mbabazi.

On 14 September, Amama Mbabazi's head of security, Christopher Aine, was arrested in Kampala. He was blindfolded, driven to an unidentified "safe house", and tortured before being released on 17 September. Iron bars and canes were used to beat him on several parts of his body.

Reports indicated at least 10 separate cases of assault, possible torture and unlawful arrest by "Crime Preventers" from September 2014 to August 2015.

## FREEDOM OF EXPRESSION

Journalists and other media workers continued to face attacks from the police as well as harassment and intimidation in the course of their work, particularly in rural areas.

On 12 January, cameraman Andrew Lwanga was assaulted by police while filming a gathering of youth activists, the Jobless Brotherhood. He sustained severe injuries, requiring hospital admission. A criminal trial against the alleged perpetrator was ongoing.

On 23 January, radio journalists Gerald Kankya and Simon Amanyire were attacked by a mob in Fort Portal, Western Region.

On 8 July, the Uganda Communications Commission issued a document to all broadcasters, cautioning against "negative and unprofessional trends such as lack of balance, sensationalism, incitement, abusive language and relying on unauthorized and unreliable sources of information". Many media observers saw this directive as an attack on freedom of expression in the run-up to the 2016 elections.

On 14 October, journalist Alfred Ochwo was arrested and subsequently assaulted by police officers after reporting on the arrest of Kyadondo East MP Ssemujju Ibrahim Nganda.

In July, disclosures by WikiLeaks revealed commercial discussions between the Office of the President and surveillance firm Hacking Team. In October, Privacy International reported on the sale and use of the intrusion malware software to the Ugandan military to target real or perceived political opponents. Privacy International also reported on the installation of FinFisher "access points" in Parliament, key government institutions and major hotels. The government denied these claims.

## FREEDOM OF ASSEMBLY

Throughout the year, numerous public assemblies organized by opposition political parties were disrupted or prevented from taking place by the Uganda Police Force. The Public Order Management Act 2013 was routinely used as the justification, with organizers often being placed under "preventive arrest".

On 9 July, Amama Mbabazi and former President of the Forum for Democratic Change (FDC) Kizza Besigye were separately arrested and prevented from participating in planned political events. Both were placed under "preventive arrest". Over the course of the following days, 14 youth activists were arrested and detained, including seven arrested at the conclusion of a peaceful press conference.

On 9 September, the police were deployed in Soroti, Eastern Region, in large numbers, ahead of a public gathering organized by Amama Mbabazi. Eyewitnesses and others reported that police used tear gas and rubber bullets against participants.

On 10 September, Amama Mbabazi was forced to abandon a consultative meeting planned in Jinja, Eastern Region, after police used excessive force to block his route and escorted him back to Kampala. Prior to his planned arrival, police used rubber bullets and tear gas to disperse several hundred of his supporters. Tear gas canisters were fired into a primary school yard.

On 10 October, Kizza Besigye attempted to travel with a convoy of his political team to Rukungiri. The Uganda Police Force prevented the planned public assembly from taking place. Kizza Besigye, along with members of his entourage, was arrested and detained. On the same day, FDC activist Fatuma Zainab was arrested and undressed by three police officers, prompting national outrage. On 15 October, Kizza Besigye was again arrested and placed under preventive arrest.

## HUMAN RIGHTS DEFENDERS

On 27 November, Parliament passed the Non-Governmental Organizations Act 2015. The new law, not yet assented to by President Museveni, imposes criminal and civil penalties on organizations for engaging in activities that are "prejudicial to the interests of Uganda or the dignity of the people of Uganda". The law fails to conform to regional and international human rights standards, including the right to freedom of association guaranteed under the Constitution.

Throughout the year, the offices of several human rights NGOs were broken into or otherwise targeted. On 30 June, the offices of Human Rights Network for Journalists-Uganda were broken into. The organization lost several computers, laptops and documents. On 17 July, the offices of Uganda Land Alliance were broken into, on the outskirts of Kampala. A security guard was killed in the course of the attack.

In July, the Uganda Registration Services Bureau began investigations into the Great Lakes Institute for Strategic Studies for allegedly "de-campaigning" government programmes.

On 17 October, the offices of Soroti Development Association and NGOs Network were broken into.

## VIOLENCE AGAINST WOMEN AND GIRLS

In May, Ugandan singer Jemimah Kansiime was arrested and jailed after releasing a music video that reportedly violated provisions of the Anti-Pornography Act 2014. A Constitutional Court challenge against the law remained pending.

## RIGHTS OF LESBIAN, GAY, BISEXUAL, TRANSGENDER AND INTERSEX PEOPLE

Attacks against persons on the basis of their real or perceived sexual orientation or gender identity continued throughout the year, with an increase in reported cases in the latter half of the year.

A draft of the Prohibition of Promotion of Unnatural Sexual Practices Bill made available in 2014 had yet to be debated by Parliament. The draft law constituted a continuation of the discriminatory ethos of the nullified Anti-Homosexuality Act (AHA) 2014. The new bill would create criminal sanctions for "promoting" so-called "unnatural sexual practices" which included consensual same-sex conduct between adults. Like the AHA, the Bill would criminalize advocacy, education and health care for the LGBTI community.

## INTERNATIONAL JUSTICE

On 6 January, Dominic Ongwen, a senior commander in the Lord's Resistance Army (LRA) was taken into custody by US forces in the Central African Republic, and subsequently transferred to the custody of the ICC. Dominic Ongwen was indicted by the ICC in 2005 for crimes committed in Gulu, Northern Region, in 2004. He faced three counts of crimes against humanity and four counts of war crimes. On 10 September, the ICC pre-trial chamber recommended to the ICC Presidency that Dominic Ongwen's confirmation of charges hearing be heard in Uganda.

ICC arrest warrants for Joseph Kony, the LRA leader, and two other LRA commanders remained in force. The men were still at large at the end of the year.

On 30 March, Joan Kagezi, head of the Directorate of Public Prosecutions Anti-Terrorism and War Crimes Division, was shot dead by undisclosed gunmen in Kampala.

# UKRAINE

**Ukraine**
Head of state: **Petro Poroshenko**
Head of government: **Arseniy Yatsenyuk**

**The year began with intense fighting in the east of the country between separatist pro-Russian and Ukrainian forces and ended with sporadic fire interrupting a precarious ceasefire. Impunity prevailed for war crimes committed by both sides. Little progress was made in investigating violations and abuses related to the 2013-2014 pro-European demonstrations in the capital Kyiv ("EuroMaydan") and in bringing perpetrators to justice. The adoption of a law creating a State Investigation Bureau was a welcome step towards creating an effective mechanism for investigating abuses by law enforcement officials. Independent and critical media and activists were unable to operate freely in the self-styled People's Republics of Donetsk and Luhansk as well as in Crimea. In government-controlled areas, media outlets and individuals perceived to express pro-Russian or pro-separatist views faced harassment. In June, a lesbian, gay, bisexual, transgender and intersex (LGBTI) Pride march in Kyiv was marred by violence despite police protection. In November, amendments to labour laws were introduced, expressly prohibiting discrimination against LGBTI people.**

## BACKGROUND

In January and February, heavy fighting resumed in Ukraine's eastern region of Donbass, as Russian-backed separatists in Donetsk and Luhansk sought to advance and straighten their frontline. Amid heavy military losses, Ukrainian forces ceded control over Donetsk airport and the area around the town of Debaltseve. More evidence emerged of Russia heavily backing separatist fighters with manpower and military weaponry, although it continued to deny direct military involvement. In February, an internationally mediated agreement was reached between the Ukrainian government and the de facto authorities of the Luhansk and Donetsk People's Republics; a fragile ceasefire ensued. In September, both sides pulled back heavy weaponry, but mortar and small gunfire exchanges were still occurring at the end of the year, resulting in further casualties. According to UN figures, the death toll exceeded 9,000 by the end of the year, including approximately 2,000 civilians. Over 2.5 million people were displaced, including 1.1 million outside Ukraine.

On 8 September, Ukraine referred the situation in Donbass to the ICC, when it lodged a declaration accepting the Court's jurisdiction over alleged crimes committed on its territory from 20 February 2014. However, Parliament failed to ratify the Rome Statute.

Right-wing groups, which had received negligible electoral support following the EuroMaydan protests in 2014, were implicated in a series of violent incidents. In July, armed paramilitaries from the nationalist organization Pravy Sektor (Right Sector) were involved in a shoot-out with police in the Zakarpattya region, resulting in three deaths. In August, during a protest organized by the non-parliamentary right-wing Svoboda party in front of Parliament, four National Guard officers were killed by a grenade. Several Svoboda activists were arrested.

Local elections were held in October and November in government-controlled territory. However, voting was postponed until later in the year in the city of Mariupol, and was not held in several towns and villages across eastern and southern Ukraine due to security concerns.

On 20 September, activists opposed to the Russian occupation of Crimea established checkpoints at the land border with Crimea, halting the overland delivery of food and other goods from mainland Ukraine. On 20 November, four electric power lines that provided over 70% of electricity to Crimea were blown up by unknown individuals, causing a blackout across the peninsula. Repair teams dispatched by the Ukrainian authorities to restore the line were blocked by anti-occupation activists. On 8 December, the blockade was lifted but power lines were not fully operational before the end of the year.

Ukraine's GDP contracted by over 12%; its currency lost over half of its value in US dollar terms, bringing further hardship to a majority of Ukrainians. Living conditions in the separatist-controlled areas continued to deteriorate markedly, with restrictions on the movement of people and goods tightened further by the authorities in Kyiv.

## TORTURE AND OTHER ILL-TREATMENT

Two years after the EuroMaydan protests, little tangible progress was made in bringing to justice law enforcement officials responsible for the excessive, unnecessary and illegal use of force. In November, the Prosecutor General's Office reported that investigations into more than 2,000 EuroMaydan-related incidents were ongoing, with criminal proceedings instigated against 270 individuals. The trial of two former riot police (Berkut) officers on charges of manslaughter and abuse of authority began in connection with the killing of 39 protesters on 20 February 2014. On 7 December, the Obolon district court in Kyiv sentenced students Aziz Tagirov and Ramil Islamli to four years' imprisonment and four years of probation respectively for beating, kidnapping and threatening to kill a protester on 21 January 2014. No other convictions were handed down for EuroMaydan-related crimes in 2015.

The International Advisory Panel set up by the Council of Europe to monitor investigations into EuroMaydan and violence in the city of Odessa on 2 May 2014 published two reports during 2015. On both occasions, the Panel found that the investigations had "failed to satisfy the requirements of the European Convention on Human Rights".

On 12 November, Parliament adopted a law creating a State Investigation Bureau, tasked with the investigation of alleged crimes committed by law enforcement officials. The law was pending presidential approval at the end of the year.

## ARMED CONFLICT

During the escalation of fighting in Donbass in January and February, indiscriminate shelling of civilian areas continued, with both sides blaming each other. Both sides committed war crimes, including torture and other ill-treatment of prisoners. There were also confirmed reports of the deliberate killing of captives by separatist fighters.

On 13 January, 12 passengers in a civilian bus were killed near the city of Volnovakha by a Grad rocket attack while waiting to pass through a checkpoint controlled by Ukrainian forces.[1] On 22 January, 15 people died when a mortar hit a trolleybus in Donetsk.[2] On 24 January, 29 civilians were killed and over 100 injured by missiles launched by separatist forces into the densely populated Vostochny neighbourhood in Mariupol.

Ihor Branovytsky was one of 12 Ukrainian people defending Donetsk airport and taken prisoner by the separatist Sparta battalion on 21 January. He was beaten unconscious during his interrogation and killed with a shot in the head by the battalion's commander, who later admitted in a phone interview to having killed 15 other captives.[3]

Members of Ukrainian forces Andriy Kolesnyk, Albert Sarukhanyan and Serhiy Slisarenko were last seen alive in footage showing them being taken captive in the village of Krasny Partizan on 22 January. They all died shortly afterwards from gunshot wounds, shot at close range.

A former prisoner reported spending several weeks in captivity in a crowded basement cell, in a building near the village of Velykomykhailivka that was used as a base by Pravy Sektor paramilitaries. Prior to his release in early 2015, he and at least 12 men and one woman had been imprisoned for varying periods of time in the same cell, and subjected to daily beatings and other ill-treatment.[4] Pravy Sektor's spokesperson confirmed the practice of imprisonment of suspected separatists by its members but denied all allegations of ill-treatment. Another anonymous source corroborated the allegations.

The Prosecutor General's Office reported that at least three criminal cases were opened into alleged abuses by members of Pravy Sektor, including abduction, beatings and extortion committed between August 2014 and May 2015, as well as the ill-treatment and disappearance of one man in November 2014, allegedly involving volunteer paramilitaries and members of the Security Service of Ukraine. All three investigations were ongoing at the end of the year.

## PRISONERS OF CONSCIENCE
Ruslan Kotsaba, a freelance journalist and blogger from the city of Ivano-Frankivsk, was arrested on 7 February after posting a video on YouTube in which he demanded an immediate end to fighting in Donbass and called on Ukrainian men to resist conscription. He was remanded in custody and, on 31 March, charged with "state treason" and "obstructing legitimate activities of the Armed Forces of Ukraine". His trial was ongoing at the end of the year.

## FREEDOM OF EXPRESSION
The media remained generally free in government-controlled areas. However, against the backdrop of the Russian occupation and annexation of Crimea in 2014 and the ongoing conflict in Donbass, media outlets perceived as espousing pro-Russian or pro-separatist views faced harassment. Broadcasters 112 Ukraine and Inter TV received formal warnings from the National Television and Radio Council for content such

as interviews and reports from separatist-controlled areas, which featured local people who expressed support for the separatists. Three consecutive warnings would result in their broadcasting licences being annulled.

Journalist Oles Buzina, who was well known for his pro-Russian views and followed by over 25,000 people on Facebook, was shot dead by two masked gunmen in front of his house on 16 April. After two suspects were arrested on 18 June, the Interior Minister Arsen Avakov announced on Facebook that the case had been "solved". Both men protested their innocence and complained of physical and psychological pressure by the investigators. Their trial was pending at the end of the year.

Four so-called "decommunization" laws were passed in May, banning the use of communist and Nazi symbols. In July, the Ministry of Justice instigated court cases seeking to ban the Communist Party of Ukraine (CPU) and two smaller parties that dubbed themselves "communist". The latter two parties – both effectively defunct – were banned on 1 October, while the CPU was banned on 16 December. It filed an appeal on 28 December.

Journalists with pro-Ukrainian views or reporting for Ukrainian media outlets were unable to operate openly in separatist-controlled areas. On 16 June, Russian journalist Pavel Kanygin was detained for several hours by local security forces in Donetsk and severely beaten before being released. He had written several reports for the Russian newspaper *Novaya Gazeta* about two Russian citizens taken prisoner by Ukrainian government forces in Donbass, in which he denounced an official Russian cover-up about them being active military servicemen.

## RIGHTS OF LESBIAN, GAY, BISEXUAL, TRANSGENDER AND INTERSEX PEOPLE
A Pride march was held in Kyiv on 6 June, following extensive negotiations between organizers and the authorities. Before and after the march, President Petro Poroshenko

spoke out strongly in support of LGBTI people's right to freedom of assembly. However, the police agreed to provide protection just one day before the event. Dozens of right-wing activists broke through police lines and attacked the march. Ten participants and three policemen were injured, and 25 attackers were arrested and later released. Pride organizers received threatening messages on their mobiles and online. Four criminal cases against anti-LGBTI protesters were opened and were still ongoing at the end of the year.

In August, a court in Odessa banned a proposed Pride march, citing the "threat to public order" and participants' safety. Instead, the organizers held a smaller, indoor LGBTI festival on 15 August, during which several masked men hurled firecrackers and smoke bombs at the organizers' office.

On 12 November, Parliament introduced amendments to labour laws, prohibiting discrimination on grounds of sexual orientation and gender identity. The move, requested by the EU as part of the visa liberalization process with Ukraine, had long been resisted by the Ukrainian legislature. The amendments were signed into law by the President on 23 November.

## CRIMEA

There was no effective investigation into six cases of suspected enforced disappearances of Crimean Tatar activists in 2014 and one confirmed case of abduction, torture and killing. This was despite a plethora of evidence, including video footage, strongly suggesting that pro-Russian paramilitaries from the so-called "Crimean self-defence force" were responsible for at least some of these crimes.

Freedoms of expression, assembly and association continued to be curtailed under the de facto administration in Crimea, after its occupation and annexation by Russia in 2014. Those expressing pro-Ukrainian sympathies faced harsh reprisals. The Crimean Tatar community was particularly affected: its public events were regularly

banned, Crimean Tatar-language media outlets were forced to close down and their leaders were subjected to regular house searches and faced criminal prosecution and detention on politically motivated charges.

The Crimean Tatar Mejlis, a representative body elected by members of the community, faced further reprisals. Its current leader, Ahtem Chiygoz, was arrested on 29 January and accused of having organized "mass disturbances" on 26 February 2014. The de facto authorities repeatedly warned that the Mejlis could be designated as an extremist group under Russian law. The two previous Mejlis leaders, Mustafa Dzhemiliev and Refat Chubarov, remained officially barred from their homeland. On 28 October, the de facto Prosecutor of Crimea announced that Chubarov could return, after a court in the city of Simferopol had ordered his arrest on 6 October for "calls against the territorial integrity of the Russian Federation".

The Crimean Tatar-language TV channel ATR was forced to stop broadcasting on 1 April, when the deadline for its re-registration under Russian laws expired. It had applied for re-registration at least four times and was consistently denied it arbitrarily. ATR resumed broadcasting from mainland Ukraine, but its reporters were no longer able to work in Crimea openly.

On 9 March, Aleksandr Kravchenko, Leonid Kuzmin and Veldar Shukurdzhiev were arrested at a small street gathering in Simferopol intended to celebrate the 201st anniversary of the birth of the Ukrainian poet Taras Shevchenko, at which they used national symbols such as yellow and blue ribbons. They were taken to a police station, released after three hours and sentenced to 40 hours of community labour each, for violating rules of public assembly. They subsequently faced harassment by members of the anti-extremism police unit, including arrests and informal interrogations. Kuzmin also lost his job as a history teacher.

Contrary to international humanitarian law, Crimean anti-occupation activists Oleg Sentsov and Alexander Kolchenko were put on trial outside Crimea. They were tried under Russian law in a military court in the city of Rostov-on-Don in southern Russia, and sentenced to 20 and 10 years' imprisonment respectively, under disproportionate terrorism-related charges. Their trials were unfair and based on testimony allegedly extracted under torture. The decision was upheld by the Supreme Court of the Russian Federation on 24 November.

1. Eastern Ukraine: Investigate deadly artillery strike on civilian bus (News story, 13 January)
2. Eastern Ukraine: Deadly attack on Donetsk trolleybus as ceasefire unravels (News story, 22 January)
3. New evidence of summary killings of Ukrainian soldiers must spark urgent investigations (News story, 9 April)
4. Ukraine: Breaking bodies: Torture and summary killings in eastern Ukraine (EUR 50/1683/2015)

# UNITED ARAB EMIRATES

United Arab Emirates
Head of state: **Sheikh Khalifa bin Zayed Al Nahyan**
Head of government: **Sheikh Mohammed bin Rashed Al Maktoum**

The authorities arbitrarily restricted freedom of expression, arresting and prosecuting government critics. A new law on combating discrimination and hatred imposed further limits on the rights to freedom of expression and association. Security forces subjected dozens of people to enforced disappearance. Torture and other ill-treatment of detainees was common. Prisoners of conscience remained imprisoned following unfair trials. Women faced discrimination in law and in practice. Migrant workers were inadequately protected by law and faced exploitation and abuse. The death penalty remained in force and there was one execution.

## BACKGROUND

In March, the United Arab Emirates (UAE)

joined the Saudi Arabia-led international coalition that engaged in the armed conflict in Yemen (see Yemen entry).

In May, the authorities denied entry to an Amnesty International representative who had been invited to speak at a construction industry conference in Dubai.

## FREEDOM OF EXPRESSION

The authorities used provisions of the Penal Code, the 2012 cybercrime law and the 2014 anti-terrorism law to arrest, prosecute and imprison critics. In July, the enactment of a new law on combating discrimination and hatred further eroded rights to freedom of expression and association. The new law defines hate speech as "any speech or conduct which may incite sedition, prejudicial action or discrimination among individuals or groups", punishable by a minimum of five years' imprisonment. It also empowers the courts to order the disbandment of associations deemed to provoke such speech and imprison their founders for a minimum of 10 years.

In February, state security officials arrested three sisters, Dr Alyaziyah, Asma and Mariam Khalifa al-Suwaidi, after they posted comments on Twitter relating to their brother, a prisoner of conscience. The women were subjected to enforced disappearance for three months; they were released in May.

In May, the Dubai Criminal Court sentenced an Indian national to one year in prison, followed by deportation, after it convicted him of blasphemy in relation to a Facebook post deemed to "insult" Islam and the Prophet Muhammad. Also in May, the State Security Chamber of the Federal Supreme Court, which hears cases related to national security, sentenced Ahmed Abdulla al-Wahdi to 10 years' imprisonment after convicting him of "creating and running a social media account that insults the UAE's leadership and the country's institutions", based on comments he had posted on Twitter.

The same court handed down a three-year prison sentence in June to Nasser al-Junaibi after convicting him on charges of "insulting the royal family" and "spreading rumours and information that harmed the country", partly on the basis of his Twitter comments criticizing as a "judicial farce" the 2013 mass trial of government critics and pro-reform advocates known as the UAE 94 trial. Many of the UAE 94 remained in prison and were prisoners of conscience, including human rights lawyer Dr Mohammed al-Roken.

## ENFORCED DISAPPEARANCES

State security forces arrested dozens of people, including foreign nationals and peaceful government critics, and subjected them to enforced disappearance. They were detained incommunicado in secret locations, in some cases for more than a year.

In August, Dr Nasser bin Ghaith, an academic, economist and former prisoner of conscience, was subjected to enforced disappearance by state security officers after he criticized "Arab dictators" on Twitter. His whereabouts remained undisclosed at the end of the year.

## TORTURE AND OTHER ILL-TREATMENT

Some of those who were formerly subjected to enforced disappearance said security officials had tortured and otherwise ill-treated them in detention. The authorities denied they had used torture, and failed to independently investigate, ignoring the recommendation in May of the UN Special Rapporteur on the independence of judges and lawyers that the government should appoint an independent committee of experts to investigate allegations of torture.

## UNFAIR TRIALS

The authorities used vague and overly broad provisions of the Penal Code, cybercrime law and anti-terrorism law to prosecute dozens of people before the State Security Chamber of the Federal Supreme Court, whose verdicts are not subject to appeal, in breach of international fair trial standards. One defendant sentenced to death by the Court was executed two weeks later (see below).

In August, a mass trial of 41 people was held before the State Security Chamber of the Federal Supreme Court. Charges included "plotting to overthrow the government and replace it with an ISIL-like 'caliphate'". The defendants included at least 21 people whom the state security forces had subjected to 20 months of enforced disappearance since their arrests in November and December 2013.

## WOMEN'S RIGHTS

Women continued to face discrimination in law and in practice. In July, a court sentenced an 18-year-old woman to nine months' imprisonment for engaging in illicit relationships with men. She was 16 years old when arrested and had been released on bail.

## RIGHTS OF LESBIAN, GAY, BISEXUAL, TRANSGENDER AND INTERSEX PEOPLE

In February, two transgender women, both foreign nationals, were charged with being disguised as women and entering a place restricted only to women. They were jailed until they each paid a fine and were then deported.

## MIGRANT WORKERS' RIGHTS

Migrant workers continued to face exploitation and abuse despite protective provisions contained in the 1980 Labour Law and subsequent decrees. The *kafala* sponsorship system made workers vulnerable to abuse by their employers.

In April, an investigative report commissioned by a UAE government agency found that thousands of migrant construction workers employed at New York University's campus in Abu Dhabi had been forced to pay steep recruitment fees and had their passports confiscated, despite university guidelines designed to ensure fair working and living conditions. Domestic workers, overwhelmingly women, remained excluded from the protections afforded to other migrant workers and faced physical violence, confinement to places of work, and other abuses. Workers who engaged in strikes or other forms of collective action faced arrest and deportation.

The authorities' intolerance of criticism of their record on migrant workers was underlined when, in March, they denied entry to Professor Andrew Ross, an expert on labour issues at New York University.

## DEATH PENALTY

The death penalty remained in force for murder and other offences, and courts continued to hand down death sentences. On 29 June, the State Security Chamber of the Federal Supreme Court sentenced Alaa al-Hashemi to death on terrorism charges. The authorities executed her on 13 July. She had been denied the right of appeal.

# UNITED KINGDOM

United Kingdom of Great Britain and Northern Ireland
Head of state: **Queen Elizabeth II**
Head of government: **David Cameron**

Plans to repeal the Human Rights Act were confirmed. The government continued its opposition to participation in EU efforts to share responsibility for the increasing number of refugees arriving in Europe. Criticism of surveillance laws gained momentum.

## LEGAL, CONSTITUTIONAL OR INSTITUTIONAL DEVELOPMENTS

In May, the Conservative Party won the general election and formed a majority government. The new government confirmed its plans to repeal the Human Rights Act and replace it with a British Bill of Rights. The UN High Commissioner for Human Rights and the UN Human Rights Committee, among others, raised serious concerns that repealing the Human Rights Act could lead to the weakening of human rights protections in the UK.[1]

In July, the government published a Trade Union Bill. If passed, the Bill would place more legal hurdles in the way of unions organizing strike action, significantly restricting trade union rights.

## TORTURE AND OTHER ILL-TREATMENT

In August, the UN Human Rights Committee raised concerns about the adequacy of the parliamentary Intelligence and Security Committee (ISC) as a mechanism to investigate alleged UK complicity in the torture of detainees held in counter-terrorism operations overseas. Concerns about the ISC's independence and the power of the government to prevent the disclosure of sensitive material led the UN Human Rights Committee to call on the government to consider initiating a full judicial investigation into the allegations.

On 30 October, former UK resident Shaker Aamer was released from the US naval base at Guantánamo Bay in Cuba and returned to the UK. Shaker Aamer had been detained without charge or trial in Guantánamo since February 2002.

In November, hearings began in the Supreme Court concerning the civil claim of married couple Abdul-Hakim Belhaj and Fatima Boudchar, who alleged that they were victims of rendition, torture and other ill-treatment in 2004 by the US and Libyan governments, with the knowledge and co-operation of UK officials. The UK government argued that the "act of state" doctrine should prevent the case from going ahead, because UK courts should not judge the conduct of foreign states (who were involved in the alleged rendition) for actions undertaken in their own jurisdictions.

## COUNTER-TERROR AND SECURITY

Broad counter-terrorism powers continued to raise concerns.[2] In February, the Counter-Terrorism and Security Act 2015 came into force, introducing new powers, including restrictions on the travel of people suspected of involvement in terrorism-related activity and exclusion from the UK of certain citizens or others with a right to live in the UK who reject government-imposed conditions on their return home. It also introduced a statutory duty, known as the "prevent duty", on certain bodies, including schools and local councils, to have "due regard to the need to prevent people from being drawn into terrorism". NGOs and civil society raised concerns about the potentially discriminatory impact of the duty.

In October, the government introduced a new "counter-extremism strategy". The strategy included plans for an Extremism Bill that would introduce new powers to tackle what it characterizes as extremism, including bans on certain organizations, restrictions on specifically identified individuals, and restrictions on access to premises used for the support of extremism. The proposals caused concern that these new powers could lead to the violation of people's rights to freedom of assembly, association, speech and privacy.

In September, the Prime Minister announced in Parliament that on 21 August a Royal Air Force (RAF) drone strike was carried out in the area of al-Raqqa in Syria, killing three persons said to be members of the armed group Islamic State (IS), including two British citizens. The government resisted calls from NGOs and parliamentarians to make public the legal guidance on which the air strike was authorized.

On 30 July, the Court of Appeal in *Serdar Mohammed v. Secretary of State for Defence* ruled unlawful the detention of an Afghan detainee by British armed forces for almost four months. The Court found that the detention was arbitrary and therefore in violation of this person's right to liberty under Article 5 of the European Convention on Human Rights, which also applies to overseas detention.

## SURVEILLANCE

Criticism of the UK's surveillance laws gained momentum over the year, with the UN Human Rights Committee, among others, expressing concerns and calling on the government to ensure that the interception of personal communications and retention of communications data are done in conformity with human rights law.

On 6 February, the Investigatory Powers Tribunal (IPT) ruled, in a case brought by Amnesty International and nine other NGOs from four continents, that the government's procedures for the "soliciting, receiving, storing and transmitting by UK authorities of private communications of individuals located in the UK, which have been obtained by US authorities" violated the rights to privacy and freedom of expression.[3] However, the IPT said such an intelligence-sharing regime was now lawful due to government disclosures made during the legal proceedings.

Following the findings of the IPT, Amnesty International and the other nine claimant NGOs brought the case to the European Court of Human Rights, arguing that the UK law governing various aspects of communications surveillance violated the country's human rights obligations, including in relation to the rights to privacy and freedom of expression.[4]

In July, the IPT notified Amnesty International that government agencies had spied on the organization by intercepting, accessing and storing its communications.[5] The IPT found a breach of Articles 8 and 10 of the European Convention on Human Rights, on account of the fact that the intercepted communications were retained for a longer period of time than foreseen under the Government Communications Headquarters (GCHQ) internal policies. The IPT also found a breach of internal policies in respect of the South Africa-based Legal Resources Centre.

On 17 July, the High Court ruled that Section 1 of the Data Retention and Investigatory Powers Act 2014 was unlawful under EU law pertaining to the right to respect for private life and to protection of personal data under the EU Charter of Fundamental Rights.

In November, the government published a draft Investigatory Powers Bill for consultation. The Bill provides for wholesale reform of surveillance and data retention laws. NGOs raised concerns that the Bill did not contain adequate human rights protections and provided for practices that threaten human rights.

## NORTHERN IRELAND

On 26 June, the Belfast High Court upheld as lawful the government's decision not to hold an independent inquiry into the 1989 killing of Belfast solicitor Patrick Finucane.

The Northern Ireland Assembly failed to introduce marriage equality legislation, making it the only UK region that failed to do so. Two court challenges to the ban on same-sex marriages were heard in the courts in Belfast in December.

The government, along with Northern Ireland political parties and the Irish government, failed to agree legislation that would have established new mechanisms to investigate deaths attributed to the conflict in Northern Ireland, as had been promised under the Stormont House Agreement.

## SEXUAL AND REPRODUCTIVE RIGHTS

Access to abortion in Northern Ireland remained limited to exceptional cases where the life or health of the woman or girl was at risk.[6] In June, the Justice Minister was reported to have submitted a draft paper to the Northern Ireland Executive on reforming the law on abortion in Northern Ireland, to allow access to abortion in cases of fatal and severe foetal impairment. This followed a consultation on legal reform which had concluded in January.

In August, the concluding observations of the UN Human Rights Committee called on the government to amend the country's legislation on abortion in Northern Ireland with a view to providing for additional exceptions to the legal ban on abortion, including in cases of "rape, incest and fatal foetal abnormality". The Committee also called for access to information on abortion, contraception and sexual and reproductive health options.

In November and December, the High Court in Belfast ruled that the existing abortion law in Northern Ireland was incompatible with domestic and international human rights law, as it prevents access to

termination of pregnancy in cases of fatal foetal impairment, rape or incest.

## REFUGEES' AND MIGRANTS' RIGHTS

The government continued its opposition to full participation in EU efforts to share responsibility for the increasing number of refugees arriving in Europe. It exercised its option not to participate in the EU's relocation scheme of 160,000 Syrian, Eritrean and Iraqi refugees present in Greece, Hungary and Italy. However, in September, following mounting public pressure, the Prime Minister announced that the country would expand its Syrian resettlement programme from a few hundred over three years to up to 20,000 places over the next five years. With respect to the situation in Calais, France, the government maintained its position of contributing financial resources primarily to secure the perimeters of the port and Channel Tunnel, while declining to accept any of the Calais refugees and migrants into the UK asylum system [see France entry].

In March, Parliament passed the Modern Slavery Act 2015, which increases enforcement powers to monitor and tackle slavery and human trafficking. The government was criticized by NGOs for its earlier decision to remove protections in the immigration rules that helped overseas domestic workers to escape situations of slavery in the UK. In response, it commissioned a review of the overseas domestic worker visa which resulted in a recommendation to reintroduce the option for these workers to change employers.

In October, a new Immigration Bill was published and included provisions to further establish what the government characterized as a "hostile environment" for undocumented migrants. If passed by Parliament, it would permit the removal of support for families who were refused asylum in a final decision and remove local authorities' duties to provide support to children leaving care at 18 on grounds of immigration status; extend the range of people who despite retaining a right of appeal may be removed from the country before the appeal has been heard; and transfer significant power from tribunals to the Home Office over decisions on whether to grant immigration bail and/or on what conditions.

Independent inspectorates continued to highlight grave inadequacies in the use of immigration detention. In March, a report by a cross-party parliamentary group found that immigration detention was used excessively.

In July, the Minister for Immigration suspended the Detained Fast Track – a process whereby many asylum-seekers are detained and have very little time to instruct lawyers or gather evidence to support their claim – following a High Court ruling, confirmed by the Court of Appeal, that the process was structurally unfair and therefore unlawful.

### VIOLENCE AGAINST WOMEN AND GIRLS

In May, the UN Special Rapporteur on violence against women issued her report on her visit to the UK. It concluded that while the government had declared violence against women to be a national priority, and had a number of strategies and action plans at a national level, in most cases initiatives had resulted in isolated pockets of good practice. The report indicated that this was due to the lack of a consistent and coherent human rights-based approach in the government's response to violence against women.

Amendments made to legislation through the Serious Crime Act 2015 included a new mandatory reporting duty for female genital mutilation (FGM), which came into force on 31 October, requiring regulated health and social care professionals and teachers in England and Wales to report known cases of FGM on girls under 18 years of age to the police.

On 29 December, a new domestic violence offence of coercive and controlling behaviour came into force, carrying a maximum of five years' imprisonment, a fine, or both.

In response to concerns raised by domestic violence organizations regarding cuts to funding for specialist women's domestic

violence services, the government announced a £3.2 million domestic abuse fund in August. However, the extent of cuts to funding of specialist violence against women services remained a major concern.

1. UN Human Rights Council: Oral Statement under Item 4 on the UK Human Rights Act (IOR 40/1938/2015)
2. United Kingdom: Submission to the UN Human Rights Committee (EUR 45/1793/2015)
3. UK: "Historic" surveillance ruling finds intelligence-sharing illegal (News story, 6 February)
4. Amnesty International takes UK to European Court over mass surveillance (News story, 10 April)
5. United Kingdom: British government surveillance programmes and interception of Amnesty International communication (EUR 45/2096/2015)
6. United Kingdom: Northern Ireland: Barriers to accessing abortion services (EUR 45/1057/2015)

# UNITED STATES OF AMERICA

**United States of America**
Head of state and government: **Barack Obama**

There was no accountability nor remedy for crimes under international law committed in the secret detention programme operated by the CIA. Scores of detainees remained in indefinite military detention at the US naval base at Guantánamo Bay in Cuba, while military trial proceedings continued in a handful of cases. Concern about the use of isolation in state and federal prisons and the use of force in policing continued. Twenty-seven men and one woman were executed during the year.

## BACKGROUND

In March, September and November respectively, the USA provided its one-year follow-up responses to the UN Human Rights Committee (HRC), the CERD Committee and the UN Committee against Torture on their 2014 priority recommendations after scrutiny of the country's compliance with the ICCPR, the CERD and the UN Convention against Torture.

In May, the USA's human rights record was examined under the UN Universal Periodic Review (UPR) process. In September, the USA accepted about three-quarters of the 343 recommendations made under the UPR process. As in 2011, the USA said it supported calls for the closure of the Guantánamo Bay detention facility, the ratification of the Convention on the Rights of the Child and CEDAW, and for accountability for torture. None had been implemented by the end of the year.

## IMPUNITY

In its one-year update to the HRC, the USA said that it prohibited torture and other ill-treatment, enforced disappearance and arbitrary detention of "any person in its custody wherever they are held", and that it held "accountable any persons responsible for such acts". Yet by the end of the year, no action had been taken to end the impunity for the systematic human rights violations committed in the secret detention programme operated by the CIA, under authorization granted by former President George W. Bush after the attacks of 11 September 2001 (9/11).

The USA also told the HRC that it "supports transparency" in relation to this issue. Yet by the end of the year, more than 12 months after the publication of the declassified summary of the report by the Senate Select Committee on Intelligence into the CIA programme, the Committee's full 6,700-page report, containing details of the treatment of each detainee, remained classified top secret. Most, if not all, of the detainees were subjected to enforced disappearance and to conditions of detention and/or interrogation techniques which violated the prohibition of torture and other cruel, inhuman or degrading treatment. Classification of the report continued to facilitate impunity and the denial of remedy.[1]

During the year, military prosecutors

reportedly learned of a cache of some 14,000 photographs relating to CIA "black sites" in Afghanistan, Thailand, Poland, Romania, Lithuania and possibly elsewhere, including images of naked detainees being transported. The photographs had not been made public by the end of the year.

## COUNTER-TERROR – DETENTIONS

Detainees held at the detention facility at Guantánamo Bay continued to be denied their human rights under the USA's flawed "global war" framework and its views on the non-applicability of international human rights law to the detentions. In its one-year follow-up response to the HRC's call for administrative detention and military commissions against Guantánamo detainees to be ended, the USA reiterated its erroneous position on extraterritoriality that "obligations under the Covenant apply only with respect to individuals who are both within the territory of a State Party and within its jurisdiction". To the CERD call to end Guantánamo detentions "without further delay", the USA responded that it did not agree that the "request bears directly on obligations under the Convention".

At the end of the year, 107 men were held at Guantánamo. The majority were held without charge or trial. About half had been approved for transfer for at least five years. Twenty-one detainees were transferred out of the base during the year to Estonia, Morocco, Saudi Arabia, Mauritania, Oman, the United Arab Emirates and the UK.

Hearings by the Periodic Review Board (PRB) continued. These administrative review proceedings, undermining ordinary criminal justice processes, apply to detainees who are not facing military commissions and have not been approved for transfer by other administrative reviews.

Pre-trial military commission proceedings continued against five detainees accused of involvement in the 9/11 attacks and charged under the Military Commissions Act (MCA) for capital trial in 2012. The five – Khalid Sheikh Mohammed, Walid bin Attash, Ramzi bin al-Shibh, 'Ali 'Abd al-'Aziz and Mustafa al

Hawsawi as well as 'Abd al-Rahim al-Nashiri, who was arraigned for capital trial in 2011 on charges relating to the bombing of the *USS Cole* in Yemen in 2000 – were held incommunicado in secret US custody for up to four years prior to their transfer to Guantánamo in 2006. Their trials had not begun by the end of the year.

Pre-trial proceedings also continued in the case of Abd al Hadi al Iraqi, who was reportedly arrested in Turkey in 2006 and transferred to US custody, held in secret by the CIA and transferred to Guantánamo in 2007. He was formally charged on 18 June 2014. His trial was pending at the end of the year.

Majid Khan and Ahmed Mohammed al Darbi were still awaiting sentencing after pleading guilty in 2012 and 2014 respectively while agreeing not to sue the USA for their prior treatment in custody. Ahmed Mohammed al Darbi was arrested by civilian authorities in Azerbaijan in June 2002 and was transferred to US custody two months later. He has alleged that he was ill-treated. Majid Khan was held in the secret CIA detention programme from 2003 and subjected to enforced disappearance, torture and other ill-treatment before being transferred to Guantánamo in 2006. Further details of his treatment in CIA custody emerged during the year, including of rape, sexual assault, beatings, subjection to prolonged darkness and solitary confinement, hanging for days from a wooden beam, and threats against him and his family.

In June, a three-judge panel of the US Court of Appeals nullified the conviction by a military commission of Guantánamo detainee Ali Hamza Suliman al Bahlul. The conviction was for conspiracy to commit war crimes, but the Court threw it out on the grounds that the charge was not recognized under international law and could not be prosecuted before a military tribunal. In September, the authorities' appeal to the Court to rehear the case was accepted and oral arguments were held on 1 December, with the ruling pending at the end of the year.

## EXCESSIVE USE OF FORCE

At least 43 people across 25 states died after police used Tasers on them, bringing the total number of Taser-related deaths since 2001 to at least 670. Most of the victims were not armed and did not appear to pose a threat of death or serious injury when the Taser was deployed.

The death of Freddie Gray in April and the one-year anniversary of Michael Brown's death sparked protests in Baltimore, Maryland and Ferguson, Missouri respectively. Similar protests against police use of force occurred in cities including Cleveland, Ohio and St. Louis, Missouri, among others. The use of heavy-duty riot gear and military-grade weapons and equipment to police the demonstrations served to intimidate protesters who were exercising their right to peaceful assembly.

Authorities failed to track the exact number of people killed by law enforcement officials each year – estimates range from 458 to over 1,000 individuals. According to the limited data available, black men are disproportionately victims of police killings. State statutes on the use of lethal force are far too permissive; none limit the use of firearms to a last resort only after non-violent and less harmful means are exhausted, and where the officer or others are faced with an imminent threat of death or serious injury.

## TORTURE AND OTHER ILL-TREATMENT

The City of Chicago, Illinois, passed an ordinance to provide reparations to over 100 survivors of torture committed by members of the Chicago Police Department from 1972 to 1991. The ordinance includes a US$5.5 million fund for survivors, a formal apology from the Chicago City Council, free college education for survivors and their families, an educational component in Chicago Public Schools on the history of torture by the Chicago Police Department, a public memorial to torture survivors and a counselling centre for torture survivors.

## MIGRANTS' RIGHTS

More than 35,000 unaccompanied children and 34,000 families were apprehended crossing the southern border during the year, many fleeing violence and insecurity in Mexico and Central America. Families were detained for months while pursuing claims to remain in the USA; many were held in facilities without proper access to medical care, sanitary food and water and legal counsel. Transgender individuals were routinely detained according to their gender at birth, leaving them susceptible to abuse, or held in solitary confinement and without access to hormone therapy.

## WOMEN'S RIGHTS

Despite legislative gains in the reauthorized Violence against Women Act, including provisions that address the high levels of violence against Indigenous women and provide protection and services for survivors of domestic violence, Native American and Alaska Native women who were raped continued to lack access to basic care, including examinations and other essential health care services such as emergency contraception. Native American and Alaska Native women continued to experience disproportionate levels of violence; they were 2.5 times more likely to be raped or sexually assaulted than other women in the country.

There were broad disparities in women's access to sexual and reproductive health care, including maternal health care. African-American women remained nearly four times more likely to die of pregnancy-related complications than white women. Over 230 bills were introduced across multiple US states seeking to restrict access to safe and legal abortion.

## PRISON CONDITIONS

Over 80,000 prisoners at any given time were held in conditions of physical and social deprivation in federal and state prisons throughout the country.

In September, a landmark settlement to a class action lawsuit, *Ashker v. Brown*, virtually eliminated prolonged and indefinite isolation in California's Security Housing Units (SHUs). Under the terms of the settlement, the overwhelming majority of prisoners held in SHUs were due to be released to general prison population units. In recognition of the harmful effects of long-term solitary confinement, prisoners who have been held for over 10 years in SHUs will be immediately transferred to a Restricted Custody General Population Unit, to begin a two-year programme to reintegrate them into the general prison population.

The release in March of an "independent" audit into the use of solitary confinement in Federal Bureau of Prisons (BOP) facilities reported a number of inadequacies in the system, including in mental health provision and re-entry programmes for those held for long periods in isolation. Its recommendations did not go far enough to improve the harmful effects the isolation regime exerts on prisoners' physical and mental health, or to bring the BOP in line with its international obligations.[2]

## DEATH PENALTY

Twenty-seven men and one woman were executed in six states, bringing to 1,422 the total number of executions since the reintroduction of the death penalty in 1976. This was the lowest number of executions in a year since 1991. Approximately 50 new death sentences were passed. Almost 3,000 people remained on death row at the end of the year.

The Nebraska legislature voted to abolish the death penalty, overriding the State Governor's veto against the bill. However, the repeal was on hold at the end of the year after opponents gathered enough signatures to a petition to have the issue put to the popular vote in November 2016. Momentum against the death penalty continued in February with the announcement of a moratorium on executions in Pennsylvania by the State Governor. Moratoriums also remained in force in Washington State and Oregon at the end of the year.

Warren Hill was executed in Georgia on 27

January. All the experts who assessed him, including those retained by the state, agreed that he had an intellectual disability, rendering his execution unconstitutional. Cecil Clayton, a 74-year-old man, was executed in Missouri on 17 March. He had been diagnosed with dementia and a psychotic disorder stemming from a serious brain injury.

The Governor of Missouri commuted the death sentence of Kimber Edwards shortly before he was due to be put to death in October. The man who shot the victim and is serving a life sentence after pleading guilty in return for avoiding the death penalty had signed a statement recanting his post-arrest statements implicating Kimber Edwards in the murder.

Kelly Gissendaner was executed in Georgia on 30 September for the murder of her husband. The man who pleaded guilty to shooting the victim and testified against his co-defendant is serving a life sentence. Numerous inmates and former correctional officials supported clemency for Kelly Gissendaner, pointing to her rehabilitation and her positive impact on prison life and prisoners.

States continued to face litigation on lethal injection protocols and problems in acquiring execution drugs. On 29 June, in *Glossip v. Gross*, the US Supreme Court upheld the use of midazolam as the sedative drug in Oklahoma's three-drug protocol. Two dissenting judges argued that the Court should revisit the constitutionality of the death penalty. Their dissent argued that the death penalty was now "highly likely" unconstitutional, including on the grounds of arbitrariness and unreliability.

After the ruling, Oklahoma scheduled the execution of Richard Glossip, one of the plaintiffs in the lethal injection challenge. Hours from execution on 16 September, and then minutes before his rescheduled execution on 30 September, the State Governor stopped the execution after it was revealed that the prison authorities had the wrong drug. It was later found that this drug had been used in at least one execution, that of Charles Warner in January. The State Attorney General sought and obtained an indefinite stay of executions and in October, his office said that it would not seek any new execution dates until at least 150 days after the completion of investigations into the execution protocol.

In October, the Ohio prison authorities announced that 11 executions scheduled for 2016 were being rescheduled for 2017, 2018 and 2019 as the state continued to seek "legal means" to obtain lethal injection drugs.

During the year, six inmates were exonerated of the crimes for which they were originally sentenced to death, bringing to 156 the number of such cases since 1973.

---

1. USA: Crimes and impunity (AMR 51/1432/2015)
2. USA: Entombed: Isolation in the US federal prison system (AMR 51/040/2014)

# URUGUAY

**Eastern Republic of Uruguay**
Head of state and government: **Tabaré Vázquez**
**(replaced José Alberto Mujica Cordano in March)**

**Little progress was made to ensure justice for human rights violations committed during the period of civil and military rule between 1973 and 1985. Gender inequality persisted, including in access to abortion and the rights of lesbian, gay, bisexual, transgender and intersex (LGBTI) people.**

## BACKGROUND

In March, Tabaré Vázquez took office promising to implement a National Plan on Social Harmony and Human Rights, and to strengthen anti-discrimination policy for LGBTI people, as well as measures to promote gender equality, among other commitments.

In March, the UN Committee on the Rights of the Child urged Uruguay to take measures to prevent, prohibit and protect children from all forms of torture or other cruel, inhuman or degrading treatment in detention, including by the police. The Committee also called on the government to tackle high rates of child poverty and improve access to quality health services, particularly for children living in the most disadvantaged and remote areas.

In October, Uruguay was elected member of the UN Security Council for 2016-17, after 50 years of absence from it.

In June, the government announced that it would continue its programme of resettling Syrian refugees. Five Syrian families arrived in Uruguay in 2014.

## IMPUNITY

In May, a presidential decree established the Truth and Justice Working Group to investigate human rights violations that occurred between 1968 and 1985. The group was to be formed of seven members having fulfilled autonomy and independence criteria throughout their careers, as well as the President and Vice-President of Uruguay.

A 2013 Supreme Court ruling remained an obstacle to ensuring justice; the ruling had overturned key articles of Law 18.831, adopted in 2011, which established that crimes committed during the period of civil and military rule between 1973 and 1985 were crimes against humanity and that no statute of limitations could be applied.

## SEXUAL AND REPRODUCTIVE RIGHTS

In August, an administrative court upheld the right of medical professionals to refuse to perform a legal abortion on grounds of conscience. The ruling resulted from a complaint lodged by a group of medical professionals against several articles of a decree regulating the 2012 legislation that decriminalized abortion and guaranteed safe and legal access to it. The court's ruling caused uncertainty over how the government would ensure the legislation's effective implementation, depending on the number of professionals refusing to perform abortions on grounds of conscience.

Abortion is decriminalized in Uruguay in all cases during the first 12 weeks of pregnancy. Decriminalization is extended to the 14th week when the pregnancy is the result of rape, and to the whole pregnancy when it either poses a serious risk to the woman's health or is a case of foetal malformation, incompatible with extra-uterine life.

## RIGHTS OF LESBIAN, GAY, BISEXUAL, TRANSGENDER AND INTERSEX PEOPLE

Investigations into the killings of five transsexual women between 2011 and 2012 showed little progress.

# UZBEKISTAN

**Republic of Uzbekistan**
Head of state: **Islam Karimov**
Head of government: **Shavkat Mirzioiev**

**The authorities used torture and other ill-treatment to suppress dissent, combat actual or perceived security threats, repress political opponents, extract confessions and incriminating information, and intimidate or punish detainees and prisoners and their families. Courts relied heavily on confessions extracted under torture, duress or deception. Prison sentences of individuals convicted of anti-state and terrorism offences were arbitrarily extended.**

## BACKGROUND

In March, President Islam Karimov was re-elected for a fourth consecutive term in office, in an election that lacked genuine political competition.

Economic growth slowed down, affected by falling commodity prices in international markets. Remittances from Uzbekistani labour migrants abroad fell by over 45%. Over 2 million labour migrants were estimated to work in Russia alone.

The authorities claimed that the country was more vulnerable to attacks as a result of the resurgence of armed groups such as the Islamic Movement of Uzbekistan (IMU), amid reports of a tactical alliance between the IMU in Afghanistan and the armed group Islamic State (IS). The authorities intensified reprisals against perceived extremists, particularly among returning labour migrants, many of whom they suspected of having travelled to Syria to fight for IS.

## TORTURE AND OTHER ILL-TREATMENT

Police and officers of the National Security Service (SNB) continued to routinely use torture and other ill-treatment to coerce suspects and detainees, including women and men charged with criminal offences such as theft, fraud or murder, into confessing to a crime or incriminating others. Detainees charged with anti-state and terrorism-related offences were particularly vulnerable to torture. Detainees were often tortured by people wearing masks.

Police and SNB officers regularly used convicted prisoners to commit torture and other ill-treatment on detainees in pre-trial detention. Under the Criminal Code, prisoners, unlike officials, could not be held responsible for torture but only for lesser crimes. A former detainee described witnessing officers and prisoners torture men and women in interrogation rooms in an SNB pre-trial detention centre, as well as in bathrooms and showers, punishment cells and purpose-built torture rooms with padded rubber walls and sound-proofing. He described SNB officers handcuffing detainees to radiators and breaking their bones with baseball bats.[1]

Courts continued to rely heavily on confessions obtained under torture to hand down convictions. Judges routinely ignored or dismissed as unfounded defendants' allegations of torture or other ill-treatment, even when presented with credible evidence.

Two men, who were sentenced in 2014 to 10 years in prison each for alleged membership of a banned Islamist party, claimed in court that security forces had tortured them to sign false confessions by burning their hands and feet against a stove. One defendant told the judge that security forces had pulled out his fingernails and

toenails. The judge failed to inquire further into the torture allegations, and admitted the confessions as evidence.

At the UN Human Rights Committee examination of Uzbekistan's fourth periodic report in July, Uzbekistan rejected allegations of the pervasive use of torture and other ill-treatment by security forces and prison staff. Uzbekistan insisted that the constitutional prohibition of torture and single mention of it in the Criminal Procedure Code conformed to the state's obligations under the ICCPR. In its concluding observations, the Committee urged the authorities to "ensure that the prohibition of forced confessions and the inadmissibility of torture-tainted evidence are effectively enforced in practice by law enforcement officers and judges".

## PRISON CONDITIONS

The practice of arbitrarily extending prison terms even for minor alleged infractions of prison rules under Article 221 of the Criminal Code led to many prisoners, especially those convicted of anti-state offences, serving de facto life sentences. Azam Farmonov, a prisoner of conscience and human rights defender who was convicted in 2006 largely on the basis of coerced witness testimony, was due to be released at the end of April after serving a nine-year sentence at Jaslyk Prison. However, in May, following a blatantly unfair and closed trial without legal representation, a court extended his sentence for another five years for breaking prison rules, in particular for verbally mocking other prisoners and not wearing appropriate identification tags.[2] He told his wife during a prison visit in July that the prison authorities had kept him in a punishment cell for 10 days in March. They had handcuffed him and repeatedly tied a bag over his head to suffocate him. He was forced to listen to the screams of prisoners being tortured in adjoining cells.

Former parliamentarian Murad Dzhuraev, who was arrested in 1994, sentenced to 12 years in prison on politically motivated charges and had his sentence arbitrarily extended four times, was finally released on 12 November.

## COUNTER-TERROR AND SECURITY

The authorities became increasingly suspicious of labour migrants returning from abroad who may have had access to information on Islam which is censored or banned in Uzbekistan, resulting in an increased number of arrests and prosecutions for "extremism". The authorities claimed that migrant workers were targeted in Russia for recruitment by the IMU, IS or other groups characterized as extremist.

In November, security forces detained dozens of labour migrants who had returned from Russia and Turkey, in raids in the capital Tashkent and several regions of the country, amid disputed claims that they were members of the banned Islamist party Hizb ut-Tahrir and had links to IS members in Syria. Human rights defenders reported that security forces used torture to extract confessions from them.

### Persecution of family members

The authorities routinely targeted relatives of individuals charged with or convicted of anti-state offences. In many cases, members of the same family were arbitrarily detained, tortured and otherwise ill-treated to force them to confess to fabricated charges, resulting in long prison sentences after unfair trials.

One woman reported how most of her male family members were serving long prison sentences after conviction of membership of a banned Islamist organization or had fled the country in fear for their lives. All had been tortured by security forces to "confess". She was regularly called to the local police station, where she was detained and beaten to punish her for being a member of an "extremist family", to reveal the whereabouts of male relatives or to incriminate them.

Former detainees and relatives of prisoners reported that *mahalla* (neighbourhood) committees compiled confidential lists of potential "suspects" for the security forces,

which led to arrests and harassment, including on the basis of planted evidence, as well as forced confessions.

Police also compiled files on members of unregistered religious communities, including information on their family members.

## FREEDOM OF EXPRESSION – HUMAN RIGHTS DEFENDERS

Freedoms of expression and peaceful assembly continued to be curtailed. In its concluding observations, the UN Human Rights Committee expressed concern about "consistent reports of harassment, surveillance, arbitrary arrests and detentions, torture and ill-treatment by security forces and prosecutions on trumped-up charges of independent journalists, government critics, human rights defenders and other activists, in retaliation for their work".

Police officers detained Elena Urlaeva, head of the independent NGO Human Rights Defenders' Alliance of Uzbekistan, in the northeastern city of Chinaz on 31 May and subjected her to torture, including sexual violence, to force her to surrender the memory card from her camera. The memory card contained photographic evidence of the use of forced labour in cotton fields. Police officers beat her, called her a traitor and stripped her naked. Male police officers and a male paramedic held her by the arms and legs while a female doctor conducted intrusive body cavity examinations to find the memory card. Police officers then took her to a local hospital to do X-rays. When she asked to use the toilet, the officers forced her to urinate on the grass in front of the hospital. They filmed and photographed her, and threatened to post the pictures on the internet if she complained about her treatment.[3] She was released without charge.

---

1. Secrets and lies: Forced confessions under torture in Uzbekistan (EUR 62/1086/2015)

2. Uzbekistan: Five more years for "violating prison rules" (EUR 62/1709/2015)
3. Uzbekistan: Defender subjected to sexual violence: Elena Urlaeva (EUR 62/1799/2015).

# VENEZUELA

**Bolivarian Republic of Venezuela**
Head of state and government: **Nicolás Maduro Moros**

Human rights defenders and journalists continued to face attacks and intimidation. Political opponents of the government faced unfair trials and imprisonment. There were further reports of excessive use of force by the police and security forces resulting in dozens of deaths, some in circumstances suggesting that they were unlawful killings. Most of those responsible for grave human rights violations during the 2014 protests were not brought to justice and there were concerns about the independence of the judiciary. Colombian refugees and asylum-seekers were deported, forcibly evicted and ill-treated. Prison overcrowding and violence continued. Survivors of gender-based violence faced significant obstacles in getting access to justice.

## BACKGROUND

Parliamentary elections in December saw the coalition Democratic Unity Roundtable gain two-thirds of seats.

In July, a draft National Human Rights Plan was issued for consultation with all sectors of society. It included proposals to reform the judiciary, prison system and security forces, as well as proposals to end discrimination and improve the rights of vulnerable groups such as Indigenous Peoples, women, children, Afro-descendant communities, domestic workers and lesbian, gay, bisexual, transgender and intersex (LGBTI) people. The consultation was ongoing at the end of the year.

The decision in 2012 by Venezuela to withdraw from the jurisdiction of the Inter-American Court of Human Rights continued to deny victims of human rights violations and their relatives whose rights had not been guaranteed in the national courts access to justice.

Interference in the judicial system by officials at the highest levels of the administration called into question their commitment to the independence of the judiciary and the rule of law. There was concern that the temporary nature of positions held by more than 60% of judges made them susceptible to political pressure.

## FREEDOM OF EXPRESSION

In June, the Inter-American Court of Human Rights ordered Venezuela to reinstate the broadcasting licence of Radio Caracas Television, which had been withdrawn in 2007. The authorities had not complied with the ruling by the end of the year.

Owners of media outlets and journalists who were critical of the authorities faced defamation charges, attacks and intimidation.[1]

## HUMAN RIGHTS DEFENDERS

Human rights defenders were attacked and intimidated.

Both President Maduro and the President of the National Assembly, among others, accused named defenders on national television of damaging the country's reputation and undermining the government. Several human rights defenders were subsequently harassed. For example, in March, Marco Antonio Ponce of the Venezuelan Observatory of Social Conflict and another 11 human rights defenders returning from presenting their concerns before the Inter-American Commission on Human Rights were followed, photographed and filmed by unidentified men in Caracas airport.[2]

In April, Carlos Lusverti, a human rights defender and professor of human rights at the Andrés Bello Catholic University, was shot and injured for the second time in 15 months, in an apparent robbery attempt.

In October, Marino Alvarado Betancourt of

the Venezuelan Programme for Education and Action on Human Rights and his nine-year-old son were attacked and robbed by three armed men in their home.[3]

In April, Víctor Martínez, a campaigner against corruption and human rights violations committed by Lara State Police, was threatened by two armed men outside his home in Barquisimeto, Lara State. The threat appeared linked to his criticism of the police; at the time of the attack he was under police protection, which he claimed was sporadic.[4]

## EXCESSIVE USE OF FORCE

In January, the Ministry of Defence issued Resolution 008610 allowing all sections of the armed forces to be deployed in public order operations. It also allowed the use of firearms to be authorized during the policing of public protests. The Resolution failed to send a clear message that excessive use of force in such operations would not be tolerated.

Excessive use of force by security forces continued to be reported and resulted in the death of 14-year-old Kluiberth Roa Núñez, who was hit by a rubber bullet fired by the security forces in Táchira State as he was walking near a protest.[5]

## ARBITRARY DETENTIONS

In September, Leopoldo López, a prisoner of conscience and leader of the opposition Popular Will party, was convicted of conspiracy to commit a crime, incitement, arson and causing damage to public property during the 2014 protests. He was sentenced to 13 years and nine months in prison. There was no credible evidence to support the charges and public statements made before his conviction by the authorities; the President called for his imprisonment, thus seriously undermining his right to a fair trial.[6]

In January, a judge ordered that Rosmit Mantilla, an LGBTI rights activist and Popular Will member, face trial on charges including incitement, arson and conspiracy to commit a crime during the 2014 protests, despite the lack of credible evidence against him. He remained in pre-trial detention at the end of

the year.

In March, Emilio Baduel Cafarelli and Alexander Tirado Lara were sentenced to eight years' imprisonment. They had been convicted of incitement, intimidation using explosives and conspiracy to commit a crime during the 2014 protests. The Public Prosecutor failed to provide evidence to substantiate the charges and the judge disregarded forensic evidence that showed neither man had handled any explosives or inflammable substances.

## REFUGEES AND ASYLUM-SEEKERS

In August, nearly 2,000 Colombian citizens, including refugees and asylum-seekers, were deported in the course of a few days, without the opportunity to challenge their expulsion or to gather their belongings. In some cases children were separated from their parents. Scores were forcibly evicted or had their houses destroyed and some of those detained were ill-treated.[7]

The deportations were in response to the deaths of three officers and a civilian in the context of security and anti-smuggling operations. At the end of the year, nine municipalities in the border state of Táchira remained under a state of emergency and the border remained closed in the states of Zulia, Táchira and Apure and in part of Amazonas.

## POLICE AND SECURITY FORCES

Although recent official data was not available, the Venezuelan Violence Observatory reported that the country had the second highest homicide rate in the region.

In July, Operation Liberation and Protection of the People was implemented by security forces to tackle the high crime rate. Reports were received of possible extrajudicial executions, excessive use of force, arbitrary arrests and forced evictions of those suspected of having committed a crime as well as their families.

According to the Ministry of Justice, a month after the operation commenced, 52 civilians had died in armed clashes with the security forces. The high number of civilian casualties, in contrast to the absence of any police injuries or fatalities, suggested that security forces may have used excessive force or carried out extrajudicial executions.

According to human rights organizations, 90% of the more than 4,000 people detained during the first three months of the operation were subsequently released without charge, suggesting high numbers of arbitrary arrests.

In August, in a community south of Valencia, Carabobo State, security forces allegedly detained all men over 15 years of age and demolished all of the community's houses, leaving at least 200 families homeless.

## IMPUNITY

Progress was slow in bringing to justice those responsible for the killing of 43 people, including security force personnel, and the ill-treatment of protesters during protests in 2014. According to the Public Prosecutor's Office, 238 investigations had been initiated by February but charges were filed in only 13 cases.

No one had been brought to justice for the killing of eight members of the Barrios family or the threats and intimidation against other family members in Aragua State since 1998.[8]

## PRISON CONDITIONS

Prisons remained seriously overcrowded despite several reforms to the system since 2013. According to the Venezuelan Prisons Observatory (OVP), prisons overall were holding over three times the number of prisoners they were designed to house. In this context, the prison authorities were unable to protect the rights of prisoners, such as the rights to health and physical integrity. Uprisings and protests, including self-harming, to demand better prison conditions remained common. OVP reported over 1,200 incidents of self-harm in the first six months of the year. In addition, it reported the deaths of 109 inmates and at least 30 injuries as a result of violence in prison facilities, during the same period. The large number of weapons in detention facilities remained

a concern.

## VIOLENCE AGAINST WOMEN AND GIRLS

Implementation of the 2007 legislation criminalizing gender-based violence remained slow due to a lack of resources. Legal aid and access to justice, as well as other effective protection measures such as shelters, had not materialized by the end of the year.

Statistics from the Public Prosecutor's Office indicated that of the more than 70,000 complaints of gender-based violence received during 2014, less than 1% went to trial. According to women's rights organizations, 96% of the cases that did reach the courts did not result in convictions.

## RIGHTS OF LESBIAN, GAY, BISEXUAL, TRANSGENDER AND INTERSEX PEOPLE

LGBTI organizations expressed concern at entrenched discrimination. There were continuing reports of violence against LGBTI people. Those responsible were rarely held to account as complaints were not investigated or prosecuted.

There was no specific provision in law criminalizing hate crimes based on sexual orientation, gender identity or expression.

## SEXUAL AND REPRODUCTIVE RIGHTS

Access to contraceptives, including emergency contraception, was limited and generally available only to those who could afford it. Abortion was criminalized in all cases except when the life of the woman or girl was at risk.

According to a 2015 report by the WHO, maternal mortality had increased to 110 per 100,000 live births. This was significantly higher than the regional average of 63 per 100,000 live births.

## INDIGENOUS PEOPLES' RIGHTS

There was no legal provision to guarantee and regulate consultation with Indigenous Peoples over matters affecting their livelihoods. Those defending Indigenous Peoples' rights reported that the right to free, prior and informed consent was not upheld by the authorities when granting licences to extract natural resources in Indigenous territories.

Concerns were raised at the slow progress of the process for the demarcation of Indigenous Peoples' territories, which started in 2011. By the end of the year, only 12% of Indigenous territory was estimated to have been demarcated.

1. Venezuela: Journalist beaten and threatened: Horacio Giusti (AMR 53/1714/2015)
2. Human rights in Venezuela before the United Nations Human Rights Committee (AMR 53/1942/2015)
3. Venezuela: Armed assault against human rights defender must be thoroughly investigated (News story, 2 October)
4. Venezuela: Human rights defender attacked again: Víctor Martínez (AMR 53/1450/2015)
5. Venezuela: The faces of impunity: a year after the protests, victims still await justice (AMR 53/1239/2015)
6. Venezuela: Opposition leader sentenced unjustly: Leopoldo López (AMR 53/2449/2015)
7. Venezuela: Concerns over grave human rights violations on the border with Colombia (AMR 53/2329/2015)
8. Venezuela: Submission to the United Nations Human Rights Committee 114th Session, 29 June-24 July 2015 (AMR 53/1769/2015)

# VIET NAM

Socialist Republic of Viet Nam
Head of state: **Truong Tan Sang**
Head of government: **Nguyen Tan Dung**

**Severe restrictions on freedoms of expression, association and peaceful assembly continued. The media and the judiciary, as well as political and religious institutions, remained under state control. At least 45 prisoners of conscience remained imprisoned in harsh conditions after unfair trials. They included bloggers, labour and land rights activists, political activists, religious followers, members of ethnic groups and advocates for human rights and social justice. Activists were convicted in new trials. The authorities attempted to prevent the activities of independent civil society groups through harassment, surveillance and restrictions on freedom of movement. A reduction in criminal prosecutions of bloggers and activists coincided with an increase in harassment, short-term arbitrary detentions and physical attacks by security officers. Scores of Montagnard asylum-seekers fled to Cambodia and Thailand between October 2014 and December 2015. The death penalty was retained.**

## BACKGROUND

A major legislative reform programme continued. Several key laws were under review or being drafted. The amended Civil Code, the Penal Code, the Law on Custody and Detention and the Criminal Procedure Code were approved by the end of the year, but a Law on Associations, a Law on Demonstrations, and a Law on Belief and Religion were not finalized. Comments from the general public were solicited. Independent civil society groups raised concerns that some of the laws were not in accordance with Viet Nam's international obligations, including those set out in the ICCPR, which Viet Nam has ratified.

The UN Convention against Torture entered into force in February, but the needed wide-ranging legal reforms for compliance were still pending.

More than 18,000 prisoners were released to mark the 70th anniversary of National Day in September; no prisoners of conscience were included.

Scores of Montagnard asylum-seekers from the Central Highlands fled to Cambodia and Thailand between October 2014 and December 2015, mostly alleging religious persecution and harassment. Dozens were forcibly returned to Viet Nam from Cambodia, with others voluntarily returning after the Cambodian authorities refused to register them and process their asylum claims. Their fate on return was not known (see Cambodia entry).

## REPRESSION OF DISSENT

Members of independent activist groups

attempting to exercise their rights to freedom of expression, association and peaceful assembly faced regular harassment, including surveillance, restrictions on movement, arbitrary short-term detention and physical attacks by police and unidentified men suspected of working in collusion with security forces. Dozens of activists were attacked, many of them before or after visiting released prisoners and victims of human rights violations, or when attending events or meetings.

In July, security forces harassed and intimidated peaceful activists attempting to participate in hunger strikes in four major cities in solidarity with prisoners of conscience. The action was organized by the "We Are One" campaign, launched in March together with a letter to the UN Human Rights Council on the human rights situation in Viet Nam, signed by 27 local civil society organizations and 122 individuals.

The authorities continued to use vaguely worded offences to charge and convict peaceful activists, mainly through Article 258 (abusing democratic freedoms to infringe upon the interests of the state, the legitimate rights and interests of organizations and/or citizens) of the 1999 Penal Code. Three pro-democracy activists arrested in May 2014 while monitoring anti-China protests were sentenced in February to between 12 and 18 months' imprisonment under Article 258 in Đồng Nai province.

Prominent human rights lawyer and former prisoner of conscience Nguyễn Văn Đài and his colleague, Lê Thu Hà, were arrested in December on charges of "conducting propaganda" against the state under Article 88 of the Penal Code. The arrest took place several days after Nguyễn Văn Đài and three colleagues were brutally assaulted by 20 men in plain clothes shortly after delivering human rights training in Nghệ An province.

Blogger Nguyễn Hữu Vinh and his associate Nguyễn Thị Minh Thúy remained held in pre-trial detention since their arrest in May 2014. They were charged under Article 258 of the Penal Code in February in connection with the blogs Dân Quyền (Citizens' Rights) and Chép sử Việt (Writing Vietnam's History), both critical of government policies and officials and since closed down.[1]

Prominent blogger and journalist Tạ Phong Tần was released in September and flown immediately into effective exile in the USA. She had served four years of a 10-year prison term on charges of "conducting propaganda" against the state.

Reports of repression of religious activities outside state-approved churches continued, including against Hoa Hao Buddhists, Catholic practitioners and Christian ethnic minorities.

## FREEDOM OF MOVEMENT

While the number of arrests and prosecutions against human rights defenders and government critics decreased from previous years, physical attacks and restrictions on movement increased. Several activists were confined to their homes. Some of those wishing to travel overseas to attend human rights-related events had their passports confiscated; several others who managed to leave were arrested and interrogated by the police on their return.

Trần Thị Nga, a member of the independent Vietnamese Women for Human Rights group was arrested by security officers on her way to meet a foreign delegation to the Inter-Parliamentary Union Assembly in the capital Ha Noi in March. Security officers beat her while she was being forcibly driven back to her home in Hà Nam province with her two young children.

## DEATHS IN CUSTODY

In March, the National Assembly questioned the credibility of a Ministry of Public Security announcement that of 226 deaths in police custody between October 2011 and September 2014, most were caused by illness or suicide. During 2015 at least seven deaths in custody were reported with suspicions of possible police torture or other ill-treatment.

## PRISONERS OF CONSCIENCE

At least 45 prisoners of conscience remained in detention.[2] The majority were convicted under vaguely worded national security provisions of the Penal Code: Article 79 ("overthrowing" the state) or Article 88 ("conducting propaganda"). At least 17 were released after completing their prison sentences but remained under house arrest for specified periods. Thích Quảng Độ, head of the banned Unified Buddhist Church of Vietnam, spent his 12th year under de facto house arrest, and Father Nguyễn Văn Lý, a pro-democracy Catholic priest, remained in prison serving an eight-year sentence.

Some prisoners were pressed to "confess" to charges in exchange for a reduction in sentence.[3]

Conditions of detention and treatment of prisoners of conscience continued to be harsh. This included lack of physical exercise; verbal and physical attacks; prolonged detention in hot cells with little natural light; denial of sanitary equipment; frequent prison transfers; and detention far from homes and families, making family visits difficult. Several undertook hunger strikes in protest at the use of solitary confinement and abusive treatment of prisoners, including Tạ Phong Tần (see above); Nguyễn Đặng Minh Mẫn, serving an eight-year sentence; and Đinh Nguyên Kha, serving a four-year sentence.[4] Nguyễn Văn Duyệt, a Catholic social activist serving a three-and-a-half-year sentence protested at being denied a Bible; and social justice activist Hồ Thị Bích Khương, serving a five-year sentence, who protested when she was not allowed to take personal belongings when transferred to another prison.

## DEATH PENALTY

The National Assembly approved the reduction in the number of capital offences from 22 to 15, as well as abolition for alleged offenders aged 75 and over. Death sentences for drug-related offences continued to be imposed. Although official statistics remained classified as a state secret, the Justice Minister was reported to have said in October that 684 prisoners were on death row. At least 45 death sentences were reported in the media. In January, the Supreme People's Procuracy was tasked with reviewing 16 death penalty cases in which the defendants alleged they had been tortured during police interrogation. In October, Lê Văn Mạnh's execution was postponed for further investigation. He alleged he was tortured in police custody.[5]

1. Viet Nam: Demand release of blogger and assistant (ASA 41/2801/2015)
2. Viet Nam: All prisoners of conscience must be immediately and unconditionally released (ASA 41/2360/2015)
3. Viet Nam: Release Tran Huynh Duy Thuc (ASA 41/1731/2015)
4. Viet Nam: Further information – prisoner of conscience Ta Phong Tan released (ASA 41/2600/2015)
5. Viet Nam: Halt imminent execution of Le Van Manh and order investigation into allegations of torture (ASA 41/2737/2015)

# YEMEN

**Republic of Yemen**
Head of state: **Abd Rabbu Mansour Hadi**
Head of government: **Khaled Bahah**

The human rights situation seriously deteriorated amid the armed conflict, which intensified in March and continued throughout the year. All parties to the conflict committed war crimes and other serious violations of international law with impunity, including indiscriminate bombing and shelling of civilian areas, killing and injuring thousands of civilians and forcibly displacing over 2.5 million people. The Huthi armed group and allied security forces also arbitrarily restricted the rights to freedom of expression, association and assembly, arresting journalists, leaders of the al-Islah political party and others, forcing the closure of NGOs, using lethal and other excessive force against peaceful protesters, and using torture. Women and girls remained subject to discrimination and abuses including forced marriage and female genital mutilation. Courts handed down death sentences and executions were carried out.

## BACKGROUND

The political transition process was derailed as Yemen became enmeshed in armed conflict. After entering the capital Sana'a in September 2014, the Huthi armed group, aided by units of the armed forces loyal to former President Ali Abdullah Saleh, extended their control over other areas in early 2015. In January, Huthis attacked government buildings and military positions, including the presidential compound, forcing President Hadi and his government to resign, and took effective control of Sana'a and other areas.

On 6 February the Huthi armed group dissolved Yemen's Parliament and issued a constitutional declaration mandating the creation of a transitional presidential council to govern Yemen for an interim period of two years. On 15 February, the UN Security Council adopted Resolution 2201, which strongly criticized the Huthis' actions and demanded that they refrain from further unilateral actions that could destabilize the political transition and Yemen's security. President Hadi, having withdrawn his resignation, relocated with his government to the Saudi Arabian capital, Riyadh, in late March, when the advance of Huthis and their allied forces into southern Yemen led to intensified armed confrontations between the Huthis and their allied forces, and armed groups that opposed them and army units loyal to President Hadi. The fighting in southern Yemen was marked by indiscriminate attacks in which both sides repeatedly fired imprecise weapons at civilian residential areas, causing civilian deaths and injuries.

On 25 March, a Saudi Arabia-led coalition of nine states intervened in the Yemen conflict in support of President Hadi's internationally recognized government. The coalition launched a campaign of air strikes on areas controlled or contested by Huthis and their allies, including Sana'a and Sa'da governorate, sent ground troops into southern Yemen and imposed a sea and air blockade. While many coalition attacks were directed at military targets, others were indiscriminate, disproportionate or directed against civilian homes and infrastructure, including hospitals, schools, markets and factories, as well as vehicles carrying civilians and humanitarian assistance, killing and injuring thousands of civilians. By the end of the year, the conflict had caused the deaths of more than 2,700 civilians, including hundreds of children, according to the UN, and the forcible displacement of more than 2.5 million people, creating a humanitarian crisis.

On 14 April, in Resolution 2216, the UN Security Council demanded that Huthis withdraw from Sana'a and other areas and surrender weapons seized from government sources. It also called for all states to prevent arms transfers to former President Saleh and the Huthi leader Abdul Malik al-Huthi, and pressed all parties to the conflict to abide by previous agreements, including the outcomes of Yemen's national dialogue and the Peace and National Partnership agreement of September 2014.

In July, forces opposed to the Huthis, supported by ground troops from the United Arab Emirates and coalition air strikes, regained control of Aden. In September, President Hadi's government partly relocated to Aden from Saudi Arabia.

UN-brokered peace talks took place in Geneva, Switzerland, from 15 to 20 December, accompanied by a temporary ceasefire, but ended without any significant breakthrough.

US forces continued to carry out drone strikes against the armed group al-Qa'ida in the Arabian Peninsula in central and southeastern Yemen, mainly in the governorates of Marib and Hadramawt.

## ARMED CONFLICT

The Huthi armed group, their allies and the various armed groups and pro-government forces that opposed them all committed serious violations of international humanitarian law, including some that amounted to war crimes, as well as human rights abuses.

## Indiscriminate and disproportionate attacks

Huthi and anti-Huthi armed groups used explosive weapons with wide-area effects, including mortars and artillery shells, when attacking civilian residential areas controlled or contested by their opponents in southern Yemen, killing and injuring civilians. During fighting for control of Aden and Ta'iz, Yemen's two most populous cities after Sana'a, both sides repeatedly fired explosive weapons with wide-area effects into densely populated civilian areas. They also conducted military operations from civilian residential neighbourhoods, launching attacks from or near homes, schools and hospitals, exposing local civilians to serious risk. The Huthi armed group and their allies laid internationally banned anti-personnel landmines that caused civilian casualties; dozens of civilians were killed or injured by landmines when returning to their homes in the second half of the year after fighting ended in Aden and the surrounding area.

Huthis and their allies carried out cross-border attacks from northern Yemen that could amount to war crimes, indiscriminately shelling Najran and other civilian-populated areas in southern Saudi Arabia.

## Attacks on medical facilities and workers

The Huthi armed group and its allies, and their pro-government opponents, attacked medical facilities, workers and patients or exposed them to serious risk by using medical facilities or their close vicinity as locations for firing positions or other military activities, particularly during fighting in and around Aden and Ta'iz. In Aden, unidentified gunmen attacked the premises of the ICRC, forcing their staff to relocate. Anti-Huthi fighters fired assault rifles from inside Aden's al-Sadaqa hospital compound and launched mortars next to the hospital, exposing patients and medics to the risk of retaliatory attacks.

In late April, Aden's al-Joumhouria Hospital was forced to suspend its medical activities because of similar actions by fighters.

## EXCESSIVE USE OF FORCE AND TORTURE AND OTHER ILL-TREATMENT

The expansion of Huthi control sparked widespread protests in Ta'iz and other cities to which Huthi forces and the pro-Huthi Central Security Forces responded with excessive force, including the use of live ammunition, arrests and torture.

In the city of Ibb, Huthis and their allied forces used live ammunition to fire at peaceful protesters on 16 February, wounding three protesters, and on 21 February, killing protester Nasr al-Shuja'.

In Ta'iz, the pro-Huthi Central Security Forces used excessive force, including tear gas and live fire, to disperse peaceful demonstrations from 22 to 25 March, killing at least eight protesters and wounding at least 30 others. Almost 300 protesters and bystanders required treatment for tear gas inhalation.

In Sana'a, Huthis and their allied forces detained three protesters on 11 February and tortured them over the following four days; one, Salah 'Awdh al-Bashri, died from injuries he sustained during hours of torture.

### Unlawful killings

Anti-Huthi forces summarily killed captured Huthi fighters and civilians suspected of supporting the Huthis. They posted videos on the internet publicizing some of these killings in Aden and Ta'iz of those they alleged were "spies" or "Huthi supporters".

### Abductions, arbitrary arrests and detention

There was a surge in arbitrary arrests, detentions and abductions of government supporters, journalists, human rights defenders and others by Huthis and allied forces loyal to former President Saleh. Many detainees were held in multiple, often unofficial, locations including private homes without being informed of the reason for their detention or given any opportunity to challenge its legality. At least 25 men, including political activists, human rights defenders and journalists, were detained by armed men in civilian clothes who said they belonged to Ansarullah, the political wing of the Huthi armed group, while attending a meeting at an Ibb hotel on 13 October. Most were later released, reportedly after being tortured, but Antar al-Mabarazi, an engineer, and Ameen al-Shafaq, a university professor, remained in incommunicado detention at the end of the year.

## Freedom of association
Huthi forces curtailed freedom of association, closing down at least 27 NGOs in Sana'a and threatening their directors and staff.

## Abuses by Islamic State
The armed group Islamic State (IS) claimed responsibility for bomb attacks that mostly targeted mosques in Sana'a seen as pro-Huthi, killing and injuring civilians. The deadliest attacks, on 20 March, hit the mosques of al-Badr and al-Hashoosh in Sana'a. They killed 142 people, mostly civilians, and injured 351. On 6 December, an IS bomb attack killed the Governor of Aden and several of his aides.

## Violations by the Saudi Arabia-led coalition
Beginning on 25 March, a Saudi Arabia-led military coalition of nine states launched a campaign of air strikes across Yemen against the Huthis and their allies. Some attacks targeted and destroyed military objectives; others were disproportionate, indiscriminate or appeared to be directly targeted against civilians and/or civilian objects, causing numerous civilian deaths and injuries. Some of the attacks amounted to war crimes.

The coalition forces' air strikes destroyed a cluster of nine houses on 3 June in the village of al-'Eram, northwest of Sa'da city, killing at least 35 children, 11 women and nine men, and injuring nine other residents. Villagers said that the strikes had continued while search and rescue efforts were under way to look for bodies and survivors in the rubble.

Despite this, both the coalition authorities and President Hadi's government failed to conduct investigations and to hold to account those responsible for this or other unlawful attacks.

Coalition forces used imprecise munitions including large US- and UK-made bombs with a wide impact radius which cause casualties and destruction beyond their immediate strike location. In Sa'da and Hajjah, they also used US-made cluster munitions, inherently indiscriminate weapons whose use is prohibited, and which scatter bomblets over a wide area and present an ongoing risk to civilians as they frequently fail to detonate upon impact.

Some coalition attacks targeted key infrastructure, such as bridges and highways. They included attacks in July that destroyed four bridges on a road linking the Sa'da governorate to Sana'a. Other coalition air strikes damaged bridges on roads linking Sana'a to Hodeidah and Marib, and Ta'iz to Aden.

Some coalition air strikes hit hospitals and other medical facilities in Sa'da governorate, injuring patients and medical workers. On 26 October, the Saudi Arabia-led coalition destroyed a Médecins Sans Frontières (MSF) supported hospital in Hayden in Sa'da, injuring seven medical workers. MSF said that another of its clinics in Ta'iz was struck by coalition air strikes on 2 December, wounding nine people, including two MSF staff. On 4 September, coalition aircraft reportedly bombed al-Sh'ara hospital at Razih in Sa'da governorate. According to MSF personnel who visited the site soon after, there was no evidence that the hospital was used for military purposes. MSF said the attack killed six patients and injured others.

In order to deny supplies to Huthis and their allied forces, the coalition imposed a partial aerial and naval blockade. This severely curtailed the import and provision of fuel and other essentials, obstructing access to food, water, humanitarian assistance and medical supplies, exacerbating the worsening humanitarian crisis.

## IMPUNITY

All parties to the armed conflict committed serious human rights abuses with impunity.

Yemeni authorities failed to hold thorough and independent investigations into past human rights violations, including unlawful killings and other serious abuses committed by government forces in connection with mass popular protests in 2011.

In September, President Hadi decreed the establishment of a national commission of inquiry to investigate all violations committed since the beginning of 2011.

## WOMEN'S RIGHTS

Women and girls continued to face discrimination in law and in practice and were inadequately protected against sexual and other violence, including female genital mutilation, forced marriage and other abuses.

## DEATH PENALTY

The death penalty remained in force for a wide range of crimes. Courts continued to impose death sentences and executions were carried out. Prisoners on death row reportedly included dozens of juvenile offenders sentenced for crimes committed when they were under 18 years of age.

# ZAMBIA

**Republic of Zambia**
**Head of state and government: Edgar Chagwa Lungu (replaced Acting President Guy Scott in January)**

The Public Order Act continued to be used to curtail freedom of assembly. Journalists were arrested for reporting on alleged corruption, while the death sentences of 332 prisoners were commuted to life imprisonment.

## BACKGROUND

Zambia held a presidential by-election on 20 January, following the death of President Michael Sata on 28 October 2014. The election was narrowly won by Edgar Lungu of the Patriotic Front. Electricity shortages led to lengthy blackouts of up to 14 hours daily, forcing businesses and mines to scale down operations and lay off workers. The Zambian kwacha lost 80% against the US dollar during the year, driving food prices up. The country's rising debt affected the provision of social services.

## FREEDOM OF ASSEMBLY

Police continued to implement the Public Order Act (POA), arbitrarily restricting freedom of assembly for opposition parties and civil society. While Section 5(4) of the POA provides for every person who intends to assemble or convene a public meeting, procession or demonstration to give the police seven days' notice, police often interpreted this provision to mean police permission is required before any public assembly can proceed.

In May, police opened a docket against opposition leader Hakainde Hichilema after he conducted a door-to-door campaign in Kamwala market in Lusaka, the capital. He was questioned by police in the presence of his lawyers for over an hour, and made to write a letter of undertaking to comply with the provisions of the POA to be spared prosecution.

## FREEDOM OF EXPRESSION – JOURNALISTS

On 15 July, police arrested Fred M'membe, owner of *The Post* newspaper, and journalist Mukosha Funga for an article they published in March. The article discussed the investigation by the Anti-Corruption Commission (ACC) of a presidential aide for soliciting a bribe from a Chinese businessman to arrange an appointment with the President. *The Post* had published a letter from the ACC to the President notifying the President about its investigation. In May, the presidential aide reported the leak to the police, who questioned the journalists before releasing them. However, on 15 July they were arrested and spent a night in custody before appearing in court, charged with publishing classified information. The journalists were released on bail the next day, which was set at over US$3,000 each.

## JUSTICE SYSTEM

In October, President Lungu pardoned Boris Muziba, Nayoto Mwenda and Wasilota Sikwibele, three prisoners from the Western Province. The three men were jailed for three years in August 2014 for "publication of false information with the intention of causing fear and alarm to the general public", under Section 67 of the Penal Code. The charges stemmed from their activities as members of a movement calling for the secession of the Western Province from Zambia. Five other men were remanded in custody since their arrest in December 2014, following the announcement in August 2013 by one of them, Afumba Mombotwa, that they would set up a transitional government for Barotseland – a region which includes the Western Province.

## DEATH PENALTY

On 16 July, President Lungu commuted the death sentences of 332 prisoners to life imprisonment, after witnessing harsh prison conditions during a visit.[1]

---

1. Zambia: Commuting death sentences a laudable first step (News story, 16 July)

# ZIMBABWE

Republic of Zimbabwe
Head of state and government: **Robert Gabriel Mugabe**

The enforced disappearance of prominent pro-democracy activist Itai Dzamara in March remained unresolved. Freedom of expression, association and assembly continued to be restricted and a number of journalists were arrested. Forced evictions continued throughout the year with thousands of informal traders being forcibly evicted by municipal police from Central Harare, resulting in clashes and arrests. The slow pace of legal reform to bring legislation into line with the 2013 Constitution restricted access to rights guaranteed by the Constitution. A Supreme Court ruling in July allowed government and private employers to dismiss thousands of workers after only giving three months' notice. No executions were carried out for the 10th successive year.

## BACKGROUND

Tension between factions of President Mugabe's ruling Zimbabwe African National Union – Patriotic Front (ZANU-PF) party continued. Factional tension also continued within the main opposition party, the Movement for Democratic Change, led by former Prime Minister Morgan Tsvangirai (MDC-T). Factionalism in the two main political parties led to the dismissal of some members of parliament by party leaders, forcing by-elections in over 20 constituencies. On 14 November, a ZANU-PF district official axed to death two other district officials in Chitungwiza following a dispute over a party restructuring exercise. The alleged perpetrator died in suspicious circumstances in police custody within days of his arrest.

In July, the Zimbabwe Vulnerability Assessment Committee reported that some 1.5 million people were in need of food aid during the 2015-2016 lean period leading up to the next harvest. The rate of formal unemployment exceeded 80%, while 72% of the population was living below the national poverty line of US$1.25 per day.

## ENFORCED DISAPPEARANCES

On 9 March, five men abducted journalist and pro-democracy activist Itai Dzamara. Despite a court ruling ordering state security agents to investigate his disappearance, there was no independent evidence to suggest the state had carried out an investigation with due diligence by the end of the year. In 2014, Itai Dzamara founded the protest group Occupy Africa Unity Square (OAUS) which was critical of President Mugabe's rule.[1]

## FREEDOMS OF EXPRESSION, ASSOCIATION AND ASSEMBLY

The rights to freedom of expression for journalists and human rights defenders continued to be restricted through arbitrary arrests, detentions and prosecutions for peacefully exercising their rights.[2]

At least 10 journalists from both the state-controlled and private media were arrested for writing articles critical of government officials and faced charges including publishing "falsehoods" under the Criminal Law (Codification and Reform) Act.

On 2 November, the editor of the state-controlled newspaper The Sunday Mail, Mabasa Sasa, and the paper's investigations editor Brian Chitemba and journalist Tinashe Farawo, were arrested after implicating some senior police officers as being part of a group behind elephant killings in Hwange National Park. The three spent two nights in detention at Harare Central Police Station and were charged with "publishing falsehoods". They were each granted US$100 bail by the court and released. They denied the charges and their trial date was set for 29 February 2016.

The assistant news editor of the state-controlled Herald newspaper, Takunda Maodza, was arrested on 3 November in Harare while investigating a story alleging that a Harare businessman was funding an opposition group known as People First composed of former ZANU-PF members. Police alleged that the journalist demanded a bribe from the businessman. However, fellow journalists reported that the journalist had refused to accept the money. He was charged with attempted extortion under the Criminal Law (Codification and Reform) Act and granted US$50 bail by the court. He denied the charges. The trial was due to continue in 2016.

On 12 November freelance journalist Shadreck Andrison Manyere was arrested by police in Harare while filming clashes between protesters and police in Central Harare. He was detained for more than four hours and charged under Section 37(1)(a) of the Criminal Law (Codification and Reform) Act with "participating in a gathering with intent to promote public violence, breach of peace, or bigotry." He denied the charges.

On 23 October, police in Rusape arrested freelance journalist Sydney Saize, Bernard Chiketo of The Daily News and Kenneth Nyangani, a correspondent for Newsday, while the journalists were covering an MDC-T protest outside Rusape Magistrate's Court. They were released without charge after police searched and interrogated them and recorded their personal details.

On 18 September, two journalists, Andrew Kunambura from the Financial Gazette and freelance journalist Emison Haripindi, were arrested by Harare municipal police while taking photos of the municipal police arresting some informal traders. The journalists were detained at Harare Central Police Station for about four hours and released without charge.

On 11 December, Pastor Patrick Philip Mugadza of the Remnant Church in Kariba was arrested by police in the resort town of Victoria Falls after carrying out a one-person peaceful demonstration. He carried a placard which read: "Mr President the people are suffering. Proverbs 21:13." The demonstration was held during the annual conference of the ruling ZANU-PF party. The pastor was charged with criminal nuisance under Section 46 of the Criminal Law (Codification and Reform) Act. He was granted an unusually high bail of US$500 and remained in custody for more than two weeks after failing to raise the money. He was released on 31 December after lawyers successfully applied for the reduction of his bail to US$50.

On 30 November, five activists were arrested by police outside the Rainbow Towers Hotel in Harare for staging a peaceful protest against Vice-President Phelekezela Mphoko's stay at the hotel for close to a year. The five activists – Tendayi Mudehwe, Dirk Frey, Irvin Takavada, Elvis Mugari and Tonderai Chigumbu – were released on 2 December after spending two nights at Harare Central Police Station. They were charged with criminal nuisance under Section 46 of the Criminal Law (Codification and Reform) Act.

On 25 July, six civil society activists from the Crisis in Zimbabwe Coalition, Chitungwiza Residents Trust and the OAUS were arrested at Harare Central Remand Prison. They were handed over to the police and charged under Section 5(2) of the Protected Places and Areas Act Chapter 11:12 with failing to comply with a directive from an authorized officer regulating conduct and movement. The six were among about 50 activists who had visited 16 informal traders held on remand after being denied bail. On 2 October, Mfundo Mlilo and Nixon Nyikadzino of Crisis in Zimbabwe Coalition and Dirk Frey of OAUS were acquitted for lack of evidence. The trials of the remaining three, Edgar Gweshe, Donald Makuwaza and Charles Chidhakwa, were continuing at the end of the year.

The government continued to impose restrictions on activists campaigning for community radio stations to be licensed. The authorities have failed to license a single community radio station since enacting the Broadcasting Services Act in 2001. At least 28 community-based initiatives were campaigning to obtain broadcasting licences in both rural and urban areas. Police blocked meetings under the Public Order and Security Act and security agents raided offices and seized material and equipment belonging to the community-based organizations. Activists campaigning for community radio licences were subjected to frequent interrogation by police and the Central Intelligence Organization after meetings and other activities aimed at setting up community radio stations.[3]

## WORKERS' RIGHTS

A Supreme Court ruling on 17 July upheld an employer's common law contractual right to terminate employment by giving three months' notice. The ruling triggered mass lay-offs by the government and by state-owned and private companies. Thousands of workers lost their jobs within days of the Supreme Court ruling as employers used the ruling to avoid going through a formal retrenchment process as set out in the Labour Act. In August, the government rushed amendments to the Labour Act through Parliament to include setting up a minimum package for retrenched workers. Unions and employers complained that they were not adequately consulted. Trade unions argued that the package did not give adequate safeguards to employees.

## FORCED EVICTIONS

Informal traders were forcibly evicted from central Harare and other town centres. In June, the government issued an ultimatum for the removal of informal traders from cities and towns with the support of the army. In July, municipal police clashed with informal traders in Central Harare in an attempt to remove them from the Central Business District. Dozens of informal traders, including leaders of the National Vendors' Union of Zimbabwe, were arrested and detained. Sixteen were charged with public violence. They were released on bail and their trials were continuing at the end of the year.

Across the country thousands of people were forcibly evicted. Some turned to the courts for protection. On 12 January, the High Court in Harare stopped the removal of some 150 families settled at Arnold Farm in Mazowe district. The families' homes had been indiscriminately demolished by police on 7 January, leaving people homeless, with no cover from the elements in the midst of the rainy season. The forced evictions had been carried out despite an earlier High Court order issued in August 2014 protecting the Arnold Farm residents from arbitrary eviction under Section 74 of the Constitution.

In July, the Harare City Council ordered the destruction of homes in areas it declared "illegal settlements" without obtaining the necessary court orders. Demolitions were carried out in the Warren Park and Westlea suburbs. These were part of settlements established by housing co-operatives.

Demolitions also continued in December when 200 structures were destroyed by the City of Harare near Kambuzuma suburb.

## LEGAL, CONSTITUTIONAL OR INSTITUTIONAL DEVELOPMENTS

On 28 October, in an unprecedented development, the Constitutional Court ordered the Prosecutor-General, Johannes Tomana, to be committed to prison for 30 days for contravening Section 164(3) of the Constitution. He was accused of repeatedly disobeying orders issued by the High Court and Supreme Court to allow private parties to pursue prosecutions for fraud and rape in two high-profile cases. The Constitutional Court ruled that in the two cases the Prosecutor-General had a statutory duty to issue the certificates for private prosecutions under Section 16 of the Criminal Procedure and Evidence Act. The 30-day sentence was suspended for 10 days on condition that within the 10 days the Prosecutor-General complied with the earlier court orders. On 4 November, the Deputy Prosecutor-General, acting on behalf the Prosecutor-General, issued the certificates allowing the private prosecutions to proceed.

The process of reviewing the country's laws to bring them into line with the 2013 Constitution continued, but at a very slow pace. Consequently, the human rights guarantees afforded by the Constitution were compromised by the continued use of old laws by police and other government departments. For example, activists were arrested and charged under legal provisions that were clearly unconstitutional and some had to turn to the Constitutional Court for redress.

## DEATH PENALTY

In July, Zimbabwe reached 10 years without carrying out any known executions.

---

1. Zimbabwe: Open letter: Investigate and resolve the circumstances around the enforced disappearance of Itai Dzamara (AFR 46/2423/2015)

2. Zimbabwe: Shooting the messengers (News story, 10 November)

3. Beyond tokenism: The need to license community radio stations in Zimbabwe (AFR 46/1613/2015)